GORDON W. PRANGE

"Mr. Prange has been called 'the dean of Pearl Harbor historians.' The accolade—with appropriate credit to his associates—is deserved."

—*Wall Street Journal*

DECEMBER 7, 1941

"Informative and entertaining . . . gripping details. . . . A colorful and dramatic account."

—*Army*

"Luminous . . . thoroughly documented and detailed yet captivatingly readable as well. . . . Highly recommended."

—*Library Journal*

"History that puts the reader mentally on the scene and emotionally feeling the disbelief and anger of that day."

—*Pittsburgh Press*

"Compelling . . . gripping . . . and featuring sound scholarship and excellent writing."

—*Booklist*

"A classic work."

—*Charlotte Observer*

"A sweeping panorama. . . . Draws on the collective memory of hundreds of individuals who were involved in the attack. . . . Uses oral history techniques to paint a vivid picture."

—*Virginian-Pilot Ledger-Star*

"What gives this particular book added flavor and helps set it apart from other Pearl Harbor histories is the devotion of the authors to seeking out and interviewing the many everyday people—military and civilian—who played heroic and largely unsung roles on Dec. 7 and the following days. . . . Highly recommended reading not only for those who participated in the great battle, but for those who would like to experience what it was really like to be there that day and the days following."

—*San Diego Union*

ALSO BY GORDON W. PRANGE

AT DAWN WE SLEPT
*with Donald M. Goldstein and
Katherine V. Dillon*

MIRACLE AT MIDWAY
*with Donald M. Goldstein and
Katherine V. Dillon*

TARGET TOKYO
*with Donald M. Goldstein and
Katherine V. Dillon*

PEARL HARBOR
*with Donald M. Goldstein and
Katherine V. Dillon*

DEC. 7 1941

THE DAY THE JAPANESE ATTACKED PEARL HARBOR

GORDON W. PRANGE

WITH DONALD M. GOLDSTEIN AND KATHERINE V. DILLON

WARNER BOOKS

A Warner Communications Company

Warner Books Edition
Copyright © 1988 by Anne Prange and Prange Enterprises, Inc.
All rights reserved.

This Warner Books edition is published by arrangement with McGraw-
Hill Book Company, 11 West 19th Street, New York, NY 10011.

Warner Books, Inc., 666 Fifth Avenue, New York, NY 10103

W A Warner Communications Company

Printed in the United States of America
First Warner Books Printing: December 1989
10 9 8 7 6 5 4 3 2 1

Cover design by Jack Ribik

LIBRARY OF CONGRESS CATALOGING-IN-PUBLICATION DATA
Prange, Gordon William, 1910–
    December 7, 1941: the day the Japanese attacked Pearl Harbor /
Gordon W. Prange with Donald M. Goldstein and Katherine V. Dillon. -
Warner Books ed.
        p.   cm.
    Bibliography: p.
    Includes index.
    ISBN 0-446-38997-8 (pbk) (U.S.A. and Can.)
    1. Pearl Harbor (Hawaii), Attack on, 1941.   I. Goldstein, Donald
M.   II. Dillon, Katherine V.   III. Title.
D767.92.P7215   1989   89-34776
940.54′26—dc20   CIP

CONTENTS

PART 3
"The Sky Was Full of the Enemy"

PART 4
"Under Constant and Continuous Attacks"

PART 5
"A Tragic Hour"

PART 6
"Back to Their Battle Stations"

PART 7
"A Date That Will Live in Infamy"

I-22: Lt. Naoji Iwasa,
PO 1/c Naokichi Sasaki

I-16: Ens. Masaharu Yokoyama,
PO 2/c Tei Uyeda

I-18: Ens. Shigemi Furuno,
PO 1/c Shigenori Yokoyama

I-20: Ens. Akira Hiroo,
PO 2/c Yoshio Katayama

I-24: Ens. Kazuo Sakamaki,
PO 2/c Kiyoshi Inagaki

Disposition of Japanese midget submarines in the Hawaiian area, December 7, 1941.

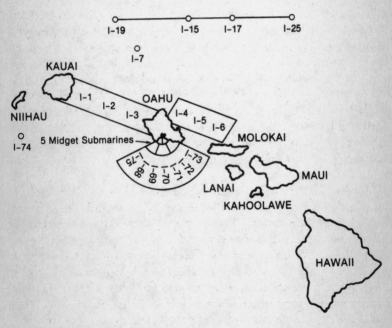

Disposition of Japanese submarines in the Hawaiian area, December 7, 1941 (Both sketches are based upon chart in Japanese Monograph No. 102).

INTRODUCTION

This is the fifth book edited from the manuscripts of Gordon W. Prange (the others were *At Dawn We Slept, Miracle at Midway, Target Tokyo,* and *Pearl Harbor: The Verdict of History*). Although other works relating to the Pacific War are in preparation, this is the last of the Prange manuscripts about Pearl Harbor, and marks the end of approximately thirty-seven years of work on the subject by Prange, twenty-five years by Dillon, and eight by Goldstein. While *At Dawn We. Slept* dealt primarily with events leading to the attack and its aftermath, and *Pearl Harbor: The Verdict of History* was concerned with responsibility on the part of various individuals, this book is about what happened that day as seen by those who were there.

Much of this volume is based on interviews available only to Prange and which have never been published before; the book has an oral history dimension. Those whom Prange interviewed include not only American eyewitnesses but many of the Japanese participants. Readers who were not yet born—or who were too young to remember—may wonder how so many people can recall the day so vividly, complete with conversations and thoughts. The current generation has no comparable frame of reference, not even their recollection of the assassination of President Kennedy.

Pearl Harbor struck with so sharp a force that it left an indelible imprint. There are few indeed who, if they were alive and of the age of reason in 1941, cannot recall where they were and what they were doing when they heard the news, and their exact role, if any, in the great drama.

By far the greatest part of the material in this book was contained in Prange's original Pearl Harbor manuscript. In searching through his files we discovered material which he did not use; if we thought it sufficiently interesting, we did not hesitate to add it. We knew that if he had the chance to write a book of this nature he would have included these items.

Times are given in the 24-hour clock, which was in use throughout the armed forces. Both American and Japanese documentation use it, and, as events move closer and closer together in the narrative, the 24-hour clock avoids any possible confusion between A.M. and P.M. All times in this book must be considered approximate, even those given in the ships' logs, which are frequently contradictory. This is not surprising, considering the circumstances of the day. As Admiral Kimmel pointed out, ". . . while these times are the best they can get, they were taken under stress."[1]

Some distances are given in meters, some in miles, depending upon whether Japanese or Americans are involved.

Some of the quotations herein concerning the Japanese may seem unduly harsh; it is impossible, however, to exaggerate the hatred the Americans, especially those on Oahu, felt toward the Japanese on December 7, 1941. These quotations are reported exactly as they were presented, and any attempt to palliate would be false to the facts.

For the reader's ready reference, the list of ships' logs in the bibliography includes the type of ship. An easy mental shortcut to the three major types is to remember that the U.S. battleships are named after states, the cruisers after cities, and the destroyers after naval heroes.

The story is arranged chronologically by incident. Instead of attempting to picture what was happening at a certain time throughout Oahu, we have devoted separate chapters to the major installations.

The book is divided into seven main sections. Part I, "Something Was Going to Happen" (Chapters 1–4), covers activities in Washington, D.C., and on Oahu on December 6. These chapters introduce many of the main characters and give the background for the events to follow. Part II, "Tora! Tora! Tora!" (Chapters 5–9), depicts the events of December 7, 1941, before the attack, including the takeoff from the Japanese carriers launching the midget submarines, the early antisubmarine actions of the destroyer *Ward*, and the radar sighting at the Opana station. Part III, "The Sky Was Full of the Enemy" (Chapters 10–13), is devoted to the first-wave attack on the U.S. ships. Among many other subjects, this part describes the destruction of the battleship *Arizona*, the capsizing of the *Oklahoma* and the *Utah*, damage to other ships and attempts on the part of the defenders to cope with the surprise attack. Part IV, "Under Constant and Continuous Attacks" (Chapters 14–18), narrates the attacks on the shore installations—Ford Island and Kaneohe Naval Air Stations, Hickam and Wheeler Fields, and so on.

Part V, "A Tragic Hour" (Chapters 19–22), is concerned with what many survivors called "the lull"—the brief respite between attack waves. In these chapters we describe, among other things, the sinking of a midget submarine in the harbor, rescue work, and attempts to prepare for the anticipated second strike. Part VI, "Back to Their Battle Stations" (Chapters 23–27), tells of the second wave, which contained such incidents as the attempted sortie of the *Nevada*, the explosion of the destroyer *Shaw*, the dramatic death of Lt. Fusata Iida, and the exploits of the few U.S. fighter pilots who got into the air. Part VII, "A Date That Will Live in Infamy," covers the balance of December 7 and a portion of December 8. This part deals with the expectation that the Japanese would attack again and that perhaps they would try to take Oahu; the myth of the third wave and other wild rumors; the shooting down of the fighter planes from the carrier *Enterprise*; the capture of the midget submariner Sakamaki, and the so-called "Battle of Niihau." This section ends with Roosevelt's declaration of war.

Many of the pictures used herein are from the collection of our colleague Michael Wenger, who has become something of an expert in this field.

The purpose of this book is twofold. First, we wanted to give the present generation a picture of exactly what it was like on one of the most significant days in American history. Second, we intended this book as a memorial and tribute to those who participated.

We hope that the three Prange works on Pearl Harbor, a trilogy, are the definitive work on the subject to date. Neither Prange nor we have ever believed that this would be the final word on the subject. There is ample room for historians of the future. Each year the government releases many hitherto classified documents. One should bear in mind, though, that a paper released yesterday is not necessarily any more valid than one released many years ago, particularly those used in evidence at the various Pearl Harbor investigations. We have discovered no recently declassified document which in any way invalidates the conclusions Prange already reached.

Space does not permit us to thank individually everyone who contributed to this work, but we want to express our special appreciation to Prange's wife, Anne, his son, Winfred, and his daughters Polly and Nancy for their support and cooperation; to our advisers Robert Levan and Ronald Schimel; to all those cited in all three Pearl Harbor books; to Masataka Chihaya for his help at the Japanese end; and to Gladys Justin Carr, McGraw-Hill Editorial Director, and Tom Miller, Editor, and their colleagues for their assistance and encouragement. And to Prange, our former teacher, we would like to say, "We did our best."

DONALD M. GOLDSTEIN, Ph.D.
*Associate Professor of Public and
International Affairs
University of Pittsburgh
Pittsburgh, Pennsylvania*

KATHERINE V. DILLON
CWO, USAF (Ret.)
Arlington, Virginia

PREFACE

Pearl Harbor was one of the worse defeats the United States suffered in its 200 years of history. Because of this, an enormous number of books and articles have been written on the subject. Most of these works look at Pearl Harbor as a political subject; few have considered it as a military engagement.

To be sure, there were misunderstandings and mistakes on the American side that contributed to the Japanese victory. As many people on Oahu cried out that day, "They caught them asleep, by God!" Failure to acknowledge this is to refuse to face the facts and to waste the lives of the Americans who died that day. But, just as surely, it would be fruitless now to review the event in a spirit of recrimination. It was human shortcomings, not betrayal, that allowed us to be taken by surprise on December 7, 1941.

Under attack, some showed themselves to be less than heroic. There was the chaplain who took off when the Japanese attacked and did not come back to his post for six days.[1] The executive officer of one ship became neurotic during the attack,[2] as did the captain of a cruiser.[3] Others performed well on the day itself, only to "come unglued"—an expression several survivors used—after the attack was over. This included at least two general officers.[4]

But for everyone who failed, hundreds rose to the occasion, performing under fire the tasks for which they had been trained. One admiral and two battleship captains died at their posts. Junior officers and enlisted men such as Ens. Francis C. Flaherty and Chief Water

Tender Peter Tomich gave their lives to save the men in their charge. Two lieutenants of the Hawaiian Air Force got their planes up and shot down seven Japanese aircraft between them. Mess Attendant Doris Miller seized a machine gun and performed so valiantly that he became the first black man to receive the Navy Cross. Untold numbers worked without panic and without vainglory, simply because that was their job.

Because this is the story of those who survived as well as those who died, it is fitting that we dedicate this book to the members of the Pearl Harbor Survivors Association, whose motto "Remember Pearl Harbor!" is as appropriate today as it ever was.

ABBREVIATIONS

AA	Antiaircraft
A-20	Army light bomber
AWS	Aircraft Warning Service
B-17	Army heavy bomber
B-18	Army medium bomber
BAR	Browning automatic rifle
BAR-6	Browning automatic rifle
CinCPAC	Commander in Chief, U.S. Pacific Fleet
CinCUS	Commander in Chief, U.S. Fleet
EST	Eastern Standard Time
FBI	Federal Bureau of Investigation
G-1	Personnel (Army)*
G-2	Intelligence (Army)
G-3	Operations (Army)
G-4	Supply (Army)

*The Air Staff used these same numerical designations, with the initial A instead of G.

IMTFE	International Miltary Tribunal, Far East
INS	International News Service
J-19	A Japanese diplomatic code
J2F	Navy utility seaplane
JN-25	Japanese operational code
NBC	National Broadcasting Company
O-47	Army observation plane
O-49	Army observation plane
OA-9	Army observation plane
OD	Officer of the Day (Army); Officer of the Deck (Navy)
ONI	Office of Naval Intelligence
Op-20-G	Security Section, Naval Communications
OS2U	Navy utility plane
P-26	Army fighter plane
P-36	Army fighter plane
P-40	Army fighter plane
PBY	Navy patrol bomber
PT	Motor torpedo boat
PX	Post Exchange
RCA	Radio Corporation of America
SIS	Signal Intelligence Service

PART 1

"Something Was Going to Happen"

December 6, 1941

CHAPTER 1

"Time Was Running Out"

Saturday December 6, 1941, was just another welcome break in routine for workers and schoolchildren in the Washington, D.C. area, a reminder to housewives that Christmas was only seventeen shopping days away. Despite the date, for the past week the thermometer had flatly contradicted the calendar. Much of the United States basked in unseasonably warm weather. "Florists delightedly reported abundant supplies of late-blooming roses, and from New England came word that the pussy willow, which usually doesn't appear until March, was budding in time to be worked into Christmas wreaths."[1] By 0800, that Saturday's temperature in Washington officially registered 46°, although a nippy westerly wind added a bite to the air.[2]

The chilling wind from the west was symbolic of the rapidly deteriorating relations with Japan which had kept many in the executive branch of the government tied to their desks. Congress, however, saw no reason to remain in session and had adjourned on Thursday December 4 for a long weekend.[3] Many in Congress looked on Japan as a nuisance rather than a menace, its navy as no match for that of the United States. Speaking that day at the opening of the welfare building at the Naval Air Station in San Juan, Puerto Rico, Senator Owen Brewster of Maine boasted that "the United States Navy can defeat the Japanese Navy at any place and at any time."[4] The public had a right to assume that Brewster's comments were reliable, both because he was a member of the Senate Naval Affairs Committee and because, as a Republican, he was unlikely to be bolstering the administration's image.

The Japanese liner *Tatsuta Maru*, the last of three ships authorized to bring Americans back to the United States from Japan and to return Japanese from the United States to their homeland, was in her fourth day at sea. Yet she carried only twenty-three Americans. And back in Tokyo women members of the American Club looked forward to December 8 (Tokyo time), when they would attend "a lecture on antique Japanese combs."[5]

As indicated by the headlines that crossed the front pages of the Washington *Post*, the Japanese were up to something: JAPANESE PLEA OF SELF-DEFENSE COLDLY RECEIVED; TOKYO SAYS TROOPS ARE BEING MASSED MERELY TO COUNTER THREAT BY CHINESE. To this, the *Post*'s editorial page snapped: "...if the Japanese expect Americans to believe such a story, they have a poor opinion of American mentality....Thus all the circumstances conspire to show that the Japanese are preparing for another snatch in their career of Asian conquest."[6]

That is why Secretary of War Henry L. Stimson decided to stay in town that day. He had hoped to escape from "this infernal hellhole they call Washington" long enough to spend the night with his wife, Mabel, at their Long Island home, Highhold. However, "as the morning wore on, the news got worse and worse and the atmosphere indicated that something was going to happen." Stimson held frequent conferences with Chief of Staff General George C. Marshall; Brig. Gen. Sherman Miles, acting assistant chief of staff, Intelligence (G-2); and Brig. Gen. Leonard T. Gerow, chief, War Plans Division. "We are mainly concerned with the supplies which are on the way to the Philippines and the additional big bombers which we are trying to fly over there and which are to start today," Stimson explained in his diary.[7]

High-level attention in Washington centered on Japan's aggressive intentions toward Southeast Asia. At 1040, the State Department received a message from Ambassador John G. Winant in London, marked TRIPLE PRIORITY AND MOST URGENT: "British Admiralty reports that at 3 a.m. London time this morning two parties seen off Cambodia Point, sailing slowly westward toward Kra 11 hours distant in time. First party 25 transports, 6 cruisers, 10 destroyers. Second party 10 transports, 2 cruisers, 10 destroyers."[8]

Capt. Roscoe E. "Pinky" Schuirmann, the Navy's liaison officer with the State Department, added in a secret memorandum to State:

Following report has been received from the Commander in Chief Asiatic Fleet dated December 6th:

British Commander in Chief China reports a twenty-five ship convoy escorted by 6 cruisers and 10 destroyers in Lat. 08–00 N. Long. 106–00 East at 0316 Greenwich time today. A convoy of ten ships with two cruisers and 10 destroyers were in Lat. 08–40 North Long. 106–20 East two hours later. All on course west. Three additional ships in Lat. 07–51 North Long 105–00 East at 0442 course 310°. This indicates all forces will make for Kohtron in Lat. 10–01 Long. 104 East.

Commander in Chief Asiatic Admiral [Thomas C.] Hart's Scouting Force has sighted 30 ships and one large cruiser anchored in Camranh Bay.[9]

Information copies of Hart's message went to the commander in chief of the U.S. Pacific Fleet (Adm. Husband E. Kimmel) at Pearl Harbor, as well as to the commandants of the Sixteenth Naval District at Manila and the Fourteenth Naval District at Pearl Harbor.[10]

The records of the White House switchboard and those kept by Secretary of State Cordell Hull's office reveal calls flying back and forth between Hull, Stimson, Secretary of the Navy Frank Knox, Marshall, Schuirmann, Chief of Naval Operations Harold R. "Betty" Stark, and other officials.[11]

Hull did not remember the details of all his telephone conversations and other conferences held during that day; however, "the Japanese large-scale military movement from the jumping-off place in Southern Indochina was very much in the minds of all of us who were called upon to consider that situation."[12] This information confirmed that the "long-threatened Japanese movement of expansion by force to the south was under way. The critical character of this development, which placed the United States and its friends in common imminent danger," was an important subject of discussion between Hull and representatives of the armed services.[13]

The implicit threat to the Philippines, then under the American flag, particularly worried these officials. Stimson and Marshall discussed whether thirteen B-17s scheduled to begin their long flight from Hamilton Field in California to Manila might be attacked over the Pacific. After careful consideration, Marshall authorized their departure that evening. He had sent Maj. Gen. Henry H. "Hap" Arnold, who commanded the Army Air Forces, to the West Coast to ensure that the planes were fully equipped to take off. "Naturally, the young men, the squadron leaders, could not be told all the various factors in the case except that we wanted them to leave as quickly as possible." Arnold phoned Marshall shortly after his arrival to say, "These damn fellows don't realize how serious this thing is." Marshall told him, "Well, you are there and they are your people. You start them out."[14]

In the Security Section of the Navy's Communications Division (Op-20-G), tension had never been higher. JN-25, the Japanese Navy's operational code, as yet unbroken, was under attack by the "first team" of the Navy's code breakers—Mrs. Agnes Meyer "Miss Aggie" Driscoll, Ens. Prescott H. "Wimpy" Currier, and Mr. Philip Cate. Those working on material encoded in a high-level Japanese diplomatic code, J-19, were, in the words of the section's chief, Cmdr. Laurence F. Safford, "batting their brains out trying to achieve solutions with minimum volume in any one key." The Americans had broken J-19, but the keys changed daily, and it was "plenty tough" to break them without a certain amount of material to work with.

Those concerned with Japan's top diplomatic code, Purple, had a technically less challenging task, thanks to the amazing mechanical system known as Magic. But the sheer volume was daunting. The very fact that the Japanese used Purple to encode a dispatch meant that it was important, and the Japanese used the code worldwide. As Safford explained, the Purple team had varied duties. It "had to code and decode messages exchanged with London and Corregidor, plot direction-finder bearings of German submarines operating in the Atlantic, and 'process' messages coming in from other parts of the world, as well as handle Purple exchanges between Tokyo and Washington."[15]

General Miles of G-2 also felt a sense of urgency that day as he said goodbye to "an old naval friend," RADM Thomas C. Kinkaid, Kimmel's brother-in-law. Kinkaid was leaving to command a cruiser division. Miles told him that he hoped he would hurry; otherwise he "did not know whether he would make it or not." By this time Miles "rated quite highly the probability of an involvement immediately, or certainly in the fairly near future, of a Japanese-American war."[16]

The Japanese Embassy faced an exceedingly trying morning. A virulently worded message from Tokyo, intended for retransmission to the ambassadors and ministers in Central and South America as well as to Ottawa, indicated the beginning of an all-out propaganda

campaign to drive a wedge between the United States and the rest of
the Americas. It read in part:

> 1. The recent occupation of Netherlands Guiana by American troops,
> or call it what you will—occupation it is, is the first example in the
> present war of the United States' invading South America....now
> that the situation is tenser, the hitherto good neighbor, the United
> States, will no longer hesitate to use arms. This at length has come
> to the surface, and we must be on the strictest alert.

> 2. Based on an agreement with France, we penetrated Southern French
> Indo-China for joint defense. Scarcely were our tracks dry, when along
> comes good old nonchalant America and grabs Netherlands Guiana. If
> she needs any of the American countries for her own interest, hiding
> under the camouflage of joint defense, she will take them, as she has
> just proven. This is a menace to the Latin American nations; so will you
> please at every opportunity, impress upon the Government and people
> of the country to which you are accredited that the United States bodes
> them naught save ill....[17]

Foreign Minister Shigenori Togo knew that no one in the Washington Embassy would be in a position to do any propagandizing.
Within approximately 24 hours, Japan's diplomats in the United States
would be, at best, under house arrest as enemy aliens.

At 1100, Saburo Kurusu, Tokyo's special envoy to Washington,
received a visit from an old friend, Ferdinand L. Mayer. The two
had once served their respective governments in Peru. Their rapport
was such that they immediately picked up the threads of old acquaintance. As Mayer later recalled, after the two had reminisced briefly
about old times, Kurusu burst into a "lengthy conversation" about
his mission. Apparently he was "extremely anxious to talk about it
with an old friend and with someone in whom he had entire confidence." Throughout their talk, which lasted an hour and a half, Kurusu
"seemed very apprehensive of being overheard by members of the
Embassy staff, repeatedly turning his head to see if anyone were
approaching."[18]

"'Fred, we are in an awful mess,'" he burst out unceremoniously.
He explained that a severe attack of conjunctivitis had delayed his
departure from Japan for two months. "This complicated the situation because time was running out, from the point of view of restrain-

ing the military element...." When he left Japan, "the Civil Government was up against it to know how to canalize the military effervescence so that it would do the least harm to American and English relations.... [They] had decided that the least harmful alternative was to allow the military to move into Indo-China since that neither directly threatened Siberia and the United States nor Singapore and Britain."

Kurusu knew that troop movements "would be regarded with great suspicion in the United States and would, inevitably, jeopardize the success of his mission." But he hoped for three weeks' grace in which to bring about "some concrete result with which the Civil Government would feel able to hold off the military."[19]

This left Kurusu in an awkward position. Obviously he could not explain this background to Hull, "who seemed to feel suspicious at once, not only at the troop movements but of the evident desire of Kurusu to arrive at results speedily." Kurusu entreated Mayer to explain the situation to Hull, and Mayer promised to do so.

The principal problems, as pinpointed by Kurusu, were "the State Department and the national sentimentality with regard to China" on the American side and the militarists' "lack of humor" on the Japanese side. But the real sticking point was how to pull the Japanese out of China. Kurusu believed that "the show was up in China, that the militarists knew this as well, or perhaps better, than anyone else and that they were all looking for a way out to save their faces." He compared the dilemma to that at the end of the Russo-Japanese war: Japan victorious but exhausted.[20]

Kurusu insisted that he expressed the real views of the military. Japan was "absolutely war-weary, had no enthusiasm for this or any other conflict, but must be restored to peaceful conditions where normal trade could be resumed." Kurusu added that "naturally, the militarists continued to bluster and roar, but that this was merely normal face-saving, particularly in the Army...." Both "the militarists' power" and pro-Axis sentiment in Japan were "definitely on the downgrade." He went so far as to say that he and "the thinking people" of Japan realized that German victory might be more dangerous for Japan than for the United States: "Germany had no intention of assisting or even permitting Japan to retain any benefits that she might derive from her Axis victory."

Mayer suggested that Japan could best improve relations between their two countries by a concrete demonstration "of her change of heart with regard to the Axis and a throwing-in of her lot with the British and the Americans."[21] Kurusu agreed, but "most ruefully" reminded Mayer of both the Anti-Comintern and the Tripartite Pacts. He had signed the latter but "had resigned as Ambassador to Germany the next day." They discussed how a change could come about without Japan's breaking its commitments to the Axis—which, as Kurusu suggested with wry humor, would offend the American government's "great interest in the maintenance and sanctity of treaties!"[22]

Mayer pointed out that the whole business boiled down to restoring mutual confidence. Again Kurusu agreed heartily, explaining that he had been "most disappointed" when the proposal for a meeting between President Franklin D. Roosevelt and former Prime Minister Prince Fumimaro Konoye had come to naught and that he still hoped for a summit conference. He realized that Japan's desire to garrison China for some time aroused American suspicions. But the United States "had taken considerable time to withdraw from Nicaragua, Haiti and Cuba. These things could not be done overnight...."[23]

Mayer reminded him that he, Kurusu, was in the same uncomfortable spot that former Ambassador Katsuji Debuchi had occupied during the "Manchurian Incident": "he was making statements in the morning to the Secretary of State which the militarists would repudiate in the afternoon...." Kurusu acknowledged this painful truth, but said that "the militarists were so much on the run and in such a difficult position that, unless hot-heads among them upset the applecart—which might be done at any time—he felt that the better element in Japan was really on the way to control the situation."[24]

While this discussion was going on, some members of the Embassy attended a farewell luncheon at the Mayflower Hotel for Second Secretary Hidenari Terasaki, who was under orders for Rio de Janeiro. Then a group of the guests returned to the Embassy. Among them was Masuo Kato, Washington correspondent for Domei, the Japanese news agency. He noticed no unusual activity and began a game of table tennis with a correspondent for *Mainichi*. Katsuzo Okumura, secretary of the Embassy, looked on for a few minutes. Then they began to speculate on whether the *Tatsuta Maru* would actually reach the United States.

"Of course it is coming," said Kato.

"I doubt it," Okumura answered. When Kato asked why, Okumura replied shortly, "It just looks that way." The two Japanese placed a dollar bet on it, but Kato did not take the wager too seriously, for Okumura had been pessimistic all along. With his reporter's nose for news, Kato asked around the Embassy whether Okumura had "any inside information on which he had based his prediction." They all assured him to the contrary. Kato snooped about for almost an hour, but saw only "the usual Saturday afternoon calm."[25]

The Embassy did a magnificent job of camouflage thus to deceive a newsman of Kato's experience, for its top personnel were far from calm. At 0656 Eastern Standard Time, the Foreign Ministry in Tokyo sent a Purple message to Ambassador Kichisaburo Nomura which the U.S. Navy Station at Bainbridge Island, Washington, intercepted between 0715 and 0720 and promptly relayed by teletype to the Navy Department.[26] This dispatch alerted Nomura to expect a reply, in English, to the proposals that Hull had submitted on November 26. This message would be sent in fourteen parts and would probably arrive the next day. "The situation is extremely delicate, and when you receive it I want you to please keep it secret for the time being," Togo instructed. He would tell Nomura later when to present it. "However, I want you in the meantime to put it in nicely drafted form and make every preparation to present it to the Americans just as soon as you receive instructions."[27] This dispatch, later dubbed the "pilot message," reached the Embassy before noon.[28]

Shortly thereafter, Tokyo amplified its instructions with another dispatch: "There is really no need to tell you this, but in the preparation of the *aide-mémoire* be absolutely sure not to use a typist or any other person.

"Be most extremely cautious in preserving secrecy."[29] Faced with the necessity for preparing a document of historic importance in a manner suitable for presentation to a major power, and forbidden to use a typist, Nomura had to call upon Okumura, the only Embassy official able to type, and that "after a fashion."[30]

Tokyo began dispatching the fourteen-part message at 0800, and 3 minutes later Bainbridge Island began to intercept it. By 1125 the thirteenth part was on its way, Bainbridge Island snaring it between 1135 and 1152. Adding to the Embassy's difficulties, Tokyo sent the fourteen parts out of numerical order. For example, parts 4 and 9 were released simultaneously at 0955. Parts 5 and 10 moved off at 0959, while parts 6 and 11 followed at 1030 and 1031, respectively.[31]

Meanwhile, the Navy Department was receiving and decoding these messages almost as fast—if not faster—than were the Japanese. Most were decoded and typed at the Navy Department, although the Army decoded parts 9 and 10, with the Navy typing them. The fact that the fourteen-part message was in English helped speed up the process.[32]

In the War Department, everyone in the G-2 Far Eastern Section who had anything to do with Magic was on duty, including the section chief, Col. Rufus S. Bratton. Although a division duty officer was present, Miles, the G-2, remained until late afternoon.[33] At about 1400 the pilot message reached Bratton from the Navy's Signal Intelligence Service (SIS), "with the usual envelope full of assorted material."[34] His office distributed it within the section, as well as to Hull, Stimson, Marshall, Gerow, and Miles. In later years, Bratton could not recall whether he or an assistant made the complete distribution, but he remembered remarking to both Miles and Gerow "that here was an indication that a reply to the State Department's note to the Japanese Government was on its way." There was no indication of just when it would be received, but they could expect it "some time in the near future. . . ." He would let them know "as soon as it started coming in. . . ."[35] Actually, at that time, some of the fourteen-part message had arrived and was in the decoding mill.[36]

On the Navy side, Lt. Cmdr. Alwin D. Kramer, who was on loan from the Far Eastern Section of the Office of Naval Intelligence (ONI) to the Translation Section of the Navy's Communications Division, usually made the top-level Magic distribution within the Navy and to the White House. But he was not exactly sure of the time when he carried around the pilot message. Relying on Navy records, he thought he did so after 1000 on December 7 with "a number of other short messages."[37] But the director of Naval Intelligence, Capt. Theodore S. "Ping" Wilkinson, was sure he saw it before he left his office on December 6 and said to Kramer, "We will be on the lookout for the message when it comes through."[38]

Capt. John R. Beardall, naval aide to President Franklin D. Roosevelt, instructed his communications assistant, Lt. Lester R. Schulz, to remain at the White House because he, Beardall, "had been advised that there would be an important dispatch for delivery to the President."[39] The Navy Department expected Japan's reply to the Hull Note within a very short time.

In the meantime, Roosevelt decided on an action he had been contemplating for several days. He approved the draft of a personal

letter from himself to Emperor Hirohito and sent it for finalizing to
the State Department with an attached handwritten note:

Dear Cordell:

Shoot this to Grew.* I think can go in gray code—saves time—I don't
mind if it gets picked up. FDR.[40]

Hull had not been enthusiastic about this approach, but in the
face of Roosevelt's decision, State could argue no longer. The Far Eastern Section examined the draft and made a few corrections. Hull asked
Dr. Stanley K. Hornbeck, his adviser on political relations, to carry
the dossier to the White House and, if possible, bring it to the President's personal attention. This Hornbeck did promptly. Roosevelt
read the draft carefully and approved the changes.[41]

Roosevelt began this historic letter by reminding the Emperor of
"the long period of unbroken peace and friendship" between the
United States and Japan, during which "our respective nations,
through the virtues of their peoples and the wisdom of their rulers
have prospered and have substantially helped humanity."[42] The President spoke of the hope of the American people for an end to the
conflict in China, and for peace in the Pacific, so that the "unbear-
able burdens of armaments could be lifted" from all people. But, he
observed: "During the past few weeks it has become clear to the world
that Japanese military, naval, and air forces have been sent to southern Indo-China in such large numbers as to create a reasonable doubt...
that this continuing concentration in Indo-China is not defensive in
its character." Therefore, the peoples of the Philippines, the East
Indies, Malaya, and Thailand "are asking themselves whether these
forces of Japan are preparing or intending to make attack in one or
more of these many directions." Roosevelt was sure that Hirohito
would understand "why the people of the United States in such large
numbers look askance" at this development. He went on:

It is clear that a continuance of such a situation is unthinkable.

None of the peoples whom I have spoken of above can sit either in-
definitely or permanently on a keg of dynamite.

---

* Joseph C. Grew, U.S. Ambassador to Japan.

There is absolutely no thought on the part of the United States of invading Indo-China if every Japanese soldier or sailor were to be withdrawn therefrom.

The President believed he could secure the same assurance from the other countries concerned, even China. He concluded on a solemn note, as one head of state to another:

I address myself to Your Majesty at this moment in the fervent hope that Your Majesty may, as I am doing, give thought in this definite emergency to ways of dispelling the dark clouds. I am confident that both of us, for the sake of the peoples not only of our own great countries but for the sake of humanity in neighboring territories, have a sacred duty to restore traditional amity and prevent further death and destruction in the world.[43]

Having seen to the dispatch of his message, Roosevelt retired to the office of his personal physician, RADM Ross T. McIntire, for one of the daily, painful treatments necessitated by a chronic sinus condition,[44] treatments in which his wife had little faith.[45]

Meanwhile, at the War Department Stimson realized by now that he could not get away for even a short weekend. He telephoned his wife, who promised to catch a train for Washington. It was well after 1300 when he took off for his local residence, Woodley, and ate a brief, belated lunch. A believer in physical fitness, he then "took a horseback ride, for I thought it might be the last one I would get for some time."[46]

Over at the Navy Department, Safford, too, called it a day. This thin, intense man had not left the office before 2200 for the past two weeks. Now, exhausted from overwork and insomnia and fearing a physical breakdown, he decided to leave at the usual Saturday closing time. Lt. Cmdr. George W. Linn, "the most experienced and most proficient cryptanalyst on the Purple watch list," came on duty at 1600 and began reworking the available portions of Japan's fourteen-part message. "There had been a mistake in the key which was set up on the machine," Safford explained. So Linn decided to find and correct the mistake "rather than clear the garble by guess and maybe make mistakes." This process, Safford knew, "would take quite a little bit of time and we simply had to throw away all the work that had been done before." At 1630 Safford checked the work and said, "There is nothing I can do but get in your way and make you nervous. I am going home."[47]

The sun set at 1646, taking with it some of the day's mildness. Newspaper readers turning to the editorial page of the Washington *Evening Star* could peruse an article by the well-known columnist Constantine Brown, headed: ALLIED FLEETS ON TWENTY-FOUR-HOUR WATCH TO MEET SURPRISE JAPANESE ATTACK IN FAR EAST.

Reports stated that the Japanese had "increased their air and submarine force in the mandated islands." Brown noted unconfirmed rumors that the Imperial Navy was "expecting assistance from abroad soon." He thought the Japanese might attempt a surprise attack against the Netherlands Indies. But whatever their next move, Brown added, there is "no doubt in the minds of military and naval strategists in Washington that the Japanese are working in closest possible cooperation with the Germans."

Then Brown underscored an idea that had haunted political and military leaders since the Nazi invasion of the Soviet Union:

> Under the circumstances military experts in Washington do not rule out the possibility of a Japanese attack against Siberia at this time.... Hence, the possibility must always be considered that the Japanese, while marking the bulk of their forces apparently for an attack against Thailand and Singapore, will make a surprise assault against the maritime provinces.[48]

Thus with the setting of the sun, estimates of Japanese intentions had come full circle: They were preparing to strike somewhere in Southeast Asia—and just possibly against Siberia.

CHAPTER 2

"Just Another Saturday"

Thousands of miles away, Saturday December 6 started at the Naval Air Station on Ford Island in Pearl Harbor with a full-scale sabotage alert at the unpleasant hour of 0200. This drill came as a result of a meeting that RADM Claude C. Bloch, commandant of the Fourteenth Naval District, had called on Thursday afternoon in his headquarters to discuss the possibility of sabotage by the local Japanese—a subject never far below the surface of Army and Navy consciousness in Hawaii. Among those attending was Capt. James M. Shoemaker, Ford Island's hearty, extroverted station commander, who decided to test his men with "a simulated surprise sabotage attack early Saturday morning." Accordingly, about 200 of his personnel participated in a very successful, smooth drill. Satisfied that any attempt at fifth column work would meet with a warm reception, Shoemaker released his men to return to the beds from which he had dragged them so abruptly.[1]

While Ford Island was thus demonstrating its readiness to counter danger from within, the most formidable carrier task force ever assembled to date was bearing down on Oahu from the north and slightly to the west, under the command of VADM Chuichi Nagumo aboard his flagship, the carrier *Akagi*. At 0530 the task force received Combined Fleet Telegram No. 775 from commander in chief of the Combined Fleet, Admiral Isoroku Yamamoto:

On 3 December I was received in audience by His Majesty and received an Imperial rescript which will be sent separately. Respect-

15

fully I relate it to you. In the audience I replied as follows: "I deeply appreciate being honored with the Imperial rescript prior to the beginning of the war. I have the honor to tell Your Majesty that every man of the Combined Fleet will, with the Imperial order in his mind, do his utmost to accomplish the aim of waging the war at any cost and justify Your Majesty's trust in them.

As Yamamoto had promised, the imperial rescript followed by Telegram No. 779:

With the declaration of war, I entrust you with command of the Combined Fleet. The responsibility entrusted to the Combined Fleet is indeed very important, as the rise and fall of the Empire depends upon it. You are trusted to demonstrate the strength of the long-trained fleet throughout the world, by destroying the enemy forces.[2]

Whereupon the diarist of the Third Battleship Division recorded: "Deeply appreciating the warm Imperial Rescript, all officers and men firmly determined to fulfill the responsibility trusted to them by the Emperor, by destroying the U.S. Pacific Fleet with utmost efforts."[3]

An hour later, the task force commenced the last of the refuelings that had made possible the long voyage from Hitokappu Bay in the Kuriles. The wind had dropped[4] and the sea was not particularly rough. Knowing this to be a period of extreme vulnerability, Cmdr. Mitsuo Fuchida, the dynamic veteran flier who would lead Nagumo's airmen into battle, watched the operation anxiously. He wore his flying togs in preparation for any emergency.

All of his pilots were similarly prepared, especially the fighter pilots who would take off from the carriers first, in the event a U.S. warship or plane appeared. But no Americans approached.[5] In fact, the U.S. Navy's dawn patrol out of Oahu had flown off southward, almost 180° in the opposite direction from the task force.[6] By 0830, the First Supply Group of four tankers, with its escort destroyer *Kasumi,* left the task force and headed northward for a rendezvous point. As they did so, the tanker *Shinkoku Maru* hoisted the signal: "Hope for your success."[7]

While Nagumo's armada was thus engaged, the island of Oahu stirred itself and began what promised to be another agreeable Saturday. There would be time for some early Christmas shopping before the big football game between the University of Hawaii and Willamette from Oregon that afternoon in the Honolulu stadium. True, headlines in the morning newspaper, the Honolulu *Advertiser,* were ominous, and the articles beneath them were no less so. A front-page story headlined AMERICA EXPECTED TO REJECT JAPAN'S REPLY ON INDO-CHINA quoted Domei: "...peace in the Far East is hanging by a very thin thread." On page six, an article headed JAPANESE NAVY MOVING SOUTH asserted that the Australian cabinet had "abandoned its weekend adjournment plans due to late advices seeming to indicate an immediate break in Japanese-American relations."[8] But it all seemed rather remote in this gracious land where, in the words of a young Army officer, Capt. Robert H. Dunlop, Jr., who loved Hawaii, "Today was like yesterday, and yesterday was like tomorrow."[9]

Weekend or not, there was considerable activity aboard the ships of the U.S. Pacific Fleet, much of it routine. At 0630, just as the Japanese tankers commenced fueling the combat ships, the destroyer *Ward* got under way to relieve the *Chew* of duty patrolling the Defensive Sea Area, which the *Ward* did at 0721.[10] Her 35-year-old skipper, Lt. William W. Outerbridge, had taken over this, his first command, the previous day.[11]

While the *Ward* was under way, the destroyer *Monaghan,* back from Maui Range, entered Pearl Harbor, her captain, Lt. Cmdr. William P. Burford, at the conn. At 0712 the *Monaghan* moored starboard side to the *Dale* in nest with Destroyer Division Two—the others being the *Aylwin* and *Farragut.* At 0830 the *Monaghan* "assumed Ready Duty in readiness to get under way on one hour's notice."[12] This assignment would keep Burford aboard the ship all day. Accordingly, his wife, "Soldier," would pick him up about 0800 on Sunday.[13]

The tanker *Neosho,* loaded with fuel, reached Pearl Harbor from San Pedro, and at 0653 a harbor pilot took the conn, guiding her to moorings off Hickam Field, home of the Hawaiian Air Force's bombers, where at 0920 the tanker "commenced discharging aviation gasoline."[14]

Ens. W. R. Maier left the seaplane tender *Tangier* with forty-two men "comprising a camping party to proceed to Camp Andrews at Nanakuli" on temporary duty.[15] Aboard the auxiliary *Argonne,* flagship of RADM William L. Calhoun's Base Force, four men reenlisted for 4-year hitches,[16] while four chiefs assigned to the seaplane tender *Curtiss* became temporary lieutenants.[17]

The tender *Dobbin* tested the general alarm at 0800 and more prosaically took on board 20 gallons of ice cream.[18] Another nest of destroyers northward of the *Dobbin*'s group included the *Ralph Talbot,* which,

like a number of the ships in Pearl Harbor, had returned from maneuvers at sea the previous day. As she moved past Hickam Field,
Cleveland Davis, a chief fire control technician, paused in his task of
checking buoys to observe to Lt. R. A. Newton, "I think Pearl is very
vulnerable, and a sneak attack could be very devastating," to which
Newton agreed. Davis had no specific reason for his remark; it was
"only an impression" that came into his head. Yet Saturday was "nothing out of the ordinary," although this veteran of 14 years' service
had duty all that day.[19]

Lt. Cmdr. J. M. Lane, skipper of the destroyer *Hulbert*, at 0930
held "Captain's inspection of personnel, living compartments, and upper decks." Then he "addressed the crew on the necessity of instant
and efficient readiness for war in view of the international situation."[20]

Another officer who sensed the possibility of imminent danger was
RADM Milo F. Draemel, commander of Destroyers, Battle Fleet.
His flagship, the light cruiser *Detroit*, had returned Friday December 5 from Fleet exercises. While Draemel could give no reason for
his fears, he later insisted emphatically that he expected the Japanese to attack on December 6. Therefore, he stayed aboard the *Detroit* until that evening.[21]

Lt. Comdr. Herald F. Stout had no such premonition, but he kept
the crew of his destroyer-minelayer *Breese* busy most of the morning
with emergency battle drills. About 20 percent of his crew of 150
were recent recruits, and he wanted them to be ready to meet any
emergency.[22]

The light cruiser *St. Louis* welcomed RADM H. Fairfax Leary,
commander of Cruisers, Battle Force, who chaired a critique of the
recently completed maneuvers at sea. The skipper of the *St. Louis*,
Capt. George A. Rood, believed that the cruisers were "in a good
state of readiness." Being tired from the exercises, Rood stayed aboard
ship all day. He had no temptation to go ashore, for he had left his
family on the mainland. "If war came, Hawaii was no place for a
family."[23]

An Annapolis classmate of Draemel was RADM Isaac Campbell
Kidd, the First Battleship Division commander.[24] At 1010 Kidd came
aboard the repair ship *Vestal* for a 15-minute official call.[25] Although
mainly intended to repair cruisers, the *Vestal* also could serve destroyers and battleships such as the *Arizona*, Kidd's flagship, which
was moored beside the *Vestal* pending repairs. Shortly after Kidd's

formal call, the *Vestal's* captain, Cmdr. Cassin B. "Ted" Young, boarded the *Arizona* to talk further with Kidd and with the *Arizona's* skipper, Capt. Franklin Van Valkenburg. While he did so, Ens. B. C. Hesser of the *Vestal* discussed with the battleship's chief engineer the nature and extent of the work to be done.[26]

Seaman 1st Class William D. Osborne, a fire control striker whose job was "cleaning, maintaining and holding morning checks in Main Battery Director number two which was situated on Main Mast aft just below the machine gun tub," remembered December 6 as "just another day in port" with everything "peaceful and serene."

When Osborne joined the *Arizona* almost exactly one year before at Bremerton Navy Yard, Washington, on his first enlistment, his initial impression of the battleship, which was in drydock, "wasn't any too good....It reminded me of a great Metal Monster." When she returned to normal, he revised his opinion. "The ship was exceptionally clean, and as the saying goes a person could eat off the deck....I was real proud to be a member of its crew."[27]

Equally fond of the great battleship was Marine Maj. Allan Shapley. He had been promoted to major only a day or so before and was on orders to return to the mainland. Despite the step up the ladder, he would be sorry to leave the *Arizona*—"the best home in the world."[28]

A flurry of activity took place aboard the battleship *Maryland* as Capt. Mervyn Bennion of the *West Virginia* and other members of an inspecting party came aboard at 0917. The Annual Military Inspection began at 0930, and Bennion departed 2 hours later. This did not signal the end of the inspection, however, for it was scheduled to continue the next week.[29]

Preinspection preparations also highlighted the day for many aboard the *Oklahoma*, so that the battleship would be ready for the admiral's inspection on Monday December 8.[30] The *Oklahoma* bustled with activity as her crew rigged awnings and otherwise policed the ship. To 1st Class Boatswain's Mate Howard C. French, December 6 was "just another Saturday aboard ship." He had no duty that day, but decided not to go ashore. He liked the battleship and had served aboard her for 9 years, turning down many opportunities for transfer.[31]

Many of her crew shared this view, among them Gunner's Mate 2d Class Edgar B. Beck. He had served since 1936 aboard the *Oklahoma*, "a clean, happy ship with a lot of spirit and rated high in athletics and gunnery....The ship had a high quota of advancement among enlisted personnel." As a plus, Beck liked duty in Hawaii. He was learning to fly and spent all he could afford taking lessons at Rogers Field—"just a little L-shaped cow pasture at the time."

When the *Oklahoma* left San Francisco for Pearl Harbor earlier in the autumn, Beck's bride of four days asked him not to go; she "had a premonition that something bad was going to happen." But it would have taken something more concrete than a wifely hunch to separate Beck from the ship where he had spent some of the happiest days of his life. Beck was not insensitive to atmosphere, however, and it seemed to him that in the first week of December "there was a lot of tension around Pearl. No one seemed to discuss it very much, but it was there hanging in the air." Nevertheless, for Beck, too, December 6 was "just another Saturday."[32]

No one in the U.S. Pacific Fleet was more dedicated, more hardworking, than its commander in chief, Admiral Kimmel. By 0800 he and his staff were at Fleet Headquarters, located at the submarine base. There he had scheduled an off-the-record interview with Joseph C. Harsch, a well-known correspondent of the *Christian Science Monitor*. Harsch had been in Europe reporting on the war in the West and was now on his way to the Soviet Union. He asked Kimmel the natural question: "Is there going to be a war in the Pacific?"

Kimmel replied in the negative. Unable to capture Moscow, the Germans had settled into winter quarters on that front. With the Soviet Union still undefeated, a Japanese attack would risk a two-front war. Kimmel added that if the Russian capital had fallen, the Japanese might well have launched an offensive. All this sounded reasonable enough to the reporter.[33]

With Harsch's departure, Kimmel turned his attention to the normal order of business, including the usual morning briefing by his efficient Intelligence officer, Lt. Cmdr. Edwin T. Layton. While Kimmel did not expect the Japanese to attack eastward into his own area of responsibility, obviously they were preparing to strike in Southeast Asia. As Layton said,

> ...we saw this movement growing; we had reports from shore observers in China, assistant naval attachés, merchant skippers, consular authorities, that they had seen these ships loading and going out, that they had been sighted going south, the merchant marine ships stating that they were going south in a convoy, and the entire movement was noted as going south.[34]

Furthermore, around 0800 Layton had received the Asiatic Fleet's report concerning its sighting of Japanese movements in that direction. So Layton considered the situation serious. Kimmel directed him to take the message to VADM William S. Pye for his comments.[35] Pye's opinion was worth having. In addition to being Commander, Battle Force, he would move up to command the Fleet if anything untoward happened to Kimmel. "The quiet, thinking type," Pye was "as bright as all hell."[36] Kimmel's chief of staff, Capt. William Ward "Poco" Smith, considered Pye "perhaps the best tactics man the Navy ever had. He spent his life at it. In fleet maneuvers at sea he could outmaneuver anyone. He always thought in terms of battleships and planned for a war in the Pacific according to the Battle of Jutland."[37]

Layton hurried to Pye's flagship, the *California*, moored in Battleship Row on the eastern side of Ford Island. There he found Pye with his able chief of staff, Capt. Harold C. Train. Both officers read the message thoughtfully.[38] Thereupon "a complete and free discussion took place as to what all this meant, not only this message but others they had seen and discussed."[39]

"What do you think of the Japanese move south?" Pye asked.

"The problem is whether the Japanese will leave their flank open or whether they will take us out on their way south," Layton replied. By "us" he meant the Philippines.

"Do you think they will leave their flank open?" Pye inquired.

"They never have," answered Layton briefly. Such was the history of Japanese military operations.

After further discussion, Pye summed up: "The Japanese will not go to war with the United States. We are too big, too powerful and too strong." He turned to Train. "Harold, do you agree?"

"Emphatically!" Train answered.

With that, Pye handed the message back to Layton. "Please thank Admiral Kimmel for this information," he requested in dismissal.[40]

Meanwhile, Kimmel and Smith, with the Fleet's operations officer, Capt. Walter S. DeLany, and the war plans officer, Capt. Charles E. "Soc" McMorris, reviewed messages and talked over the current situation. They reviewed Kimmel's memorandum, "Steps to be Taken in Case of American-Japanese War Within the Next Twenty-four Hours," and brought it up to date. This was not a war plan, merely a checklist to remind the admiral and his staff of what should be done if war broke out.[41]

The immediate problem was whether to keep most of the units

currently in Pearl Harbor, especially the battleships, in position or send them to sea. Obviously, as long as the Fleet remained at its moorings, the Japanese could pinpoint its location. Nonetheless, for a number of reasons, notably the absence of carrier cover, Kimmel decided against a sortie.[42] None of the Pacific Fleet's three carriers was available. The *Saratoga* was on the West Coast undergoing repairs and overhaul.[43] The *Enterprise*, with three heavy cruisers and nine destroyers, was headed back toward Oahu from Wake Island, while the *Lexington*, with an escort of three heavy cruisers and five destroyers, was on course for Midway.[44] In Kimmel's judgment, to send the battleships to sea "without air cover for any prolonged period would have been a dangerous course." In Pearl Harbor they would have the protection of the Army's antiaircraft defenses.[45]

During this conference, Layton appeared with a brief summary of his talk with Pye and Train.[46] He also reported, either then or shortly thereafter, "that they were burning papers outside of the Japanese consulate." But such reports had come to Kimmel several times during 1941, and there was nothing to indicate that this day's action was of particular significance.[47]

This was not the opinion of Lt. Col. George W. Bicknell, assistant G-2 of the Hawaiian Department. He had received word at about 1700 on Friday December 5 that the consulate had begun burning papers and so reported at the Hawaiian Department's staff meeting, which convened on December 6 at 0800. Bicknell thought this was "a most interesting fact," and told his colleagues "that it was very significant in view of the present situation."[48]

Lt. Gen. Walter C. Short, commanding general of the Hawaiian Department, did not attend this staff meeting, where his chief of staff, Col. Walter C. Phillips, presided. Short later recalled that his G-2, Lt. Col. Kendall J. "Wooch" Fielder, passed this information along to him but "apparently did not consider it a matter of importance."[49]

While these high-level staff meetings were in progress, at 1130 Nagumo's task force headed south toward Oahu, increasing its speed to 20 knots. Ten minutes later, the *Akagi* signaled a message from Yamamoto virtually identical to that which Admiral Heihachiro Togo had given before the historic Battle of Tsushima in the Russo-Japanese War: "The rise and fall of the Empire depends upon this battle. Every man is expected to do his utmost."[50]

The diarist of the Third Battleship Division recorded the emotions of the enthusiastic officers and crew:

This signal flag of "Z" reminds us of the signal flag of "Z" which was hoisted in the sea battle of the Japan Sea thirty-eight years before. Nothing more contents us, as sailors, than to look at the same signal hoisted up when we are about to meet the enemy Pacific Fleet on the Pacific Ocean. There is none who does not make up his mind to accomplish the great deed comparable to those accomplished by his ancestors, thereby making the Empire everlasting.[51]

Thoughts of attack from within rather than without continued to trouble the minds of many on Oahu. Kaneohe Naval Air Station's commanding officer, Comdr. Harold M. "Beauty" Martin, had been warned the previous day "indirectly that the possibilities of sabotage were unusually imminent." So on this Saturday morning at personnel inspection he addressed his men "on the possibilities of this particular danger." He emphasized the standing orders, "mostly with a view of keeping the people in the alert status that they had been for some time."[52]

Martin was a popular, respected commander. "He was known to be strict but fair." Aviationist Machinist Mate 1st Class Walter J. Curylo remembered after more than 20 years, "His eyes seemed to be smiling all the time."[53]

Aviation Machinist 3d Class Guy C. Avery considered Martin "the finest Naval officer I have ever known." He was "genuinely concerned with the welfare of even the lowest rated men under his command." Avery was standing directly in front of Martin and thought that his commander looked "intensely nervous" as he spoke words which Avery never forgot: "Men, I have called you together here this morning to tell you to keep your eyes and ears open and be on the alert every moment. You are probably the nearest into war that you will ever be without actually being in it."[54]

After Martin had dismissed the men, "a very heated discussion broke out." In talking over Martin's warning, a seaman named Morris "belittled the intellectual and technical abilities of the Japanese, asserting that if they were so reckless as to attack the U.S. they could not possibly survive longer than two weeks." Avery tried to convince Morris and his supporters "that their judgment was beclouded by wishful thinking." He argued "that any nation with enough ability to design and build a war machine could also employ it intelligently." But Morris proved the better debater and made Avery "appear ridiculous," much to the amusement of their shipmates, all of whom, apparently, agreed with Morris's views.[55]

Across the island at Hickam Field, its commanding officer, Col. William F. Farthing, called a meeting in his office on the subject of security. Among those attending was Capt. Brooke E. Allen, in acting command of a squadron of bombers. "By this time security against sabotage was almost an obsession," he said later.[56]

Nevertheless, Allen had a few words on the general subject of preparedness for a group of lieutenants he rounded up later in the morning. These young men were working with the B-18 bomber, which flew at about 120 knots and carried only two .30 caliber machine guns—one in the nose, one in the belly. These fliers had never used a real bomb. In fact, they had been practicing against the target ship *Utah* with sheet metal and water missiles.

With conviction, Allen exhorted, "You guys should think of yourselves as captains and be prepared to accept the duties and responsibilities of captains."

"Good heavens, a *captain!*" thought 2d Lt. Vernon H. Reeves blankly. In those days of slow promotion, a captaincy was "a far-off dream" for a second lieutenant.

After Allen released them, the pilots crowded around the bulletin board, where they scanned a notice announcing that henceforth no more than 50 percent of any organization might be absent from the post at any one time. That would put a crimp in weekend leaves.[57]

At Schofield Barracks, Maj. Gen. Maxwell Murray, in command of the Twenty-fifth Infantry Division, had taken measures a few days before just in case of combat rather than sabotage. He "never dreamed that there was a possibility of carriers." He thought that there might be a surprise raid by what, in disregard of naval terminology, he called "boat." To avoid possible slaughter from Japanese bombs dropping into the magazine area while hundreds of men were drawing ammunition, Murray "violated the usual regulations regarding ammunition by moving all infantry ammunition except high explosives into the company barracks." Thus on this Saturday morning his men had available "as much as 30 rounds of ammunition in the belts...ready for immediate action."[58]

But in the opinion of Pvt. Philippe A. Michaud of the 515th Signal Aircraft Warning Regiment, Schofield was "more like a campus or a training base" than an offensive or defensive military installation. Maneuvers were held periodically, but these were "Civil War type skirmishes back in the cane fields; the posts were defended against saboteurs (never against an enemy soldier, or air attack somehow) by men who had never fired a gun." Michaud's impression was that Schofield reacted to alerts "by having more surprise inspections of the footlockers, and cutting the grass a little closer."[59]

Schofield was fine as far as housing was concerned—"very well kept, picturesque, and spotless." To Michaud, however, it appeared that the installation lacked "a real military mission. It was as though the troops there were training for a war that was going to take place somewhere else." Undue emphasis was placed "on sports competition between outfits." Michaud had transferred from Hickam, where

> ...the competitive emphasis was more on gunnery and bombing. At Schofield, baseball, football, boxing, basketball, all the sports were pursued with a vengeance....Anyone with athletic ability and who really wanted to be a soldier did not stand a chance. He would be drafted and forced into a rigorous sports training schedule, and be excused from other duties.[60]

Michaud's actual duty post was as an operator of early-warning radar, the model SCR-270, "a mobile set with maximum range of 150 miles," located at Kaaawa, on the northern tip of Oahu. The station, 7CU, "was set up on a knoll, with the mountains at our backs, and to our front, the highway, and about 400 yards away, the ocean." Michaud came off duty from the 0400 to 0700 shift. With his colleagues, he spent the "beautiful and pleasant" morning cleaning the equipment and grounds.[61]

Meanwhile, at the opposite end of the island, in downtown Honolulu, Takeo Yoshikawa was at work early in his quarters in the Japanese consulate compound. Yoshikawa, alias Tadashi Morimura, was the spy the Japanese Navy had planted in the consulate, where he held the titular post of chancellor. Over a period of months, Yoshikawa had worked out a routine, and this morning he followed it as usual. After checking the weather with a particular view to flying conditions, he breakfasted and carefully read the Honolulu *Advertiser*. He also glanced hurriedly through the *Hawai Nippo*, but as usual it contained little information of any use to him. Shortly after 0800, he went to his office, where he performed a few routine chores. At around 1000 he set out for Pearl Harbor to fulfill his latest instructions from Tokyo:[62] "Please wire immediately re the latter part of my #123 the movements of the fleet subsequent to the fourth."[63]

The cited message, dated December 2, had requested a daily report on the "warships, airplane carriers, and cruisers" in port, as well as whether or not "observation balloons" had been placed over Pearl Harbor and whether or not the warships had been provided with "antimine nets."[64] Correctly interpreting Tokyo's phraseology as barrage balloons and antitorpedo nets, Yoshikawa had been at work on the problem ever since. About 1300 he brought to the consulate the results of the morning's observations and prepared a draft for the approval of Consul General Nagao Kita, his superior.[65] The message read in part:

> At the present time there are no signs of barrage balloon equipment. In addition, it is difficult to imagine that they have actually any. However, even though they have actually made preparations, because they must control the air over the water and land runways of the airports in the vicinity of Pearl Harbor, Hickam, Ford and Ewa, there are limits to the balloon defense of Pearl Harbor. I imagine that in all probability there is considerable opportunity left to take advantage for a surprise attack against these places.
>
> 2. In my opinion the battleships do not have torpedo nets. The details are not known. I will report the results of my investigation.[66]

Kita approved the dispatch and directed Yoshikawa to encode it and send it off immediately. After Yoshikawa had encoded it, the consular chauffeur, Ichitaro Ozaki, drove him to the commercial telegraph office in Honolulu to send the message.[67]

This was exactly the sort of information that Nagumo needed as his task force plunged toward Oahu and which such a fine American intelligence officer as Layton would have given almost anything he possessed to have seen on Saturday December 6. But when Kimmel released his staff for lunch, Layton had no idea that the local consulate was assuring Tokyo that "a considerable opportunity" existed for "a surprise attack" on Oahu's military installations.

As he joined a group of staff officers awaiting him, Capt. Willard A. Kitts, Jr., the Fleet gunnery officer, sang out, "Well, here comes Layton with his Saturday crisis!"

"What's up?" Several officers put the question with one voice.

"There is a sighting message on the Japanese for the Gulf of Siam," answered Layton. "I have just delivered it to Pye and returned it to Kimmel."

"What do you think of the situation?" inquired Cmdr. Maurice E. "Germany" Curts, Kimmel's communications officer.

"The situation is extremely serious," Layton replied. "I don't know about you gentlemen, but I expect to be in my office tomorrow."

"Come off it, Layton! You said that last Saturday!" grinned a colleague.

"The situation this week is far more serious than last Saturday," countered Layton. With this sobering thought, the group began their lunch.[68]

About this time, Curts's assistant, Lt. (jg) Walter J. East, strolled with Cmdr. Roscoe F. Good past the headquarters building on the way to their own midday meal. East had duty all that day and would be up until 0400 Sunday decoding messages. From their gist so far, he had no doubt that war was coming, "but we thought if it came to Pearl it would be a sub attack."[69] Good was assistant operations officer under DeLany and was highly respected among his peers. "A little Scottie" of a man, "full of ideas and initiative"—thus Layton characterized him.[70] Cmdr. Arthur C. Davis, Kimmel's aviation officer, termed Good "as near as possible to being the perfect naval officer."[71]

As was natural with two such dedicated men, their eyes strayed irresistibly to Battleship Row, with its double-moored vessels sparkling with fresh paint and polished brasswork. "What a beautiful target that would make!" remarked Good.[72]

CHAPTER 3

"An Air of Tenseness"

Roosevelt was already in his place at the hospitable White House dinner table when at 2000 his thirty-two guests filed in. It was a mixed group ranging from VADM Sir Wilfred and Lady French, in the United States on business, to two young White House aides. The wife of Assistant Secretary of State Breckenridge Long sat at the President's right, Lady French at his left. Farther down the table were the President's son and daughter-in-law, Capt. and Mrs. James Roosevelt, and an old friend, Mrs. Charles S. Hamlin. To the latter, the President "looked very worn... and after the meat course he was excused and wheeled away. He had an unusually stern expression."[1]

Ferdinand Mayer took Special Envoy Kurusu to dine with him at the home of F. Lammot Belin, a former ambassador to Poland. As Mayer later recalled, they had scarcely seated themselves at table when Kurusu received a telephone call advising that Roosevelt "had sent a personal message to Emperor Hirohito, hoping that a peaceful solution could be found." A long-time diplomat himself, Kurusu recognized that "this was a very clever move on the part of the Government; that the Emperor could hardly say 'no', nor could he say 'yes', and that this would cause many headaches in Tokyo and give much food for thought."[2]

Kurusu also repeated for the benefit of Belin, whom he had never met before, almost everything he had said to Mayer that morning, with a frankness that "astonished Mr. Belin beyond measure." They agreed that the only way to swing Japanese-American relations rightabout would be for Japan to renounce the Tripartite Pact. Again Kurusu agreed in principle, but he knew that this would be exceedingly difficult. He and

28

others "realized perfectly that Germany was trying to make of Japan an Italy in the Pacific, and...he hoped and prayed that they would not be successful. He had no illusions that, in the event of a German victory, the Germans would take the Netherlands East Indies for themselves and give nothing to Japan." Kurusu spent 4 hours with Mayer and Belin, although he had ordered his car for 2200, and the chauffeur sent in a reminder that the Embassy expected him back.[3]

Masuo Kato of Domei dined at a Chinese restaurant near Union Station with Ichitaro Takata of the Osaka *Mainichi*, along with Kato's assistant, Clark Kawakami, and the latter's wife. In effect, this was a farewell party for Mrs. Kawakami. Her husband was an American citizen, but she was not, and she planned to return to Japan on the *Tatsuta Maru*. On their way home from the restaurant, they discussed what they would do if war came and they were interned. "I may write a book," said Kato. Takata promised to teach Kato to play the difficult Japanese game of *go*. "I'll send you plenty of whisky," pledged Kawakami, laughing.

Kato accepted Kawakami's invitation to visit him at his home the next day, and his friends parted with him at the National Press Building. There an International News Service (INS) reporter asked him if he knew that "the President had sent a message to the Emperor appealing for peace." Kato thought the American was joking, but a hasty check confirmed that Roosevelt had indeed sent such a message, although the contents had not yet been released. So Kato cabled Domei in Tokyo immediately.[4]

By midnight, the Embassy's decoders had finished the first thirteen parts of Tokyo's fourteen-part message. This accomplished, the Embassy councillor let them go home, leaving a duty officer in charge.[5]

The Americans did much better. By 2030 or 2045 Safford's men had decoded these same messages, the necessary copies had been made, and Kramer had them in folders ready for delivery to the "usual recipients" of Magic messages on the Navy side: Knox; Stark or his flag secretary; Wilkinson; RADM Richmond Kelly Turner, chief of the War Plans Division; the director of the Far Eastern Section of ONI, Cmdr. Arthur H. McCollum; and the White House. Reading the segments thus far received, Kramer gained the distinct impression "that this note was far and appreciably stronger in language than earlier notes had been and that it indicated a strong probability that the Japanese were concluding any further negotiations."[6]

Kramer phoned those on his distribution list, letting them know by a few cautious words that he had something important they should see at once. He could not reach Stark and Turner.[7] Admiral and Mrs. Stark, with his former flag lieutenant, Capt. Harold D. Krick, and Mrs. Krick, had gone to the National Theater, where a revival of *The Student Prince* was playing.[8] Turner was sure he had been home all evening,[9] but his phone did not answer. Kramer's last call was to Wilkinson, explaining in veiled terms what he had in hand that "should be delivered at once" and what deliveries he proposed to make. Wilkinson approved his suggestions, whereupon Kramer made one last call—to his own home, asking his wife to act as chauffeur.[10]

The request did not seem unusual to Mary Kramer, because she knew that official cars were in short supply and she had driven her husband on his rounds several times before. She abandoned the Christmas gifts she had been wrapping on the floor, left the children with the maid, and set off. When Kramer joined her, he had "an air of tenseness about him." And she was surprised when at each stop he asked her to "drive right up to the lighted entrances." Usually they hunted a nearby parking place.[11]

Their first stop was the White House Office Building, where Kramer learned "that the President was entertaining at the moment" and Beardall was at dinner at Wilkinson's home. Kramer told Lieutenant Schulz that he would show the message to Beardall when he reached Wilkinson's home and that probably Beardall would call him then to find out if the President had seen the document. Then Kramer left with Schulz the locked pouch containing the White House copy of the messages.[12]

Beardall having alerted Schulz to this delivery, the lieutenant immediately carried the pouch to the White House, where he sought and received permission to go up to the second floor. "Someone from the usher's office" escorted him to Roosevelt's study, announced him to the President, and withdrew.

Roosevelt was seated at his desk, with his confidant Harry Hopkins "pacing back and forth slowly, not more than 10 feet away." Informing the President that he had the material Kramer had brought, Schulz removed from the pouch the document of about fifteen typewritten pages and handed it directly to Roosevelt. Schulz had not read the material and thus could not judge for himself its content or importance. He could only wait the approximately ten minutes Roosevelt took to read it. When he had finished, the President gave the papers to Hopkins, who also read them silently and then returned them to Roosevelt. "The President then turned toward Mr. Hopkins," Schulz recalled, "and said in substance—I am not sure of the exact words, but in substance—'This means war.'"[13]

Hopkins agreed, and they fell into a brief discussion about the deployment of Japanese forces. Hopkins expressed the opinion "that since war was imminent, the Japanese intended to strike when they were ready, at a moment when all was most opportune for them... when their forces were most properly deployed for their advantage." He made some mention of Indochina, "because the Japanese forces had already landed there and there were implications of where they should move next." Roosevelt remarked that he had sent a message to the Emperor which in effect requested withdrawal of Japanese troops in Indochina.

Hopkins observed "that since war was undoubtedly going to come at the convenience of the Japanese, it was too bad that we could not strike the first blow and prevent any sort of surprise." Roosevelt nodded and answered, to the best of Schulz's recollection, "No, we can't do that. We are a democracy and a peaceful people." Then the President "raised his voice," and Schulz remembered his next words definitely: "But we have a good record." From this Schulz gathered "that we would have to stand on that record, we could not make the first, overt move. We would have to wait until it came."[14]

Roosevelt started to phone Stark, but learning that Stark was at the theater, decided to wait until later, because "he did not want to cause public alarm by having the admiral paged." He could reach Stark "within perhaps another half an hour in any case." Thereupon he returned the document to Schulz, who left the study.[15]

While Roosevelt and Hopkins mulled over this latest intercept, the Kramers drove to Wardman Park on Connecticut Avenue to deliver Knox's copy. Kramer had little to say, but his wife spoke in a soothing murmur "about the children" and her plans for "a decent meal when he got home." Tomorrow would be Sunday, and she hoped that he "could sleep round the clock."

Mrs. Kramer remained in the car, and her husband took the message to the Knox apartment. Mrs. Knox and "a civilian business associate" of Knox's from the Chicago *Daily News* were in the room, so Knox, who was "very security-minded," read the despatch in silence for about 20 minutes. Part of the time Kramer "sat next to him in a corner of the room" and then "engaged in general conversation with the other two people present."[16]

Finishing his perusal, Knox instructed Kramer to be at the State Department the next morning at 1000 when Knox would be meeting with Hull and Stimson.[17] There went Mary Kramer's hope that her husband could sleep late on Sunday.

The time was within a few minutes of 2200 when Kramer emerged from the Knox apartment. The next stop was the Wilkinson home in Arlington, Virginia. Again Mrs. Kramer waited in the car, but within a few minutes Wilkinson came out to the car and brought her in to wait with his guests.[18] The Wilkinsons were giving a small dinner party, the guests including Miles, Beardall, their wives, and two French officers.[19]

Mrs. Kramer thought she must have looked ludicrous in her old sweater and skirt amid "all those beautifully gowned and meticulously groomed people." She and the others sipped coffee and drinks while Wilkinson, Miles, Beardall, and Kramer went into the library.[20]

There they read and discussed the intercept. They agreed that "this was a diplomatic message...that resembled the diplomatic white papers" and that "it was a justification of the Japanese position." On the basis of these thirteen parts, Wilkinson was not sure that the Hull-Nomura conversations would be broken off, and he "did not think diplomatic relations would be broken. It is one thing to break off current negotiations and another thing to break off diplomatic relations." The talks had been broken off before and then resumed.[21]

The reading and discussions in Wilkinson's home kept the men occupied until almost half past midnight, when the Kramers drove to his office. There he returned the documents in his possession to the safe. He remained in his office some 10 or 15 minutes, checking with the watch officer "to see if anything new of interest or importance had come in," including the anticipated fourteenth part. Upon the watch officer's negative reply, Kramer could do no more that day.[22]

By the time he reached home, Kramer was too tired to eat, so he went straight to bed, instructing his wife to wake him if he had a phone call. Mrs. Kramer picked up the bright clutter of Christmas wrappings, checked on the children, and followed her husband to bed.[23]

In the War Department, Bratton had a less complicated schedule than Kramer. The thirteen parts were available to him some time between 2100 and 2200. Bratton's first action was to call the officer on duty at SIS to ask what the chances were of the final, fourteenth part being received later that night.

"No, there is very little likelihood of that part coming in this evening," the officer replied. "We think we have gotten all of that message that we are going to get tonight."[24]

Realizing that the intercept was of primary interest to Hull, Bratton gathered up the secretary's folder, "put it in the pouch, locked the pouch and personally delivered it to the night duty officer in the State Department," telling him that this was "a highly important message as far as the secretary of state was concerned" and that it should be sent to his quarters. The duty officer assured Bratton that he would do this. Bratton obtained a receipt and returned to his own quarters about 2300. He called Miles's home, leaving a request that his chief return the call.[25]

Miles phoned Bratton about half an hour later. Like Bratton, Miles considered that the thirteen parts had "little military significance." His phone call was merely to assure himself "that the full reply would be disseminated the next morning" and that both he and Bratton would be in their offices then.[26]

There appeared to be no reason to deliver the document to Marshall, so he and his wife enjoyed a quiet evening in their quarters at Fort Myer, where they "were leading a rather monastic life."[27] Earlier in the autumn Mrs. Marshall had fallen, breaking four ribs, and had not regained her full strength by the first week of December. So she had spent a few days recuperating with friends in Florida, returning to Fort Myer on this Saturday, December 6.[28]

The Starks and their guests returned from the theater to the admiral's quarters around 2330. Informed that the White House had called, Stark went to the second floor study where his White House phone was located, staying about five or ten minutes.[29] He had no independent recollection of the conversation, but he was certain that if Roosevelt had intimated that the thirteen-part message meant the imminence of war "or anything new, or indicated any action, it would have stirred me into immediate action."[30] When he came back downstairs, he remarked in effect "that conditions with Japan were in a critical state.[31] Krick saw nothing unusual about Stark's "appearance or demeanor" as a result of his call from the White House. The CNO "was very much as he always is, apparently not disturbed."[32]

About the time Stark hung up the phone, General "Hap" Arnold was addressing the commanders and staffs of the 38th and 88th Reconnaissance Squadrons at Hamilton Field in California. In the next hour or so, these men would begin a trans-Pacific flight in their B-17s, their first stop being Hickam Field, their final destination Clarke Field in the Philippines. Arnold reminded the officers that the international situation was grave, with war possible at any moment. Before they completed their trip, "they might run into trouble...and they might have a fight on their hands."[33]

"If we might face a war situation on our trip, why don't we have the bomb sights and machine guns for our aircraft aboard, instead of having them shipped by surface vessel?" asked Maj. Truman H. Landon, in command of the Thirty-eighth Reconnaissance Squadron.

Arnold agreed that this equipment should indeed be aboard the aircraft, and accordingly the bomb sights and machine guns, still in their packing boxes, were loaded aboard the B-17s.[34]

However, not only were the machine guns inoperative, being packed in cosmoline and not bore-sighted, but the aircraft carried no ammunition.[35] The reason for this was, in Arnold's words, "a question of gasoline or ammunition for that long 2400-mile hop.... Somebody had to weigh...the certainty of arriving there by providing sufficient gasoline against the probability of their using their machine guns and not getting there by carrying that extra ammunition." And in warning the fliers, Arnold thought of possible trouble "somewhere on the other side of Hawaii." He "did not visualize the fight in Hawaii or this side of Hawaii."[36] Moreover, skeleton crews of pilot, co-pilot, engineer, navigator, and radio operator manned the planes, and these crews would have been insufficient to fight even if the guns and ammunition had been ready to fire.[37]

Aboard the destroyer *Akigumo*, Chigusa had a rather better idea of what the next day might bring. As executive officer, he considered himself in the light of the ship's "mother"—her father being the skipper. Like a good "mother," Chigusa wanted to do something special for the crew, for he was by no means optimistic that he or any of them would be alive when another full day rolled around. So he asked the men what they would like for lunch. The unanimous choice was *ohagi*—rice paste covered with sweetened bean jelly. Sugar being scarce in Japan and even aboard ship, this dish was a special treat, and Chigusa watched the men dig in, wistfully pleased to see their enjoyment. If the good fortune which so far had blessed the Japanese abandoned them now, this could well be their last lunch.[38]

CHAPTER 4

"A Wonderful Evening"

Honolulu Stadium presented a rollicking, carefree scene early in the afternoon of December 6. More than 24,000 spectators, including high-ranking military personnel, roared their delight as the Bearcats from Willamette University, Oregon, tangled with the Rainbows of the University of Hawaii in the annual Shrine football classic. Pageantry, music, and color packed this pigskin show. With a crack Marine band in the lead, fifteen bands marched on the field in procession shortly after 1300. They played "Hawaii Ponoi," a favorite tune of the islands. Fireworks followed, and "a miniature parachute floated to earth bearing the Hawaiian flag." Then the massed bands blared forth "The Stars and Stripes Forever," more fireworks exploded in showers of sparks, and yet another parachute wafted down, unfurling the American flag.[1]

Among those attending was Col. Robert H. Dunlop, adjutant general of the Hawaiian Department, and his wife Ruth. The game was not the best the Dunlops had ever seen, but they enjoyed it.[2]

For many of the Army and Navy on Oahu, business went on as usual. Shortly before the massed bands began their procession, Admiral Kimmel and some of his officers went to a lunch which was in effect a continuation of the morning's staff meeting. They talked over "the possibilities of this and that in connection with the situation" until about 1400 or 1500, when the admiral dismissed them and went home.[3]

Kimmel's communications officer, "Germany" Curts, stayed in his office all afternoon, keeping a close check on all communications, because he was somewhat apprehensive about conditions in general and the Pacific situation in particular.[4]

In the basement of the old administration building near 1010 Dock, Cmdr. Joseph J. Rochefort and his skilled colleagues at Combat Intelligence Unit "Hypo" were restless, "for we didn't know what was going on. We thought that something might be under way that we did not know about." They "had a big huddle" on Saturday afternoon. Rochefort's interceptors had lost track of six Japanese carriers. This, of course, was the result of the Nagumo force's strict radio silence.[5]

Aboard the *Maryland*, a lieutenant (jg) was suspended from duty for 5 days "for improper performance of duty as Communications Watch Officer," having failed "to deliver a despatch to the Commander, Battleships." But righteousness had to wait upon expediency. He was "restored to duty for the duration of the Annual Military Inspection and Damage Control Practice" scheduled for December 8 and 9.[6]

Beginning at 1400, Commander Burford put his destroyer *Monaghan* through a brief but comprehensive series of drills—fire, collision, fire and rescue.[7]

2d Lt. Grover C. White, Jr., of the Signal Corps, obtained permission from Maj. Kenneth P. Bergquist, the control officer, to operate the Aircraft Warning System (AWS) stations on Sunday morning December 7 from 0400 to 0700 only. The schedule normally ran from 0400 to 1100 on weekdays, the remaining three stations picking up the duty from 1300 to 1600. The Hawaiian Department had prescribed no training on Sundays, so the radar personnel had been doing this on their own. White's request, therefore, was not to cut operating hours—merely to avoid an extra stint. Some of the men were developing eye trouble from the oscilloscope.[8]

At Camp Malakole, an antiaircraft unit, Sergeant of the Guard June D. Dickens stared out to sea at the movements of a Japanese fishing craft. It ventured within 50 yards of shore, and Dickens could see two men swimming toward him. They were not supposed to be in that area, so he unlimbered his .45, walked to the beach, and called out that if they came any closer he would shoot to kill. The Japanese trod water uncertainly and then swam back to their boat. Dickens at once mounted a machine gun and spotted two BAR (Browning automatic rifle) men with loaded guns. He shouted to the Japanese that if they came back, he would open fire. Three or four times the vessel returned into the general area, but it stayed out of range. Dickens was highly suspicious of the local Japanese, and of the Chinese too, for that matter.[9]

Everyone at Kaneohe except duty squads knocked off at 1300. Radioman 3d Class R. R. Moser went downtown and bought Christmas presents, arranging to have them mailed directly from the stores. "Since busses to Kaneohe seemed to run on a semi-annual basis," he returned to the naval air station early.[10]

Fort Kamehameha lifted a sabotage alert that had been in effect since December 3 and went back to "normal peacetime routine." Named for Hawaii's national hero, Fort "Kam" was "smart and sort of a showplace." The installation began at the southernmost end of Hickam Field and could be entered only by passing through the main gate at Hickam and driving the length of the airfield. Fort Kamehameha was part of Pearl Harbor's defenses, protecting it from the east side of the channel while Fort Weaver guarded it from the west.[11]

Pvt. William B. Daniels, a native son of Hawaii, who had been on station since May of 1941, thought it was "probably the most beautiful post on the island of Oahu." It was small enough to have "a homelike atmosphere," but it had most of the amenities of a larger installation— an Army band, a drum and bugle corps, a chapel, post exchange, beer garden, gymnasium, and swimming facilities. Furthermore, Daniels was proud of his unit, the 41st Coast Artillery Battalion, which in competition earlier that year had fired its 8-inch guns to victory for the trophy which Secretary of the Navy Knox awarded for the best score in the entire Coast Artillery Corps.[12]

Fort Kamehameha's training program was good:

> We had instructions on nomenclature and general maintenance of our guns. We fired them about once a month for target practice. We had thorough training and target practice for both .30 and .50 caliber machine guns. We had basic infantry training and took weekly hikes of five miles or more. We had morning calisthenics and daily drill and evening retreat parade about twice a week....In our post emergency plan every man knew his own gun position or assignment to cover....[13]

However, "almost every outfit was undermanned. This meant that when we had a seacoast alert we would be shorthanded on the antiaircraft guns, and when an air alert took place we would concentrate on antiaircraft defense and consequently our seacoast defenses would suffer." On this particular Saturday, Daniels was not worried about either training or shortages. Armed with a pass and looking forward to "a nice restful day on Sunday," he went to Honolulu and spent a few hours with some of his hometown buddies.[14]

A few of the men from the radar station at Kaaawa, including Michaud, went to the nearest town, Kaneohe. There Michaud "got a haircut from a Japanese lady barber," mailed Christmas cards to the mainland, and bought a few trinkets to send to his nieces and nephews.[15]

1st Lt. Charles W. Davis, adjutant of the Second Battalion of the 27th Infantry Regiment, officiated at a football game between two service teams at Schofield Barracks. After the game, he passed the rest of the afternoon with his wife, Joan, who was seven months pregnant with their first child. Then he returned to his duty post, an unorthodox location under the stadium at Roosevelt High School. His battalion's job was to guard Honolulu's vital installations, such as the waterworks, electrical substations, and telephone system.[16]

Another officer who had been officiating at Schofield was Capt. James W. Chapman of Headquarters Squadron. As he and his wife reached a point in the road that gave a fine panorama of Pearl Harbor and its ships, Mrs. Chapman remarked, "If the Japs really are going to attack Hawaii, this would be the ideal time, for there sits the entire Pacific Fleet at anchor." The Chapmans talked over the possibility, which was much on their minds. The captain "had no doubt that we would eventually be subjected to an aerial attack, but did not expect it for 7 December."[17]

The various football games were in full swing when, at about 1400, the FBI in Honolulu finished translating the transcript of a long telephone conversation held on December 5 between a Tokyo newsman, who originated the call, and Mrs. Motokazu Mori, wife of a Honolulu dentist.

After the opening courtesies, the newsman said, "I received your telegram and was able to grasp the essential points. I would like to have your impressions on the conditions you are observing at present. Are airplanes flying daily?"

"Yes," replied Mrs. Mori, "lots of them fly around...."

"Are they large planes?"

"Yes, they are quite big."

"Are they flying from morning till night?"

"Well, not to that extent, but last week they were quite active in the air."

The newsman inquired, "I hear there are many sailors there, is that right?"

"There aren't so many now," Mrs. Mori answered. "There were more in the beginning part of this year and the ending part of last year...."

"Are any Japanese people there holding meetings to discuss U.S.-Japanese negotiations being conducted presently?" the reporter continued.

"No, not particularly," Mrs. Mori rejoined. "The minds of the Japanese here appear calmer than expected. They are getting along harmoniously." She assured him that the American community did not "look with suspicion on the Japanese," adding, "We are not hated or despised. The soldiers here and we get along very well. All races are living in harmony." She also informed her listener that "the current tense situation" had brought about "nothing which stands out" except that Honolulu was "enjoying a war building boom."[18]

"Do they put searchlights on when planes fly about at night?" he asked. Upon her "No," the journalist switched subjects. After a number of questions and answers about the current U.S.-Japanese political situation, he inquired, "Do you know anything about the United States fleet?"

"No, I don't know anything about the fleet," returned Mrs. Mori. "Since we try to avoid talking about such matters, we do not know much about the fleet. At any rate, the fleet here seems small. I don't [know if] all of the fleet has done this, but it seems that the fleet has left here."

"Is that so? What kind of flowers are in bloom in Hawaii at present?"

"Presently, the flowers in bloom are fewest out of the whole year. However, the hibiscus and the poinsettia are in bloom now...."[19]

At this point, the conversation became "badly mixed up with static."[20] A few more exchanges followed—the local sale and brewing of sake, the number of first- and second-generation Japanese in Hawaii, and the drafting of some of the latter into the U.S. Army—then the newsman closed with "Best regards to your wife," not realizing that he had been talking with Mrs. Mori instead of her husband.[21]

When Robert L. Shivers, the FBI's special agent in charge at Honolulu, read the transcript, he was fairly sure that the conversation "appeared to have some hidden meaning" because the topics under discussion "would not ordinarily warrant the expense incurred" in an 18-minute Tokyo-to-Honolulu telephone call. Therefore, he phoned the two Intelligence officers with whom he worked most closely: the Fourteenth Naval District's Intelligence officer, Capt. Irving Mayfield, and Colonel Bicknell.[22]

Mayfield was not in his office in the Alexander Young Hotel, so Shivers talked with Lt. Denzell Carr, one of ONI's Japanese experts, gave him the main points of the Mori call, and asked him to contact Mayfield. When the latter received the information, "he was sure there was some hidden message which would be of value if they could only decode it, but that there was nothing in the message in line with previous information indicating Japanese movements."[23]

At about 1800 Mayfield telephoned Layton, asking if he would be in his office the next day. When Layton said that he expected to be there, Mayfield requested him to stop by his office on the way. Layton wanted to know if he could do anything, to which Mayfield replied, "No, there is nothing you can do here because I haven't got the material, and I won't have it until tomorrow morning, but I would like to have you stop in here because I have something that I want your opinion on."

Of course, when Sunday morning rolled around, Layton and Mayfield were otherwise occupied. Layton heard nothing further about the Mori call until he appeared before the Navy Court of Inquiry on September 9, 1944.[24]

Bicknell had left the Federal Building where he, like Shivers, had his office, at around noon, and Shivers could not reach him until about 1700. "George, I've got something awfully important here. You'd better hurry down." Bicknell hastily drove downtown from his home in Aiea. "What do you make of it?" Shivers asked, handing him the Mori transcript.[25]

Bicknell did not like the look of it. For one thing, Dr. Mori "was already on our suspect list" and had been "ever since we had a list."[26] And "why should any newspaper spend this much money on the blooming of the flowers in Hawaii?" So Bicknell promptly phoned his immediate superior, Fielder.

"Wooch, I have something very important here and I'd like to show it to the general."

"Well, you can't do it tonight," responded Fielder, "because he is going to a party out at Schofield."

"You tell him I have something very important!" snapped Bicknell, his sense of duty overcoming protocol. "Never mind the party at Schofield! You call him and see what he says about it and call me back."

Within three minutes, Fielder returned the call: "The general will give you ten minutes to get out here." This did not give Bicknell much time to drive from downtown Honolulu to Fort Shafter, so he hurried off immediately. He reached Fielder's residence, which was next door to Short's, at around 1900. He noticed that Mrs. Short and Mrs. Fielder were already seated in the general's car, "champing at the bit, waiting to go to the party."[27]

Fielder read the transcript and then said, "...we had better go over and see General Short." Sitting on Short's porch, the three men discussed the document. They agreed that it was "very suspicious, very fishy," but they "couldn't make heads nor tails of it."[28] However, Bicknell averred "that he knew Mori, that he suspected Mori and for that reason he was rather positive that it meant something."[29]

"I think this is a pretty good picture of what is going on in Hawaii today," said Short. That, thought Bicknell, "was just the trouble with it; it was too accurate a picture." The very things he "considered most suspicious seemed to be everyday affairs" in the minds of his two superiors.[30] He had the impression that they thought him "rather perhaps too 'intelligence-conscious,' and that this message was quite, quite [sic] in order, that it did describe the situation in Hawaii as it was, and that possibly there was nothing very much to get excited about."[31]

Feeling somewhat frustrated, Bicknell took the document to his office, where he studied it for about an hour. Then he locked it in his safe and returned home to dinner.[32]

While Shivers and his service colleagues mulled over the Mori telephone call, Yoshikawa set out around 1500 for what was to be his last scouting of the U.S. Pacific Fleet. He took a taxi to Aiea, where he had a good overall view of Kimmel's ships, and then he drove down to the Pearl City pier. After a careful check, he returned to his office to work up his findings into a report. Once again Kita approved his draft. Yoshikawa personally processed it and took it to the commercial telegraph office for dispatch at 1801:[33]

1. On the evening of the 5th, among the battleships which entered port were *Wyoming* and one submarine tender. The following ships were observed at anchor on the 6th:

9 battleships, 3 light cruisers, 3 submarine tenders, 17 destroyers, and in addition there were 4 light cruisers, 2 destroyers, lying at docks (the heavy cruisers and airplane carriers have all left).

2. It appears that no air reconnaissance is being conducted by the fleet air arm.[34]

There were several mistakes in this message, but Yoshikawa reported accurately on the essentials: the number of battleships present, the absence of carriers, and the lack of aerial reconnaissance. Well satisfied with his work, he decided to spend the rest of the day relaxing in his quarters. Meanwhile, a pit in the yard blazed merrily with the contents of a wheelbarrow full of papers and other material from the code room. This was the only time the sharp-eyed consulate chauffeur, Ozaki, ever saw any material taken from the code room. At about 1900, just before darkness fell, he crushed the last ember.[35]

Oahu moved serenely into a pleasant evening of routine duties, family life, and happy gatherings of good friends. Lt. Cmdr. Samuel G. Fuqua had head-of-department duty aboard the *Arizona*. As damage control officer, he was responsible for "the watertight integrity of the ship and to keep it afloat in case of damage in battle."[36] Having no duties, Major Shapley went swimming at Waikiki that afternoon and then dined downtown. Although he had to wait an hour to catch a boat back to the *Arizona*, he was aboard by 2300.[37]

Commander Young and Ensign Hesser finished their conferences on the *Arizona* and secured the *Vestal* for the day. Young granted his crew 50 percent liberty, but stayed aboard and dined in his cabin. Hesser joined the other officers in the wardroom, where they discussed the danger of war with Japan. Ens. Fred Hall, the assistant communications officer, who had been run ragged all day with messages "flying back and forth so fast they couldn't swing it," prophesied that the Japanese would hit Pearl Harbor. "They will attack right here," he declared. No one pressed him for details; it was just another "bull session" comment.[38]

To Chief Boilermaker John Crawford that evening aboard the *Vestal* was notable for another reason. "That Saturday, December 6, 1941, was the only Saturday while I was in the Navy that I was sober." He was scheduled for the 2400–0400 watch. Even though CWO C. V. Smith agreed to stand Crawford's watch for him, he decided to take it easy. He went ashore to Bloch Center for a beer or two, returning to the *Vestal* by 2300.[39]

Bloch Center was relatively new. Since its opening at the Navy Yard in August, "probably one quarter of the men who formerly went to town ceased to go to town." At the center the men could drink beer, play billiards or pool, or go to boxing matches or the movies.[40]

Capt. F. W. Scanland, skipper of the *Nevada*, lived with his wife in Honolulu, so he was not aboard. But Lt. Lawrence E. Ruff was present. Mrs. Ruff was not in Hawaii, because the lieutenant considered the situation too serious to bring her out to the Islands. So he watched the movie on shipboard and retired about 2230 with the idea of rising early to attend morning mass on the hospital ship *Solace*.[41]

Lt. Comdr. Harold F. Pullen left his destroyer, *Reid*, early in the afternoon to be with his wife and two children in their cottage in Honolulu near the beach. That evening he gave a dinner party at the Pearl Harbor Officers' Club for the commander of his destroyer division. Skippers of all the destroyers were there with their wives. After dinner, there was dancing. Such occasional parties were "the only social life we had," recalled Pullen.[42]

This particular club was a favorite spot, especially on Saturday evenings, when about 250 turned up for dinner and some 450 for the dancing. Dinner cost $1.00, and if one came after dinner, there was no charge. These functions cut off at midnight, for Territorial laws prohibited the serving of liquor after that hour.[43]

Admiral Bloch played golf that afternoon and returned home by 1730, "very tired." After dinner, he read a book and was in bed by 2030 or 2100.[44] Such early hours were not unusual for the admiral, who admitted that he "could not stay awake" after 2130.[45]

Another "early-to-bed type" was RADM William Rea Furlong, in command of Minecraft, Battle Force, who lived aboard his flagship, the old minelayer *Oglala*.[46] "Jesus, that was some tub!" exclaimed Crawford, with a shout of laughter at the memory.[47] Furlong played host to several Navy captains at luncheon aboard his "tub." His afternoon and evening passed without incident, and he retired not later than 2200, because he would be on duty the next morning.[48]

Ens. John R. Beardall, Jr., son of the President's naval aide, went to Honolulu on shore leave from the light cruiser *Raleigh*. He returned at around 0115, in "not the best shape...but not the worst."[49]

RADM William L. Calhoun, Commander, Base Force, left his flagship, the *Argonne*, for his home in Honolulu—the first time in 7 days that he had spent an evening at home.[50] Astern the *Argonne*, the minesweeper *Tern* was in harbor for upkeep and overhaul. "We didn't even have a .45 revolver aboard," said Baker 1st Class Emil Johnson, who spent the day doing routine chores. The *Argonne* was showing a movie that night, but Johnson had seen the picture, so he wandered up dock to a beergarden for a glass or two. He was back aboard and in his bunk by 2130 or 2200.[51]

The tanker *Neosho* finished discharging fuel at Hickam at 1910. By 2140 she had moored starboard side to F4, Ford Island, and at 2259 started discharging gasoline.[52] Ashore on Ford Island, Shoemaker turned in early, anticipating a morning golf engagement with Mayfield.[53] Elsewhere on Ford Island, RADM Patrick N. L. Bellinger, commander of Patrol Wing Two, was already in bed, having been confined since Tuesday with the flu. Sunday December 7 would be his first day up.[54]

Joan East, wife of Lieutenant East on Kimmel's staff, spent her time taking care of her 4-month-old daughter Susan, buying supplies, washing dishes, and cleaning their first-floor apartment in Honolulu. Her husband had duty at headquarters until 0300 Sunday morning; then he would remain at the BOQ to sleep, so he should not be home until around noon on Sunday. Therefore, Joan asked her mother, who lived in the Colonial Hotel in Honolulu, to stay with her over Saturday night.[55]

Lt. Comdr. Doir C. Johnson of the *West Virginia* was on shore patrol duty in Honolulu; in fact, he had lived in the Alexander Young Hotel the entire week. That afternoon he saw his skipper, Captain Bennion, whom Johnson admired and respected highly. The two men chatted for a few moments in the hotel lobby and then parted. Johnson was a busy man that afternoon and evening: "A group of ships were in from sea, the boys had been cooped up for a spell and now they were breathing the air of Honolulu again with its joints and gals and their pockets full of money. There was some trouble that night with the boys."[56]

Not, however, as much trouble as might have been anticipated, considering the thousands of soldiers and sailors stationed on Oahu. Short's provost marshal, Lt. Col. Melvin L. Craig, was home by 2200. Nothing happened to warrant sending for him, so he spent an uninterrupted night at home.[57]

Saturday was the "busy night" for the Honolulu police, and their chief, William A. Gabrielson, was "around every Saturday night checking up." He found conditions on December 6 to be neither better nor worse than on any other Saturday night—"they were just normal."[58] Some 700 men took advantage of the overnight facilities offered by the Army and Navy YMCA, which had available 400 beds and 375 cots.[59]

Their discussion with Bicknell made the Shorts and Fielders over an hour late for their engagement.[60] They, among others, stopped on their way to the Schofield Officers' Club at the home of Lt. Col. and Mrs. Emil Leard for cocktails. There Short took the two old-fashioneds which were all he permitted himself.[61] Then they moved on to the club, where they, Phillips, and Maj. Gen. Durward S. Wilson of the 24th Infantry Division were among those who attended "Ann Etzler's Cabaret"—an annual charity dinner dance which "one of the very talented young ladies had worked up."[62] The Shorts and Fielders left the club between 2230 and 2300 and went straight home. As they drove past Pearl Harbor, all its lights gleaming, Short remarked in unconscious echo of Commander Good, "What a target that would make!"[63]

Maj. Robert J. Fleming, a member of Short's G-4 who functioned as the general's personal troubleshooter, attended the same party with his wife. As they drove home, they too noted the glittering display of ships. "They had their signal lights blinking back and forth. Collectively they looked like a huge Christmas decoration."[64]

Kimmel, Pye, and Draemel attended a small dinner party of about a dozen close friends given by Admiral and Mrs. Leary at the Halekulani Hotel.[65] Kimmel mentioned to Draemel that he had an invitation to drop by the Japanese consulate to drink champagne. Deeply distrustful of the Japanese, Draemel urged the admiral against going, and Kimmel assured him that he would not.[66]

Kita frequently entertained officers and businessmen at stag parties of around fifty. Short went once or twice out of courtesy, staying only long enough to pay his respects. Bicknell went to most, for in his position he could not afford to neglect any opportunity to improve his knowledge of the consulate and its personnel. These occasions were "really wet parties. A bottle of scotch at each place and a geisha girl pouring it out." One of these functions ended with the geishas tossing one of Honolulu's most dignified businessmen in a blanket.[67]

This was not the sort of entertainment to appeal to Kimmel, a somewhat stately man who would accept one drink and make it last for an entire cocktail party.[68] A friendly get-together with a few colleagues and their wives was much more to his taste. Even so, he left the hotel early, about 2130. After the 20- or 25-minute drive to his quarters, he went straight to bed.[69] He planned to rise early and play golf with Short.[70]

At least two individuals had especially pleasant memories of that evening. After supper, at Kaaawa, Michaud and his fellow enlisted men chipped in and one of their number went to Kaneohe to buy "a case and a half of beer, and chips." The men sat in the mess tent and played cards and drank beer until late at night. They "roared at ribald jokes and listened to the *Hit Parade* on the radio." Some came in for "much kidding and envy," being due for rotation to the mainland in a few months. "It was a wonderful evening, with everyone in a good mood."[71]

Lieutenant Reeves and a buddy left Hickam for Honolulu at approximately 1700. They hit a number of spots, ending at the Royal Hawaiian Hotel for a party. Reeves remembered the evening as "the best time I had had in Hawaii thus far."[72]

Captain Allen, whose instructions so awed Reeves that morning, gave a dinner party at the Hickam club for a Navy friend from Samoa who was staying with Allen that weekend. A group returned to Allen's quarters where they drank and threw darts until 0500, when one man left and the rest fell into bed.[73]

Bicknell was in no such mellow mood, still "feeling pretty well frustrated" over the Mori experience, when about 2000 he received a call from Lt. Col. Clay Hoppaugh, signal officer of the Hawaiian Air Force: "We have a flight of B-17s coming in from the mainland. Will you put station KGMB on the air all night so the planes can home in on the signal?"

"Why don't you have KGMB on the air every night and not just on the night we have airplanes flying?" Bicknell exploded. "You folks have the money to do it."

"We'll talk that over some other time," Hoppaugh replied. At the moment, they had no choice. Bicknell phoned KGMB and made the arrangements. The station did not know the reason for such requests, but the Army Air Force paid for this service.[74] It was a little late to worry about the security aspects; by this time it was common knowledge that when KGMB played music all night, military aircraft flew in the next morning.[75]

Word of the incoming flight reached various people in various ways. Lt. Col. James A. Mollison, chief of staff of the Hawaiian Air Force, was at a dinner party in the home of Lt. Col. William C. "Cush" Farnum when he received notice, at about 2230, that a call had come for him from San Francisco saying that twelve B-17s would arrive in Oahu from the mainland at 0800 the next morning. Mollison in turn called the duty officer to give him the estimated time of arrival. Since Mollison wanted to be sure he would be at the tower when they came in, he left the party immediately and went straight home.[76]

Farnum was in charge of maintenance of supply and engineering at Hickam. Part of his job was to service B-17s being ferried to the Philippines and to send them on their way as quickly as possible. So he alerted his civilian chief clerk, Henry Ortner, as well as the maintenance crews. Farnum knew that by morning all would be ready—the big gasoline trucks, the Aqua System,* and about 200 or 300 crewmen.[77]

Colonel Dunlop received similar information when he dropped in on the officer of the day at his office while on his way to a movie with his wife and son, Lt. Robert H. Dunlop, Jr. The colonel tried to reach Colonel Phillips but could not do so until about 2300, when Phillips returned from Schofield. After Dunlop told him of the incoming flight, Phillips asked, "Bob, is there anything else you want to tell me?" Dunlop replied, "Tige, there isn't another thing."[78]

Equally detached from such unexpected, late-night duties as well as from social obligations, Capt. George R. Sampson, assistant signal officer at Fort Shafter, stayed home and played Chinese checkers with his wife, Lucille.[79]

Layton spent what was left of his afternoon mowing the lawn at his home beyond Diamond Head. That evening he and Mrs. Layton went to his brother-in-law's apartment for a cocktail and then on to the Royal Hawaiian Hotel for dinner and dancing. At midnight, the band struck up "The Star Spangled Banner." As Layton snapped to attention, he had to control a sudden impulse to shout "Wake up, America!" and shake his countrymen out of their complacency. He did not fear for Hawaii, but he believed that war was coming in the Far East very soon.[80]

About an hour earlier, an equally dedicated officer of another uniform stood on deck of the carrier *Akagi*, where engines roared as mechanics tuned up aircraft in preparation for the forthcoming attack. For months Cmdr. Minoru Genda, air staff officer of the First Air Fleet, had devoted virtually every waking thought of his probing, in-

* Gasoline stored in tanks underground with water under it providing the pressure.

novative mind to perfecting the tactical plans for the forthcoming attack. Now, suddenly, as he climbed the ladder to the bridge, he "felt very refreshed, as if all the uncertainties were cleared away." Worries and doubts vanished, leaving his mind "as bright and clear as a stainless mirror."[81]

Genda's colleague and long-time friend, Commander Fuchida, removed his flying suit in preparation for a few hours' rest and visited the wardroom for a last-minute word with Lt. Cmdr. Shigeharu Murata, who would lead the torpedo bombers, and Lt. Cmdr. Shigeru Itaya, the leader of the fighter aircraft. He urged them, and a number of the other fliers present, to get a good night's sleep. He followed his own advice and retired around 2200. Despite the responsibility resting on his shoulders, he slept soundly. "I had set up the whole machinery of attack, and it was ready to go. There was no use to worry now."[82]

Aboard the carrier *Soryu,* Sublt. Iyozo Fujita, a young fighter pilot, had an attack of nerves. This would be his first combat mission, and he expected it to be his last. Before going to bed, he calmed himself with several bottles of beer; then he took a bath so that he could go into battle fresh and clean, like the samurai of old.[83]

Cmdr. Kyozo Ohashi, senior staff officer of the Fifth Carrier Division, remained in the *Shokaku*'s operations room, tuned in to KGMB for any clues to the situation on Oahu. Everything seemed normal, and he began to relax. He heard nothing to hint that the Americans had discovered the task force. That being the case, the Japanese might well achieve surprise.

But the *Shokaku* and her sister ship the *Zuikaku* had only been in service since August and September, respectively, and their airmen could not match in experience their seasoned counterparts in the First Carrier Division (*Akagi* and *Kaga*) and the Second Carrier Division (*Soryu* and *Hiryu*). So Ohashi could not predict how his newly trained airmen would react under fire. He divided the feelings of the officers and crews aboard the *Shokaku* and the *Zuikaku* on the eve of the attack into three principal categories:

First, there were those who were virtually unmoved by the special mission of attacking Pearl Harbor, who considered the operation as their God-given duty, and who faced the immediate future with grim stoicism. Into this class fell most of the older staff officers and key pilots.

Secondly, there were those who thought the Pearl Harbor operation would succeed, but who were apprehensive about the final outcome of the war. They wondered what was going to happen after the initial phase was over. Into this class fell the more intelligent of the younger officers who tried to look at things from a long-range viewpoint.

Finally, there were those who were nervous and afraid of what lay ahead. This class included the newer officers, the young trainees, and those of the crew who could only glimpse snatches of the overall plan.[84]

At about the time Fuchida tumbled into bed, the Japanese submarine I-26 reached a point on the great circle midway between Hawaii and San Francisco. Almost immediately the submarine's skipper, Comdr. Minoru Yokota, spotted the navigation light of an American vessel. Running on the surface, the I-26 overtook the ship and then kept in position slightly to its fore. Yokota's prey was the small wooden craft Cynthia Olsen. It would have been an easy mark for the I-26, which was one of Japan's best and newest submarines, finished on November 6, 1941. But Yokota had strict orders not to fire until the aerial attack on Pearl Harbor had begun, and he was conscious of his responsibility not to start anything prematurely. So he continued to stalk the Cynthia Olsen throughout the night.[85]

Yokota's self-restraint would have reassured Nagumo's airmen, for they, especially Fuchida, entertained serious doubts as to the wisdom of submarine participation in the attack. They did not see what the undersea operation could possibly accomplish that would outweigh the risk of untimely detection.[86]

Some 50 miles from the entrance to Pearl Harbor, the waters churned briefly as the submarine I-22 broke the surface. Aboard her was Capt. Hanku Sasaki, in command of the Special Attack Force of five mother submarines, each carrying a two-man minisub. According to plan, the midgets would slip into Pearl Harbor and await the air attack before commencing their own action. Ideally, they would strike between the first and second waves of aircraft, but if necessary, they would wait until nightfall to attack, then circle counterclockwise around Ford Island, escape from the harbor, and rendezvous with the mother submarines some 7 miles west of Lanai Island.[87]

Sasaki fervently hoped to be able to rescue the midget submariners, but the young men had little hope or expectation of emerging alive. Therefore, they were more interested in "how to make a final stand" on the island with the pistol and samurai sword each carried and in how to destroy their own small craft so that the Americans could not salvage them and thus learn about these secret weapons.[88]

As the *I-22* cruised steadily toward Oahu, Sasaki could see the lights at the entrance to Pearl Harbor itself. Searchlight flashes swung intermittently over the sky, the only evidence of enemy activity. This, together with the sight of the *I-20* nearby, boosted Sasaki's spirit with "a feeling of confidence and a renewed hope that the attack would be successful." Sublt. Keiu Matsuo, aboard the *I-22* to observe and study this operation, begged to go with Lt. Naoji Iwasa, leader of the midget submariners, and his mate, Ens. Naokichi Sasaki. But Iwasa assured him that their minisub had neither room nor air for three men. In any case, Captain Sasaki would not hear of it. Matsuo's mission was to learn all he could about midget submarines and their operation so that he could carry on the program in case all the others were killed. The Navy could not spare him.[89]

Shortly before embarking, Iwasa called in the maintenance crew. After thanking them for their efforts, he said, "Now I am going to leave the ship with everything in good condition....I think the war will last a long time and in its course midget subs will be used more and more. I expect you to do your best in future operations."

Just before Iwasa entered the midget, he and Captain Sasaki met on the bridge of the *I-22* to discuss the operation once more. Sasaki gave Iwasa final instructions and his exact position, pointing out all the factors to be considered in entering Pearl Harbor, which now lay directly ahead. Then Iwasa and Ensign Sasaki crawled down into their midget submarine. At this point they were within 10 miles of Pearl Harbor. Just before the *I-22* released the minisub, Captain Sasaki called Iwasa on the intersub telephone to say, "Congratulations in advance on your success. I hope you will do your job well. Good luck!"

"Thanks a lot for taking me so close to the harbor," Iwasa replied. "I will attack without fail." Once more they exchanged regards, and Iwasa, reconciled to his probable death, added, "I wish you to look after my private affairs." Then it was time to disconnect the lines between mother ship and midget.[90]

Aboard the *I-24*, Ens. Kazuo Sakamaki wrote what he expected would be a last letter to his parents, bathed, and donned his uniform. Then he and his partner, CWO Kiyoshi Inagaki, visited all the sections of the mother submarine, bidding farewell to officers and crew. The skipper, Lt. Comdr. Hiroshi Hanabusa, reminded Sakamaki that his minisub's gyroscope was out of order. "What are you going to do?"

Sakamaki knew all too well the difficulty, indeed the virtual impossibility, of navigating with an inoperable gyroscope, but he and Inagaki had no intention of throwing in the sponge. ".We will go," Sakamaki declared, whereupon Hanabusa, catching fire from the young man's enthusiasm, shouted with him, "On to Pearl Harbor!"[91]

PART 2

"Tora! Tora! Tora!"

December 7, 1941

The Preattack Hours

CHAPTER 5

"That Rather Hectic Morning"

While Hawaii's last carefree parties were under way in an atmosphere of friendly chatter, laughter, and dance music, most of Washington slept the deep sleep of the early morning hours. Soon trucks would rumble through the towns and cities of the mainland United States, dropping heavy bundles of the bulky Sunday newspapers.

Page one headlines in *The New York Times* told of Knox's pride and confidence in his department: NAVY IS SUPERIOR TO ANY, SAYS KNOX... SECRETARY'S ANNUAL REPORT CITES COMMISSIONING OF 325 NEW SHIPS, 2059 PLANES. In a story datelined Washington, December 6, this newspaper reported:

> The United States Navy, now in the midst of a record expansion program and recently placed on a war footing with full personnel manning the ships of three fleets, has at this time no superior in the world, Secretary Knox stated tonight in rendering the annual report of the Navy Department....
>
> "I am proud to report," Secretary Knox wrote, "that the American people may feel fully confident in their Navy. In my opinion, the loyalty, morale and technical ability of the personnel are without superior. On any comparable basis, the United States Navy is second to none."[1]

However, he warned, "the international situation is such that we must arm as rapidly as possible to meet our naval defense requirements simultaneously in both oceans against any possible combination of powers concerting action against us."[2]

The Washington *Post* quoted RADM Clark H. Woodward: "The Japanese have a fine navy, but it is decidedly inferior to the American Pacific Fleet in heavy ships....Japan's greatest weakness is in her air forces." The admiral predicted that if the Soviet Union collapsed, Japan would move both north and south, counting on Nazi help. And another article suggested that the German battleships *Von Tirpitz* and *Gneisenau* might be en route to the Pacific "as a surprise addition to the Japanese fleet," which could be one reason why Japan was refusing to reach an agreement with Washington.[3]

There were a few tidbits of information about Europe. Effective December 7, Great Britain declared war on three of Hitler's allies—Finland, Roumania, and Hungary.[4] And the marriage of King Leopold III of Belgium to a commoner, Mary Lelia Baels, was announced.[5]

Concerning the course of events in the Pacific, commentators took positions ranging from cautious optimism to a resigned fatalism. Among the former was Constantine Brown:

> Much of the credit for averting a clash with Japan at this time, with its obviously incalculable consequences, must be given to Secretary of State Cordell Hull. It is, of course, premature to say that war in the Pacific has been avoided altogether, for the situation continues to be strained and dangerous. But while betting a little over a week ago in the highest Washington circles was 10 to 1 that the guns would be barking before the end of last week, there is now a strong feeling that the Pacific crisis has been postponed, at least for a while.[6]

Owen L. Scott took the other position, writing in a retrospective tone:

> If and when shooting starts in the Pacific, there will be little argument about the responsibility. Probably never in history have the responsible officials of one nation been as patient in dealing with another nation as President Roosevelt and Secretary of State Cordell Hull have been with Japan.

Scott pointed out how the United States had sent oil and other materials to Japan over the years: "It is almost as though this country had built up an army, navy and air force in Japan, only to find that its own creation was turning out to be an enemy."[7]

The hours of sleep in Washington were those of business in Tokyo.

At about 1500 Japan time (0100 EST), Ambassador Grew was listening to San Francisco radio station KGEI when he heard its report that the President "had sent or was sending a message to the Emperor," but "no information was given as to its substance or the channel of transmission." Grew promptly phoned the Embassy's councillor, Eugene H. Dooman, to stand by. The ambassador assumed that the Japanese had also picked up the radio message, because KGEI's beam "went all over Japan."[8]

While Grew awaited official confirmation and instruction, the Foreign Office at 1638 local time (0238 EST) sent off the long-awaited fourteenth part of Tokyo's reply to Washington's proposals of November 26. U.S. Navy Station S at Bainbridge Island, Washington, intercepted this between 0304 and 0310 EST and teletyped it in Japanese code to the Navy decrypters in Washington, D.C.:[9]

> Obviously it is the intention of the American Government to conspire with Great Britain and other countries to obstruct Japan's efforts toward the establishment of peace through the creation of a New Order in East Asia, and especially to preserve Anglo-American rights and interests by keeping Japan and China at war. This intention has been revealed clearly during the course of the present negotiations. Thus, the earnest hope of the Japanese Government to adjust Japanese-American relations and to preserve and promote the peace of the Pacific through cooperation with the American Government has finally been lost.

> The Japanese Government regrets to have to notify hereby the American Government that in view of the attitude of the American Government it cannot but consider that it is impossible to reach an agreement through further negotiations.[10]

This message arrived at its destination, the Japanese Embassy, between 0700 and 0800. The duty officer tried to summon the personnel of the Cable Section, but was unable to reach them.[11]

The Americans were much more expeditious. When Kramer reached his office at about 0730, he found the message ready for him.[12] While Kramer prepared the packets for his morning delivery, his immediate chief, Commander McCollum, arrived and was "trying to digest" the first thirteen parts when Captain Wilkinson sent for him. The two officers mulled over these messages until an orderly informed Wilkinson that Admiral Stark was now in his office. "Well, come on," said Wilkinson, "let's go and see the chief." So a brief three-way discussion ensued. Shortly after they parted, Kramer brought McCollum the now-complete set of messages. McCollum immediately returned to Wilkinson and "pointed out to him the difference in the tenor of the language of the 14th part from that of the others." The two men hurried back to Stark "and pointed out to him the virulence and tenor of the language."

Someone remarked "that it looked right there that that was enough to indicate that we could expect war." Wilkinson suggested "that an additional warning be sent to Pearl Harbor"; however, "nothing was done at that time."[13]

Although Stark realized that the fourteenth part "was in much stronger, more definite language" than its predecessors, as he later explained, "...we had come to the conclusion previously that we considered Japan likely to attack at any time in any direction....It was a confirmation, if anything."[14]

While these three officers talked over the situation, Kramer stopped by on his way to his 1000 appointment at the State Department, in accordance with Knox's instructions of the previous night. He was relieved to find Wilkinson with Stark, because his chief could "carry the ball." This would save Kramer the time he would otherwise spend in explaining matters to the CNO.[15]

Kramer left the Navy Department at about 0930 and delivered the President's copies of the morning's crop of messages to the White House.[16] Within half an hour, Beardall took them to Roosevelt, who was still in his bedroom. Beardall was not normally on duty as naval aide on Sundays, but on this particular morning he went to the White House on his own initiative in case the fourteenth part should come in. Roosevelt and Beardall exchanged no conversation about the content of the dispatches, for they never discussed Magic. To the best of Beardall's recollection, the President made only one comment, in substance: "It looks like the Japanese are going to break off negotiations."[17] This was the logical deduction, because the dispatch neither declared war nor severed diplomatic relations.

Having made his White House delivery, Kramer walked over to the ornate State Department building, arriving at Hull's office at "almost exactly 10 minutes of 10." About five minutes later, Knox arrived, and Kramer gave him the packet, "pointing out what new traffic was in the folder which he had not seen the night before."[18] Then Knox disappeared into Hull's conference room. After exchanging a few brief words with an Army courier and Hull's private secretary, Kramer hurried back to the Navy Department, reaching his office at about 1020.[19]

On the Army side, Bratton arrived at his office some time between 0700 and 0800 and received the fourteenth part at approximately 0830.[20] He processed it and then read the whole document through "to see just exactly what it meant." His reaction was similar to Stark's. He considered the entire fourteen parts "relatively unimportant, in view of the other messages which preceded it, especially the one ordering the destruction of the Japanese codes and ciphers." Therefore, the message was "merely the formal announcement couched in diplomatic language* of a break which, from the evidence, seemed inevitable." Thereupon he released it for delivery to the authorized recipients, among them the State Department.[21]

Meanwhile, in Tokyo, Ambassador Grew was preparing to present Roosevelt's personal appeal to the Emperor. At approximately 2100 Japan time (0700 EST), he received "a very brief, urgent message from Mr. Hull saying an important message for the Emperor was then being encoded" and for Grew to be ready for it.[22]

The anticipated message was delivered to the Embassy at 2230 Tokyo time (0830 EST), just as Bratton in Washington received the fourteenth part of the Foreign Ministry's intercept. The Roosevelt telegram "was officially stamped as having been received at the Japanese telegraph office at 1200 hours and was marked 'triple priority,' dispatched 6 December, 2100 hours (Washington time)."[23] Obviously the Japanese had held it up for 10½ hours, although the Japanese post office normally handled telegrams 1 hour after receipt.[24]

Grew assumed that "when the message came it was probably turned over to certain authorities of the Japanese Government, who could have readily decoded it, because it was in what we called our nonconfidential code,...the gray code which was perfectly open to anybody, and...that the military authorities did not want this message to get to the Emperor at that time."[25]

He was not far wrong. The delay was caused by an arrangement between Lt. Col. Morio Tomura, of the Army General Staff's Communications Section, and Tateki Shirao, chief of the Ministry of Com-

---

* Of course, by "diplomatic language," Bratton meant the language of diplomacy; it was far from diplomatic in the popular conception of the word.

munications' Censorship Office. On November 29, Tomura had asked
Shirao to delay by 5 hours the delivery of all incoming and outgoing
cables except those of the Japanese government. On December 6,
this schedule was changed to 5 hours one day, 10 the next, making
December 7 a date for 10-hour delays.[26]

Grew had already asked the Foreign Ministry to stand by, and
now he sent a telephone message to Foreign Minister Togo's secretary, asking for an appointment around midnight. The secretary de-
murred at first—Was the matter so urgent that it could not wait until
the next day? Ultimately, however, he made the appointment. As soon
as Roosevelt's message was decoded and typed, Grew took it to Togo's
official residence and met with the Foreign Minister at about 0015
December 8 (1030 December 7 EST).

Grew read the message aloud and then handed Togo a copy. He
asked for a personal audience with the Emperor, which was his right
as an ambassador. He "did not want any doubt as to getting it in his
hand." At first Togo quibbled—he would like to study the document
first. But the ambassador countered firmly, "I am making a definite
application for an audience with the Emperor." Finally, Togo agreed,
"I will present your request to the Throne." Grew left Togo at about
0030 (1030 December 7 EST), returned to the Embassy and went to
bed "rather late."[27]

A message of quite another character was occupying the attention
of the Army and Navy in Washington: "Will the Ambassador please
submit to the United States Government (if possible to the Secretary
of State) our reply to the United States at 1:00 p.m. on the 7th, your
time."[28] Station S at Bainbridge Island intercepted this at 0437 and
relayed it to Washington, where the Navy decoded it and sent it to
the Army for translation and typing.[29]

The intercept came into Bratton's hands while he was still reading
the fourteen-part message. "This immediately stunned me into frenzied
activity because of its implications."[30] The physical presence of the
fourteen-part message in Washington "had little significance," in Bratton's
opinion, because the Japanese ambassador was under orders to prepare
it for delivery and then hold it "pending further instructions." Now came
this activating intercept, which "was peculiarly worded, and the impli-
cation was inescapable that it was of vital importance."[31]

The idea of danger to Pearl Harbor did not occur to him, but "the
one o'clock message" convinced him that "the Japanese were going

to attack some American installation in the Pacific area."[32] So he "just wiped everything else" out of his mind and turned his office over to his assistant, Lt. Col. C. Clyde Dusenbury.[33]

Having no authority to send a warning message, Bratton hastened off in search of someone so empowered. But neither Marshall, Gerow, nor Miles was in his office. Even if Miles had been in, he "could not issue a command message." Under pressure of his sense of urgency, at about 0900 Bratton telephoned Marshall's quarters. An orderly informed him that the general had gone horseback riding.

"Well, you know generally where he has gone," answered Bratton. "You know where you can get ahold of him?"

"Yes, I think I can find him," replied the orderly.

"Please go out at once, get assistance if necessary, and find General Marshall....Tell him who I am and tell him to go to the nearest telephone, that it is vitally important that I communicate with him at the earliest practicable moment," Bratton instructed. The orderly agreed to do so.

Bratton then telephoned Miles at his home and told him what he had done. He urged his chief to "come down to the office at once," because Bratton assumed "that General Marshall would want to see him and talk with him." Either Miles or Bratton—he could not quite recall which—called Gerow with the same request.[34]

Kramer found the activating dispatch, usually referred to as "the one o'clock message," waiting for him, fully translated, when he returned to his office from the State Department. It did not rouse in him such strong reactions as in Bratton, but he recognized that it was important and instructed his chief yeoman to prepare another set of folders so that he could make immediate delivery. During the 5 minutes this process required,[35] Kramer made some quick calculations in accordance with a standard procedure that had been established in McCollum's office. McCollum explained, "...when any dispatch of which time was an element came in, we immediately converted that time to not only our own time but usually set up Washington time, West Coast time, Honolulu time, Manila time, and Tokyo time." This last was included because the Japanese Navy ran exclusively on Tokyo time. Such a time comparison could help "keep track of... whether it was sunset or sunrise, or moonset."[36]

Kramer had had previous experience as a navigator, and navigation was one of his hobbies. So he made a navigator's time circle "to get a picture of how this 1 o'clock Washington tied up with the movement of the big Japanese convoy down on the coast of French Indochina; in other words, to get an idea of whether it was evening or midnight or early in the morning around Kota Bharu." Instead of figuring the West Coast time, he used Greenwich Mean Time, as well as the special 10½-hour zone for Hawaii. Kramer's primary interest was in the South China Sea zone, where he calculated that the designated time would be "probably 2 or 3 hours before dawn," which was "the normal time to institute amphibious operations." In contrast, 1300 EST would be 0730 in Honolulu, and on the basis of past experience, Kramer estimated that this would be "the quietest time of the week aboard ship at Pearl Harbor." 0730 was "the normal time for the piping of the crew to breakfast," and usually only the men on watch would be topside.[37]

In addition to the one o'clock message, Kramer's folders contained a few other dispatches, one conveying Tokyo's "deepest thanks" to Nomura and Kurusu for their "endeavors and hard work." Another instructed that, after deciphering part fourteen, the one o'clock message, and the two telegrams of thanks, the Embassy should "destroy at once the remaining cipher machine and all machine codes" plus "all secret documents."[38]

This, along with the one o'clock message, struck Kramer "as forcibly indicating an acute crisis," the nature of which he was uncertain. While these dispatches "did not positively mean war," they did "indicate an extreme likelihood of war."[39]

The folders were sealed, and he was about to leave on his rounds when the watch officer sent in "a plain language Japanese message," which, from the English word "stop" at its end, Kramer recognized as implementing the so-called hidden word system of dispatches which Japan had established on November 27.[40] Hastily scanning the message, he spotted the code word for England and dictated to his chief yeoman "the sense of the message," which thus read: "Relations between Japan and England are not in accordance with expectation."[41] So hurried was Kramer that he did not notice the word "*minami*," the code word for the United States. Kramer explained that *minami* was "a very common word in the Japanese language. It simply means 'south.'" But "*Koyanagi*," the code word for England, was a proper name and readily caught his eye. Not until after the attack did he learn of the inadvertent omission.[42]

While Kramer and his yeoman were preparing the "hidden word" implementation for inclusion in the packets, the Army sent over a few last-minute intercepts. One of these was an expression of appreciation for the efforts of Counselor Sadao Iguchi, his staff, and Kurusu's first secretary, Shiroji Yuki. Another, dated December 6, asked for facts about the AP and UP reports that Roosevelt had "wired a personal message to His Majesty the Emperor." Since the packets had already been reopened to receive the "hidden word" implementation, Kramer also stuffed in these latest intercepts.[43]

The resealed packets in hand, Kramer proceeded to Stark's office. McCollum was still with the CNO and came to the door. Kramer stressed the one o'clock message, pointing out the "tie-up of the time, 1 o'clock Washington, with the scheme that had been developing for the past week or so in the Southwest Pacific with reference to Malaya and the Kra Peninsula." He also mentioned that this would be 0730 in Hawaii, but neither officer saw any special significance in that hour.[44] However, they decided that this message was so important that, although normally the Army delivered to the State Department, it would take too long to go through channels. Therefore, Kramer would drop it off at State on his way to the White House, and McCollum would tell Bratton what they had done. This conversation between McCollum and Kramer took place at about 1030 or 1035 and lasted not more than about 10 seconds.[45]

While Kramer hastened off, McCollum took Stark's copy to the CNO, directing the admiral's attention to the fact that 1300 EST would be 0730 in Honolulu and

> ...very early in the morning in the Far East...and that we didn't know what this signified, but that if an attack were coming, it looked like...it was timed for operations out in the Far East and possibly on Hawaii....We had no way of knowing, but because of the fact that the exact time for delivery of this note had been stressed to the ambassadors, we felt that there were important things which would move at that time.[46]

Nevertheless, "Pearl Harbor as such was never mentioned." The opinion of McCollum and, he presumed, of most officers "was that at or near the outbreak of war with Japan, we could expect a surprise attack on the fleet." This had been "the major assumption" for some time.[47] But, while McCollum knew that the Fleet was operating somewhere in the Pearl Harbor area, he was under the impression that the Fleet had gone to sea and had so informed Bratton a few days before.[48]

Meanwhile, Kramer walked to the State Department, covering the distance in about 10 minutes. He delivered the message to one of Hull's private secretaries, the usual recipient of Magic. Another man was present, and although he, like Kramer, wore civilian clothes, Kramer recognized him as an Army courier. Kramer spoke of the time element: "The principal point of that was the conviction...that the Japanese intended to carry out their plans against Kota Bharu, with the intention and purpose of forcing the hand of the Thai Premier, Pibul."

No one suggested that the time in Hawaii might presage an attack on Pearl Harbor. Kramer mentioned the 0730 hour "purely in passing and...primarily for the benefit" of those "who might not be familiar with the ships' routine or Fleet routine on a Sunday morning." He made only a "general remark to the effect that 7:30 on a Sunday morning was probably the quietest time of the week." He especially wanted to convey to Knox, who was with Hull, that this would be "a few hours before sunrise at Kota Bharu." From State, Kramer moved on to the White House and then back to the Navy Department.[49]

Hull, in conference with Stimson and Knox, was already "very certain that the Japs [were] planning some deviltry." They all wondered where the blow would strike. As Stimson recorded in his diary, "Today is the day that the Japanese are going to bring their answer to Hull, and everything in MAGIC indicated they had been keeping the time back until now in order to accomplish something hanging in the air [Stimson's capitals]." The three secretaries remained in conference until lunchtime, "going over the plans for what should be said or done." The "main thing," in Stimson's opinion, was to hold the Americans, British, Dutch, Australians, and Chinese together. Hull and Knox expressed their views, which the orderly-minded Stimson insisted they dictate to a stenographer.[50]

So far, General Marshall had received no word of anything extraordinary taking place. He had gone to bed early, slept through the night, and woke up "thankful that no news had come in that was sufficiently urgent to call me to the office in the middle of the night."[51] Mrs. Marshall did not yet feel well enough to be up and about, so they had a late breakfast in her room, the general eating on a tray at her bedside. Then he ordered his horse for his usual Sunday morning ride.[52]

To the best of his recollection, he rode for an hour or less, "at a pretty lively gait...down on the experimental farm where the Pentagon now is."[53] Clocks in the War Department showed nearly 1030 when he returned Bratton's call. The colonel explained that he had "a most important message" that Marshall "must see at once." He offered to bring it out, but Marshall answered, "No, don't bother to do that. I am coming down to my office. You can give it to me then."[54]

Ironically, the message causing such a dither in American circles had not yet reached its nominal destination, the Japanese Embassy. Secretary Yuki reported for work at about 0900, at which time Okumura was "typing like mad" on parts one through thirteen of Tokyo's long message. The fourteenth part was waiting, but the cable office personnel did not show up until around 1000 to begin work on it.

By the time the one o'clock message came in, Okumura had finished the first thirteen parts, but his product was too messy for presentation. In the belief that he had plenty of time to meet the 1300 deadline, he began to retype it, with the aid of an interpreter. Neither one was an expert typist, and feeling under pressure, both made several mistakes. They also received a few correcting cables, nothing major, but enough to necessitate another retyping.[55]

Luxuriating in a semiholiday, reporter Masuo Kato slept in. He began his breakfast of delicate brown griddle cakes, "with plenty of butter and maple syrup," at roughly the same moment the one o'clock message reached the Embassy. Then he began work on two news stories. Col. Kenkichi Shinjo, the assistant military attaché, had died of pneumonia, and his funeral would be held on this Sunday, December 7. Kato's second story summarized the international situation. He estimated that there was still a one-in-three hope for peace between Japan and the United States.[56]

Secretary Terasaki, in whose honor the luncheon of the previous day had been given, also allowed himself a few hours' relaxation. For several weeks he had been putting in 18- to 20-hour days, so his American wife, Gwen, was glad of the break. The Terasakis rose late and sipped coffee while their 9-year-old daughter, Mariko, read the comics. Gwen suggested dining out of town, for the weather was mild. The diplomatic circuit did not offer much in the way of plain American cooking, and Gwen wanted a real southern Sunday dinner of fried chicken and sweet potatoes, such as she remembered from her girlhood in Tennessee. So Terasaki, Mariko, Gwen, and her mother, who was visiting them, piled into Terasaki's new Buick convertible and drove to an excellent country restaurant, a happy and animated family.[57]

Far from happy was Bratton, waiting impatiently for Marshall to arrive at the War Department. Meanwhile, he discussed "this whole business" with Miles, who had reached his office shortly after Bratton phoned him.[58] Both the fourteenth part and the one o'clock message made a deep, immediate impression on him. Taken together, they "meant two things: (1) That war is very likely, because of the language used by the Japanese, and (2) something is going to happen coincident with 1 o'clock Washington time."[59]

Marshall entered his office at about 1125, and very shortly thereafter Miles and Bratton joined him, Bratton clutching the one o'clock message in his hand. Marshall had the entire fourteen parts before him and read the whole message aloud. Both Miles and Bratton made vain attempts to interrupt him and show him the one o'clock message.[60]

At last Marshall put down the fourteen parts and accepted Bratton's offering. Neither Miles nor Bratton had cause to complain of their chief's reaction. He had no doubt "that that 'one o'clock' had some very definite significance. When they specified a day, that of course had significance, but not comparable to an hour. Something was going to happen at one o'clock....it was a most remarkable message."[61]

He asked the two intelligence officers what they thought it meant. Both answered that they "were convinced it meant Japanese hostile action against some American installation in the Pacific at or shortly after 1 o'clock that afternoon." At approximately that stage of the discussion, General Gerow and Col. Charles W. Bundy, head of Pacific Affairs, War Plans Division, came in, and they concurred in this assessment.[62]

The consensus was that the Japanese probably would invade Thailand, "but it might be any one or more of a number of other areas." So Miles "urged that the Philippines, Hawaii, Panama, and the West Coast be informed immediately that the Japanese reply would be delivered at one o'clock that afternoon, and to be on the alert."[63] There was no discussion "on that rather hectic morning" of what hour in those locations would coincide with 1300 EST. As Miles said later, "We wanted to get the hour out to the overseas departments and let them translate it into their own time."[64]

Marshall pulled a piece of scratch paper toward him, picked up a pencil, and dashed off a longhand message. He then called Stark on the White House phone, informing the CNO "in a guarded way" of the messages he had in front of him and what he proposed to do.[65] Coincidentally, Stark had been discussing the one o'clock message with "Pinky" Schuirmann. The admiral told Marshall that he hesitated to send any more warnings, because "we had sent them so much already."[66]

Miles and Bratton still urged that Marshall send out the warnings,[67] and within a minute or two, Stark called back. He had decided there might be "some peculiar significance in the Japanese Ambassador calling on Mr. Hull at 1 p.m.," so Stark "would go along" with Marshall in sending out the information. He asked if Marshall's "communications were such that he could get it out quickly," because his own were "quite rapid when the occasion demanded it." Marshall replied that he believed he could "get it through very quickly." Stark requested that he "include in the dispatch instructions to his people to inform their naval opposites."[68]

Marshall did so and then gave his draft to Bratton, with instructions to take it to the message center for dispatch "at once by the fastest safe means." Some brief question arose as to whether he should take it to Gerow's office for typing, "but time was then pressing" so they decided to let it go out first. As Bratton was leaving the room, Gerow called after him, "Tell them to give first priority to the Philippines if there is a question of priority."[69]

Within minutes, hearing "some commotion over in the code room," Lt. Col. Edward F. French, officer in charge of the War Department Signal Center, left his office to see what was going on. There was Bratton, draft in hand. French had "never seen him more excited."[70]

"The Chief of Staff wants this sent at once by the fastest safe means," said Bratton.

French glanced over the draft and answered, "Well, will you help me get this into readable script? Neither I nor my clerk here can read General Marshall's handwriting."

Bratton took back the paper, and standing beside a typist, dictated the message while the man typed. This took approximately 1 minute.[71] The message read:

Japanese are presenting at one pm eastern standard time today what amounts to an ultimatum also they are under orders to destroy their code machine immediately. Just what significance the hour set may have we do not know but be on alert accordingly. Inform naval authorities of this communication. Marshall.[72]

Bratton glanced at his watch and noted the time—about 1158. Leaving French to process his message, he returned to Marshall's office. "Go back and find out how long it is going to take for this message to be delivered to the addressees," the Chief of Staff directed him. Bratton hastened back to the message center and put Marshall's question to French. After "a little figuring mentally," the latter stated, "It will take about 30 or 40 minutes for it to be delivered to the persons to whom it is addressed." Bratton returned to Marshall and relayed French's estimate.[73]

Promptly at 1200, the message went off to the Caribbean Defense Command, to Manila at 1206, and to the Presidio at 1211.[74] But on checking, French found that atmospheric conditions had cut off the channel to Honolulu since around 1030, and even interfered with San Francisco. He considered turning the message over to the Navy, which had more power on one channel, but decided that the Navy was probably having the same atmospheric difficulties. Moreover, if the Navy handled it, the message would have to go first to Pearl Harbor instead of direct to Fort Shafter. French decided that commercial service could provide quicker transmission. He had a direct teletype to Western Union in Washington, which could relay the message to San Francisco and there turn it over to RCA, who would send it to Honolulu. Therefore, at 1217 he sent the dispatch to Western Union.[75]

1217 in Washington; 0647 in Honolulu. In 10 minutes, Hawaii's sun would rise on December 7, 1941.[76]

CHAPTER 6

"About to Launch a Blow"

At the precise moment that December 6 gave way to December 7 at Pearl Harbor, two seamen from the battleship *California* suffered minor injuries while at work.[1] These incidents seem to have been the most exciting events to occur in Pearl Harbor between midnight and 0100 that Sunday. Then the ships settled into sleep, except for those officers and seamen on routine night duties.

Aboard the tanker *Ramapo*, moored starboard side to Dock No. 12, workmen were placing four PT boats on deck for shipment to Manila.[2] The destroyer *Ward*, on channel entrance patrol, was "maneuvering on various courses and speeds."[3] The *Ward* was "an old 'four-piper' of World War I vintage" which could barely make 30 knots. Professional sailors mixed with "civilians-in-uniform" to comprise a crew typical of those destined to man U.S. destroyers throughout the coming war. Her new skipper, Lieutenant Outerbridge, was very proud of her.[4]

Only a few miles away—7 miles off the channel entrance—the Japanese submarine *I-16* released the first of the midget submarines, manned by Ens. Masaharu Yokoyama and Petty Officer 2d Class Tei Uyeda.[5] "Yokoyama was the most handsome of the midget submariners," recalled Capt. Takayasu Arima, who had been Yamamoto's liaison officer with the midget submarine project. "When he smiled, he looked like an innocent child." But he was a hard worker and had a lot of raw courage.[6] Although of a gentle and retiring disposition, he was no stranger to responsibility, having become the "man" of his family at the age of 9, when his father died, leaving six sons and five daughters.[7]

Most of the officers and men who did not have overnight leave were back on the ships in Pearl Harbor by 0100, when shore leave expired. One seaman just made it under the tape to the heavy cruiser *San Francisco*, "brought aboard under the influence of intoxicating liquor."[8] But it was exceedingly rare that the shore patrol brought in men "for their own good," as the log of the *Maryland* expressed it demurely.[9] Most of the latecomers—and they were few—straggled in on their own steam, having overstayed leave from minutes to several hours.[10] Men began to return from shore patrol duty and others to leave the ships for the same job.[11] It was just another early Sunday morning in Pearl Harbor.

But not outside of it. At 0116, 9 miles off the channel entrance, the submarine *I-22* released Iwasa's midget on what all concerned hoped and believed would be a mission of destruction. To the Japanese, there seemed a good chance that Iwasa and his comrades could enter the harbor and damage a number of ships. Visibility was good, the moon almost full, and the American forces obviously were not on the alert. On the other hand, the tiny craft were admittedly fragile, and when a torpedo was fired the lightened bow headed for the surface, exposing the conning tower. And defects in the communications system were such that all but Yokoyama's minisub lost contact with the mother submarines after launching.[12]

Aboard the carriers, some 200 miles to the north, mechanics had been routed out at 0030.[13] Cmdr. Naohiro Sata, air officer of *Kaga*, had not slept at all, being much too busy making final preparations and rechecking everything personally. "Everything was dark aboard the carrier, and except for moonlight, there were no lights on the flight deck," he recalled. "Officers and men moved hurriedly about like elves in a dark forest."[14] Sata's counterpart aboard the *Zuikaku*, Cmdr. Hisao Shimoda, allowed himself a few hours' sleep, but he, too, rose with his maintenance crews to supervise their preparation of the planes. He had explained to them the importance of properly placing the aircraft, for they would be launched in the order of their positioning.[15]

Upheld but not lulled by his almost exalted sensation of calm assurance, Commander Genda checked the visibility and the condition of the sea and examined all incoming radio information.[16]

At 0150, the task force received a message from the Naval General Staff crammed full of valuable data. It began, "The Naval General Staff is firmly convinced of success."[17] This was a nice touch, for the Naval General Staff had fought against the Pearl Harbor attack until Yamamoto forced the issue by threatening to resign. Now Capt. Sadatoshi Tomioka, chief of the Operations Section of the Naval General Staff, one of the plan's most convinced opponents, had dictated this message to encourage the First Air Fleet "to dash to their objective."[18] The dispatch continued:

1. . . . In the evening of the 5th (local time), *Utah* and a submarine tender entered the harbor. Ships in port on 6th are: nine battleships, three light cruisers, three seaplane tenders and seventeen destroyers, in addition to four light cruisers and two destroyers in the docks. . . . All heavy cruisers and carriers were out of the harbor. . . . No unusual condition was observed concerning the fleet. . . .

4. Telephone contacts made with Japanese and civilians on Oahu from 1330 to 1400 today reported Oahu was very calm and no blackout.

5. . . . No indication of small type planes' activities in the Hawaiian area.[19]

Yoshikawa had incorrectly reported that the *Wyoming* entered port on December 5, but Tokyo correctly relayed the ship as the *Utah*. Bicknell would have been highly interested in paragraph 4. At the very time when he was analyzing the Mori call with General Short and Colonel Fielder, someone on Oahu had informed Tokyo that everything was "very calm," with no blackout in effect.

This message gave the First Air Fleet a satisfying picture, except, of course, for the disappointing confirmation that Kimmel's carriers were absent. At 0200, another message from the Naval General Staff relayed Yoshikawa's information that neither barrage balloons nor antitorpedo nets were in use in Pearl Harbor. For obvious reasons, the Operations Section did not repeat Yoshikawa's indiscreet remark that there was still time to make a surprise attack.[20]

Fifteen minutes later, the third minisub was detached from its mother, the *I-18*, 12.6 miles off Pearl Harbor. The crew consisted of Ens. Shigemi Furuno and Petty Officer 1st Class Shigenori Yokoyama.[21] Evidently Furuno did not expect to emerge from this adventure alive. On his last leave, his father scolded him for wearing civilian clothes, and Furuno replied with a smile, "When I return home, I shall be in a white casket." He seemed attracted rather than repelled by the idea of an early death. His favorite song, which he caroled when in high spirits, contained the line, "I'll come back surely in a small casket."[22]

At 0257, the *I-20* sent off Ens. Akira Hiroo and Petty Officer 2d Class Yoshio Katayama in their midget submarine.[23] Hiroo was the youngest of the group and very enthusiastic.[24] Barely 22, he had a boyish sense of fun. Before leaving Japan, he had remarked to some staying behind, "The ice cream sold at Honolulu is especially fine. I will bring you some when I come back." A hoot of laughter greeted this promise. Undaunted, Hiroo told them he looked forward to landing on Oahu and engaging "in some hot action" with his revolver and sword.[25]

Last to launch was Sakamaki, leaving the *I-24* at 0333, following the discussion about his defective gyroscope.[26] From the moment of release, it was obvious that Sakamaki had a "jinx ship" on his hands. The trim was not working well, and the minisub threatened to surface. Sakamaki did not fear death—he fully expected to die in this engagement—but he did fear the consequences should any blunder of his prematurely disclose the presence of Japanese forces in the area. And he was only 10½ miles from the entrance to Pearl Harbor.

As the little craft bounced up and down, now submerged, now on the surface, Sakamaki and Inagaki scrambled back and forth hauling ballast from stem to bow. This took a long time, because the inside passage was very narrow. Finally, Sakamaki brought the minisub to the surface long enough to take sights on Pearl Harbor. Then he took her down and proceeded toward the harbor, using his magnetic compass.[27]

Meanwhile, at 0200, the minesweepers *Crossbill* and *Condor* left Pearl Harbor and commenced operations.[28] At 0342, the *Condor* was approximately 1¾ miles south of the entrance buoys when her officer of the deck, Ens. R. C. McCloy, noticed "what, in the darkness, appeared to be a wave." He summoned Q.M. 2d Class R. C. Uttrick. Examining this phenomenon through binoculars, "they both were convinced that what they saw was the periscope of a submerged submarine." Helmsman Seaman 1st Class R. B. Chavez could see the wake, but not the periscope itself. The men estimated the distance as around 50 yards.

The submarine was headed toward the entrance buoys and on a

collision course with the *Condor*. It turned "sharply to port," and simultaneously the minesweeper turned to starboard. This incident took place "in a defensive sea area where American submarines had been restricted from operating submerged." At 0357, the *Condor* blinkered to the *Ward*, the channel entrance patrol destroyer, "Sighted submerged submarine on westerly course, speed 9 knots."[29]

Outerbridge was in his cabin when he received the message, and he promptly went out on the adjoining bridge, where he found his executive, Lt. H. T. Doughty. Fully aware of the critical relations between Japan and the United States, Outerbridge thought it likely that this was a genuine sighting. At 0408, the *Ward* went to general quarters and came as close to the *Condor* as it could without fouling the *Condor*'s sweeping gear. Then the *Ward* moved off, slowed to 10 knots, and searched by sonar.[30] After about an hour's fruitless search, Outerbridge contacted the *Condor* by radio to ask, "What was the approximate distance and course of the submarine that you sighted?"

The *Condor* replied, "The course was about what we were steering at the time, 020 magnetic, and about 1000 yards from the entrance apparently heading for the entrance."

This information convinced Outerbridge that he had been searching in the wrong direction, so he headed westward toward Barber's Point. By this time he wondered if the *Condor* actually had seen a submarine; therefore, he radioed the *Condor*, "Do you have any additional information on the sub?"

"No additional information," the *Condor* answered.

"When was the last time approximately that you saw the submarine?" Outerbridge countered.

"Approximate time 0350, and he was apparently heading for the entrance," the *Condor* replied.

"Thank you for your information," Outerbridge radioed courteously. "Notify us if you have any more information."[31]

Outerbridge continued to search "in the restricted area outside the buoys." But the crew of the *Ward* saw and heard nothing, so at 0435 Outerbridge secured from General Quarters, planning to let his men sleep late after tumbling them out of their bunks at such a beastly hour. Now dubious that the *Condor* had seen anything except, perhaps, a buoy, he did not report the incident.[32]

Neither did the *Condor*, nor the radio station at Bishop's Point, which also picked up the conversation. The *Condor*'s skipper thought "that the identification at that time was not positive enough to make a report to other than the Senior Officer Present Afloat," who was Outerbridge. Bishop's Point transcribed the exchange, but because "the conversation was solely between the ships and was not addressed to the Section Base and no request was made that it be relayed,... [it] did not relay or report it to higher authority."[33]

The Americans concerned were thinking in terms of a standard-sized submarine, and it is quite likely that the *Condor* had spotted a minisub whose skipper hoped to slip into the harbor with the mine-sweepers. This might well have been Yokoyama, whose sector covered an arc roughly from directly off the harbor entrance to Barber's Point.* In any event, this submarine escaped for the time being; it could very well have entered the channel with the *Condor* and the *Crossbill* when the protective net opened to admit them at 0458, not closing until 0846. In a pinch, the sub could have edged in under the net, which extended to a depth of 45 feet, whereas the deepest part of the channel was 72 feet. The midget submarines measured 20 feet from keel to conning tower, so this gave some 7 feet of leeway under the net.[34]

Meanwhile, Nagumo's carriers gradually awoke to full life. Cmdr. Takahisa Amagai, air officer of the *Hiryu*, rose at 0330. Like his opposites on the other five carriers, Amagai had three main duties this morning: first, to ensure that the planes were operational; second, to be sure that the airmen had the latest information and were fully briefed; and third, to get the planes off the carriers when the time came.

Amagai's four officer assistants checked the aircraft and reported to him, thus covering the first responsibility. For the second, Amagai personally reviewed the latest information about conditions in Pearl Harbor. Everything seemed to be normal, although he worried about the missing American carriers. Not only was the absence of these prime targets a keen disappointment, but "if they were not in Pearl Harbor, where in hell were they?" Could they be in ambush, waiting to deliver a counterpunch? This prospect also bothered the *Hiryu*'s skipper, Capt. Tomeo Kaku, and his boss, RADM Tamon Yamaguchi, the aggressive commander in chief of the Second Carrier Division (*Soryu* and *Hiryu*).

Despite being busy with his practical duties, Amagai did not forget the symbolic. He ordered *sekihan* prepared for breakfast, a mixture of

---

* See chart following Contents.

rice and beans traditionally eaten to celebrate a birthday, wedding, or festival, and therefore appropriate to celebrate the forthcoming attack.[35]

Another early riser aboard the *Hiryu* was Lt. Heita Matsumura, leader of the carrier's torpedo group. Automatically he adjusted his *masuku*, a lightweight mask that many Japanese wore over their noses and mouths to avoid inhaling or exhaling germs. Matsumura wore a *masuku*, however, because he wanted to spring a surprise on his shipmates. Since leaving Japan, he had been sprouting a mustache under cover of the *masuku*. He had mixed motives for cultivating this adornment. First, on September 22 his wife, Keiko, had given birth to their first child, a daughter, Hisako, whom Matsumura had seen only once. Somehow he felt that sporting a mustache would make him feel more like a man, as befitted a new father. Second, this would be his own way of signaling the start of the war. Third—and no doubt most weighty—"just for the fun of it." He planned to unveil his mustache at an appropriate moment this morning. However, his first thoughts were serious as he made his way to the *Hiryu*'s forequarters to bow before the Shinto shrine.[36]

Aboard the *Hiryu*'s sister ship, the *Soryu,* Sublieutenant Fujita pulled on a complete outfit of clean clothes and pocketed a picture of his deceased parents. In a fatalistic mood, he checked his plane, obtained current information from the *Soryu*'s weather station, and presented himself to Lt. Masaharu Suganami, leader of the *Soryu*'s fighter pilots of the first wave. This officer had no instructions for Fujita, who would participate in the second wave, so for the moment Fujita became an onlooker.[37]

Husky Lt. Tamotsu Ema had passed a restless night aboard the *Zuikaku.* His dive-bomber group under Lt. Akira Sakamoto had the mission of hitting Wheeler Field. Ema had heard that this fighter base had potent antiaircraft batteries, and he wondered if he would emerge alive. He told himself that if he died, "it would be for the Emperor and the Homeland." The sentiment failed to exhilarate him. He was 28 years old, with a wife and month-old daughter he dearly loved. Definitely he did not want to die.[38]

Lt. Yoshio Shiga of the *Kaga* was "one of the most handsome officers in the Japanese Navy." More to the point, he was a good fighter pilot.[39] He had slept soundly and awoke eager for action. He had worked up "a good deal of animosity against United States and Great Britain," especially the former. Now he and his comrades "were about to launch a blow to satisfy our long grudge." Like Fujita, he donned clean clothing from the skin out and headed for breakfast.[40]

When a warrant officer of the maintenance division knocked on Lt. Keizo Ofuchi's door aboard the *Akagi*, Ofuchi "strongly thought that we had come to the last end." This did not mean that he thought his last hour had come, but that the Naval General Staff had canceled the attack. All along he had anticipated that the negotiations in Washington would succeed; moreover, the whole operation seemed to him like some fantastic dream. In fact, he was winging his way to Oahu as a dive-bomber observer before this sense of unreality left him.[41]

Among the late risers was Fuchida, who got up at about 0500. In dressing, he varied the standard uniform by putting on long red underwear and a red flying shirt. Before the task force left the Inland Sea area, he and Murata, leader of the torpedo bombers, had bought similar red garments, reasoning that the color would hide any wounds they might receive in the forthcoming engagement. Both men had highly personal qualities of leadership and feared that the sight of their blood might dismay and demoralize the other flight leaders.

Murata, clad in full flying togs, was already at breakfast when Fuchida entered the wardroom. "Good morning, Commander," the wiry, invincibly good-natured torpedo ace greeted him. "Honolulu sleeps."

"How do you know?" asked Fuchida.

"The Honolulu radio is playing soft music," answered Murata. "Everything is fine."[42]

Breakfast aboard the *Akagi* was a "combat meal" of *nigirimeshi*— a plum inside a rice ball, the whole wrapped in bamboo skin—washed down with green tea.[43] Fuchida was a good trencherman and did full justice to this repast. As he ate, he noticed that the sea had become unusually rough. He and all the other pilots present could not help worrying about the takeoff.

Following breakfast, the flying officers went to the briefing room, located under the flight deck. Here was posted all the information concerning the operation—weather, time of takeoff, position of the targets, everything that could bear on the success of the attack. Before the formal briefing began, Fuchida spoke with Murata and the leader of the fighter pilots, Itaya, about the problems imposed by the heavy seas. Had the carriers been on maneuvers in such rough conditions, takeoff would have been postponed. Under the circumstances, however, there was no such option. Fuchida feared that they might lose a number of aircraft during takeoff, but, as Itaya said, "Even if we lose several planes during the takeoffs, it won't make any difference. We will attack anyway."[44]

After this interlude, Fuchida went up to the operations room to report to Admiral Nagumo, who was waiting with his chief of staff, RADM Ryunosuke Kusaka. The air commander saluted and announced, "I am ready for the mission." Nagumo rose, gripped Fuchida's hand, and replied, "I have confidence in you." Returning to the briefing room, Fuchida passed Genda in the gangway. For an instant their eyes met; no words were spoken or needed. Fuchida grinned, Genda patted his shoulder, and the air commander continued on his way. The *Akagi's* skipper, Capt. Kiichi Hasegawa, was already there when Fuchida arrived, as were Masuda and the other flying officers. Nagumo, Kusaka, and Genda entered within minutes.[45]

Masuda conducted the proceedings and reviewed the general plan. Fuchida gave the main talk, discussing overall attack methods, with special emphasis on those of the high-level bombers which he would lead personally. He stressed the importance of the operation and all it could mean for the destiny of Japan. Murata and Itaya had a few encouraging words for their torpedomen and fighter pilots, respectively, and Hasegawa offered his best wishes for all concerned. Nagumo spoke last, seriously and briefly. He wished them all the best of luck and promised that he would pray for their success.[46]

This ceremony over, one by one Fuchida's key men saluted him and reported in the order in which they would take off from the *Akagi:*

"Air control flight ready!" That was Itaya, the keen-minded but somewhat solitary leader of the fighters.

"Horizontal bomber flight ready!" This from Lt. Izumi Furukawa, whose personal efforts had done so much to improve the high-altitude bombing program.

"Torpedo flight ready!" So spoke Murata, whose flippancy was only exceeded by his aggressiveness.

"Attention!" barked Fuchida, and all the fliers snapped to. Fuchida saluted Hasegawa and said, "Ready!" Thereupon Hasegawa gave the order, "Take off according to plan." Saluting Hasegawa once more, Fuchida turned to his flight officers and ordered, "Take action!"

Nagumo and his staff officers stood nearby, taking this all in. The commander in chief's expression was not that of a man who expects his prayers for success to be answered. It was a study in doubt.[47]

The atmosphere aboard the *Kaga* was tense with the knowledge that this attack would trigger war. Sata briefed his fliers in much the same vein as did Masuda, ending, "This is a chance that comes once in a lifetime. Everyone should do all in his power to perform his duty." Then Capt. Jisaku Okada encouraged his men to live up to the best traditions of the Japanese warrior and to the teachings they had received during their training.[48]

The *Kaga*'s pilots checked their air charts with the carrier's position and made the necessary adjustments. Having memorized them, they erased all positions from the charts, so that if they should be shot down and captured, the Americans could not use these charts to locate the Japanese carriers. "The important thing," said Shiga, "was to remember the route back."[49]

Briefings aboard the other carriers followed much the same lines. Amagai gave the *Hiryu*'s airmen the latest word on the situation at Pearl Harbor and emphasized exactly where to find the carrier on their return from the attack. Following Amagai, Captain Kaku gave a short pep talk, bearing down on the seriousness of the forthcoming war between Japan and the United States. He urged every man to do his duty to the utmost.

Amagai hoped to keep his officers and crew relaxed, and in this aim Matsumura contributed by appearing without his *masuku*, revealing his new mustache, much to the amusement of his fellows.[50]

Ema enjoined his men aboard the *Zuikaku* that they should attack Wheeler Field against the wind, so that smoke from the bombing would not obscure the targets.[51] Shimoda expressed his conviction in the success of the attack. If all concerned did their very best, heaven would bless their efforts.[52]

On the *Zuikaku*'s sister ship, the *Shokaku*, flagship of the Fifth Carrier Division, air officer Cmdr. Tetsujiro Wada and the squadron leaders gave brief instructions, and senior staff officer Ohashi spoke a few words of encouragement.[53] Finally, RADM Chuichi "King Kong" Hara, the division commander in chief, urged his men to "keep smiling" and, more seriously, exhorted them to adhere to the rules of warfare and attack only military objectives.[54] On the basis of the information available to them, both Hara and Ohashi were fairly sure that Hawaii was not on the alert and that the attack would be a success.[55]

CHAPTER 7

"To the Point of Attack"

Around 0230, Lt. Kermit A. Tyler awoke in the quarters he shared with Lt. Charles H. MacDonald in the Haleiwa area. He dressed quickly, made himself breakfast and coffee, and then scrambled into his car for the drive of some 35 miles that would take him to Fort Shafter. A fighter pilot, unmarried, Tyler was happy in Hawaii and liked his duty as executive officer of the 78th Pursuit* Squadron. Normally his work hours were more civilized than from 0400 to 0800, but he had drawn duty as pursuit officer at the Information Center.[1]

As he sped through the blackness, Tyler turned on his car radio, picking up the same soft Hawaiian music that convinced Murata that Hawaii slept unsuspecting. To Tyler it meant something quite different. Recently, Lt. Morris Shedd, a friend and a bomber pilot, had told him that "any time that they play this Hawaiian music all night long, it is a very good indication that our B-17s were coming over from the mainland, because they use it for homing." Obviously, a flight of the big bombers was en route to Oahu.[2]

Tyler was on time to begin work, but, as he explained later, "I did not know what my duties were. I just was told to be there and told to maintain that work."[3]

Located in a two-story building that looked to Tyler like a converted barracks, the Information Center was the nerve center of the Aircraft Warning Service. On the first floor, a table about five times the size of a bed held a large map of the Hawaiian Islands and the

---

* The name "Pursuit" was changed later to "Fighter" for all such units.

surrounding air space. During duty hours, a group of enlisted men stood around the table, marking on the map information telephoned from the radar stations. Each of these plotters had a phone that connected him to one particular station, and when he received the position of a sighting, he marked it on the board with a movable arrow indicating the direction of the flight. In addition, another telephone operator manned a separate line for nontechnical calls. To one side stood another enlisted man, known as the "historical plotter." This soldier kept a record of sightings and also carried a small plotting board on which he marked the position of aircraft as yet out of range of the main board. From a large balcony at second-floor level, the controller and pursuit officer on duty could look down on all this activity.[4]

The controller was in charge. He would determine the necessity for sending up fighter aircraft to intercept an unidentified flight, and he would instruct the pursuit officer "to order so many squadrons off and tell them where to send them." To help him contact the fighter squadrons, the pursuit officer had a small switchboard that could reach those organizations.[5]

Theoretically, it was all very impressive, but on the morning of December 7, 1941, it was an exercise in futility. "The crux of the entire problem was the identification of approaching aircraft," Tyler stressed. "For the information that came in from the outlying radar stations was useless unless it was evaluated."[6] There was no way to do this, however. The radar equipment could not distinguish friend from foe. And as yet neither the Navy, the bomber command, nor the local civil defense organization had assigned a liaison officer to the Information Center. Hence the center personnel had no way of telling whose aircraft was being reported. There would have been no Army Air Corps officers assigned to the Information Center had it not been for the initiative of Maj. Kenneth P. Bergquist, technically the operations officer of the Hawaiian Interceptor Command, which had not yet been formally activated. The operation of the Aircraft Warning Service was under the Hawaiian Department's signal officer.

Bergquist's instructions to the pursuit officers had been verbal and unavoidably vague: "...they were to go down there during the times I specified, acquaint themselves with the whole setup as far as they possibly could, and if anything went wrong they were to notify me."[7]

To Tyler, "radar was so new that the word was unknown to me several weeks before Pearl Harbor."[8] He had been through the Information Center once with a group of officers on an orientation tour. His first and—up to December 7—his only duty there had been from 1200 to 1700 on Wednesday, December 3. At that time he and the telephone operator were the only persons present. Having no instructions, Tyler telephoned Bergquist for clarification. This took a certain amount of courage on his part, for he considered Bergquist "very energetic, dedicated, very busy and somewhat unapproachable."[9] Bergquist told Tyler that they were trying to get the Information Center set up and that they "were leading off by furnishing personnel to man it." Thus Tyler got the idea that he was there for training. Bergquist informed him that "if any of our planes went down we might, by radar reports, be able to tell where they came down," and Tyler "would be able to assist in that." The major further said that Tyler "was to help locate aircraft that might be in trouble."[10]

This left Tyler little the wiser. But it did not matter; Wednesday afternoons were free time for most of the Army personnel on Oahu, so he had little to do beyond familiarizing himself with the setup. That was the extent of Tyler's background, experience, and training as pursuit officer when he walked into the Information Center at 0400 on December 7.[11]

He was rather surprised to find five plotters already in position around the table, one for each of the mobile stations on Oahu, as well as the historical plotter and the administrative switchboard operator, Pvt. Joseph McDonald, who had been on duty since 1700 Saturday evening. There was no sign of a controller—not too surprising, for Bergquist considered that no Army officer on Oahu except himself and Maj. Lorry N. Tindal were really qualified as such. Tyler settled down for what promised to be another boring session, broken only by a few scattered arrows on the board over the next 2½, almost 3, hours.[12]

Of the five mobile radar sites—Opana, Kaaawa, Kawailoa, Koko Head, and the backup station at Fort Shafter—Opana, located near Kahuku Point on the northern tip of Oahu, was considered the best.[13] Its 270-B unit was mounted on two van-type trucks, only a few feet from the officer's war tent where Pvts. Joseph L. Lockard and George E. Elliott were sleeping. They and their fellow soldiers who manned the Opana Mobile Station lived about 10 miles away at Kawailoa, but they had been sent out to Opana Saturday afternoon "just to be on the unit in case any prowlers or anyone should come around. It wasn't a regular guard post or a walking post or anything of that nature, but it did call for two men to be present at all times at the unit." They did not have to stay awake all night, but they did have to rise in time to go on duty to operate the radar station itself at 0400.[14]

The young men kept busy Saturday afternoon repairing the oil pump on the generator motor in the power plant. When the alarm clock roused them at 0345, they hastily dressed and finished work on the oil pump. This ran them a little late, and they went on the air at 0415.[15] Another soldier was supposed to be on duty also—a "motor man" with the duty of maintaining and operating the engine and generator. But he did not show up, a circumstance that did not unduly surprise Lockard. As he remarked tactfully later, "Very few people like to get up at 4 o'clock on Sunday morning."[16] The more experienced of the two in the radar field, Lockard operated the oscilloscope, which registered visual echoes of planes picked up at a maximum effective distance of 130 miles. Elliott observed and acted as plotter.[17]

This Sunday was developing into an unusually dull morning. Normally around twenty-five targets appeared in the early hours; today there were few, if any, certainly none worth reporting to the Information Center.[18]

The radar watchers and recorders on Oahu had been on the job an hour and a half when, some 220 miles to the north, the Japanese heavy cruisers *Tone* and *Chikuma* each sent aloft a single-engine, Zero-type reconnaissance seaplane. These aircraft, which carried a pilot, observer, and wireless operator, were the only two of that type with the task force. With a roundtrip capacity of 800 to 1000 miles, this type of aircraft had the longest range of any Japanese shipborne reconnaissance plane. The *Tone*'s scout was to reconnoiter Lahaina Anchorage. The scout submarine *I-72* had on the previous day advised that the U.S. Fleet was not in this harbor, but the Japanese were taking no chances that their information might not be absolutely current. After scouting Lahaina, this plane was to patrol south of Pearl Harbor in search of U.S. ships, especially the carriers. The *Chikuma*'s plane would double-check Pearl Harbor and make a last-minute report of ships in the great anchorage and weather conditions over the target. Neither scout would directly overfly their targets, but would stay approximately 5 miles to the side.[19]

As the two scouts took the air, "there was a little mess on board the other ships, taking these two planes for enemy planes," Genda remembered, "but in a minute they proved to be ours, and the slight commotion was settled."[20]

Takeoff of the first wave of attacking aircraft would not wait on the reports of the scouts. Fuchida was to receive the results en route, either by direct pickup or from the *Akagi*. As soon as the briefing was over, Nagumo and his key staff officers, among them Kusaka, Senior Staff Officer Cmdr. Tamotsu Oishi, Genda, Navigator Cmdr. Gishiro Miura, and, of course, the *Akagi*'s skipper, Captain Hasegawa, mounted the bridge. "I have brought the task force successfully to the point of attack," Nagumo told Genda. "From now on the burden is on your shoulders and the rest of the flying group." Genda replied confidently, "Admiral, I am sure the airmen will succeed." From that moment until after the attack, channels bowed to expertise. Genda gave the orders; Nagumo and Kusaka approved them.[21]

A strong east wind was blowing. "Waves bounce over the bow of the ship," recorded Chigusa aboard the *Akigumo*, some 500 meters aft of the *Shokaku*. "Since about 0100 big noise of airplane propellers is heard."[22] The Third Battleship Division's diarist observed briefly that visibility was "suitable for flight," adding, "Pretty rough sea."[23]

This was a considerable understatement. When Fuchida reached the command post on the upper flight deck, he found Masuda very worried about the heavy pitching and rolling, so strong that high waves were splashing water over the flight deck. Masuda cast a dubious glance over the angry ocean and asked, "What about this rough sea?" But it was much too late for second thoughts, so Fuchida answered, "I have already given the word for action." Then he said his goodbyes to those on the command post, including the ship's paymaster and doctor, who had come up from below to watch the takeoff, and strode toward his plane.[24]

Before taking off, each flying officer and crewman tied around his head a *hachimaki*, a white cloth traditionally so bound when a Japanese embarked on a project of great moment requiring courage and determination. The *hachimaki* the airmen wore were marked with the symbol of the Rising Sun and the legend, "Sure Victory." Then the men pulled on their flight helmets.[25]

The *Akagi*'s senior maintenance crewman approached Fuchida, a *hachimaki* in his hand. "All of the maintenance crew members would like to go along to Pearl Harbor," he said. "But since we cannot, please take this *hachimaki* from us as a symbol that we are with you in spirit." Knowing very well how much he and his fellow fliers depended on the unsung work of these men, Fuchida thanked their representative warmly and bound the scarf over his helmet.[26]

It was still dark; the sun had not yet risen, and the sky was heavily overcast. Maintenance men were busy with last-minute checkups. Like the other airmen, Lt. Jinichi Goto personally inspected his plane to make sure that it was airworthy, fueled, and fitted with ammunition. Satisfied that his torpedo bomber was in perfect shape, Goto exchanged goodbyes and good wishes with those nearby. He was neither nervous nor pessimistic. The fact that the Americans had not detected the task force gave him confidence that all would go well. Somehow, too, he felt sure that he would survive and return safely to the *Akagi*.[27]

"The takeoff was postponed about twenty minutes owing to the weather conditions," recalled Matsumura. During this interval, maintenance crews shouted encouragement, and the fliers in turn sung out their promise of "certain success."[28]

As the moment of takeoff approached, each carrier and its escort vessels turned eastward into the wind for about 15 minutes, raising speed to 24 knots to ensure proper wind velocity for takeoff.[29]

Ofuchi acted as takeoff officer aboard the *Akagi*, signaling with flags to each pilot when he should start his run. "It was difficult to figure the pitch and the roll and to get each plane off at the exact second when it was most propitious," he explained.[30]

The fighters were scheduled to take off first. With a one-man crew and no bomb load, they needed only a comparatively short run. So, on the *Akagi*, attention centered on Itaya as his plane lifted off. Suddenly the Zero dropped out of sight. Ofuchi gulped. Quite aside from the loss of Itaya, it would be an ill omen indeed if the first plane off crashed into the sea. "But he made it and soared upward like a great bird." The first aircraft was aloft "in first-rate order." Surely this augured well.[31]

All six carriers launched simultaneously. Shiga, aboard the *Kaga*, had hoped to be the first in the air so that he could be "the first man to go to war against the enemy," but Itaya beat him to the punch. Shiga was not the sulky type, however. Like all the fighter pilots, he was in high spirits. And he had complete confidence in his Zero, despite its lack of armor, for it had excellent maneuverability, long range, and good firepower. So he looked forward to a duel with an American pursuit plane. He took off smoothly, although, like Itaya's, his Zero dipped briefly on takeoff. Then he recovered and swung outboard—the second man in the air. It was a great thrill for the eager young pilot.[32]

The *Hiryu* was "pitching and rolling a good deal" under "a sea of cloud," according to Lt. Kiyokuma Okajima, who led the Fourth Air

Control Group of fighters.[33] Still, 1st PO Kazuo Muranaka, piloting the second plane of the first group, took off quite easily, "owing to the relatively strong wind." Peering over the side of his fighter, he could see the *Hiryu*'s senior officers and his shipmates lined up on both sides of the flight deck, waving flags and caps.[34]

With the last fighter airborne, the horizontal bombers followed, Fuchida in the lead. The high-level bombers, carrying a crew of three and one bomb weighing roughly a ton, had a built-in capacity for trouble, especially in view of the restricted runway space and the heavy seas.[35] But everything went well, although Lt. Heijiro Abe, leading his group off the *Soryu*, did not have room for a really good run and his bomber dropped sickeningly before it clawed itself aloft.[36]

Lt. Cmdr. Takashi Hashiguchi, a calm and gentle person who listened more than he spoke, led the *Kaga*'s horizontal bomber group. He considered the takeoff a routine matter. His superiors thought so well of this veteran of 10 years' flying experience that he had been selected as Fuchida's substitute should anything untoward happen to the latter either before or during the forthcoming attack.[37]

The last horizontal bomber barely cleared the deck when the dive bombers commenced to rise, under the leadership of Lt. Cmdr. Kakuchi Takahashi of the *Shokaku*. A big man, a little slow on the uptake, and so ruddy that his friends nicknamed him "*Aka-san*" (red-faced), he was also an expert dive bomber and solidly dependable. Like all the fliers, Takahashi carried a map of Oahu, a pistol, a knife, and a waterproof cork jacket, the latter to give a slim chance of survival in case he had to ditch at sea, for these men wore no parachutes. The planes held certain emergency equipment—a life raft and a pump to inflate it, a first-aid kit, and a small supply of food and water.[38]

Taking off under the rough sea conditions was difficult for Lt. Iwakichi Mifuku, also of the *Shokaku*. In his haste to gain altitude, he penetrated the cloud cover and lost sight of the preceding planes' lights, so he hastily dropped below the clouds to join the formation.[39]

Lieutenant Ema, on his first combat mission, also had some difficulty in making formation because of the clouds, so much so that he worried lest he and his comrades overshoot Oahu. He remembered that some of the bombs bore a message that enthusiastic crewmen had brushed on them—"The bombs which will start the war between Japan and the United States"—and he was conscious of his great responsibility.[40]

The last of the attacking planes to lift off were the torpedo bombers, heavily loaded with their missiles and three-man crews, under Murata's dynamic leadership. Fuchida described him as "a real comedian; everyone loved him. . . . He could melt any tense atmosphere in a minute." In addition, he was unquestionably Japan's ace torpedoman, fearless and cool under pressure.[41]

When Goto came to his moment of takeoff, the gravity and drama of the situation overcame his serenity. As his plane lumbered forward, followed by the farewell waves of his shipmates, the intensity of the moment and the thought of the tremendous mission ahead, as well as the poignancy of parting, brought a sudden welling of tears to his eyes.[42]

In contrast, Lt. Atsuki Nakajima of the Soryu "felt nothing particular. It was just like the usual training flights."[43] Lt. Ichiro Kitajima of the Kaga entertained unpleasant recollections of the occasion: "The takeoff on that morning was very hard; the planes were too overloaded; the carrier rolled and pitched a good deal, and it was still too dark for the takeoff."[44]

Matsumura experienced "a strange, eerie sensation" as his plane lifted off the Hiryu's flight deck and plunged down briefly into the darkness and mist: "I had a feeling as I took off that the darkness would envelop me completely and that I would never return." This feeling left him in seconds when he realized that his bomber "was getting upward in the still dark sky."[45]

The entire launching had taken only 15 minutes—better time than the task force had achieved in any practice maneuver. Under the circumstances, takeoff had been perfect, except for one fighter that crashed. Although the plane was lost, a destroyer rescued the pilot.[46]

One final group of planes remained to be launched—thirty-nine fighters, composed of three each from the Akagi and the Kaga, six from the Soryu, and nine each from the Hiryu, the Shokaku, and the Zuikaku—as protection for the task force should any American pursuit craft appear to dispute the air space. These planes guarded the carriers in relays, roughly half on deck and half aloft close to the flattops, within 10 kilometers in each direction.[47]

VADM Gunichi Mikawa, commanding the support force, which consisted of the Third Battleship Division and Eighth Cruiser Division, watched from the bridge of his flagship, the battleship Hiei. He was amazed at the speed and skill with which the aircraft took to the sky and formed into groups. "The formation of the first group of attacking planes was a truly beautiful sight," he said later.[48] Chigusa, too, "was much impressed" as he watched from the *Akigumo*. "All the crew of my ship were on deck waving their caps and hoping for the success of the planes as they were taking off."[49]

For about 15 minutes the aircraft circled on the outboard side of the carriers, Fuchida's orange light easily distinguishable from the yellow lights of the flight commanders. Then, at around 0620, Fuchida led his horizontal bomber group across the *Akagi*'s bow, the signal to set course for Oahu, and the first wave headed south.[50]

Meanwhile, when the final torpedo bomber soared off, the task force turned south at roughly 24 knots. All those concerned expected many of the attacking planes to be badly shot up, so the carriers should be as near the scene of action as they safely could. While on this southbound run, deck crews worked ceaselessly to bring the remaining aircraft from hangars to flight decks. Aboard the *Kaga*, this operation lagged some 15 minutes, because the carrier's elevators were old and slow. All told, roughly an hour elapsed before the takeoff of the second wave.[51]

Several officers took advantage of this interlude to issue final instructions and exhortations. Lt. Takehiko Chihaya, in command of the Eleventh Dive Bomber Group, rounded up his pilots and observers. Among them was Ofuchi, now released from his extra duty as the *Akagi*'s takeoff officer. Ofuchi had immense respect for his leader. "Lieutenant Chihaya was broadminded, brave and daring—a silent type who never boasted," although he had racked up an excellent combat record in the China theater. Now Chihaya informed his men that as yet no new information had come in about the enemy. He stressed that they must remember the planned position of the task force, so that they could find their home carrier after the attack.[52]

Just before Chihaya clambered into his plane, Genda gave him a strict order to report as promptly as possible the nature and strength of the antiaircraft fire encountered. Genda was thinking ahead. If this attack proved successful, it might be possible and advisable to mount a second. On the degree of American antiaircraft effectiveness would depend whether or not such a second major strike would include torpedo bombers. Chihaya had plenty to think about—to lead a dive-bomber group, deliver his own missile, report to Genda, and, in addition, lead back the fighters after the attack.[53]

An Eta Jima classmate of Chihaya's, Lt. Fusata Iida, counseled his fighter pilots on the *Soryu* in a Spartan vein. Iida was one of the naval air arm's most promising young officers. So intelligent that he graduated from Eta Jima with an imperial prize, he had also been the best tennis player in his class and excelled at baseball. "Iida was tall and very handsome," said Shiga. "We all wondered how he could stay single so long." His gentle disposition and even temper won him the nickname "*Ojosan*" (daughter),[54] yet he was, in Fuchida's words, "brave, with a strong fighting spirit; skillful in combat."[55]

Now he posed a rhetorical question: "What are you going to do in case you have engine trouble in flight?" Before anyone could speak up, he answered his own query: "In case of engine trouble, I will fly straight to my objective and make a crash dive into an enemy target rather than an emergency landing."[56]

At 0705, the carriers repeated the maneuver of turning into the wind and increasing speed. The morning was growing brighter, but clouds still limited the ceiling to roughly 1 mile, with visibility about 12 miles.

This second wave was no mere mop-up operation. The Japanese had decided to divide the aircraft into two sections because the full complement could not become airborne quickly enough for one big strike. A single mass attack would have been ideal from the standpoint of surprise and maximum damage, but the first planes aloft would have had to circle for an undue period, thus wasting time and fuel.

Nagumo and his staff, as well as the key airmen, expected the second wave to suffer considerable damage because, by the time it struck, the Japanese would have lost the element of surprise. With the Americans aroused and waiting, the sky over Oahu could be a deadly obstacle course of antiaircraft shells and U.S. fighter planes. This expectation of heavy losses was the main reason why the second wave contained no torpedo planes. These slow-moving, almost defenseless aircraft depended heavily on surprise and an unobstructed view of the target. By the time the second wave reached Pearl Harbor, smoke from the first strike should be rolling over the ships and airfields, making a clear sighting extremely difficult, if not impossible.

At 0715, Lt. Saburo Shindo of the *Akagi*, a first-rate pilot, was the first man off. He would lead the thirty-six fighter aircraft—nine each from the *Akagi*, the *Kaga*, the *Soryu* and the *Hiryu*[57]—and then observe battle results. Shindo possessed "a very logical mind" but was somewhat phlegmatic. He "did not have any particular feeling" that morning; Pearl Harbor was just another air operation as far as he was concerned.[58]

The horizontal bombers flew off next. All were from the Fifth Carrier Division, the *Shokaku* and the *Zuikaku* each contributing twenty-seven. Their leader, Lt. Cmdr. Shigekazu Shimazaki, also headed the entire second wave. He was a command pilot. Nerves had seemingly been omitted from his construction, and he functioned at his best under fire.[59] In personality he was somewhat like his brother-in-law and close friend, Takahashi—"a good solid type with a fine sense of humor, but not too bright; very practical and a good leader."[60]

Sublt. Zenichi Sato, a unit leader of the *Zuikaku*'s horizontal bombers, had been the carrier's takeoff officer for the first wave. Now, despite the lightening skies, the heavy clouds caused him "much apprehension" about the ability of the pilots to maintain the planes in proper position.[61] His shipmate Lt. Jozo Iwami worried because just before takeoff someone told him that the position of the carriers shown on the plane navigation charts was not accurate. These charts were printed upside down, with a view toward concealing the carriers from the Americans should one of the charts fall into their hands, but this maneuver also confused the Japanese who had to use them. Iwami's thoughts centered on the problems of leading his squadron to Oahu and getting them safely back to the *Zuikaku* when the attack was over.[62]

The dive bombers came from the First and Second Carrier Divisions—eighteen each from the *Akagi*, the *Soryu*, and the *Hiryu*, twenty-six from the *Kaga*. At their head flew Lt. Cmdr. Takeshige Egusa of the *Soryu*, whom Genda termed "the Number One dive-bombing pilot in all Japan."[63] His close friend Fuchida considered Egusa "perhaps the bravest of all Japanese naval pilots." A clever man whom everyone trusted, Egusa "never knew the meaning of the word 'quit'; he never complained."[64]

Lt. Zenji Abe, squadron leader of the *Akagi*'s dive bombers, had engaged in no battles worthy of the name in China, so he considered himself a newcomer to combat. "I was nervous, mixed with some excitement of going to unknown enemy territory for the first time in my life."[65]

Lt. Michio Kobayashi, commanding the *Hiryu*'s Fourteenth Group, experienced the only mishap of the second-wave takeoff. His bomber developed engine trouble and had to be withdrawn. Kobayashi was one of the most skilled dive bombers, and his absence could make a difference. He begged permission to follow the attacking force as soon as repairs had been completed. He pleaded that for want of his bomb "an American ship might escape." But Captain Kaku was adamant. A lone bomber without fighter cover would be easy pickings for an American interceptor. The petty officer in charge of Kobayashi's bomber was so ashamed that he came to the bridge and apologized profusely for not having kept the plane in tiptop shape.[66]

Complete launching of both waves had taken 90 minutes. Meanwhile, at 0630, the battleships *Hiei* and *Kirishima* and the heavy cruisers *Tone* and *Chikuma* each sent up three patrol planes. Four searched east, another four west, to warn Nagumo of the possible approach of American ships or planes. Another four headed south, to seek U.S. submarines and, if found, to bomb them. With both attack waves aloft, the task force turned south and advanced to about 180 miles north of Oahu.[67]

After the aircraft departed, the ships maintained strict radio silence. All hands remained at their battle stations with lookouts on a double alert. "Radio operators were glued to their seats listening for any possible indication of the enemy," recalled Amagai. The task force must rely on the radio, the fighters circling above, and the patrol aircraft to spot a possible counterattack, for these Japanese ships had no radar.[68]

Nagumo watched his air armada disappear southward. Beside him stood Kusaka, "filled with deep emotion" despite his usual Buddhistic calm.[69] For a few minutes Genda stayed on the bridge, savoring his pride in the skill and efficiency displayed by the takeoff. Then he went to the control room to await Fuchida's attack signal. Cheering deckhands, some frankly weeping with emotion, waved their caps until the planes disappeared. Now all of them, from Nagumo down channels, could do nothing but wait.[70]

CHAPTER 8

"Suitable Dawn for the Epoch-Making Day"

While the Japanese were making their final preparations for the attack, the stores and supply ship *Antares* lumbered her way toward Pearl Harbor, a lighter in tow. The *Antares* was, in the words of her skipper, Cmdr. Lawrence C. Grannis, "one of those Hog Island ships with no armament that did very well if it made 9 knots." Grannis was nearing the end of a long, tiring trip from Palmyra and Canton islands after delivering supplies and about 240 workmen. The *Antares* had sighted Diamond Head at 0130 and passed the Barber's Point Light at 0545.[1]

Grannis had been on the bridge since 0230 and was awaiting with considerable eagerness the arrival of both the tug that would take over the lighter and the harbor pilot who would guide the *Antares* to her moorings in Pearl Harbor. As he watched, "the sun came up in all its glory, and the dawn and morning were especially beautiful." Suddenly he spotted something peculiar almost submerged in the water. He did not know quite what to make of it, for it did not look like any submarine he had ever seen. Yet it must be one, for its conning tower was showing. The strange undersea craft was "obviously having depth control trouble and...trying to go down."[2]

The log of the *Antares* recorded as of 0630: "Sighted suspicious object bearing 227°. True, distance about 1500 yards on starboard quarter."[3] Grannis passed this information to the *Ward*, requesting that the destroyer investigate.[4] Before the *Ward* could act, Ens. William Tanner, piloting a PBY on routine morning patrol, glimpsed the floundering object. Deducing that this was an American submarine in distress, at 0633 he dropped two smoke pots near the object, to help guide the *Ward* on what Tanner assumed was a rescue mission.[5]

The *Ward*'s helmsman was the first aboard her to see the "suspicious object" the *Antares* had reported. At first, it looked to him like a buoy; then he and Lieutenant Goepner "decided probably it was a conning tower of a submarine, although we didn't have anything that looked like it in our Navy," and they had never seen anything like it. So Goepner called to Outerbridge, "Captain, come on the bridge!"

Outerbridge immediately spotted the conning tower awash; probably, he thought, the skipper believed his craft was completely submerged. The sub was making about 12 knots—"fairly fast." Outerbridge had no doubt that the intruder was unfriendly, whether German or Japanese he could not tell. However, it was making no aggressive moves, which somewhat puzzled him. "She is going to follow the *Antares* in, whatever it is," he decided.[6]

The sighting came at 0637. Within 3 minutes, Outerbridge acted. Not only was the object unmistakably a submarine unlike any American craft, but Outerbridge had orders to attack any submarine in the restricted area.[7] He ordered General Quarters at 0640, and his men tumbled out of their bunks once more to their battle stations. The *Ward*'s gunner, a chief petty officer, asked, "Captain, what are we going to do?" Outerbridge assured him, "We are going to shoot."[8]

The destroyer plunged toward the submarine, "all engines ahead full," as her crewmen brought up ammunition and loaded the guns. When the *Ward* reached some 50 yards abeam the target, she commenced firing. The first round, from No. 1 gun at 0645, "missed, passing directly over the conning tower." Then No. 3 gun fired "at a range of 50 yards or less," striking the submarine "at the waterline...the junction of the hull and conning tower." Several members of the crew saw the damage, "a square positive hit" with "no evidence of ricochet."

This seemed "to shake up the sub," which heeled over to starboard and "appeared to slow and sink." Then it apparently passed under the *Ward*'s stern and ran into "a full pattern of depth charges" set for about 100 feet. "The submarine sank in 1200 feet of water.... There was a large amount of oil on the surface where the depth charges exploded."

At 0646 Outerbridge ordered "Cease Fire" and broke off the depth-charge attack. Later he described the midget sub: "Cylindrical tube about 80 feet long with small oval-shaped conning tower. It has no deck. It was painted dark green and was covered with moss indicating that it had been at sea for a considerable period."[9]

Meanwhile, Tanner, although plagued with doubts, remembered his own orders to sink any unauthorized submarine in the defensive sea area, and he bombed the submarine. Patrol Wing Two claimed the sinking.[10] So did Outerbridge, reporting to the Fourteenth Naval District at 0651: "We have dropped depth charges upon sub operating in defensive sea area."

Almost immediately, however, he reflected to himself, "Well, now, maybe I had better be more definite." He later explained his reasoning: "...we did fire and if we said we fired, people would know it was on the surface, because saying it was a sub and dropping depth charges, they may have said it might have been a blackfish or a whale." So, at 0653, he sent off an amended message: "We have attacked, fired upon, and dropped depth charges upon submarine operating in defensive sea area." Outerbridge was sure that his destroyer had knocked off an unfriendly submarine, but he had no idea that its presence heralded a mass air attack such as the one then bearing down on Oahu.[11]

While this burst of activity was taking place off Oahu, the all-night musical program that KGMB was sending out for the benefit of Landon's B-17s was of considerable help to the first wave of oncoming Japanese fliers. "On the way to Oahu my plane's observer informed me that a Hawaii radio station was broadcasting routine morning music," recalled Mifuku. "This made me feel sure that we could make a surprise attack."[12]

Muranaka turned the switch of his "radio-detecting instrument" to pick up Oahu and heard something he would never forget: "There happened to come in a lovely teenage girl singing a Japanese song 'Come on a Pony' [*Menkoi Kouma*]. Thinking about what would happen to such lovely children and what a change in their lives would occur only an hour and a half later, I couldn't listen to it any more and turned off the switch."[13]

Lt. Heijiro Abe also heard *Menkoi Kouma*. But the child's song which so touched Muranaka brought Abe only reassurance. Routine morning music from Oahu meant that the attack force most probably had not been detected; hence a surprise attack would be possible. Then unbidden images and memories sprang to mind: "Impressive were the beautiful clouds colored by the rising sun. It reminded me of the cloud formations I saw in the dawn attack of January 1, 1938, in south China—clouds that rolled over the horizon like a huge pile of red rocks." While he could and did appreciate the beauty of the sunlit clouds, he worried over the feasibility of level bombing should that cloud cover persist over the target.[14]

Goto's confidence had increased with each passing mile; nevertheless, as his group from the *Akagi* sped nearer and nearer to Oahu, the sky grew ever more overcast until it seemed to him that fate itself flew with them. He became quite apprehensive lest they miss their target.[15]

Leading his torpedo group from the *Hiryu*, Matsumura absorbed the glory of that sunrise: "Soon the eastern sky brightened and each cloud ball was distinctly marked by bright side and shadow, sunbeams coming down through breaks in the clouds straight onto the blue sea. It was the suitable dawn for the epoch-making day, I felt at the time."[16]

Little imagination was required to transform the red disk of the sun with its shafts of light into a symbolic representation of Japan's naval flag. The sight so inspired Fuchida that he stood impulsively. Looking behind him, he saw his first wave droning along, its formation perfect, throwing off reflections from the sun's rays. He drank in the spectacle for several minutes, thrilling with pride; then he sat down and became once more the practical leader. At just past 0700 he tuned his receiver to KGMB and instructed his pilot to use the music as a homing beam. Fuchida had ambivalent feelings about the heavy cloud coverage below at some 5000 feet. True, it provided excellent screening, but it might cause his men to overfly Pearl Harbor and alert Oahu's defenses; conceivably they could miss the island itself.[17]

Fuchida had no way of knowing that not only had the midget submarines triggered premature action, just as he and other airmen had feared, but U.S. radar was beginning to track his first wave. Roughly the first 2 hours of Tyler's duty at the Information Center were so dull that he whiled away the time writing letters.[18] In fact, no plots were recorded until about 0610. Then Hawaii's skies began to wake up, and "a number of plots or indications, some arrows, appeared on the board to show that there was aircraft flying around the islands."[19]

In about half an hour, blips became fairly numerous. Between 0640 and 0651, the station at Koko Head recorded four sightings, all south of Oahu. The backup station at Fort Shafter picked up something at 0652 off Barber's Point.[20] Probably these represented the U.S. Navy's dawn patrol.

At roughly the same time, three stations began to sight aircraft coming toward Oahu from the north. Kaaawa logged in five plots between 0646 and 0654.[21] Of course, there was no way to tell whether these were five separate aircraft or a time track of the same plane. In any case, evidently the sightings made little or no impression on the men operating that particular station. Michaud was not on duty, but he ate breakfast and chatted for at least an hour with the three who had been covering Kaaawa. They were still together when they saw the first aerial combat, and they made no remarks about the activities of the morning.[22]

Kawailoa registered four blips to the north, at 0648, 0650, 0651, and 0652, respectively.[23] The Opana chart, in Elliott's handwriting, recorded nine sightings from 0645 to 0700, at distances ranging from 18 to 74 miles. These blips made so little an impression on Elliott that he did not remember them until they were called to his attention when he appeared before the congressional committee in February of 1946. He did not believe they could have been multiple sightings, since "there was no exceptional echo on the scope." And he could not remember whether they had been telephoned to the Information Center.[24] It is very possible that these three stations—Kaaawa, Kawailoa, and Opana—had picked up traces of the reconnaissance plane from the *Chikuma* on its way to scout off Pearl Harbor.

Shortly before 0700, Tyler walked over to the historical plotter to see what he was doing and noticed several markings on his chart that were too far out to record on the main board. Among them he noticed two plots north of Oahu, one south of Molokai, and another south of Maui. "Having seen the plotters work once before with about the same general layout," he stated some 2 weeks later, "this did not seem irregular to me."[25] Almost certainly the plane south of Maui was the *Tone* scout, about to size up the situation at Lahaina anchorage.

Meanwhile, Outerbridge's morning continued to be action-packed. During the engagement against the minisub, the *Antares* noted that a "Japanese-type Sampan was within 500 yards of submarine when sighted."[26] Two minutes after the *Ward* ended her depth-charge attack, Outerbridge turned his attention to this vessel, "one of these large white sampans." Sampans were not supposed to be "lying out there in the defensive area," so Outerbridge pursued it toward Barber's Point. There the sampan halted, and her captain "came up waving a white flag." Outerbridge "thought that was funny."[27] However, one can imagine that a commercial skipper who has witnessed at close

hand action involving ship's gunfire, depth charges, and aerial bombs
and then has been chased by a destroyer might well consider it pru-
dent to show a flag of truce.

The sampan chase began at 0648 and took some minutes, in the
course of which at 0703 the *Ward* "established sound contact on enemy submarine." Two minutes later she dropped depth charges and
almost immediately saw "black oil bubbles 300 yards astern."[28]
Outerbridge discounted this incident; he barely mentioned it in his
official testimony, and later he remarked, "I did not have too much
faith in oil bubbles."[29] At 0703 and 0735 he advised that the *Ward*
had intercepted a sampan, was escorting her into Honolulu, and requested, "Please have Coast Guard send cutter to relieve us of
sampan."[30] This was normal procedure when the Navy caught a sampan in the defensive sea area. The Coast Guard promptly sent a cutter,
and Outerbridge returned to his patrol duties.[31]

While the *Ward* was thus occupied, on the dot of 0700 the plotters at the Information Center's main board, the historical plotter,
and the telephone operators manning the station lines folded up their
equipment and left, leaving only Tyler and McDonald. This prompt,
wholesale exodus surprised Tyler, but he said nothing to these men,
because his instructions were nebulous and the center was still in its
birth pangs. He did not realize that McDonald—in a telephone cubicle and out of Tyler's sight—was still there. So the lieutenant settled down for what he assumed would be a solitary vigil until his tour
of duty expired at 0800.[32]

Opana's normal duty hours had ended at 0700 also, and Lockard
began to shut down; however, Elliott wanted to get in a little more
practice on the oscilloscope. Lockard agreed "that we might as well
play around because the truck had not come in yet to take us back to
camp."[33]

Elliott was at the scope, with Lockard looking over his shoulder,
when "an unusually large response" appeared in a northerly direction at a distance of 136 miles. "It was so large, in fact," said Lockard,
"that I checked the equipment to determine whether it was the fault
of the equipment or actually a flight of some sort."[34]

Lockard took over the scope, because this blip was "just something completely out of the ordinary." Elliott went back to the plotting table, recording the sighting at 2° True. The time was now 0702,
and the flight had moved to within 132 miles.[35]

More than a little awed by this echo, which he estimated to represent more than fifty planes, Elliott suggested that they report it to the Information Center. At first Lockard laughed at Elliott and told him he was crazy. Their tour of duty was over. But Elliott argued the point. Even if these were U.S. Navy planes coming in, "if the Army were to send up interceptors, it would make a very fine problem." Finally, Lockard gave in to the pleas of his eager trainee; he could send it in if he liked.[36]

The Opana station had two telephones, one the tactical line direct to the plotters, the other the administrative line. Elliott tried the former first, but no one answered. So he picked up the second and reached McDonald. Elliott's voice quivered with nervousness, for the blip "was very big and it was very noticeable and it was just something out of the ordinary." From his cubicle, McDonald could not see Tyler and assumed he was alone. So he told Elliott that "there was nobody around there, and he did not know what to do about it." Elliott asked him "to get somebody who would know what to do and pass on the information," whereupon the two privates broke the connection.[37]

McDonald wrote down the information. Then, checking the clock in the next room to log in this conversation, he saw Tyler sitting at the plotting table. He took the message to the lieutenant and read it aloud: "Large number of planes coming in from the north, three points east." Impressed both by Elliott's message and manner, McDonald said, "It's the first time I have ever received anything like this, and it looks kind of strange." He added, "Do you think we ought to do anything about it?" He even suggested recalling the plotters: "...they didn't have much practice there all along, and when this fellow called in he expressed it to be 'an awful big flight.'"[38]

McDonald called Opana back, and Lockard replied, repeating Elliott's message. McDonald turned to Tyler, saying, "Sir, I would appreciate it very much if you would answer the phone." So Lockard informed Tyler "that we had an unusually large flight—in fact, the largest I had ever seen on the equipment—coming in from almost due north at 130 some miles."[39]

Tyler's first reaction was relief—the B-17s were coming in safely, and from the correct position—no sure thing in those early days of transocean navigation. Such a flight might very well be the largest Lockard had ever seen.[40] He reflected that there was an almost equal chance that the large echo might signal the approach of U.S. Navy carrier planes. He was not in a particularly alert frame of mind—"in fact, just the opposite, because we had been on the alert about a week before, and the alert had been called off."[41]

Tyler pondered for a moment and then told Lockard, "Well, don't worry about it."[42] After the lieutenant had hung up, McDonald inquired, "What do you think it is?" Tyler replied, "It's nothing."[43]

By that time—approximately 0715—the blip showed the planes at 88 miles.[44] Fuchida's pilot was guiding the first wave in from the Hawaiian music being broadcast for the benefit of Landon's B-17s, which indeed were approaching Oahu only a few degrees off the Japanese course. Beneath the music, Fuchida heard what sounded like a weather broadcast. Holding his breath in concentration, he heard: "Averaging partly cloudy, with clouds mostly over the mountains. Cloud base at 3500 feet, visibility good. Wind north, 10 knots." Fuchida relaxed gratefully. Had he planned it himself, the timing could not have been better. He had been worrying over how to predetermine the weather over his target, and the Americans had solved his problem.[45]

Having received Tyler's dampening reply, Lockard wanted to shut down, but Elliott insisted that they continue to operate the scope. So they kept on tracking the large blip, posting it every 3 to 6 minutes. At 0730, the planes had reached the 45-mile mark.[46]

In Washington, the clocks stood at 1300—the hour Nomura had been instructed to deliver Tokyo's long message to Hull at the State Department. However, the Japanese Embassy staff had not finished preparing the document. Part 14 had been decoded for half an hour, but Okumura was still pecking his way through the clean copy of the full message. Nomura "impatiently peeked into the office where the typing was being done, hurrying the men at work." Obviously they would not be able to meet the deadline, so Nomura had to ask Hull for a brief postponement.[47]

RCA messenger Tadao Fuchikami reported for work at 0730. By chance, he selected for delivery the messages stuffed into the pigeonhole marked Kahili, the district that covered Fort Shafter, among other destinations. One of the documents Fuchikami picked up was Marshall's message advising of Japan's 1300 deadline. It had reached RCA at 0733—already 3 minutes too late—and it was not marked priority.[48]

At that same minute—0733—Fuchida's first wave was 35 miles away.[14] Aboard the *Akagi*, Kusaka sat in front of the maps in the operations room, awaiting the reports of the reconnaissance aircraft hovering over Lahaina anchorage and Pearl Harbor. They came in almost simultaneously, first the scout from the *Tone*: "The enemy fleet is not in Lahaina anchorage." That removed the last, lingering possibility of catching the U.S. ships in Lahaina's deep waters. Then, most important, the *Chikuma* plane came in: "Cloud ceiling over the enemy fleet, 1700 meters. Its density, scale 7. 0308." With the same time designation, 0308 (0738 local time), the *Chikuma* scout verified the presence of the U.S. Fleet in Pearl Harbor. At this, wrote Kusaka, "Instinctively Admiral Nagumo and all of his staff officers looked at each other and could not suppress their smiles."[50] Of equal importance to Fuchida, absorbing the reports as they came to his aircraft, the *Chikuma* scout reported that ten battleships, one heavy cruiser, and ten light cruisers were in harbor and gave their locations.[51]

The timing was excellent. At 0738, the first wave was 25 miles from Oahu, and it closed to 20 miles at 0739.[52] At that point, Lockard and Elliott lost the blip "in the permanent distortion we had, due to bad echoes from the mountains surrounding us." The two young men shut down the station and went outside to await transportation back to camp.[53] When the truck arrived shortly thereafter, they took the station log with them. "We were very proud of the reading that we had gotten; that is, the distance out," explained Elliott, "and we brought it along, not knowing what was taking place, but it was just the fact that the reading was a very good reading. We brought it back to show off, so to speak." Clutching their piece of history, and quite pleased with themselves, they stowed their gear in the truck, scrambled in, and rode off in modest triumph to their camp for breakfast.[54]

CHAPTER 9

"We've Made It!"

While the two young men at Opana were tracking the mysterious blip toward Oahu, Outerbridge's message of 0653 announcing that he had attacked a submarine was stirring up action through channels.

Lt. Cmdr. Harold Kaminski, a World War I "retread" recalled to active duty a little over a year before, had the watch for the Headquarters, Fourteenth Naval District that morning. He was officer in charge of Net and Boom Defenses. He had been on duty since 1600 Saturday, with somewhat nebulous duties: "to take care of anything that turned up pertaining to the district."[1]

Kaminski was not happy over the watch officer situation, for he believed that "the station could not function efficiently" with just one officer present. Moreover, the enlisted man on duty that morning was, in Kaminski's opinion, "perfectly useless," for he, like the other operators, had not received "the proper instructions at the telephone," nor did he, or they, understand the teletype.[2]

This conscientious officer did not like the international situation any more than he did the watch arrangements. As early as November 10, 1941, he had issued a directive to the Net and Boom Defenses to be "in a state of readiness and on station."[3] And he was fighting against moving into the district housing area; it reminded him "of Tokyo or Yokohama," and he was "a little scared of it." He told the Roberts Commission frankly, "That area is right above the oil tanks, and I do not think that officers of any importance, or anybody, as a matter of fact, should be in those houses."[4]

So he was not a man to shrug off Outerbridge's message when he received it at about 0712. His instructions were that in the event of an emergency, his first calls should be to the district chief of staff and the commandant's aide. Unable to reach the latter by phone, he telephoned the Fleet duty officer and read the message to the assistant, Lt. Cmdr. R. B. Black.[5]

The staff duty officer that day, Cmdr. Vincent R. Murphy, was in his quarters dressing when Black passed the word to him. "Did he [Kaminski] say what he was doing about it?" asked Murphy. "Did he say whether Admiral Bloch knew about it, or not?"

"No," answered Black.

"While I'm finishing dressing, call him and see what he's doing about it, and whether or not he's called Admiral Bloch."

By the time Murphy had dressed, Black was back on the line. He "had dialed and dialed," but Kaminski's line was busy. "All right," said Murphy, "you go to the office and started breaking out the charts and position of the various ships; I'll dial one more time and then I'll be over."

Accordingly, he phoned, but the line was still busy. Then he dialed the operator, instructing him to tell Kaminski to call him immediately, and to break in on any conversation the district duty officer might be holding "unless it was of supreme importance."[6]

Black and Murphy could not reach Kaminski because his line was very busy indeed with official business. On Kaminski's own initiative, he sent a message to the ready duty destroyer *Monaghan,* with a copy to the *Ward*: "Get under way immediately and contact U.S.S. *Ward* in defensive sea area." Then he phoned Bloch's chief of staff, Capt. John B. Earle.[7]

Mrs. Earle answered the ring. "I want to speak to Captain Earle," said Kaminski in "a very excited voice." From his manner, Mrs. Earle knew at once "that something important had happened."[8] When Earle took over the receiver and Kaminski told his story, the captain's "first impression was that it was just another of those false reports which had been coming in off and on for a period...of a year. We had been having many false reports of submarines in the outlying waters," he explained, "but this seemed to be a little bit more serious. Apparently there had been an actual attack made." He could recall no previous incidents when shots had been fired or depth charges dropped.[9]

Therefore, Kaminski stated that Earle "was quite astounded and said he could not believe it. He asked for this confirmation...and he made several remarks at that time that he was astounded and that it was unbelievable, and made various other remarks."[10] He instructed Kaminski to call the district operations officer, Cmdr. C. B. Momsen, while he, Earle, would contact Bloch, which he did at 0712. After listening to the details, the admiral asked, "Is this a false report, or do you know anything about it?"

"Well, this is the dispatch," replied Earle, and read it aloud. Still not sure "whether it was a bona fide report or whether it was a sound contact," Bloch instructed Earle, "Find out about it." The two officers "discussed the matter over the telephone five or ten minutes to try to decide what was the reliability of this word and what steps should be taken." They decided to await developments, because Kimmel had already been notified.[11] After Bloch hung up, Earle began to shave and dress, while Mrs. Earle started to prepare breakfast.[12]

At virtually the same time—between 0712 and 0720—Kaminski received the Ward's message about the sampan. Discovering that the Coast Guard had received and acted on this information, Kaminski did nothing further about it.[13] When Earle received this message, it relieved his mind about the Ward's submarine dispatch. He could not understand why, "if it had been a serious situation...Ward was proceeding now apparently to leave her post without any particular fear and escorting a sampan to Honolulu."[14]

Meanwhile, Murphy reached his office to find the telephone ringing. Lt. Cmdr. Logan Ramsey, operations officer of Patrol Wing Two, was on the line to forward word he had just received from the duty officer on Ford Island, Lt. Dick Ballinger: One of their planes on intertype tactics had sunk a submerged submarine 1 mile off the entrance to Pearl Harbor. Ramsey knew that the Navy's patrol aircraft covering the operating areas were "carrying live depth charges and had specific orders to sink any submerged submarines sighted outside of the submarine sanctuary and without a close escort."

Ramsey asked Ballinger to secure confirmation of the sighting, for it seemed to him that someone might have made a mistake, that "a drill message of some variety...had gotten out by accident."

When Ramsey relayed this to Murphy, the latter replied, "That's funny, we got the same sort of message from one of the DDs on the inshore patrol."

"Well," answered Ramsey, "you had better get going and I'll be down at my Operations Center soon."

Hanging up, Ramsey donned slacks and aloha shirt and drove the three-quarters of a mile from his quarters to the administration building on Ford Island which housed the Operations Center. He did not consider the morning's reports "as definite information of any enemy attack." But he drew up a search plan for the PBYs "under the conditions prevailing that day." He postulated this on the Naval Base Air Defense Operating Plan, which called for a search to the northeast sector as first priority, because Ramsey and others figured that would be the most likely approach direction for a Japanese attack.[15]

Scarcely had Ramsey broken the connection when Kaminski called Murphy to advise that Bloch had been notified of the *Ward*'s action, the ready duty destroyer had been ordered out, and the standby destroyer had been instructed to get up steam.

"Had you any previous details or any more details of this attack?" Murphy asked.

"The message came out of a clear sky," replied Kaminski. "There was no word of preliminary search or chase of any kind."

Murphy then telephoned Kimmel. The CinCUS had arisen about 0700 to prepare for the golf game he played with Short every other Sunday. He had neither dressed, shaved, nor breakfasted when Murphy reached him, but he promptly replied, "I will be right down."

Kimmel was "not at all certain that this was a real attack." He later explained, "...we had so many reports, false reports of submarines in the outlying area, I thought, well, I would wait for verification of the report."[16]

Unaware of all this activity, most of Oahu's citizens and its transient service population awoke to what they expected would be the usual Sunday of rest and recreation. At Police Chief Gabrielson's residence, the pet dog whined so incessantly and piteously that he roused the whole family—something he had never done before and never did again.[17]

Captain Davis's wife, Joan, an exceptionally beautiful woman who "looked just like Hedy Lamarr,"[18] arose in the darkness of early morning to feed a puppy a friend had left in her care. This accomplished, she still felt sleepy and went back to bed.[19]

In Capt. "Poco" Smith's apartment near Fort De Russy, his wife, Betty, went downstairs early to start the morning coffee. While it heated, she went out to bring in the morning paper, but it had not yet arrived.[20] By an odd chance, the Honolulu *Advertiser*'s press had broken down at 2000 the previous night,[21] thereby starting many a reader's day off on the wrong foot.

Kathleen Bruns Cooper rose early to attend mass in the outdoor theater at Pearl Harbor with her parents, her brothers, David and John, and her sister, Betty. At 19, Kathleen had been married for four months to Frank "Bud" Cooper, an officer aboard the submarine *Pollack*. Of that four months, she and her husband had been able to live together only one. She accepted this as only to be expected in the Navy. Indeed, she knew no other way of life, being the daughter of Capt. Henry Bruns, engineering officer of the Fourteenth Naval District. For the moment, she was content to be back under the parental roof, her blue Plymouth convertible tucked safely away in the family garage.

This was to be the last day of the current separation, for the *Pollack* was due back at her berth in Pearl Harbor at 1100. Only one cloud lurked on Kathleen's horizon: the long-drawn-out tension between the United States and Japan made a Pacific war seem possible. But it might not last long if it came at all. Just the night before, Mrs. Stanley P. Moseley, wife of Bud's skipper, had declared at a small party for submarine wives, "We can lick the Japanese with our hands tied behind our backs." Everyone had agreed.[22]

Many, like Kathleen, prepared to answer the cheerful ring of church bells. Already at dawn the service of holy communion had begun in St. Andrew's Cathedral at Queen Emma Square. By 0730, members of St. Clement's Episcopal Church were also partaking of the Lord's table in the parish house chapel at Wilder Avenue and Makiki Street. The Reverend Peter Chang of the Korean Community Church had prepared a sermon on the subject, "Love Your Neighbor as Yourself," Pastor Arthur Hormann of the Lutheran congregation near the Punchbowl had selected as the title of his discourse, "What Seek Ye?" The devotional hour for the First Methodist Church carried the prophetic heading, "The Transforming Touch."[23]

Some aboard ship also turned their thoughts to worship. Lieutenant Ruff got up at 0630 to attend mass aboard the hospital ship *Solace* anchored north of Ford Island. Father Drinnan from the *Nevada* was going to hear confessions aboard the *Solace*, so Ruff joined the priest in a motor launch and chugged off. Upon reaching the *Solace*, Ruff waited in the officers' lounge for Father Drinnan to finish hearing confessions and serve mass.[24]

Seaman Osborne of the *Arizona* had only to change from T-shirt and white shorts to Class A's to be ready for mass. At that moment, a cleaner assigned to F Division compartment, where Osborne was standing, asked his help in carrying a trash can up to the incinerator on the boat deck. Osborne obliged, and the two young men took their place in line to dump the trash.[25]

Since Navy nurse Lt. Ruth A. Erickson was not scheduled for duty, shortly after 0700, with her hair still in curlers, she pulled a morning coat over her pajamas and sauntered to the nearby one-story dining room. There she treated herself to papaya, scrambled eggs, and bacon. A full breakfast was a luxury after the quickly bolted toast, fruit, and coffee of the normal working day.[26]

2d Lt. C. B. Drake, USMC, shared the watch aboard the *California* with Ens. Tom Nicholson. The ship had sent off the early Catholic church party and the regular Sunday players called the "Dawn Golf Patrol." The two young men discussed the possibility of a Japanese-American war. "For all we know the Japanese may be on their way right now," Nicholson said.

"Well, if they are, you and I as the watch officers on the Flagship of Commander Battle Force, Pacific, ought to be the first ones to know," answered Drake. Ens. Herb Jones relieved Drake at the watch, and the lieutenant went to breakfast.[27]

Major Shapley was one of the fairly early risers aboard the *Arizona*. He skipped his usual shower. The *Arizona*'s baseball nine, of which Shapley, the leading hitter in the Fleet, was coach and first baseman, was scheduled to tangle that day with the nine from the carrier *Enterprise* for the championship.[28] The *Enterprise*, three heavy cruisers, and nine destroyers formed Task Force Eight, which was returning after delivering some Marine aircraft to Wake Island. VADM William F. Halsey, the task force commander, expected to enter the Pearl Harbor channel at 0730 that morning, but head seas had delayed fueling the destroyers, so when dawn broke the *Enterprise* was still about 200 miles at sea.[29]

Shapley climbed into his Marine uniform—he could change to baseball togs later, he assumed—and helped himself to a stack of pancakes topped with eggs.[30]

At 0700, the assistant quartermaster of the watch for the *Nevada* roused Ens. Joseph K. Taussig, Jr., who had the forenoon watch.[31] Taussig was only 21 years old, but he was more conscious than many Americans twice his age of the tensions between the United States and Japan. "In fact, I had been weaned on the subject," he wrote years later. In April of 1940, his father, a rear admiral, had been reprimanded for testifying to a joint congressional committee that, in his opinion, if current trends continued, "war with Japan was inevitable."

Young Taussig was by no means convinced that the *Nevada*, or any other U.S. battleship, was capable of a truly effective antiaircraft defense. In fact, "...from the point of view of an anti-aircraft officer, immediately responsible for the laying and firing of the ordnance, I can testify with vim, vigor, and conviction that we couldn't hit the broad side of a barn except at point-blank range," he wrote. Taussig continued:

> Reasons: (1) Fleet gunnery doctrine. Through the combined effects of economy engendered by the late depression, and a propensity to judge everything "in competition," the Fleet gunnery exercises were always conducted under "canned" conditions. The target was almost always a sleeve towed by a utility type aircraft (either ship based or land based), which always slowed up the towing plane immeasurably. The few "drone" firings that I had heard of (I never saw one) were exceptions. The "rules" themselves allowed us to refuse to shoot if (a) the plane was approaching outside of a very limited scope of bearings (b) if the altitude was higher than an extremely low ceiling (c) if the target exceeded a certain limited speed (I think we were not required to fire at a plane going over 108 knots. My memory is not exact, but I believe that 108 was the order of magnitude.)

Taussig had other reservations of a technical nature, although in his opinion training was excellent: "We could man the guns (and did) in a time frame which was almost immediate; we could, and did, replace casualties without any interruption in firing; and we could load and shoot on local control...at a rate of speed which people not involved would not believe."[32]

On this particular morning, however, the only question on Taussig's mind was this: Had the Stars and Stripes of the correct size been ordered for the raising of colors at 0800?[33]

Sgt. Robert G. Crouse was not detailed to duty on the morning of December 7, but he knew that a flight of B-17s was due in and that his services as supply sergeant would be useful at the Hawaiian Air Depot. So he rose early, breakfasted, and walked to the supply hangar. There he stood chatting with several other enlisted men and civilian employees while awaiting the big bombers.[34]

Captain Allen was somewhat reluctantly awake. It seemed to him that he had barely fallen asleep when the phone rang. A trans-Pacific operator was on the line: Would he accept a call from Mrs. Allen in Florida at 0700? Agreeing to stand by, the captain made a pot of coffee. The call came through somewhat later. Mrs. Allen wanted to know if she should come out to Hawaii. Some problems had arisen in connection with travel. Uneasy about the current situation, Allen asked that she not make the long trip across country to San Francisco until matters had cleared up. After exchanging goodbyes with his wife, Allen fell back into bed.[35]

Capt. James W. Chapman of Headquarters Squadron at Hickam was already up, having volunteered to give his baby son, Stephen, his early bottle. He had to rise early in any case, because a rifle firing competition was scheduled for that morning between the officers and NCOs of Headquarters Squadron. "Entry fee 50¢, winner take all."[36]

Across the island at Kaneohe, Aviation Machinist Avery awoke to "one of the prettiest, calmest springlike mornings one is ever apt to see." After he dressed, for a moment he "gazed out to sea and was particularly impressed by the tranquility of the whole scene: the placid waters, the soft gentle breeze which one could feel on the cheeks but was not enough to disturb the water, the bright sun and the dream-inducing quietness."

Luxuriating in the twin thoughts that, being Sunday, there was no routine work to do and he had no watch to stand, Avery dropped back on his cot. "All was well with the world!—so I thought!"[37]

Commander Rochefort of Combat Intelligence packed steaks into his car, preparing to set out on a picnic with his wife, daughter, and mother-in-law. But he had an uneasy feeling and found himself curiously reluctant to leave the house. "I had a premonition that something was wrong," he recalled.[38]

Meanwhile, the cloud cover was so thick that Fuchida's fliers were practically over Oahu before they saw the island. Lieutenant Ema was so worried about possibly missing it that he experienced a surge of relief, bringing with it the conviction of success.[39]

The beauty of the island and the calm that seemed to brood over it so impressed Sublt. Toshio Hashimoto, a dive-bomber observer from the *Hiryu*, that the thought flashed across his mind: "This island is too peaceful to attack!"[40] Much the same idea came to Sublieutenant Mifuku when he saw the "very calm and picturesque scenery of the green island dotted with red, blue and yellow roofs of houses." Were they really going to attack this beautiful island?[41]

One of the men in Murata's group of torpedo bombers caught Lieutenant Goto's attention and pointed downward. Goto, his observer, and his radioman peered in the direction indicated. There lay Oahu dead ahead. The sight gripped Goto with sudden exultation: "We've made it, now just you wait!" he silently addressed the unsuspecting Americans below him.[42]

In contrast, as Lieutenant Matsumura saw the "white-surfed northern tip of Oahu through a break in the clouds," behind his new mustache he "swallowed a tense feeling of coming into enemy territory."[43]

Fuchida was too busy with his duties as leader for on-the-spot self-analysis. "Ha!" he exclaimed in gratification at the first glimpse of land. But the weather conditions forced him into a prompt command decision. The plan called for an approach to Pearl Harbor from the northeast, flying over the mountains and down the eastern side of Oahu. However, in view of the heavy cloud cover over the mountains, Fuchida decided to follow the west coast and approach the target from the south. He did not need to radio the change to the pilots; they were under instructions to follow him.[44]

"This is the north point of Oahu," Fuchida told his pilot, Lieutenant Mutsuzaki. He ordered "*Tenkai*" (Take attack position), instructing Mutsuzaki to look for American interceptors. As the pilot opened the canopy, the wind snatched off the *hachimaki* which his girlfriend had given him. Mutsuzaki was very proud of that scarf, and this incident struck the rest of the pilots as hilarious. They often recounted in wardroom bull sessions how the first Japanese casualty of the air war was Mutsuzaki's *hachimaki*.[45]

The change of plan that followed almost immediately was totally unpremeditated. The Japanese had worked out a careful system of rocket pistol signals. If surprise was achieved, Fuchida would fire one "black dragon" signal, whereupon Murata's torpedomen would attack first, in the hope that their slow planes could release their torpedoes and escape before the Americans reacted. The horizontal bombers would follow, and last the dive bombers, lest the smoke from their attacks on the nearby air bases impede the aim of the other bombers. But if the Americans were ready and waiting, Fuchida would fire two flares at 2- or 3-second intervals. In that case, the vulnerable torpedo planes would follow while the other bombers were engaging the enemy. In either event, surprise or no surprise, the fighters would dash in as a group to clear the skies of American interceptors.

Having seen neither American aircraft of any type nor any signs of antiaircraft activity by 0740, Fuchida was convinced that the Japanese had indeed achieved surprise. He seized his rocket pistol and fired one "black dragon." Instantly he saw that a fighter group leader, Lt. Masaharu Suganami, did not lead his planes into their prearranged position, having missed the signal. So, after allowing some 10 seconds to elapse, he repeated the flare.

Oddly enough, it was the deliberate Takahashi who acted precipitately. He misjudged the time between signals, thought this was the double flare betokening an alert enemy, and led his dive bombers down for their strikes on Ford Island and Hickam Field.[46]

More than two decades later Fuchida was still upset with the "stupid" Takahashi, as Fuchida called him. But at the moment he had to live with the mistake and soon realized that it mattered little, if at all. "Commander, look! I see Pearl Harbor!" cried Mutsuzaki excitedly. Fuchida squinted along the valley, and as he did so, the clouds parted to give him a perfect view.[47] Later, for the benefit of the Japanese press, Fuchida described the moment: "Through the opening in the clouds, I saw Pearl Harbor, glistening in the sun. 'God must be with us,' I thought. 'It must be God's hand which pulled aside the clouds directly over Pearl Harbor.'"[48]

Through his binoculars, Fuchida saw a sight to thrill any navy man—Battleship Row with seven great ships at their moorings. "What a majestic sight, almost unbelievable!" Fuchida said to himself. But seven was two less than the Honolulu consulate had reported on Saturday and the *Chikuma* scout had confirmed that morning. What about the other two? Actually, both observers had counted the target ship *Utah* as a battleship, and Fuchida did not notice the *Pennsylvania* in drydock. However, what was one battlewagon more or less in the circumstances? Fuchida's only real regret was the absence of carriers.

His spine tingled with excitement. He knew that the entire Japanese Navy waited for his next move. Spread across the Pacific, commanders of the Second, Third, Fourth, Fifth, and Sixth Fleets, poised for action, waited. Aboard the battleship *Nagato* in the Inland Sea, Yamamoto and his staff waited. In the Navy Club in Tokyo, key members of the Naval General Staff, gripped with apprehension, waited. Aboard the *Akagi*, nerves tense, Nagumo, Kusaka, and Genda waited, as did every other man aboard every ship of the task force.

At a spot "somewhat off Lahilahi Point," at 0749, Fuchida gave his radio operator, 1st Flying Petty Officer Tokunobu Mizuki, the attack signal, "To, To, To," the first syllable of totsugekiseyo (charge). The radioman hit his key so that all the first-wave planes got the word.[49]

As Mizuki rapped out the "charge" order, Mutsuzaki guided the plane in a sweep around Barber's Point. According to available information, this location bristled with antiaircraft guns, and Fuchida expected that his men might encounter a heavy barrage, but nothing happened. At precisely 0750, Fuchida heard both Murata and Takahashi order "Tsu, Tsu, Tsu," which had much the same meaning as "To, To, To" but was applicable to individual groups. Still no sign of enemy attack! So at 0753 Fuchida ordered: "Petty Officer Mizuki, send a telegram to the fleet: 'Successful surprise attack made stop.' Okay? Check up your transmitter and send it so that it can reach Tokyo." Thereupon Mizuki clicked out the famous code words "Tora, Tora, Tora" (Tiger, Tiger, Tiger).[50]

Nagumo could not be called the demonstrative type, and through the practice of Zen Buddhism, Kusaka had schooled himself to an almost complete control of his reactions. But both men had been for months under the nerve-shattering necessity of planning, training for, and leading a mission in which neither one genuinely believed and which both feared could end in disaster. Now, in the exquisite release from tension, tears rolled down Kusaka's cheeks unchecked and unrepented, as he and Nagumo clasped hands in a moment as silent as it was emotionally charged. Against all the dictates of common sense, against all the unpredictable odds, the task force had caught the Americans unawares.[51]

PART 3

"The Sky Was Full of the Enemy"

December 7, 1941

(0753–0835)
The First Wave:
Attack on the Ships

CHAPTER 10

"Japanese! Man Your Stations!"

As soon as Fuchida gave his general attack signal, *"To, To, To,"* Murata gave a similar order, *"Tsu, Tsu, Tsu,"* to the torpedomen. At a point northwest of the Marine base at Ewa Field, they split into two main groups, in accordance with carefully worked-out plans. Murata and Kitajima each led twelve planes from the *Akagi* and the *Kaga*, respectively, to the southeast and then turned north and northeast over Hickam Field. At the same moment, Lt. Tsuyoshi Nagai from the *Soryu* and Matsumura from the *Hiryu* headed for the ships moored on the west and northwest of Ford Island.[1]

The group from the First Carrier Division (the *Akagi* and the *Kaga*) was subdivided into units of three planes, all three to attack the same American ship, for the Japanese assumed that more than one torpedo would be required to sink a battleship. The unit leaders were officers expert in all aspects of aerial torpedo warfare, whereas the follow-up pilots were mostly petty officers of less experience and skill than the leaders. The Second Carrier Division could not furnish enough torpedo aircraft to permit three-plane units, so the torpedo bombers from the *Soryu* and the *Hiryu* flew by twos.

As Murata's group overflew Ewa Field, Goto, leading the second unit, could see the parked aircraft sparkling in the sunlight. There was no sign of any activity on the ground. "Perhaps the Americans are still at Sunday breakfast," he speculated.[2]

Even as the Japanese deployed, the U.S. Navy's telephone lines were still humming with conversations generated by the *Ward's* adventures. Ramsey called Murphy back, wanting to know if he had

113

any further instructions. Murphy did not, but he told Ramsey that "it might be wise for him to make his search planes available in case the Admiral wanted them." No sooner had they hung up than Kaminski phoned about the *Ward*'s experience with the sampan. After securing the details, Murphy called Kimmel to relay this latest information.[3]

Meanwhile, Admiral Furlong strolled along the *Oglala*'s deck waiting for his "boy" to call him to breakfast. "It was a most beautiful morning," he recalled. "Everything was perfect—bright sunshine, a clear day, everything quiet and peaceful." Across Battleship Row he could see that near the stern of each battleship the quartermaster was carrying the flag aft, and with him there was a bugler standing by to sound "To the Colors."

Glancing up to the right, he noticed a plane coming over the northern end of Ford Island. Rather idly he watched it fly across the island. Suddenly it dropped a bomb below the hangars on the southwest tip of Ford Island near the water's edge. The missile did no damage, and assuming the aircraft to be American, Furlong reacted only with anger and disgust. "What a stupid, careless pilot, not to have the releasing gear for his bomb properly secured!" he exclaimed mentally. Then the pilot turned hard to port and flew up the channel between Ford Island and the *Oglala*, so close that, said Furlong, "I could have hit him with a spud."[4]

As the plane sped by, "I saw the rising sun," the admiral stated, "and I knew it was a Japanese plane." He shouted to his men, "Japanese! Man your stations!" But the order was unnecessary, he testified with pride, "because the men also had heard this explosion and they were busy manning their stations and closing all the doors and manning all the stations immediately and manning the guns." Thus, thanks to Takahashi's misinterpretation of the attack signal, the first missile dropped at Pearl Harbor came from a dive bomber instead of a torpedo as planned. A second bomb followed the first within seconds, setting fire to a building on Ford Island.[5]

While preparing breakfast, Mrs. Earle "heard a terrific explosion and ran to the front window in time to see the hangar on Ford Island go up in smoke and flame." She screamed for her husband, who hurried to the window, "one half of his face lathered." He stood beside his wife and watched horrified as planes flew over their home and swooped down on the ships, dropping their missiles. "It's an attack!" he shouted. Hastily finishing dressing, he rushed to his car and sped to his office.

Mrs. Earle hurried upstairs to rouse her niece, Barbara Deibert, who was visiting them. She had been to a dance the night before and was sleeping so soundly that her aunt had to shake her into consciousness. "Get up, Barbara, we are being attacked!" Only half awake, Barbara sputtered, "Why—the very idea!"[6]

Aboard the *West Virginia*, Ens. Roland S. Brooks saw the same smoke and flame and thought there had been an internal explosion on the *California*, moored southernmost of the battleships and the closest to the patrol plane hangars on Ford Island. He ordered "Away Fire and Rescue Party." Hundreds of officers and men rushed topside.[7] Brooks's mistake was as timely as it was providential.

When Murata's torpedo planes flew past Barber's Point, they lined up in single file, flying at an astonishingly low altitude. Over Hickam Field they were a mere 40 to 50 meters, and as they approached the southeast loch, they dropped to about 20.[8] Hovering overhead with his Second Air Control Group of fighters to intercept enemy aircraft, Shiga had a perfect view. "They moved so slowly they looked like ants crawling along the ground," he described the scene. "The U.S. Fleet in the harbor looked so beautiful...just like toys on a child's floor—something that should not be attacked at all." No such qualms bothered the torpedomen. Shiga "saw the splash in the water and a torpedo streaking for a battleship...just like a dragonfly laying an egg on the water."[9]

The torpedo was Murata's, his target the *West Virginia*. Goto saw it score a direct hit and watched the other two planes of Murata's unit attack the same battleship.[10]

Commander Johnson always remembered a young ensign sprinting down the *West Virginia*'s deck to pull the alarm for General Quarters. "He did it in one bounding gesture and scarcely missed stride as he sped on to his battle station." Moving as fast as he could toward his own battle station on the bridge, Johnson came upon a 5-inch .25 caliber antiaircraft battery. It was manned and had ammunition in the ready box, but the gun captain seemed confused. "What fuse setting shall I put in these shells?" he asked. Johnson had no more idea than the gun captain, but he gave him an educated guess. As he said later, "I thought the best thing to do was to get the guns going and worry about the exact setting later."[11]

Racing up the starboard passageway to the bridge, the *West Virginia*'s navigator, Lt. Cmdr. T. T. Beattie, caught up with Captain Bennion.

By this time, three torpedoes had struck the battleship, and she was listing badly.[12]

Meanwhile the Second Carrier Division's torpedo planes sped on toward the other side of Ford Island. As Matsumura approached, it seemed to him that, contrary to the *Chikuma* scout's report, the vessels in that location were cruisers rather than battleships. Absorbed in his attempt to resolve this question, he "unconsciously went down so low as to stir up leaves of sugar cane and at the same time felt the warm air of an unending-summer land."

Discovering that indeed no battleships were west of Ford Island, Matsumura decided to ignore the lesser targets at those moorings and head for the east side where bigger game awaited him. To his astonishment, he saw one of Nagai's torpedomen launch a missile against the *Utah*. This made Matsumura furious, for he had specifically told his men not to waste a torpedo on the target ship.[13]

The culprit was Nakajima, who thought he saw Nagai attack the *Utah* and followed his lead. "During the training period identification of ships was stressed, but I failed in a time of real fighting," he lamented in retrospect.[14]

Chief Davis was on his way from his bunk aboard the *Ralph Talbot* to the shower room in a state of nature when he happened to look out a port. He saw two torpedoes heading toward the *Utah*, hit, and explode. As the attacking planes pulled up, Davis recognized the Rising Sun insignia. Flinging on a cravanette—a combination topcoat and raincoat—Davis sped for the destroyer's Combat Information Center to get the communications and gun control in action.[15]

Directly forward of the *Utah* lay the light cruiser *Raleigh* in Berth F-12. Seaman 1st Class Frank M. Berry was standing watch on the port side quarterdeck, the officer of the deck (OD) at his side, when they noticed a plane "flying very high," but they thought nothing of this circumstance. The OD asked Berry if they "should call the AA battery for a practice drill." Then another plane came in quite low and dropped something "a little beyond midstream." Berry asked the OD what was dropping. "I don't know," he answered, but he called the antiaircraft men to their guns, assuming this to be "part of a routine air-raid drill."

At that moment, approximately 0755, a torpedo struck the cruiser at frame 58, flooding the forward engine room and Nos. 1 and 2 fire rooms. Fortunately, there were no personnel casualties. Berry ran for the ship's alarm, but it did not go off because "the electricity went the first thing."[16] The explosion blew the crew of the church boat, which had been standing by, into the water, but they "climbed back on the ship and went to their gun stations." The OD "did not know whether he was swimming or walking as there was so much water on the deck."[17]

The concussion awakened Ensign Beardall, who hurried to the quarterdeck in his red pajamas just as a plane passed over and "banked around to the left," he recalled. "One of the first things I saw when I came topside was those big red balls...and it didn't take long to figure out what was going on." Beardall's antiaircraft battery went into action within 5 minutes, because all of the Raleigh's 3-inch guns had their ammunition in the ready boxes.[18]

Capt. R. Bentham Simons "had not spent a night off the Raleigh in the sixteen months prior to the attack." At that moment, still wearing a pair of blue pajamas, the skipper was reading the morning paper in his cabin. "I felt a heavy concussion," he remembered, "and looking out of the cabin airport I saw water boiling abreast of number two stack." Immediately he ran to the signal bridge and "then climbed the ladder to the anti-aircraft control station." He found the battery just going into action. "Give those yellow bastards hell, boys!" he shouted. With that, he went back to the signal bridge, where he could best direct the defense.[19]

When Nagai turned away from the east side of Ford Island, he swung south and followed Murata's course. He hoped to hit the American flagship, Pennsylvania, in dry dock, but realizing that the mooring slip would interfere with his torpedo, he turned his attention to the nearby cruisers.[20]

A sailor standing beside Furlong aboard the Oglala pointed and said to his captain, "There is a torpedo coming." As Furlong remarked later that month, "Of course, I could do nothing about it. The ship was moored, and you could just look at it." The torpedo went under the Oglala and struck the Helena, scoring a double hit for the Japanese.[21]

The Oglala's log recorded the scene graphically. The torpedo "exploded under the bottom on the port side....The force of the explosion lifted up fireroom floor plates and ruptured hull on port side. Fireroom started flooding rapidly; personnel secured fires, closed water-tight doors, and abandoned fireroom."[22] The Helena's log observed, "At about 0757½, a series of three heavy explosions felt nearby. At about 0758, ship rocked by violent explosion on starboard side."[23]

Her crewmen were already racing to their stations, thanks to an alert sailor, Signalman 1st Class C. A. Flood, who had spotted a plane, recognized it as Japanese, and notified the officer of the deck.[24]

At Battleship Row, Goto led his three-plane group so closely behind Murata's that their strikes were virtually simultaneous. Goto was some 500 meters away from the *Oklahoma* when he released his torpedo at a height of about 20 meters. Flying over the battleship, his plane was lower than the crow's nest. The speed of the plane exceeded that of the missile, but watching rearward, his observer saw the strike and shouted "*Atarimashita* [It struck]!" Goto looked around, saw a huge waterspout and also watched his two companions likewise launch their torpedoes against the *Oklahoma*.[25]

The huge ship so absorbed the shock that Boatswain Adolph M. Bothne "did not even feel the ship shake." He was preparing to send his side cleaners to their work when the mate on the Sixth Division screamed, "Get the guns covered; them Japs are bombing everything in sight!" Bothne hurried to the loudspeaker on the main deck aft of midships and "passed the word for General Quarters and set material condition Zed."*[26]

Electrician's Mate 1st Class Irvin H. Thesman was in the power room, ironing a pair of dungarees, when the public address system blared out: "Man your battle stations! This is no shit!" Such language over the PA was unprecedented, but Thesman thought the *Oklahoma* was having just another drill. So he picked up a bag of tools and a flashlight and jogged toward his station in the steering gear compartment. As he did so, he heard a loud "Hrump" and felt the *Oklahoma* jolt. "What the hell are they firing the big guns in the harbor for?" he wondered.[27]

Swabbing up coffee which someone had spilled in a mess area, Seaman Stephen B. Young thought this was a crazy time to hold a drill and paid no attention until he heard General Quarters. As he hurried along toward his battle station in the upper starboard power hoist room in the No. 4 14-inch gun turret, amid other men running and pushing in their haste to reach their stations, he felt the ship quiv-

---

* A damage-control measure whereby the crew closed all openings except the hatches necessary to do battle.

er. Then the lights went out, and he had to grope his way down a ladder, reaching the deck below as the emergency lights came on. Another ladder, a heave of the deck, and once more the lights went out. Young managed to reach his duty station where some sailors were climbing into the turret. "Stay below, men," the officer in charge directed them. "Below the armored deck. These 14-inch guns are no good against planes. I'm going topside to see what's going on." His men never saw him again.[28]

So rapid, so well organized had been the Japanese attack that all this action and much more took place while Murphy was still on the telephone giving Kimmel the word about the *Ward* and the sampan. Murphy's yeoman burst in on him: "There's a message from the signal tower saying the Japanese are attacking Pearl Harbor and this is no drill." Immediately Murphy relayed this to Kimmel.[29] The admiral slammed down the receiver and ran outside.[30]

The Earles' new home next door as yet had no shrubbery, so the lawn gave an unobstructed view of Battleship Row. There Kimmel and Mrs. Earle watched as the planes flew over, "circling in figure 8's, then bombing the ships, turning and dropping more bombs." They "could plainly see the rising suns on the wings and could have seen the pilots' faces had they leaned out. Fierce fires were burning on the ships." Even with the scene being enacted before their eyes, they were almost unable to believe the "unbelievable," the "impossible" sight.

The Earles had become very fond of their neighbor, quite aside from their respect for him as commander in chief. Amid her own shock and horror, Mrs. Earle ached with pity for the admiral who stood beside her "in utter disbelief and completely stunned," his face "as white as the uniform he wore." Kimmel said later, "I knew right away that something terrible was going on, that this was not a casual raid by just a few stray planes. The sky was full of the enemy." Gazing toward Battleship Row, they saw "the *Arizona* lift out of the water, then sink back down—way down." Neither uttered a word; the scene was beyond speech.[31]

The strike on the *Arizona* that transfixed Kimmel and Mrs. Earle may have come from the torpedo plane which, having dropped its missile aimed at the *Arizona*, angled upward over the *Nevada's* stern at the exact moment the battleship's twenty-three-man band struck up "The Star Spangled Banner" and the Marine color guard began to raise the flag. The Japanese rear gunner loosed a burst of machine-gun fire. By some freak of chance, he missed a solid target of twenty-five or thirty men, but ripped the flag as it slid along the pole. The bandsmen kept right on playing. Not until they finished the last note did they break for cover and speed to their battle stations.[32]

The torpedo—or another one—sped under the repair ship *Vestal* and, in Chief Crawford's words, "tore the bottom out of the *Arizona.*" Crawford had awaked to the sound of machine-gun fire and explosions. Someone shouted, "Jesus Christ, the Japanese are attacking us!" And a sleepy voice countered, "Throw him in his damn bunk, the bastard's drunk!"[33]

Consuming his eggs and pancakes, Shapley felt "a terrific jar." He thought one of the 40-foot boats had dropped off the crane to the fantail, so he ran topside to check on it. There some sailors were standing at the *Arizona*'s rail watching the planes speeding across the harbor. One of them remarked admiringly, "This is the best goddamn drill the Army Air Force has ever put on!"[34]

These reactions were more characteristic than isolated. By this time it was obvious for miles around that hot action of some sort was taking place at Pearl Harbor, but such was the ingrained sense of security, so accustomed was Oahu to the racket of military aircraft and mock gunfire, that many assumed that the armed forces were engaged in unusually realistic maneuvers.

The noise awoke Joseph Harsch, who had interviewed Kimmel on Saturday morning. He roused his wife to say, "Darling, you often have asked me what an air raid sounds like. Listen to this—it's a good imitation."

"Oh, so that's what is sounds like," she murmured. Then this seasoned war correspondent and his wife dropped back into slumber, while the story of the year broke around them.[35]

Blake Clark, an associate professor of English at the University of Hawaii, was living at the time with former Territorial Governor Walter F. Frear and his wife. They were at breakfast when the Frears' Japanese houseman ran in exclaiming, "Plenty plane outside! Come see!" He led them to the back porch, where they could see the aircraft overhead and the smoke from antiaircraft fire. "That's good," remarked Frear with satisfaction. "We *ought* to get ready."

A neighbor dashed in crying, "We're under attack! The Japanese are bombing Oahu!"

"Oh, no, it's only practice," Frear reassured her. "Don't get excited, Claire."[36]

From his apartment in the Halekulani Hotel, Admiral Pye could view "the general direction of Pearl Harbor." Hearing gunfire, he looked out the window. Seeing bursts of AA projectiles, he said to Mrs. Pye, "It seems funny that the Army would be having target practice on Sunday morning."[37]

Mrs. Anna Kahanamoku was taking a shower when she heard what she assumed to be gunnery practice. Someone had told her that "every time a battleship fired those 16-inch guns it cost the taxpayers $30,000." She began to count off the booms disapprovingly.[38]

So outlandish was the idea of a Japanese air strike on Oahu that Honolulu's Mayor Lester Petrie watched it for half an hour and still "couldn't believe it." He stated some days later:

> It looked to me very much like a practice smoke screen. The smoke was right on the ground, going right over the entrance to the harbor, and I thought that was a perfect demonstration. I got my glasses out and saw the fire burning on the ground, didn't see any fire coming from the hangars, and they seemed to be intact, and I could see the shells exploding in the air, the clouds, black clouds that they make. And then I saw the detonation possibly of bombs which I thought at the time were mines that we might have been setting off outside the entrance.
>
> Then I got a little suspicious....[39]

Waiting to attend mass aboard the *Solace*, Lieutenant Ruff heard the firing and reflected, "Oh, oh, some fool pilot has gone wild."[40]

Harold T. Kay, an officer in the National Guard, was attempting unsuccessfully to persuade his wife, Ann, to return to the mainland with the three children, aged 9, 11, and 13, "due to the tensity of the situation." A few years later he related vividly:

> ...during our argument, why, the house began to shake, and I told her to go downstairs to find out what the kiddies were doing, that I had never heard them make a noise like that before. And she tore downstairs and came back and reported that they were not doing anything; they were quietly eating breakfast.
>
> So I told her to go outside and see what was happening. The house was still shaking, and large booms, and so forth, and she came running back and said, "Well, it's war all right."

Kay seized his high-powered binoculars and went out to see for himself. The Kay home was on top of Alewa Heights and commanded a clear view of Pearl Harbor, Hickam, and "the various forts along the sea front." Kay had not the slightest doubt what was going on and dispatched his wife to "check on the radio to see whether any alarm had gone out." But she found that the radio was only playing church music. Whereupon Kay tried unsuccessfully to reach the radio stations and the police. Eventually, he got "the civil emergency operator who could not believe the report that Pearl Harbor was being attacked, but finally agreed to make inquiry upon urgent request."[41]

Even Outerbridge, who had good reason to be aware of unusual activity in the area, had trouble realizing what was happening as he stood on the *Ward*'s bridge with Doughty. "Look at those planes over there," exclaimed Doughty in surprise, "they are coming straight down!"

"Yes, sure makes it look realistic," Outerbridge agreed, believing this to be U.S. carrier aircraft practicing bombing runs on the oil tank farms. Then booming sounds reached their ears.

"They shouldn't be blasting that road on a Sunday morning," said Outerbridge. He assumed that workers were dynamiting a road under construction between Pearl Harbor and Honolulu. Not until heavy smoke began to roll upward did he realize what was taking place.

The *Ward* remained on patrol doing figure eights to avoid Japanese fire. "What was good enough for Dewey was good enough for me," Outerbridge commented later.[42]

Seaman Osborne experienced a strange dichotomy. He and his comrade, waiting to dump trash aboard the *Arizona*, watched the explosions on Ford Island and recognized the planes as Japanese. "It still did not dawn on us that we were being attacked by the Japanese. We returned the trash can to the compartment and set it in its normal place as though nothing was happening."

When "the call for Air Defense came over the PA system," he ran for his air defense station "near the forward magazines below the armored deck." He had just put his leg through the armored deck hatch when General Quarters sounded, so he changed his destination to his battle station, which was "on the mainmast aft just under the machine gun nest." This was on top of the mainmast. As he hurried along, he wrote later, "I noticed holes being punctured in the deck alongside of me. It did not dawn on me at that time that it was strafing from enemy planes that were causing the holes to appear."[43]

The bursts of AA fire these witnesses saw or heard testified that some individuals had reacted very promptly indeed, as Matsumura discovered when he reached Battleship Row and loosed his torpedo against the *West Virginia*. Cruisers and destroyers moored along the dock machine-gunned his plane as it flew past, but he got off his torpedo. His observer called out: "It is running—ready—it hits!" With that, Matsumura "listed the plane greatly to watch the torpedo hit. A big waterspout went up over the stack of the ship....Indeed it was a great sight!"

He ordered his observer to take a picture (*"shashin o utsuse"*), but the man thought he had used the word *"ute"* and thus mistook Matsumura's instruction as an order to fire. He opened up with his machine gun and cut off the antenna of his own plane. "By this time, enemy AA fire had begun to come up very fiercely; black bursts were spoiling the once beautiful sky," Matsumura remembered. "Even white bursts were seen mixed up among them; this might have occurred as some rash boys fired training shells instead of war shells. Because of the fierce AA fire some torpedo planes were set on fire but nonetheless dashed bravely forward."[44]

Lt. Masanobu Ibusuki, a Zero pilot from the *Akagi,* admitted that the American counterattack was more rapid and fierce than expected, but it "did not seem systematic and seemed to be carried out at random in order to get rid of fears." Therefore, he claimed, "we fliers did not mind it and were rather stirred up to dauntless action." Most of the American fire came from ships, "very little from bases and land installations."[45]

The destroyer *Hulbert,* moored at the submarine base, claimed, "Shot down Japanese torpedo plane" at 0758. The destroyer-seaplane tender *Thornton,* across the dock, confirmed this claim.[46]

Ens. William S. Finn, torpedo officer aboard the nearby submarine *Dolphin,* "was eating a poached egg in the wardroom when one of the boys started screaming and hollering." He ran to the control room to find an enlisted man pointing up the hatch into the sky. Finn had to grab the man by the arms and shake him to get any sense out of him.

Finn reached the bridge in time to see a Japanese plane laying a torpedo in the water. He dropped back to the control room and sounded the alarm. Neither Finn nor the sailors with him could find the key to the ammunition locker to get the .50 caliber machine guns in action, but the chief of the watch shouted, "My God, this is war! Let's break the damn lock!" Thanks to this sensible thought, the *Dolphin's* "machine guns, automatic rifles, and rifles were manned and firing at enemy aircraft" by 0800.

Finn was justly proud of his machine-gun training—"I could dismantle a machine gun and put it back together again blindfolded"— and he sent off a couple of bursts before he realized that he was the only officer aboard. This jerked him back to a sense of responsibility: "My God, what am I doing firing this gun? I'd better command the ship."[47]

At that same moment, the destroyer *Selfridge* "brought down in flames" two Japanese aircraft.[48] The PT boats in cradle aboard *Ramapo* likewise "opened fire with .50 caliber machine guns and downed one enemy aircraft" at 0800.[49] The old gunboat *Sacramento* reported somewhat more modestly that at 0802 her "AA machine-gun fire aided in destroying enemy torpedo plane crossing astern distant about 200 yards."[50]

At that same instant, the *Nevada* swung into action under her senior officer present, Lt. Cmdr. Francis J. Thomas, with Taussig as acting air defense officer. "Machine guns opened fire on torpedo planes approaching on port beam. Members of crew state one enemy plane brought down by NEVADA machine gun fire 100 yards on port quarter."[51]

It is impossible to determine which of these early reports represented an actual kill. Cool, exact observation was too much to expect under the circumstances, and naturally, each ship was eager to claim the honor of retaliating. Thus, by 0802, the ships in Pearl Harbor claimed six kills, yet actually the Japanese lost only five torpedo planes in the entire first wave,[52] and the torpedo action was by no means over. But it had gone far enough that as Murata winged away he could radio the *Akagi*: "Torpedoed enemy battleship. Serious damage inflicted."[53]

Genda counted receipt of this message the happiest moment of his life: "This was the result of our long, hard training." No doubt remained that the whole attack would be successful. But the bridge appeared outwardly calm. Nagumo and his officers "exchanged glances," and Nagumo permitted himself a faint smile—the first Genda had seen on the admiral's face since the sortie from Hitokappu Bay.[54]

CHAPTER 11

"Great Ships Were Dying"

The *Nevada* was preparing to get under way when a torpedo struck her port bow, at about frame 40.[1] "The plane came in very close, about midway of the channel, and dropped his torpedo and then turned right," related Ens. John L. Landreth, who was in the antiaircraft directory. "After we got the torpedo, it evidently didn't cause a great deal of jar, not as much as we expected; but it did jar loose her synchronizer from the range finder," and the battery had to go temporarily to local control.

Landreth did not see the attacking plane shot down, but "understood it was hit when it turned away and went astern," where a man with a machine gun "riddled the plane and it crashed aft" of the battleship.[2] This casualty, as well as the torpedo plane the *Nevada* had shot down about a minute before,*may have been from Kitajima's group from the *Kaga*. After loosing his torpedo, Kitajima saw one of his command planes "set on fire and crash near the torpedo-releasing point and another one also on fire to the right." Kitajima felt "a great regret...to see them lost."[3]

Acting as the *Nevada*'s air defense officer, Taussig was at his battle station when a missile went through his thigh and hit the ballistics computer in front of him. In the shock, Taussig felt no pain. He observed in a detached way that his left foot had lodged under his left armpit.[4] Despite all efforts to remove him to a battle dressing sta-

_____
* See Chapter 10.

125

tion, "he refused to leave...and insisted on continuing his control of the AA battery and the continuation of fire on enemy aircraft."[5]

This promising young officer survived, but he spent the rest of World War II in the hospital recovering from his wounds received at Pearl Harbor.[6]

Down in the forward dynamo room, Chief Machinist Donald E. Ross forced his men to leave when smoke, steam, and heat made their stations untenable. He performed all their duties singlehandedly until he became blind and fell unconscious.[7]

Very few ships could retaliate as promptly and effectively as the *Nevada*. By 0802, the minesweeper *Grebe* had recognized the planes as Japanese and prepared "to repulse attack." But one can sense the frustration in her log entry:

Main battery, consisting of two .30 Calibre LEWIS machine guns, eleven SPRINGFIELD repeating rifles, model 1906, and six U.S. Navy pistols. All ammunition except that for pistols and rifles had been turned in to ammunition depot. Sent messengers in search of ammunition. Served out all available small arms to Officers and men. Issued steel helmets and gas masks to all hands.

By the time they had completed this exercise, the first wave was over.[8]

Leo F. Storm, an 18-year-old mess cook aboard the destroyer-minesweeper *Perry*, was washing dishes in the galley, the radio tuned to "Singing Sam, the Barbasol Man," when the Japanese struck. He ran to man his station on a .50 caliber machine gun, only to find the guns "under wraps and all gummed up with heavy preservative grease." The Japanese flew low to strafe the *Perry*, but, said Storm, "...we just stood there, helpless, watching good targets go by during the first wave."[9]

No one was more upset than Grannis, aboard the *Antares* off the harbor entrance, as a fighter plane circled low to strafe. The pilot "grinned one of those typically arrogant Japanese grins of the time" and shook his fist at Grannis. "So damned mad" because his only weapons, two machine guns, could not be elevated, Grannis cried out to one of his seamen, "Throw a spud at him!" The man replied despairingly, "I'm sorry, Captain, but I don't have any more."[10]

With each passing moment, more and more people were drawn into the drama. A series of explosions sent the Bruns family rushing to the windows. They did not have to wonder what was going on. Their house was close to the harbor, and the Japanese flew so low that the Brunses could see the goggled faces of the pilots peering down.

"We will all be killed!" thought Kathleen Cooper. Still in her teens and in the first year of marriage, she was by no means ready to die. "I'll be killed, and Bud will marry again!" Years later she smiled at the memory of this incongruous reaction. "The idea made me absolutely furious," she admitted. This anger sustained her throughout the attack. Her father had to leave for his post of duty and hurried away with a hasty caution, "Don't leave the house!"[11]

Another woman who reacted with fury was Peggy Hickock Hodge. When she and her husband heard the first bombs, Hodge was so sure it was an exercise that as he prepared to go to his duty post he took along his Portuguese grammar to study for an upcoming test at the University of Hawaii. However, a call from Fort DeRussy "told him it was the real thing and he disappeared for days."

Mrs. Hodge was seven months pregnant, although her doctor had been sure she would not carry the pregnancy so far. Listening to the voice of her old friend, announcer Webley Edwards, on the radio and watching the Japanese planes overhead and the puffs of AA smoke only ten blocks away, she "got madder and madder. No little enemy soldiers were going to stop me from having a baby now, by golly!"[12]

"Gee, Ford Island is certainly at it this morning!" remarked a Navy nurse, as a wave of aircraft smashed the Sunday quiet. Then the nurses at their breakfast heard rapid gunfire, and violent concussions shook the building. This went far beyond the usual drill. "We had no idea what it was," said Ruth Erickson. "We just froze there in our seats."

At that instant the corridor telephone shrilled, and Chief Nurse Gertrude B. Arnest snatched it up. Ruth "had an eerie feeling that something was wrong" even before Nurse Arnest cried out, "Girls, this is the real thing! Get into your uniforms at once!" They scattered in all directions. Ruth ran out of the dining hall, following a corridor whence she could see the Japanese planes flying up the Pearl Harbor channel. "It seemed so low I could have called the Japanese pilot by name had I known him."

She leaped into her quarters and pulled on a uniform. Nothing could better indicate her sense of haste and agitation than the fact that she did not stop to put on her cap—that symbol which meant so much to a dedicated nurse like herself. As she ran across the street to the hospital, she flipped curlers from her hair. "Shrapnel was falling all over the place and why I did not get hit I do not know." She did not pause to dodge the shrapnel. "I made a beeline for the hospital because I wanted to get under cover as fast as I could."[13]

In later days Kimmel did not recall who, if anyone, called for his official car. Probably his longtime driver, Machinist's Mate 1st Class Edgar C. Nebel, "a fine lad and always on the job day or night," had used his own initiative. Kimmel leaped in almost before Nebel braked to a halt, and as the car sped off, Capt. Freeland A. Daubin, commanding Submarine Squadron Four, jumped on the running board. The car pulled up at Fleet Headquarters at the submarine base at approximately 0805.[14]

At that moment the *California*, flagship of Admiral Pye's Battle Force, sustained her first damage—two torpedo strikes "portside at frame 110." She was moored singly "starboard side to berth F-3," somewhat southward of the other battleships, with the tanker *Neosho* between her and the double-moored *Maryland* and *Oklahoma*.[15]

Captain Train, Pye's chief of staff, felt the twin impacts—"not a loud explosion, rather a dull one, in fact." One of those details that stick in a person's mind at such moments clung to Train's memory. The *California*'s air officer came up to his battle station on the bridge with his face dripping oil. "He was a funny sight," said Train, "because he had stuck his head out the porthole when the general alarm went off and the two torpedoes that caused the explosion had splashed him with oil."[16]

Racing to his post, Marine Lieutenant Drake passed Ensign Nicholson. Remembering their exchange earlier that morning,* Drake yelled, "Where in hell did you get the word?"[17]

But the *California*'s plight was far from amusing. Ens. Edgar M. Fain directed counterflooding measures which prevented her from capsizing, but salt water from the harbor poured into her fuel tanks, cutting off light and power.[18] In the flooded air compressor compartment, Machinist's Mate 1st Class Robert R. Scott refused to leave his post. "This is my station and I will stay and give them air as long as the guns are going." He gave his life at this task.[19]

Throughout the next crucial minutes, men labored to perform jobs

* See Chapter 10.

that normally were mechanized. Twenty-three-year-old Ens. Herbert C. Jones organized a group to supply ammunition to the antiaircraft battery. Although mortally wounded, he refused to be carried away from the action. In a burning passageway, Radio Electrician Thomas J. Reeves, 46 years old, helped keep the ammunition moving until he was killed by the smoke and flames. Lt. Jackson C. Pharris was more fortunate. He repeatedly risked his life moving ammunition along and dragging men to safety from the flooded compartment. Although severely injured and twice overcome by oil and fumes, he survived.[20]

Not all the Japanese torpedoes struck home. One dropped at about 0800 hurtled between the *Raleigh* and the *Detroit*, about 25 yards from the latter's stern, to bury itself harmlessly in the mud.[21] Nevertheless, by 0805 the *Raleigh* listed heavily to port, thanks to the torpedo that did hit. Despite counterflooding in several compartments, the list continued. Captain Simons immediately directed efforts to save his ship from capsizing. The noise of the *Raleigh's* guns firing at the enemy planes crisscrossing over her portion of the harbor forced him to transmit orders by messenger.

From the bridge Simons "noted that the UTAH, close aboard, was turning over very rapidly and that the heavy beams placed about her anti-aircraft guns were rolling down on the unfortunate members of the crew as they came up the hatches."[22]

Realizing that his ship was capsizing, the *Utah's* Chief Water Tender Peter Tomich remained at his emergency post until he had assured himself that all boilers were secured and the other sailors had left the station. His devotion to duty cost him his life.[23]

Aboard the *Breese*, almost directly across the channel from the *Utah*, Commander Stout saw the old target ship roll over. One of the *Breese's* crew yelled, "They've got the *Utah!*" Stout's silent response was, "We're losing a ship of little account, but there are people on it—our people."[24]

Stout was one of those who, like Osborne aboard the *Arizona*, had great difficulty in comprehending what was happening that morning. He had been up since 0700 and was at breakfast when he heard the alarm gong. He hastened topside "to give the gangway watch hell for sounding General Quarters on Sunday," for he had issued a ship's order forbidding this practice, so that his officers and crew could sleep in. A gunner's mate 1st class was scheduled for the watch, and Stout's irritation increased when he found the man not at his post.

Looking around for the gangway watch, he saw a plane drop a bomb on Ford Island, but merely reflected, "I always knew one of those screwy aviators would pull a stunt like that." A number of men aboard the *Breese* were running about, and Stout wondered, "What in the hell goes on here?" About 15 seconds later, a plane came from the direction of Ford Island on the starboard side of the *Breese* at masthead height and seemed headed directly for the ship. Her machine gun amidships on the deck house opened up. Still under the impression that some of Ford Island's naval aviators were practicing, Stout asked himself in dismay, "Why are the boys shooting at that plane?" He saw ripples in the water as the aircraft flew in, but did not recognize them as the result of strafing.

As Stout stood in perplexity on the *Breese*'s starboard side, he heard a sound like riveting, and chips of paint from the deck flew up. The plane flew over, revealing its red insignia, and Stout knew the truth: "He's a Jap! We're in the midst of an attack—that's war!" Reality hit Stout just before the *Utah* began to turn over.[25]

The destroyer *Blue* was moored well beyond Ford Island, almost in the north end of the harbor. Four ensigns—Nathan F. Asher, M. I. Moldafsky, J. P. Wolfe, and R. S. Scott—were in the wardroom when they received word from the bridge that Japanese aircraft had torpedoed the *Utah*. They took their stations, Asher commanding the *Blue* as senior officer present. The destroyer "opened fire with .50 cal. machine guns" at 0805 and 2 minutes later with the 5-inch .38 caliber guns of the main battery.[26]

Asher could not explain how his men "got their ammunition from the magazines to the guns in the fast and swift manner that they did." Some of the crew had awakened with hangovers but later asserted that "they had never sobered up so fast in their lives."

The *Blue* maintained continuous fire until the No. 4 ammunition hoist stopped. The gun captain from No. 1 gun hurried to the No. 4 ammunition handling room to try to repair the damage. When the hoist still balked, he dropped to his knees and prayed, "Oh, Lord! Oh, Lord! Make this gun ammunition hoist work just this once!" As he prayed, tears streaming from his eyes, a tall black sailor who was stationed in the handling room gazed down at him and said mildly, "Why, Smith, you got the oil turned off." Galvanized, the gun captain jumped to his feet, tossing skyward a grateful, "It's all right, Lord, I got it now."[27]

Cmdr. Carl K. Fink of the light cruiser *St. Louis* broke the news of the attack to his skipper, Captain Rood. "Fink came busting into my quarters," said Rood, "and awakened me by shouting, 'Captain, there is some kind of a raid on.'" Rood evaluated Fink as "one of the best Executive Officers any ship was ever blessed with," so he wasted no time in questions, especially in view of the fact that, as he jumped out of his bunk, he heard "sounds like the loud twanging of guitar strings." He slipped his uniform over his pajamas, put on his cap, popped into a pair of slippers without stopping for socks, and bounded up to the bridge. There he saw machine-gun bullets hitting the ship from strafers overhead.

Rood was immensely proud of his crew's quick reaction to the attack. "No one had given the word 'commence firing,' which is the most sacred command given in battle at sea and given only by the captain of the ship." But December 7, 1941, was the exception to virtually every rule, and Rood was highly pleased that "the men went right after the enemy without any orders from anyone. That morning no one had to tell our officers and men what to do. They did it on their own."

Admiral Leary's flagship, the light cruiser *Honolulu,* berthed alongside the *St. Louis,* plus a large dock warehouse, obscured the view of the *St. Louis*'s gunners, so an old dock force chief went to the fantail and signaled with his arms when to fire on the oncoming Japanese planes. "And it paid off," said Rood. "The boys splattered one of those torpedo planes with a full load of fire. When they hit him, it sounded like thick pancake batter smacking against the wall. The barrage cut the head of that torpedo right off. The plane crashed into the water, and when he did, the torpedo shook lose and also landed in the harbor."[28]

Meanwhile, the crew made frantic preparations for sortie—neither a simple nor a speedy task. The *St. Louis* was to have been in port for about a week for major boiler repairs. The repairmen had cut a hole about 4 feet in diameter in her side, through which they could pass gear in and out. This hole had to be welded closed during the bombing and strafing. What is more, wooden scaffolding stood on the after director station main deck for the repair and installation of antiaircraft equipment. Rood's men knocked down that scaffolding without waiting for orders, and it bounced around on the deck—"some pretty good-sized beams, too. But no one got hurt."[29]

At the same time, matters were rapidly deteriorating aboard the

Oklahoma. After passing the word for General Quarters, Bothne "went back to see why the anti-aircraft batteries were not firing, and the ready boxes were still locked on the port side." Then he went forward seeking the fire and rescue chest at the stack. Finding that it too was locked, he "went amidships to the gear locker and picked out a hammer and a cold chisel" to knock the locks off.

At that instant, as Bothne related shortly thereafter,

> a third torpedo hit in the middle of the ship, and the ship started to list noticeably then. I had to walk uphill to go to the starboard side, and after they had the ready boxes open there and the ammunition out they had no air to load the guns, and one of the men said there was no fire locks on the guns.

By that time the ship was listing heavily to port. Having noticed no action aboard the *Maryland*, moored inboard of the *Oklahoma*, Bothne and the men near him decided to go over to *Maryland* and get her guns going. They had reached the blister edge when Bothne called out for everyone to stay where he was.

Some 150 men were thus "perched along the blister ledge" when "the ship seemed to hesitate, to be stationary." Then another torpedo struck. The *Oklahoma* "bounced up, and when she settled down she turned."[30]

In this crisis, two of the *Oklahoma*'s personnel, 22-year-old Ens. Francis C. Flaherty and Seaman 1st Class Richard Ward, two years younger, won posthumous Medals of Honor for remarkably similar actions. Flaherty refused to abandon ship and stayed in a turret holding a flashlight, enabling the turret crew to see their way to safety. Ward also remained behind so that the beam of his flashlight could aid his shipmates in escaping.[31]

Gunner's Mate Beck was heading for his battle station in turret No. 4 amidships when the *Oklahoma*'s list became so noticeable that he decided there was no point in reaching the turret. "For we were not going to fire those 11-inch guns. And by now it was clear that we were going over." It would make better sense to help as many men as possible through the shell hoist, now their only means of escape. He knew that when the ship listed completely the 14-inch shells on the shell platform would break loose from their lashings and roll across the deck. They weighed roughly 1400 lbs each and would crush to death anyone in their path.

With the help of some shipmates, Beck pulled men up the hoist until they had to abandon the effort. Soon the shell projectiles scattered across the shell hoist and blocked its passage. "By then the place was a confused mess of 14-inch projectiles."

Beck and his buddies reached the turret, climbed into the gun chamber room, and then entered the fire-control booth. Finding the overhanging hatch open, Beck dove into the harbor. In retrospect, he estimated that another 5 minutes would have been too late, for water was already coming into the turret.[32]

Seaman Young grabbed the bulkhead of the power-handling room. He had been sure that the *Oklahoma*'s armored deck would withstand bombing, but he had not thought in terms of torpedoes. Then someone cried out and pointed to the portside bulkhead where water was pouring in. The deck began to tilt, and gear began to spill out of the lockers. The habit of his job still held Young. "All our breakfast dishes must be breaking," he said. A nervous titter arose, and he added, "Don't laugh, they'll take it out of my pay."

He peered up the ladder into the shell deck above and saw the shells break loose, rumbling down on men trying to scramble up the tilting deck. But he called down reassuringly, "They're just counterflooding to get us back on an even keel so they can fire the guns." This seemed to satisfy his buddies briefly; then came the call, "Abandon Ship!"[33]

The order came from the senior officer aboard, the ship's executive officer, Cmdr. Jesse L. Kenworthy. With the ship listing almost 35° and continuing to slip still further, it became obvious that the *Oklahoma* was going to roll over. He "climbed over the boat deck toward the starboard side." From men scrambling up "from below through hatches and gun ports," he learned that the ship was flooding.

On the starboard side, Kenworthy met the ship's first lieutenant, Lt. Cmdr. W. H. Hobby. The two men concluded "that the ship was fast becoming untenable and that an effort should be made to save as many men as possible." Kenworthy ordered "Abandon Ship" and directed the men "to leave over the starboard side and to work and climb over the ship's side out onto the bottom as it rolled over."[34]

Boatswain's Mate French also sensed that this latest torpedo would prove fatal to the battleship which had been his home for nine years. His men had been so eager to reach their battle stations that they bypassed the ladders, jumping from one deck to the other. "They bounced on top of one another like balls and then sped to their battle stations." Now French began to shoo the approximately one hundred men of his division up the ladder. "Get topside; the ship is going to turn over!" he shouted.[35]

By the time French reached the second deck, loose equipment was sliding across it: "mess tables, lockers, buckets, clothing—anything that was not screwed to the deck was flying across to the other side." There French met a Reserve ensign on his way forward. French tried to stop him: "Sir, you can't get out up forward." But the young officer hurried on, saying, "I've got to get to my room." French never saw him again. "He could have gotten to his room," he explained, "but he couldn't have gotten out from there."[36]

French was now alone; his men had beaten him topside. He made his way to S Division "right at the break of the deck" and thence to the main deck. The *Oklahoma* had not yet rolled over, and French could stand on the deck, albeit with some difficulty. Suddenly a bomb exploded nearby, sending a huge wave washing over the deck. The weight of the water knocked French down and almost drowned him, but he struggled to his feet in time to see Petty Officer 2d Class "Smoky" Struthers, "a real bruiser" from French's division. "How are you doing, Smoky?" he panted.

"OK, Howard," he replied; then he calmly jumped over the rail and swam over to the *Maryland*. French waited to see him reach the nearby battleship, where a big sailor pulled him up on the armor ledge. Satisfied that Struthers was safe, French went to the boat deck, both because "it was normal to seek the highest level" and because the boats and life jackets were there.

He was on the boat deck when the *Oklahoma* took her last big list. Knowing she was going over, French walked against the roll until he reached the bridge keel. About fifty men were walking around the bottom, but many struggled in the oil-covered water near the ship. He called for life jackets and threw them to the men, including a group of five who were supporting a wounded comrade. With the help of the jackets, they succeeded in reaching Ford Island.[37]

"Commander, it doesn't look like they left us much to fight with," French remarked to Kenworthy, who was standing beside him.

Kenworthy made no reply. "He tried to say something but couldn't," French reflected. "His face was ashen and gray. He was in such a state of shock he could not talk."

French himself was stunned, but the events of the last few minutes were too much to take in. "I was so shocked I couldn't get scared," he remembered. "The enormity of it all was all-embracing." For years thereafter he would awaken in the middle of the night reliving the horror of that day. For the moment, however, he had a job to do.

Spotting a 50-foot motor launch, still secure, resting on the bottom of the ship, he continued to address Kenworthy: "I'll see if I can get that boat loose." Still the executive officer made no reply, and shortly thereafter French lost contact with him.[38]

Bothne and most of the sailors with him slid down the side into the water, where he was fortunate enough to find a motor launch. He and his companions took two boatloads of men to safety.[39]

Beck swam to the starboard side of the 14-inch gun turret, which was about level with the harbor surface. He climbed aboard the turret, where he remained waist deep in the water. He had been inside the *Oklahoma* throughout the action; now he looked about him. "For the first time I realized what a terrible blow we had received. . . . It was an awesome situation." Wherever he looked, he could see nothing but smoke and flame. His initial instinct was to stick with the ship, for he felt sure she would not explode and could not sink much further, hence suction could not pull him down. Then, being a good swimmer, he wondered if he should not trust himself to the water, but he asked himself, "Where in the hell shall I swim to?"

As if in answer, about a hundred yards into the channel he spotted one of the *Oklahoma*'s catapult planes which had broken loose from the aft part of the ship. It had capsized and was floating upside down, but the pontoons would serve as a temporary life raft. So Beck swam to the plane and hung chest-deep to the pontoon, with two other men, one on each side of him.

They had no sooner settled into position than a Japanese strafer, whether a fighter or bomber Beck did not know, sped up the channel. "We heard him roar up behind us before we heard the pip, pip, pip of his bullets splashing into the water. The pilot was so close when he shot that the machine guns on each of his wings took out the man on my right and on my left." Without a sound they slipped into the channel, killed instantly.[40]

Marine Sergeant Thomas E. Hailey was among those who dived overboard at the order "Abandon Ship." He struggled through the heavy oil atop the water to the *Maryland* and pulled himself aboard by a line hanging over the side. After helping several of his shipmates to follow him, he spotted an unmanned AA gun and soon had it blazing away with an all-*Oklahoma* crew.[41]

Mrs. Earle watched the grim scene from in front of her home. "Then slowly, sickeningly, the *Oklahoma* began to roll over on her side, until, finally, only her bottom could be seen. It was awful, for great ships were dying before my eyes! Strangely enough, at first I didn't realize that men were dying too."[42]

A sense of false security upheld Thesman when the *Oklahoma* began to list. The harbor was shallow and "one could always counterflood." However, the ship continued to roll. Soon lockers toppled over, and spare parts that had been stacked high in the steering gear compartment crashed down. Thesman and the six sailors with him ducked and dodged frantically to avoid being hurt.

At 25, Thesman was the oldest man present and felt responsible for his juniors, among them two brothers whose older brother was also aboard the *Oklahoma*. "My immediate concern was that one of these kids might panic and that I would have to take care of him if he did."[43]

Fortunately, no one panicked, but of course everyone felt considerable apprehension. Thesman described the situation eloquently:

> And now the whole realization of what was happening began to dawn on me and the rest of the men. Shortly, too, water began coming in through the ventilation system, and our immediate objective was to stop up the vent ducts and retard the flow. We stuffed these ducts with mattresses, blankets or anything we could lay our hands on. The water in time started to get high but not enough to drown us. We had a damage control chart on the bulkhead and we decided that at the highest point within the compartment we could still stay above the water line.

They lost all concept of time—if anyone had a watch, it had stopped. Next they lost light when someone dropped the only flashlight. As the water rose, the men began to peel off some of their clothes to be ready for whatever might happen next.[44]

Many miles out at sea off Oahu, 0800 brought an end to the long patience Commander Yokota of the submarine *I-26* had been exercising. He had received no news concerning the air operations at Pearl Harbor, but he knew the scheduled time for the attack. In sublime faith—quite justified—that the project had begun, he brought the *I-*

26 to the surface. At an estimated distance of some 2000 meters from his prey, the *Cynthia Olsen*, he ordered an over-range shot from his 15-centimeter gun to halt the little wooden ship. However, she continued coming toward the submarine. Thereupon the *I-26* fired a torpedo, which missed.

This time the *Cynthia Olsen* stopped, and Yokota could see the crew hastily lowering her two lifeboats. He waited chivalrously until the last crew member had scrambled into the second boat before he began to work on the ship, submerging and surfacing from time to time. The *I-26* launched a second torpedo but relied primarily on the gun. The stubborn little vessel kept the submarine hammering away for approximately 5 hours before rolling over on her port side. Yokota did not actually see her sink, but he had no doubt that she did. Then he ordered his submarine to his predesignated patrol area, roughly midway between the Hawaiian Islands and San Francisco.[45]

CHAPTER 12

"Through the Smoke and Flames"

During these early minutes of action, Murata's torpedo bombers had occupied center stage. Fuchida's high-level bombers were not far behind, however, and they inflicted much of the damage with which the first wave could credit itself.

After giving his *"Tsu, Tsu, Tsu"* attack order for the high-altitude bombers, Fuchida fell back, trading places with the No. 2 plane in his group of five, the better to observe the action. The pilot and bombardier of plane No. 2 were, respectively, 1st Flying Petty Officers Akira Watanabe and Yanosuke Aso, the best in the Japanese Navy in their fields, invariably winning first prize in bombing contests.[1]

As they neared the target area, Fuchida admired the rapidity of the American antiaircraft counterattack. He doubted if the Combined Fleet would have reacted so quickly; the Japanese "had a suitable character for the offensive but not for the defensive." Even as he so reflected, his plane vibrated "as if struck with a club."

"Commander, that one was terrible!" Mutsuzaki exclaimed. "Is everything all right?"

Mizuki reported holes in the fuselage and the steering wire half shot through. "Lt. Mutsuzaki, can you control the plane?" Fuchida asked anxiously.

"Everything is all right," Mutsuzaki reassured him.[2]

Turning his attention outward, Fuchida observed the No. 3 plane, alongside his own, drop its bomb prematurely. Throughout training, that bombardier had had trouble with the timing of his release. "That damn fellow has made the same mistake!" Fuchida fumed. He shook

138

his fist at the culprit and knocked it against his own head to indicate his opinion of the bombardier's intelligence. Then, noticing gas blowing out of the plane, he scribbled "What happened to you?" on a small blackboard, holding it up so that the offending bombardier could read it through his binoculars.

The man replied by this same primitive intercom, "Received a hit under the fuselage," indicating by gestures that this had loosened his bomb. Remorseful for having misjudged his comrade, he directed him to return to the carrier. He scribbled back, "Only extra tank destroyed. I will follow the group," and bowed repeatedly as he held up the message. Fuchida was practical enough to realize the uselessness of a bomber with no bomb tagging along; however, he appreciated the man's esprit de corps and nodded permission.[3]

He was impatiently watching the lead plane for the release signal when shreds of fluffy clouds covered the target area. Aso's face popped up in his cockpit, and he waved to indicate that he had missed the opportunity. He banked to make another try.[4]

In the meantime, at least two of the high-altitude bombers had gone for the *Vestal*. CWO Hall, who only the previous night had predicted a Japanese attack on Pearl Harbor,* was the *Vestal*'s officer of the deck when the first planes flew over. He immediately recognized the Rising Sun insignia and rapped out the order, "Sound General Quarters." The quartermaster only stared as if doubting Hall's sanity. "Goddamit, I said 'Sound General Quarters.'!" thundered Hall. "Those are Jap planes up there!" Without further ado, he pulled the signal himself.[5]

By 0800, the *Vestal* had all guns manned, and opened fire 5 minutes later "with 3-inch A.A. and machine guns." At that moment, a bomb struck the *Vestal* "at frame 110 port side" and "a second hit at frame 44 starboard side." Each bomb killed one man and wounded several.[6]

The first bomb landed forward, killing Chief Boatswain's Mate "Billy" Duane, the first man to lose his life aboard the *Vestal*.[7] "This bomb landed on the fore part of the ship," Hesser remembered, "penetrated the superstructure, went down through the mess deck, down into a steel storeroom where steel supplies were kept, and there it detonated. The force of the bomb was so great it twisted steel and brass bars four to eight feet in length like pretzels."[8]

---

* See Chapter 4.

"The second bomb hit aft," said Crawford, "and went through the carpenter's shop—port side—then went seven more decks right down through the damn ship and into the mud and never exploded. Had that son-of-a-bitchin' bomb gone off down there in all that mud it would have blown the guts right out of the *Vestal*."

Crawford was trying to reach topside when Moulder 1st Class "Red" Ferguson called out, "Help me get the hatches closed." Knowing well the importance of watertight security, Crawford joined Ferguson and managed to close some of the hatches. Then Crawford continued on his way topside and aft.[9]

Hesser had been checking the steering engine in case the *Vestal* had to get under way, and he was headed aft when the second bomb struck. Unlike Crawford, he believed this bomb detonated in the water after passing through the bottom, for "the ship took a severe jolt after the bomb had gone through."

Hesser pulled a sailor out of the wreckage and carried him to the after dressing station in the optical shop off the well deck. Both the ship's doctor and dentist were ashore, and a pharmacist's mate 2d class named Baker was tending the wounded, although he was bleeding from a severe wound in his calf. Hesser urged him to seek medical aid, either ashore or aboard the *Solace*, but Baker refused: "I will stay here until I take care of my shipmates." So Hesser wrapped up Baker's calf as best he could and left him to his work.[10]

Fuchida was swinging from the south of Pearl Harbor to come in north again for his second bombing run when a tremendous explosion sent fire and smoke a good 1000 meters high. He described the scene: "The smoke and flame erupted together. It was a hateful, mean-looking red flame, the kind that powder produces, and I knew at once that a big powder magazine had exploded."

Fuchida's aircraft was at approximately 3000 meters, but it rocked from the concussion and the pull of the suction in the afterblast. At least one U.S. battleship was out of the reckoning. "Joy and gratification filled my heart at the time," he said, "for I knew now that our mission would be a success."[11]

The Japanese credited Petty Officer Noboru Kanai, a crack bombardier from the *Soryu*, with the astounding hit that sank the *Arizona*.[12]

Hiding with his shipmates behind the *Oklahoma*'s antiroll keel, French was looking directly at the *Arizona*. "There was an awful blast and a terrific concussion, but the force was upward instead of out. The foremast tilted forward, took a crazy angle and the ship went down immediately. I could see parts of bodies in the foremast rigging." He reflected fearfully that all the debris from the explosion would have to come down somewhere. "I thought I had checked in for the last time, and I said a prayer for my family."[13]

To Fink, aboard the *St. Louis*, "the explosion of [the] *Arizona* seemed almost unreal....The explosion seemed to have a focal point, with huge red flames shooting from all angles. It was the most horrifying thing I have ever seen."[14]

Minutes before the explosion, Seaman George D. Phraner had been manning his station on a 5-inch gun forward when the gunner's mate sent him aft to bring ammunition. The order saved his life. He and some of his comrades were in the aft magazine when the forward magazine exploded. Everyone in his gun crew was killed.

Lights went out, and smoke began to creep through the corridors. Fortunately, Phraner knew the *Arizona* well, having been with her for a year, and he was able to grope his way topside. Burning oil surrounded most of the ship, but the water aft was still free. Phraner and a few shipmates jumped in and swam to Ford Island.[15]

Twenty-one-year-old Lloyd Coole was in the *Arizona*'s No. 3 turret when he felt the ship "bounce and shake like a leaf." The blowers began discharging smoke and gas. "I crawled out of there in a hurry.... The ship was a mess. Wounded were lying all over the place. I saw one man crawling around without any clothes on—they had all been blown off. He fell into the water and drowned."

When the word came to abandon ship, he and some other sailors slid a large life raft into the water, which by that time was close to the quarterdeck. Finding no paddles in the raft, the men tried to paddle with their hands, but the the raft refused to budge. A few of the men climbed back aboard, but Coole "didn't want any part of the ship anymore." Despite the wind which seemed to be blowing flaming oil in his direction, he made it to shore.[16]

Seaman Osborne and a friend, Bob Seeley, were manning the No. 2 director on the mainmast when the explosion sent "debris and what appeared to be bodies flying through the air." They tried to contact someone over the battlephones but could get no answer. Osborne saw the foremast burning "and once in a while through the smoke forward caught a glimpse of men trying to get down off the foremast."

Then came the command to abandon ship. On the way down from

their post, the two men saw no one until they reached the search-light platform, where they saw "a couple of bodies, one of which was a Marine officer." Osborne avoided a flaming hole at the bottom of the mast. There on the main deck men were wounded and in shock. In the Marine Compartment, he wrote, "was what appeared to be a pile of debris, but looking closely through the smoke and flames I could make out bodies mixed in with the burning debris. It was impossible to get to the bodies because of the flames."[17]

The body of the Marine officer Osborne saw on the searchlight platform no doubt was that of Lt. Carlton E. Simonsen, where Major Shapley had carried him. Shapley had scrambled up the ladder to his battle station "in the secondary battery control in the director, up in the mainmast," along with Simonsen and thirteen enlisted men. At a point on the ladder about 87 feet up, Japanese planes strafed Shapley and his men. Simonsen fell back abruptly into Shapley's arms. The sudden dead weight could have knocked a less athletic and alert man off the ladder, but Shapley caught himself and his comrade. He "boosted him up to the searchlight platform and found he'd been instantly killed by a burst of machine-gun fire." The strafing also killed three or four of the enlisted men.[18]

Shapley continued up the mainmast, about 180 feet above deck, where he had "the best seat in Pearl Harbor to watch the attack." Soon it became apparent to him that the situation was impossible. The little group of Marines could not elevate the ten guns in the secondary battery high enough to hit the Japanese planes, and if they fired level, they would strike Ford Island on one side or the harbor on the other. The Arizona was already burning badly, and Sgt. John Baker asked the question that probably was in everyone's mind: "What are we going to do, cook up here?"

Shapley ordered his men to go down and try to save themselves. He, too, began to descend, stopping at the searchlight platform to determine that Simonsen was indeed dead, as he had assumed. He had just verified Simonsen's death when Kanai's bomb hit the magazine.

Shapley had a vague sensation of being catapulted into space. Faced with a 100-foot enforced dive, he kept his self-possession. "I had better go in feet first or head first," he decided. He had no recollection of hitting the water, but suddenly he was swimming, stark naked. The concussion had whisked away every stitch of his clothes.[19]

Among the Marines scrambling down from the mainmast was 20-year-old Cpl. Earl C. Nightingale. Someone ahead of him impeded

his progress. This man walked with arms outstretched, blindly grop-
ing his way; severe burns had temporarily deprived him of sight.
Nightingale also noticed a big, husky cook sitting on the deck. He
was staring blankly at the stump where a leg had been blown off,
watching his life pump out through severed arteries. Charred bodies
lay everywhere.

Nightingale spotted Commander Fuqua on the quarterdeck, assisting men to leave the ship. Nightingale anticipated that he would need
no help in reaching shore, because he was an excellent swimmer with a
lifeguard certificate and was in top physical condition. When he reached
the quarterdeck, he began taking off his shoes in anticipation of swimming to Ford Island.[20]

Then he found himself in the water, too dazed to remember how
he got there. When he came up the first time, shock had paralyzed
his arms and legs. Some of his buddies hanging on to a pipeline between the *Arizona* and Ford Island cheered him and encouraged him
to swim over, but in his bemused condition he only smiled and winked
at them. He was, however, conscious enough to be terrified of going
under again, especially fearing that concussion from a bomb or torpedo exploding under water might kill him. He felt himself sinking
and wondered if he would drown. The sensation was not unpleasant—
not a bad way to go, if one's time had come. Then he jerked himself
alive: "How ridiculous! I'm young and have so much to live for!"[21]

As Shapley struck out for Ford Island, he encountered a couple of
his shipmates floundering in the water, Nightingale among them. "Put
your arms on my shoulders," the major instructed them, "and don't
struggle or I'll bang you!"[22]

Nightingale knew Shapley well and considered him "a great guy."
He never looked better to the corporal than now, and Nightingale clung
to him gratefully.[23] During Shapley's efforts to reach shore, bombs striking the water compressed his body so forcefully that he retched with
nausea. "I'm going down," he gasped. "Let go!" Slowly he slipped under, and Nightingale also went down. As the waters parted the two men,
Nightingale saluted.

Shapley went down only a few feet before striking bottom. He
pushed up again, pulling Nightingale along with him.[24] By this time,
the corporal began to regain the use of his limbs and thought he could
carry on alone, so he pushed Shapley away. The major thought Nightingale had panicked and was struggling against his efforts at rescue.

"Knock it off, goddamit!" he snarled. Whereupon he grabbed Nightingale again and pulled him toward the pipeline.[25] There they and a few others clung for a moment; then Shapley helped them ashore on Ford Island.

There, 200 or 300 men stood in forlorn groups, "all burned like steaks, no clothes, just burned like lamb chops," Shapley remembered. "The only thing I could see was their eyes, lips and mouths. Their mouths were reddish; their eyes looked watery. Everything else was black. They were moaning and walking around in a daze. They were in a state of shock and would not suffer deeply until they came out of it. I don't recall anyone keeling over, though many of them may have been dying by degrees."[26]

Over a thousand of Shapley's shipmates died in that ghastly moment of destruction, including Admiral Kidd and Captain Van Valkenburg.[27] Their deaths left Fuqua senior officer aboard. He had been engaged in firefighting, although the hoses had no water. He and his damage-control men were attempting "to keep the fire back by dipping water from the side in buckets and by the use of CO_2 fire extinguisher." Somehow they were able "to keep the fire from spreading aft" long enough to "pick the wounded off the deck and place them in boats to transfer them to Ford Island."

Fuqua was thus occupied when "a tremendous mass of flames" erupted to about 300 feet. It rose forward "and shook the ship aft as if it would fall apart like a pack of cards." Immediately Fuqua realized that the forward magazine had exploded. By about 0820, the Arizona's guns had ceased firing. Since "the ship was no longer in a fighting condition," Fuqua ordered "Abandon Ship" and devoted his attention to the only constructive work possible under the circumstances—rescuing the wounded and transferring them to Ford Island.[28]

Aboard the Solace, still waiting for mass, Lieutenant Ruff heard a frightful sound "like a powerful and heavy wind blowing through thick foliage." He raced to the starboard side of the officers' lounge to look out. The Arizona was erupting in a huge cloud of smoke and flame. As he watched in horrified bewilderment, a plane snarled overhead and banked, revealing the red ball on its wings. Thus Ruff realized for the first time what was going on.

Almost immediately the priest dismissed his flock, and Ruff caught the launch to return to the Nevada. From the little boat he had an excellent view of enemy action above. Seeing antiaircraft fire from the ships "belting lead at them right and left," he asked himself, "What

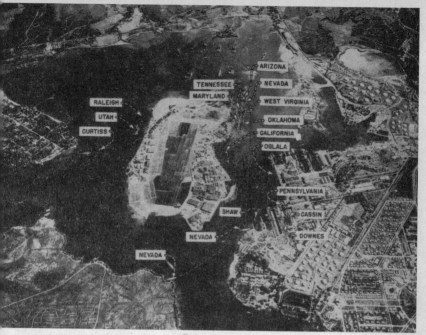

Aerial view of Pearl Harbor showing location of battleships.
(*National Archives—Prange File*)

This aerial view taken on an October morning in 1941 shows Pearl Harbor much as Fuchida saw it a scant two months later. Dominating the scene is Ford Island, flanked by the famed "Battleship Row" to the island's left. (*National Archives—Michael Wenger*)

B5N2 Type 97 attack plane of the second wave pulls up and away from *Shokaku*'s flight deck in the early morning light of 7 December. (*Smithsonian Institution—Michael Wenger*)

The raid in the opening moments. At far right, smoke boils up from the seaplane ramp at the Ford Island NAS. Across Ford Island on Battleship Row, a gargantuan water column rises alongside *Oklahoma* as the stricken vessel sustains a torpedo hit. A B5N2 attack bomber from *Soryu* pulls up over the island after launching its torpedo against the ships on the northwest shore. (*U.S. Naval Historical Center—Michael Wenger*)

The target/gunnery training vessel *Utah*, a converted battleship, takes two torpedo hits early in the raid and capsizes almost immediately. (*National Archives—Michael Wenger*)

U.S.S. *Arizona*'s forward magazines detonate shortly after 0800 hours, 7 December 1941. (*National Archives—Prange Files*)

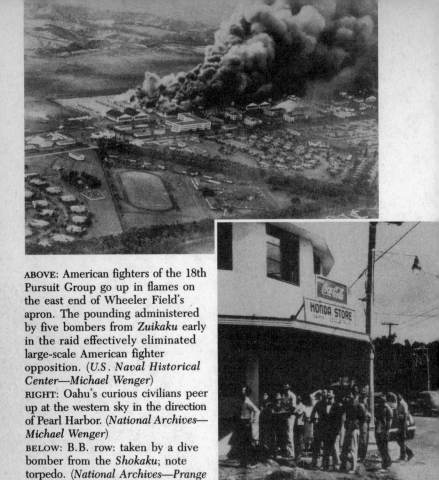

ABOVE: American fighters of the 18th Pursuit Group go up in flames on the east end of Wheeler Field's apron. The pounding administered by five bombers from *Zuikaku* early in the raid effectively eliminated large-scale American fighter opposition. (*U.S. Naval Historical Center—Michael Wenger*)

RIGHT: Oahu's curious civilians peer up at the western sky in the direction of Pearl Harbor. (*National Archives—Michael Wenger*)

BELOW: B.B. row: taken by a dive bomber from the *Shokaku*; note torpedo. (*National Archives—Prange Files*)

ABOVE: Sometime after 10:30 A.M., the seaplane tender *Avocet* and yardcraft *YT-146* lent aid to the beleaguered *Nevada*, playing water on the still smoldering fires, started by five bomb hits on the forward part of the ship. (*National Archives—Michael Wenger*)

RIGHT: The smoldering ruins of Hangar 6 on Ford Island relatively early in the raid, probably around 9:00 A.M. (*National Archives—Michael Wenger*)

BELOW: Beyond the small seaplane tender *Avocet* in the foreground, *Nevada* beaches on Hospital Point, ending her gallant sortie shortly after 9:00 A.M.) with the Stars and Stripes still flying proudly from her stern. *Avocet* would later go to *Nevada*'s aid, battling the fires that raged through the forward part of the ship. (*National Archives—Michael Wenger*)

A bombardier's view of Battleship Row during Commander Fuchida's horizontal bombing attack. At left, splashes in the water around *Arizona*'s fantail mark bomb impacts. At right, fuel oil hemorrhages from the torpedoed *West Virginia* and *Oklahoma*, both of which are in danger of capsizing. (*U.S. Naval Historical Center—Michael Wenger*)

With fires raging through the forward part of the ship, *West Virginia* slowly settles to an upright position as a result of counterflooding, which saved her from the same fate as *Oklahoma*. (*National Archives—Michael Wenger*)

Amidst the chaos of the raid, personnel on leave struggled to return to their stations. At far left two men in mufti have just debarked from a small launch which carried them to Ford Island. The oil fires from the other burning battleships now threaten *California*, which is listing to port and burning from a bomb hit amidships. (*National Archives—Michael Wenger*)

Japanese torpedoes find their mark on the Pacific Fleet's battle line. Torpedo tracks and concentric concussion rings are clearly visible to the left of the battleships. At the far end of Battleship Row, *California* has just taken a torpedo hit. Circled at left is one of Lieutenant Commander Kakuichi Takanshi's Type 99 carrier bombers pulling out of its bomb run over Ford Island. (*U.S. Naval Historical Center—Michael Wenger*)

As personnel dressed in skivvies approach one of Ford Island's landing docks during the lull between attack waves, a towering billow of dense smoke rolls upward from the stircken vessels on Battleship Row. *Neosho* at far right, loaded with aviation fuel, backs well away from the oil fires threatening her berth at Ford Island. At left, *California*—holed by two torpedoes—has a pronounced list to port. (*National Archives—Michael Wenger*)

Burning oil from the battleships to the north totally engulfs the stern of *California* and forces her crew to abandon both ship and efforts to keep her afloat. (*National Archives—Michael Wenger*)

in hell is keeping those Jap planes up there?" Then he understood; the shells were exploding too far beneath the planes to do much damage.

Small as the launch was, it did not escape Japanese notice; a strafing pilot bracketed a furrow of bullets on each side.[29]

Crawford had scarcely reached his destination on the *Vestal* when "that big *Arizona* blew up like a million Fourth of Julys." Crawford flew through the air and landed in the main channel. He did not know how high the explosion flung him. "But, by God, it was high enough, because I was stunned when I hit the water, and my right hand and the left side of my face were burned."

A small boat picked him up and took him to "the old liberty landing" at Aiea. There Joe Fisher, the Navy's lightweight boxing champion, gave him a pound of butter to smear on his burns. As soon as Crawford got his bearings, he tried to organize some fellow refugees into a patrol. "For you didn't know what those Goddamn Japs were going to try next."[30]

The explosion flung overboard about a hundred of Crawford's shipmates, including Commander Young, the *Vestal's* skipper. Looking across to the *Arizona*, Hesser could see men still standing at their gun stations completely surrounded by fire and smoke; then suddenly they keeled over. "They were dead," said Hesser, "there was no question about them being dead."[31]

Commander Smart, too, "could see the men on [the] *Arizona* walking on deck and burning alive. They had their helmets on, their clothes were all seared off. Actually they were only recognizable because of their helmets. They were a ghostly crew as they walked out of those flames. And then they just dropped dead."[32]

Tons of debris rained down on the *Vestal's* decks: "Part of the ship, legs, arms and heads of men—all sorts of bodies were lying around on our ship," said Hesser.[33] The deadly shower included "coins of various denominations all over the deck, large valves, fittings, people (intact) were blown over." Incredibly, some of these men were still alive. "The whole business was just plain weird and in fact unbelievable," recalled Smart. "Everybody thought the whole Fleet was going to Jesus."[34]

Among the wounded was Hall, who had to relinquish his post as officer of the deck to an ensign fresh out of college. But Hall insisted on going to his battle station to carry out his duties as best he could.

Another young ensign, nicknamed "Speedy" because, said Hesser, "he was one of the slowest mortals ever," jumped overboard and struck out for shore. About halfway there he realized that he had forgotten his wallet. So he swam back to the *Vestal*, ran to his quarters, found his wallet, dived overboard again, and this time reached shore. Hesser reflected that it was just as well the skipper did not witness this performance.[35] Young was "very much a career officer" who "expected a lot of his officers and men."[36]

About this time, with the ship afire and flooding, someone ordered "Abandon Ship." The new OD placed some men in a boat alongside and was going down the gangway himself when he came face to face with Young, dripping with oil and water. "Where the hell do you think you're going?" he inquired ominously.

"We're abandoning ship," the OD replied.

"Get back aboard ship!" Young thundered. "You don't abandon ship on me!" With that he climbed aboard, the OD following him. Young spotted Hesser, an old and trusted friend, and directed him, "Hesser, take over the deck. Get these people out of the boat and don't let any more off the ship."[37]

Young and Hesser were standing near the rail of the ship, down on the quarterdeck, when they saw a plane glide down and drop a torpedo. It struck the water and raced toward the *Vestal*. "It went under the water after it was launched," Hesser remembered, "but we could see its wake, and it headed right for us." Someone observed fatalistically, "Well, here it comes."

It seemed too much to hope for a repetition of the *Vestal*'s earlier escape from a torpedo. Although not a man given to dramatics, Young impulsively turned to his shipmate and said, "Goodbye, Hesser."

"Goodbye, Captain," Hesser replied.

To their astonished relief, the torpedo struck not the *Vestal*, but the *Arizona*. "We did not actually see the torpedo pass under the *Vestal*," explained Hesser, "but it had to in order to hit the *Arizona*, and that torpedo hit the *Arizona*, believe me." The missile could have made comparatively little difference in the condition of the battleship, already wrecked by the explosion of her magazine, and it actually did the *Vestal* a favor. The concussion "almost knocked us flat," said Hesser, "but the second torpedo saved our ship." It snuffed out the fires on the *Vestal* "as though it had been done by a giant hand."[38]

Debris from the *Arizona*, including burning powder and oil, poured down on the *Tennessee* and started fires in her stern and port quarter.

"These fires and the subsequent wetting caused considerable damage to the ward room and the officers' quarters in this vicinity." In addition, high-level bombers registered two hits on the *Tennessee*. One struck Turret III, where it "wrecked the high catapult and penetrated the roof of the turret. The bomb broke into large pieces but did not explode. The explosive charge spilled in the turret and burned."

The second bomb struck Turret II and "split the hoop on the center gun, rendering it inoperative." This bomb did explode, and fragments "caused casualties on the machine-gun stations."[39]

A fragment of this bomb flew across to the *West Virginia* and killed Captain Bennion.[40] This circumstance was all the more bitterly ironic because the *West Virginia* had already taken far worse direct punishment than did the *Tennessee*. Beattie reported a few days later:

> At this time the ship listed at least five or six degrees and was steadily listing more to port. The Captain and I went to the conning tower, our battle station, and at this time dive-bombing attacks started to take place and numerous explosions were felt throughout the ship. Upon testing all communications with central station and to the guns, we found they were disrupted. I suggested to the Captain as long as our communications were in the battle conning tower that we leave there and attempt to establish messenger communication and try to save the ship. We went out on the starboard side of the bridge discussing what to do.[41]

In the meantime, Lt. Claude V. Ricketts, although ill, made his way topside from the wardroom. He knew that in all likelihood few damage-control officers were aboard. "Captain, shall I go below and counterflood?" he asked.

"Yes, do that," Bennion replied.

As Ricketts went below, he saw men bringing wounded "up the hatches forward." The ship now listed so heavily that "it was impossible to walk without holding on to something."[42] With the able assistance of a boatswain's mate named Billingsley, Ricketts began counterflooding, which, with the cables linking the *West Virginia* to the *Tennessee*, saved her from capsizing.[43]

Commander Johnson was hurrying to his battle station, worried because so few of the *West Virginia*'s guns were manned and operating, when the battleship took two bomb hits. Both were duds, but one "landed in the crew's galley and blew them all to hell," according to Johnson.[44] It passed within 20 feet of Seaman John Matheson's battle station on an antiaircraft fire director, but he could not remember it hitting.[45]

The bombs came from Lt. Heijiro Abe's high-altitude group from the *Soryu* on their second run over the target area, smoke having prevented a good sighting on the first attempt. As Abe remembered, his unit of five aircraft delivered one hit each on the *Tennessee* and the *West Virginia*, with three near misses, his own effort among the latter. The second five-plane unit dropped five near misses in perfect echelon alongside the *Nevada*. Abe was sure that the hit on the *West Virginia* caught her squarely amidships. "Huge explosion after the hit and began to list slowly," he recorded on a sketch drawn from memory. Probably he saw the result of one of the seven torpedos that slammed into the *West Virginia*. During both his first and second runs, Abe "felt shocks caused by AA shell blasts nearby," but his group soared away undamaged.[46]

On the bridge, Bennion suddenly doubled up and moaned. Beattie "saw that he had been hit in the stomach, probably by a large piece of shrapnel, and was very seriously wounded." Bennion sank to the deck; Beattie loosened his collar and "sent a messenger for a pharmacist's mate to assist the Captain."[47]

Others hastened to the scene, including Johnson, who took in the situation at a glance. A chief pharmacist's mate named Leak was caring for Bennion as best he could, but the captain "was all full of blood and obviously in very bad shape." Hoping to move him to a safer place, Johnson hurried off and returned with Mess Attendant 2d Class Doris Miller, a towering black man who was well known throughout the ship, being the *West Virginia*'s heavyweight boxing champion. The muscular Miller would be just the man to lift his captain, should that be advisable.[48]

However, Ricketts, who also had reached the captain's side, decided that Bennion "would be better off with as little handling as possible," and Leak concurred in this judgment. Nor did Bennion want to be moved. Despite his great pain, he remained conscious, asking alert questions about the condition of the ship. "He was particularly concerned about the fires on board and the oil on the surface of the water." Ricketts "assured him that everyone was doing everything possible to fight the fire and control the damage."

Nevertheless, fire crept closer, and Bennion insisted repeatedly that the officers and men with him should leave him and go below. This was the one order of Bennion's that his subordinates deliberately disobeyed. When the flames "broke out around the after part of the bridge structure," Ricketts finally had to permit the captain to be moved "because of the suffocating smoke and the approaching fire." Shortly thereafter, Leak said, "Mr. Ricketts, the captain is about gone."[49]

When Ens. Victor Delano rounded up another officer, a seaman, and Miller to man two idle machine guns on the conning tower, he meant Miller to handle the ammunition while the others did the firing. Not content with such a relatively passive role, Miller, although completely untrained with the weapon, seized one of the guns. To Delano he appeared to be enjoying himself, smiling for the first time since winning the heavyweight title.[50]

Johnson was so impressed with Miller's courage, coolness, and initiative that he recommended him for the Navy Cross.[51] On May 27, 1942, Admiral Chester W. Nimitz pinned the award on Miller—the first black "to receive such high tribute in the Pacific Fleet" in World War II.[52]

CHAPTER 13

"A Terrible Hour"

Ruth Erickson bounded up the steps onto the lanai of the hospital's administrative building, breathing a silent "Thank God I made it!" In retrospect, she could neither describe nor explain the force which for a moment held her bolted to the spot and then just as mysteriously released her. She ran into the building and down the corridor to the orthopedic dressing room. Finding the door locked, she called to a nearby corpsman, "Run to the OD's desk and get the key! Hurry!"

To Ruth, waiting impatiently, the seconds dragged. Would the man never return? "That morning every moment seemed like a life-time. But he actually arrived right fast." As she unlocked the door, she ordered, "Draw water into every container possible." Then she began sterilizing instruments.

She was none too soon. The first casualty reached her dressing station about 0820—a sailor with a bullet wound in the abdomen. He received emergency treatment to combat shock and loss of blood before surgery. Despite the expert care, he died some 2 hours later.

Immediately after his admission, other patients began to pour in, far too many for the forty beds in the ward, although some of the orthopedic patients voluntarily gave up their beds to the wounded. There was no time to change the linen; the incoming casualties went straight into the vacant cots.[1]

Aboard the *New Orleans*, 19-year-old Seaman Andrew Singer was grateful that the cruiser was berthed next to an enormous dockside crane. Japanese pilots swooped down on the ship so closely that Singer could see their faces. Then, to avoid the crane, they had to pull up, which ruined their aim. Singer ran to his battle station at a forward 8-inch gun. He and his shipmates smashed open ammunition boxes with fire axes and cut away the awning for an unobstructed view of the attackers.[2]

Suddenly the power went out. In an attempt to cut the *New Orleans* loose, a seaman had chopped through the electric cable. This necessitated moving the ammunition by hand. Singer joined the line of men feeding the 5-inch guns. Chaplain Howell Forgy moved among them in the darkness. As a "sky pilot" he could not man a gun or even handle the missiles and powder, but he could offer encouragement: "Praise the Lord and pass the ammunition!" The fine swing of the words stuck in men's minds and inspired one of the war's best remembered songs.[3]

Plenty of targets remained, including Fuchida's group of high-level bombers, which had swung out in a great circle almost over Honolulu for another run over Battleship Row. Smoke obscured the *Nevada*, Fuchida's original target of choice, so he scrutinized the scene below, seeking a pristine objective. The fourth ship, a "*Maryland* type" in the inner row, apparently had not been damaged, so Fuchida ordered the lead plane to shift the target to this vessel.[4]

The *Maryland* had commenced firing early. Seaman 1st Class Leslie Short was perched in his machine-gun station high aloft in the mast, having decided that this would be a quiet spot to write letters and address Christmas cards. He was thus occupied when the attack began. Breaking out the nearby ammunition, he fed it into the nearest machine gun and fired at two torpedo planes within range. He was certain that he struck the first, which fell in the direction of the hospital, and he thought he winged the second but could not be sure.[5]

By the time Seaman 2d Class Harlan C. Eisnaugle reached his battle station on the *Maryland*'s port side "up in the superstructure just below the bridge," the *Oklahoma* was listing. Eisnaugle described the scene aboard the *Maryland*:

Men were screaming and trying to get aboard our ship and get out of the water. When I got to my gun, there were a few of the others there. We threw the gun cover over the side of the gun tube. And stood there cussing and crying at the Japs! You would be scared for a while and then you would get mad and cuss. After awhile we finally got ammo up to our gun. But we had to put it into clips before it could be fired. I don't know how long a time this was. But the

Oklahoma had rolled over on her side. And the harbor was pretty well afire by this time. The smoke and fire was all around us.

Eisnaugle got his gun loaded and in action, and the *Maryland*'s 5-inch guns were firing, too.

Then somebody yelled planes overhead. We trained the gun around and started firing. One of the planes fell up in front of us off Ford Island. I don't know who hit it, but it was one down. We got a hit in the forecastle from a bomb. I don't know whether it was one of that group, or one of the others. We done a lot of firing, but you don't know whether you hit them or someone else. For when you are loading the gun under these conditions, you are acting from instinct. For you are scared and you do your job from the drills you have been doing.[6]

At Fuchida's order, "Release!" pilots, observers, and radiomen shouted. Aso's plane dropped its missile first. Fuchida stretched out flat on the floor of the cockpit and opened the slot to observe the progress of his group's four bombs. He held his breath as the missiles became smaller and smaller. Two puffs of smoke and flashes of fire appeared on the ship's deck. "Two hits!" Fuchida shouted exultantly. The other two missed, sending up waterspouts near the target.

Fuchida scrambled to his feet and ordered his bombers back to the carriers. His own remained, however, to direct operations still going on and to observe results.[7]

Later, on his estimated damage chart, Fuchida indicated "serious damage" to the *Maryland*.[8] No doubt the Japanese leader would have been less pleased with himself and his group had he known just how little effect they had had on the *Maryland*. One bomb tore a large hole in the forecastle awning and inflicted moderate damage in the compartment below. The other hit below the waterline at frame 10, where its explosion caused flooding so that the *Maryland*'s bow settled some 5 feet. The ship did not even require drydocking and was fully repaired by December 20, 1941.[9]

The *California* was in much worse shape, for the torpedoes had caused massive flooding. Small wonder that when Admiral Pye boarded his flagship he was "visibly stunned by the attack."[10] Pye had made good time from Honolulu, for the manager of the Halekulani Hotel promptly offered a lift to Pye and Leary. So leaving word for the driver of his staff car, who was on the way, Pye and Leary set out. Pye found his boat waiting for him at the dock, where two staff officers joined him. Arriving at the battleship, Pye went immediately to the bridge, where he consulted with Train "as to the orders which had been given and found that he had complied with the orders which were included in our battle book."[11]

While they were thus conferring, more planes came over, and the noise drove Pye and Train into the flag conning tower, where each could hear what the other was saying. About 10 or 15 seconds later, bombs fell near the *California*. "There was one definite explosion and at least three which appeared to be near hits."[12]

The *California*'s log records that at 0825 her 5-inch AA battery opened fire on horizontal bombers. "Ship shaken by four near bomb hits." Four minutes later, the bomb that Pye described struck "topside, abreast casement #1, frame 59, penetrated main deck and exploded on second deck causing large fire. Ship listed 8° to port; commenced counter-flooding starboard voids."[13]

Train recalled: "This bomb went right through the deck of the *California* and exploded in the vicinity of the sick bay and killed about a hundred men."[14] This hit, coming on top of the torpedo damage already sustained, caused serious concern lest the *California*, like the *Oklahoma*, turn turtle. In addition, the near misses threatened the gasoline the *California* carried forward for her seaplanes and motorboats.[15]

When Johnson left Captain Bennion in good hands aboard the *West Virginia*, "the noise and confusion was tremendous," he stated. "I got hold of a flashlight and went below to some of the lower decks to see what I could and try to find out what was going on. Dirt and smoke were as thick as clouds everywhere, and I can assure you that no one was doing anything very useful and productive."

Everywhere Johnson looked, he saw wounded men. He especially remembered "a nice-looking kid who had his arm and shoulder blown off. One would have had to tie up every artery in his body to save him." Attempting to rescue the wounded posed an immediate problem, and Johnson joined others in assisting them off the battleship and into launches.[16]

Lt. (jg) F. H. White and Doris Miller teamed up and were "instrumental in hauling people along through oil and water to the quarterdeck, thereby unquestionably saving the lives of a number of people who might otherwise have been lost."[17]

The launch from the *Solace*, with Ruff aboard, reached the *Nevada* safely, and Ruff directed the helmsman to swing under the *Nevada*'s stern as a protection against the Japanese. As soon as Ruff clambered aboard the battleship, the launch sped off to the *Arizona* to aid in removing the wounded and take them to the hospital ship.

Ruff hurried toward his duty station as communications officer. But finding that Captain Scanland and other senior officers were not on board, he realized that he and the other junior officers present would have to assume unusual responsibilities. Moving forward, Ruff located the officer of the deck, Ens. "Pops" Jenkins, in the damage-control station under the galley.

Continuing forward, Ruff reached the conning tower, where he checked on all the personnel present and tested the communications circuits. Commander Thomas, the command duty officer, was the senior officer present; however, he was at his battle station several decks below, near the tube that ran up and down inside the ship. As soon as they were able to communicate, Ruff proposed that Thomas take charge of the ship below, while he, Ruff, handled the topside duties.[18]

The first-wave attack was still under way when Kimmel jumped out of his car at his headquarters. As he hastened to his office, he wasted no time or energy on futile reflections as to what this would mean to his own career. "My main thought was the fate of my ships, . . . to see what had taken place and then strike back at the Japs."[19]

Members of his staff joined him, some early, some not until the second wave, depending on how far they were from Pearl Harbor and how quickly they received word of the attack. One of the first was Lt. Walter East, the assistant communications officer. He had been up until 0330 decoding messages and had had only 4 hours' sleep in the BOQ when Commander Black routed him out about the *Ward*'s attack on the Japanese submarine. East was hauling on his trousers when he heard "a lot of noise and explosions." Looking out the window, he saw a low-flying plane with "one of the biggest damn torpedoes hanging under it" that he had ever seen. As he watched it, the pilot threw up his right wing, exposing a red disk. East's eyes popped. "That's a Jap!" he exclaimed to himself. Hastily pulling on shoes and blouse, he dashed to headquarters, staying as close to the buildings as he could.

About 5 minutes after the first bomb, he phoned his wife, Joan. "Hi, how are you, Walter?" she sang out cheerfully.

"Take it easy, everything is under control," he assured her cryptically. And with that he slammed down the receiver.

"Now that's strange!" Joan reflected. Equally strange was the absence of the Sunday morning newspaper, and Joan had an uneasy feeling that something was wrong somewhere. Glancing about, she saw several Army officers in a nearby compound, discussing how best to reach their duty station. They told her what was happening and cautioned her not to try to go to Pearl Harbor. With her baby to consider, Joan had no intention of endangering her life unnecessarily. "Oh, don't you worry!" she exclaimed emphatically.[20]

East's immediate superior, Commander Curts, was one of the early arrivals at Fleet headquarters, having risen about 0700 to read the newspaper, only to find it missing. Curts especially enjoyed the Sunday edition, so he went out to look for it several more times. At about 0745 he strolled some 50 yards to the beach area to see if anyone there had the *Advertiser*. He was thus engaged when he saw a plane with a red disk on its wings flying toward the naval base. Immediately recognizing the Rising Sun, he uttered within himself a heartfelt "the dirty sons of bitches!" and asked himself in wonder, "How the hell could they be so arrogant and bold as to attack Pearl Harbor and at the same time strike the Kra Peninsula?"—for such he assumed the Japanese were doing.

Almost immediately he saw a huge puff of smoke in the direction of Pearl Harbor, some 6 miles from his home, and heard a loud explosion. Having seen and identified the Japanese aircraft, he had no trouble with the logic of the situation: "No plane with the red ball of the Rising Sun of Japan could be over here unless it was on an offensive mission."[21] Moreover, Curts "had been apprehensive for a long time...about the danger of Japan starting a war without formal declaration."[22]

Curts called out to a number of Navy officers who lived in the same apartment building, "Let's get the hell going and get over to Pearl Harbor." He paused long enough to race home to tell his wife that Pearl Harbor was under attack and that she should head for the hills with their son Daniel. A full week passed before he saw them again, a week in which he did not even know where they were.

He shot off in his car at about 70 miles per hour, encountering no interference on the way beyond a few Japanese strafers who landed only one solid hit which neither disabled the car nor interfered with Curts's high-speed drive to his post of duty.

He described the atmosphere there as one of "no hysteria but ordered dismay."[23] At least one important message had already gone out. Murphy had ordered "Enemy air raid Pearl Harbor. This is not a drill" sent to the CNO in Washington, to the commander in chief, Asiatic Fleet (CinCAF) in Manila, and to U.S. forces at sea.[24]

Briefly, Curts stood with Kimmel and "Poco" Smith at the windows watching the attack, trying to determine just how effective it was and from what direction the aircraft were coming. They could see Murata's torpedo planes flying toward their objectives and dropping their missiles, but they could not see the actual strikes. They could hear the explosions, however, and see the waterspouts and clouds of smoke arising from the stricken ships. Just as one of the attacking aircraft crossed mid-channel, gunfire struck it, and it dived into the water.

There was not much of a constructive nature that these officers could do, but they attempted to establish communications with the areas under attack and to send messages to the ships at sea advising them of the attack and to take action accordingly.[25]

At 0816, Headquarters advised all ships and stations: "Hostilities with Japan commenced with air raid on Pearl." This message was repeated to the CNO. One minute later Kimmel ordered Patrol Wing Two, "Locate enemy force."[26]

As Curts stood beside Kimmel watching the attack, a .50 caliber machine-gun bullet crashed through the window and struck Kimmel on the chest. Fortunately, it had spent its force and dropped harmlessly to the floor after leaving "a dark splotch" on the admiral's white uniform. Kimmel picked it up and said softly, "It would have been merciful had it killed me."[27]

The first inkling that Smith and his wife Betty had of anything out of the ordinary was a sound like "a terrible thunder shower and a high rushing wind." The captain had just begun to shave when the phone rang. It was Murphy with the message from Headquarters, "We are under attack from the Japanese."

Smith relayed the awful news to Betty and prepared to leave. Aghast at the possibility that she might never see him again, she begged, "Take me with you!"

"Oh, I can't do that," he answered, "but I will go by way of King Street to avoid the traffic." He rushed out, and Betty would not see him again for over two weeks, and then only for 1 hour on Christmas Day. He scrambled into the black LaSalle he had bought in Annapolis in 1939 and drove pell-mell through the still largely empty streets. As he neared Pearl Harbor, he could see the Japanese "bombing hell out of the place." He parked his car on the Headquarters lawn away from the danger of falling masonry. Some nearby Marines were loading their rifles and firing them hopefully but ineffectually at the attacking planes.[28]

Smith estimated that he reached Headquarters at about 0820, at which time "all ships seemed to be firing. The sky was full of bursts. I could see those long before I got down there. The *Arizona* had already been hit and was smoking. Not only the batteries were firing, but men and machine guns and rifles were all over the tops of buildings and out in the park and everybody was shooting."[29]

Capt. Arthur Davis, Kimmel's air officer, had been preparing to play tennis with some friends when his yeoman telephoned him from Headquarters: "Captain, get out here right away, the Japanese are attacking Pearl Harbor!"

Utterly astounded, Davis shouted *"What?"*

"Captain, I ain't shittin' you," the yeoman replied earnestly, and hung up.

Davis piled into his "beat-up Cadillac roadster" and drove to Headquarters at top speed. On the way, he kept repeating to himself, "The goddamn fools! The goddamn fools!" He thought the Japanese "plain crazy" for attacking American territory. "Whatever they might achieve temporarily by striking Hawaii, they'll live to regret the day they were born."

On the brief drive to Pearl Harbor, Davis was too occupied combining speed with safety to pay much attention to externals, but he could hear the roar of planes and the explosion of bombs. As he left his car and hurried toward Headquarters, he noted a number of officers, enlisted men, and civilians standing around irresolutely and gazing into the sky. "These people looked like a bunch of old sick crows."

Davis laconically summed up his impression of conditions inside the building: "Confusion." It seemed to him that in these early moments, Kimmel was "utterly shocked and crushed by the attack." No one gave Davis any orders, so he seized his telephone in an attempt to reach everyone who had anything to do with naval aviation. Davis's first order of business was to try to get as many U.S. Navy planes as possible into the air to seek out the Japanese carriers and attack them.[30]

Captain DeLany, the Fleet operations officer, agreed that the attack was "a real crusher" to Kimmel, whom he saw that morning when he reached his office about 0830.[31] DeLany himself was totally taken aback, for he "never would have expected that the Japs would attack Pearl Harbor as they did."[32] When Black called to tell him what was happening, at first DeLany failed to recognize Black's voice and "attempted to exchange some light talk back and forth across the telephone."[33] He chaffed, "If you want me back at Headquarters, don't kid me." Finally convinced that Black meant business, DeLany scooped in Commander Good and a colleague who had just come on a nearby court to play tennis. The three drove to Headquarters together, Good and his partner still in tennis shorts.[34]

By the time they arrived, the first wave was tapering off, and the Americans could assess the fate of the ships on Battleship Row. When word reached Kimmel that the *Arizona* had blown up, the *Oklahoma* had capsized, the *California* was gradually sinking, and the rest were damaged in varying degrees, he groaned like a man under torture, as indeed he was. "It was a terrible hour for Kimmel and a frightful blow," Davis recalled sympathetically. "He loved his ships like any true sailor, and now many of them were gone. But most of all he bitterly regretted and mourned the loss of his officers and men."[35]

Singly and in groups, the Japanese aircraft that had attacked Battleship Row left the scene and headed for their rendezvous point, their mission accomplished. After circling Pearl Harbor once, the *Kaga's* high-level bombers picked up some fighter aircraft at the rendezvous point and then turned their noses toward the mother carrier.[36] Kitajima missed the group and had to leave with only one plane from his own unit. On the way back, he "kept a strict alert against pursuing enemy planes but with no events."[37]

Murata, Goto, and other torpedomen rendezvoused "off the westernmost extension of Oahu." They circled the point several times until about a dozen torpedo planes were on hand, as well as a number of fighters. Then they flew back to their carriers, maintaining "no particular formation."[38]

After the torpedo attack, Matsumura lost contact with his follow-up aircraft from the *Hiryu*. On the way to the rendezvous, he met one of the *Soryu's* torpedo bombers; then one by one Matsumura's men joined until they numbered about ten. Matsumura asked, "How were your torpedo attacks?" Each replied, "Direct hit on a battleship." Recalled Matsumura, "We were wild with joy." So far as he could tell, the only damage to the group was a shot-up landing wheel on one of the *Soryu's* planes.

On the way back to the carriers, they spotted what Matsumura believed at the time to be "an enemy transport plane" but which they later realized was a B-17. They did not challenge the American aircraft, for they were not equipped for plane-to-plane combat.[39]

As they winged homeward, Nagumo's torpedo and high-level crews had reason for elation. The devastation they had inflicted on the battle line of the U.S. Pacific Fleet had cost Japan no high-altitude bombers and only five torpedo planes.[40]

PART 4

"Under Constant and Continuous Attacks"

December 7, 1941

(0745–0835)
The First Wave:
Attack on the Shore
Installations

CHAPTER 14

"This Is Not Drill"

On Ford Island, Ramsey had completed a search plan to be employed in case the reported sinking of an enemy submarine should be confirmed.* Awaiting firm information one way or the other, he stood at a window of the Command Center watching the color guard as it prepared to hoist the flag. The duty officer, Lieutenant Ballinger, stood watching at another window.

At roughly 0755, Ramsey heard the unmistakable scream of an aircraft going into a dive. He assumed the pilot to be "a young aviator 'flathatting.'" As a solid, professional pilot, he was much irritated by this apparent disregard for flying safety. Turning to Ballinger, whose window commanded the better view, he snapped, "Dick, get that fellow's number, for I want to report him for about sixteen violations of the course and safety regulations."

Each man peered closely out his window. "Dick, did you get his number?" Ramsey asked.

"No, but I think it was a squadron commander's plane, because I saw a band of red on it," replied Ballinger.

"Check with the squadrons and find out which squadron commanders' planes are in the air," Ramsey ordered.

Scarcely had the words left his mouth than Ballinger exclaimed, "I saw something black fall out of that plane when it completed its dive." With that, an explosion resounded from the hangar area.[1]

That was all Ramsey needed to take in the situation. He had long

---

* See Chapter 9.

believed "that the most likely and dangerous form of attack on Oahu would be an air attack," and the potential enemy to make such an attempt "was obviously and solely Japan." What is more, the Japanese were right on Ramsey's estimated schedule, for he assumed "that the most dangerous period was approximately one hour before sunrise and approximately two hours after sunrise in the morning; and approximately the same period with reverse overlaps in the evening."[2]

So with theory turned reality, he told Ballinger, "Never mind the squadron commanders. That was a Jap plane and a delayed action bomb." Whereupon Ramsey sped across the hall to the radio room, where he ordered all radiomen on duty to send out the plain English message, "AIR RAID, PEARL HARBOR. THIS IS NOT DRILL." This was at exactly 0758.[3]

Immediately, Ramsey dispatched a second message ordering all planes in the air "to proceed and search the section 315 to 360 degrees from Pearl Harbor to maximum practical distance." He followed this up by assigning a search sector to certain aircraft that had been conducting joint tactics with submarines off Lanai. Then he issued similar orders "to the various units" in accordance with the search plan he had just drawn up. All this took a very few minutes, and by 0805, he had received acknowledgment from the airborne planes.

These vital messages on their way, Ramsey telephoned Admiral Bellinger to inform him, "The Japanese are attacking!" Understandably skeptical, the admiral shot back, "You wouldn't kid about a thing like that?" Ramsey finally convinced his chief and turned away from the phone to observe the torpedo attack.[4]

Mrs. Bellinger heard her husband ask, "Is it really?" When he hastily explained matters, she was still incredulous, repeating to herself, "They wouldn't dare!" But as she looked out the window, she saw Japanese planes diving on the moored ships. Obviously, "they" would and did dare.

She roused her daughters, Patricia, 14, and Eleanor, 11, and rushed them downstairs. The Bellinger quarters had been constructed in part on an old fort, with the basement designated as a shelter area. They did not pause to dress, but Patricia snatched up a lipstick as they ran. The girls had often played hide-and-seek in the shelter; now games were forgotten as women and children, almost all in their night clothes, began to stream in. "They were white-faced," said Mrs. Bellinger. "I kept thinking, what if this caves in and we're covered up. Will I be able to stand it?"[5]

Ramsey told his group, "We can't do much now until this attack is over. Therefore let's become observers so we can size up the Japs and evaluate their tactics." At first he thought the torpedomen could not succeed, dropping their missiles in such shallow water. Then he saw several torpedo wakes and perforce revised his opinion. "Their accuracy was uncanny," he recalled. "Evidently they were further advanced than the U.S. in torpedoes and torpedo planes."[6]

Seaman 2d Class Victor Kamont had arisen early because he was on duty that morning. He and his comrades fell in for muster at 0745 in front of the administration building. At 0755, the men heard "the drone of aircraft in the distance, getting closer and closer all the time. As they came into view, the general feeling was that the navy was having maneuvers again."

One aircraft came in just above the barracks, so close that Kamont could see the pilot's face. At the same instant, the bombardier released his bomb, which "hit the hangar at the tip of the island, demolishing it along with the guard on duty and the planes in the hangar."

An aerial gunner's mate first class yelled, "Meatball! Meatball!" Then the men "fully realized that it was the Japanese attacking." Chaos reigned "in mind if not in body" as the men raced for their gun lockers and for cover. They received immediate orders to report to their duty stations. "The ramp was a shambles, damaged aircraft and bomb craters all over the place."[7]

CPO Thomas E. Forrow had been up since 0530 so that he could linger over Sunday breakfast in the chiefs' mess, chatting with his buddies before reporting to the aircraft communications tower for duty. He was walking toward the tower with Chief Aviation Pilot Roy Crocker when they heard aircraft engines and saw three flight levels approaching from the northeast. "What's the Army doing up so early on a Sunday?" they asked one another. Suddenly Murata's torpedo bombers dropped for their runs; Forrow and Crocker could see the "meatballs" on the wings. "I don't know what I thought," Forrow said in retrospect. "We were just paralyzed with the sight."

Out of this momentary stupor, the two men ran for the tower. They had covered about 50 yards when one of the bombers started strafing. "Bullets were coming from everywhere." Both men dived into a ditch about 3½ feet deep that ran horizontal to the flying field. There they stayed for about 10 minutes, while the Japanese continued to strafe.[8]

Storekeeper 3d Class Jack Rogo, assigned to clerical duties at Ford

Island's supply depot, noted with approval that the morning was "mild and sunny." He put on undress whites, the uniform of the day for Sunday, and was breakfasting in the mess hall when the attack began. "I felt some anxiety when I heard the bombs explode and felt the concussions," he wrote years later. "However, the scuttlebutt started that the Army was holding maneuvers. Even though the bombings persisted, I only gave it a passing thought. This was the general atmosphere prevailing in the mess hall."

When he finished breakfast, he strolled out onto the lanai of the main building and looked northeast along Battleship Row. The *California* was listing, the *Arizona* burning, "and the acrid smell of smoke was was in the air." A plane flew overhead, and Rogo waved at the rear gunner who returned the wave. Rogo wrote:

> I know this sounds naive, but when I saw the Rising Sun insignia on the plane I knew it was not one of ours, but not knowing airplane recognition or markings I still did not know or realize who were doing the bombings. I don't know how long I watched the attack, but I do know I was absolutely fascinated by the aircraft making their torpedo runs and the dive bombers coming in from higher altitudes. About this time it sunk into my thick skull that this was for real: Battleship Row was really ablaze.[9]

With some obscure desire to keep his whites clean, Rogo returned to his quarters and changed into dungarees. Someone ordered him into the mess hall, which was the safest place in the vicinity, being on the first floor of the concrete-and-steel main building. He and several other sailors crawled under the mess tables, since there was nothing else they could do at the time.[10]

Lt. Cecil D. Riggs, staff medical officer of Patrol Wing Two, was breakfasting with his wife in their quarters when he heard the first explosion on Ford Island, and they wondered what was up. Another and even more ominous sound, which proved to be a torpedo slamming into a battleship, brought Riggs outside on the run. He was in time to see another torpedo plane wing over his quarters. The rear gunner—perhaps the same man who exchanged waves with Rogo—waved at Riggs. The doctor dashed back indoors, flung on his uniform and hurried to his "old beat-up Buick—about a $50 job that had no license plates for Honolulu." He lived only 100 yards from the *Arizona*'s mooring and drove within half that distance on his way to the dispensary. The torpedo attack was still going strong, the ships' guns firing back defiantly.

Casualties began reaching the dispensary within 5 minutes. A young machinist who had been machine-gunned while in the hangar area had two wounds, one in the left groin. He was still conscious, though bleeding internally. Riggs and his medics gave him plasma at once, but he died at 0822.

In these initial moments, so many wounded came in so fast that Riggs and his colleagues had no time for intensive treatment. They gave morphine shots, then marked foreheads with Mercurochrome to indicate that the patient had received the drug.[11]

Lt. Cmdr. Charles Coe, Bellinger's war plans officer, had established a ritual for Sunday mornings. Around 0800, he would get up, collect his 5-year-old son, Chuck, and make the family's breakfast of pancakes. Mrs. Coe and their 8-year-old daughter, Charlotte, stayed in bed until summoned to the feast. Coe was talking himself into arising and putting this program into operation when he heard a plane fly over and then the bomb strike at the other end of Ford Island. Unlike many, Coe did not have to see to believe; as war plans officer, he was sensitized to the situation in the Pacific. Immediately, he shouted to his wife, "Get up, the war is on!"

The Coes scrambled into bathrobes and slippers, hastily dressed the children, and the four ran for Bellinger's nearby quarters. As they sped on, they could see the torpedo planes coming in to bomb Battleship Row, the Rising Sun plainly visible. "They were not more than a hundred feet above me," Coe recollected. He was furiously angry, "but I did not have time to be scared. There was simply too much to do."[12]

First order of priority was to get his family into the air raid shelter. But on that score, Chuck had other ideas. He had no intention of missing the excitement by being cooped up in a cellar. Quite fearless, and delighted by the dipping planes and super-Fourth-of-July fireworks, he slipped away, his father in hot pursuit. Chuck was as swift and elusive as quicksilver, and Coe spent a few breathless moments chasing him down while Japanese planes swooped and circled, machine-gunning the area.

Coe shepherded his son inside just as Bellinger bounded down the stairs, zipping up his trousers. "Come on, Charlie!" he said. "Let's get down to headquarters."

"Admiral, at least let me get my pants on," replied Coe. "I'll drive down in my own car."

Whereupon Bellinger took off for his office "like a bat out of hell," and Coe ran back to his quarters for suitable clothing. When almost at his door, he experienced a strange and horrifying sensation: "It just took my breath. There was a sudden pressure wave or massive air movement, like a 16-inch salvo going off a few feet away. First the terrible concussion and then the deafening roar of the detonation which followed." For a brief moment Coe halted, paralyzed, as superstructure parts, steel plating, and other debris from the exploding *Arizona* littered his lawn. One piece of steel "about the size of a brick came right through two layers of wood" into Coe's garage and dropped on the bumper of his car. "Had this hit me on the outside of the building, I wouldn't be here today," he said later.[13]

The almost simultaneous fate of the *Oklahoma* was just as frightful to Coe:

> The capsizing of the *Oklahoma* was to me a sight beyond all belief. It was in fact the most awful thing I had ever seen. To watch this big battleship capsize and to see only her bottom sticking up out of the water like the back of a turtle and to realize that U.S. officers and men were still in there—well, I just couldn't believe it. It made me realize as nothing else that war had come to Hawaii.

Coe plunged indoors, pulled on trousers and shirt, and drove "hells bells" toward the administration building. On the way, he passed people running in all directions. "Officers and enlisted men were making a beeline to their stations, and civilians, women and children, were dashing for the safety of air raid shelters. There was also a hell of a noise overhead and out in the harbor. The sky was thick with planes, and machine guns were chattering madly."[14]

No man was more closely involved with Ford Island, its installations and men, than the station commander, Captain Shoemaker. He had no duty scheduled for that morning, however, and rose at 0700 to give himself time to shower, breakfast, and dress before joining Captain Mayfield for a game on the Oahu Golf Club's course. He was dressing when he heard "boom-booming and bang-banging outside and the roar of planes, and wondered what in hell was going on." His two sons looked outside, and in great excitement, the younger, Tom, shouted, "Dad, those are Japanese planes!"

Shoemaker verified this statement and phoned his headquarters to ask, "What's going on?" A lieutenant replied, "The Japanese are attacking."

"Sound General Quarters!" Shoemaker ordered. Hurriedly he finished dressing, pausing only to instruct his family to go at once to the Bellinger shelter. Then he started off in the little black Model A Ford sedan parked near his quarters. The Navy-owned vehicle was for use only in emergencies, but under the circumstances no one was likely to quibble at Shoemaker's driving the official car.

At the seaplane parking area, scarcely a plane was left undamaged, and the hangar was "burning like a forest fire." Oddly enough, Shoemaker seemed to be alone on the scene: "Hell, there wasn't a goddamn soul in sight at the time but me." Soon, however, he spotted a petty officer and some sailors trying to find a sheltered spot. Shoemaker put them to work, ordering, "Pull the good planes away from the fire." About that time, the Ford Island fire brigade drove up, but they could do little to stop the flames, because the *Arizona* had sunk on the water mains.[15]

Meanwhile, Ramsey's historic message had reached the aircraft carrier *Enterprise*, on her way back to Pearl Harbor from Wake Island. Admiral Halsey and his flag secretary, Lt. H. Douglas Moulton, were sipping their second cup of breakfast coffee when Moulton picked up the ringing telephone: "Moulton...*What?*...Roger!" Turning to Halsey, he relayed, "Admiral, the staff duty officer says he has a message that there's an air raid on Pearl!"

Halsey leaped to his feet. "My God, they're shooting at my own boys! Tell Kimmel!"[16]

Shortly after 0600 that morning, Halsey had sent eighteen scout planes ahead "to see that there were no possible hostile craft" between the *Enterprise* and Pearl Harbor. This, in Halsey's words, "was a protection for my own force, with, of course, the full knowledge that I would, if I saw anything, report it to high authority, not for action but for information." It was normal for carriers to send their planes in ahead before the mother ship entered port. In this instance, to maintain radio silence, Halsey did not notify Pearl Harbor of this flight. He assumed their approach lanes "and everything else" would identify them as friendly. Now he naturally jumped to the conclusion that someone had mistaken his scouts for a raiding party and had opened fire. The volatile admiral was "very much perturbed," and although his staff tried to persuade him otherwise, he did not believe them until the second message came in, this one from CinCPAC headquarters repeating Ramsey's warning.[17]

At 0615, Halsey had sent off his assistant operations officer, Lt. Cmdr. Bromfield B. Nichol, in an aircraft piloted by Cmdr. Howard L. Young, who commanded the *Enterprise* air group, to give Kimmel a confidential report and to make berthing and logistical arrangements for the task force.[18]

Later Nichol related their adventure to Halsey, and it would be difficult to improve on the graphic account which the latter gave to Admiral Hart's investigation:

> ...as they approached Pearl he [Nichol] saw all the anti-aircraft in the air. His first impression was, "My God, the Army has gone crazy, having anti-aircraft drill on Sunday morning." They got in a little bit closer and he saw a plane playing around and he thought, "Here's one of these fresh, young Army pilots coming down, playing around, breaking orders." He said just at that time he happened to be looking at the wing and saw a piece of the wing begin to fly off. Just then the plane went by and almost took his head off. He looked up and saw a red ball on it. Then he tried to unlimber his gun and couldn't get it unlimbered. They then went through the damnest amount of anti-aircraft fire and bullet fire he had ever seen, before or since, and finally got in to the field at Ford Island.[19]

Making his way around the island to assess damage and initiate corrective measures when necessary, Shoemaker saw this plane heading in and was on hand when it landed. The "completely surprised" and "no end befuddled" officers demanded, "What the hell goes on here?"

Shoemaker hustled them into his car and briefed them as he drove them to the Naval Air Boat Landing to catch a boat to CinCPAC Headquarters.[20]

Not all of Halsey's scouts were so fortunate as Nichol and Young. Five aircraft fell either to American antiaircraft or to Japanese Zeroes. Thirteen came in safely to either Ford or Ewa, and after the attack, they were sent out to hunt for the Japanese carriers or to check on reports of Japanese ships off Barber's Point.[21]

Meanwhile, from his ditch, Forrow saw the *Arizona* blow up. "So many things were happening, the explosions of the torpedoes, the bombs bursting, the fires, the dense black smoke from the oil, ships going over." Making a quick dash, he reached Central Control in the base of the tower, which escaped with only the glass shot out of it. There he picked up the phone and broadcast that Ford Island was under attack.[22]

Kamont and his comrades kept busy filling in bomb craters and moving aircraft to relative safety. They removed the machine guns from the planes and mounted them "in vises on the portable work benches. It proved very effective after the wheels were chocked up. This was all done amid continued strafing and bombing runs."[23]

Shoemaker's prime worries that morning were the dangers of fire and explosions of fuel supplies. At the gasoline pier, wooden pilings were on fire, and he hastily directed a nearby sailor to pour water over them. Then he drove to the tank farm. These huge tanks stored gasoline, not oil, and if they caught fire, heavy loss of life and property would result. So Shoemaker was relieved and gratified to discover that as soon as the attack began, an ensign of his command had turned on the water sprinklers above the great tanks. This example of common sense under pressure pleased Shoemaker immensely, and later he was able to have the young man awarded the Navy Cross.[24]

Above all, Shoemaker feared a possible explosion of the tanker *Neosho*, moored at Berth F-4 dangerously close to the battleships. This was adjacent to the tank farm, and at 0750 the *Neosho* had just finished "discharging aviation gas to Ford Island," maintaining a strict security watch.[25]

The *Neosho*'s skipper, Cmdr. John S. Phillips, a short but commanding Virginian somewhat resembling actor James Cagney, had been strolling on deck when a plane droned overhead and screamed into a power dive.

"Have our Navy fliers gone completely nuts?" Phillips demanded of an officer standing nearby. "Practicing dive bombing over a live target before eight o'clock on Sunday morning?"

As the aircraft curved out of its dive, Phillips saw the red sun on its wings.[26] General Quarters at 0800 rapidly brought the crew to their stations, and at 0810 the *Neosho*'s AA battery commenced firing. By 0842 Phillips had his ship under way "to clear focal point of attack and to clear Channel" for the *Maryland*. He hoped to take the tanker across channel to Berth M-3 at Merry's Point.[27] Danger to and from the *Neosho* had not ended, but the immediate peril it posed to Ford

Island was over, and Shoemaker credited Phillips with "a magnificent job."[28]

While all this was going on, Ramsey telephoned Kaneohe Naval Air Station, instructing the operator not to disconnect him under any circumstances. He wanted above all things to send out every available patrol plane to locate the Japanese carriers. Since Takahashi's dive bombers had destroyed at least half of Ford Island's carrier-based planes and had complete command of the air over that installation, Patrol Wing One stationed at Kaneohe was Ramsey's only hope.[29] It proved vain, for by that time, Kaneohe was in even worse shape than Ford Island.

CHAPTER 15

"Somebody Is Going to Pay for This!"

Located on Mokapu Peninsula, Kaneohe Naval Air Station was one of the newest of Hawaii's military installations, and it seemed to Radioman Moser to have been "in a constant state of building" ever since he arrived on station early in July. "Barracks *were* finished, administration buildings were completed, etc. However, between our hangar and the hangar to our west, was a deep excavation for installation of service utilities. Such excavations were constantly going on in an effort to get the station completed."[1]

As station commander, "Beauty" Martin had had "to make do with very little." When he first set up shop, being woefully short of officers, he wrote to a colleague at Pearl Harbor asking that more be assigned to him. The reply was crisp and definite: "There ain't none. Make 'em!"[2]

As of December 7, he had under him naval personnel totaling 31 officers and 303 enlisted men, as well as a Marine contingent of 3 officers and 93 men. He controlled no aircraft except one utility plane, an OS2U. Kaneohe's thirty-six patrol aircraft belonged to the commander of Patrol Wing One, Cmdr. Knefler McGinnis, who reported to Bellinger. On December 7, 1941, three of these PBY-5s were under repair, three were on patrol, four "were moored in Kaneohe Bay at about a thousand yards apart....The remaining planes were parked on the ramp except for four which were in No. 1 hangar." To protect these aircraft, Martin had only machine guns and rifles.[3] Kaneohe had had the temporary protection of some Army antiaircraft guns, but these had been rolled back to their home sites on December 5.[4] As for readiness, Machinest Guy Avery described Kaneohe's predicament:

> There were no gun emplacements for defense. Even the landing mat was not yet completed. The only arms on the station were the three or four dozen Springfield 30–06's and probably half a dozen BARs. All securely locked in the armory. Of course there was a pair of machine guns in each of the PBYs..., but these flying boats were unmanned at the moment....[5]

None of these considerations worried Avery as he stretched out fully clothed on his cot, savoring the luxury of a Sunday morning's idleness. A lone plane passed overhead and returned. "To hell with the Army!" Avery thought. "Every day is the same to them."

Almost immediately, however, a discrepancy struck his sensitive ear: "...the sound was that of an air-cooled radial engine. The Army used only liquid-cooled in-line engines at that time. The Navy used radial engines only but did not drill on Sundays." This thought sped through Avery's mind "in a split second." The mysterious plane called for investigation, and Avery sprang to the window. He heard a burst of machine-gun fire and saw the Zero strafing the little utility plane. Other Zeroes were "just beginning to fan out over the heart of the station and opening fire promiscuously."[6]

He shouted to Morris, with whom he had argued the previous day about a possible conflict with Japan and who was still asleep, "The Japs are here! It's war!"

Armored in his conviction of Japanese inferiority, Morris replied sleepily, "Well, don't worry about it, Avery. It'll last only two weeks."

Avery glanced at his watch: The time was exactly 0748. Being a person who liked to be precise as to facts, Avery was always "scrupulously careful" to synchronize his watch with "the Naval Observatory time-tick," and he had no doubt of its accuracy. Hence, judging from later reports which he read, he was certain that the Japanese made their initial attack on Kaneohe no later than 0748, a good 7 minutes before they struck Pearl Harbor.[7] Fuchida agreed that this might well have been so.[8] In any case, according to Avery, "Our OD called nearby Bellows Field to warn them and to ask for help but his call was regarded as a practical joke—but only for a few minutes, then it was too late."[9]

A Kaneohe contractor, Sam Aweau, had a similar experience. He phoned both Bellows and Hickam that the Japanese were attacking, but no one believed him.[10]

While Morris was dressing, Chief Machinist Woodrow Wilson Beard returned from breakfast. Looking at Avery with "a startled expression," he exclaimed incongruously, "Men, we are all veterans!" He rather spoiled the effect by adding, "Do you think this is really it?"

Avery assured him that this was indeed "it" and suggested that they get out of the bungalow before the Zeroes attacked it, since they were strafing "individuals, autos, parking lots and even residences" on the main part of the station. Later Avery reasoned that "their purpose had been to test the station's defenses and to create a maximum of confusion in advance of the bombers." For the moment, he and his comrades took refuge on the beach in a small sandbagged building left from "some military drill of weeks before." From that vantage point they watched the early attack.[11]

Martin was drinking a cup of coffee in his quarters and was about to make some hot chocolate for his 13-year-old son, David, who sat at a big window, reading a newspaper. Around 0745 they heard the drone of approaching planes but thought little of it, for Martin assumed they were aircraft from the *Enterprise* coming in to land.

David pressed his nose against the pane for a better look. "Dad, those planes have red circles on them," he reported. Martin walked over to see for himself. He noticed that the aircraft made a right-hand turn, which was "contrary to the station flight rules." They flew at a height of about 800 feet and approached "almost head-on." As the fuselage came into view, Martin could confirm that David was correct—they bore the Rising Sun.

He tossed on his uniform over his blue silk pajamas and ran for his car, slamming the door just as the firing commenced. He raced to his office at 50 miles per hour, his tires screeching painfully at every turn. From the corners of his eyes he could see people rushing to their windows and out of doors trying to determine what lunatic was driving so recklessly in their 15-mile-per-hour residential zone on a Sunday morning. Martin parked his car some distance from his command post and ran for it amid a splat of bullets.[12]

The roar of engines "disrupted the usual Sunday quiet" for Aviation Machinist Mate Curylo and his wife. They left their breakfast and went out onto the porch of their quarters to see what was going

on. Their first sight was "a Jap Zero making a firing run on Baker
Control, the new Seaplane radio control tower, not yet in commission." Curylo had been stationed aboard ship in Shanghai, so he was
familiar with the "meatball" emblem on Japanese aircraft. Now he
recognized it, but he could not believe what he saw.[13]

Many on Kaneohe were so accustomed to aircraft noises that this
early warning did not interrupt their slumbers. As Moser explained,
"the sound of planes buzzing the station wasn't really anything new.
Planes from nearby Bellows Field often buzzed us (seemingly just for
kicks). But machine guns have a very awakening effect."

That sound brought Moser and his barracksmates out of the sack.
"Someone saw a car explode and burn behind the barracks at approximately the same time that a plane passed the windows of our barracks,
so close that the rising sun was unmistakable. It seemed as though everyone yelled 'Japs' in unison."[14]

Aviation Ordnanceman 2d Class R. M. "Bert" Richmond slept especially soundly, for he had been on duty until 0200, after which he retired in the ready room of the hangar. He "awakened next morning to
the rattle of machine gun fire and the roar of fighter planes coming low
over the hangar." By the time he pulled on trousers and shoes "men
were running everywhere, getting guns and ammunition out of planes
and ordnance rooms, bullets were ricocheting around the hangar. Some
of our planes were burning. Men were shouting orders and cursing."

One group set up a machine gun on a temporary mount outside the
hangar door, some firing, some feeding the gun, others running between
gun and ordnance room for ammunition, and then belting it. "Skinny
Grisham, my chief, arrived and started, among other things, to get two
planes out of the hangar. The next I can remember of him, he was sitting on the deck, holding a shattered leg to stop the bleeding, and still
shouting orders."[15]

Lieutenant Dunlop, son of Short's adjutant general, was assigned
to duty with Battery D of the Sixteenth Coast Artillery Regiment.
The regiment was quartered at Fort de Russy, an installation which,
from the standpoint of location and facilities, would have ranked high
on any list of the most desirable military posts under the American
flag. Located in a beautiful setting about 200 yards from the Royal
Hawaiian Hotel, it boasted "dream quarters, our own beach, our own
recreational facilities, swimming pier, and a magnificent officers' club."

On December 7, however, Dunlop was in no position to enjoy de

Russy's plush facilities. He and another young lieutenant, Eugene Delle Donne, were sharing a far from palatial shack at Ulupau Military Camp at the south end of Kaneohe Bay. This camp was a part of the Coast Artillery's searchlight program and also part of the defense position on Ulupau Head which overlooked the bay and ocean. Dunlop had a rifle and understood that in an emergency he would function as an infantry-man until the Infantry itself took over.[16]

Dunlop appreciated the chance to sleep an extra hour or two that Sunday, since for the past week he had risen at about 0530 and put in 12-hour work days, from 0600 to 1800, helping to build a camp at Fort Hasey. Delle Donne was not in the shack that morning, so Dunlop had it to himself. He had barely awakened when someone knocked at his door. He had a vague idea that something was wrong, for he had awakened to the noise of aircraft engines and was quite sure the planes could not be a regularly scheduled exercise at Kaneohe. He knew their habits fairly well, and they seldom flew on Sunday.

"Come in," Dunlop invited. The man who entered was a young PFC, an Amish lad from Lancaster, Pennsylvania, "dark-haired, clean-cut, a good soldier."

"Wake up, lieutenant," he said, "the Japanese are attacking the is-land." Surprising as the statement was, Dunlop accepted it instantly, for the PFC was a serious individual not given to leg-pulling and so respon-sible that of his $30 monthly pay, he sent $27 home to his family. So Dunlop skipped all expressions of incredulity, asking only, "Where have you just come from?"

"We've just posted the man on the top of the hill," he answered, referring to Ulupau Head.

Dunlop nodded. "Go back to headquarters," he directed. "I'll be there in three or four minutes."[17]

The lieutenant dressed hurriedly and then set out over the three-quarters-of-a-mile of rough road to his post, acutely aware that his green Buick coupé, 6 years old but highly polished, must be clearly visible from the air. He still had not learned that Pearl Harbor was under attack, only that some sort of attack had taken place, the mag-nitude of which he did not know. The gates of Kaneohe Naval Air Station were only some 200 yards from Dunlop's Headquarters, and as he approached, he could hear the sounds of combat.

"How could this have happened?" he asked himself. The United States had maintained a garrison of all branches of the service in Hawaii "from the days of annexation for the sole purpose of countering an aggressive threat to the Islands and the west coast of the United States." His reflections gave Dunlop a strange feeling of isolation. Driving past an engineer barracks, he saw little apparent activity and wondered if, after all, this was a false alarm.[18]

He parked his conspicuous car under some foliage and entered his headquarters, a mere pine shack still under construction. There a sergeant named Sovicki, one of Dunlop's finest NCOs, punctured any hope that there had been a mistake. Sovicki was slightly given to nervousness and had a bit of a language problem, so he had some little difficulty in getting across the precise details of what had happened. But Dunlop understood all too well the main thrust of the message. Japanese aircraft had appeared, coming fairly straight up the coastline and attacked Kaneohe with machine guns. So far they had dropped no bombs. Except for the five men in the Headquarters—Dunlop, Sovicki, and three others—all the men of this outfit were at their emergency posts, knew that this was no maneuver but war, and would fire at any target of opportunity.

Dunlop asked for a volunteer to man the telephone, a task more dangerous than it sounded, for the little wooden building could be a tempting, inflammable target. "It was then," reminisced Dunlop, "that for the first time I realized what a truly noble figure the American soldier is." He knew these men to be of humble backgrounds, with little education, but nothing was wrong with their courage. Every hand shot up without hesitation. Dunlop chose Pvt. Manuel Rita, a second-generation Portuguese-American, a good athlete and rifleman. Then the rest went outside to scout around and try to determine more accurately just what was going on.

Dunlop and a corporal named Goforth were passing a pile of lumber when three or four Japanese dive bombers came over. To Dunlop, they seemed to be "extremely skillful...in bringing their aircraft from a normal bombing height down to a height of 400 feet in an incredibly short period of time." He and Goforth stood there wondering at the sheer brazenness of the attack. After these bombers passed, Dunlop counted fifty bullet holes in the lumber pile.

The two men then joined the others and sought shelter in the brush. A sergeant asked what on the surface was a silly question: "Shall we shoot at them?" After all, they had only their observations to go on; they had received no word that a state of war existed between the United States and Japan. But this was a case where actions most definitely spoke louder than words, and Dunlop replied, "Shoot at them with everything you have."[19]

By the time Martin reached his administration building at Kaneohe, "the first plane on the water had begun to burn."[20] About that time, Kaneohe received the message from Ford Island that Pearl Harbor was under attack. To which the recipient replied indignantly, "What the hell do you think they're doing *here*?"[21] This and other exchanges with Ford Island disposed of Martin's initial thought that the attack "might have been an isolated raid" on Kaneohe.[22]

He could not help wondering how his personnel, many of them new to the service, would react to this, their initial combat experience, which was a heavy one, because after the first Zero attack, dive bombers had joined in. However, Martin's officers and men did him proud: "It was remarkable. There was no panic. Everyone went right to work battling back and doing his job."[23] Indeed, Martin reported, "their conduct was a trifle too reckless and their disregard for danger undoubtedly increased the number of casualties. It was necessary to constantly urge the men to scatter and take cover because most of them were so intent on repulsing the attack that they were disregarding enemy fire."

Martin also extended high praise to the civil service and contractors' employees, all of whom "displayed extreme gallantry in their disregard of personal danger." He particularly cited the civil service telephone operator, a Mrs. Spencer, who "rushed to her post of duty and manned the switchboard throughout the day. Her calmness and her initiative were of tremendous value."[24]

As the planes that were parked next to the hangars caught fire, Curylo jumped into his car and drove toward his squadron VP-14s' hangar. He picked up a shipmate, Frank J. Brown, but, wrote Curylo, "en route we were forced to abandon the car and proceed on foot due to enemy planes strafing moving cars. In the hangar area some of our planes were burning and plane crews were battling the fires while others were removing the planes' machine guns and ammunition. All this time we were under constant and continuous attacks by enemy planes."[25]

From his barracks, Moser could see smoke from the burning planes on the ramp. He and his comrades "wanted to get going," but realized that to go out in the open would be "sheer suicide." They descended to the first deck, where the master at arms, a 20-year-old boatswain's mate, had "just emptied his Colt 45 trying to hit a Zero." In the barracks to the north, Marines were firing 30-30 rifles from windows at the low-flying aircraft, without success.

Moser and his buddies moved from barracks to barracks under cover of the walkways, but when they reached the mess hall, "already a mess from strafing," they knew they would be "sitting ducks" if they went outside. When the last plane of the first wave disappeared, they all sprinted for the hangars and planes. Some were so mad they cried at the sight of the burning aircraft. One was full of holes and leaking gasoline, but it was not on fire, so they pushed it across the street and tried to hide it between two buildings.

Moving to the ramp area, they found more burning aircraft and pushed one into the bay to put out the fire. The wing of another was in flames; they threw a line around the float, and with a ramp tractor pulled off the wing "in a blinding explosion of gasoline."

Meanwhile, ordnance people were issuing rifles and submachine guns and breaking locks on ammunition dumps. This was about all they could do. Firefighting continued, but in Moser's opinion, the situation was "really hopeless."[26] Undoubtedly, one reason that firefighting was so ineffectual at Kaneohe was that its only fire truck had fallen victim to the first bomb.[27]

While Avery watched the Zeros strafing, the general alarm sounded. Within a few minutes, he and those with him could see squadron men trying to move the blazing PBYs to protect those as yet untouched. As they did, Beard looked to seaward and groaned, "Oh, oh! Here comes the heavy stuff. Now we'll see the fireworks!"

They did indeed, for bombs hit, among other targets, the hangar that housed explosives. As the resultant heavy black smoke arose, Morris exclaimed, "Don't you know somebody up there is dead? Believe me, *somebody* is going to pay for this!" Avery tried a feeble witticism to the effect that he would detail Morris to collect the bill, but it fell flat.

"After the bombs were dropped," wrote Avery, "the Zeros left the bombers and flew around over the station. They zoomed, circled and strafed. The air over the station was now in confusion."

Suddenly everything quieted down and the "All Clear" sounded. Avery and his group retired to the bungalow and began to assess damage to the utility plane. One young man was "too nervous to be any help at all, but no one resented his inactivity because we knew his circumstances. His wife was at home alone on the other side of the station. She was bedridden and helpless, having just come from the hospital where she had undergone serious surgery." The young husband could not learn "how she had fared nor get any word to her of his own safety. The man was pitiful."[28]

So, in fact, was the entire Naval Air Station. When the Japanese of the first wave soared off, they left Kaneohe in far worse shape than Ford Island.

CHAPTER 16

"Tearing the Place to Pieces"

Although it was Sunday, a fair amount of activity was going on at Hickam Field, home base of the Hawaiian Air Force's bombers. Brig. Gen. Jacob H. Rudolph, in command of the Eighteenth Bombardment Wing, had planned a flight of some B-18s, obsolescent but still usable, to indoctrinate "some of the youngsters who had not finished B-18 training." So twenty-four men were in the hangar preparing to wheel out the B-18s for 0800 takeoff.[1]

Sgt. Ralph T. Ullrich, assigned to the 22d Matériel Squadron, reported for duty at Hangar No. 15, the base engineering shops, at about 0730. "Practically everyone else" was there, too. Sunday duty was not customary, but they had to complete a job on a B-24 they had been working on Saturday evening. Then, too, "they expected some more airplanes in in the morning, and we had orders that the entire crew would come out and report for duty."[2]

The anticipated planes were Major Landon's eleven B-17s.* At about 0745, Colonel Mollison telephoned the Hickam control tower to ask if they had heard anything from this flight. The tower operator reported being in contact with some of the incoming pilots, "but the static was so bad that they could not make out what they were trying to say"; however, the flight should come in at about 0810. Mollison began to dress, timing himself to arrive at the tower by that hour.[3]

Colonel Farthing had already been at the tower for nearly 2 hours, for he expected the B-17s at about 0600. As base commander, he

---

* See Chapters 3 and 7.

wanted to be there to greet them. He had nothing to do with "the tactical defense of the field," but everything to do with its housekeeping. He knew, however, that Hickam had no antiaircraft, no air raid shelters, and no slit trenches. Nor could the latter have been dug in a hurry; Hickam rested on a coral foundation that resisted all measures short of power equipment, and any deep digging would soon encounter Hickam's low water level. The field's guard force of several hundred men was armed with pistols and had no access to machine guns. Most of the latter "were sighted for the defense of the airplanes against sabotage."[5]

Farthing passed the time talking with Lt. Col. Cheney Bertholf, adjutant general of the Hawaiian Air Force, while the base operations officer, Capt. Gordon Blake, stood by.[6]

A slight error on the part of a young navigator had delayed the arrival of the B-17s. Daybreak found them about 100 miles away. The navigator realized that Landon's lead aircraft was "abeam Oahu either to the north or the south." He opted for the latter and recommended a turn to the right. Being a well-qualified navigator himself, Landon carefully checked the navigator's log and the radio signal coming in from Honolulu. As a result of his calculations, he decided that Oahu lay south instead of north, so he ordered a left turn of 110°. The choice was fortunate; Landon later estimated that a right turn would have brought his plane nose-to-nose with Fuchida's incoming air armada.[7]

The Hickam tower commanded a full view of the sky and the surrounding area. Farthing saw a plane slide down the runway at Ford Island and take off. Out at sea he noticed a destroyer bumping along on patrol. Below him spread the broad expanse of Hickam Field. Across the way, officers, enlisted men, and their families slept in their homes or barracks. Hickam's bombers—twenty B-17s, thirty-two aging B-18s, and twelve A-20s—sparkled in the sunlight, bunched close together as an antisabotage measure. The display looked more deadly than it actually was, for only six B-17s, six A-20s, and seventeen B-18s were operational, and the airworthy Flying Fortresses might not be there much longer, for Hawaii was under orders to send all of them to the Philippines.[8]

Although not on duty, William H. "Bill" Heydt and Harry H. Byrd, both supply sergeants in the Eighteenth Ordnance Company, rose at about 0600 in anticipation of an early morning double date. They put on

Class A uniforms; then, their own mess hall being painted, they walked the five blocks to the main Air Force mess for breakfast. They ambled back to their barracks and changed into dazzling white sharkskin suits.

"You wait here on the steps, and I'll be right back to pick you up in my car." With that, Byrd trotted off for his red Chevy roadster with its white wire wheels.

While Heydt waited, he idly watched "a cloud of planes" coming down from the north. When they reached Pearl Harbor, he saw "black things" drop down and reflected, "Oh, boy, someone will catch hell."[9]

At the Air Depot, Sergeant Crouse and his companions heard the roar of planes, and one of the civilians remarked in disgust, "The damn Navy must be on maneuvers again this morning."[10]

Lt. Howard F. Cooper, in command of Headquarters Squadron, Seventeenth Air Base Group, awakened to the sound of loud explosions. Peering out, he saw smoke arising from Pearl Harbor and thought that "it was very strange to have...the Navy practicing on Sunday morning right in the harbor."[11]

Busily shaving, Mollison felt more curiosity than alarm at an explosion that sounded to him like a bomb. "That's a damn funny thing," he told himself. A second explosion was unmistakably that of an aerial bomb, whereupon Mollison decided that the Marines must be conducting a drill and "that someone had inadvertently let one go." In that case, "someone is in deep trouble and there will be hell to pay."[12]

Charles J. Utterback, head foreman of the District Engineers, located at Fort Kamehameha Base Yard, happened to be walking toward Mat A, "the main mat at Hickam Field, air side," when he heard the initial explosion, and "the first thing that I thought was the dynamite blew up, because we were loading the dynamite."[13]

This tendency to seize on a familiar, rational explanation was quite common that morning. However, when Ullrich and his colleagues at Base Engineering went outside seeking to determine the source of the planes overhead and "some explosions over near the Navy sector," one of the men remarked, "If that's fooling I'll believe anything."[14]

Even Farthing and those with him at the tower, with their panoramic view, were momentarily deceived:

While we were in the tower we saw many Navy ships, or what we took to be Navy ships, flying off the island and coming around to the Navy base at the east of the island, and we heard a bunch of airplanes diving in, coming from about 10,000 feet with the clouds. We knew they were not Army planes, and we thought it must be Marines. They dived down on Pearl Harbor. I saw a black object leave the first and hit with an explosion. The first plane turned its wings up and I could see the Rising Sun on its wings. That airplane immediately came to Hickam Field.[15]

Bertholf ran down the tower to give the alarm. Farthing followed him just in time to hit the dirt and stay there for the remainder of the first attack wave. He was the only person on the mat at the time, and a Zero fired on the tempting target, but missed.[16]

Aircraft which seemed to Crouse "to come from every direction" opened up with machine guns:

Some of the planes were so low in their strafing operations that you could almost see the expression on the Jap's face. It was an old expression to anyone familiar with the Japanese. One that you couldn't quite figure out; whether he was laughing at you or an expression of agony in doing something he hated to do![17]

Flinging a bathrobe over his pajamas, Mollison ran out of his quarters to find out what was going on. He was just in time to see a Zero speed down the street firing indiscriminately. At the same instant, Captain Allen erupted from his quarters, his bathrobe flying open over his nude body. He shook his fist after the Zero, threw his arms skyward and shouted, "I *knew* the little sons of bitches would do it on a Sunday! I *knew* it!"

"Brooke, this is no place for us to be," Mollison called to him. "Let's get into our clothes and get going." Having done so, the two officers hastened to their respective posts.[18]

Mollison's next-door neighbor, Col. "Cush" Farnum, a heavy sleeper who was somewhat deaf, was the last person in his household to learn what had happened. His wife, Louise, and son, William C., Jr., were already up when Sgt. John "Red" Davis, who dated their maid, invaded Farnum's bedroom and shook him awake: "Colonel, this is it!"[19]

Cpl. Nicholas Bongo of the 58th Bomb Squadron (L) had dropped into his cot in "Tent City" at 0700 after being released from guard duty 1 hour before. Like Farnum, he was dead asleep when "the dropping of bombs and machine-gun fire" awakened him. Looking out, he saw an airplane banking away from the tent "with a large red ball painted underneath its wing." Much more rapidly than some of his seniors, Bongo knew that the base was under a Japanese attack.

He could see the dive bombers "dropping bombs and strafing the base, the hangars, the new concrete barracks and the parking lot outside of the barracks." Several men in his group had pistols and shot at the low-flying airplanes, but to no avail. The base chapel, across the street from where Bongo stood, "received a direct bomb hit." So did the tent in which he had been sleeping.[20]

Lieutenant Reeves, one of the officers Allen had lectured the previous day on responsibility, saw from a window an aircraft that seemed to be sprinkling toothpicks on the roof of Hangar No. 9. In fact, a Japanese bomber had just sent the roof up in splinters. As Reeves wondered, "How can this be?" a plane sped by his window, its wingtip almost touching the ground. It appeared to be targeting the door of the Officers' Club.

"My God!" thought Reeves admiringly, "the guy is awful good to be able to do that. He must be an expert. I couldn't do it. I don't know anyone who could do it." His astonishment at the pilot's skill overrode the obvious fact that the man was attacking Hickam Field.

"Who can this terrific pilot be?" Reeves asked himself. Turning to some of his companions, he said, "He must be a German." Then he did a mental doubletake: "What in hell is a German doing with red disks on his plane? He should have swastikas." Japan was too far away for the plane to be Japanese. At this reflection, the uncomfortable idea crossed his mind, "Germany is still farther."

The incredible truth finally dawning on Reeves and his friends, they jumped into khakis, took their sidearms, hastened outside, and began to shoot at the planes. Reeves had no hope of success: "If we have to win the war with this damn thing, we'll never make it," he said in disgust.[21]

Standing near Mat A, Utterback saw "a lot of planes" fly directly overhead, very low, and at "just cruising speed." One of the men with Utterback recognized them as Japanese. The first of the planes Utterback saw dropped a bomb that missed its evident target, the repair hangar, and hit the kitchen adjacent to it.

The men with Utterback "seemed to be dumbfounded." Being a World War I veteran, he knew what to do and told them to take cover. They dove into a ditch along the Fort Kamehameha highway. Eventually, "some Army officers appeared on the scene," and their leader instructed Utterback to take his men to "the old mortar casement." Finding it locked, they hid behind it until the first-wave attack on Hickam had ended.[22]

This initial attack on Hickam Field came from two groups of dive bombers from the *Shokaku*. Their assigned mission was "to dive-bomb carriers in the harbor and, if they are not there, to attack Hickam air base," and then strafe until "friendly fighters" came to take over the job. Accordingly, since no carriers were at moorings, after seeing waterspouts "going up from a cruiser" moored on the opposite side of Ford Island from Battleship Row, Lieutenant Mifuku and his comrades dive-bombed hangars at Hickam and "then strafed parked planes on the base."[23]

Ullrich at Hangar No. 15 figured that the aircraft came in at about 200 feet. "Just then there was an explosion occurred near us, and we all scattered. Some of us went through the hangar, and there was a number of explosions in there. When the dust and everything settled, what of us [sic] were on our feet yet, we run outside, and then they began machine-gunning us."

When this strike ended, Ullrich and his friends who had been outside went back into the hangar to help move the wounded out. Later Ullrich estimated his unit's casualties at 20 percent. Equipment had suffered much less than he expected: "I lost a few grinders, drill presses; that's about it. Practically all my welding equipment was ruined." The resultant fire was small.[24]

The attack caught the twenty-four men who were readying B-18s for a training flight. The bombing and strafing killed twenty-two and "cut the legs off the other two."[25]

At his post, Crouse was wounded in the ankle. "I crawled into the doorway of the hangar for some protection but found that one of the Jap pilots had the same idea to enter with a bomb at practically the same time." So he inched along the curb for about 200 feet. As he did so, he heard a sound that brought back childhood memories: "About twenty-five feet to my left was a hangar being built of galvanized tin. Every time one of these strafing planes would cross it reminded me of how we would throw crushed stone on a tin roof just to hear the noise."[26]

Lieutenant Cooper scrambled into some clothes and took in the situation at a glance: "Dive bombers were tearing the place to pieces, blasting everything." He noticed two flights of high-altitude bombers. "When they were over Pearl Harbor, they dropped their bombs,

and the formation was perfect, so perfect, and the timing of the dropping of the bombs was so perfect" that Cooper could "follow them
down in V formation right...to the impact." He remarked how efficiently the two types of bombers, dive and high-level, worked together: "It was a methodical system whereby they wouldn't bomb any of
their own planes."

Having more immediate duties than watching the action over Pearl,
Cooper grabbed his steel helmet and gas mask and went to the hangar
line. There his first sergeant informed him that all their men were out of
the barracks. Instructing the sergeant to keep the men separated, Cooper looked about. "Of course the damage seemed considerable at the
time."[27]

Bill Heydt also watched as bombers attacked the ships in Pearl
Harbor. He counted six that had dived before the first one swung
around, displaying the Japanese insignia. Incongruously, he asked himself, "What are the Japanese doing here on a Sunday morning?"

He heard a sound like hail and saw five or six men running and
then "roll over like rabbits shot with a gun blast." Dashing to his room
to change into uniform, he awakened everyone still asleep in the barracks, shouting, "The Japs are shooting the hell out of us and they're
using real bullets, so get your asses out of bed before I roll you out!"

In case of emergency, Heydt and his men were to report to the
bomb dump, load the bombs on trailers, and proceed to the airstrip
to arm all available aircraft. In the tiers of the dump, Heydt found "a
Little Lord Fauntleroy of a second lieutenant" crying with fear and
nerves. "Lieutenant, get your ass out of here," Heydt scolded him.
"You're supposed to be an officer, and you're to lead these men."
Retorted the lieutenant sullenly, "Well, I don't want to get shot."[28]

Captain Chapman of Headquarters Squadron and his wife had an
unusually good view, for their bedroom overlooked a part of Battleship Row. "I will never forget the feeling of shocked unbelief as I
watched the planes dive," Mrs. Chapman reminisced, "and recognized with sick horror the red circle on their wings, still too frozen
with shock to do anything but stare until concussion from a bomb
caused the ceiling light fixture to drop onto the bed."[29]

In addition to their own sons, aged 5 years and 13 months, the
Chapmans had house guests, a Navy wife whose husband was at sea
and her two daughters, one 5 years old, the other 11. The Chapmans
had discussed, "idly of course," what to do in such circumstances, and
these casual conversations paid off. They hurriedly dressed, grabbed "a

bottle for the baby and some crackers and milk for the children," and barricaded themselves in the maid's room on the first floor, the room with the least amount of exposed glass.

Meanwhile, Chapman changed into uniform and headed for his duty post in the Headquarters building. A young clerk-typist asked, "Sir, may we break out a couple of windows so that we can shoot at them?" Chapman approved the request, although they had nothing available but 1903 Springfields. He instructed a young soldier who had never fired a rifle before how to load and aim.[30]

When Colonel Phillips, the Hawaiian Department's chief of staff, heard the first bombs, his immediate reaction was, "This is Sunday. What can this be? We planned nothing."[31] Evidently he had not resolved this when Mollison telephoned him from Headquarters that the Japanese had attacked Oahu. "You're out of your mind, Jimmy," he protested. "What's the matter, are you drunk? Wake up, wake up!"

The very sane, sober, and wide-awake Mollison swallowed his irritation as best he could and held the phone open so that Phillips could take in the sounds of conflict. "I can hear it, I can hear it," Phillips said. "What do you want me to do?" Then, inspiration seemed to dawn, and he continued, "I'll tell you what, I'll send over a liaison officer immediately." Mollison's jaw dropped, and so, at that very moment, did the ceiling of his office.[32]

In the meantime, General Martin, coming down to breakfast, "heard a very violent explosion in the vicinity of Pearl Harbor" and ran to the door to investigate. The action was taking place less than a mile from his home, and Martin immediately recognized the attacking aircraft as Japanese. He rushed inside and telephoned Brig. Gen. Howard C. Davidson, in command of the Fourteenth Pursuit Wing, "to tell him to get his pursuit ships in the air just as fast as he could." Davidson replied that they, too, were under attack and "were struggling to get their ships in position so they could get off."

After trying unsuccessfully to reach General Rudolph, Martin drove to his headquarters to find his staff assembling rapidly.[33] Martin's ashen face and grim expression showed how deeply the attack had shocked him. "Martin thought things had gone to hell in a handbasket," said Mollison. "It was all so hard to believe, it was almost beyond comprehension." The general automatically started upstairs to his office, but Mollison, having improvised a working area on the first floor, halted him.

"General, don't go up there," he cautioned. "It is too dangerous.

If you stay down here at least you'll have two ceilings between you and the enemy."

Martin recognized the good sense of this and took over Mollison's desk, while assistants rolled in another for the chief of staff.[34]

The general had but one burning ambition at the moment—"to try to get the carriers." So he called Bellinger on the field phone that connected their offices. The bombardment was so heavy the two men could scarcely hear one another; however, Bellinger told Martin that he "had no information whatever...as to which direction to go to find the carriers."[35]

Colonel Farnum urged his light gray Mercury toward his office. "We either get through this or we die," he told himself, jumping out of his car to join his officers and men fighting fires, dispersing gas trucks, and helping the wounded. On a bright green patch of grass several yards square in front of Headquarters, he found the body of his inventory section chief, a master sergeant, "an excellent soldier, good-looking, well-built, and a wonderful person." Velvety petunia blossoms and the ever-present red hibiscus framed his body, which was naked except for khaki trousers; his bare toes pointed to the sky. His clear blue eyes were open, and his face looked upward "with a normal expression in every feature." Little blood was visible beyond a small stain on the sergeant's shoulder. He might have stretched out to relax for a moment, except that his head lay several feet from his body. Farthing thought that a large piece of shrapnel had beheaded him quickly and smoothly, "as though he had been struck with a knife so whitehot it had coagulated his blood on the spot."[36]

Allen rushed to the hangar line with two objectives—to get his B-17 in the air and bomb the enemy carriers and, meanwhile, to save as many of Hickam's own aircraft as possible. This would be no simple matter, for Takahashi's dive bombers were "knocking the hell out of everything." The first bomb that Allen saw scored a direct hit on a repair hangar.[37]

Another struck a supply building; yet another smashed into the enlisted men's mess hall, located in the main barracks. Thirty-five men died instantly; others emerged in a state of confusion and shock. As they stood outside in dazed groups, a fragmentation bomb fell among them, leaving mangled bodies in a pool of blood.[38]

Targets of no conceivable military value, such as the base chapel and the enlisted men's beer hall, were shattered. A bomb struck the

Small point, but illustrative of the movie's storytelling license: in early December it was not the whole Japanese fleet that had gone missing to U.S. intelligence, it was four carriers. So Admiral Husband Kimmel didn't say to his aide, "The entire fleet could be rounding Diamond Head right now, and we wouldn't know a goddam thing about it?" but rather, "Do you mean to say they"—meaning the four ships—"could be rounding Diamond Head, and you wouldn't know it?"

A controversial figure in the Pearl Harbor saga was a mess attendant on the *West Virginia* named Doris Miller. Cuba Gooding Jr.'s portrayal of him rubberstamps the legend while ignoring other versions of the Miller story. In the movie, Miller comforts the dying Captain Mervyn Bennion, then locks onto an antiaircraft gun, blasts away and makes a kill. In reality, Miller, the ship's boxing champion, who was regarded as something of a bully, was recruited to help move Bennion out of harm's way. A man who *did* comfort the captain was Ensign Victor Delano, and it was Delano who managed to get two machine guns working forward of the conning tower, then showed Miller how to operate one.

Nearly 60 years after the attack, Delano, 81, remembers, "I didn't see any planes shot down from our ship. If Miller did get one, it was an accident. He didn't know how to shoot that gun." Some survivors recall Miller as more of a nuisance on deck than a hero, but regardless, the Tale of the Intrepid Messmate was passed along, and Miller was awarded the Navy Cross. He should have.

died later in the war when the ship he was on was sunk. Says Bruckheimer: "Whether or not he shot down one or two planes, or no planes at all, he was a brave and honorable man who risked his life for his fellow sailors and his country."

We might have known the filmmakers were playing loose with President Roosevelt when they cast someone other than

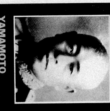

YAMAMOTO
(PLAYED IN THE FILM BY MAKO)
The admiral's reasons for the attack were more subtle than those shown onscreen

MILLER
(PLAYED BY CUBA

DOOLITTLE
(PLAYED BY ALEC

AP, HULTON ARCHIVE, HULTON-DEUTSC

Edward Herrm
Voight's impe
ty, his action
things—Roose
not a hallway,
then there's th
chair. During
attack in the
struggles to l
upon his lily-l
courage in th
screenwriter
old show-biz

Some of the movie's harshest critics have been nonetheless wowed by its centerpiece battle scene. It is, surely, stunning. It is also confusing: you can't tell which boat you are on, which airfield you're at, what's blowing up. In a sense, this mimics the horrifying confusion of the day. But it doesn't allow you to understand what happened and how quickly it happened: 40 minutes for the first wave of the attack, 36 for the second, the last Japanese planes heading north by 9:30 a.m. And, of course, in a PG-13 film the imagery can only hint at the gruesomeness of the carnage. Photographs from the day show the true hell of Pearl Harbor—blown-apart boats and bodies, oil fires everywhere, the sea aflame. Bay's bay is, by contrast,

ROBERT D. BRA[...]

movie but a Bratton-like figure named Thur-man. This is presumably because, were he playing Bratton, he would never have told his superiors that he felt Pearl was in gravest

guardhouse; the prisoners so unceremoniously freed promptly joined forces with a sergeant who was trying to mount a machine gun.[39]

Pvt. Francis Gutzak saw another bomb hit the firehouse and was sure the strike was deliberate, to hinder the base's firefighting capability.[40]

Spotting a bulldozer-type tractor, Crouse decided to crawl across the road to it. There he lay for what seemed to be several hours, but which could not have been more than a few minutes. He had a good view of the high-level bombers dropping their loads. "Each one of these bombs seemed to be coming directly for me, but must have landed several miles away as none ever landed close."

Soon a young soldier, not more than 17 years old, crawled under the tractor beside Crouse. As he was in full uniform and wore a .45 at his belt, Crouse deduced he had been on guard duty. The boy looked at Crouse's wound, then at his .45, and asked, "Do you think it will do any good?" Crouse doubted it, but replied, "It sure wouldn't hurt to try." So he started to shoot whenever a Japanese plane came over.[41]

Allen got together the best crew he could improvise and scrambled into a B-17. Its guns were in position, and they readied them for firing. Engines two, three, and four started promptly, but number one would not take hold, so Allen taxied across the field on three engines, still trying to start number one.[42]

While he was thus occupied, the dive bombers left Hickam to the Zeros and headed for the rendezvous point.[43] Their mission over Ford Island finished, Shiga and his Second Air Control Group had arrived on the scene. Shiga strafed Hickam three times, coming down as low as he dared, some 120 feet. After each run, he swung into the black cloud of smoke and came in again from the east. He strafed a B-17, noting that this big aircraft was very difficult to set afire.[44]

At this unpropitious time the B-17s from the mainland began to appear. CPO Harry Rafsky, Admiral Calhoun's enlisted aide, watched them and said to himself, "Jesus Christ, the Japanese are really coming in now!"[45] The impression was natural under the circumstances, and even Allen, himself a B-17 pilot, briefly made the same mistake when the first of the incoming bombers flew over the hangar line. He had never seen a B-17E before. Knowing that these approaching aircraft did not belong to the Hawaiian Air Force, he wondered, "Where did the Japs get four-engine bombers?"[46]

The mistaken identity was mutual. Seeing a group of planes flying toward him from Oahu, Landon assumed "Here comes the air force out to greet us." No sooner had he framed the thought than the welcoming committee opened fire. "Damn it, those are Japs!" barked Landon's intercom. His own plane's guns packed away, Landon could not retaliate, but he managed to lose the Japanese in the cloud cover.[47]

Lt. Bruce G. Allen brought his B-17 into Hickam safely.[48] Capt. Raymond T. Swenson was not so fortunate. A Japanese shot touched off his bomber's magnesium flares, and the tail burned off as it landed. "When it stopped," said Mollison, "the plane was standing up like a penguin." All of Swenson's crew made it to safety except 1st Lt. William R. Schick, a flight surgeon, shot while running from the wrecked plane.[49] Swenson's bomber probably fell victim to Lt. Ibusuki, a Zero pilot from the *Akagi*, who made five strafing runs on Hickam's Flying Fortresses; he also claimed, "With other planes, I shot down a flying B-17."[50]

Landon informed the Hickam tower, "I have ample fuel to proceed to Hilo Field* if necessary." Captain Blake replied, "You can land at Hickam, but three Japs are on your tail and the antiaircraft fire is erratic and dangerous."

Landon decided to take the chance, and after dodging the Japanese a second time, managed to land at about 0820.[51] Shortly thereafter, an apparition materialized before Mollison's desk, asking "Where do you want me to go?" It was Landon, so pale and grimy that Mollison did not recognize him at once, although he had known him for years.[52]

Other B-17s came in, scattered all over the island. Lt. Frank Bostrom received landing instructions from Hickam, but no hint of what was happening, so he was well into the mess before he realized that something was wrong. The Pearl Harbor batteries cut loose at him, and Bostrom hid behind a cloud while he tried to figure out what could be going on. After about 15 minutes, he called Hickam again, and this time the tower ordered him to stay clear. At this point, six Zeros jumped him and chased him all around Oahu, shooting out two of his engines. But Bostrom stuck with his plane and managed to bump to a landing on the Kahuku Golf Course.[53]

Kathleen Cooper had a clear view of Hickam Field, about half a mile from her parents' quarters. To her horrified eyes, the field looked like "a great sea of flame about a mile long." Strangely enough, the gruesome sights and sounds did not frighten her. Instead, "I had an utter feeling of horror, helplessness and anger, consuming anger. If a

---

* Located on the "Big Island" of Hawaii.

Japanese pilot had walked in the house, I would have tried to kill him," she declared.[54]

So would anyone on Hickam at the time, but the first wave had left the field in no condition to retaliate.

General Martin took great pride in the behavior of his men,

> because practically without orders they immediately rushed to the positions, grabbed the ships, got them out of the concentration, got them into the dispersion area, and took such steps as were indicated by the conditions existing at the time. Both officers and enlisted men. I am extremely proud of their conduct under those circumstances, which were most unusual and trying.[55]

Not everyone had the temperament to be a hero. "There was confusion plus when the attack came," recalled Farthing. "Men were simply petrified and frightened stiff."[56] Farnum remembered, but did not name, an officer of fairly high position who "went all to pieces after the attack and had to be sent back to the states on a stretcher."[57]

Then there was the pathetic PFC from Hickam who also had to be evacuated to the mainland, "crying and combative," for years of neuropsychiatric care, "hallucinating Pearl Harbor again and again."[58]

CHAPTER 17

"Bedlam and Bombs and Bullets"

Col. William J. Flood had been on Oahu since March of 1940 as A-4 (supply officer) of the Hawaiian Air Force when, in November of 1941, he assumed command of Wheeler Field.[1] His long-time friend, Brig. Gen. Howard C. Davidson, had commanded both the base and the Fourteenth Pursuit Wing, but while he was on temporary duty in the States, the decision was made to split the assignments. Davidson became the tactical commander, while Flood took over the base.[2]

The job was very much to Flood's liking. Himself a command pilot, he understood aircraft and airmen. "No one bothered me, and I didn't ask for anything special." Wheeler itself was "an excellent base, neat, tidy, really beautiful and well run." However, it was in a very exposed position. A public road ran alongside the base, so that "one could spy on it almost at will."[3]

About 125 protective bunkers had been built for Wheeler's aircraft—U-shaped walls made mostly of earth, 8 to 10 feet high—enough for the main elements of the fighter force.[4] Unfortunately, by direct orders of General Martin's Headquarters, the planes had been removed from these bunkers and "concentrated so they would be easier to guard against sabotage."[5]

Flood respected Martin as "a fine person and a damn good pilot," but he mistrusted this policy, so he asked Martin for permission to keep the aircraft dispersed in their bunkers. "Well, Flood, no," Martin replied. "The orders are to concentrate the planes." Further inquiry produced a reason: Dispersal might alarm the local populace.[6]

So on the morning of December 7, Wheeler's fighters, like Hickam's bombers, were lined up in the open. Again as at Hickam, the display gave a rather false impression of power. Of 140 fighter aircraft on hand, 87 were modern types, P-40Bs and P-40Cs, and of these, 35 were out of commission. The remaining aircraft were obsolescent, 39 P-36s and 14 P-26s, of which 20 and 10, respectively, were airworthy.[7] And the fighters able to take the air could not have engaged in combat, for the ammunition had been taken out of the planes and stored in the hangar as another antisabotage measure.[8]

Base security against attack was practically nonexistent. Wheeler had no antiaircraft guns, no air raid shelters, and no trenches. The perimeter guards were armed with rifles. The entire base could produce no more than five machine guns. These were mounted on top of the big hangar and the barracks.[9]

Sgt. Mobley L. Hall, a crew chief of Headquarters Squadron, Eighteenth Pursuit Group, recalled that no instructions had been issued covering an attack from without, only against sabotage: "...that was to investigate, and if anybody was fooling around, give them a chance to halt three times, as usual, and then, why, shoot. Those instructions we always gave the sentries."[10]

Although a bachelor, as base commander, Flood rated a large home on Wheeler. Finishing his breakfast, he went out on his patio to read his newspaper. "All at once," he remembered, "I heard this awful whang." A second "whang" brought him out of the patio to investigate.[11] He saw a bomb hit near the depot area, and as with so many others that morning, his "first reaction was that it was an accidental bomb due to someone having been out on maneuvers, or something like that."[12]

Wheeler was situated "right in the saddle of the two mountain ranges of Oahu," somewhat elevated, so Flood could "look right down on Pearl Harbor." Seeing huge billows of smoke rising over the harbor, he went indoors for his hat. By the time he returned, the Japanese had struck in force. Flood

saw all those bastards bombing and strafing the base, the planes, the officers' quarters, and even the golf course. I could even see some of the Japanese pilots lean out of their planes and smile as they zoomed by. They were that damn low—just a few feet above the ground really, not much higher than a man's head. Hell, I could even see the gold in their teeth.[13]

The Davidsons were up and about early. Mrs. Davidson and the two older children, Stewart and Mary, were indoors, but the active 10-year-old twins, Julia and Frances, had gone outside to play on the lawn. The general was shaving when he heard "a terrific roar" of aircraft engines and reflected, "That's those damn Navy pilots jazzing the base."

The explosion of bombs drove that idea out of his head. Hastening outside, he saw Japanese dive bombers ripping Wheeler apart. To his horror, the twins were racing gleefully around the lawn. Completely unaware of danger, they were busily collecting the fascinating shining objects that bounced around—empty cartridges from the attacking aircraft. Davidson helped his wife snatch the girls indoors and then dashed away to direct operations.[14]

Sergeant Hall, at his quarters in "the new defense housing project" at Kemoo Farms, knew something was wrong when he heard the first bomb drop. He had no idea what was going on, but his orders were clear: "I was supposed to report to my place of duty." So he drove his car "down to the hangar to see what was happening, and it was as I arrived there that the bombing was going on." Although he recognized the nationality of the low-flying planes, it all still seemed illusory: "I did not believe it was real."[15]

Capt. Charles A. Kengla and his wife had not yet arisen when their 3-year-old son, Charles, Jr., who had been waiting for the Sunday-school bus, bolted into the room, shouting with excitement: "Daddy, there are planes and they go up and come down and they drop round things that go boom!"

Kengla catapulted up as his phone rang. It was his mother-in-law, Mrs. Durward S. Wilson, asking, "What goes on, Charles?"

"The Japs are bombing the hell out of us, that's what's going on," he replied. And at that moment, the enemy machine-gunned his house.

Mrs. Kengla remembered ever after the sharp contrast between the confidence and safety she had felt and this horrible moment when the fact struck home—Oahu was under attack. "There was a psychological factor of impregnability about Hawaii," she said. "There was no doubt about that." Now their psychological Rock of Gibraltar had collapsed. "You have no idea of the terrible helplessness we felt with our ships and planes destroyed. You cannot describe it—you have to feel it."[16]

M.Sgt. Fred Brown, chief clerk of Air Corps Supply, rose at 0730 to turn on the radio to KGMB and then climbed back into bed. About half an hour later, the sudden burst of noise outside brought him to the window in time to see the gas storage dump on the southwest corner of the field go up. This dump held all of Wheeler's inflammables, such as gas, turpentine, and lacquer, so it leaped into sky-licking flames. All too aptly, from the radio came a popular song of the day, "I Don't Want to Set the World on Fire."

Brown shepherded his wife and mother-in-law out of their brick duplex two streets from the flight line into a metal-roofed garage across the road. Then he hurried toward his office. On the way, Wheeler's Intelligence officer snapped him up to help round up undesirables.[17]

Cpl. Franklin Hibel of the Fourteenth Pursuit Wing's Public Relations Office had just reached for an aloha shirt when the Japanese pounced on Wheeler. He first saw a plane with a fixed undercarriage. For a minute the pilot with his huge goggles looked like "a creature from another world." Machine-gun bullets crashed through the shattered windows of Hibel's barracks, into walls and footlockers, and ricocheted off concrete pillars into the bunks. "All was bedlam and bombs and bullets after that."

Hibel ran outside where families were emerging from their quarters into the chaos. Japanese aircraft sweeping over the hangar line blasted nearby tents housing men of the 78th Pursuit Squadron. As each bomber delivered its deadly load, it circled and swung into the target again to strafe:

> Those two-seater jobs came in crawling, pulling out almost in slowmotion from their shallow dives. They came so close that you could see the expression on the faces of the gunners riding backwards in the rear seats of those open jobs.[18]

These were the men of Lt. Akira Sakamoto's twenty-five dive bombers from the *Zuikaku*. Their mission was to dash for Wheeler Field as soon as Fuchida gave his deployment order and to put the base out of action as promptly as possible to prevent U.S. fighter planes from taking off and intercepting the first wave.

Wheeler, basking in the bright morning sunshine, was "a beautiful and quiet sight," according to Lieutenant Ema. In view of what impended, the scene was "almost fantastic." He could see no sign of activity whatsoever. Intelligence briefings had advised that Wheeler had 250 planes, but only about half that number were visible. However, these were lined up neatly—an ideal target.[19]

As befitted a leader, Sakamoto led his group of nine bombers for the first strike. Ema had a perfect view as Sakamoto's planes dropped their bombs for direct hits. Flames and debris soared skyward. Having been briefed that Wheeler had heavy antiaircraft batteries, Ema was dumbfounded to note that the only resistance came from two machine gunners firing gallantly but ineffectively.

As Ema turned to make his dive, his mind briefly turned back to 1936 when as a midshipman he had visited Schofield Barracks, adjacent to Wheeler. But he had no time for reminiscences of more peaceful days. As many on the ground noted, the bombers came in very low. In fact, two of the planes in Ema's group struck telephone wires and returned to the carrier with short bits of the wire wrapped around their wheels. After each dive bomber dropped its missile, it returned four or five times to strafe. After about 20 minutes of action, they soared away toward the *Zuikaku,* with not a single plane lost or damaged.[20]

Petty Officer Muranaka of the *Hiryu* had a fine view as he flew his Zero toward its target:

> There was a group of dive bombers over Wheeler Field lining up in a single row with its leading planes already in dive, while torpedo planes crawled low below the clouds. Level bombers were still seen heading to the west as a black group in the air. There were no enemy planes in the air at all, no AA fires from the ground were seen as yet. It was indeed a thrilling scene.

His group headed for Wheeler. "Through breaks in the clouds flashes of fire caused by hits on hangars were seen." A short time before, Muranaka had been troubled at the thought of children being hurt. Now, looking back at his comrades as their Zeros droned after him, he "could see them grinning with sharp eyes hungry for good games." Forming in a single file, they dropped down for the attack. "Wheeler air base was already a sea of fire."[21]

Driving into this scene of flame and ruin, Flood felt bitter anger: "To think that this bunch of little yellow bastards could do this to us when we all knew that the United States was superior to Japan!" Grief and horror at the fate of many of his enlisted men soon piled on top of his fury. "The bombers slammed right into the barracks," he said, "and killed about 200 soldiers in their sleep." Others were badly wounded, and some were maimed for life.

In addition, Sakamoto's bombers destroyed Hangar No. 2, and another bomb struck the middle of the Post Exchange. "After the attack, there just wasn't a PX."[22]

Davidson recalled that the dive bombers also hit one of the mess halls and attacked the fire house. The furious bombing of the baseball diamond led the general to believe that the Japanese were working from an old blueprint showing estimates of future building, which had included a projected fuel supply base on the site of the ball field.[23]

Flood remembered the Zero strafing as less destructive than the bombing. "The fighter attack and the strafing frightened hell out of people, but it did not hurt as many as the bombing did." He added, "Boy, you could hear those bullets zinging all over the place. A fighter plane would swoop in, make his head-on pass, and the bullets would hit the cement and whine and zing off just like in the movies. It's a wonder that any of us came out alive."[24]

At Hall's hangar, "everybody...seemed to be there and doing everything as rapidly as possible." His own plane, an AT-6, was in the hangar, for Hall had only recently put a new engine in it. The little trainer burned completely when the hangar took a bomb, while the second AT-6 and an OA-9, exposed on the line, escaped damage.[25]

Davidson stated that the biggest difficulty that day was "to try to get the guns loaded." Guns were in the planes, but the hangar where the ammunition had been stored as a protection against sabotage was afire, and the ammunition "exploded like firecrackers."

With no means of repelling the attack, Wheeler's officers and men could only hope to save as many of the aircraft as possible by hauling the undamaged fighters away from those on fire. Even this proved more difficult than anticipated, because the Japanese marksmen had shot the tires off a number of the otherwise airworthy planes.[26]

Small wonder that Takahashi radioed the *Akagi* jubilantly: "Bombed Ford Island, Hickam and Wheeler. Terrible damage inflicted."[27]

At least two young men had no intention of confining themselves to relatively passive measures like saving aircraft to fight another day. They wanted to fight right then, that day, December 7, 1941.

Lt. George S. Welch, assistant operations officer of the 47th Pursuit Squadron, and Lt. Kenneth M. Taylor, a pilot of the same outfit, were permanently stationed at Wheeler; however, their squadron was on temporary duty at Haleiwa Field for gunnery camp. As Welch explained, Haleiwa was

> a very short, sandy field originally used as an emergency landing field, and probably about six months before the war started they had chopped down a few trees and were allowing fighter squadrons to operate out of there as an emergency field to practice shortfield landings; and a month before the war started, the 15th Group, of which the 47th Squadron is a part, was sending each squadron out there for two weeks in rotation to operate off of the field in simulated combat conditions.

The officers and men on temporary duty there had to bring their own tents and other equipment, for Haleiwa had no installations.[28]

On Saturday, Welch and Taylor abandoned this rather forlorn spot in favor of making the rounds in Honolulu, at Hickam, and at Pearl Harbor. They ended up at the Wheeler Officers' Club and joined an all-night poker game that did not break off until nearly 0800.[29]

When the first bomb hit, Taylor "thought a Navy man had probably gone off the main route," so he paid no attention until the second explosion. Then he and Welch went outside just as the Japanese began machine-gunning the club.[30] Taylor ran for his car while Welch waited, meanwhile watching the action. When Taylor pulled up, Welch jumped in, and they sped off for Haleiwa and their P-40s. As they drove, the Japanese "were machine-gunning all around."[30]

They reached Haleiwa to find that the attackers had "passed right over it, apparently they didn't notice its existence or didn't know that we were using it." This was just as well for Haleiwa, because the planes "were lined up in a perfect line right down one side of the field. . . . At Haleiwa we had no revetments, and we just parked them there just to look nice, and also to keep them bunched so we could guard them easier."[31] Evidently someone at Wheeler had alerted Haleiwa, because crewmen were already loading the fighters when Taylor and Welch pulled up. Welch noticed the ranking officer present, Lt. Robert Rogers, getting out of his car, having driven in from his quarters at Wheeler.[32]

Technically, Rogers was in charge, because Major Austin, the squadron commander, was on leave, hunting deer on Molokai. However, Welch and Taylor awaited no one's permission to take off. Upon telephone instructions from interceptor control to proceed to "Easy"—Barber's Point—at 8000 feet, they headed in that direction, but saw no Japanese aircraft. Communication was poor, so receiving no order to the contrary, they went to Wheeler with the view to loading up with .50 caliber ammunition. Haleiwa had only .30 caliber.

All this had taken time, and by the time Welch and Taylor reached Wheeler, the first-wave attack was over.[33]

At roughly this same moment, Bellows Field received its initial strike, one that caused remarkably little disturbance. Like Haleiwa, Bellows housed a squadron of fighters "for a month's aerial gunnery practice." They had only come in the previous day, and as was customary when such pursuit craft came in on a Saturday afternoon, they received a more thorough than usual cleaning. So the guns had been dismounted from most of the P-40s. Lt. Col. Leonard Weddington, the base commander, was not sure what percentage were fueled, but it was not the practice to refuel them on such occasions.[34]

Pfc. Raymond F. McBriarty of the 86th Observation Squadron was about to go to church when, at approximately 0830, a single aircraft came over from the sea "and fired on the shore." McBriarty had no idea that Oahu was under heavy attack. To him the bullets sounded like "blanks that the U.S. Army uses, and the ship looked like the AT-6 trainer the Army has." One of his barracksmates asked him what it was, and McBriarty "told him it was a plane with two red balls." Thereupon McBriarty "proceeded to go to church."[35]

At Barber's Point, the Marine base at Ewa Field had been attacked well before Welch and Taylor flew in that direction. The heavy drone of aircraft engines brought the officer of the day, Capt. Leonard Ashwell, from his breakfast, and he recognized the planes at first sight.[36] He bounded back into the mess hall, shouting, "Air raid...Air raid! Pass the word!" Then he ran toward the flight line, noting the time as he did so—0753.[37]

The attackers concentrated on the parked aircraft—mostly scout bombers—"using explosive and incendiary bullets from extremely low altitudes."[38]

Cpl. Duane W. Shaw, Ewa's fire truck driver, had been up for about half an hour and was fully dressed when he and his comrades in the barracks heard approaching planes. At first, they thought maneuvers were under way. "We really got the message, however," said Shaw, "when one of the Japanese planes tattooed the barracks with bullets."

The Marines pelted outside "in nothing flat." Initially somewhat frightened, Shaw soon became so busy that he had no time to think about the danger. He and his buddy, Cpl. Carl Hines, jumped into the fire truck, of 1930 vintage, intent on reaching the blazing aircraft. Shaw feared that the planes burning at the end of the runway were beyond help, but he hoped to save such valuable equipment as guns and spare parts. As he pressed the truck to its 42-mile-per-hour limit, bullets shattered the windshield, though miraculously the men escaped being cut by flying glass. Bits of metal from the hood of the dull red vehicle shivered skyward. More bullets hit the truck's rear and ricocheted past Shaw's ears.

The next strafer shot the rear tires off, and Shaw's race ended abruptly. He and Hines abandoned ship and bolted across the runway, taking refuge behind a stack of crates. "These contained airplane parts," Shaw recalled, "and we found plenty of company behind them."

A nearby pilot remarked, "A man ought to draw double flight pay for a ride like that." Shaw could still grin in reply. But he sighed as he looked toward his ruined vehicle. Then he brightened a bit. "Sure looks like I'm going to get a new truck!"[39]

Shortly, many of the Japanese who had finished with Hickam and Wheeler descended on Ewa. Lieutenant Okajima led six fighters from the *Hiryu* in several strafing runs until "in the last strafing the second plane of my direct command got holes in its fore fuel tank, therefore I with other planes headed back to the ship escorting that plane."[40]

Muranaka had been having a bad time over Ewa. When he reached the target area, he saw four or five planes on fire on the ground and began to strafe from the west toward the coast. "When I squeezed the trigger, confidently aiming at one of them parked there, 20-mm. tracer bullets which we nicknamed 'ice candy' fired from both wings of my plane. They overshot the target, however."

Disconcerted, Muranaka zoomed up and tried again, only to fail again. This was his first experience in strafing planes on the ground.

By this time, many U.S. aircraft were blazing, but Muranaka's group made at least eight strafing runs. Certain "large-type planes" seemed difficult to set on fire, and Muranaka wondered if this might be because the Japanese had already used up their fifty rounds of 20-mm ammunition per gun.[41]

On his last run, Muranaka "felt successive shocks of hits.... Looking around inside the cockpit, I found fuel running out fiercely beneath the gauge plate. I immediately thought that the fuel pipe was broken. The leader's plane was heading north along the coast line; we were going back."

He had not yet released the additional fuel tank, which he thought was good for another hour's run. He also should be able to squeeze another hour or two from the fuselage tank and the wing main tank. That should be enough to take him back to the carriers, about an hour-and-a-half's flight to the north.

Muranaka made up his mind to return alone at cruising speed, lagging behind the others. One of his fellows edged his fighter close, obviously worried about Muranaka, and the latter looked at him with deliberately knit brows.

At that moment, Muranaka saw "ahead to the left what appeared to be two American carrier-borne reconnaissance planes flying southward over the coast line." Forgetting his instructions "that a plane with fuel running out should never be speeded up nor slowed down lest possible fire running out from the exhaust pipes set fire to the plane," he pushed the throttle to catch up with the lead plane.

Having done so, he drew attention to the American planes, but the leader, after momentarily turning toward them, continued northward in view of the damage to Muranaka's plane. Soon thereafter, fuel ceased to leak from the damaged fighter, and, signing that he was all right, Muranaka took his normal position within the group.[42]

In contrast to Muranaka, Shiga from the *Kaga* strafed Ewa with relative ease. His most lasting memory of Ewa was of "a gallant soldier on the ground attempting to shoot us with his pistol, to whom I paid a good respect."[43] This was Pfc Mel Thompson at the Main Gate sentry booth, who emptied his .45 skyward, cursing the while that he had nothing more powerful.[44] It was a perfect vignette of mingled valor and ineffectiveness.

CHAPTER 18

"It's the Real Thing, Boys"

The sudden air strike surprised and stunned General Short and his ground forces as much as it did the Navy and the air forces. "I heard the first bombs, and my first idea was that the Navy was having some battle practice, either that they hadn't told me about or that I had forgotten that they had told me about," Short testified. "...When some more dropped I went out on the back porch to take a look at what was going on, and about that time the chief of staff came running over to my quarters around three minutes after eight, and said he had just received a message from Wheeler or Hickam, or both—I have forgotten—that it was the real thing."[1]

Phillips did not mention his call from Mollison* and said that he received the word from the G-1 (personnel officer), Lt. Col. Russell C. Throckmorton: "This is attack. Attack!"

"It must be," replied Phillips, "because we have nothing planned today."[2]

Phillips may have confused Throckmorton with the department adjutant general, Col. Robert H. Dunlop. The latter had arisen at about 0730 in anticipation of the customary telephone notification that the oncoming officer of the day had reported for duty in his office shortly before 0800. The call came through as expected, and the colonel, having no additional orders for the new OD, was about to hang up when a terrible racket arrested him in midmotion.

"What in the world is this?" the OD exclaimed.

---

* See Chapter 16.

"I haven't the least idea," answered Dunlop. "You know as much about it as I do. I'll call you back and let you know what it is."

"What on earth is going on?" Mrs. Dunlop asked. "Do you suppose Burgin* is having a shoot on Sunday morning?"

Gazing toward Pearl Harbor from their second floor bedroom window, the Dunlops could see planes bombing the Naval Base and Hickam Field, 2 miles away. "Ruth, this is no practice," said Dunlop. "This is the real thing." Nevertheless, as was the case with so many, the fact did not fully penetrate his consciousness. At that moment, the phone rang again. "We are under hostile air attack by the Japanese," reported the caller, Colonel Bertholf.

"You can't be serious, Cheney," Dunlop protested, still incredulous.

"I was never more serious in my life," Bertholf answered.

Dunlop promised to phone Short immediately, but first he called Phillips: "I have just gotten word from Cheney Bertholf that Hickam Field is under hostile attack by the Japanese."

"Oh, my God!" Phillips groaned.

"Tige, I am giving it to you just as I see it," Dunlop emphasized. "You can hear it from your window."

"I know, Bob," Phillips answered.

Then the Dunlops dressed hurriedly. "Bob, this is war and all of our good times are over," Mrs. Dunlop said sadly. "Go to your office and come back in forty-five minutes and I'll have a cup of coffee for you."[3]

Having received word, Phillips shouted the news to his family and ran next door to tell Short that Oahu was under attack and to recommend "that the troops move out under Alert No. 3 at once."[4] This would move the state of alert from antisabotage to defense against an all-out attack. Short readily agreed, for, as he said, "I didn't know how serious the attack might develop. If they would take a chance like that, they might even take a chance on a landing of troops, and so I sent everybody to his battle station."[5]

Throckmorton had been up since 0700, in anticipation of a golf foursome with Kimmel, Short, and another officer, scheduled to tee off at 0800. At his breakfast he heard "all the ruckus." Like Short and Phillips, he wondered what was going on, because the Army had no exercise planned for that morning, and "the Navy was usually quiet

---

* Maj. Gen. Henry T. Burgin, in command of the Hawaiian Department's Coast Artillery.

on Sundays." An explosion behind his house brought him out to find that a Navy shell had made a large crater in his yard. "You could put a jeep in it," he recalled. "In fact, it was the one thing that convinced me a war was on." Staring at the hole, he reflected, "Well, hell, this is it!"

Rushing back indoors, he called to his wife, "Sybil, get the dog and head for the basement! We are being attacked!" He threw on some clothes and made for his office only 400 feet away.[6]

Lt. Col. Morrill W. Marston, Short's G-4, had just pulled on his boots, intending to go for a horseback ride at Aliamanu Crater when he heard loud explosions. He thought it was dynamite blasting, but Mrs. Marston, seeing the smoke from Pearl Harbor, said, "With that much smoke there is danger that this is the real thing."

Just in case her estimate should be correct, Marston sent her and their two Japanese maids into the basement. A U.S. Navy shell landing in front of the nearby Headquarters removed all doubt. Too curious and interested to remain in the basement, the women emerged to watch. One of the maids remarked with awed fascination, "Just like the movies!"[7]

Marston's good friend and titular assistant, Major Fleming, Short's troubleshooter, was propped in bed playing with his 4-year-old daughter when, as he wrote, "All hell broke loose. I thought Aliamanu had blown up." He remained bewildered until Marston telephoned him to say, "This is no drill. Get to headquarters pronto!"

This did not take very long, for the Flemings lived on Fort Shafter. Short instructed Fleming to report to Kimmel at Pearl Harbor. He gave no further instructions. "The Old Man was calm but in a hell of a hurry." He presumed that Short meant for him "to play it by ear."[8]

Colonel Craig, Short's provost marshal, rose early and dressed in his riding togs for his customary Sunday morning ride. He went out to look for the newspaper, and finding it had not yet been delivered, he returned to his room. That was when he heard shellfire and assumed "that it was artillery firing falling short," although he "didn't know whether the Coast Artillery were having target practice or not." Then from his window he saw Phillips, clad in uniform, walking up the street. Suddenly Phillips "took up the double-time...toward Headquarters," so Craig followed. He did not realize that an attack was in progress until he reached Headquarters, where Phillips informed him "that Alert No. 3 was in effect."[9]

Although Phillips ran for his post, Throckmorton beat him out by a head, and others streamed in almost immediately. A crisis threatened to develop when Maj. "Swede" Henderson, the Headquarters commandant, rushed in, panting, "Where are the keys to the forward echelon?"[10]

He referred to the huge cavern dug in Aliamanu Crater, about one-third of the way between Fort Shafter and Schofield Barracks, for use as a command post in the event of an attempted invasion. Under about 15 feet of rock, it was, as Dunlop described it, "quite a place, but not a spot for anyone with claustrophobia."[11]

The keys to this advance Headquarters were locked up in the safe of Lt. Col. William N. Donegan, the G-3 (operations officer), and Donegan had not yet arrived from early mass. No one present knew the combination, but Throckmorton took a wild chance born of desperation. He twirled the dial several times at random, and no one was more surprised than he when it swung open. "God led us by the hand," said Throckmorton. "We could go to the crater and get to work."[12]

Dunlop manned one of the Headquarters telephones, calling Department and Hawaiian Air Force staff officers and commanders. Since he wanted to round up as many as possible without long-winded explanations, he shouted into the phone, "Get on the job at once and go to your office! It will all be explained later." Some wanted page, line, and verse before budging; others caught on at once: "Yes, yes. I can hear it. I'll be right down."

An officer's radio nearby played church music in the background. "What a hell of a contrast to the real thing going on!" Dunlop recalled. "It was all too macabre." Soon the hymns gave way to urgent instructions: "Get off the roads and stay off!" "Don't block traffic!" "Stay at home!"[13]

A number of officers who lived off base arrived at Headquarters somewhat later, although they became aware of the attack almost simultaneously. Dunlop's senior assistant, Maj. Kenneth E. Thiebaud, lived at St. Louis Heights, where he and his wife, Vivian, planned a quiet weekend, since Mrs. Thiebaud was due to return stateside shortly for an operation. The major was in bed when he heard the Japanese flight coming in over Kolekole Pass. At first glance he recognized them as Japanese. "Get some food and head for the hills," he told his wife and 13-year-old daughter, Jane Caroline, for he expected an attempted invasion to follow the air strike.

He drove through Wheeler on his way to Shafter. The Japanese were still bombing, and craters in the road made driving slow and hazardous. He could not resist the temptation to park for 5 minutes or so near Pearl Harbor to observe, but he could not see much because of the thick smoke. The first wave had passed over and the second wave was almost upon Oahu when Thiebaud pulled up at Headquarters.[14]

Colonel Bicknell awoke before 0800 at his home on Aiea Heights to a "popping noise" that sounded to him like "the Chinese shooting off firecrackers." So he got up, looked down toward Pearl Harbor, and saw puffs from AA shells bursting in the air. A plane with a red disk streaked in from the direction of Diamond Head and dived toward the harbor. Suddenly it burst "into a great ball of fire" and dropped into the waters. "It seemed to me," Bicknell remembered, "that I was looking at some fantastic movie."[15]

From the lanai of his home, "two miles behind Pearl Harbor and 900 feet above it," he had a panoramic view of the action against Kimmel's ships, and that added to his astonishment.[16] As he told the congressional committee that investigated the disaster some years later, "Well, naturally, when you are looking out of your window on a peaceful Sunday morning and see a battleship blow up under your eyes, you are pretty apt to be surprised."[17]

By that time, his wife, Dorothy, had joined him on their lanai. He turned to her and announced, "The war is on!"[18]

Bicknell was not conscious of talking to himself, but later his wife asked him, "What in the world were you mumbling about these 'poinsettias and hibiscus' while all this fighting was going on?" Then he remembered wondering, on December 7, whether the reference to those flowers in the Mori telephone call* might not have contained a code for certain types of ships.[19]

But these reflections did not interfere with Bicknell's actions. First, he called his OD in downtown Honolulu, Lt. Jiro Iwai. "Pearl Harbor is under attack by the Japanese. Alert the command!" Next, Bicknell called the OD at Shafter to tell him, "There is an air attack on Pearl Harbor." Bicknell did not know who answered the phone. "But whoever the dimwit was said this: 'Go back to sleep, you're having a bad dream.'"

As Bicknell left his house, his wife handed him a packet. "I have fixed you a lamb sandwich; you may not be back for lunch." She had underestimated badly; she did not see her husband for eight days.

Before reporting to his office in the Dillingham Building, Bicknell

---

* See Chapter 4.

drove to Shafter in search of his immediate superior, Colonel Fielder, reaching the post at about 0820. There he saw wounded men lying on stretchers on the lawn before Tripler Hospital, which at that time was located in front of Shafter. Already men were digging slit trenches on the parade ground of beautiful Palau Circle with its palm trees and ring of neat buildings—the Headquarters and officers' quarters. On his way, Bicknell saw Short, who seemed "in a state of animated confusion." The general knew that Pearl Harbor was under attack, but since the harbor was not visible from Shafter, he knew little or nothing concerning the progress of events. "What's going on out there?" he asked.

"I'm not sure, General, but I just saw two battleships sunk," Bicknell replied.

Staring incredulously, Short snapped, "That's ridiculous!" With that he walked away.[20]

Capt. George P. Sampson, the department's assistant signal officer, who lived in Honolulu, received the first word when another officer phoned him to say, "Something unusual is going on and you had better get over to Headquarters. There might possibly be an attack."

Sampson was astonished at this idea, but drove to Shafter "down School Street at great speed." Soon he saw the attack going full blast but just could not believe it. "We were in a state of mind not conditioned to the event at the time." But he had his own immediate duty: "Get to my Command Post at once."

He found no great confusion there. "People were apprehensive, yes, and unsure, but during the day they were generally too busy to be much concerned about the dangers that faced them."[21]

The Japanese concentrated heavily on the Navy and the Hawaiian Air Force, so the communications system between Army units suffered relatively little damage. Colonel Powell and his colleagues soon had everything under control and operating satisfactorily between Short's Headquarters and the other elements of his command. But one colonel became quite unsettled. He wandered in and out of the communications section, grousing, fretting, and generally getting in everyone's way.

Finally, Sergeant Jack Carney reached the limit of his endurance. He looked the colonel squarely in the eye and exploded, "If you'll get your ass out of here we'll get some communications going!"

Sampson held his breath, visualizing a court martial in the making. But no bolt of lightning struck the sergeant, and the colonel was big enough to take the rebuke with good grace.[22]

According to Short, "the only officer of any rank who observed the planes before they actually dropped a bomb" was Col. A. E. "Empie" Potts, who commanded the 98th Field Artillery at Schofield Barracks. Potts "saw this group of planes as they came over Wheeler before they started their dive,...and he thought it was a bunch of Navy or Marine dive bombers just doing a little practice."[23] Soon, however, bombs began to fall, and Potts and his wife could recognize the Rising Sun insignia. Potts left at once for his post, leaving his wife with their 10-year-old son, David, a teen-age Korean maid, and her baby. During the raid, a house three doors away was hit.[24]

General Murray, who had recently more or less bootlegged some ammunition into readily accessible spots at Schofield,* planned to take a horseback ride and went to the window to check the weather. He heard a dive bomber coming over his quarters and ran to his front door, watch in hand, so that he could report the pilot "for coming so low into an occupied area." Even when he saw the first bomb drop, he still thought "there was some crazy aviator dropping a practice bomb on the dump there." When the bomb exploded, light dawned on Murray, and he took his wife and daughter to shelter in the barracks.

As information began to come in from Short's Headquarters, Murray decided to move out the artillery of the 25th Division. They began to draw ammunition at 0820. Murray went to his office and moved his staff in with him, for the frame building offered the only available protection against the heavy machine-gun strafing. A bomb landed in Murray's front yard but did not strike the house. From his office, the general phoned the infantry to "get the machine guns on the roof," but they had anticipated the order and were already firing. As far as Murray knew, however, they had no effect.[25]

These infantry machine guns had gone into action even before General Wilson, in command of the 24th Infantry Division, had reached his Headquarters, about a 5-minute drive from his home.[26] Hearing the thunder of the attack, Mrs. Wilson assumed, as did many other Army people, that the Navy was holding maneuvers. She remarked disapprovingly to her husband, who was in bed, "I think the Navy has gone too far, having exercises like this on Sunday." She slipped into a dress and went outside to watch the excitement. What she saw made her stomach turn over: planes with the Rising Sun on their wings swooping down for the kill. She could see the pilots looking out of their cockpits, grinning like "Oriental devils—arrogant, mocking grins."

---

* See Chapter 2.

Wilson, joining her, was so surprised that he "had little feeling." Mrs. Wilson felt "too astonished to be afraid at the moment." She recalled, "I was not terrified; I was plain numb. We all felt perfectly safe in Hawaii, and, golly Moses, here came this fantastic attack!"[27]

In the home of Colonel and Mrs. Leard, two members were up early. Mrs. Jeane King, Mrs. Leard's mother, had given her grandson, 6-year-old Bob, his breakfast. Bob was something truly special in the Leard household, "a beautiful youngster" born to the Leards after fifteen years of marriage. Suddenly the house began to shake and the windows rattle, all of which frightened Bob into scrambling into his father's bed.

The Leards got up hastily and went out in the yard. Planes were flying around extremely low, and they could hear the rat-tat-tat of machine guns. "This is a hell of a time for the air force to be putting on a maneuver," Leard complained to his wife. "And they have even gone to the extreme of camouflaging their planes!" He added, "I think those are machine guns in the alley behind the house." Whereupon he went to investigate.

Just as he returned, a young lieutenant came running down the street, calling, "Colonel, this is the real thing! You better get your things and get going." At that moment, a Japanese plane flew dangerously low between Leard's house and the one next door, the goggled pilot leaning out of the open cockpit. Suddenly this plane shot upward, cutting a branch off the top of a palm tree.

As Leard took off for his office, he said to his wife, "You better get dressed, ole lady. If I don't see you again, you have been a delightful companion."[28]

Moody, a majestic white cat, the pet of Lt. Col. Allen F. "Skinny" Haynes's household, slept at the foot of the colonel's bed that morning when a boom resounded. Moody shot up in the classic arched-back posture of a Halloween cat, every hair at attention, his tail the size of a brush. "He looked like the caricature of a cat," recalled Mrs. Haynes. She gazed at him in astonishment. She assumed the noise came from a gun on the post announcing reveille, and Moody usually took post sounds in stride. A second thunderous explosion shook the house, and Moody disappeared in a streak of white.

"What do two reveille guns mean, an extra special alert?" Mrs. Haynes asked her husband.

"I don't know," he replied uneasily, "but I think I had better find out."

Then came the sound of planes; perhaps the Navy was having maneuvers. At that moment, their 12-year-old son popped in. "Jimmy, go out and see what this is all about," his mother requested.

Jimmy ran outside and flashed back. "Mother, those are Japanese planes," he shouted.

"Nonsense, they couldn't be," she scoffed.

His parents followed Jimmy back outside to see for themselves, stopping between two tall pines on each side of the front walk. Pine needles showered down, and for a fleeting moment they entertained the grotesque notion that firecrackers were exploding in the tree. When they discovered that machine-gun bullets were zinging through the branches, they scurried back into the house, still incredulous. "I wasn't frightened," said Mrs. Haynes. "It was so very interesting, I wondered what was going to happen next."[29]

Haynes dressed quickly and rushed to Headquarters of the 25th Division for which he served as G-2. Headquarters wanted more information about the attack, as well as current instructions, so Haynes drove to Shafter to get the word from Short or someone on his staff. As he and his driver moved down Kamehameha Highway, a bomb struck a car behind them and blew it up. They also saw the *Oklahoma* capsize.

When Haynes reached Shafter, he saw Short "running up and down one of the streets like a chicken with its head cut off." Haynes learned that the general's staff considered the situation serious and that Short had ordered a full alert with all that it implied. Throckmorton wanted him to remain for a while, but Haynes was eager to get back to his Division Headquarters.

After briefing General Murray, Haynes hurried home to check on his family. "I still think this is one of General Short's little pranks," Mrs. Haynes observed skeptically. But he gave her the true picture and suggested that she go to the home of a friend at Haleiwa, where thick trees would provide some protection.[30]

Nothing was going on at the Information Center as Lieutenant Tyler's tour of duty approached its end, so at about 0750 he stepped outside. "I got a breath of fresh air, and I actually saw the planes coming down on Pearl Harbor; but even then, I thought they were Navy planes; and I saw antiaircraft shooting, which I thought was practicing antiaircraft." Shortly after 0800, Sgt. Eugene Starry telephoned from Wheeler Field that the base was under attack. Tyler immediately directed Private McDonald to call the Control Center men back to duty.[31]

On their way back to Kawailoa from Opana, Lockard and Elliott, the two privates who had logged in Fuchida's first wave, were mildly surprised to encounter a truck similar to theirs carrying some of their colleagues with full field equipment. The truck was "going very fast back toward the unit." The driver of the outgoing truck blew his horn and slowed down, wanting to ask the other driver why they were going back, but "they simply blew their horn and went on very fast." Lockard and Elliott "thought something was queer" but had no idea what.[32]

Passing on, they "noticed all this black oil smoke in the sky." They knew it came from the harbor and "thought there might have been some sort of an accident or a fire." At Kawailoa they found out about the attack and promptly connected it with the sighting they had picked up and recorded.[33]

They turned their tracking record over to 2d Lt. John Upson, who commanded the two platoons at the camp. There was no time for breakfast; they had to pack their field bags and return to Opana.[34]

Lt. Stephen G. Salzman, communications officer of the 98th Coast Artillery at Schofield, was in bed when he heard aircraft passing over his quarters. Although not an airman, he had long been interested in the air arm, and these "didn't sound like American planes." So he threw a towel around himself and went outside. Recognizing the aircraft as Japanese, he ran to the switchboard in an unsuccessful attempt to reach the commanding officer. "Just about that time they opened up over Wheeler Field."

Salzman shouted to some nearby officers that this was an attack. He "threw on a pair of coveralls and a pistol" and ran to the regimental barracks area, where he found the men already drawing ammunition. Picking up some pistol ball, he alerted the drivers at the motor pool and then headed for the regimental communications shop.[35]

Sgt. Lowell V. Klatt, in charge of wire communications for the First Battalion of the Ninety-eighth, was having breakfast when he heard planes coming in over Kolekole Pass right over the mess hall. The men paid little attention, "figuring it was some of either Wheeler Field or Hickam Field planes that were out on maneuver or something like that." Then the men heard concussions and machine-gun fire in the vicinity of Wheeler. Klatt testified:

...at that, why, we all ran out and stood out around the yard watching to see what happened. At first we didn't know just what to expect, and as we saw smoke and flame coming up from Wheeler Field and as these planes would tear over the barracks, why, we would see them cut loose with their machine guns, and numerous places there was splinters flying....[36]

Klatt instructed his detail "to get their packs, get the trucks down and be ready to take off." While they were thus engaged, they received instructions from Salzman to go to the battalion command post and set up communications. Klatt supervised the loading of his truck and drove it with his men aboard to the command post, about 3½ miles away on the other side of Wahiawa. On the way, he related, "we passed Hickam Field and we could see that it was all in flames, and we could see these planes diving down and concussion of bombs, and so forth, and so it looked very real to us." Very shortly after they reached the command post, Salzman joined them, saying, "It's the real thing, boys."[37]

The men were busy establishing communications when, at about 0825, Salzman heard "what sounded like two planes pulling out of a dive over Kam Highway." Grabbing a Browning automatic rifle from one of the men nearby and "a couple of clips of ammunition," he ran outside, Klatt behind him. Klatt, too, snatched up a BAR. Both men dropped to their knees "to study the planes and make sure there were no friendly pursuits in the air." At that moment, one of the Japanese planes opened up with its machine guns. The attackers peeled off, one to the right, the other to the left, to avoid a high tension line, and as they did so, the two Americans "cut loose with the Browning automatics." Salzman was "too mad to be scared," and Klatt was sufficiently coolheaded to remember the action in detail. Within "two seconds at the most," they heard "this crash and a blast." They had shot down the second plane, the one that had swung to the left. The first pilot, heading right, pulled away so fast that he avoided danger.[38]

Salzman and Klatt could not see the crash, because the plane went down around the corner of the building. They ran to investigate but could not approach very near because "the heat was terrific" from the burning plane and spilled gasoline. After the plane had burnt itself out, they examined the wreck. Discovering that the engine was of American manufacture, for a hideous moment Salzman thought he "had made a mistake" and worried until later Air Corps Intelligence determined that the aircraft was indeed Japanese. Klatt believed that the two Japanese in the plane had been killed instantly, for their badly burned bodies "were just all crashed down in the cockpit."[39]

It was one of the communications anomalies of that morning that Lt. Charles Davis, from his temporary duty post under the Honolulu stadium, had no difficulty in reaching his wife, Joan, at their Schofield quarters. Under normal conditions, 5 or even 10 minutes were necessary to reach any of the military establishments from Honolulu, yet on this of all days not more than 30 seconds elapsed before he heard her voice and could tell her, "The Japanese are attacking Pearl Harbor." The individual who alerted Davis—he never knew who it was—had said, "The Japanese are attacking Wheeler Field." But the stadium stood on high ground, and from the track, Davis could see for himself the smoke and black bursts of AA fire from Pearl Harbor. Joan Davis, of course, had heard planes overhead but assumed Wheeler Field was conducting maneuvers until she saw the Rising Suns.

"I'm OK," Davis continued, "but I don't know when I'll see you again. Go next door...until someone takes care of you."

Mrs. Davis was frightened, but managed to conceal this fact from her husband. Pulling a heavy coat over her house robe, for the air seemed chilly to her, she followed Davis's advice and went to the home of Lt. Col. Peter Salgado, where she stayed until the attack was over.

Shortly after his call to her, Davis moved with his battalion command post to Fort Shafter. "One could feel the tension and astonishment in the air," he remembered, "but there was neither chaos nor panic."[40]

At Camp Malakole at Barber's Point, Lt. Willis T. Lynam of the 251st Coast Artillery was preparing to accompany his captain to church—"they were going to dedicate our chapel"—when he took a telephone call from the wife of another lieutenant, who was absent. She told him "that there was a lot of noise, and she said a lot of big black things [were] dropping around the place up there at Wahiawa, which is near Schofield Barracks. We could hear the sound of explosions."

Lynam assured her that "it was just a practice bombing on the north side of the island by the air corps." She hung up; Lynam stepped outside, "looked toward Pearl Harbor, and saw bursts of high explosive in the air." At the same time, three aircraft circled low toward the camp. Rushing back indoors for his glasses, Lynam recognized them as Japanese. At the battalion executive's order, he alerted the battalion, ran to the battery, "and went to work."[41]

This he did to such good purpose that his machine gunners shot down one plane definitely. Another, "a question mark...seemed to have some trouble getting away." The claimed kill had dipped to about 75 feet at its lowest point; "it was almost pointblank range both ways," Lynam testified. Struck near "the junction of the wing and the fuselage... the plane made a climbing turn to the left and wheeled out and kept dipping down...and struck the water some distance out."[42]

Sgt. June Dickens, who on Saturday had warned Japanese swimmers away from Malakole,* stepped off the guardhouse porch in time to see this action. The two Japanese planes "were going directly down California Street in Malakole....They seemed to have picked out the ammunition dump as their target." The stricken aircraft "banked down and went into the ocean."

Dickens also spotted a four-engine bomber and "couldn't quite make out what it was," so he decided not to fire on it. As he prudently observed, "If you don't know what the plane is, you don't want to shoot at it; it might be your own."[43] Which, in this case, it undoubtedly was.

The sound of aircraft engines at about 0745 did not bother Col. William J. McCarthy, who commanded the First Battalion, 55th Coast Artillery at Fort Kamehameha. Planes in and out of Hickam habitually flew over his quarters, but now "the bombing and explosion and the tat-tat-tat of machine guns" aroused his curiosity. "My first reaction was that this is a funny time for the Air Corps to start trouble. I got out just in time to see a single-seater Japanese plane flying over my quarters." He had no trouble identifying it: "There was the insignia, the red ball, and his two machine guns were both going."

The telephone operator could not enlighten him as to what was taking place, but obviously the situation called for action. He drove off to alert the batteries.[44]

One of those he contacted was Battery B, but its commanding officer, Capt. Frank W. Ebey, had anticipated him. Ebey was sitting on his lanai reading Stephen Vincent Benét's *John Brown's Body*. He had just reached "the surprise at Shiloh Church" when, in his words,

---

* See Chapter 4.

...I first heard this commotion. I thought it was a Navy plane, but we were on an anti-sabotage alert, so I got my gun and went up to the battery. I did not think we were being attacked. I just stayed there, and the first indication was a plane dove at me, letting go machine guns at me, and I saw dive bombers coming down on Pearl Harbor, and I knew what it was.

Naturally, he was "sort of stunned," but he lost no time in ordering the machine guns moved from the supply room to the tennis court behind his quarters. The supply sergeant was already there with some ammunition, and they opened fire. Ebey was sure of the time, for he checked his watch—it was 0813.[45]

Several civilian engineers were taking inventory at the Fort Kamehameha Base Yard, for they were scheduled to take over the yard shortly for their own operations. Hearing "quite heavy aviation noises," Albert L. Brenckman "looked up and saw these green planes with torpedoes under them, flying very low and circling out toward Pearl Harbor." At the first explosion, he "jumped in the nearest ditch and stayed there during the first strafing." He candidly admitted that this "seemed like hours," but probably it was about fifteen minutes.[46]

His colleague, Edwin St. J. Griffith, "saw a plane coming in a westerly direction about 100 feet or possibly more above us, which swooped down and machine gunned the place while it was in flight, and then swung around." Despite the bullets, the men decided this must be some sort of military maneuver; then they saw another plane drop a bomb on Hickam Field and recognized the attackers as Japanese.

In a wild burst of normality, the official in charge of the inventory asked Griffith to call their immediate boss, George A. Sisson, "and ask him...whether he wanted us to continue in this inventory." After attempting to contact first Sisson and then Col. Bernard E. Robinson, Griffith finally reached Colonel Theodore J. Wyman, Jr., who said, "Use your own judgment."[47]

Charles Utterback summed up reaction that morning in grim testimony to the Roberts Commission: "The only thing I heard that morning, sir, was 'They caught them asleep, by God.'...I think I heard that comment 50 times that day."[48]

Daniels, the Hawaiian-born private, remembered the events at Kamehameha very clearly. He was eating breakfast with the rest of his outfit in the mess hall and "thinking about getting ready for church...

when all of a sudden the thundering roar of a zooming plane and the ear-splitting noise of machine-gun fire shook us from our serenity.... We looked at each other with startled expressions on our faces and then we all seemed to jump up together and scramble outside, curious to see what was going on."

Someone shouted that the plane that had strafed had the Rising Sun on its wings. Daniels thought the man was joking; "this must be some sort of maneuvers." Then the air-raid siren sounded and cut off abruptly. Later Daniels noted that the clock on the administration building had stopped at 0755, and someone said that the electricity had been shut off.[49]

Orders came quickly to get their rifles and equipment, secure ammunition from the supply sergeant, and report to their gun positions. Only one clip apiece was available for the rifles. "By this time the sky was becoming full of black puffs of smoke from antiaircraft guns. Then a huge cloud of black smoke came rolling in from Pearl Harbor and there were planes all over."

The men ran up the company street, where someone ordered them to evacuate women and children from the officers' quarters and take them to a bunker for shelter.

> Some women were afraid to come outside. Others wanted to wait for their husbands to come and get them. Still others were slightly hysterical or perhaps a little panicky and were worried more about their children than themselves. I remember one young mother running while trying to shelter two small heads, one in each arm, crying, "My poor babies, my poor babies!"

The men cleared the houses, put the women and children in an underground shelter, and at the same time "took care of the civilian workers on the post. Most of these were Japanese and were put under guard."[50]

The gun position Daniels and his colleagues manned was Battery C, equipped with 12-inch mortars, located adjacent to the channel at the end of the Hickam runway. When they reached their position, they found "that no one had the keys to the ammunition storage. All we could do was to fire at the strafing planes with our one clip of ammunition in our rifles, while waiting for someone to get the keys." These were found about 15 minutes later, and the men could set up their machine guns.

An incendiary bomb landed near them, "and the flames seemed to go a hundred feet in the air." A sergeant crawled over to a couple of men who were not taking adequate cover, warning them to look out for shrapnel. "There was an embankment right in back of us which was part of the gun bunker. Someone picked up some fragments that hit there and showed them how close they were coming. Everyone was more cautious after that."[51]

Col. Eugene B. Walker, in command of Kamehameha and other harbor defense installations, attempted a novel form of camouflage. At the east side of Kamehameha was a huge acreage of barren red clay soil. On a windy day a mild storm of red dust would fill the air. Sisal had been planted in an attempt to dispose of this nuisance. But on the morning of December 7, Walker ordered vehicles to run over the sisal and stir up as much dust as possible to camouflage the fort and Hickam with a dust storm. Daniels thought this could have been effective had the wind been stronger. "As it was, there was just enough red dust in the air to make us more miserable. By the next morning we looked like a bunch of red-faced Indians."

Real war had come to little, showcase Fort Kamehameha, and suddenly everyday life became precious. Daniels thought of his family and how much he would like to see them just once again. And he "would like the opportunity to go to church just once more."[52]

PART 5

"A Tragic Hour"

December 7, 1941

(0835–0855)
The Lull between Waves

CHAPTER 19

"A Heart-Breaking Scene"

"The lull"—this is what eyewitnesses, almost unanimously, called the period of roughly half an hour between the end of the first-wave attack and the beginning of the second-wave attack. It was a lull only in the sense that no bombs were falling, no machine guns were strafing. Otherwise, few moments of the day encompassed more activity.

Officers and men continued to struggle toward their duty stations. Among them was Kimmel's flag secretary, Lt. Cmdr. Paul C. Crosley, who with his wife, Betty, lived in northeast Honolulu a little farther out than most officer families. He was about to pull on his boots for his usual Sunday morning horseback ride when Headquarters phoned him about the attack.[1] Immediately, he called Layton that he would pick him up. Layton had barely hung up from his own first notification, at which his initial reaction was, "Jesus! We were sure looking in the wrong direction!"[2]

When Crosley's Cadillac pulled up at Layton's quarters, Betty Crosley, a skillful driver, was at the wheel. She sped her passengers at 60 miles per hour on a back road to Pearl Harbor. All three were silent. "We weren't talking about anything," said Crosley in retrospect. "I just wanted to get there." In the distance they could see the Japanese planes dipping down and great billows of smoke.

Somewhere along the way a motorcycle policeman gave them an escort, and Mrs. Crosley "covered the fifteen miles in ten minutes." Near Pearl Harbor, traffic had snarled into a huge jam, but without pause she whipped the car off the road and sped around the jam and on her way. As she brought the car to a halt, her husband ran into

Headquarters.[3] A few days before, he had watched Kimmel walk up to a chart in his office and say in effect, "I wonder what those rascals are up to now?"[4] Today he and his staff knew the answer.

The first wave had passed when Layton, hastening to his office, encountered Captain Kitts, who at lunch on December 6 had greeted Layton with a quip about "his Saturday crisis."* Now he hailed Layton generously: "Here's the young man we should have listened to."

McMorris, too, observed graciously, if grimly, "If it's any satisfaction to you, you were right and we were wrong."[5] Layton could take no satisfaction in his vindication. "There was an air of complete and utter shock about the place," Layton recalled. "It was like you had had a bad dream and woke up in the middle of it saying that it was just a bad dream. Only it was not. It was true. The dream was bad. And everyone was having it right then and there."

In his office, where his yeoman had commenced logging data, Layton's principal objective was to gather all the information possible about the Japanese carrier force. But even Rochefort at Combat Intelligence, whom Layton phoned, could not help in that respect.[6]

Despite his "premonition that something was wrong,†" Rochefort was as surprised as anyone else when cryptanalyst Lt. Thomas H. "Tommy" Dyer phoned to tell him, "We're under attack."

"Are you kidding or not?" Rochefort asked suspiciously. At Dyer's emphatic "No!" Rochefort hurried to his office in the basement of the Fourteenth Naval District's administration building. His men had lost all communications and could not trace the Japanese immediately, but all concerned did the best they could with their usual efficiency. "The idea was, let's get organized and get the war on."[7]

Captain Davis clung to his telephone, trying to locate the enemy carriers; however, at the back of his mind nagged a suspicion that it would be just as well if he did not succeed. As a career air officer, he had little doubt that the Japanese "would have hammered the hell out of our surface ships without adequate air cover."

He felt exceedingly sorry for Kimmel, who, he recalled, "was just numb. He kept sitting around, staring glass-eyed into space."[8] To Lieutenant East, however, Kimmel seemed "very haggard and pale, but relatively calm."

---

* See Chapter 2.

† See Chapter 9.

What momentarily staggered East was the sight of one of his colleagues in communications, a big Naval Reserve ensign, "freshly caught and brand new,...pulled out of college somewhere," reading the Sunday comics. He had only been in position for a few days. Catching East's eye, he asked, apparently in all seriousness, "Is it always like this on Sunday morning?"[9]

The officers and men stationed at the Marine barracks, Navy Yard Pearl Harbor, charged with perimeter defense, had their own communications problems trying to contact outlying sentry posts. Vibrations from explosions interrupted service at the Navy Yard switchboard, and, of course, it seemed quite likely that the sentries were ignoring their phones in favor of firing at the enemy.

The attack forced an immediate and complete change of orientation on the Marines, whose plans and preparations were basically to counter "a commando type of attack mounted against the Navy Yard by a hostile formation already ashore." Defense against air attack was purely incidental. Local terrain made perimeter defense relatively simple, except at the gates, where ornamental concrete gatehouses had been erected to help conceal open machine-gun emplacements. Crews to man these guns came principally from the Marine "A" Company, others from the post band, although the usual battle assignment for bandsmen was as litter bearers.[10]

Changing of the guard was taking place when the sergeant of the outgoing guard, who had served in Shanghai, said to the OD, "Sir, those are Japanese war planes."

"By God you're right!" exclaimed the OD. "Music, sound 'Call to Arms'!" At the sound of the bugle, with no formal command, the Marines in guard formation began to fire their rifles.[11]

Lt. Col. William J. Whaling was sharing a room with Maj. James Monaghan in a friend's nearby quarters. "Jerry, don't you think the Admiral is a little bit inconsiderate of guests?" he asked quizzically when the noise awakened him. Seeing smoke through the window, he added, "This thing is so real that I believe that's an oil tank burning right out in front there."* Dressing and hurrying outside, in front of the Marine barracks he found Col. Elmer Hall. "Elmer, this is a mighty fine show you are putting on," he remarked admiringly. "I have never seen anything like it."

---

* Later he discovered that the "oil tank" was the *Arizona*.

"It's so fine and real," snapped Hall, "that, look at those Japs...."[12]

Still thinking in terms of their basic war plan, Marine officers and senior NCOs fanned out to discover "what was going on in the security system and whether anything like a ground attack was apparent."[13]

Admiral Calhoun, in charge of Shore Patrol, among his other duties, reached the main gate at Pearl Harbor at about 0825:

> It was necessary to clear a way for me as traffic conditions were quite crowded. On one or two occasions I had to get out of one car and into another car and I passed many officers and men returning to their ships. Realizing the importance of getting these men off promptly to their commands, I stopped long enough to talk to the beach guard and patrol officer on the dock and saw that both were being efficiently and properly handled and the people were readily and rapidly being returned to their ships.[14]

Those he saw were "awed and somewhat surprised by the events of the morning, but they were all a well-behaved, very sober group of officers and men, who had only one desire and that was to return to a ship in which they could render service."

Many years before, Calhoun had commanded the destroyer *Young*, which had been wrecked. Now, as he made his way toward 1010 Dock, he remembered how West Coast newspapers "had commented on drunkenness and published cartoons of drunken men and officers" in connection with that disaster. So as soon as he reached his flagship, the *Argonne*, at about 0845, he dispatched his flag secretary, Lt. E. P. "Bud" Southwick, and his flag lieutenant, Lt. Harry Johnson, "to go to the various landings and in the yard and circulate among the men with exactly the idea of seeing what was their conduct." They as well as the beach guard officer on duty at the Fleet landing reported "that the conduct of all hands was excellent."[15]

Calhoun's chief of staff, Cmdr. Allen G. Quynn, lived with his wife in the Pleasanton Hotel in downtown Honolulu, for their son and two daughters were at school on the mainland. When the bed began to shake that morning, Mrs. Quynn suggested, "Maybe there's an earthquake."

"You're always thinking the worst about things." With that, her husband dismissed her notion. But the shaking continued, and the phone rang. The force's medical officer, Dr. W. H. "Babe" Michael, had called to ask, "Do you have your radio on?" At Quynn's negative, he added, "Well, you had better turn it on, because Pearl Harbor is under attack."

After confirming this with the radio, Quynn gulped a cup of coffee, and Lt. Cmdr. Thomas Fowler, in command of a minesweeper, picked him up. When they reached 1010 Dock, "the harbor was a mass of fuel oil, smoke and flames." Looking down the dock, he saw the *Oglala* heeling.[16]

This list had reached about 5°. The engine room was flooding, however, and the waters were "spreading aft rapidly. In the absence of pumping facilities, ship could not remain afloat much longer." So it was decided to tow her astern of the *Helena* to prevent further listing and "to clear the range" for the *Helena*'s guns.[17]

Captain Bruns had instructed his family to stay in the house, but after gathering together to say the rosary, they no longer took orders literally. Soon the two boys went down to the docks to offer their services. From time to time, Kathleen Cooper ventured into the back yard—the scene of her wedding in August. Once, she saw a seaman clad in blue dungarees with a rifle across his back. He looked not a day over 18, "frightened to death" and "shaking all over." Mrs. Cooper felt so sorry for him that she invited him into the house to keep him out of danger and to give him a chance to pull himself together. Even as she did so, she worried a little, lest taking a man from his duty station might be considered a form of treason.

Shortly thereafter, Bruns snatched a moment to come home and tell his family what had happened. "Most of our ships in the harbor have been hit and are down," he said. With that, he wept in frustration. Kathleen had never seen her father cry before. The sight made her "absolutely desolate," and she could only hug him in voiceless sympathy.[18]

Certainly Pearl Harbor and its adjacent area presented a sight to wring a much harder heart than Bruns's. Much of the activity centered at 1010 Dock, where many wounded managed to swim ashore, some burned, some shot, all bleeding and in pain.[19] Chief Rafsky, Calhoun's enlisted aide, had been waiting at the commandant's boat house to go on duty when the attack struck. Commandeering a car, he sped to the Waikiki section to round up staff members. Among those he brought to the *Argonne* was Dr. Michael, who changed into

---

* See Chapter 11.

his uniform and came back to the dock, where he organized a working party to handle the wounded. He set the Base Force Band to its wartime mission of stretcher-bearing. They carried many wounded men aboard the *Argonne*, where Dr. Michael used the warrant officers' mess as an emergency operating room. In addition, many, with all or part of their uniforms blown or burned off, boarded the *Argonne* in search of clothing.[20]

Many small craft darted to and fro, hauling survivors out of the water. Two brothers from the *West Virginia*, "Red" and "Chippy" Woods, ran a motor launch between the dangerous, oil-covered waters around the ships, bringing men to 1010 Dock. "Had it not been for some of the men who got these small boats and started to rescue people, a lot more boys would be resting now on Red Hill," said Rafsky. At the dock, Lieutenant Southwick organized a retrieving party to take these men to the *Argonne* or the Naval Hospital, using any available vehicle, even dump trucks.[21]

Meanwhile, heavy reverse traffic was going on, as officers and men crowded the dock attempting to reach their duty stations. Some, too impatient to wait for a launch, jumped into the harbor and swam to their ships.[22]

Gordon Chung-Hoon, star Annapolis halfback of a few years past, found that he could not carry the ball for the Navy on this occasion. He and others assigned to the *Arizona* could not get to the stricken battleship, "because she was in flames, there was burning oil all around her and people were trying to get off."[23]

Fuqua had commenced rescue operations aboard the *Arizona* while the first attack was still on. "With the assistance of a rescue boat from the U.S.S. *Solace*, approximately 100 men who were burned and wounded were transferred to Ford Island."[24] Ens. W. J. Bush and several others from the *Arizona* "got three boats clear of the oil fire on the water and picked up the men in the water who had jumped to get clear of the fire. We took several boatloads of badly burned and injured men to Ford landing and continued picking up men in the water between ship and the shore. I took a boat alongside...[the] *Arizona* and waited until everyone gathered at the stern had been taken off."[25]

The *Vestal*'s crew fished a number of refugees from the *Arizona* out of the water. "Those boys were covered with oil from head to foot and most of them were burned so badly you could take your hand, start at their forehead and end at their toes and fold their hide back like you were peeling an orange," Hesser related, shuddering at the recollection more than twenty years later. Each *Arizona* survivor aboard the *Vestal* received a shot of morphine and a mark on his forehead to tell the doctors that the shot had been given. Then they were transferred to a hospital or to the *Solace* as rapidly as possible.[26]

As Major Shapley from the *Arizona* wandered about Ford Island, his clothes blown off, a Navy wife of his acquaintance, trying in a distracted way to be helpful, gave him a red scarf about two feet long and a foot wide, and a jar of Heinz pickles. Armed with this unlikely emergency gear, Shapley headed toward the airfield in search of a machine gun. A CPO spotted him and called out, "Hey, come here, Major." He escorted Shapley to a nearby building, gave him some clothes, a full glass of whiskey, and sent him to a dugout. After the whiskey, Shapley lost track of the scarf and pickles.[27]

Those from the *Arizona* who, like Seaman Osborne, had escaped with little or no injury helped the wounded to the quay and into launches to take them to Ford Island. "I can always remember the smell and the feel of burned flesh sticking to my hands and arms from handling the burned men," Osborne wrote. "We put the wounded into pickup trucks that were at hand to take them to medical aid."

Their missions accomplished, Osborne and his comrades went to the basement of a nearby house, where women and even children were caring for minor injuries. Osborne had only a small cut on his hand, "caused by some flying object," and the hair on his head, arms, and legs was singed. But he was completely covered "with oil, blood, burned flesh and water." A little later he received some clothes brought from one of the officers' homes nearby.[28]

All of Commander Coe's personal clothing, as well as that of his wife and children, went thus to those who had lost their own in the attack. "Much of our clothing was simply used to swab oil off the people who managed to crawl out of Pearl Harbor's waters."[29]

Casualties almost swamped Lieutenant Riggs, Patrol Wing Two's staff medical officer, who converted the Marine barracks and the main mess hall into emergency hospitals. In the space of an hour and a half, they treated some 300 men suffering from a wide variety of wounds as well as traumatic shock. Fortunately, Riggs had plenty of supplies, and a few ships' doctors, unable to reach their posts, offered their services.

Since May, Riggs had trained his corpsmen in double-time work, and this paid off as the men went about their tasks with swift efficiency. Many of the men who brought in wounded wanted to stay and help, but they had to return to their ships. "They showed no particular fear other than normal anxiety. There was no panic at all," Riggs remembered.

Ambulances plied between his makeshift hospital and the ships or hangar areas. A car hit one of these ambulances carrying about ten ambulatory patients, knocking it over on its side. Some twenty sailors nearby set it back on its wheels, and off it went again for Riggs's location. When the ambulance pulled up, its engine had lost all its water. "You must use sea water," Riggs told its corpsmen. "We need the fresh water."[30]

Mrs. Riggs arrived at Ford Island's new BOQ, where she fell to work taking care of frightened women and children, as well as officers and men from the ships. Soon she was helping to conjure up, as if by magic, huge pots of steaming, nourishing soup.[31]

The hospital patio was full of patients, many beyond medical help. Commander Ramsey's 16-year-old daughter, Mary Ann, knelt beside first one man after another, recording names and murmuring a few soothing words. In many cases, she offered a cigarette and held the young man in her arms as he took a last drag, sighed, and slipped into death. Gently she laid the body back, covered it with a blanket, and went to comfort the next dying patient.[32]

Seaman Kamont never forgot the dreadful scenes at the mess hall and barracks:

> Men, women and children were crying. They were also bringing in the wounded that were pulled from the flaming bay. Some of these men looked beyond help, burned flesh and bone showing through the oily mess. Some of these men were half clothed, raw meat just hanging from their bones. Some cried like babies, babbling for their mother, father or loved ones. It was a sickening sight to be part of.[33]

Emerging from Ford Island's Central Control, Chief Forrow walked toward one of the hangars. Seeing many men milling around aimlessly, some burned, some oil-covered, some simply dazed, Forrow led them to a steel hangar and called the pharmacies to send medical aid. They responded in minutes and set up a first-aid station. A number of Marines congregated around the hangar asking what they could do, so Forrow had them collect the patients and bring them under cover. These men were moaning and mumbling incoherently. "It was a heart-breaking scene to have witnessed. There were probably 1000 men around there." One man wore skivvies and a captain's coat. "Captain, go over to the hangar where there is shelter," Forrow suggested. The man looked at him dazedly and answered, "I am no captain. I just found this coat." Recognizing that he was suffering from shock, Forrow led him into the hangar.[34]

At the Naval Hospital, Lt. Ruth Erickson scarcely noticed the lull in the attack. Doctors and nurses worked frantically around operating tables. Corpsmen ran up and down corridors carrying anything the emergency demanded. Ambulances wailed in and out; stretcher-bearers rushed in with load after bleeding load and then raced off for the next patients. Lt. Erickson could not sort out all of her impressions; it was like watching a movie reel speeded up to the point where the frames ran together into a featureless blur. One inescapable memory was the stench of burned flesh. "I can still smell it after thirty years and I think I always will," she said.

But there was pride amid the horror. "Hospital personnel who had not been too motivated by their daily routine in the past, rose to the challenge of that terrible emergency and performed miracles," she declared. "Some of the corpsmen one would not expect it of worked as though it was their last day on earth. The attack brought the very best out of them."[35]

CHAPTER 20

"What Is Going to Happen Next?"

On the *Antares'* bridge, Commander Grannis seethed with anger and frustration. The ship had two machine guns aboard, but neither could be elevated, so the officers and crew could do nothing about the Japanese fighters that strafed the *Antares'* deck. "I could hear the bullets zing and whine when they hit the steel of the ship," he remembered.

His young paymaster, always of a serious disposition and now "worried as all hell," did nothing to improve Grannis's temper. Strictly in accordance with Navy regulations, the paymaster bundled together all his government funds and all his accounts into a sealed bag. Fearing that the *Antares* would be sunk, he came up to the bridge to ask Grannis for permission to throw the container overboard. "No, hang on to the bag," replied Grannis. "We aren't sinking yet."

The young man disappeared below, only to emerge about 15 minutes later. "Don't you think I ought to throw the bag overboard now, Captain?" he asked anxiously.

Grannis's patience snapped. "Go away, and don't bother me again!" he snarled.[1]

Suddenly, out of the thick, black pall of smoke from Pearl Harbor burst what Grannis called "one of the most beautiful sights I ever saw": a destroyer making about 30 knots as it left the channel and hit the open sea. The water, bright in the early morning sunshine, piled high on each side of the destroyer in impressive bow waves. "It was a prideful moment," Grannis added, "for in spite of the Japanese advantages of surprise and superiority in the air, that destroyer came out like a bulldog ready to fight and every part of her spoke defiance."[2]

Almost certainly this was the *Helm*. At 0817, 4 minutes after passing the entrance-gate vessel, she sighted the conning tower of an enemy submarine on the starboard side of the channel entrance, northward of Buoy No. 1. The intruder promptly submerged, but the *Helm*, passing the entrance buoys at 0818, "increased speed to 25 knots, turned hard right toward enemy submarine," which had popped back up into sight again. The *Helm* experienced a temporary setback when she "lost steering control due to short circuiting of main contact relay." But she "shifted to hand steering" and opened fire on the submarine off Tripod Reef, where it "appeared to be touching bottom on ledge of reef and in line of breakers." The *Helm* scored no hits, and while still under fire, the submarine slipped off the ledge and submerged. The *Helm* proceeded on her way, "firing intermittently at enemy aircraft and searching for submarine."[3]

The target that escaped the *Helm* was the *I-24*'s minisub holding Sakamaki and Inagaki. Somehow, despite the inoperative gyroscope, Sakamaki had managed to guide his minisub this close to the target area, only to strike the reef three times while attempting to enter the channel. Peering through his periscope, he found an American destroyer only 50 meters distant. Although he could not identify her, undoubtedly this was the *Helm*. He could see her crewmen running to and fro on her deck. He was fairly sure that he could have torpedoed this destroyer, but he was gunning for bigger game than a mere destroyer. His orders specified that he enter Pearl Harbor and torpedo either a battleship or a carrier. His own target of choice was the U.S. Pacific Fleet's flagship, the *Pennsylvania*. Unaware that the *Pennsylvania* was in drydock, he planned to torpedo her or, if that failed, to ram her or at the least some other capital ship. Circumstances canceled this lofty ambition. Either the *Helm*'s attack or the midget's smashing against the reef destroyed one of the torpedo-firing mechanisms and knocked Sakamaki senseless.[4]

The *Helm* was the first ship to clear the harbor, but others were speeding preparations either to sortie or to defend themselves against whatever else might be in store. Aboard the submarine *Dolphin*, enlisted men carried ammunition to the guns and checked to see if anyone had been wounded. Lieutenant Finn asked himself, "Now, what is going to happen next?" The dismaying, if logical, reply seemed to be that the Japanese would bomb Kimmel's nearby Headquarters in an attempt to knock out with one stroke the admiral and all his key staff officers.[5]

Lt. H. G. "Steve" Corey had no thought except to reach the destroyer *Henley*, of which he was executive officer, as soon as possible. He had awakened to gunfire, seen the flames from Pearl Harbor, and flipped on the radio in time to hear the announcement: "All military personnel are under orders to return to their stations immediately." Incongruously, "the station dipped right back into music as if nothing was happening."

His skipper, Lt. Cmdr. Robert Hall Smith, who lived nearby, picked up Corey and they raced toward the Area Landing. They had arranged to keep their whaleboat at this locale, anticipating that in case of emergency, "there would be too much chaos" at the Fleet Landing. Smith pulled into a nearby parking lot and tossed his car keys to the attendant with a hurried, "Get them to my wife when you can."

As they ran toward the whaleboat, the Hawaiian woman who operated a hot-dog stand near the landing screamed, "Halt!" She brandished a rifle which she pointed at the two officers. Convincing her of their identity, they hurried on to the whaleboat. There the *Henley*'s engineer and the coxswain of the whaleboat awaited them. They all climbed in and looked across the bay. To their dismay, the *Henley* was steaming off. The officer of the deck, Lt. Francis E. Fleck, Jr., had gotten the destroyer under way at 0830.[6]

When the first wave winged away, Commander Stout of the *Breese* thought the Japanese had gone for good, but he kept the 4-inch-gun crews busy getting ammunition for the machine-gun crews. At 0825, the *Breese* received a signal to get under way, and officers and men worked hard to prepare to move. Soon, said Stout, "I was ready to haul tail but I couldn't." Since the *Breese* was "inside next," the skipper of the destroyer-minelayer *Ramsay*, Lt. Cmdr. G. L. Sims, objected to the *Breese*'s move. The *Ramsay* was moored to starboard nearby, and Sims feared that when the *Breese* pulled out she would set the *Ramsay* adrift. Since Sims ranked Stout, the latter had to keep his ship in position for the time being.[7]

The destroyer-minesweeper *Zane*, moored immediately south of the *Breese*, seems to have been the first to note that American ships were not alone in the harbor. Her log recorded at 0830, "Sighted enemy submarine 200 yards astern of U.S.S. *Medusa* at berth K-23."[8] Two minutes later, Kimmel's Headquarters alerted all ships present, "Japanese submarine in harbor."[9] The seaplane tender *Curtiss*, for one, did not need official word of the enemy's presence. At 0836, she sighted a periscope "on starboard quarter, distance 700 yards." She opened fire with her Nos. 2 and 3 guns and three machine guns.[10] Two minutes later, the repair ship *Medusa* observed the submarine firing a torpedo "south of berth X23." This was probably the torpedo that Captain Simons of the *Raleigh* reported as having "detonated near a pile driver at the Deperming Station without doing any damage." The *Medusa* brought her Nos. 5 and 6 guns to bear against the submarine.[11]

Simons saw the periscope off the *Raleigh*'s port quarter "on the far side of the channel leading to the Yacht Club and near the Deperming Station." The *Raleigh* "hoisted the submarine warning signal but did not shoot as some of our own ships were in the line of fire, and also because the ships in the immediate vicinity of the submarine were doing a good job on it."[12]

Since 0827, the ready-duty destroyer *Monaghan* had been under way, having been ordered to sea to support the *Ward*.[13] In any case, under the circumstances, Burford, the *Monaghan*'s skipper, "wanted to get out of that damn harbor as fast as possible." He had the *Monaghan* on a southwesterly course between Pearl City and Ford Island, when, at 0839, his signalman directed his attention to the *Curtiss*, which had signaled a submarine sighting.[14]

Thinking in terms of standard submarines, which were much too large to operate in Pearl Harbor's shallow water, Burford reacted with incredulity: "Well, *Curtiss* must be crazy," he scoffed.

"That may be, Captain," the signalman admitted, "but what is that down there?" He pointed off the starboard bow, and Burford saw what looked like "an over and under shotgun barrel" at about 1200 yards. "I don't know what the hell it is," he declared, "but it shouldn't be there." With that, he ordered flank speed to ram.[15]

Almost simultaneously, the intruder "commenced surfacing in damaged condition." The *Curtiss* claimed to have hit it "directly with both 5″ and .50 caliber shells."[16] The seaplane tender *Tangier* also spotted the submarine about 800 yards off her starboard bow and fired off six salvos from her No. 1 AA gun, but ceased fire "due to fouling of target by the *Monaghan*."[17]

"It was a hectic few minutes," Burford remembered. "We were pushing our boilers so hard it's a wonder we didn't wreck them. We violated every damn principle in the book."[18] The *Medusa*'s log described what happened next. The *Monaghan* "brushed its starboard side and bottom about amidships against the submarine's starboard topside and conning tower, shoving the submarine out of sight."[19] Somehow the victim managed to fire its second torpedo, which passed the *Monaghan* "about 50 yards on starboard beam."[20] It, too, detonated harmlessly against the shore.[21]

As the minisub passed under the *Monaghan*'s stern, the destroyer dropped "two depth charges which exploded at 30 feet depth." To put down "ash cans" in such shallow water risked blowing off the *Monaghan*'s stern, and in fact the explosions lifted it clear of the water. "But I had to depth charge close to my own ship under the circumstances if I were going to destroy that sub," Burford explained in retrospect.[22]

The surface fire and the depth charges had effectively finished this particular midget submarine. When the Americans raised it several days later, they discovered that a 5-inch shell had decapitated the captain and blown him "into a mass of crumpled steel."[23]

Such was the force of the *Monaghan*'s drive that after ramming and depth-charging the sub, she raced pell-mell toward a dredge with a large derrick aboard, moored on the west side of the channel. Burford hastily "backed engines emergency." The *Monaghan* slowed, but not enough to prevent striking the dredge and sustaining "slight damage to starboard plates forward above waterline at frame 38." This occurred at 0843. Burford backed his destroyer off, in the process running aground "in soft bottom on shoal off Beckoning Point." Within 2 minutes, however, he had backed the *Monaghan* clear of the shoal, and the destroyer proceeded on her way seaward.[24]

So did the nearby destroyer *Dale*, under way since 0837 with Ens. F. M. Radel in command. Radel had halted her while the *Monaghan* dropped the depth charges.[25]

At the precise moment that the *Monaghan* attacked the midget submarine, outside the harbor the *Ward* dropped two depth charges and continued the antisubmarine search with sound gear.[26] Outerbridge's destroyer may well have spotted Sakamaki's floundering minisub. Sakamaki claimed to have had several encounters with depth-charging destroyers that morning, but he was understandably vague about times.[27]

Another destroyer on her way out of harbor was the *Blue*, which got under way at 0847 with Ensign Asher in command.[28] "When we got abeam where the *Utah* had been torpedoed we noticed a lot of wood floating on the water," he recalled. He presumed that this came from the *Utah*'s topside after she capsized. "We stopped our engines so we would drift through it without causing any damage to our hold plating."[29]

All these events were out of the sight of those on the other side of Ford Island. One of these men, Gunner's Mate Beck of the *Oklahoma*, had been clinging to the pontoon of an overturned aircraft. After the plane sank, Beck swam around in circles until he spotted a whaleboat upside down in the water. He swam to it and hung on. He was almost at the end of his strength and feared that if anything happened to the whaleboat he might drown. "By this time I figured that I had already been given my chance," he remembered.[30]

His shipmate, French, had managed to work a boat loose from the *Oklahoma* and into the water. He entered the launch with about twenty men, of whom he was the senior. But the starter was dead and the engine would not respond. So with no motive power except the current, French guided the launch down channel. It drifted slowly just ahead of the burning oil atop the water. As the boat floated down to the gasoline dock, French made a bow-on landing. Everyone got out, and French tied up the boat. In a few minutes the fire came down channel and burned the boat to a crisp.

French and another enlisted man were standing beside the *Neosho* when one of the officers cried, "Cast off my lines." They did so, and the *Neosho* swung out into the channel.[31]*

Aboard the *Arizona*, Fuqua "made a thorough search of the after part of the ship, which was accessible for wounded and uninjured personnel." Then he directed that the *Vestal*'s forward lines be cut. He understood that her men "cut their own after lines."[32]

According to the *Vestal*'s log, this action began at 0830,[33] when the last Japanese planes were just pulling away. A lieutenant commander whose name Crawford could not recall but who "everyone thought was a damn screwball" proved himself a brave man by arming himself with an axe and cutting the lines connecting the *Vestal* to the *Arizona*.[34] A tug pulled her bow away from the wrecked battleship. Then the *Vestal* started to list to starboard; the shipfitter and blacksmith shops were filling with water.[35]

Another ship that required moving was the *Oglala*. "Extensive flooding of engineroom was reported," and while "the forward crews' bunkroom was dry...flooding was spreading aft rapidly." Moreover, the ship was listing some 5°. "In the absence of pumping facilities, ship could not remain afloat much longer." To prevent further listing, and to clear the range for the *Helena*'s guns, Admiral Furlong determined to move his flagship clear of the cruiser.[36]

---

* See Chapter 14.

He sent men to handle the *Oglala*'s lines. Looking across the channel, he saw, between the two ships and Ford Island, "a dredge with two small contractor's tugs." They were well within hail, and "by hallooing and motioning" he ordered the tugs to come alongside the *Oglala*. They pushed her astern of the *Helena* and secured her to the pier.[37]

Meanwhile, Ruff was preparing to move the *Nevada* out of the harbor. In the most favorable of circumstances, the sortie of a battleship from Pearl Harbor was a real undertaking, requiring 2 hours to build up steam, several tugs to nudge her into position, a specially trained civilian harbor pilot, an experienced, skillful captain, and a navigator. None of these requirements could be met at the moment, so Ruff did the best he could, with excellent cooperation from the two engine rooms and from the helmsman at the wheel, Chief Quartermaster Robert Sedberry.[38] In the last minute of the first wave, Chief Boatswain Edwin J. Hill directed the men who cast off the lines from the mooring quay. As the *Nevada* drifted loose, Hill swam to the ship.[39]

From his post in the conning tower, Ruff established two landmarks on Ford Island to help him navigate the *Nevada* into the main channel. Just before getting under way, he heard a voice crying out, "Let me in, let me in!" He opened both doors of the conning tower, but no one was there. Again came the shout, "Let me in!" Then Ruff discovered that the voice came from below. There was Thomas, who had climbed up the 80-foot tube from below. Ruff and his men removed the floor gratings, opened the hatch, let Thomas in, and briefed him thoroughly on what had taken place above while he was below.[40]

The *Nevada* was officially under way at 0840, with Thomas at the conn and Ruff acting as navigator in the conning tower. The starboard AA conveyor being out of commission above the main deck, men passed ammunition to the battery from the main deck by hand.[41]

As the *Nevada* crept past the *Arizona*, the intensity of the heat forced the *Nevada*'s gunmen to turn their backs and hug the shells close to their bodies lest the heat explode the missiles. Someone tossed a line to three survivors from the *Arizona* in the water nearby. They climbed aboard the *Nevada* and helped man one of her guns.

Seeing the *Arizona* in her dreadful condition was "a terrible shock" to Ruff. In spite of his absorbing duties, he could not help gazing at the fire-swept vessel and wondering about the fate of his many friends and Academy classmates aboard her.[42]

While the *Nevada* had some success, Lt. W. B. Pendleton, navigator of the minesweeper *Tern*, had no luck in his attempts to move his ship. She had been undergoing overhaul and upkeep prior to a scheduled trip to the mainland to pick up some barges and tow them back to Oahu. Some of her men went on deck to get water pumps; others cut hawser lines linking the *Tern* with the dock. "Everyone was hollering and yelling do this and do that, but they were all pitching in," recalled Baker 1st Class Emil Johnson. "No one shirked his duty." The fire room men got the boilers going, but the *Tern* did not get up enough steam to move for approximately an hour.

Johnson saw the *Nevada* slipping down channel and reflected, "Well, there's one that's going to get away." But he and his shipmates were too busy to pay much attention to what was happening elsewhere.[43]

Lt. Cmdr. Edward E. Berthold and Lt. Levi Knight, gunnery officer and chief engineer of the *West Virginia*, respectively, reached Pearl Harbor at about 0830 and caught a launch out to the battleship, which was sunk at the bow and on fire in several sections. Her ruptured fuel tanks were releasing oil that ignited on the surface, to the danger of swimmers and small boats. Beattie ordered Berthold to flood the forward magazines, lest the *West Virginia* suffer the fate of the *Arizona*. On reaching the second deck level, however, Berthold found it already flooded from port to amidships, blocking passage to the third deck. As Berthold returned to the main deck to report this to Beattie, he searched the smoke-filled compartments for wounded but found none.[44]

Lt. Cmdr. Doir Johnson, helping to evacuate the wounded, did not believe the *West Virginia* would be habitable much longer. "The ship was burning like a forest fire," he said. At first he could not determine exactly what was burning so fiercely, and then he realized it was the paint. "You see, we had a coat of paint an inch thick on this ship," he explained. "Instead of chipping it right down to the steel in the past, they painted one more coat right over the old one until it stood there an inch. And with the turpentine and the chemicals mixed into that paint it burned readily."

On the port side—the side facing the Pearl Harbor channel—the leaked oil was burning furiously. Oil had spilled also on the starboard side, next to the *Tennessee* and Ford Island, but it had not yet caught fire. This was the only avenue of escape, and Johnson feared it was only a matter of time before the starboard oil also ignited.[45]

CHAPTER 21

"We Wanted to Fight "

On Ford Island, officers and men strove to cannibalize planes and get them into the air to search for the Japanese carriers. Spare parts were in short supply, and the old paymaster in charge of them could not shake off the administrative practices of years. "I won't issue supplies without a signed receipt," he declared. Informed of this bottleneck, Admiral Bellinger, normally the most good-natured of men, lost his temper, rounded up a group of Marines, led them to supply, and ordered them, "Boys, take what you want."[1]

What Bellinger himself badly wanted was information as to where the first-wave attackers had gone so that he could notify Halsey, in the hope that the *Enterprise* task force could catch up with the raiders. Of course, Bellinger had no idea that this would be asking the *Enterprise* to take on six Japanese carriers. Coe tried to secure the necessary information from a direction finder on the other side of Oahu. "We just had to find out where the enemy was coming from and where he was at the time," said Coe. "But our communications were badly demoralized, also our combat forces." The direction finder showed that the Japanese were flying on a line running north and south, the supposition being that they had come from the north and were returning in that direction. However, the U.S. forces "simply were not in a position to retaliate."[2]

One of the Marines on Ford Island picked up a Japanese girl wandering about and brought her to Chief Forrow, asking "What shall I do with her?"

In no mood to give any Japanese the benefit of the doubt, Forrow replied, "Chain her to a tree."

"I maid, no spy!" protested the terrified girl. "Japanese, yes, but maid, no spy!"

"It makes no difference," declared Forrow. "Chain her to a tree so we know where she is."

"That's fine with me!" answered the Marine, and fastened her to a nearby eucalyptus.

Forrow went off to report this incident to his commanding officer, who followed Forrow back to inspect his catch. The CO recognized the frightened captive as the maid of a Navy family and ordered her released.

This matter settled, Forrow helped break out machine guns to be used against the next attack, which most on Oahu confidently expected.[3]

Over at Kaneohe, efforts concentrated on firefighting. Salvage operations were going so well that "Beauty" Martin allowed himself the hope that the hangar could be saved.[4]

Six aircraft from the *Enterprise* landed at Ewa, beginning around 0835. "They came down in the normal method of identification and procedure and came to our field," explained Ewa's commanding officer, Marine Lt. Col. Claude A. Larkin, "and we took them aboard." He ordered them up again as soon as possible, and they did not return to Ewa. To the best of Larkin's knowledge, they went to Ford Island.[5]

Alerted by the single aircraft* and a warning from Hickam, Bellows prepared for a possible resumption of the attack. "The ground defense noncommissioned officers reported the ground defense units to the armament storerooms where their weapons were located. The reserve of the main guard...assembled by the runway and deployed for antiaircraft fire."

About a hundred men were armed, the but machine gunners were not yet able to mount their weapons for AA fire.[6] Moreover, Bellows was authorized no ammunition, so men of the 298th Infantry, Hawaiian National Guard, had to go to "the crater" to secure ammunition belted for machine-gun fire "out of the 86th Squadron Reserve."[7]

---

* See Chapter 17.

When Welch and Taylor landed their P-40s at Wheeler, everyone's primary objective was dispersal of the field's aircraft, and the two fighter pilots encountered a little difficulty in obtaining the gas and .50 caliber ammunition they requested. "We had to argue with some of the ground crew," said Welch. "They wanted us to disperse the airplanes and we wanted to fight." They won the argument barely in time.[8]

Sergeant Hall found that one of Wheeler's AT-6s, parked next to the OA-9, was "still in a whole piece." He pulled it off the ramp with scarcely time to finish his task.[9]

After his brief encounter with Short,* Bicknell drove to his office in the Dillingham Building. He found his office personnel issuing small arms and ammunition. Robert Shivers of the FBI was there, "flabbergasted and scared all the way through." They decided to start rounding up Japanese suspects but had to delay putting this plan into operation, for they could not reach the provost marshal for trucks and guards.[10]

Capt. Wesley C. Wilson, executive officer of the Eleventh Tank Company at Schofield, later estimated, "It took me an hour and a half to realize that fighting was going on and I was right in the middle of it....I had the impression that the United States was so big and strong that no one would dare to attack it."[11] He was still in this somewhat bemused state when, at about 0845, he reported to Short. "He made the impression of a man who had a great load of responsibilities suddenly thrust upon him," Wilson remembered. In a calm, quiet voice he told Wilson that the operating sections had gone to the tunnel and he was to report there. So Wilson did so, at the back of his mind the uneasy suspicion that the Japanese were already on the beaches.[12]

Most of Short's staff went to the Advance Headquarters. His chief of staff, G-1, and adjutant general remained at Fort Shafter. "None of us were running around wringing our hands," recalled Throckmorton. "We had too much to do."[13]

"Retired Army officers living in Oahu called in constantly offering their services," said Dunlop, "and we needed help so I took many of them on."[14]

At the Hawaiian Air Depot on Hickam Field, "all officers reported at Headquarters to assist in fire fighting, salvaging material, and to help in any other way possible. Approximately 100 civilian employees reported for duty after the first raid."[15]

---

* See Chapter 18.

Lieutenant Reeves was disproportionately concerned about his beloved new Studebaker, a two-toned job to match his uniform. He moved it next to a bomb crater on the principle that lightning would not strike twice in the same place. His buddies yelled to him to "leave that damn car alone" and take shelter.

They all decided they had better get to the hangar area. As they approached, a middle-aged colonel shouted at Reeves, "Do something, Lieutenant! Do something!"

"What should I do?" countered Reeves.

"I don't know," the colonel retorted, "but do *something!*"

This exchange somewhat shook Reeves's faith in his senior officers.[16]

Leaving his B-17, Major Landon found much confusion at all levels of command. When he went to Headquarters, Hawaiian Air Force, to inform the staff of the direction from which he thought the Japanese aircraft had come, he was disappointed at the lack of interest shown in receiving such information. Nearly everyone was preoccupied fitting liners into their steel helmets. In Landon's opinion, they should have been expending every effort toward locating and attacking the Japanese carriers.[17]

It is possible that these men had just received Short's order to place in effect Alert No. 3, which postulated an all-out attempt to take Oahu. According to General Wilson, Schofield received the alert order at about 0850.[18]

In any case, some at Hickam were thinking in terms of counterattack, notably Captain Allen, who was still trying to persuade the balky No. 1 engine of his B-17 to turn over when the first-wave attack ended. "I observed ammunition bomb trucks being pulled out of the ammunition storage area loaded with bombs," he explained. "The thought occurred to me to try to load the bombs so I could attack any enemy ships in the vicinity." Allen and his men had taken aboard three or four bombs before the Japanese came back.[19]

Allen had seen the two trailers that Sergeant Heydt supervised loading at the bomb dump. Heydt pushed the driver off one of the trucks and drove it himself to the flight line. The sight there appalled him: "busted fuselages, wings dropping on the ground, tires flat, engines falling out of the wings." He could not recall seeing a single B-17 in condition to take the 600-pound bombs that his two tractors were hauling.

Momentarily at a loss, Heydt reflected, "I wish there was someone in authority to tell me what to do with these bombs, for there are no planes to put these bombs in." As if in answer to his thought, a rather short major came trotting up. "Sergeant, you'll have to take these bombs back and get 300-pound bombs," he directed, "because they're going to bring out the A-20s."[20]

One of Captain Chapman's Headquarters Squadron soldiers, a very young man, "became quite nauseated, with the usual result." When Chapman expressed sympathy, the soldier replied, "Sir, when that last row of bombs came so close, I swallowed my chew." After he walked off, Chapman's sergeant remarked, "That youngster never had a chew in his life!" But both men appreciated the boy's attempt to explain away his momentary weakness.[21]

With the disappearance of the first wave, Sergeant Crouse realized how intense was his pain and how much blood he was losing. He decided to crawl out from under the tractor where he had taken shelter and seek help. "What I was going for I knew, but *where* I didn't know," he wrote. "I hadn't crawled very far when luck was with me again! Some soldier was using his private car as a make-shift ambulance. He spotted me and picked me up just as the second 'wave' was getting under way."[22]

Civilian Honolulu found itself drawn into the drama at various times and by various means. At breakfast at the Army and Navy YMCA, servicemen who had stayed there overnight crowded the dining room. "Every table, every stool, every chair was filled," said Executive Secretary Weslie T. Wilke, "and when the radio announcement came that all men were to go back they dropped their knives and forks and left. In two minutes they were gone. . . . Every man Jack left for his post, even though hardly any of them believed at that moment that it was anything but an alert."[23]

Mrs. Jessie S. Peet's car radio said something about an attack, but she assumed army maneuvers were under way. The little grocery store where she stopped for a small bottle of cream was "in a dither of excitement," and outside people were squinting skyward.

On her way home she picked up a bewildered sailor hurrying up the road, under instruction to report to his quarters. A little farther along she scooped in four other sailors. But Mrs. Peet and her passengers "still thought it was a sham." Anything else would be "impossible. . . fantastic." As they neared Pearl Harbor, armed soldiers halted the car and then, seeing the five sailors, waved it on.[24]

Toy Tamanaha, a contender for the flyweight boxing champion-ship of the world, awoke to the sound of bombs, but he, too, thought it just another maneuver. He strolled to a café for breakfast. Some-one mentioned that a war was going on, but no one paid attention. When he and some friends left the café and walked down the street, he still could not believe that war had come.[25]

One reason for skepticism may have been the fact that not until 0840 did the local radio directly state that an attack was in progress. At some 17 seconds after 0804, KGMB interrupted a concert to recall all Army, Navy, and Marine Corps personnel to duty. The station repeated the announcement at 0805 and 0830. At 0832, police and firemen were called to duty. Then at 0840 came the first reference to an attack: The enemy planes bore the Rising Sun insignia on their wingtips, and some enemy aircraft had been shot down.[26]

Pearl Harbor sent the Hawaiian Medical Association an urgent call for ambulances. Within minutes, doctors and volunteers were gut-ting over a hundred trucks of every description and refitting them with prepared frames that could hold four litters apiece. In an amaz-ingly short time, these makeshift ambulances were speeding toward Pearl Harbor.[27]

High school student Daniel Inouye was dressing to go to church. As was his custom, he had the radio on. Suddenly an announcer, who "sounded almost frantic," interrupted the music, shouting something about Pearl Harbor being bombed, and this was not an exercise.

His tie still in his hand, Inouye and his father ran outside and looked toward Pearl Harbor a few miles away. The enemy had evidently fin-ished the bombing run and were heading toward Diamond Head in the direction of the Inouyes' home. For young Inouye, the sight of the red sun on those planes "was the end of the world." He had a brief premo-nition of the burden this attack would bring on Americans of Japanese ancestry like himself. "Those dirty Japs!" he muttered.

Inouye was a member of Civil Defense, and shortly he received a call to report to his first-aid station, where he had charge of stretcher-bearers. Arriving at his post, he found the station burned down, not by Japanese bombs, but by malfunctioning U.S. antiaircraft shells.[28]

Although many citizens of Honolulu were naturally convinced that their city was under Japanese attack, these American shells accounted for the damage the city suffered that day. One such brought tragedy to Toy Tamanaha. He and his friends had stepped into the Cherry

Blossom Sweet Shop to buy Popsicles when one of those erratic shells blew up the store, throwing Tamanaha into the street. "I was conscious," he said later. "I just sat there, looking at my legs. They were all mangled. Then I just lay down on the street and blacked out." He awoke in a hospital, both legs amputated.[29]

Teenager Tsuneko Ogure was waiting for a bus when the building across the street burst into flames. She did not know what had happened, and a nearby policeman told her only that no more buses would be running that day. At this news, she hurried back home in tears of disappointment. She had been looking forward to the picnic her sophomore class at the University of Hawaii was holding that day and especially to seeing "the skinny, 17-year-old American private" who sat in on her creative-writing class. The two were not romantically attached, but she liked this "funny-looking guy in the GI glasses" who shared her ambition to write "The Great American Novel." Ten years later, the former soldier, James Jones, would publish *From Here to Eternity*.[30]

CHAPTER 22

"Terrible, Simply Terrible"

Roosevelt spent the hours from 1000 to 1200 of December 7 in the company of Admiral McIntire, his personal physician. Like the other members of the close White House circle, McIntire knew that the President was "deeply concerned over the unsatisfactory nature" of the Hull-Nomura-Kurusu talks, and on this morning, Roosevelt "made it clear that he counted only on the usual evasions" when Hull met with the envoys.[1]

The President received his first scheduled visitor of the day, Dr. Hu Shih, the Chinese Ambassador, at 1230 in his study in the residential section of the White House. He informed Hu Shih that he wished to read to him parts of a letter he had just sent to the Emperor of Japan. Roosevelt was obviously pleased with himself as he pointed to a word here, a phrase there, saying, "I got him there; that was a fine, telling phrase. That will be fine for the record."

Then he continued, "If I do not hear from the Mikado by Monday evening, that is, Tuesday morning in Tokyo, I plan to publish my letter to the Mikado with my own comments. There is only one thing that can save the situation and avoid war, and that is for the Mikado to exercise his prerogative. If he does not...there is no averting war.

"I think," Roosevelt added, "that something nasty will develop in Burma, or the Dutch East Indies, or possibly even in the Philippines. Now those fellows"—referring to Nomura and Kurusu—"are rushing to get an answer to Secretary Hull's most recent notes; in fact, I have just been told that those fellows have asked for an appointment to see Secretary Hull this noon. They have something very nasty under way."

Hu Shih left the White House at precisely 1310—0740 in Honolulu.[2] After his departure, Mrs. Roosevelt "was disappointed but not surprised" when her husband sent word that he could not join her and their luncheon guests. She told them "she was so sorry but the news from Japan was very bad." Thirty-one people would sit down to lunch—relatives, old friends, and some officials—none of sufficient political importance to make the President's attendance mandatory. In those tense days, social occasions imposed a certain strain on him. Despite his outgoing disposition, "the fact that he carried so many secrets in his head made it necessary for him to watch everything he said, which in itself was exhausting."[3]

Following the morning's conference with Hull and Stimson, Knox returned to his office at about 1130. He summoned Stark, who soon arrived with Turner. They conferred for at least an hour. The meeting had ended and the three men were standing beside the desk of John H. Dillon, Knox's civilian confidential assistant, when an officer from Naval Communications hurried in with a message. Dillon remembered that it read "something like 'We are being attacked. This is no drill.'"

Knox exclaimed, "My God, this can't be true; this must mean the Philippines." But the office of origin—CinCPAC—left no room for misunderstanding. "No, sir; this is Pearl," Stark replied.[4]

Knox immediately telephoned the White House. The call went through to Roosevelt's study, where the President was lunching with Harry Hopkins, at 1340. Knox repeated the message, adding that he had no further details but would keep Roosevelt advised. Hopkins was incredulous and, like Knox, "thought there must be some mistake.... surely Japan would not attack in Honolulu."

Roosevelt spoke of his "earnest desire to complete his administration without war," adding "that if this action of Japan's were true it would take the matter entirely out of his hands." For in that case, "the Japanese had made the decision for him."

He thought that "the report was probably true." This action was "just the kind of unexpected thing the Japanese would do and that at the very time they were discussing peace in the Pacific they were plotting to overthrow it."[5]

While Roosevelt and Hopkins were discussing this astounding development, Okumura at the Japanese Embassy finally completed his laborious typing of Japan's fourteen-part message at 1350—50 minutes beyond the deadline of 1300.[6] Embarrassed and distressed, but with no idea that Japan had attacked Pearl Harbor, Nomura and Kurusu reached the State Department at 1405. This was 0835 at Oahu.

The two envoys had scarcely seated themselves in the diplomatic waiting room when Roosevelt phoned Hull to inform him, "There's a report that the Japanese have attacked Pearl Harbor."

"Has the report been confirmed?" asked Hull.

"No," replied Roosevelt.

Neither had any real doubt of the information's truth. Roosevelt advised Hull to receive the envoys but to mention nothing about Pearl Harbor, merely "to receive their reply formally and coolly and bow them out."[7] However, when Hull hung up, his first instinct was to refuse to see them. But on "the one chance out of a hundred" that the report was false, he decided to do so. At 1420, in the company of Joseph W. Ballantine, he received Nomura and Kurusu with a coldness that contrasted to his usual courtesy. He did not even ask them to sit down.

Nomura explained that he had been instructed to deliver the note at 1:00 p.m. and apologized for the delay; the Embassy had needed more time to decode the message. Hull wanted to know "why he had specified one o'clock." Nomura answered "that he did not know but that that was his instruction." Thereupon Hull emphasized "that anyway he was receiving the message at two o'clock."

After reading two or three pages, Hull asked Nomura "whether this document was presented under the instructions of the Japanese Government. The Ambassador replied that it was." The Secretary of State finished reading the document with which, of course, he was already familiar. Then he spoke with chilly contempt:

I must say that in all my conversations with you during the last nine months, I have never uttered one word of untruth. This is borne out absolutely by the record. In all my fifty years of public service I have never seen a document that was more crowded with infamous falsehoods and distortions—infamous falsehoods and distortions on a scale so huge that I never imagined until today that any Government on this planet was capable of uttering them.

Hull lifted his hand to silence any protest and nodded toward his door. The envoys walked out with heads down, Nomura obviously "under great emotional strain."[8]

The ambassador did not learn of the attack until he reached the Embassy. He noted in his diary, "...*this might have reached Hull's ears during our conversation*" (Nomura's italics).[9] Nomura had not expected war to break out so suddenly, and the attack both surprised and stunned him. He had never anticipated that the Japanese would launch such an operation.[10]

No one would have guessed from the atmosphere in the Japanese Embassy that the Imperial Navy had just won a major victory. Domei correspondent Kato found it more like the funeral of Colonel Shinjo, which he had just left. Failure hung heavy in the air.[11] Secretary Terasaki, who had returned to the Embassy following his family dinner, telephoned his wife to lament, "Oh, it's terrible! Why did they do such a terrible thing? Japan is doomed."[12]

The word filtered through the White House to Mrs. Roosevelt's luncheon guests. An usher leaned over the shoulder of Capt. Frank E. Beatty, Knox's aide, and murmured, "Captain Beatty, the Secretary's office would like you to come to the phone. They said it was urgent." Making his excuses to his luncheon partner, a young WREN* on leave, and to Mrs. Roosevelt, he went to pick up the call. Dillon informed him of the attack, adding that Knox wanted him at the office as soon as he conveniently could make it.

Finding that the luncheon party had broken up, he told his wife that they must leave quickly. He dropped a hint to the WREN; he "feared that her much-planned-for leave was drawing to an unexpected termination and that she should phone her Embassy as soon as possible." With a courteous farewell to Mrs. Roosevelt, the Beattys went on their way. Beatty told his wife what had happened as she drove him to the Navy Department.[13]

The rest of the luncheon party "stood around in stupefied knots—there was nothing to say—it was absolutely incredible," Mrs. Hamlin wrote. "The guests seemed to melt away—nobody bothered to say goodbye to anyone."[14]

Mrs. Roosevelt heard of the attack from an usher when she and her guests went upstairs. She saw her friends off. Later she wrote, "The information was so stunning that there was complete quiet, and then we took up our next occupation in a kind of vacuum."[15]

Among the few whom Roosevelt notified personally was Hu Shih.

---

* Women's Royal Naval Service.

His voice flustered the ambassador, because the President had never called him before. "Hu Shih, I just wanted to tell you that the Japanese have bombed Pearl Harbor and Manila," he said. He sounded "very much excited and very angry and worked up." "It is terrible; simply terrible," he went on. "Since you were the last person I talked to before this happened, I thought I ought to call you and tell you about it."

Hu Shih hung up in a most thoughtful mood. Despite all that this development could mean to his nation, which had resisted the Japanese so long and so heroically without military allies, he did not rejoice. Instead, he marveled at human nature: "There is a definition of the Infinite that applies differently to different kinds of people. To the religious man, the Infinite is God. To the mathematician, Infinity is a certain symbol...; to the astronomer, Infinity is something else. To me, Infinity is the stupidity and foolishness of man."[16]

Roosevelt also telephoned the news personally to Stephen T. Early, his press secretary. Early was still in his bathrobe and had been reading in his second floor room. Mrs. Early and the three children—Stephen, Jr., a student at the University of Virginia, Helen, and Thomas—were downstairs.

In a radio interview over Washington station WWDC in the spring of 1944, Early described what happened: "The President was on the line. He said, 'The Japanese have attacked Pearl Harbor from the air and all naval and military activities on the Island of Oahu, the principal American base in the Hawaiian Islands. You had better tell the press right away.'" The President added incongruously, "Have you any news?" The question struck Early as "funny," and he replied, "None to compare with what you have just given me, sir."

Early immediately called to his wife to get pen and paper and take down the message, "not more than ten key words." Both were thoroughly surprised and shocked, especially because, as Mrs. Early stated, "the two Japanese diplomats were still negotiating with the State Department."[17]

The White House switchboard connected Early with the three news agencies—Associated Press, United Press, and International News Service in Washington. The time was precisely 1422. "This is Steve Early," he said. "I am calling from home. I have a statement here which the President has asked me to read." Then, "in low, clear tones, with ice-cold composure," he gave them Roosevelt's statement: "The Japs have attacked Pearl Harbor, all military activities on Oahu Island. A second air-attack is reported on Manila air and naval bases."

Early closed the conversation by informing the news associations that he was going directly to the White House. "I will tell you more later." His statement so confounded one of the editors that he checked back to make sure of Early's identity and that he had heard the message correctly.[18]

Early summoned his car from the White House garage and dressed as rapidly as possible. When the chauffeur, Frank Mohun, did not bring the official auto promptly, Early said to his wife, "Come on, we'll take our own car and drive down 16th Street. You watch for Frank and I'll do the driving."

Their Pontiac burned rubber pulling away. Mrs. Early not only watched for the White House vehicle, she kept an uneasy eye on the speedometer. Sixty miles per hour in the city did not coincide with her idea of safe driving. Neither spoke on that mad run of about 8 miles from Shephard Park. Early was much too busy at the wheel and Mrs. Early too occupied in looking ahead for Mohun. About half-way to the White House the two cars met, swung around and stopped at the curb. Early transferred to the White House auto and sped on his way, while Mrs. Early took the family car home.[19]

Stimson was having a late lunch at his home, Woodley, when the President telephoned him. In "a rather excited voice," he asked, "Have you heard the news?"

"Well, I have heard the telegrams which have been coming in about the Japanese advances in the Gulf of Siam," Stimson answered.

"Oh, no," Roosevelt came back quickly. "I don't mean that. They have attacked Hawaii. They are now bombing Hawaii."

Stimson recorded his reaction in an understatement: "Well, that was an excitement indeed."[20]

It was the first Sunday on the White House switchboard for a new operator, Jessie Gill, who manned the lines alone. The switchboard began to flash as though everyone in the nation were trying to phone the President. The overworked newcomer summoned Louise Hack-meister, the White House chief operator, who rushed to the scene.[21]

The President's secretary, Grace Tully, was "trying to relax from the grind of the past weeks" in her apartment at 3000 Connecticut Avenue. She was reading the Sunday papers when "Hacky" telephoned. "The President wants you right away," she said crisply. "There's a car on the way to pick you up. The Japs have just bombed Pearl Harbor."

"I was simply too stunned to have any reaction and I had no time to think," Miss Tully said in retrospect. "The President needed me. He had confidence in me. My only objective was to get to the White House as fast as I could." She dressed hurriedly and "jumped to like a fireman going down the pole."[22]

A telephone call awoke Capt. James Roosevelt, USMCR, from a nap in his home in Washington. Someone at the White House informed him of Pearl Harbor and told him that his father wanted him right away. So he hurried off as fast as he could. The first thing that he noted when he saw his father was: *"Why, Pa's wearing an old sweater of mine!"* (Roosevelt's italics). Then Captain Roosevelt became aware of the President's "extreme calmness—almost a sad, fatalistic, but courageous acceptance of something he had tried to avert but which he feared might be inevitable."

"Hello, Jimmy. It's happened," his father greeted him. The President was too busy to talk to his son, merely instructing him to stand by in case he could be of any assistance.[23]

As Early reached the White House driveway, he encountered H. R. Baukhage, noted commentator of the NBC Blue Network. The latter's opening gambit, "Baukhage talking..." was almost as familiar to a generation of news-conscious Americans as the President's "My friends...." During World War I, Early and Baukhage had served together in Paris on the Army newspaper *Stars and Stripes.* Baukhage had already heard the news about Pearl Harbor. "Steve, you want to get as much as possible of this out as quick as you can," he said. "Can I install a mike in the newsroom?"

Early hesitated briefly, because this privilege had never been granted before. But Baukhage was "a wonderful guy," a favorite of Roosevelt, and an honest, trustworthy newsman. Furthermore, the whole situation was without precedent. So Early replied, "Yes. I'm going up to the President in a few minutes." Baukhage hastened to take advantage of the precious authority and called his studio to dispatch an engineer to set up a microphone.[24]

A. Merriman Smith, White House correspondent for the United Press, was shaving when his wife informed him "rather puckishly" that, according to the radio, "the Japanese bombed Hawaii." Smith nearly knocked her down as he shot out of the bathroom. By an odd chance, he lifted his telephone precisely as his Sunday night editor called him with instructions to go to the White House as fast as he could. Smith grabbed a tie and coat and dashed for his car. A few blocks from his home he hailed a motorcycle policeman. "Officer, the Japs have just attacked us in the Pacific and I've got to get to the White House right away," he said. "How about an escort?"

"Why, those little bastards!" the policeman exclaimed, and willingly convoyed the newsman. They made the 6 miles from Arlington to the White House in less than 10 minutes.

Smith remembered that afternoon as "the most rapid succession of world-shaking stories in the memory of the oldest old-timer in the newspaper business around Washington. . . . Men spend an entire lifetime in press association work without ever handling one flash story. I had four in four hours."[25]

Miss Tully reached the White House within 20 minutes of Miss Hackmeister's call. The driveway was "already swarming with extra police and an added detail of Secret Service men." News and radiomen also were "beginning to stream into the Executive Office Wing." Hopkins, Knox, and Stimson were with the President. Steve Early, Admiral McIntire, and a few others bustled about their duties. As she walked in the front door, the atmosphere struck her as one of regret, almost of apology. Everyone seemed to be on the verge of saying, "We're sorry," and she felt like saying it, too. "After all, we were Americans gathered together in a tragic hour and we were all in the same boat." Miss Tully spoke briefly with Steve Early and Admiral McIntire, but, as she recalled, "it was no time for conversation."[26]

Shortly after noon, Marshall had told Col. John R. Deane, secretary of the General Staff, that he expected to see the President at 1500 and that Deane should arrange to keep the office open and have some of the commissioned and civilian personnel report for duty."

At about 1330—0800 at Oahu—a Navy enlisted man, "out of breath," rushed into Deane's office with a penciled note. Deane recalled the wording as "Pearl Harbor attacked. This is no drill." He immediately telephoned Marshall, who was at lunch. The general directed Deane "to contact Hawaii if possible and verify the message." Before Deane could do so, "another and more official message came, indicating the correctness of the first message." Marshall was back in his office within 10 minutes.[27]

In the Far Eastern Section of G-2, Lt. John B. Schindel heard the news from Commander McCollum, from the same section of ONI. Schindel scarcely had 2 minutes to recover from his shock when Colonel Bratton walked in. Goggle-eyed, Schindel blurted out the message. Bratton threw up his hands and cried, "Oh, my God!"[28]

Totally exhausted when he left work on the afternoon of December 6, Commander Safford "slept the clock around—with 4 extra hours to boot." He was eating breakfast when a Navy wife telephoned him "that the Japs were bombing Pearl Harbor and was her husband in danger?"

Safford firmly believed that a message had been received that clinched the fact that Japan meant to go to war with the United States and Great Britain. Moreover, he was upset over several warning messages that had not been released. So he decided to stay away from his office, where he kept "a detective-model .38 and shoulder holster" in his desk. He feared that if this weapon were within reach, he would have murdered Admiral Noyes and even tried to shoot Stark.[29]

At Griffith Stadium, some 27,000 people, among them young Ens. John F. Kennedy, watched gleefully as quarterback Sammy Baugh passed the Washington Redskins to a 20–14 victory over the Philadelphia Eagles. Sports columnist Shirley Povich of the Washington *Post* was in the press box near Pat O'Brien of the Associated Press. Late in the first quarter, O'Brien received a message from his office: "Keep game short. Unimportant."

Curtail coverage of the last Redskin game of the season? In *Washington?* "What the hell you mean unimportant; it's a damn important game," he wired back. The prompt reply explained AP's sudden loss of interest in the game: "Japs just kicked off. War now."

No public announcement to that effect boomed over the loudspeaker. Later, Redskin owner George Preston Marshall explained, "No announcement of hostilities was made because it is against the policy of the Redskins management to broadcast non-sport news over the stadium's public address system."[30]

Despite this, as early as the first half a hint of something unusual seeped through the crowd as the PA system paged various notables. "Admiral W. A. P. Blandy is asked to report to his office at once." Someone handed Secretary of Commerce Jesse Jones a note in his box on the 50-yard line, and he departed instantly. "The Resident Commissioner of the Philippines, Mr. Joaquin M. Elizalde, is urged to report to his office immediately."

Little murmurs of curiosity rippled through the stands, but for the most part, the spectators kept their attention on the field, where their beloved Redskins were fighting what, so far as they knew, was the most important battle of the day.[31]

PART 6

"Back to Their Battle Stations"

December 7, 1941

(0855–0955)
The Second Wave

CHAPTER 23

"The Japanese Bombers Swarmed Down on Us Like Bees"

As the second wave of Japanese aircraft sped toward Oahu, Sublt. Iyozo Fujita wondered how the first wave was faring. He had no way of knowing, for the fighter planes were not equipped to receive radio messages.[1] The bombers, however, had receivers capable of picking up the messages Fuchida sent to the *Akagi*. Lt. Keizo Ofuchi, one of the *Akagi*'s dive-bomber squadron leaders, heard Fuchida's "*To, To, To*" and knew that the first wave was about to attack. Ofuchi had been too busy on the flight to spare many thoughts from checking the wind speed, drift, and other such technical details as would enable his group to perform its postattack mission of guiding the fighter planes back to the carriers. Still, the sound of music from a Honolulu radio broadcast was welcome. He could not identify the songs because he did not understand English, but the sound indicated to him that all was well in the Pearl Harbor area.[2] Lt. Saburo Shindo, leading the fighter pilots, also determined that the first wave was launching its attack by picking up radio broadcasts from Honolulu.[3]

Lt. Zenji Abe, squadron leader of a dive-bomber group from the *Akagi*, had been nervous and excited at the prospect before him. He relaxed when he heard Fuchida's "*Tora! Tora! Tora!*", which meant that the first wave had achieved surprise.[4]

Approximately 1 hour later, the men of the second wave caught their first glimpse of Oahu. The sight charmed Ofuchi. The beauty of Oahu from the air "completely amazed" him. "The green island, the blue sea, the white surf" made this "the most beautiful scene" of his experience. "For an instant I forgot my mission, just soaked up the beauty of the scene below and regretted that it could not last."[5]

Lt. Jozo Iwami, leading a level bomber group that would strike Hickam, "had expected more hell surrounding the island because of the first-wave attack." But everything was so quiet that for a moment he doubted that this was indeed "the target island."[6]

Fujita was almost over Oahu before he saw it, and he tensed up: "*En garde*, we are now entering enemy territory," he told himself.[7]

Fuchida, who, as befitted a leader, would remain on the scene until the last, heard the roar of the incoming aircraft and Shimazaki's attack order: "*To, To, To!*" He noted the time: 0854 local.[8]

In one important respect, this second strike was no replay of the first. The element of surprise was gone, and the "lull" between waves had given the Americans the opportunity to muster their own defenses. As Abe's dive bombers headed for Pearl Harbor, "fierce AA barrages began to close in." He added with candor, "This gave me the cold shivers."[9]

In contrast, Sublt. Zenichi Sato relaxed somewhat when he realized that what at first glance he had thought to be aerial dogfights over Pearl Harbor were AA barrages, especially when he saw "white blasts," indicating "that even practice shells were being used."[10]

When Ofuchi first saw the huge balls of smoke above the clouds, he thought they were barrage balloons. As he flew closer, he realized that they were the tops of huge columns of smoke. Crossing the island, he noted some ships outside of Pearl Harbor and reflected that the second wave really should add these "free ships" to their bag.[11]

Shindo led his fighters at 6500 meters. Because of the strong AA fire, he moved them up to 8000 meters in the attempt to divert attention from the more vulnerable dive bombers.[12]

Fuchida knew that, with a few notable exceptions, the pilots of the second wave were not quite equal to those of the first. And he had anticipated that he might have to give the attack orders for Shimazaki to relay. However, it soon became evident that the second wave was doing fine without his help, so he decided not to interfere and confined himself to observing the action.[13]

Egusa's dive bombers did not have individually assigned targets. They were to polish off whatever ships the first wave had not disabled, and this they could not determine until on the scene. Also, having only one bomb, the pilot could not afford to drop it unless he had a target in clear view.[14] This was easier in theory than in practice, for a heavy pall of black smoke obscured the sky over the harbor. Egusa's men observed a useful rule of thumb: Assuming that any ship not firing its AA guns had already been destroyed, they attacked only those still able to put up a fight.[15]

A case in point was the seaplane tender *Curtiss*, which opened fire at 0853 and attracted an inordinate amount of Japanese attention over the next half hour.[16] Indeed, logs indicate that the dive bombers devoted much of their action to the ships anchored in the Middle and East Lochs and along Ford Island opposite Battleship Row. The repair ship *Medusa* and the destroyers *Conyngham* and *Tucker* were firing by 0855. At 0900, three bombs dropped a mere 20 feet off the *Medusa's* port quarter.[17]

The seaplane tender *Tangier* claimed to have brought down one of the attackers—"shot away plane's tail assembly"—in these early minutes. The destroyer-minesweeper *Zane*, too, recorded: "Enemy plane shot down directly overhead, bomb landed close aboard stern of U.S.S. *Perry*."[18]

Observer Chihaya, in command of the Eleventh Group of dive bombers from the *Akagi*, had good cause to click off to the flagship, "Enemy defensive fire strong." This message gave Genda abundant food for thought. Chihaya was no alarmist, and if he called the AA strong, he meant exactly that. So Genda decided that if the task force's top brass agreed to a third major wave, no torpedo planes would be included. Those slow aircraft would be easy prey to accurate fire.[19]

A plane piloted by Lt. Mimori Suzuki of the *Akagi* dove on the *Curtiss's* starboard beam at 0905 and "was hit badly and burst into flames." It crashed into the No. 1 crane, "where it burned completely." The blast effect and heat knocked the No. 3 gun temporarily out of action and set afire the starboard boats aft.[20].

A number of ships claimed this kill, among them the *Aylwin*, under way down channel. The *Aylwin* had just taken a bomb on her port quarter, "throwing the stern against a buoy."[21] The destroyer *Patterson* credited herself with a direct hit on the plane that crashed on the *Curtiss*. So did the *Blue* and *Tangier*.[22] The light cruiser *Detroit* likewise took a bow: "One plane under DETROIT AA fire was set on fire and crashed on the CURTISS."[23]

The *Raleigh's* log did not record any part in this action, but her skipper, Capt. R. Bentham Simons, reported that a bomber approaching on the *Raleigh's* starboard quarter took a hit from her after 1.1-inch gun. "This plane burst into flames and crashed on the aircraft tender CURTISS where it started a big fire."[24]

Whoever did hit this particular dive bomber, Lt. Cmdr. Herald F. Stout of the *Breese* observed that it was burning furiously before it struck the *Curtiss*. "This was a dead man's landing," he said. The pilot must have perished before impact.[25]

Meanwhile, two bombs dropped 25 to 50 yards off the *Detroit's* port quarter.[26] At 0908, a bomb landed less than 100 yards from the *Raleigh*, and the plane machine-gunned the light cruiser. A second missile struck at frame 112.[27] Simons described the result:

> The bomb that hit us went between the gun crews of the after three-inch and the after one-point-one guns. It hit a three-inch ready ammunition box a glancing blow, missing a man by inches. It then went through a man's locker in the carpenter shop, through a bunk in the living quarters under the carpenter shop, through an oil tank, pierced the hull of the ship on the port quarter below the water line and exploded on the harbor bottom, doing further damage to the hull. In its path through the ship, this bomb missed our aviation gasoline tanks, containing three thousand gallons of high test gasoline, by about ten feet.[28]

The after compartments flooded, and the *Raleigh's* list increased. Crewmen hoisted out her planes by hand and sent them to Ford Island with an aviation detail.[29]

At that same moment—0908—the *Curtiss* brought down a plane that was "flying low over bow of ship, from starboard to port."[30]

Meanwhile, on the other side of Ford Island, at 0900, five bombs fell about 50 yards off the bow of the seaplane tender *Avocet*, but none exploded.[31] The light cruiser *Helena* escaped damage at that same time. "Several bombs exploded alongside, several near misses, no direct hits." The *Helena's* heavy AA fire "appeared to cause planes to veer off. One dive bomber which veered off was raked by 1.1 and .50 cal. and was seen to fall in flames near Hospital Point."[32]

Moving slowly down the channel was a potential victim so satisfying that seaplane tenders and even light cruisers faded into insignificance— the *Nevada*, doggedly plunging toward escape. The opportunity not only to bag a battleship but to cork the channel made the *Nevada* the target of a lifetime. "Ah, good!" gloated Fuchida, as his plane banked steeply to give him a better look. "Now just sink that ship right there!"[33]

"The Japanese bombers swarmed down on us like bees," said Ruff. "Obviously they were trying to sink us in the channel."[34] Ensign Landreth estimated that ten or fifteen bombs missed the *Nevada* before the Japanese found the range.[35] Then several bombs struck the forecastle and exploded below decks, one or two near the crew's galley. "Fires broke out forward and amidships."[36]

Chief Carpenter's Mate James J. Curley was "knocked out," overcome by the smoke "coming up from the officers' quarters."[37]

A few minutes later Admiral Pye, "having been informed that there were submarines in the channel, and being afraid that if she were torpedoed there it might block the channel, ... sent her a signal not to go out."[38]

At that moment, Ruff and Sedberry had their hands full trying to pass through the narrow space between the dredge *Turbine* in midstream and a pipeline running out from Ford Island. By "some real twisting and maneuvering" they squeezed the battleship through.

Now Ruff faced a dilemma. He could not disobey orders and take the *Nevada* out, but equally he could not leave her in the channel to block traffic. After consulting together, Thomas and Ruff decided to take her as near as possible to Hospital Point on the east side of the channel.[39]

Two minutes after receipt of Pye's instruction, another bomb hit the forecastle, killing an unknown number of men and hurling Chief Boatswain Edwin J. Hill overboard to his death. At the same time, there were numerous near misses.[40] "Their bombs jolted all hell out of the ship," recalled Ruff. "My legs were literally black and blue from being knocked around by the explosions.... I could see the Japanese bombs—big black things—falling and exploding all around us."[41]

For Landreth, the "most noticeable" strike was the one that went through the directory platform:

One plane came in and dropped one short. We could see that one go short and land in the water. Another one came in a little too far to the left and dropped it over us, and the third one came in right between these, and we could see before he did that it was going to be fairly close, and when he dropped it the bomb came right directly at our directory, and we were certain it was going to hit us. It

hit about a foot from the director and went through the director platform, went through the navigation bridge deck, went through the
signal bridge and down into the captain's cabin and exploded somewhere probably below the captain's cabin, caused great damage in
personnel in casemate 4 and casemate 6, just went below and was
stopped by the third deck, armor deck.[42]

Admiral Furlong saw the *Nevada* "give quite a heave" and reflected
to himself, "Well...there she is in the channel and there is going to
be trouble if that ship sinks in the channel." So he sent the two tugs
that had been assisting the *Oglala* to help nose the *Nevada* over toward Hospital Point.[43]

The boatswain operating at the stern of the *Nevada* sent a message to Ruff reading in essence, "Because we may lose radio communications, wave your hat as a signal and I will drop anchor." Despite
his exposed position, the boatswain kept a diligent lookout for Ruff's
signal.[44]

At 0910, Ruff backed the engines, waved his hat, and the anchor
dropped. He had grounded the battleship "between floating drydock
and channel buoy #24, starboard side to beach" on an even keel. The
"intense smoke" made the exact position "not definite." This accomplished, Thomas stepped up action of the damage-control parties. Ruff
left the conning tower and made his way aft to the quarterdeck. There
he briefed the skipper, Captain Scanland, when he came aboard at
0915.[45]

Five minutes later the two tugs moored alongside, and within another 5 minutes all men who were not manning the guns—which kept
up an intermittent fire on the Japanese planes—were busy fighting
flames aboard, while casualties were transferred to the hospital ship
Solace or to the nearby Naval Hospital.[46]

The *Nevada* was not the only battleship to attract Japanese attention. Ofuchi selected as his target the one "in the extreme south of
the anchorage." The bombers flew in groups of nine but bombed each
target in single file. "During the dive, I didn't give a damn what happened," Ofuchi observed later. "It was a feeling of complete surrender to fate. But after the bomb was released and we leveled off, I got
scared."[47]

If Ofuchi recalled the position of his target correctly, he was after
the *California*. He must have missed, however, for Admiral Pye, who

was aboard her, remembered no direct hits during the second wave.[48] Nevertheless, at 0900, the ship was "violently shaken from cause undetermined and there followed issue of smoke from starboard side gallery deck." Five minutes later Capt. J. W. Bunkley came aboard and assumed command.

The *California* attempted to launch her planes, but one capsized in the process. Officers and men lowered the other over the side, and Ens. S. M. Haley taxied it to Ford Island. At this time, a "large patch of fuel oil…was ignited and commenced drifting toward ship."[49]

His flagship gradually sinking, and believing his proper place to be at sea, Pye told Train to get the staff together so that they could "shift over to any other ship of the force that could get out." A boat had already drawn alongside to take them off when Pye received a signal from Kimmel that no more ships should sortie.[50]

Lt. Shohei Yamada of the *Akagi* was "a very big fellow for a Japanese, about six feet, and a cheerful and brave pilot of a dive bomber." He made a practice of always selecting a top-priority target. So now he dove toward what appeared to be "the most fierce barrage of AA fires." As he glided toward it, he found the fire came from a battery, not a ship, and pulled out to seek a more profitable target. Spotting the U.S. Pacific Fleet's flagship, the *Pennsylvania*, in drydock and apparently untouched, he directed his entire squadron toward her. In accordance with his habit, he went for the big one.[51]

At 0907, a bomb hit the *Pennsylvania* "at frame 83, starboard side of boat deck," killing two officers and eleven men. Two other bodies were unidentified. Thirty-eight were wounded, fourteen missing. Material loss was surprisingly light—the No. 9 5-inch .51 caliber gun and the No. 3 clipping room were wrecked, with further damage to casemate No. 9, the crew's galley, compartment A-704, and stateroom A.

In addition, "Fire engulfed both USS CASSIN and USS DOWNES."[52] These two destroyers were berthed at the dock's head. By 0930, their magazines and torpedo warheads were exploding, and the *Cassin* rolled against the *Downes*.[53]

One of Yamada's group scored a direct hit on the destroyer *Shaw* as she lay in the nearby floating drydock and left her, in Furlong's words, "ruined and wrecked," burned completely from the bridge forward.[54] The resultant explosion was awesome. "I couldn't describe it," said Ensign Smart of *Vestal*. "It was just a great big whoof!"[55] "When the *Shaw* blew up, I was in Admiral Kimmel's office," said

Major Fleming, "and I never want again to see a look on a man's face as I saw on Kimmel's."[56]

Ensign Asher, bringing the *Blue* down channel, thought this was "the ammunition dump going up." Three or four planes were attacking the *Blue* while this action was going on, but none of the bombs struck her.[57] In contrast, the *Blue's* log declared, "Four planes fired on with main battery were later seen to go down in smoke. It is claimed that two of these planes were definitely shot down by this vessel." One crashed on the Waipio Peninsula; the other was the plane which fell on the *Curtiss*. The *Blue* further claimed that of two aircraft diving on her, the *Blue's* machine guns brought down one near the Pan Am landing at Pearl City.[58]

"When the crew saw that plane down, they stopped shooting and proceeded to pat each other on the back," Asher related. "Then the chief gunner's mate went back there, thinking there was a casualty because he did not hear the firing. Then they went back to their battle stations and continued fire."

When the *Blue* was abeam of Weaver Field, Asher increased her speed to 25 knots. A minesweeper loomed up in front of the destroyer. Asher did not see its paravane, ran through it, and believed he cut it in two.[59]

At some point in the action, Asher threw his field glasses at one of the diving planes. "I do not know what my motive was," he admitted. "I just was kind of mad."[60]

His was not the only illogical action of the day. Lt. Cmdr. Robert H. Smith and Lt. Steve Corey, vainly attempting to catch up in their whaleboat with their destroyer, the *Henley*,* which had cleared the channel at 0900, made for the *Selfridge*, which was their squadron flagship as well as being the nearest destroyer. Finding that the *Selfridge* "wasn't going anywhere," they chugged off in search of a more suitable ship from which they might hope to transfer to the *Henley*. "The dive bombers were coming out of everywhere. The shrapnel was like rain," Corey reminisced. "We picked up the whaleboat's seat cushions and held them over our heads, as if they'd protect us from being creamed."[61]

Certainly plenty of action was happening nearby among the ships in nest with the *Selfridge*. At 0908, the *Conyngham* noted, "One plane

---

* See Chapter 20.

attacking on starboard bow was shot down by nest and crashed in direction of Schofield Barracks."[62] Three minutes later the *Dale* "shot down enemy dive bomber with .50 caliber machine gun fire."[63] Less modest, the *Tucker* claimed to have bagged three, two crashing on a hillside. The other "disappeared over low ridge smoking and flaming badly."[64]

Definitely, the East Loch was no place to be in an open whaleboat with no protection but her seat cushions.

CHAPTER 24

"The Desperate Urgency"

Lt. Cmdr. Harold F. Pullen, skipper of the destroyer *Reid*, had been a prey to bewilderment, anxiety, and frustration ever since his stepdaughter, Peggy, had come running in from the beach where she had been taking an early morning swim and called, "Daddy, you had better come out here and look."

"What's the matter, Peg?" he asked.

"There's some shooting going on," Peggy answered.

Pullen accompanied her to the beach, looked in the direction of Pearl Harbor and saw "what looked like dozens of antiaircraft bursts in the sky." His first thought was a surprised, "They're shooting in the danger zone!" And he suggested, "Let's go back and turn on the radio."

They switched it in it time to catch one of the local broadcasts: "There has been a sporadic air attack on Pearl Harbor. All military and naval personnel report to your stations."

Pullen snatched up the phone and called his gunnery officer, passed on the word, and added, "Pick me up on your way to Pearl Harbor." Since all of his uniforms were aboard the *Reid*, he dressed hastily in civilian clothes, including a Hawaiian straw hat.[1]

It was not exactly a mad dash, for the car was "an old beat-up Chevy that could go only about forty miles an hour." They encountered little or no traffic as they passed Fort Ruger, where AA guns were barking skyward. "We drove right by Aloha Tower and there was a Coast Guard cutter with its small 3″ guns blazing away at the Japanese. They were at General Quarters and really working at it."

Pullen recalled the strange contrasts of that ride to Pearl Harbor: "The quietude and calm of an Hawaiian dawn and yet the pounding noise of the guns. The vacant streets and yet the deep ominous feeling that something very serious was taking place without knowing exactly what it was. And with all this, the desperate urgency to get to one's ship."

As the old car made its way through the main gate at the Pearl Harbor Navy Yard, Marine sentries recognized the two officers and saluted. The Chevy was only one of many civilian autos "running helter-skelter into the yard bringing officers to their posts."

At Officers' Landing, Pullen and his companion had their first clear view of Battleship Row. "My God, it looks like a movie set!" Pullen exclaimed. The remark was not flippant; it expressed in everyday terms the strange sensation of unreality so many experienced that day. He described the scene:

> The water was afire; the *Arizona* was ablaze; the smoke rose high and black over the Navy Yard; then there was that umbrella of black bursts overhead, and straight ahead the pyre of burning ships, with huge, terrific black clouds of burning oil. Interspersed with the explosion of the bombs and guns was the speed of the flames moving across the water and directing long fingers of flame at me.

He added, "The thought hit me like a truck: 'Is my ship in *that?*'"[2]

The second wave was well under way by the time Pullen reached Pearl Harbor. Another latecomer was Admiral Draemel, the Fleet's destroyer commander. He had been on his way to the golf course when Mrs. Earle telephoned the news to Mrs. Draemel, who called the golf course. Draemel received the message when he arrived and immediately headed for Pearl Harbor, where he caught a launch for his flagship, the *Detroit*. From the light cruiser's position, Draemel could not view the whole scene of destruction, but he could see enough to fill him with horror and fury. "It made me almost sick," he said later.[3]

The *Detroit's* bridge should have given Draemel a clear view of the action on her side of Ford Island. At 0910, three planes attacked the destroyer tender *Dobbin*, in nest nearby. Three near misses landed "on starboard quarter, astern and port quarter." Fragments from these bombs killed one man and wounded four, two of them critically.[4]

Two minutes later the *Curtiss* took another hit when a plane "diving steeply on starboard beam" scored a strike near the No. 1 crane that exploded below decks. The hangar, main deck aft, and the No. 4 handling room caught fire and sent off billows of smoke. The flames and smoke from the handling room put the No. 4 gun out of action. The ship took a list to starboard, and her crew began making preparations either to abandon ship or run around. Those aboard the *Curtiss* had the satisfaction of seeing the attacking plane, badly hit, crash some 1000 yards off her port beam. She also claimed credit, at 0913, for shooting down two dive bombers at close range "which fragmented in air."[5]

Stout credited his *Breese* with one of these kills. Earlier attempts had been somewhat frustrating. Stout had been spotting fuse ranges, starting with 12-second fuses at a twenty-rounds-a-minute rate of fire. The gunners came close, but they kept hitting behind the target. Stout blamed this difficulty on the fact that peacetime training had never employed a target anywhere near the speed of the Japanese dive bombers—the sleeve in the target tow cut down the rate of speed.

With a little adjustment, the gunners caught in their sights a plane heading for the *Curtiss*. When it was about a mile away, they scored a direct hit on the fuselage. "This shell went off on contact and blew the Japanese all to hell," Stout recalled. "It fragmentized the bastard. The engine kept right on going, but the plane disintegrated in a ball of fire with parts of it coming down like leaves from a tree in autumn." Stout's men set up a rousing cheer: "Yeah, we got the S.O.B.!"[6]

Meanwhile, the *Breese* had been preparing to sortie and at 0917 got under way, steaming out of the harbor at 0942.[7]

The *Tangier*, too, continued to be a focus of Japanese attention. At 0913, one bomb dropped off her port bow that struck Ford Island and one dropped off her starboard bow. This second missile exploded, splintering the No. 1 gas delivery boat and the No. 3 motor whaleboat, which was on skids on the boat deck; it also shattered the glass of the pilot house window. One minute later, bomb fragments from a heavy explosion "off starboard side aft, close aboard" pierced two staterooms, wounding six men.[8]

Counterflooding had commenced aboard the *Raleigh* when another bomber dove from the northeast at 0920, releasing a missile that exploded harmlessly between the ship and the beach.[9] Despite this narrow escape, the *Raleigh's* condition was serious. She was settling and had taken a bad list to port. "Our after deck was awash," Captain

Simons wrote later, "and it seemed probable that the ship would capsize. The normal draft of nineteen feet full load had increased to a
maximum draft of thirty feet due to enemy action. However, there
was still fifteen feet of water under our keel."[10]

Aboard the minesweeper *Perry*, where crewmen had been working
to free the machine guns of preservative grease, someone poured gasoline on the gun at Seaman Storm's battle station. Storm thought the *Perry*
shot down two planes during the second wave, but the *Perry's* log
does not confirm this impression. In addition, Storm remembered that
"an old chief was shooting a Browning automatic rifle at the planes.
He was mad clear through, but he probably didn't hit anything." Storm
conceded that his own contribution "certainly was unheroic. I was
just scared to death."[11]

The *Curtiss* came under fire again at 0925, when three planes "attacking from ahead dropped one bomb close aboard to starboard and
two under the stern with no apparent damage, rear buoy sank." Although the *Curtiss* had incurred no further damage in this assault,
she was in bad shape. The after engine room was out of commission
and had to be evacuated "due to smoke and broken steam line and
water overhead." By 0936, fires had been located "on boat deck starboard, in number 4 handling room, in hangar, shops and office spac-
es, main deck aft" and in one living compartment.[12]

The destroyer *Aylwin* was headed out of harbor under the command of Ens. Stanley Caplan, a chemist in civilian life. His officer
component consisted of three other ensigns almost as green as himself. The combined sea experience of all four was less than two years.
The enlisted crew was almost as sparse, for many of the *Aylwin's* petty
officers had gone ashore for the weekend. She had only "one signalman, one quartermaster, and two radiomen." Skeleton crews manned
the guns, and engineers were so scarce that not one of them dared
leave his post.

In view of the heavy dive-bombing attack going on in their area,
the ensigns had little hope of taking their destroyer safely out to sea.
But Ens. Burdick H. Brittin donned a steel helmet, organized a repair party, and stripped the ship for action. They tossed overboard
everything not absolutely essential—even drums of lube oil and the
accommodation ladder. After much difficulty and maneuvering, the
Aylwin broke into the open sea at 0932.[13]

At 0930 a plane crashed in the Middle Loch 500 yards off the destroyer-minelayer *Montgomery's* port beam. This ship sent a boat to the site to rescue the pilot and take him prisoner. The would-be rescuers found one man alive, but he resisted their efforts so strenuously that one of the boat crew shot him.[14]

The ships on the other side of Ford Island continued to take equal or even greater punishment. At 0910, dive bombers attacked the ships moored at Pier 19. A bomb falling within 25 yards of the destroyer *Cummings* wounded three men. At that unpropitious moment, or soon thereafter, Cmdr. L. P. Lovett, commander, Destroyer Divisions Three and Five, reported aboard the *Cummings* for temporary duty, as his flagship, the *Cassin*, had been destroyed.[15]

That same bomb or another launched simultaneously struck the water about 30 feet off the port quarter of the repair ship *Rigel*, moored alongside the *Cummings*. Numerous fragments peppered the *Rigel's* shell plating, leaving "approximately fifty jagged holes through plating from ½" to 4" in diameter." The warrant officers' stateroom suffered minor damage.

Another bomb hurtled down at roughly the same time, splashing "approximately 20 feet off port bow, passing through stern of #2 MTB and exploding under water." There was no apparent damage below the waterline, but seven men were injured.[16]

Shrapnel and bomb fragments also struck the heavy cruiser *New Orleans*, which opened fire "with 1.1" batteries forward and aft."[17] The heavy cruiser *San Francisco*, moored next to the *New Orleans*, made no attempt to keep track of actual times, her log reflecting only that several bombs dropped clear of her.[18]

Three missiles from this series of attacks landed in the water almost straight ahead of the bow of the *St. Louis*, moored between the *San Francisco* and the light cruiser *Honolulu*, flagship of the Pacific Fleet's cruisers.[19] Then another bomb struck the pier about 15 feet from the *Honolulu's* side "at frame 40. It penetrated dock and exploded under water." The force of this explosion opened two of the *Honolulu's* oil tanks to the sea, causing considerable flooding with both oil and water. The *Honolulu* credited herself with the possible downing of one of the attacking planes at this time.[20]

So did the *St. Louis*, whose bow rose on the swell of water from the bomb's explosion.[21] This gave the *St. Louis* "a terrific jolt," and the blast knocked down Commander Fink, the cruiser's executive officer. Officers and men had been working frantically to make the ship

Nevada proudly stands down the channel during her famous sortie. Just moments later, she came under attack by 21 Aichi Type 99 carrier bombers from *Kaga*. (*National Archives—Michael Wenger*)

An immense tower of water thrown up by a bomb near-miss enshrouds *Nevada*'s bow during the desperate attempt by *Kaga*'s aircraft to sink her in the harbor entrance channel. Fire already rages amidships from a bomb which penetrated the boat deck and detonated in the crew's galley. (*National Archives—Michael Wenger*)

The only large vessel to leave the harbor during the attack was the light cruiser *St. Louis,* seen here making the turn to port around 1010 Pier at about 9:40 A.M. (*National Archives—Michael Wenger*)

The shambles left behind at Kaneohe Bay NAS by the first-wave fighters from *Shokaku.* At least four PBY-5 patrol bombers burn out of control on the ramp beside Hangar 1. (*National Archives—Michael Wenger*)

U.S.S. *Shaw* explodes after fires detonate her forward magazines. Incredibly, the ship received repairs and returned to carry the fight to the Japanese. (*National Archives—Prange Files*)

Curtiss burns after being struck on her starboard aircraft crane by a Japanese dive bomber. View taken from *Tangier*. (*National Archives—Michael Wenger*)

Bomb racks empty, a B5N2 Type 97 carrier attack plane from *Shokaku* flies past Kaneohe Bay NAS after completing its run over the target. (*Smithsonian Institution— Michael Wenger*)

An Aichi Type 99 carrier bomber of the second attack wave releases its 250-kilogram bomb somewhere over Pearl Harbor. (*National Archives— Michael Wenger*)

With its starboard wing afire, an Aichi Type 99 carrier bomber of the second attack wave falls to American antiaircraft fire over Pearl Harbor. (*National Archives— Michael Wenger*)

An antiaircraft barrage from the aroused Americans greets the second-wave attackers over Pearl Harbor. This photo illustrates well why both Americans and Japanese experienced difficulty in seeing their respective targets. (*National Archives—Michael Wenger*)

"... The flag was still there..." A bullet-ridden American flag waves defiantly near the "Big Barracks" at Hickam Field. (*National Archives—Prange File*)

Panoramic view of "Battleship Row" on the afternoon following the raid. The ships from left to right are: *Oklahoma* (capsized)/*Maryland*; *West Virginia* (sunken, but upright)/*Tennessee*. (*National Archives—Michael Wenger*)

U.S.S. *Arizona*, 12 December 1941. Though the sunken ships in Pearl Harbor may have demoralized some of the Americans on Oahu, the sight of the Pacific Fleet's battered front line unquestionably filled many Americans with the "terrible resolve" so dreaded by Isoroku Yamamoto. (*National Archives—Michael Wenger*)

At center, *West Virginia* sits in the Pearl Harbor mud several days after the raid. *Tennessee* (to her right) lies relatively undamaged, but wedged between *West Virginia* and the mooring quays to starboard. Navy Yard personnel finally had to resort to dynamite blasting to free the trapped *Tennessee* on 16 December. Visible at left is the upturned hull of *Oklahoma*. (*National Archives—Michael Wenger*)

Clock recovered from U.S.S. *Arizona* during salvage operations in 1942. (*Smithsonian Institution— Michael Wenger*)

U.S.S. *Oklahoma*, following righting operations during 1943. Salvage crews from the Pearl Harbor Navy Yard turned the capsized battleship upright with a series of shore winches on Ford Island connected by cables to giant wooden struts erected on the hull of the ship. Though refloated and partially repaired, *Oklahoma* never returned to action. In 1947, while being towed back to the ship-breakers on the West Coast, she sank in a storm. (*U.S. Naval Historical Center—Michael Wenger*)

ready to sortie, and now Rood directed the engine room, "Make preparations for getting under way. Full power, emergency."[22]

At 0931, the *St. Louis* began backing out in the direction of the capsized *Oklahoma,* Rood at the conn, with Fink and the navigation officer, Lt. Cmdr. Graham C. Gill, on the bridge.[23] Originally, Rood planned to move directly down the south channel, but seeing the *Nevada's* ordeal, he feared she might block the channel. So as the *St. Louis* began to move, he thought it would be a good idea to steam completely around Ford Island and he notified Admiral Leary aboard the *Honolulu* what he intended to do. Leary considered that Admiral Pye, as commander, Battle Force, should be informed, so he answered, "Notify *California.*" Rood looked over at Pye's flagship, saw that she was sinking, shrugged his shoulders and thought, "What's the use?" So he did not bother to notify the *California* but returned to his original plan and maneuvered southward. This brought the *St. Louis* through burning oil that had leaked from the *Oklahoma,* as well as through the many men struggling to keep afloat in the oily waters. Rood could only hope fervently that he would not run down any of them.[24]

When the *St. Louis* reached a point roughly between Drydock No. 1 and the seaplane tender *Avocet,* moored at the Naval Air Station Dock, Rood realized that a steel cable linking a dredge to shore was directly across his course. There was no time to maneuver, and if he did not cut the cable, it might well scrape along the bottom of the ship and foul her propellers. So he called for "Emergency Full," even though he knew that the *St. Louis* did not yet have enough steam up. But he wanted the cruiser at all available power. What she had was enough, for she "hit that cable a smashing blow and snapped it like a violin string."

Further down the channel, Hickam Field was burning with frightening force. The smoke was blowing westward so thickly across the channel that Rood, his officers, and men could scarcely see. Rood sent for smoke helmets and everyone possible donned one. As the cruiser neared the outer channel, however, the smoke lifted and she steamed under it.[25]

Early in the second attack action, an enlisted man aboard the tilting *Vestal* turned to Ensign Smart. "Mr. Smart," he observed, "the Japs are strafing us and have been torpedoing us, the ship's been hit and is sinking, we may have to abandon ship, and the oil on the water is on fire and I can't swim." He paused for breath, fished an envelope out of his pocket and flourished it. "And here is a letter from my wife's lawyer who says that if I don't pay this bill for $18.00, he's going to make trouble for me!"[26]

By 0910, Commander Young had maneuvered the *Vestal* to a position southeast of McGrew's Point, and her crew had the fires under control, except in the lower hold. But her situation continued to deteriorate. She was settling, and her list to starboard increased.[27] Finally, at 0945, Young remarked to Ensign Hesser, "The ship is getting into bad shape. We had better beach her." So the *Vestal* dropped anchor at Aiea and came to rest in the mud, in 11 feet of water. The fire in the lower hold, Compartment A-9, "the after bulkhead of which is the forward bulkheading of the forward magazine, compartment A-6-M, raised the temperature of the magazine." Thirty-seven charges of powder had been removed when the fumes overcame three men and this operation had to be discontinued.[28]

Admiral Furlong's flagship, the *Oglala*, was listing so badly that the sailors could not maintain a good footing to man the guns. With no further contribution to the battle possible, Furlong's primary concern was to save the lives of his men. So he ordered "Abandon Ship."[29] Men slid "off the deckhouse out to the dock at about 45 degrees with their guns, and they set up their guns on the dock, and the doctors and many of the crew set up there receiving the wounded and the injured from the battleships."[30]

Furlong was the last to leave; in fact, the *Oglala* had begun to turn over just as he left her at about 1000. She rolled toward the dock, and the admiral stepped from his bridge toward the dock. His chief of staff was already ashore and gave him a hand; otherwise he might have fallen between the ship and the dock.[31]

Such mutual assistance efforts as those of the *Oglala's* doctors and crewmen were taking place despite the continued Japanese attack. At 0920, the old gunboat *Sacramento* sent her No. 1 motor launch to the *Oklahoma*. It returned with two survivors, "after landing about 25 others in place of safety."[32]

The minesweeper *Tern* got under way at 0943 with a racket from her engines, her boilers having been cold. As she moved down channel amid oil and debris, headed for Battleship Row to render assistance, Baker 1st Class Emil Johnson saw many small boats picking up survivors. The *Tern* herself took aboard two from the *Chew*, thirty from the *Oglala*, and thirteen from the *West Virginia*.[33]

The situation aboard that battleship, which Furlong had considered "the best ship in the Pacific Fleet,"[34] was worsening by the minute. "Either you got off the ship or you stayed there and fried," said Commander Johnson. He had just about decided to follow the first alternative, as many of his shipmates were doing, when up over the bow of the battleship scrambled one of Johnson's academy classmates, named White. "What the hell he wanted aboard ship, I don't know," reflected Johnson, "because we were all getting off as fast as possible." Speed was vital, because oil was burning on the water on the port side, and when it spread to the starboard side they would be trapped.

A few minutes after White came aboard, Johnson stripped down. "About all I had on was my class ring." He and his classmate dived off the starboard side and struck out for Ford Island. "White was swimming right along with me and grunting like a walrus," Johnson remembered.

Johnson reached Ford Island completely covered with oil. He headed straight for a barracks and seized a pair of trousers—whose he neither knew nor cared.[35]

At 0952, the *Trever*, "an old four-stacker that had been turned into a minesweeper," picked up Smith and Corey "from motor whaleboat for transfer at sea." The two officers from the *Henley* did not realize that the attack was almost or completely over, and they still hoped to catch up with their destroyer.[36]

In a fever of impatience to reach the *Reid*, Pullen spotted his gig, the ship's cook at its controls. As all available personnel were manning the guns, the cook had decided to do his bit by taking the gig to the dock on the chance of picking up some of the *Reid*'s officers.

As the little craft headed out, Pullen saw in the water what he took to be heads of men swimming, but which turned out to be hundreds of shell containers. Putt-putting northward, they heard "the slap-slap-slap of machine gun bullets on the water," so Pullen suggested to his gunnery officer, "Let's get down in the boat." This they did, pulling their Hawaiian straw hats over their eyes, "as if they would give us protection," Pullen chuckled in retrospect. "Then everything seemed to drop back to nothing," he added. "Either we were not the targets or they were damn poor shots."[37]

In fact, the attack on the ships had ended. Pullen came aboard the *Reid* at 0955, at which time her log recorded, "All enemy planes disappeared; sounded cease firing." Pullen could be thankful that the *Reid* had suffered no casualties.[38]

When he and his gunnery officer went over the fantail, he found almost everyone deaf from the noise, but every man was at his station. "Skipper, everything is under control," one of his officers told him. The *Reid* had come into the harbor only the previous week for major overhaul, "with stern lines down, boilers dismantled, valves being reground and magazines locked." So Pullen feared she would not be able to sortie for long hours. However, the chief engineer assured him, "Captain, we can get going in half an hour." This officer, a lieutenant (jg), had been senior officer aboard during the action. "I couldn't believe my ears," Pullen reminisced.[39]

The second wave, like the first, lasted approximately an hour, and from the Japanese point of view, this second strike against the ships had been highly successful. But Fuchida, hovering overhead in his horizontal bomber, would have to await completion of the concurrent attacks against the airfields before he could assess results—and their cost.[40]

CHAPTER 25

"A Mass of Twisted Wreckage"

CPO Charles A. Russell, chief quartermaster of the submarine *Argonaut*, left his wife, daughter, and two sons barricaded behind mattresses in the living room when he "hopped into a car with some other guys" on the way to the submarine base. He reported for duty, but no one, including himself, knew what he could do about the second wave raging overhead.

So he went topside on the signal tower to see what was happening. There he found the commander in chief. "Kimmel was just standing there with his hands clasped watching the destruction. Hell, there was nothing the man could actually do. All the guns of the fleet were manned, the fleet was fighting back as best it could."

Russell's reaction was that of a man caught in some catastrophe of nature. "It was like being engulfed in a great flood, a tornado or earthquake. The thing hit so quickly and so powerfully it left you stunned and amazed."

A blazing Japanese plane went by so closely that Russell could see the pilot clearly:

He was alive and seemed to be trying desperately to get free from his plane. He looked as though he were having fits in that cockpit. Maybe it was because he had several bullets in him. If he did, he continued to wiggle and jerk himself out of that cockpit. But he was unable to do so and plunged to his death.

Russell stayed in the tower 15 or 20 minutes and then went below to fortify himself with some coffee. He still had no idea what he could do that would be constructive.[1]

On Ford Island, Jack Rogo nibbled raisins in his shelter under a mess table. From that position he could look out a window into the sky. "All at once a Japanese plane flew by with its wing burning furiously. This was the plane that hit the fantail of the U.S.S. *Curtiss*." Feeling "quite nervous and scared," he wondered how close the bombs were coming to the mess hall.

Suddenly, he was tired of his inactivity and decided he would "rather be out where he could see what was going on than hiding under a mess table." When a call came for volunteers, he was "ready and willing" to go to the small-boat landing and help pull the wounded ashore and get them to the dispensary.[2]

After helping cast off the *Neosho's* lines, Bosun's Mate French went to Ford Island's administration building. "There was mass confusion in that building that morning. There was no order, no control, no authority. People were milling around like so many lost sheep." Quite soon he reflected that the Japanese might try to bomb buildings, so he went outside to a parking lot on the main channel side.

There he had a perfect view of the action. He saw the *Cassin* and the *Downes* erupting "like a Fourth of July deal. Only it was a thousand times as great." He watched anxiously as "one dive bomber after the other peeled off and went after the *Nevada*. She hesitated and shuddered," he recalled, "and I thought she was a goner, but she made it down channel."[3]

Admiral Bellinger happened to be on the telephone to General Martin when the *Nevada* drew opposite the administration building. Like French, Bellinger thought the battleship was "a goner" and broke into the conversation to exclaim, "Just a minute! I think there is going to be a hell of an explosion here."[4]

The sortie of the *St. Louis* gave French "a great thrill." He described the scene enthusiastically:

The ship was moving beyond all knots I had ever seen in the channel. Booms were rigged out with boats as booms, a gangway was rigged over the side and these were wiped clear on the pier at Ford Island. . . . In fact, she almost hit Ford Island. Actually I wondered what kept her from hitting bottom. Everyone on that ship seemed at their battle stations and no one seemed to give a damn as that cruiser dashed out to sea.... That skipper was really moving and it looked as though no one but God himself was going to stop him.[5]

At the dispensary, patients had been placed around the inner perimeter of the sick bay patio adjacent to the administration building. At around 0930, Commander Riggs happened to glance up and saw three dive bombers almost directly overhead. They peeled off to attack the nearby ships. However, the third plane seemingly overcorrected in entering his dive and "came down in a crab position"— that is, sideways. At about 2000 feet, this plane dropped a bomb that went through the concrete walkway of the patio.

Riggs was under the impression that it exploded,[6] but others agree that it was a dud. Captain Shoemaker stated that it dug down deeply "and frightened everyone silly because they thought it might explode at any time."[7] Rogo saw the crater as he was leaving the dispensary after helping to deliver a load of wounded. "My God, what if it blows?" he asked himself.[8]

Nevertheless, the impact was sufficient to explain why Riggs thought the bomb had gone off. Two sailors were just emerging from a stairway when the concussion blew open a heavy glass door, knocking one of the men back down the stairs.

Some 10 minutes later, the senior medical officer, Cmdr. Lewis Iverson, reached the base hospital. Like so many others, he had been playing golf when he received word of the attack. At Wheeler Air Field, Japanese strafers sped him on his way.[9]

Rogo did not recall having heard General Quarters sounded, but for some reason he left the infirmary and headed for his official battle station at the Supply Department building. What he saw so burned itself into his consciousness that he could describe it in detail over twenty years later:

The panoramic view of Pearl Harbor from the roof was breathtaking.... To my right, across the channel was the USS *Shaw* all twisted in her dry dock. To my right on Ford Island lay the wreckage of our seaplane hangars with all of their windows blown out, and our seaplanes in a mass of twisted wreckage. Ahead of me the USS Nevada, listing, was steaming out to sea. She never made it and was beached at the mouth of the main channel. To my left was Battleship Row. I cannot remember the names or the positions of the ships now, but they were all damaged, listing, sunk, and some turned bottom up. Behind me, looking across Ford Island I could see the bottom of the USS *Utah* rising from the water and the damaged fantail of the USS *Curtiss*.

Appalled, he asked himself, "Where in the hell were our planes?"— the "our" encompassing the Army and Marine Corps as well as the Navy. He could find only one comfort: "Thank goodness the carriers were still at sea."[10]

Ford Island had escaped in the second attack with remarkably little damage, possibly due to a Japanese error. After Shimazaki gave his deployment order, his horizontal bombers veered slightly eastward and headed for a point about 5 miles northeast of Kaneohe. There they split into three groups. One group of eighteen from the *Shokaku* swung around Kaneohe to the east and south and then turned due west to attack Ford Island.[11]

This group was under the command of Lt. Tatsuo Ichihara, whom Fuchida described in later years with obvious affection as "a big wrestler, a good person."[12] Something went wrong, however, and Ichihara had to send back to Nagumo's flagship a most disappointing message: "We attacked the enemy's airfield with little success." According to Genda, Ichihara and his bombers missed their target.[13]

Another detachment of nine horizontal bombers from the *Shokaku* attacked Kaneohe from the northeast, while the third group consisting of twenty-seven bombers flew past Kaneohe to the east several miles, continued across the southeast tip of Oahu, and then turned west and north and attacked Hickam from the southeast. These planes were from the *Zuikaku* under Shimazaki's personal leadership.[14]

Shindo's thirty-six fighters, however, already had deployed to seize control of the air so that the bombers would have a clear field. The fighters' secondary mission was to machine-gun any American planes they could find on the ground. Just before they came over Oahu, they split into two groups. Nine planes from the *Soryu* under Lt. Fusata Iida and nine from the *Hiryu* under Lt. Sumio Nono turned sharply eastward and struck Kaneohe from the northwest. The second group— nine from the *Akagi* under Shindo's leadership and nine from the *Kaga* led by Lt. Yasushi Nikaido—proceeded southward until it was just northeast of Hickam, and then it attacked from almost due east.[15]

Fujita led the second unit in Iida's group. As they neared the combat area, the awesome smoke and flame of combat came into view, and "AA fire was so thick in places you could almost *walk* on it," Fujita declared. He added, "My one thought was to do a good job and hope to God I got through alive."[16]

Over Kaneohe the eighteen fighters subdivided, Nono's nine remaining behind to strafe that base, while the *Soryu* aircraft sped on to Bellows.[17] Flying in V formation of three units of three planes each, they began working over Bellows at about 0900 for about 15 minutes.[18]

Private McBriarty "ran from church down to the section" when "whistles blew around the camp." He snatched his gun from the armament shack, another man some ammunition. They mounted the gun in an aircraft and were loading it when the attack began. McBriarty "hit the dust," and then, as the first sweep passed him, he "crawled in the cockpit, and... expended 450 rounds on them."

One Japanese plane "was coming down, just came right down the runway, didn't seem to have any objective at all, just fired on the ramp. Well, I know I hit that," said McBriarty, "...I could see holes going in the fuselage behind the pilot, but I doubt whether I got him."[19]

Another fighter dived straight for McBriarty's aircraft, his tactics causing the American to take a dim view of Japanese flying efficiency. "I fired right into its motor, and after he came out of his dive he pulled awful hard on the stick, not as any regular pilot would do, and I might say he was an awful poor pilot," because in trying to correct his fire, the Japanese "gave it too much rudder from one side and then too much rudder on the other side, and he completely missed his target."

McBriarty had the impression that most of the attacking pilots were inexperienced, "from the way they banked their ships. They skid all around. They really were rugged with the controls, really pretty rugged with them."[20]

Nevertheless, Iida's men, however awkward with the controls, set fire to a gasoline tank truck, sprayed a few holes in roofs, damaged one O-49 and one O-47, wounded one man, and shot down an officer of the 44th Squadron trying to take off. Two others were able to get their wheels up, only to be shot down promptly.[21] The base commander, Colonel Weddington, looked on with horror, and later recounted,

I personally watched, wondering what would happen if the pilot was hit while taxiing, whether the airplane would just go on off, over the island, or whether he would die there, or whether he would groundloop, or what would happen. . . . Six different airplanes made passes at him and seemingly never hit him, but when he got on the runway and started to take off, they got right square behind him, and just as he got off, shot him down in flames; and he was turning, trying to give them a bad target, and crashed into the beach and burned there.

The other one that they shot down taking off, I did not see take off, because there were some of them making passes at the position I was in at that time, and I ducked. I had seen him taxiing down, however. They shot him down in the same manner, except that he was not so badly shot up, landed in the water about three quarters of a mile to a mile down the beach, and swam ashore. He was not killed.[22]

All nine fighters poured machine-gun bullets into a B-17 that had "landed about midrunway and went off the end of the ramp." The Flying Fortress was already "a complete washout" when the Japanese attacked it, and three of the crew were wounded. As soon as they could, Bellows men took the guns out of the B-17 to use for ground defense.

About 5 minutes after the fighters winged away, McBriarty's O-47 took off with the object of following the Japanese out to sea. But the engine "was acting sort of rough" and they had to give up the chase.[23]

Evidently satisfied with their brief strike on Bellows, the *Soryu* fighters sped back to Kaneohe. Fujita soon realized that their mission of air control was superfluous, for no American planes were visible aloft. Iida's men could confine their efforts to strafing during and after the attack of the *Shokaku's* bombers.[24]

Aviation Ordnanceman Bert Richmond thought the latter were friendly until he saw them drop their missiles. Then he ran from the hangar toward some ditches. He was still running when the bombs detonated and the concussion knocked him down. Despite his jumping nerves, he noticed that the marksmanship of this group seemed very poor.[25]

Cmdr. "Beauty" Martin later stated that most of the second-wave bombs fell "on the southern side of the hangars and on the southeastern corner of No. 1 hangar. This attack destroyed the planes in the hangars. The fire engine ignited the hangar itself."[26]

The Zeroes "cruised around over us, firing sporadically at any likely target," recalled Aviation Machinist Guy Avery. Barely skimming rooftops, they strafed "individuals, residences and autos." The Zeroes particularly harassed "the firemen who were fighting the blazes among the squadron planes standing on the ramp." One of the Japanese headed for Avery's bungalow. "On one of his passes he was extremely low and right in front of me....he looked down at me, laughed and said something which I could not hear." But he was near enough that Avery "could see his teeth and the motion of his lips quite distinctly." However, the pilot ignored the men and concentrated on their J2F aircraft, scoring two hits.[27]

Radioman R. R. Moser heard someone cry out, "Take cover!" So he and a buddy sought shelter on each side of an I beam. A Zero strafed them and sped past. The two sailors emerged, only to hear another "Take cover!" within seconds. Brief as the interval was, an ensign had taken over the I beam, so Moser slipped "behind the rear of an ammunition truck parked in the hangar doorway."[28]

Kaneohe had no antiaircraft guns, but machine guns and rifles had been distributed,[29] and the men put up the best defense they could. Aviation Chief Ordnanceman John W. Finn manned a machine gun and, although wounded, continued firing until he received a direct order to stop and seek treatment for his wounds.[30]

Aviation Machinist Mate Walter Curylo observed one man shooting at the strafing fighters with a .45, and another firing a Browning automatic rifle (BAR), "using a squadronmate's shoulder for a gun rest. The latter was deaf for several days." In retrospect, Curylo characterized such measures as "futile and ludicrous," although symbolic of the men's instinct to fight back.[31] Nevertheless, Fujita admitted to being "terribly nervous" as he swooped down to strafe, and one of the makeshift defenders shot a hole in his plane's left wing.[32]

One of these men fighting valiantly with the weapons at hand was an aviation ordnanceman named Sands, a sailor of the old school, and worthy of his chief, Finn. He stood about 6 feet and had a nose somewhat the worse for an old fracture. Although he impressed Avery as "an arrogant extrovert," he had "a large circle of friends" who considered him "a rugged citizen, but a darn good person to have around."[33]

Iida's Zero swept near the station armory as Sands emerged from the side door, a BAR in hand, "just in time to get off a burst of fire at the passing plane." He yelled back to the men inside the armory, "Hand me another BAR! Hurry up! I swear I hit that yellow bastard!" The Zero circled again and fired on Sands, who grabbed a fresh

BAR and "emptied another clip in the brief moment of his opportunity," somehow escaping Iida's bullets, which "pockmarked the wall of the building." Meanwhile, the rest of Iida's group "had reformed and were headed toward a mountain gap known as Gunsight Pass... directly in line with Pearl Harbor." Iida's Zero sped after them, gasoline spraying from behind it.

Suddenly, the fighter leader seemed to realize that he could not make a recovery.[34] No doubt he remembered the Spartan word he had spoken to his comrades at takeoff—if he had engine trouble in flight, he would head for his objective and "make a crash dive into an enemy target rather than an emergency landing."*As the other planes of his group edged up to discover what was wrong, Fujita saw him point first to himself, then to the ground, indicating that he was indeed going to crash dive. Then he signaled for the others to disband formation. Perhaps he thought they would stand a better chance operating individually.[35]

Guns blazing, Iida sent his Zero screaming back toward the armory. One of Kaneohe's sailors shouted, "Hey, Sands! That son o'bitch is coming back!" Avery described what happened next:

> Sands grabbed a rifle from the hands of a man who had started toward the door and plunged out into the Zero's line of fire. Bullets were striking the ground all around him. He emptied the rifle at the roaring Zero which was coming on in a constantly descending line of flight as though the pilot intended to crash at the fighting sailor's feet. Lt. Iida ceased his fire a moment before passing over Sands' head and continued in a straight line of gradual descent until he struck the ground.[36]

Avery was convinced that Iida was dead before impact, for he flew directly into Sands's fire and apparently lost control of the Zero, which crashed into a road winding up a round, flat-topped hill on which stood the married officers' quarters. It struck the pavement about 5 feet below one of the homes, "skidded across and piled up against the embankment at the opposite side. The engine was torn from the fuselage. It rolled across the lawn and came to rest against the wall of the house." Avery could not see the actual crash, but "there was good indication that the plane had become inverted." Iida's body was "hor-

---

* See Chapter 7.

ribly torn and broken,"[37] but the Americans had no difficulty in identifying him from his effects. He wore a leather jacket with identification on the back, and "a belt of a thousand stitches," traditionally made by Japanese girls for presentation as good luck charms. His scarf, imprinted with "his name and rank, the motto 'Certain Victory,' a Japanese flag and a poppy," lay near the wreckage. Richmond, who with two or three comrades had rushed to the scene, "picked it up and got back to the business at hand."[38]

Sick with horror, Fujita watched Iida's plunge: "As his plane plummeted earthward, I, who loved him like a brother, felt weak and useless for I could not help him. Tears rolled down my cheeks as I saw my dear friend diving to his death. The last I saw of Iida was his plane crashing straight downward in the midst of a flaming hangar on Kaneohe Air Base."[39]

Fujita had made a natural mistake, probably compounded of poor visibility, wishful thinking, and coincidence. Moser, standing in the hangar doorway, heard someone call out excitedly, "We got one!" He stepped outside to watch the crash. "Then the lights went out. I learned later that one of the high level bombers had laid an egg squarely in the center of our hangar."

Moser had "a very dull feeling" as he sat on the hangar deck "looking the wrong way," with pieces of asbestos hitting him on the head. He could not stand, but on his hands and seat scooted backwards about 30 or 40 feet. Until he saw the red streak he was leaving behind him, he did not realize that he had been hit. Minutes later, he found himself in sick bay, "taken there by Ensign Gillette in his Cadillac convertible." They arrived just as Marines were bringing in Iida's body. At this point, Moser lost consciousness again.[40]

One other Japanese plane went down near Kaneohe, crashing "off Kailua Beach some distance at sea." In addition, Martin stated, "Several other planes appeared to be giving off a vapor mixture which looked as it might be leaking gasoline."[41]

In strictly military terms, the Japanese could consider Kaneohe a bargain-counter operation. In addition to the damage to the ground installations, they had destroyed twenty-seven PBYs and damaged another six. Of Kaneohe's thirty-six Catalinas, only three out on patrol remained whole.[42]

As to the end of the Iida story, it would be difficult to improve on Avery's words:

Lieutenant Iida's...body was taken up in a galvanized iron garbage can, not entirely out of disrespect—although heaven knows we despised him and his kind to the limit that day—but because we had no more suitable facility at hand....The garbage can with its revolting contents was left on the front walk outside the sick bay entrance for the remainder of the day. We had sixteen of our own corpses awaiting care in the improvised morgue, and besides, there was nothing more that could be done for him then. Many of our own men were very indignant because he was given a dignified military funeral and interment along with those Americans who died that tragic day.[43]

CHAPTER 26

"This Time Our Aim Was Better"

As soon as Iida crashed to his death, Fujita re-formed the group and led it toward Wheeler. In addition to his assigned mission of machine-gunning Wheeler's fighter aircraft and installations, he and his comrades now had the personal impetus of avenging their fallen leader.[1]

But the *Soryu* group never reached Wheeler. Suddenly, Fujita heard firing behind and above them. Several American fighters—Fujita estimated their number as six to nine—were speeding to the attack.[2] This was the handful from Haleiwa who managed to get aloft in time to participate in the second-wave action. Lieutenant Welch was sure that four fighters besides himself and Taylor took off, and possibly six, including Lt. Robert Rogers and 2d Lt. Harry W. Brown.[3]

In the course of the ensuing dogfight, Fujita set fire to an American fighter below him. He did not see it crash, so could not claim a kill, but from the black smoke pouring out of it, he was sure that at least it was out of the fight.[4] This may well have been the action in which Lts. Louis M. Sanders and Gordon H. Sterling, Jr., engaged. A Japanese fighter set Sterling's plane afire, but the American continued to fight. Sanders closed in to assist him, although he had a Japanese on his own tail. All four aircraft headed down—first the enemy Sterling was chasing, then Sterling's badly hit aircraft, with Sanders's target in pursuit, and finally Sanders. According to American accounts, only Sanders pulled out of this four-plane dive.[5]

At Schofield, a large, excited group of spectators watched as 2d Lt. Philip M. Rasmussen engaged another Japanese in single combat over a pineapple field at Wahiawa. The Japanese handled his aircraft skillfully and peppered Rasmussen's plane, shooting the American's radio equipment to pieces. But Rasmussen hung in and sent down his opponent, to the great delight of his audience on the ground. When Rasmussen landed, he discovered that the enemy had shot away the rudder of his plane and filled the fuselage with holes.[6]

Lieutenant Brown saw Rogers in a dogfight with two Zeros and shot at the one on Rogers's tail. One of Brown's guns jammed; in a fury he pounded it with his fist, got it back in action, and shot down his target, which crashed in the sea off Kahuka.[7]

This could have been the dogfight that Private Michaud saw from the SCR-270 station at Kaaawa. He was off duty that morning, "sitting around after breakfast" with his buddies when they heard planes coming over the range. This was unusual, not only "because of the hour on a Sunday," but because "fliers usually followed the coast." The men did not recognize the first plane to appear, but the second was a P-40. The men ran outside to watch just as the P-40 "gained and made a pass at the other. The first plane turned back toward the island" and the watchers admired this display of skillful flying. "Those crazy bastards are really having a dogfight, aren't they?" remarked one of Michaud's comrades.

On the P-40's second pass, it let go with "two long bursts of machine gun fire, and the lead plane went down into the ocean a mile east of us. No survivors. The P-40 went back westward, over the mountains." The Americans at this isolated radar station had not yet received word of the attack and "were completely at a loss for an explanation." After some discussion, they decided to report this peculiar incident to the Information Center. "The Japs are bombing us!" came the reply. "Get the station back on the air!"[8]

Meanwhile, an American fighter shot up Fujita's engine, but somehow he kept airborne and fighting. He noted proudly that "the Zero fighter handled beautifully and consistently outmaneuvered the U.S. fighter planes." Still, after a few more minutes Fujita banked his wings as a signal to the other *Soryu* fighters to head for the rendezvous point.[9]

Since these men from the *Soryu* failed to reach Wheeler, those who machine-gunned the base must have been Nono's group from the *Hiryu*. No sooner had Sergeant Hall pulled his AT-6 off the ramp than the Japanese struck again and, as Hall said economically, "then I left. There was nothing then I could do because I thought the airplane was burning, and then we all went to work on the fire and tried to get the hose to put the fire out."[10]

Nono's fighters were all that Wheeler had to contend with in the second wave. Indeed, General Davidson stated, "We did not have very much of a second attack." He added the somewhat disparaging opinion: "Our second attack was more or less shooting off the additional ammunition that they had left from some other attack as they came by Wheeler Field on their way out."[11]

These second-wave fighters came back while Welch's and Taylor's P-40s were taking on ammunition. The attackers came in at such a low altitude that their faces could have been recognized had anyone on the ground known them. The crews loading Welch's and Taylor's aircraft ran for shelter, but the two fliers promptly took off, their planes rolling over dollies and running into boxes of ammunition. As they soared skyward, loose rounds lying on their wings flew in all directions.[12]

From that point on, Taylor admitted, "things got kind of jumbled. . . ." He described the action as best as he could:

I took my plane around and took off right into them so they could not run me down too easily. I made a nice turn out into them and got in the string of six or eight planes. I don't know how many there were. I was in them. I was on one's tail as we went over Waialua, firing at the one next to me, and there was one following firing at me, and I pulled out. I don't know what happened to the other plane. Lieutenant Welch, I think, shot the other man down.[13]

Welch confirmed Taylor: "We took off directly into them and shot down some. I shot down one right on Lieutenant Taylor's tail."[14]

Fort Kamehameha claimed its share of Japanese fighter kills. Private Daniels and two other soldiers had just gotten a .30 caliber machine gun in action when "a low strafing plane came right down in front" of them. They opened fire and saw their tracers inches behind the aircraft's tail. A lieutenant bustled up and reprimanded them for firing "at one of our own planes. He told us to be more careful, because we had lost enough of our own planes already."

The men did not take this reproof without protest, pointing out that they had seen the Japanese insignia; moreover "he could not have been diving down that close to the ground and strafing if it was one of ours." As if to underline the force of these arguments, another fighter attacked them. "We opened fire and this time our aim was better," Daniels wrote. "It looked like we hit him but apparently not in a vulnerable spot because he went back up."

A few minutes later, someone detailed the three men to board a truck and go after more ammunition. "Just as we were leaving we saw a Japanese Zero come down and crash right on the water's edge, just outside the channel. We wondered if he had some of our lead in him."

Further down the company street, they saw another Japanese plane out of control. It crashed into the ordnance building, killing Sergeant Brown of the 41st Coast Artillery, who had tried to take cover under the building's eaves. Either this pilot or another—Daniels was not sure which—killed Edward F. Sullivan in this same area—"the first to die for our country in this area."[15]

No doubt this action accounted for the gruesome sight that met Colonel McCarthy's eyes when he reached the battery at the lower end of Oahu Point:

> ...a Japanese plane had just struck a tree and caromed off the first tree and struck into a wall at my right at the ordnance machine gun shell....The pilot was dead...stuffed in the tree, but the plane was on the ground, and the engine went around the ordnance shop. In caroming off he struck several men who were in the road. One man was completely decapitated. Another man apparently had been hit by the props, because his legs and arms and head were off, lying right on the grass. The pilot was dead, as I say, in the plane.[16]

Daniels and his friends hurried back toward their battery with the ammunition, but on the way they had to take cover under the truck to escape strafing planes. After these roared away, the men took off in the truck once more. They passed their barracks, which had been hit again. The mess hall was in ruins:

> There was a huge hole in the roof of the kitchen and the bomb had exploded inside, shattering the big cast iron stove and hot water boilers. All the large 50 gallon cooking pots were full of shrapnel holes and the wall was knocked down that separated our kitchen from the shower room and latrine.

After checking to be sure no wounded were lying in the ruins, the three soldiers hurried on to the battery.[17]

At the Kamehameha Base Yard, a colonel asked for volunteers, and Mr. Utterback sent "a bunch of men" to dig trenches and carry water to locations with no water facilities. While this detail was out, at about 0900, Utterback "noticed a couple of our small fighter planes flying very low after the Japanese planes." Utterback "hollered at the gunner from Fort Kamehameha to quit firing because it was one of our own planes."[18]

Mr. Brenckman conceded,

We were largely disorganized. We had no place to go, so we gathered by the old trench battery in Fort Kamehameha, and while we were there trying to find a safe place—which we did find for the women—the second attack occurred. The machine-gun bullets were shooting around, and we went to one of the magazines, and so far as I could see they just repeated the same tactics..., but it was too hard for us to see anything definite....I would say that was about 9:30 or thereabouts.[19]

The first Lieutenant Reeves and his friends at Hickam saw of the second wave was the dive-bombing attack on Pearl Harbor. "Look," he said, "they're laying off of us and giving the Navy hell." And he wondered, "How in hell can the Navy survive?" A pilot himself, he watched with respect the tactics of the dive bombers: "How can they go in so fast, keep boring in so low, and escape?"

One answer to the escape question, as he and his companions noted with chagrin, was that the American AA seemed consistently to shoot behind the target aircraft. In fact, Reeves did not see a single Japanese plane shot down all day. Although sorry for their naval colleagues taking such a beating, these Hickam pilots could not help feeling thankful that their field was not on the receiving end.[20]

This respite was short-lived, for within minutes "additional enemy planes arrived in a second raid of greater intensity and duration than the first," in the words of the Hawaiian Air Depot Engineering Department's Journal of Events and Production Report. "It was necessary for Depot personnel to rapidly evacuate the Depot area and seek shelter as best they could in adjacent areas."[21]

Shimazaki's high-level bombers and their fighter escort led by Shindo and Nikaido had arrived. Shindo had little to say about his part in this operation. A man of logical mind but rather colorless personality, he was not the type to indulge in heroics on the spot or in colorful reminiscences. In view of the fierce AA fire, he had only one chance to strafe. Having done so, he left his fighters and flew over Pearl Harbor at low altitude to observe battle results; then he took off for the rendezvous point.[22]

Lieutenant Iwami, leading his high-level bomber squadron from the *Zuikaku*, also found the defense a nuisance: "The enemy AA fire proved accurate, and they came close to us even when flying over clouds." What is more, air conditions made identification of targets difficult and interfered with his men's aim.[23]

Sato tried to level-bomb Hickam at 3000 meters but failed in his first and second attempts. Eventually, he made a third run and released his bombs. By this time, he was able to relax somewhat in spite of the AA barrages. He also became "rather excited to see the confusion in the harbor, in consequence my piloting of the plane became rather loose, to the extent that I was warned by my observer, to my great shame."

Others shared his nervousness and excitement to the full. One of the observers snapped away with his Aimo camera for what should have been a valuable pictorial record. But when, back in Japan, he sent the film to be developed, it came out blank. "He had forgotten to wind the screw of the camera."[24]

Nevertheless, Shimazaki's men were not too jittery to inflict heavy damage. At the Air Depot, "one hit was registered on the partially completed engine repair building, additional hits were made on the repair docks, and two bombs severed the main power feeder cable to the engineering shops...the new main shop building, the equipment repair building, the new steam plant, and the partially completed armament buildings suffered only minor damage." Machine-gun fire killed the purchasing clerk for Depot Supply, Philip W. Eldred.[25]

Two hangars took direct hits and "looked as if they were being lifted right off the ground," said Allen.[26] At the parade ground, where men were trying to put some machine guns in working order, Lieutenant Cooper

> ...could imagine that the high-altitude bombers were close overhead because of the anti-aircraft fire just blasting the skies, and it was all black, and before I knew it they had probably dropped their second bomb load from high altitude, and that's what sprayed the large barracks... and splattered on the ball diamond and the parade ground.[27]

Concussion from a bomb exploding on the diamond lifted Colonel Farnum's car right off the road. "This was the first time in my life that I had ever been near a bomb explosion," said Farnum. "It was a shattering experience." He got out, shook himself, and after determining that he had not been hit, eased his car homeward to drop it off and then he would hurry to Headquarters for an official car. He could not imagine why the Japanese should waste bombs on the base-ball field, but later decided that they might have thought there was an underground fuel supply on the site.[28]

As he entered his home, his 7-year-old son jumped into his arms and inquired wide-eyed, "Daddy, is this war?" Gently, Farnum put the boy down and then told his wife and son to stay inside the house. He added, "I cannot do anything for you now. I must go to the general's office, but I shall be back as soon as I can."

Mrs. Farnum accompanied her husband to the door and as he was stepping outside, the nose of a U.S. Navy AA shell whizzed by his shoulder and embedded itself in the driveway. Sparing it a glance, Farnum alternately walked and ran to Hawaiian Air Force Headquarters. General Martin was on the telephone talking to someone in Washington. The general's side of the conversation was not exactly illuminating, consisting of such remarks as "I don't know....I don't know how many.... No, we don't know where they came from."

Mollison gave Farnum a Government car with orders to "get out and get everything dispersed."[29]

Meanwhile, on the flight line, Allen and his crew were loading bombs in his B-17 when Zeros and dive bombers, apparently finished at Pearl Harbor, strafed the area. Allen hustled his men behind a bull-dozer, but one man panicked and ran for the hangar line. A Zero "lit-erally ripped his head off." The B-17 Allen had hoped to use was too badly damaged to fly. "One engine was completely shot up and one wheel was shot from under it."[30]

Searching for another B-17, Allen saw "a mild-mannered private first class who was an orderly room clerk" climb into a B-18, mount a machine gun in the nose and blaze away at the Japanese. All the while the B-18 was on fire. The last Allen saw of the man, he was still firing as flames engulfed the plane. Allen never found out whether he lived or died.[31]

Bullets zinged overhead as Sergeant Heydt, his men, and the ma-jor who had just directed him to exchange their load of 600-pound bombs for 300-pounders* flattened themselves under the trailer. This particular strafing came from dive bombers, and they were still over-head when one of Heydt's men, Micken O'Neal, began to roll out

---

* See Chapter 21.

from under the trailer. He barely escaped with his life, and the men learned a valuable lesson: "Don't uncover until enemy planes are out of sight."

After these aircraft vanished, the group crawled out and the major got back to the business at hand: "We need 300 lb. bombs for the A-20s." And the captain of Heydt's outfit, who had appeared from somewhere, added, "Now we're going to have to go back and unload these 600 lb. bombs."

"Oh, no, we don't!" retorted Heydt firmly. "Just follow me." So under his direction they drove the trailer alongside a B-17. "Dump the bombs!" he ordered. He estimated that the job did not take more than a minute, for they all expected further strafings.[32]

The group returned to the bomb dump and loaded on the 300-pounders. "I never saw men working so fast in my life," Heydt remembered. They returned to the flight line in time to see a sergeant climb through the bomb bay of a B-17, up into the turret, and fire a machine gun at the strafing planes. Heydt saw two of that group of Japanese crash into the side of a hill.

He and his men loaded the 300-pound bombs into the A-20s, and then, as the strafing continued, they took off for the grass on the other side of the field. "We ran like scared rabbits," Heydt reminisced. He jumped into a crater in the middle of the field, only to find four men already in it. "Get out, there's no more room in here!" they yelled.

"OK," answered Heydt, and he hit the grass nearby. A private first class, "one of the best men on the crew," dropped to the earth just in front of him. The Japanese strafers spotted them. "They put their bullets right along my hip pocket," Heydt said. "They drilled a gutter on my right side about four or five inches deep and about the same width wide." He gave silent thanks to God and then looked up and saw that the guttering bullets had run straight up his comrade's back, almost splitting him in two, changing what had been a fine young soldier into "a mass of blood, bone, flesh and excreta with his head split right down the middle." Heydt vomited and crawled away. "Memory hurts," he whispered, almost thirty years later. "Memory hurts."[33]

The car serving as a "makeshift ambulance"* sped Sergeant Crouse through the second wave to the base hospital for first aid, "which included a shot of the most precious whiskey" Crouse had ever swal-

---

* See Chapter 21.

lowed. From there he was transferred by GI ambulance to Tripler General Hospital. Crouse recalled the trip vividly:

> En route to the Hospital, which was four or five miles, I think all four of us patients, if alive, still remember every bump in that road. One patient, a Lieutenant, who was a navigator aboard a B-17, kept us amused by "cussing" every bump and the driver alternately.

Later Crouse met him aboard ship going back to the States; the lieutenant who had kept up their spirits had lost both legs.[34]

Courage sprang up in many places that day, some of them unpromising. Mollison remembered an enlisted man who had been a constant malingerer. He was a private on December 7, recently having been demoted from PFC. Mollison was about ready to give up on him and recommend his dismissal from the service. But the challenge of combat galvanized the man. He seemed to be everywhere, "staunch as a combat veteran," issuing guns and ammunition, noticing the Japanese bullets only to curse at them.

Nor did Mollison ever forget another enlisted man, "an old punch-drunk prize fighter" who was useless for any work beyond such mentally undemanding details as cutting grass. "However," said Mollison, "during the attack he responded with tremendous courage. He got hold of a field gun and fired it at the Japanese planes first from his hip and then from his shoulders. Of course he was killed, but everyone remembered his valor."

Mollison also praised Hickam's civilian employees who worked through the attack. "They stood at their lathes and their other instruments until they dropped."[35]

Some of the Japanese targets at Hickam seemed to make such little sense that Private Gutzak, for one, was under the impression that after the first wave "the Japanese could not see their targets. They were just bombing at random" during the second attack.[36] Farthing disagreed heartily. He was sure that every bomb "had its target, and the man knew where it was going to be put." Nevertheless, a postattack survey of damage sites only deepened the puzzle until someone came up with a set of 2-year-old blueprints that fit the pattern: "It showed that the last two hangars were not built and that the control tower was an officers' club. The control tower got no fire and the last two hangars got none. All the rest of the hangars were shot at."[37]

Ofuchi's was one of the dive bombers that, having emptied their bomb racks, leveled off and strafed Ewa Field, which the Japanese usually called Barber's Point. There Ofuchi saw several Japanese aircraft shot down. A U.S. fighter was mixed up in the melee of planes over Barber's Point, but Ofuchi could not see what became of it.[38]

Two U.S. fighters were involved—the indestructible Taylor and Welch. Having learned that Ewa was under attack, they left Wheeler to give the Marines a hand. "At that time there was a whole string of planes looking like a traffic pattern," Taylor recounted. "We went down and got in the traffic pattern and shot down several planes there. I know for certain I had shot down two planes or perhaps more; I don't know."[39]

Welch confirmed that he "went back to Ewa and found some more over Barber's Point and engaged them there." After that, he went back to Wheeler and then returned to Barber's Point. He scoured the skies for a 5-mile radius from that location but found no more enemy planes, although he kept aloft for about 45 minutes. "Then there was no more action."[40]

CHAPTER 27

"A Mixed-Up Affair"

As the second wave broke over Pearl Harbor, doctors, nurses, corps-men, and patients at the Naval Hospital scrambled for cover. Some patients dived under their beds; others scuttled under tables. Lt. Ruth Erickson had just settled a wounded man into a cot on the lanai when the planes struck. She was much too absorbed and busy to succumb to fear. When one aircraft seemed to fly directly over her head, she spared it only an absentminded "Oh, that one just missed me!"

The hospital escaped direct bombing, but a Japanese plane crashed into the laboratory just off the orthopedic ward and sheared off a quar-ter of the building.

The beaching of the *Nevada* at Hospital Point imposed an additional burden on the hospital. A number of sailors dived off her and swam ashore. Between wounds received aboard ship and the fires spreading over the harbor, many of these men were in pitiful condition as they tried to walk the short distance to the hospital. Some did not make it; others collapsed as soon as they reached the building. These men were among the worst of the burn cases treated that day.

The former nurses' quarters became improvised morgues. These had been pleasant rooms, each with its little lanai, which the nurses had vacated on December 1 because planned expansion of the dry-docks would require the space. Now corpsmen filled these rooms with the dead. "It all seemed like a hideous nightmare," said Ruth Erick-son. "But it was real, happening then and there."[1]

Dr. John J. Moorhead, a specialist in traumatic surgery at Post-Graduate Hospital in New York and medical director of that city's transportation system, was scheduled to speak at Honolulu's Mabel L. Smyth Auditorium at 0900. This "lean, gray, intense little soldier with a genius for getting things done right" had served with distinction in France as a lieutenant colonel in World War I. He was credited with discovering "many of the modern methods of treating wounds of all sorts." So a number of Honolulu's doctors and nurses looked forward to his lecture entitled on "The Treatment of Wounds."[2]

The news that Oahu was under attack came over the car radio while another doctor was driving Moorhead to the auditorium, but somehow it did not cross his mind that this circumstance might de facto cancel his lecture. He faced an almost empty auditorium, but commenced gamely, although shells were dropping outside. He had just begun with a quotation from the Bible—"Be ye also ready, for in the hour that ye know not, the Son of Man cometh"—when an emergency call came: Tripler Hospital urgently needed doctors. Moorhead and his entire audience headed for Tripler, where the wounds expert and his team of surgeons operated almost without pause for 11 hours. By the end of the day, the indomitable doctor was back on active duty as a full colonel.[3]

Sergeant Crouse had only praise for Tripler and its staff, regular and augmented. "In the hospital miracles were being performed. In my opinion, all the doctors, nurses and orderlies who were on duty there the next few weeks deserve some kind of special medal." Crouse remembered especially one nurse "who seemed to be putting extra effort into her work and trying extra hard to make us smile." Later he learned that she had been engaged to a lieutenant from Hickam, and they were to have been married on Christmas. But the lieutenant was killed in the attack.[4]

Captain Chapman of Hickam's Headquarters Squadron helped carry a wounded man into the Hickam Hospital. As they put him down, Chapman recognized the patient in the next cot as one of his own men, a confirmed goofoff. Only the previous day Chapman had turned him down when he had asked to be relieved from KP so that he could play on the basketball team. Now he lay on a hospital cot, so still and white that Chapman bent over him to see if he was dead or only unconscious. The man's eyes flickered open momentarily, and he said, "Captain, you've got to get me off KP so I can fight those damned Japs." His wound was so serious that he had to be evacuated to the mainland, and Chapman never saw him again, but he always remembered the man's "spirit and quick wit."[5]

So far ignored in all the excitement and tragedy was the Japanese consulate. Unaware of what was happening, the consular personnel expected to enjoy the usual leisurely Sunday. As was customary, one of the maids set Consul General Kita's breakfast on his dining room table and then wakened him at about 0830. All he expected to do that morning was play golf with Vice Consul Okuda and a friend, Tsunetaro Harada. Another maid found a note on Yoshikawa's table directing her to put his breakfast on the table and then go home. This was normal; he usually left some such message on Saturday nights.[6]

Consular clerk Richard M. Kotoshirodo, a local resident of dual nationality, first heard the noise of battle around 0900 and walked to the consulate to find out what was going on. Kita, Okuda, Treasurer Kohichi Seki, and the chief of the code room, Sainon Tsukikawa, were already there "and appeared to be worried." At first Kotoshirodo "could not believe Pearl Harbor was under attack," but in view of the fact that the puffs of smoke erupting in the sky were black, not white, he told Kita that this must be a real attack.[7]

As he did so, a memory flashed into his mind. Occasionally during the past year, Kita had suggested that Kotoshirodo consider going to Japan to live. If he wished to do so, Kita would make all the arrangements. "Christ!" Kotoshirodo exclaimed to himself. "Kita probably knew!" But on mature reflection, he doubted this. Many dual citizens like himself were having to decide between the United States and Japan in 1941. For Kotoshirodo it was no contest—he never gave a thought to leaving the Islands.[8]

When Yoshikawa heard the racket, he assumed maneuvers were under way. He showed up shortly after Kotoshirodo, his hair tousled, his sport shirt and trousers wrinkled. He remarked that it was "a noisy morning." He wanted to go to the Pearl Harbor area and inspect the situation for himself, but Kita refused to let him out of the consulate.

Seki was worried on Kotoshirodo's behalf and expressed his hope that "things would not go too hard" for him. Fervently hoping the same, Kotoshirodo left the consulate after about half an hour and went home.[9]

The second-wave attack was still in progress when Mrs. Peet delivered the five sailors in her car to Pearl Harbor. Someone promptly directed her to return, and she "wheeled back towards home with the shots and noise growing dimmer."[10]

To Mrs. Molly R. Kenny, a young housewife living on Aiea Heights with an excellent view of Pearl Harbor, Hickam, and Fort Kamehameha, it seemed "as if the world were coming to an end." The scale was so grand that it swallowed personal fear, but although she felt physically sick, she was furiously angry. At about 0930 she went to the kitchen to prepare coffee for herself and those with her. She found the lights were off, and that made her "madder than ever."

She and her companions decided they might be safer at a small reservoir about 100 feet away in a cane field, and they had dashed about half that distance when what she thought was a bomb, but was probably a shell, dropped in it.[11]

At roughly this same time, a guard came to the home of Colonel "Empy" Potts with instructions that Mrs. Potts, her son, her maid, and the maid's baby should "stay in quarters and lie on the floor when the planes came over." An hour or so later, an officer from her husband's outfit arrived to tell them "to go at once to his house within about six miles from Schofield. We had to go so near the bombing that we made 35-miles an hour down the post street."[12]

"Soldier" Burford, wife of Commander Burford of the *Monaghan*, kept close to the radio and caught a few details about the attack. She knew that the *Monaghan* was the ready-duty destroyer; hence Bill must be in the thick of the action, but she kept her composure. Seeking comfort in her Bible, she instinctively turned to the Twenty-Third Psalm. "I not only read it once," she said, "I read it again and again. I prayed, too, and I prayed *hard*."[13]

Nancy Shea, wife of Col. Augustine Shea of the Army Air Corps, was the author of *Army Wife*, that useful volume which for five printings had made life easier for young women marrying into the Army. As of December 7, a companion book, *Navy Wife*, which she had written in collaboration with Ann Briscoe Pye, wife of Admiral Pye, was ready for its final checking. That task would have to wait as Mrs. Shea and a Filipino servant "made a sort of shelter of trunks topped by a mattress in the garage." A piece of shrapnel "carried away part of one of the trunks." The two hurried to the house "and crawled under it."[14]

Mrs. "Skinny" Haynes was just backing her car into the back alley preparatory to loading some canned goods when a shell fell on the opposite side of the hedge. She sped on to the home of friends at Haleiwa as her husband had suggested. From this point and for the rest of the day, Mrs. Haynes had a feeling of being pushed from pillar to post. She reached Haleiwa in time to join her friends for a belated breakfast; just as the toast popped up, a phone call came for the women to return, since they would be safer on the post. Back at Schofield, Mrs. Haynes had started breakfast once more when some soldiers arrived and instructed her, "Get over to the barracks, you will be safer there." She went, still regretfully thinking of breakfast.[15]

Mrs. Emil Leard had scarcely finished dressing when an orderly came to the door, telling her, too, to go to the barracks at the end of the street. She should take with her blankets, pillows, valuables, and any concentrated food available. He cautioned her to walk slowly and keep under the eaves of the houses, because the Japanese had been strafing.

Mrs. Leard estimated the time as about 0900 when she, her son Bob, and her mother, Mrs. King, reached the intersection of the main street at Schofield. Cars were hurrying by, and ambulances were speeding past, sirens wailing, headed toward and from the hospital about half a mile northward up the street.

At the barracks, the three entered a day room. There sat a soldier, "just a youngster; he couldn't have been over seventeen at the most." He wore a helmet and full field pack, and was busy stamping Christmas cards. He turned to Mrs. Leard and said wistfully, "I hope someone will mail these for me."

Moving to another day room, they found some forty or fifty women and children from the 21st Infantry. A bomb exploded nearby, and everyone dropped to the floor. A chaplain escorted them to a larger room and tried to calm them down by leading them in singing hymns. "The kids were frightened stiff, clinging desperately to their mothers."[16]

What seemed to Mrs. Chapman at Hickam to be a break in the action encouraged her and her children to go outside their shelter to see what would happen next. A "reconnaissance vehicle" drove up and a soldier jumped out and said, "Ma'am, all dependents have to leave the Post, pack some things and take your children and go. Go now—it's orders!"

"But, where?" asked Mrs. Chapman.

"Up to the Shelter in the Mountains."

Mrs. Chapman knew that a shelter was under construction but had no idea whether it had been completed or even where it was located. And how could she get there, wherever it was? "I have no car," she told the soldier. "I'll have to wait until my husband brings our car."

The man would not accept this excuse for delay. "No Ma'am—

orders are, you've got to go, this is war—just take one of those cars out there in the lot."

"But they belong to my neighbors, I can't do that!" protested Mrs. Chapman.

"Oh yes you can!" he declared firmly. "This is war, you can commandeer any car you want and you must go."

"Are you sure I can commandeer any car?" persisted Mrs. Chapman.

In his relief that she showed signs of yielding, the soldier overlooked the fact that he had crawled out on a limb and reassured her, "That's the law, ma'am, this is war and you can." As he started to leave, she grabbed his arm and declared, "All right, if we must go, we will, but if it's OK to commandeer any car, I commandeer this truck and we'll go in that!"

The dismayed GI argued; Mrs. Chapman repeated his own words to him. Just how long the impasse would have lasted who knows, but during the argument Captain Chapman drove up, and the soldier made good his escape. The Chapmans hurriedly packed some necessities in the car and drove away. As they left the field, a lone plane shot at them, and ricocheting bullets knocked six holes in the left front door. "Smoke hung over everything, planes were burning or at crazy angles up and down the mat, huge craters were everywhere on the mat...," so their last glimpse of Hickam that day was "a very depressing one." They had planned to go to the home of friends, but the MPs refused to permit them to drive into Honolulu. Eventually, a "charming and hospitable family" of total strangers took them in. Mrs. Chapman considered that they were exceedingly fortunate, especially by contrast with those who did indeed go to the shelter.[17]

At roughly 0930, Colonel Mollison sent his wife, his 14-year-old son, Douglas, and his two daughters, Molly and Betsy, 12 and 7, respectively, to the Oahu Country Club. He could not go with them, for he had just received instructions to move the Hawaiian Department Headquarters to the crater, with a deadline of 1430.* The job of making the crater even partially usable by that hour was "a real back-breaker," for the old ammunition tunnels had neither communications nor housekeeping facilities.[18]

General Short estimated that he left Fort Shafter for the Army's command post at about 0840, leaving Phillips with instructions to call Gen-

---

* See Chapter 18.

eral Marshall in Washington.[19] The call went through at around 1900 (1430 EST) and, from Phillips's recollection, contained few specifics. "General Marshall, this is Colonel Phillips, Chief of Staff, Hawaiian Department stating that General Short, who is now on reconnaissance, has directed me to call you and give you the situation. We are now being attacked by Japanese planes. Hickam Field, Wheeler Field, and Pearl Harbor are being attacked."

Marshall broke in to ask, "Did you get my message?"*

Upon Phillips's negative reply, the Chief of Staff asked that he continue with his description.

"Some hangars and planes have been destroyed. Our casualties have not been heavy. All troops in the Department are now moving to their field positions," Phillips continued.

"Keep me informed," Marshall ordered, and they broke the connection.[20]

By 0950 (1520 EST), the Hawaiian Department was in a position to send off a preliminary report to The Adjutant General in Washington:

Japanese enemy dive bombers estimated number sixty attacked Hickam Field Wheeler Field Pearl Harbor at eight am Stop Extensive damage to at least three hangars Hickam Field and to planes caught on ground Stop Details not yet known Stop Raid lasted over one hour Stop Unconfirmed report that three ships in Pearl Harbor badly damaged Stop Marine airfield EWA also badly damaged Stop More details later. End [signed] Short.[21]

As the Japanese planes disappeared from sight, the defenders of Oahu tracked them, attempting to establish the direction of flight and, hence the location of the carriers. "We tried very hard," wrote Michaud. "We felt that we were on trial in this matter. We felt that the Hawaiian command had not placed sufficient faith in radar prior to this, and I believe we were still regarded as gadgeteers. We were not successful, since flights went out in all directions." He was not sure what good the knowledge would have done. "It took heroes to go up in what we had left, and if they had found the Jap fleet, God only knows what they could have done about it."[22]

At the Opana Station, which unknowingly had tracked the Japa-

* See Chapter 5.

nese in, Private Lockard found "an enormous amount of activity" when he and Elliott returned at about 0910. "It was going every which way— away from it and back to it." The men in the station "were covering more than their sector in order to get every bit of information they could." But he saw no plot of the returning planes.[23] Private Elliott agreed that it was "pretty much of a mixed-up affair....And I think that what happened was that they had plots here and there, and it was just almost impossible to keep up with all of the targets as they left the island of Oahu."[24]

At the Control Center at Fort Shafter, matters were no better. Lieutenant Tyler's scheduled relief never showed up,[25] so he remained on duty.[26] At this time, he was "busy with the squadrons," but he remembered that the plotting board was "very much confused."[27] When Major Tindal arrived, he agreed: "There were so many plots on the board, all at once, that it was hard to ascertain any single path, or any definite pattern of airplanes returning. However, to the southwest of the island, there were very definitely two tracks to the southwest, ending in a couple of circles, oh, about 30 or 50 miles out."[28] These circles were about 10 miles apart.[29]

Nevertheless, at 1018, Kimmel's Headquarters sent a message to the three task forces: "Search from Pearl very limited account maximum twelve VP searching from Pearl. Some indication enemy force northwest Oahu. Addressees operate as directed. Comtaskforce Eight to intercept enemy. Composition enemy force unknown." However, the northward search was not made because "the task force at sea, before they could organize a search to the northward, and from information which they had obtained, decided that the most profitable area to search was to the southward."[30]

Commander Layton saw Kimmel at about 1030 or 1100; the admiral was still seeking information on the enemy carriers. "Kimmel seemed calm and collected," Layton remembered. "But he looked shocked by the enormity of the thing that was happening to his command and by the fact that his world was blowing up around him." Of course, Layton could not tell him exactly where the Japanese carriers were. According to current findings, they could be either north or south of Oahu, either 180° or 353°.[31]

When RADM John H. Newton, commanding Task Force Twelve, received word of the attack, he assumed that the enemy must be to the north of Oahu, "inasmuch as approach on Pearl Harbor from any other direction would probably have disclosed their presence by passing through or near our normal operating areas." From his flagship, the heavy cruiser *Chicago*, he signaled the *Lexington* to cancel the scheduled flight delivering aircraft to Midway Island some 50 miles away; he notified Kimmel of this action, giving his position. Shortly thereafter, Newton received orders to report to Admiral Halsey, commanding Task Force Eight. Upon Halsey's orders "to join him in the vicinity of Oahu," Newton set course for that locality. At approximately 1000 or 1100, he received a message from Halsey "to the effect that I was to assume enemy carriers about 200 miles South of Oahu at that time and retiring on the Marshalls. My orders were to intercept and destroy." So Newton changed course "to the eastward of Johnston Island."[32]

Newton's immediate superior, VADM Wilson Brown, had just arrived at Johnston in command of Task Force Three, consisting of his flagship, the heavy cruiser *Indianapolis*, and five destroyer-minesweepers. When he received word of the attack, he realized that his force was "in a quite exposed position" to possible submarines. The *Indianapolis* had just recovered her planes when Brown received orders to rendezvous at a point about 500 miles to the northwest. He estimated that it was around noon when he received orders from Halsey giving indications that "led to the conclusion that the enemy might be withdrawing from a given position southwest of Pearl Harbor toward Jaluit, which would have put the *Indianapolis* practically on the line." So instead of joining the rest of the task force, they proceeded back toward Johnston.[33]

Admiral Halsey, aboard the *Enterprise*, was "close aboard Kaula Rock" southward of Niihau Island. At first estimating that the Japanese carriers might be north and west of Kauai, he sent up six planes from his cruisers to scout the area and then fly on to Pearl Harbor. One of these scouts claimed that he contacted an enemy fighter; he did not report this to Task Force Eight but to Admiral Bellinger when he reached Ford Island. "If he did have contact with an enemy plane," Halsey remarked later, "it was probable that this was the Japanese plane that landed on Niihau."[34]*

The "confusing and conflicting reports" that inundated the *Enterprise* enraged Halsey. Some, "giving so-called radio bearings and the suspected position of the carriers," he recognized as genuine. Others

_____

* See Chapter 33.

were so lurid that he could not decide whether they were "phony or excitable."[35] Messages "about battleships four miles south of Barber's Point and sampans flying the American flag and coasting up and down the eastern Coast of Oahu...and parachute troops landing, and describing their uniform and the marks on their sleeve—I just threw those into the discard, didn't pay any attention to them."[36]

Indeed, some of these messages would have upset a far more phlegmatic individual than Halsey. They were not meant to be deliberately misleading, any more than were the rumors that generated them. Colonel Fielder, Short's G-2, later submitted a chronology of various reports received throughout the day. The morning's crop from the Combat Intelligence Worksheet included these three items:

1025.   Parachute troops landing near BARBERS POINT—at JENSEN and CANNEL ROAD....

1040.   Parachute troops reported at BARBERS POINT. Unverified.

1132.   Parachute troops have landed on North Shore and have been identified as wearing blue coveralls with red discs on left shoulder. BURGIN. Unverified.[37]

The *Maryland* picked up the latter rumor at 1143,[38] and it was widely reported. The Patrol Wing repeated it at 1146: "Enemy troops landing on north shore. Blue coveralls with red emblems."[39]

"Well, what was the truth of the matter?" Layton asked rhetorically. He explained that an American, whose name he did not know, had taken off from Rogers Airfield and "was flying—fat, dumb and happy all by himself—when suddenly a Zero pounced on him and began shooting his plane. So the only thing the poor devil could do was bail out. And he happened to be wearing blue coveralls with a red insignia on the back advertising some local oil company."[40]

The Navy section of Fielder's report at 1037 had three "troop ships escorted by enemy planes" off Barber's Point.[41] The *Maryland* logged the report of an "enemy tanker" to the south at 1112. Fifteen minutes later, the *Maryland* recorded, "Eight enemy ships reported at Latitude 21°10″N, Longitude 160°16″W."[42] From the coordinates given, almost certainly the "eight enemy ships" were part of Task Force Eight, which as of 0800 on December 7 was at latitude 21°11″N, longitude 161°00″W.[43]

All this was little more than a hint of the rash of rumors that would break out that afternoon and evening.

The welter of action, confusion, and rumor passed over at least one head. Mary Lee, attractive wife of Maj. "Swede" Henderson, slept through the entire attack. At about 1030 she dashed over to the Dunlops' home and dumbfounded the household by asking, "What has happened?"[44]

PART 7

"A Date That Will Live in Infamy"

December 7–8, 1941

Postattack

CHAPTER 28

"They Didn't Have Their Right Bearings"

"The outer channel of Pearl Harbor was blasted right out of the coral and is as straight as an adze," said Rood. A speed limit of 8 knots had been imposed on warships using the channel, lest heavy wash smash smaller craft against the coral. Captain Rood took the *St. Louis* through it at 22 knots. He fully anticipated that Japanese submarines would be lurking offshore, waiting to knock off ships attempting to escape from the harbor. But he decided that his best chance was to burst out with all possible speed.

Well down the channel, almost to the sea, Rood happened to look off the starboard bow at an angle of some 45°. Two torpedoes were headed directly for the *St. Louis*, one a short distance behind the other. "I thought that this was it, my ship was going to get smacked good and proper," Rood reminisced. For a few brief seconds, resigned to the seemingly inevitable, he called out to Commander Fink, "If you want to see a ship torpedoed, come take a look!"[1]

Fink had seen so many things already that day—bombings, strafings, ships set afire, blown up, and capsized—that a few torpedoes more or less did not have quite the impact one might expect. Like his skipper, he reflected, "Here's where we're going to get it!"[2]

Meanwhile, Rood's mind worked at supersonic speed: "What the hell am I going to do? If I stop, I'll sure get it. And the channel is so narrow I can't take any evasive action. And if I happen to get hit in the lower part of the channel, my ship will block it and cause all sorts of difficulties." There was only one course open: "I'll just give the ship everything she's got. That's all I can do now." So he ordered "Emergency Full."[3]

At 1004 the *St. Louis* changed course "to left and right and settled on 25 knots to avoid two torpedoes approaching starboard beam."[4] Suddenly, with "a terrific explosion," the missiles struck the coral near Buoy No. 1 and went off. Rood decided the submarine skipper must have been trigger-happy. "Had he waited another minute or two, he would have hit us for sure."

Rood could see the conning tower of a midget submarine about 1000 yards on the starboard quarter. Immediately the *St. Louis* "commenced firing with five inch battery. The first two salvos were believed to have hit conning tower of submarine." As the cruiser swung away from this engagement, Rood found himself heading directly for two minesweepers. They were much too close to avoid, so he kept the ship going full steam and passed between them, smashing the heavy sweep. "I guess I scared hell out of both of them," he reflected.[5]

The *Blue,* steaming nearby, obtained a sound contact on a submarine apparently headed for the *St. Louis* and dropped two depth charges. "Upon a return to the spot where the attack was made, a large oil slick was noticed on the surface of the water."[6] About this time, Rood received a message that the enemy force was some 31 miles to the south and returning on Jaluit. Although well aware of the risks involved, he set course and ordered the destroyers *Blue, Phelps,* and *Monaghan* to join the *St. Louis* to act as an antisubmarine screen.[7]

The other destroyers outside the harbor kept busy with underwater contacts. Lieutenant Outerbridge aboard the *Ward* saw no submarines during this period, but the *Ward* made many "good metallic contacts" that gave "a good sharp echo."[8] Her log shows four such attacks between 1020 and 1150, one of which might have hit the mark, for when at 1127 she dropped four depth charges, she "sighted heavy oil slick on surface." The 1150 engagement was less encouraging; "none of the charges exploded."[9]

The destroyer-minesweeper *Wasmuth* put down one "ash can" at 1023, "results negative," but 13 minutes later she let go another. This time "large oil slick appeared just after depth charge exploded...3.4 miles from Pearl Harbor entrance."[10] The *Chew* reported a supersonic contact "1000 yards west of entrance buoys" at 1030. She released a depth charge that did not explode. The *Chew* had three more contacts between that time and 1214.[11] At 1139, the *Cummings*'s sound operator reported "propellor noises...close aboard." She sent over two depth charges and recorded, "Unusual quantities of oil observed in vicinity of second attack. Contact could not be reestablished."[12]

The *Breese* had a particularly busy half hour beginning at 1108 when she followed a motor torpedo boat "to spot where a periscope had been sighted." She dropped two depth charges 7 minutes later and proceeded with her supersonic search. At 1133, the *Breese* picked up and tracked "submarine on port bow," loosing five depth charges 2 minutes later. "A great deal of debris and oil was observed in the wake of the explosions."[13]

The *Trever* cleared the entrance buoys at 1005 and commenced antisubmarine patrol,[14] Smith and Corey of the *Henley* still aboard her. Over an hour later they found the *Henley*, but Lt. B. A. Fuetsch, the *Trever*'s navigator and temporary senior officer, refused to let Smith and Corey have the *Trever*'s whaleboat, which he was saving for his own skipper—if and when he showed up.* The two *Henley* officers decided to swim to their ship. Cutting off their trousers at the knee—for they needed their pockets for their wallets and ID cards—they plunged in. This dramatic effort fizzled, because the *Henley* was drifting as fast as they could swim. So they had to scramble back aboard the *Trever*. After a brief time to catch their breaths, they tried again, this time successfully.[15] The *Trever*'s log recorded this action sedately: "1140 Maneuvering to approach HENLEY life raft to transfer Captain and Executive Officer of HENLEY. 1150 Transfer completed."[16]

All Smith wanted to do was sit on his favorite stool on the bridge and relax for a few minutes. The stool was gone. "I threw it over the side," a seaman told him.

"Now why in hell would you do that?" marveled Smith.

"Because it was made of wood, and wood's inflammable," the sailor replied.

Smith recalled resignedly, "It was one of those crazy rules we had picked up from the British."[17]

The ships remaining in harbor were just as busy as those outside—rescuing personnel, preparing to sortie, and attempting repairs. At 1002, with Admiral Pye's permission, Capt. J. W. Bunkley, skipper of the *Cal-*

---

* "Lt. Cmdr. D. M. Agnew, in command of *Trever*, transferred aboard from *Wasmuth* at 1634" (log of *Trever*, December 7, 1941.)

ifornia, ordered her temporarily abandoned because of danger from the fuel oil fires burning on the surface of the water. However, by 1015 the flames had cleared the ship, so the order was canceled and battle stations were remanned.[18]

When Pye received the signal from Kimmel that the battleships were to remain in port until further notice, Pye and his staff went to Fleet Headquarters for instructions.[19] "I need you men," said Kimmel, and directed them "to remain with him and assist him" pending further orders.[20] Accordingly, "Commander Battle Force shifted flag and staff to Submarine Base."[21]

At 1010 the *Detroit* got under way, Capt. L. J. Wiltse at the conn, Lt. Cmdr. R. E. Elliott, navigator, on the bridge.[22] As she passed the *Raleigh,* "standing out with Admiral Draemel aboard," Captain Simons, his officers and men "gave her a hearty cheer though it seemed that we ourselves would capsize at any minute."[23] The cheers were premature, for at 1015 Kimmel issued an order, "Do not send any more cruisers to sea." [24] The *Detroit* received the order at 1050, and Captain Wiltse had to moor his ship. But by 1115 she was under way again, and at 1155 Kimmel directed all cruisers and destroyers to sortie "as soon as practicable" and "report to Comtaskforce One [Draemel] in Detroit." At 1200, the *Detroit* cleared Pearl Harbor and began forming the task force.[25] While she was moving down the channel, one of her officers came aboard the *PT 20* from a motorboat. The motor torpedo boat chased the *Detroit* hopefully but failed to stop her.[26]

The *Raleigh,* which so gallantly cheered the *Detroit,* was in exceedingly bad shape, and Simon's problem was to keep her from capsizing. He ordered her two planes hoisted out, and they took off on a 200-mile scouting trip. Then he jettisoned the catapults along with "torpedo tubes, all torpedoes, booms, ladders, boat skins, chests, stanchions, anchors, chains, etc., about sixty tons in all." As the electricity and steam power were out, all this work had to be done by hand. Simons made a chart showing where everything had been dumped; subsequently, everything was recovered.

At around 1100 Simons received a report "that there was someone inside the capsized UTAH pounding on the bottom." He sent a carpenter named Tellin with an acetylene cutting outfit to the old target ship, "where he cut a hole in the bottom rescuing one man. This man, after taking a deep breath, insisted upon going back in the hole to look for shipmates, but found none there."[27]

Deep in the capsized *Oklahoma,* Thesman swam to the tiller room to see if it had less water and better ventilation than the room where he and his men were trapped. One look convinced him that they were better off where they were. The water would rise by the hour rather than by the minute, and while it did, they could cling to the equipment for safety. They began banging out "S.O.S." against the bulkhead.[28]

At 1050 the *Tern* steamed over to the *West Virginia* to help fight fires, a task that kept the *Tern's* men busy throughout the rest of the day and night.[29] Oil from the nearby *Arizona* kept bubbling out, and on the water it shot up flames 2 to 3 feet high. As soon as the *Tern* came to a halt, a number of survivors from the battleships climbed aboard. "Many of these boys were badly stunned. They didn't have their right bearings. Some wanted a place to go to get away from the *Arizona.* Some thought that the aft magazines of the ship might blow up."[30]

At 1005 the *Curtiss* transferred some seriously wounded men to the hospital ship *Solace.* By 1012, the *Curtiss* was nearly on an even keel, but water on her second and third decks caused her to list alternately to port and starboard.[31]

Ensign Landreth recalled that when the *Nevada* reached her final position, "the activity subsided. We looked around, and we couldn't get communications with the guns, and everything apparently was abandoned on the boat deck. Of course we had had great casualties.... The signal bridge was ablaze, and had gone up to the navbridge and coming up on top of our own platform." This fire continued for quite some time "and practically destroyed most of the structure up there."

Finally, there was time to take the badly wounded Ensign Taussig to a fairly comfortable spot. Despite her severe damages, the *Nevada* did not order "Abandon Ship." On the contrary, officers who had not been aboard were coming on duty and organizing firefighting parties, under the handicap of having no water on the boat deck. "We were trying to get all the ammunition out of the ready boxes to keep them from exploding," Landreth explained. "On the port side we did get all ammunition out. On the starboard side there was one ready box that exploded." The engineers were having trouble getting water up to fight the fires. Landreth went below to try to get up some ammunition. By this time other officers had come aboard and taken charge of the antiaircraft battery.[32]

Captain Scanland sent Ruff to Kimmel's Headquarters to report personally to the admiral and his staff on the condition of the *Nevada*. They were very interested and plied him with questions as to when the battleship could be ready for duty and the number of casualties she had suffered. "Kimmel seemed calm enough," said Ruff, "but it was obvious he was sorely shocked and in a state of mind of wondering how in the world the whole thing could have happened." His staff appeared to be "very occupied in figuring out ways and means of retaliating against the Japanese."

Ruff returned to the *Nevada*, but soon Scanland sent him back to Kimmel with another report as new information developed. Unfortunately, this news was bad. At first the *Nevada*'s officers had estimated that she was not too heavily damaged, but upon further inspection it developed that the ship had been much harder hit than originally thought.[33]

Indeed, the *Nevada*'s log reveals an appalling situation:

> One torpedo hit port bow, at least 6 bomb hits on forecastle forward of #1 turret, at least 2 bomb hits forward of stack in bridge structure, and at least 2 aft of stack in boat deck. Forecastle to forward of #1 turret wrecked, including all anchor handling gear. Wardroom and officers' country forward on main deck wrecked....All spaces below and forward of wardroom flooded. Navigating and signal bridge structure completely gutted by fire....Captain's cabin, Captain's office, and officers' galley completely wrecked and burned. Casemates 4 and 9 wrecked. Broadside gun #9 out of commission. Canteen destroyed....Ship's galley wrecked as well as boat deck above where bomb penetrated....[34]

The chief engineer of the *Reid* had not quite been able to make good his pledge to "get going in half an hour," but at 1043 she "was under way and ready to answer all bells." As she moved toward the outer channel, the gunnery officer got an axe and chopped off the locks to the magazines, for who knew what action might lie ahead. "Passing the *Utah* was a shock," Pullen remembered. "Even though it was a target ship, it was a shock to see her in such bad condition."

Pullen called for flank speed—30 knots—although usually any destroyer in Pearl Harbor held speed down to 10 knots. "Boy, I'll bet I catch hell for this," he reflected. At 1120 the *Reid* cleared the channel and Pullen drew a deep breath of relief. Somewhat illogically, he had the idea "that with deep blue water under the keel, we were safe." The *Reid* joined Draemel's task force and did not return to Pearl Harbor until December 10.[35]

Perhaps the only ship hoping to get in rather than out was the *Antares*, which had seen so much early action. However, Commander Grannis was under orders to stay out of Pearl Harbor for fear of blocking the channel. So he requested, and received at 1054, permission to enter Honolulu Harbor. This the *Antares* did at 1130, mooring 16 minutes later. As soon as Grannis reached shore, he telephoned his wife that he was safe. He asked her to call the wives of *Antares* personnel with the assurance that there had been no casualties among them.[36]

All these activities aboard ship, in and out of harbor, had been practical and sensible, if somewhat hectic. But even as these events were going on, there developed one of the most irrational of the day's manifestations—the myth of the "third attack." On ship and ashore, the high and the low believed in this nonexistent wave as firmly as, perforce, they believed in the all-too-real first and second waves. General Short declared, "I would say at that time a definite attack was at 11:30."[37] On the basis of Short's report to Marshall, the Chief of Staff advised Roosevelt: "Enemy Air Attack resumed 11:00 a.m., much less intense than former attack."[38]

Admiral Calhoun thought that there had been a third wave, but that "it did not get home." He saw no damage "except possibly machine-gun strafing." He added, "I believe the third wave was principally sent in to photograph."[39] So deep-rooted was this "third wave" illusion that after his inspection trip to Hawaii immediately following the attack,* Secretary of the Navy Frank Knox returned to the mainland convinced that the Japanese had indeed attempted a third strike. On December 19, he assured the graduating class at the U.S. Naval Academy:

> The third assault came two hours after the first one. With all the resources that were left to the same Army and Navy, we were ready, and that attack never got home. It encountered, as it approached Pearl Harbor, such a barrage from every gun and every ship that the enemy planes had to sheer off, and not a single torpedo found its mark or did the slightest damage to our ships or to our equipment ashore.[40]

Eyewitnesses and ship logs alike make positive assertions about this "third attack," which would be convincing if one did not know

---

* For an account of Knox's visit to Oahu, see *At Dawn We Slept*, Chapter 69.

that by this time the Japanese aircraft were well on their way back to the carriers and indeed some had already landed. Col. Francis H. Miles, Jr., had been at Shafter on December 7, 1941, "from which place he had a grandstand seat for the attack on Hickam Field and Pearl Harbor." Yet on January 20, 1942, he made this statement to Secretary of War Stimson:

> The third attack came at about 11 to 11:25 A.M. Seven of our P-40 pursuit planes which had not been destroyed at Wheeler Field were in the air. They were faster and much more maneuverable than the Japanese planes and succeeded in shooting down eleven Japanese planes and damaging four more. As a result of this action by our pursuit, the damage on the third attack was very light.[41]

Some comments reveal clearly that a certain amount of taking-for-granted was involved. For example, Mr. Brenckman at Fort Kamehameha stated, "about 10:30 or 11 another attack occurred, and all we could see were tracer bullets." But he saw no actual attack "after the first two."[42]

One can readily understand how, on that morning, trigger-happy defenders might shoot indiscriminately at anything in the sky and how observers at a distance might postulate another attack. But how can one account for such detailed testimony as that of Harold T. Kay, the National Guard officer at Aleiwa Heights? Gathering up such "armament" as he had, he headed with his family for a large reservoir behind his house. He thought reservoirs might be targets of attempted sabotage and he "might serve some useful purpose" by guarding this one. In obvious sincerity, he asserted later:

> At the hour of about eleven o'clock planes flew very low over our hilltop in a direction headed toward the other side of the island, up through the Nuuana Gap, probably 40 or 50 planes in that flight, and they flew very low, and they bore a very close resemblance to pictures that we had seen of the German 2-engine Stuka bomber. They bore no insignia, and were a very dark, gray-black color.
>
> About an hour after that, or about 45 minutes after that, approximately the same number of planes flew back, some going down the valley, letting go some of their bombs, a few over the Diamond Head area, and then others, passing directly over our heads about 200 feet

above us. On the return trip, we were able to observe some fighter planes escorting the bombers, and on the fighter planes one could observe the Japanese "rising sun" insignia, but these bombers still did not have any insignia that we could observe, and they were just immediately over our heads. They flew back toward Pearl Harbor and then went out to sea.[43]

The Kays were convinced that "the great majority" of the aircraft they saw that morning were German. Kay based this identification on pictures appearing in current newspapers, magazines, and books. "The planes considered to be German were black and dark gray in appearance, without any insignia. The planes deemed to be Japanese bore a round circle insignia, with a splash of dull color within this circle." Under the influence of a long-standing American delusion that Japanese made poor fliers, Kay reported: "The planes appeared to be operated with the skill and experience exceeding that attributable to the Japanese in general, leading to the conclusion that the attack was lead [sic] by German pilots of considerable war experience from the type of attack technique involved."[44]

Ships' logs show that something in the sky triggered heavy fire. At 1040 the destroyer-minelayer *Tracy* recorded, "Air attack continued by smaller group of planes." Others firing within the next 20 minutes were the *Maryland*, the auxiliary *Sumner*, and the submarine tender *Pelias*.[45] The *Dolphin* was more circumspect: "Single enemy plane flying high overhead drew heavy fire. This ship did not fire as plane was well out of range as we are exercising great care not to fire on planes which are not identified as enemy."[46]

At 1100 the destroyer-minelayer *Sicard* declared, "Horizontal bombing attack commenced on battleships," ending 10 minutes later.[47] The *Maryland* and the *Conyngham* promptly opened fire.[48] The *St. Louis*, out of harbor, joined in at 1115 when "five enemy aircraft" were spotted "on port beam position." She ceased fire 2 minutes later.[49] Just as the *St. Louis* opened fire, the *Helena* "received reports from Observation Post No. 10 that planes were attacking from 148° T." At that time, the cruiser "observed planes flying over at high level in general northerly direction believed to be enemy planes observing or high bombing. No bombs observed. Opened fire on this formation with 5″ battery."[50]

Another flurry of activity began at roughly 1125 when the *Ramapo* noted "enemy planes passed over to starboard." The *Maryland* and the *Sumner* began blazing away.[51] The *Pelias* claimed a portion of a kill:

> 1125.   Opened fire on enemy plane approaching from ahead. This plane, which was being fired at by seven or eight .50 caliber machine guns from different ships including PELIAS was struck while over the Navy Yard at an altitude of approximately 500 feet, was seen to radically alter course, with smoke issuing from its exhaust; it zoomed up, then was seen to disappear over the yard.[52]

At 1130 the destroyer *Dewey* reported that the air attack was over,[53] but others did not agree. Three minutes later the *Pelias* opened fire again, this time "on enemy formation of four planes crossing the bow."[54] The *Sicard* claimed that at that very moment "horizontal bombers" were attacking "heavy ships," but 2 minutes later "Bombers withdrew, followed at short intervals by single attack of five planes each, horizontal bombers, keeping high."[55] Even as the "enemy" withdrew, the *Sumner* fired on five planes "dead ahead."[56] Ten minutes later, the *St. Louis* on her patrol "sighted three enemy aircraft...and commenced firing." She ceased abruptly within a minute.[57]

What may rank as the most astounding entry of this period came from the light cruiser *Phoenix*. At 1144 she speeded up to 30 knots "to escape attack while leaving Pearl Harbor," adding, "several Japanese bombers had the letters 'USA' painted in white on them."[58]

Evidently it occurred to none of these understandably jittery men that the aircraft were marked "USA" because they were American.

CHAPTER 29

"What a Welcome Sight!"

Unaware that the Americans thought they were engaged in a third attack wave, the Japanese pilots sped home to their carriers. Most of them experienced little difficulty, thanks to improved weather and careful calculations.[1] In fact, Petty Officer Muranaka of the *Hiryu* sighted the task force much earlier than he had expected. "When I saw again our ships which I had thought I wouldn't see again, I felt I was choked with tears of joy," he remembered.[2]

Recovery of the first-wave planes began at roughly 1010.[3] The swells ran high, so landing was difficult and took so long that some aircraft almost ran out of gas.[4] Lieutenant Goto recalled that the *Akagi* "was pitching and tossing a good deal and the sea was rough." Nevertheless, he thought that his own difficulties "might have been due in part to the release from tension which had been very high during takeoff, but had decreased considerably by the time I returned to the *Akagi*."[5]

In the rush to recover the first wave and to clear the decks for the second, several badly damaged planes had to be shoved overboard. In addition, a few of the aircraft had been "fairly well shot up." Goto's torpedo plane had taken three holes; another had twenty. There were no wounded pilots among the torpedo group. But a petty officer observer on one of the level bombers was badly wounded. "The first aid group gave him immediate attention when his plane landed and he was taken at once to the ship dispensary. He died that night, however, aboard the *Akagi* and was buried at sea."[6]

After landing, the fliers gathered on the flight deck near a blackboard about 8 by 6 feet in size marked with a chart of Pearl Harbor and the ships moored therein. Pending Fuchida's return, Murata, leader of the torpedomen, collected reports from all the pilots. As initial assessments were posted on the blackboard, "the general atmosphere was one of great excitement with most pilots and observers going wild with joy over the success of their mission." They agreed, however, that all things considered, "the reaction of the U.S. Fleet units was surprisingly quick," and "had the attack not been a surprise, conditions would have been very difficult."[7]

As soon as Murata finished his official chores, Commander Genda, Nagumo's air staff officer, pounced on him: "Hey, Butsu,* I never heard such a good message as the one you sent!"

"Is that right?" Murata returned. Briefly, he described his own torpedo strike and then added a typical touch in his role of comic: "I saw the enemy's bullets chasing all around me. 'Oh, oh,' I thought, and flew out of there!"[8]

Fighter pilot Ibusuki landed aboard the *Akagi* convinced that the long, hard training for Operation Hawaii had paid off and that such training was never futile. "Thorough training and planning are the most essential factor for a successful raid. . . . The offensive is the best way of the defense, and to forestall the enemy is most essential." Still, the pilots and crews "were most displeased that they failed to destroy the American carriers at their base." Many argued that they should seek out and attack these flattops. Others proposed "an after-the-attack reconnaissance" over Oahu.[9]†

On his way to the *Kaga*, Lieutenant Shiga also reflected that "a regrettable thing was that we missed the American carriers, the most important objective of the attack." He flew back alone and landed after the *Kaga*'s torpedo planes and high-level bombers had returned.[10]

The carrier had lost five of the former and none of the latter, which were ordered to prepare for conversion to torpedo bombers in case of an encounter with American ships. Scouts were sent up to look for enemy submarines, and a plane from the *Akagi* landed on the *Kaga* to collect photographs.[11]

All the first-wave planes were put in the hangar and refueled, but the bombs were not returned to their racks. Commander Sata, the

---

* Murata's unfailing good nature won him the nickname "Butsu (Buddha)."

† For a thorough discussion of the arguments pro and con another major attack, see *At Dawn We Slept*, Chapter 65.

Kaga's air officer, interrogated all the first-wave pilots. They stressed two points: (1) the success of torpedo bombing in shallow water, and (2) the success of the armor-piercing bombs. "They were enthusiastic and joyous."[12]

Aboard the *Soryu*, "in spite of a good deal of pitching and rolling all planes successfully made landing on the flat top of the ship. Even those green pilots who had trained the carrier-landing only for a month could make successful landing," stated Lt. Heijiro Abe. As with the First Carrier Division, Abe ordered his bombers prepared to make a torpedo attack to meet the possibility of an American carrier strike.[13]

That anticipation was by no means confined to the airmen. Admiral Mikawa aboard the battleship *Hiei* knew that the Japanese had not located Kimmel's carriers, and he rather expected them to appear and attack. But he did not fear such an encounter, believing that the task force could take care of itself.

Some air units had reported a U.S. flying boat trailing them back to their carriers; however, a later report claimed that it had been shot down. Mikawa decided that, in that case, the prospect of an aerial counterattack had been considerably diminished.[14]

Lieutenant Okajima of the *Hiryu* and his fighter unit had been flying alone toward the task force when his "radio-direction finding instrument" picked up a dive-bomber group and were able to join it. "By that time the weather was getting better; there was only a thin, intermittent cloud sea." The sky was clear over the carriers when Okajima reached the *Hiryu*. A warning that B-17s were coming to attack sent fighters into the air, but no Flying Fortresses appeared.[15]

At the session around the *Hiryu*'s blackboard, Okajima related his exploits with relish. "He had a big time shooting up planes on the ground, and...he shot down several planes which were just taking off from the runways," Amagai remembered.[16]

Lieutenant Hashimoto found everyone aboard the *Hiryu* eager to hear about the attack, but not so eager as to skip channels—each pilot or observer (whoever was senior) to his squadron commander, squadron commander to flight commander, flight commander to the *Hiryu*'s skipper. Then each squadron commander also reported to the captain. These initial debriefings took place on the flight deck. Hashimoto felt very bad because he had to admit that his bomb had missed the target. But no one could question the overall success of the attack, and the fliers "were wild with joy."[17]

Commander Amagai, the *Hiryu*'s air officer, worried about the returning men who might be wounded, so he had the medical officer standing by with everything in readiness. But there were no wounded. Several planes did not return, however, and some came back with a dozen or more holes. The men who did make it back were "bubbling with confidence."

On his own initiative, Amagai ordered preparations to reservice all planes immediately and reload them in the event of a U.S. counterattack or of Admiral Nagumo's deciding to launch another blow against Oahu.[18]

By the time Lieutenant Matsumura's torpedo plane landed on the *Hiryu*, many had already returned. Matsumura assured a maintenance man who hurried up to his aircraft that the plane was in good condition and stopped long enough to tell him a little about the successful torpedo attack. Then he went to the bridge to join his fellow fliers, who were in high spirits.[19] When his turn came to speak, he had one complaint—double mooring had prevented the torpedo bombers from getting at the inboard battleships.[20]

After Muranaka landed, he counted eight bullet holes in his plane. The one that had pierced his fuel tank was "an ordinary type." He did not like to think of the result had it been an incendiary or a tracer.[21]

When word reached the *Shokaku* that surprise had been achieved, her officers, including her skipper, Capt. Takatsugu Jojima, judged that the Americans must have suffered heavy damage, "but at the same time our losses, too, would reach a considerable number." So they were relieved when planes began to return safely and land "in an orderly manner."[22]

Commander Takahashi, leader of the first-wave dive bombers, touched down with telephone wire wrapped around the landing gear of his aircraft—material proof of how low he had flown in the postbombing strafing. A fighter pilot from the *Zuikaku* ran short of fuel and had to land on the *Shokaku;* later he flew on to his own carrier.[23]

As rapidly as the planes returned, maintenance crews prepared them for further action. The flying officers repaired to the flight deck where Admiral Hara, commander in chief of the Fifth Carrier Division, his senior staff officer, Commander Ohashi, and other staff officers awaited them. Commander Wada, the air officer, conducted the questioning. The pilots reported the general problems they had confronted and the probable results of the strike.

Unlike a number of other officers, Ohashi did not fear attack from U.S. carriers, reasoning that if they had not been far afield, they would have sent up aircraft to intercept the attackers. He did fear a land-based strike from Oahu, however.[24]

Lieutenant Mifuku likewise "was afraid of a counterattack by land-based air forces," and for that reason, he did not consider the possibility of a third strike, "although morale of the fliers and the condition of the planes was such as to enable another attack."[25]

In his pretakeoff speech, Admiral Hara had instructed his men emphatically to confine their attack to military targets. He questioned the returning pilots closely as to whether they had aimed at any civilian target. All answered "No" except one, who admitted strafing naval houses near an airfield. Hara was annoyed, not only because the man had disobeyed orders, but also because he himself would prefer to fight a clean war between warriors.[26]

Lieutenant Ema brought his dive-bomber down aboard the Zuikaku, "relieved and glad" to be alive. But he made a mental reservation that the task force was not yet out of danger; the Americans might counterattack. The Zuikaku's officers were jubilant when the first reports came in, and with Operation Hawaii an obvious success, Ema and his colleagues believed that they had given Japan at least a fighting chance in the war that would ensue.[27]

Meanwhile, Commander Shimoda, the Zuikaku's air officer, examined the first-wave planes. Few had been shot up, which Shimoda attributed to their having struck only land targets. He ordered the planes into hangars and prepared for another attack: "Such a step was only common sense."[28]

According to Matsumura's figures, the first-wave recovery was completed at 1047, and by 1130, the second wave was coming in.[29] Characteristically, Lieutenant Shindo took the return to the Akagi in stride: "On the way to the carrier I felt easy just like a training flight flying on the radio-guided course."[30]

Others were neither so fortunate nor so phlegmatic. During the latter part of the attack, Lieutenant Chihaya had informed the Akagi, "Gasoline tank hit by machine gun fire. Will return at once." Almost immediately he changed his mind. As flight leader of the Akagi's second-wave dive-bombing group, he had a clear duty to stay with his men and lead them back. This he managed to do, although almost out of gas when he touched down on the carrier.[31]

Lieutenant Ofuchi, one of Chihaya's group, also had evidence of American marksmanship when he landed. He counted four holes in the wings of his plane, each 8 to 10 inches across.[32]

The fierce AA fire delayed Lt. Zenji Abe in making rendezvous. "Being anxious to get safely back to the carrier, relaxing after the attack—this might be a natural human feeling for ordinary people—I sent a signal requesting guidance from the carrier for the return." The situation proved not so serious as he had expected, and he was ashamed of himself. There was "a good deal of pitching and rolling, particularly the latter because of the strong wind," but all of his group landed aboard the *Akagi* without incident.[33]

Several aircraft failed to return to the *Kaga*, and in addition, several were badly shot up. The reports of the fliers were much the same as those of their colleagues in the first wave, with one important difference: "The second attack wave pilots reported fierce antiaircraft fire which the first wave did not report," said Air Officer Sata.[34]

At the rendezvous point, Lieutenant Fujita's fighters picked up three dive bombers and then headed back to the carriers. Fujita was not too sure where the carriers were, but took a position to the right of the bombers and proceeded northward. His engine, which had been severely damaged in the dogfight, began to give him trouble. "It almost stopped running about twenty times," he recalled, "but always managed to cough itself back into fair shape." He was very much worried that he would not make it back to the task force. "A hell of a way to die after surviving the attack and the bitter dogfight above Oahu!" But eventually he spotted the carriers—"What a welcome sight!" He was not sure what happened to the three dive bombers; they might or might not have made it back.

As soon as his group landed on the *Soryu*, they reported to the carrier's skipper, Capt. Ryusaku Yanagimoto, on the bridge. All of the *Soryu*'s flying officers were there, as were Admiral Yamaguchi and his staff. Fujita recounted his experiences, adding that he doubted whether U.S. forces would be in a position to launch an aerial strike against the task force.[35]

The *Hiryu*'s second wave, like the first, brought back no wounded men, but Amagai noted that their aircraft were in much worse shape than those of the first wave.[36]

Muranaka agreed that the *Hiryu*'s second-wave planes came back having sustained what he called "pretty damage." However, he had little time either for reflection or rest after his own first-wave efforts. A report came in "that six enemy flying boats were approaching." Muranaka was one of six fighter pilots ordered aloft as air cover. Having been in a state of tension all morning, he had a splitting headache but was able to finish "the three-hours-long patrol without any hitch." If he and his fellow pilots saw any U.S. aircraft, Muranaka did not mention it.[37]

All the *Shokaku*'s planes returned, although thirteen of them had bullet holes.[38] Her sister ship, the *Zuikaku*, lost one dive bomber and its crew. After managing to land safely on the *Zuikaku*'s "rolling and pitching" deck, Lieutenant Sato stopped by the radio room, where he heard this bomber, which had become lost, appealing for directions. Unwilling to risk thus revealing the task force's position, the carrier did not break radio silence. "Finally they sent a message to the effect that they ran out of fuel and were going to crash into the sea after saying '*banzai*' three times." Sato, hearing this, was "full of deep emotion."[39]

The *Zuikaku*'s decision was tactically sound, for Oahu had picked up the dive bomber's message. General Short drew a somewhat optimistic conclusion therefrom:

> We have reason to believe that they [the Japanese] lost a complete squadron on account of the message the Navy picked up from a squadron commander sent in to his carrier saying that he was lost and he was out of gas; so there is a possibility that there was a complete squadron lost in addition to what was brought down.[40]

Fuchida remained over Pearl Harbor until about 1000 to observe and photograph results. The nature and extent of the damage was difficult to assess because of the heavy smoke. He was just about to leave when a fighter plane, which Mizuki, the radio operator, recognized as belonging to the *Zuikaku*, closed in. Japan had no radar at this time, so it was difficult for a single-seater to fly over water for a long distance. Therefore, the plan was devised that returning bombers would rendezvous with fighters and escort them to the carriers. The presence of this *Zuikaku* fighter made Fuchida wonder if some more fighters might still be in the area, so he headed for the rendezvous point, where he picked up another stray.[41]

During his flight back to the *Akagi*, Fuchida was mentally preparing for a third major strike. He would like to repeat attacks on a few of the battleships and other vessels in the dockyard area. More important, now was the time to put the shore installations out of action, and in particular to bomb the fuel tanks. He had noticed them during the action but had not attacked them; he had his assigned mission and he stuck with it. However, if he and some of his men could return and destroy the American fuel supply, the United States could not effectively carry out its strategy, whatever that might be. So he was furiously frustrated on landing on the *Akagi* to discover that, while Nagumo and his staff were delighted with his briefing on the results of the attack, the admiral had no intention of renewing the fight.[42] He had accomplished his mission beyond his wildest dreams, and at the astonishingly low cost of twenty-nine aircraft—three fighters, one dive bomber, and five torpedo planes in the first wave; six fighters and fourteen dive bombers in the second.[43] In exchange, they had destroyed 165 American aircraft of all types, sunk or damaged eighteen ships, and left 2403 Americans either killed outright or mortally wounded, in addition to 1178 less critically wounded.[44]

By approximately 1214, all aircraft that could return had done so. At roughly 1300, the task force commenced withdrawal.[45]

Meanwhile, the Americans were making determined but futile attempts to find Nagumo's forces. From Bellows, one O-47 started out in the direction of Kauai.[46] This was probably the aircraft in which McBriarty took off about 5 minutes after the last Japanese plane disappeared.*

Commander Young of the morning's *Enterprise* air group ascertained that thirteen of the planes had landed safely. He received orders to send up nine of these planes "to search a sector 330°–030° distance 175 miles," while the remaining planes were to investigate reports of Japanese surface ships and sampans south of Barber's Point, "and if found, to attack with bombs and gunfire." This was approximately 1020.

Young asked and received permission to station himself in the Ford Island Field Control Tower to direct communications with these planes and with the *Enterprise,* for at the time a Coast Guard officer was the only officer on duty. But the low power of the transmitter prevented him from communicating with either the aircraft or the carrier. This group, of course, made "no contact" with any Japanese ships.[47]

---

*See Chapter 25.

In accordance with joint planning, the Hawaiian Air Force turned over its bombers to the Navy's control.[48] But discovering that the Navy had not yet given the four A-20s a mission, General Martin personally gave them one: Try to find the carrier south of Barber's Point. These light bombers took off at 1127. They, too, failed to find anything in that direction.[49]

A large ship was in the designated position—the heavy cruiser *Minneapolis*, returning to Pearl Harbor from the fleet operating area.[50] She picked up the report of carriers in a location very close to her, and her skipper prepared a message for Kimmel reading "No carriers in sight." Somehow the radioman garbled it as "Two carriers in sight." Luckily, the fifteen scout bombers that Halsey sent to the area recognized the *Minneapolis* and withheld their fire.[51]

After dispatch of the four A-20s, Hawaiian Air Force Headquarters received "a map that had been recovered from a pilot that had been shot down on the edge of Fort Kamehameha." This map showed a number of courses to a point northwest of Oahu. As other aircraft were put in commission a little after 1200, Martin sent them off to the north, but they found nothing.[52]

One genuine contact took place in those late morning hours. At 1135, the heavy cruiser *Northampton*, flagship of Halsey's cruiser commander, RADM Raymond A. Spruance, reported from about 15 miles west of Kauai:

Section attacked by enemy single seat monoplane, engagement lasting about 20 minutes. Enemy plane made total of seven attacks diving from above or to the side of the scouting section. On all diving attacks presented an exceptionally good target as he squashed down toward the section. Apparently enemy speed 275 miles or better. Enemy plane broke out in smoke and departed.[53]

Shortly after the attack on Hickam ceased, Captain Allen found an airworthy B-17 and loaded it with bombs. He was just about ready to take off when he received orders from General Rudolph that he must wait for a fighter escort. This delayed takeoff until about 1130. The first of the three B-17s preparing for flight "jammed his propeller on takeoff and was unable to get off." Thus it happened that Allen was the first of the two Flying Fortresses in the air. Capt. "Blondie" Saunders followed.[54]

One of his crewmen, S/Sgt. Bernardino Tortona, was "all steamed up." He inquired indignantly over the intercom, "Who the hell do those little yellow bastards think they are?" He added boastfully, "We'll win this war with a couple of B-17s" and heard Saunder's skeptical laugh.[55]

Although loaded and airborne, Allen's B-17 was not really combat-fit. Two life vests that he checked were riddled with bullet holes. He had interplane communications with Saunders but none with the ground. The two B-17s were under instructions "to attack two enemy carriers reported about 35 miles south of Barber's Point." They had no better luck than their predecessors. Having no further information, they began a search southwest and northwest. After about two or three hours, Saunders's bomber developed engine trouble and had to turn back. Allen kept on until evening.[56]

By this time, Oahu had one definite piece of information. The big radio direction finder at Lualualei "had gone out of commission due to a failure of communications." Commander Rochefort was inclined to attribute the trouble to "just excitement of various people pulling out plugs." So he and his men had to rely on the station at Heeia. From that source Rochefort learned at about 1030 that "Commander Carrier Divisions" headed the enemy forces, and as of 1040, one carrier had been identified as the *Akagi*.[57]

However important, this news was of little practical value to Oahu's defenders. They were less interested in who led the attack force than in the current location of his ships and whether they would be back to renew the assault.

CHAPTER 30

"Rumors Were Coming In Fast and Furious"

Back on Ford Island, Jack Rogo learned that Chief Storekeeper Bonnett wanted help in putting up AA defenses at the paint storage building. Although uncomfortably aware that this building was very inflammable, to say the least, he joined Bonnett and three other men on the roof. Bonnett, "a quiet, unassuming man,...was setting up a machine gun with the experience of an ordnanceman. It is men in the U.S. Navy like Chief Bonnett," wrote Rogo years later, "who calm men's fears and exude confidence."

Calm and confidence were precisely what these men needed, for "rumors were coming in fast and furious. 'The Japs were landing at Hickam Field,' 'They are landing on Oahu,' 'They are landing north of us.' We couldn't tell truth from fiction, but we were going to be ready." Rogo swapped his pistol for a Springfield .30 caliber rifle. "The waiting game starts. The U.S.S. *Arizona* is close by and we watch it burn and burn and burn."[1]

Many on Oahu feared—indeed were confident—that the Japanese would return to polish off the remaining ships and installations, even try to take over the island. This belief motivated defense activities and lent color to such rumors as Rogo mentioned. Lieutenant Riggs at the Ford Island dispensary thought that the Japanese might attempt a landing. He evacuated all the seriously wounded to hospitals, using the trucks and ferries that Captain Shoemaker placed at his disposal. By 1130, only some of the slightly wounded remained, and the dispensary was ready for whatever new demands might be made on it.[2]

Howard French and many other enlisted men who had escaped

from the ships to Ford Island thought the air raid was just the initial attack. The Japanese probably would be back to renew the assault or would land the next day.[3]

Mrs. Bellinger with other women and children remained in the air raid shelter long after the real danger had passed. The admiral sent word to see how they were; they were hungry. Enlisted men, some of whom had come to the shelter toward the end of the attack, raided the pantry shelves of the officers' homes and brought back canned goods. They passed around tomato juice, each taking a sip. One man said as he opened a can, "You better take this, you don't know when you'll eat again." The first can Mrs. Bellinger received contained candied yams.[4]

Bellinger himself told Kimmel around noon that he "expected another attack at any time."[5] But whether the Japanese came back or not, they had left some problems that called for immediate, practical measures. Ford Island's landing strip had to be cleared, so civilians and sailors fell to and in about 2 hours picked up approximately 3 tons of scrap metal.[6]

There were "thousands of stragglers on Ford Island from the battleships," many badly shocked, in pain, oil-soaked, and frightened. "And they were trigger-happy," Shoemaker pointed out. "Many wanted to get hold of a rifle or machine gun and fire at random." The supply officer opened the clothing store and let them take what they needed. And somehow he fed them all—"not well, but he fed them." He boiled water from the swimming pools.[7] Rogo vividly recalled "dry sandwiches and coffee made from chlorinated swimming pool water. We were hungry so it was delicious. For a few days afterwards, we had chlorinated coffee and chlorinated soup."[8]

This practical action—boiling water meant for swimming before using it for drinking purposes—may have triggered one of the more persistent rumors of the day: "Do not drink any water. The Japanese have poisoned the water." When this warning flashed around Hickam, "of course everybody became thirsty," Lieutenant Reeves remembered, "and asked, 'What can we do?'" To which someone answered brightly, "Why, hell, get a case of beer and use it for water."[9] Captain Wilson at Schofield listed this as one of the four principal rumors of the afternoon.[10]

This tale reached Hawaiian Department Headquarters and "upset everyone." Col. Edgar King, the department surgeon, told Dunlop, "I am not surprised, but it is going to raise hell with the whole command. What you have to do, Bob, is to see to it that all the water is boiled."[11]

As late as 1822, the *Maryland*'s log recorded, "Water at Ford Island reported contaminated."[12]

As at Ford Island, the Marine Barracks took on a formidable task of feeding and clothing large numbers of men. The mess sergeant had to ask for help. All his messmen and even some of his cooks had snatched rifles and gone outside, he complained bitterly, "practicing being heroes and to hell with the mess hall." Someone remembered the Barracks brig—the holding brig for all the men in the Fleet who had been convicted by General Court Martial of serious offenses and who were awaiting transportation to mainland prisons. About twenty of these prisoners were marched to the mess hall and put to work. Not a single man caused trouble. In fact, some worked so hard and so intelligently that later their sentences were commuted subject to good behavior.[13]

Shortly after noon, the Naval Hospital appealed for extra space for some of the less seriously wounded patients. The Marine Barracks took a number of them. The PX, the beer hall, and the staff NCO Club could be cleared without too much trouble, and two barracks squeezed their men into one, turning the other over to the injured.

The Fleet Marine Force Supply Depot and the Post Quartermaster handed over fresh clothing to any officer who showed up in an oil-soaked uniform. Sailors were directed to the Receiving Barracks for uniforms and dungarees.[14]

One of those who obtained pants and a shirt from the Marine Barracks was Major Shapley. After pulling on these fresh clothes, he went to a friend's quarters. Finding no one at home, Shapley spread out the Sunday newspaper on the lanai, dropped down, and slept for almost 10 hours.[15]

At the submarine base, men continued to crawl out of the water, many half naked and covered with oil. Commander Curts told any number of officers and enlisted men to go to his room in the BOQ and help themselves to his clothes. By evening, they had cleaned him out. Meanwhile, he got in touch with the Army and asked for clothing to be shipped to Kimmel's Headquarters. Before long, two trucks arrived loaded with pants and shirts. Curts always remembered this as an example of interservice cooperation when the chips were down.[16]

Most of Curts's colleagues at Fleet Headquarters, including Kimmel and his chief of staff, Captain Smith, expected the Japanese to renew the air attack and then attempt a landing.[17] So did Captain Davis, the Fleet aviation officer.[18] Commander Layton, the Fleet Intelligence officer, estimated that the enemy would return to attack the oil tanks. "They were all right above ground and in plain sight. Such an attack would have required no special strategy by the Japanese," he explained. "All they had to do was fly some of their high level bombers over and drop their bombs. And if the oil had leaked out into the harbor it would have created a hell of a mess."[19]

The Honolulu radio stations had been broadcasting periodic warnings to all civilians, such as "Do not use your telephone. Stay off the streets. Keep calm. Keep your radio turned on for further news." The alert continued with a number of well-meant but alarming orders:

> Get your car off the street. Drive it on the lawn if necessary, just so you get it off the street.

> Fill water buckets and tubs with water, to be ready for a possible fire. Attach garden hoses. Prepare to take care of any emergency.

> Keep tuned to your radio for details of a blackout which will be announced later.

> Here is a warning to all people through the Territory of Hawaii and especially on the island of Oahu. In the event of an air raid, stay under cover. Many of the wounded have been hurt by falling shrapnel from anti-aircraft guns. If an air raid should begin, do not go out of doors. Stay under cover. You may be seriously injured or instantly killed by shrapnel falling from anti-aircraft shells.[20]

Small wonder that, according to Curts, "one of the main problems after the attack was to turn down the hysteria on the civilian side." He called the radio stations and told them sternly to "knock off the damned foolishness"—quit sending out messages that were disrupting the civilian population.[21]

At about this time, 1145, the Army G-2, with General Martin's approval, ordered Honolulu stations KGU and KGMB off the air, not to keep down panic, but "because enemy aircraft were using the beam to come in by." Shortly afterward, the stations at Hilo on Hawaii and Lihue on Kauai were cut off. "Thereafter, all radio stations went on the air only for short intervals to broadcast announcements approved by this section dealing with military and civilian defense."[22]

Of course, far from homing in on KGU and KGMB, Fuchida's airmen had long since left the area. But for most of the afternoon, some

4hips in the harbor kept reporting and firing on nonexistent or misidentified aircraft. The repair ship *Rigel* noted at 1200, "Continued bombing attack," which was "discontinued" at about 1320.[23] The 1200 to 1600 shift aboard the *New Orleans* recorded, "Continued firing intermittently at Japanese planes."[24] The *Maryland* "Sighted enemy plane on port beam" at 1229, and at 1355 "Commenced firing on enemy plane." Four times during the afternoon this battleship recorded "unidentified aircraft."[25] Officers and men aboard the *Maryland* stayed at their battle stations until after dark, "for we kept thinking that they would be back," wrote Seaman Eisnaugle. "For the rumors were that they were making landings around the Island."[26]

From this point on throughout the afternoon the stream of rumors that began to trickle that morning burst into full spate. The story of blue-clad paratroopers continued to pop up and was taken seriously enough for Shafter to receive an inquiry at 1320 "re orders to shoot on sight wearers of blue denim." While this was being checked, Chief of Staff Phillips ordered "no soldier to wear blue denim." Ten minutes later, a landing party was reported between Barber's Point and Nanakuli; the invaders were "being fired on by our P-40s."[27] When the word reached Fleet Headquarters that Japanese were landing at Barber's Point, Lieutenant East thought that they might well take over the entire island.[28]

Military police reported paratroopers near the water tower on St. Louis Heights.[29] Investigation turned up nothing more deadly than a kite tangled in a tree.[30] A sampan was supposed to be about to land near Lualualei; an unverified story had "quite a number of parachutists" landing in Pauoa Valley, near Mt. Tantalus. All this while, many Army offices were in the process of moving to the advance Headquarters at Aliamanu crater. One can understand why, toward evening, an Army colonel had to be relieved "due to mental condition."[31]

The Hawaiian Air Force contributed its bit to the general confusion, noting "enemy planes" approaching Pearl Harbor and "flying low overhead" from 1113 to 1129. At 1310, the Hawaiian Air Force claimed that the "last flight of bombers at 1130" had dropped a bomb in the Capital Grounds and Richard Street, leaving a hole 8 by 2 feet.[32]

The Navy was not backward in its offerings. "Four Japanese transports" were off Barber's Point. Paratroops were landing on the North Shore. Three telephone messages at 1319 conveyed these tidings: "Enemy sampan about to land at Naval ammunition depot.... Enemy landing party off shore Nanakuli. Friendly planes diving at them....Op-1 Southeast enemy and friendly planes in dogfight."[33]

At 1452, the Fourteenth Naval District Control Post Watch Officer's Log recorded, "Received report that five transports were sighted off Lualualei discharging troops in small craft. At this point," the log continued, "checks on the above obviously false reports began to come in, and the aircraft warning circuit was temporarily cut out in order to eliminate confusion since it was then believed that enemy agents were making false broadcasts."[34]

Kimmel echoed this belief when he wrote to Admiral Stark on December 12: "The Fifth Column activities added great confusion and it was most difficult to evaluate the reports received."[35] Even had there been a local "fifth column," Oahu's defenders would not have needed its help in generating a state of confusion on December 7, 1941. Well-meaning error was quite sufficient.

Tracking down such rumors kept Lieutenant Davis busy far into the night and for several days thereafter. Having moved with his infantry battalion from the high school to Shafter, he was put to work checking out the scuttlebutt. It was said that arrows had been cut in the cane fields so the Japanese would know where to bomb.[36] Considering the size of Pearl Harbor relative to an arrow cut in a cane field, this tale was illogical, but it was widespread nonetheless.[37] An equally well-known tale claimed that some of the Japanese whose bodies were recovered wore class rings from the University of Hawaii and other American colleges. Admiral Bloch admitted to hearing this story: "and probably [I] have been unwise enough to repeat it once or twice, but so far as I know the reports are unsubstantiated."[38]

Another of Davis's assignments read, "Japanese paratroops are landing at the water tank in the fields above you. Investigate." So off again he went with his half-ton truck and about eight soldiers, only to draw a blank. When people began to wonder how these stories got started, someone came up with another rumor by way of explanation: "A sergeant of German background in the Headquarters of the Hawaiian Department was feeding these messages into official channels."[39]

Hard work, much of it heartbreaking, was going on in Pearl Harbor. At 1300 the *Sicard* set up .50 caliber machine guns, having received ammunition from the West Loch. "Battle stations manned and landing force organized to repel boarders."[40] Aboard the *Maryland*, Eisnaugle lost track of time until a cook "came around with some boiled eggs" about 1300. The boatswain's mate in charge of Eisnaugle's division asked that each man "kick in a little change to buy our new 'shipmates' some toilet articles and things of necessity to live on until they could be re-outfitted. For they didn't have a thing!" These were the men who had taken refuge on the *Maryland*.[41]

Shipfitters from the *Tern* and other small vessels were working on the *Oklahoma*, cutting holes in her sides with torches to rescue men trapped. "Some of these boys were still alive, but practically out of their minds." Some died when the torches cut through, because smoke seeped in and used up the oxygen in the compartments.

All this made Emil Johnson and his shipmates hate the Japanese. "I would have killed any one of them if I could have gotten my hands on one of the bastards," he declared. "Hell, we couldn't believe it, because the Japanese envoys had been down on the dock only a week or so before and there was the ambassador in Washington talking peace."[42]

Sickened by the fate of his comrades aboard the *Oklahoma*, Gunner's Mate Beck heartily echoed Johnson's sentiments. "There was a deep, powerful thirst for revenge on the part of every enlisted man. I wouldn't have given any Japanese a second of mercy after Pearl Harbor."[43]

Chief Crawford watched men "hauled out of the water like fish" and brought to Aiea Dock. "Most of them were all wrapped up by the time they got ashore and no one knew who they were. They were stretched out there on Aiea Dock like so many sacks of wheat." A cold rage seized him. "If I could have gotten my hands on any one of those Japanese," he declared, "I would have crushed him like an insect!"[44]

Aboard Crawford's ship, the *Vestal*, Ensign Hesser walked over her decks. Among the litter of debris he spotted a roll of bills—$260 in various denominations, obviously blown from the *Arizona*. Hesser wondered how the money had made it over undamaged. He also spied a drawer from a crewman's locker. In it he found a number of letters addressed to a sailor on the *Arizona*, as well as one the boy had started to write to his mother the previous night. Hesser remembered that it ended something like this: "I am going to turn in now, Mother, I'll finish this tomorrow." Hesser dried these letters and kept them. After the war, he delivered them to the sailor's father, a judge in New York City.[45]

About midafternoon, Commander Johnson and several others went back aboard the aft part of the *West Virginia*. "But there was not much we could do, because everything was burned to a crisp. There was nothing on that ship that was functioning at the time. You couldn't cook a meal on it, you couldn't fire a gun on it. The vessel was in very bad shape." He added, "Had the Japanese come back the next day, *West Virginia* would have been totally unable to fight back." He thought that if they returned and landed, they could take over Oahu. But he was not sure they would try.[46]

The *West Virginia* was receiving help from a humble source—"a little garbage scow." The scow's crew of five men kept her powerful hoses going for 48 hours without relief, breaking up the oil fires on the water.[47]

The *Nevada* had her fires under control by 1530 and 20 minutes later removed her dead—two officers and twenty-seven men. The flames broke out again at 1830 and did not come under control until 2300.[48] The *Shaw*, too, fought fire until 1530. "As soon as it was safe to get aboard, started removing remains and getting depth charges out of racks."[49]

The destroyer tender *Dobbin* sent a motor launch at 1535 to the northeast point of Ford Island to take survivors of the *Arizona* to the Fleet Landing. At 1730 she took aboard 200 men from the *Raleigh* for food and temporary berthing.[50]

The *Raleigh* was still in bad shape, but her captain was ready and willing to help others. At about 1215, Simons heard a voice over the auxiliary radio "reporting that six enemy transports were landing troops on the north side of Oahu, clad in blue denim"; later paratroopers might be expected. So Simons sent all the men he could spare to the Air Station, taking with them rifles, machine guns, pistols, and ammunition. He learned later that these reports were false.

At 1713 the tug *Avocet* came alongside the *Raleigh* "supplying electricity and steam, and hot coffee and sandwiches." This was the first food Simons had eaten since the previous night, "though the crew had been provided for."[51]

That afternoon and early that evening, a submarine scare triggered considerable action. "We all thought that there was another submarine in the harbor at the time," said Kimmel.[52] At 1508 the *Curtiss* "reported sighting submarine."[53] Then at 1715 the *Case*, on her way out of the harbor, depth-charged what she thought was a sunken submarine.[54] An hour and twenty-five minutes later the *Hulbert*, steaming down channel, sighted "what appeared to be submarine periscope on starboard beam off Berth F-6, commenced steaming ahead and astern over area in attempt to ram."[55] Fourteen minutes after that, the *Maryland*'s log noted, "Submarine periscope reported south end of Ford Island."[56]

The ships on patrol outside Pearl Harbor were equally concerned about submarines and with much better cause, for in addition to the five midget submarines—at least two probably sunk already and one disabled—seven of Japan's finest large undersea craft were stationed in a fan-shaped sector south of Oahu.*Commander Outerbridge expended all of the *Ward*'s depth charges. When the *Chew* relieved the *Ward* at 1245, Outerbridge took his destroyer into the West Loch and renewed his supply. At 1640 he took her out again, fully anticipating plenty of action. He thought the Japanese would attempt a landing on Oahu and greatly feared that they could conquer the island.[57]

About half an hour before relieving the *Ward*, the *Chew* made a supersonic contact, dropped two depth charges, and heard one explode. She doubled this at 1515, when she "made supersonic contact in defensive sea area west of entrance buoys. Dropped four depth charges, two explosions heard."[58]

At 1300 the *Aylwin*, steaming on the *Detroit*'s starboard beam at some 600 yards, "reported sighting two torpedo wakes passing toward and astern of *Detroit*." Soon the *Detroit* spotted two explosions on the horizon, which the observers assumed had been caused by these torpedoes' end-of-run detonation.[59] In the midst of this excitement, Draemel received a message to the effect that Japanese troops were landing at Nanakuli Beach. He led his entire force to that part of the island only to draw a blank. Draemel was under orders to rendezvous with Halsey, and this false alarm delayed the encounter until 1643.[60]

Another cruiser on a similar fruitless errand was the *St. Louis*. At 1205, Captain Rood received a signal from Kimmel's Headquarters which, to the best of Rood's recollection, read: "Enemy ship five miles south of Barber's Point." So Rood changed direction and sped off to this location. On the way, from 1213 to 1234, the *St. Louis*'s guns banged away at "enemy aircraft." The cruiser had scarcely swung into her new course when there lifting over the horizon was a ship headed almost due east toward Barber's Point. "There are the Japanese!" Rood thought with satisfaction. "My boys were at General Quarters and

---

* See chart, following Contents.

itching to knock hell out of them." Fortunately, Rood recognized the approaching ship as the *Minneapolis*, which thus had another narrow squeak.[61]

She was not the only lucky American vessel. The destroyer-minelayer *Gamble*'s No. 1 gun opened fire at 1632 "on a surfacing submarine." The first shot fell short; the second failed to fire. The submarine promptly submerged and sent up an emergency signal identifying herself as the U.S.S. *Thresher*.[62]

Possibly the strangest case of mistaken identity came shortly after Halsey had launched fifteen planes to search 200 miles south and west of the *Enterprise*. One of the pilots advised the *Enterprise* that he had sighted an enemy carrier and cruiser, giving the latitude and longitude. Halsey promptly sent up his eighteen torpedo planes, four scout bombers, and six fighters.[63]

The pilot who claimed this contact also reported "that he had dropped two bombs on this carrier, which was zigzagging at high speed, and then had been chased some eighty miles downwind." Admiral Brown's position being within 90 miles of the coordinates, Kimmel's Headquarters directed him "to get the carrier." Brown promptly replied that he believed the ship bombed was the *Portland*. So Headquarters radioed the heavy cruiser, which was with Admiral Newton's *Lexington* force, "Were you bombed this afternoon?" The *Portland* replied, "Yes, a plane dropped two bombs narrowly missing me astern."

When the pilot in question, a man with "a very fine reputation," reached Oahu that night, virtually every member of Kimmel's staff questioned him. He declared "he knew it was a Japanese carrier because he saw the Rising Sun painted on her deck." He added "that this carrier had the plan of a heavy cruiser painted on her deck as camouflage."[64] It later developed that the "cruiser" accompanying the "carrier" was the destroyer *Porter*.[65]

Naturally, when the attack force that the *Enterprise* had dispatched reached the reported location, "nothing was there." So Halsey directed them to proceed on and land at Ford Island; however—most fortunately for them—the torpedo planes and scouts returned to the *Enterprise*, but the fighters proceeded to Ford, with disastrous results.[66]*

The *Enterprise* herself escaped at least an attempted bombing when Captain Allen spotted "this beautiful carrier" far below his B-17. Mis-

---

* See Chapter 32.

taking her for an enemy flattop, he went into a bomb run and pulled out just in time. "God had a hand on me," he said later, "because I knew this was not a Jap carrier." He turned northward, but finding nothing, swung back southward. He saw the *Enterprise* again, much nearer to Oahu, and two Navy Wildcat fighters flew up for a look at him. Satisfied, they let him proceed back to Hickam, leaving the *Enterprise* safe to carry out a war career second to none.[67]

CHAPTER 31

"Everybody Thought the Japanese Would Be Back"

So much had happened in so short a time that to some of the survivors it seemed like many hours had passed, instead of little over two, when the attack ended. As Avery and his companions walked back to their bungalow following the "All Clear" signal, one man asked, "Is it time for dinner?"

Avery glanced at his watch and replied, "Hell, it's a long time yet before chow."

"They can shoot up the whole damn station if they like," his friend shot back, "but if they put that galley out of commission I'm gonna be mad like one devil!"

When chow time did roll around, the men did not have to go to the mess hall; a truck came around with hot coffee, corned beef sandwiches, and pork and beans. Avery was grateful for this evidence of Cmdr. "Beauty" Martin's concern for his men's welfare at a time when "there were other weighty problems demanding his attention." But Avery could not partake:

> I was so stimulated by the excitement that I had no desire for either
> food or water until supper-time the following Thursday, and I did
> not take even a moment's sleep until after 0400 Thursday morning....
> Not a morsel of food, nor a drop of liquid of any kind, yet I remained
> alert and energetic.

Nor did nicotine keep him going; Avery was a nonsmoker.[1]

While the chow truck was at the bungalow, a messenger arrived to say that Martin, in anticipation of a Japanese landing party, had

342

ordered a change of uniform. "Each man was to bring two suits of whites to the mess hall to be dyed." No dye being available, the whites were dipped in "very strong, boiling hot coffee. They came out a dark brown." Nearby, at the armory, "Sands and his shipmates were in high glee. They gladly reenacted their roles in the duel," describing every detail of shooting down Iida for the benefit of Avery and others who had come to ask about it.

Back at the bungalow, Avery discovered that the army had moved in two AA batteries, "manned by reservists with less than 90 days of Regular Army experience." Most appeared to be between 18 and 22 years of age. They arrived at about 1400, and Avery conceded that they set up in an efficient manner.[2]

Radioman Moser awoke about 1600 as he was being put into an ambulance that took him and three other wounded men to the Territorial Hospital in the town of Kaneohe. "This later caused some consternation among state-side friends who knew Territorial as a mental hospital and didn't know that we had been taken there because of lack of hospital facilities at the air station."

Moser needed expert care, for he had been hit in many places, the most serious wound being "just below the belt line on the southeast side while traveling north. This had cut the main artery in the right leg." During his stay in the hospital he received fifteen blood transfusions which came from a mixed bag of donors—six Japanese, five Caucasians, two Chinese, and one each Filipino and Korean.[3]

This mixture of blood was a tribute to community solidarity. An emergency call for plasma brought hundreds to Queen's Hospital in Honolulu, much faster than the doctors could take the blood. Donors stood in line for hours: white, brown, black, and every imaginable tint in between—huge Hawaiian workmen, dainty Chinese girls, white-collar workers by the busload, field and dock laborers, and Japanese by the hundreds, the older generation clad in black in token of respect.

Soldiers and sailors tried to sneak through the line twice. The entire crew and some of the passengers from the Dutch ship *Jagersfontein*, which happened to be in Honolulu Harbor, showed up. A group of prostitutes gave blood and then begged to help with the work. The center gratefully set them to clean-up tasks. Former Governor and Mrs. Frear waited their turn. That morning Mrs. Frear and her little Japanese housemaid had wept in each other's arms; now she stood in line, composed and smiling. When a nurse tactfully hinted that at

78 and 72, respectively, Frear and his wife were somewhat over the 50-year age limit for donors, Mrs. Frear pushed the objection aside. "It ought to be very good blood," she protested. "It has lasted us a long time!"[4]

Many spent the afternoon looking for wounded, taking them to hospitals, and helping men to get to their units. The hospital at Hickam had limited facilities and was overflowing, so Lieutenant Reeves personally drove his car back and forth to Tripler Hospital.[5]

Laurence Nakatsuka of the Honolulu *Star-Bulletin* hurried off to see what news he could gather at the Japanese consulate, having wrung a reluctant consent from editor Riley H. Allen, who feared for the safety, even the life, of his AJA* reporter "on that tumultuous morning."[6] He had covered the consulate a number of times and was friendly with Kita and Yoshikawa.[7] At first Kita refused to admit that Japanese were attacking Oahu, let alone give Nakatsuka a statement. The reporter had to rush back to the office for a copy of the day's extra and present it to Kita as confirmation.[8]

Meanwhile, Shivers of the FBI discovered that the consulate was not guarded and still had telephone service. "I tried to find out who could properly take over that duty there and I could not find anybody who would do it," he said, "so I instructed the Chief of Police to place a guard around the consulate for the protection of the consul general and the members of his staff and the consular property."[9]

Around 1215, Chief Gabrielson turned the job over to Captain of Detectives Benjamin Van Kuren and Lt. Yoshio Hasegawa of the Records Division. Taking along Capt. Robert Kennedy and two detectives, they soon reached the consulate. Uniformed policemen armed with sawed-off shotguns "were patrolling on the outside boundaries of the consulate." Two of these guards escorted Van Kuren and Hasegawa to the rear of the building. There in the driveway stood Kita, "dressed in a pair of gray slacks and a light-colored, short-sleeved, sport shirt, open at the neck." He was holding the *Star-Bulletin* extra with its scarehead WAR! OAHU BOMBED BY JAPANESE PLANES, and talking to Nakatsuka. When Van Kuren informed him that the police were establishing a guard over the members of the consulate, he merely nodded acknowledgment.[10] This cool reaction was typical. "Kita," said Kotoshirodo, "was the type who could be sitting on top of a volcano and still maintain a calm, detached and aloof attitude."[11]

---

* American of Japanese Ancestry.

The little group entered the office building through the rear door. A nearby room was closed and locked. Van Kuren asked Kita to open it. The Consul General knocked several times before the door opened.[12] Behind it Yoshikawa and Tsukikawa had been busily burning papers. Yoshikawa had hopped to this task as soon as Nakatsuka confirmed that an attack was in progress. He burned one code and his coded material in a wash tub in the code room. This was as much of his own papers as he had to get rid of, because he made a practice of destroying material periodically to keep his files clear as well as to avoid the obvious risks involved in having too much of it on hand. He helped Tsukikawa with the other papers and let Kita, whom he took to be a policeman, keep hammering at the door until he was sure everything of importance had been burned.[13]

Not only these two men, but Okuda, Consular Secretary Kyonosuke Yuge, and Treasurer Kohichi Seki were in the code room. Kita and Hasegawa explained that the newcomers were police officers. Van Kuren ordered his men to search each member of the staff "in order to prevent the concealment of weapons or dangerous drugs on their persons."[14]

The smoke-filled room produced one "bellows type envelope that was full of papers that had not been destroyed." This Van Kuren and his men later brought to the FBI, who passed it along to Naval Intelligence.[15] As for the consulate's telephones, the lines "had gone dead or something," as Shivers slyly expressed it.[16]

While these dramatic events were taking place in the office building, John Mikami drove up in his taxi. Although not formally a consulate employee, this elderly driver frequently chauffered various members of the staff, including Yoshikawa. This morning, war or no war, he was ready to fulfill his engagement to take Kita and Okuda to the golf course. He asked one of the police guards to inform Okuda of his arrival. Okuda sent back a message not to wait; he "probably would be unable to play golf that day."[17]

Another individual of Japanese extraction was trying hard not to let the war overcome his performance of duty. Throughout the morning, RCA messenger Tadao Fuchikami had patiently inched his motorcycle toward Shafter. Thanks to the monumental traffic jam and the National Guard and police roadblocks, he did not jump off his machine at the Shafter message center until 1145.[18]

The Army clerk kidded Fuchikami "for having this red circle on his arm....he had better take that off or somebody might take him for a

Japanese."[19] Among the messages he delivered was General Marshall's warning to Short concerning the deadline of 1300 EST for Nomura to present Japan's final note to Hull.*

This message wended its way to the code room, where Lt. J. H. Babcock decoded it. The clear copy did not reach Colonel Dunlop in the Adjutant General Section until 1458.[20] The contents filled him with a half-ironic, half-disgusted amusement, and he barked out a bitter laugh. "The damn thing won't do any good now," he reflected. Then he handed it to a nearby officer with the order, "Get this to General Short at once. Take it right to him."[21]

While it was on its way, a copy reached Colonel Phillips. In discussing the contents with Capt. William B. Cobb, an officer of the Judge Advocate General Department on duty in Phillips's office, the chief of staff remarked that this "must be the message to which Gen. Marshall was referring, and which he asked me if I had received."† Soon after this, Cobb heard Phillips telephoning the contents to Short.[22]

Meanwhile, the department signal officer, Lt. Col. Carroll A. "Cappy" Powell, called in his friend Major Fleming and asked him to carry a message to the general. When Fleming asked him "why in hell he didn't deliver his own messages," Powell explained that he "had had a couple of run-ins with the general." So he did not want to be the one to give Short this dispatch because "General Short would probably go through the roof and land all over him." Fleming, he continued persuasively, "knew General Short better than he did" and probably "would be safer from the flak." Fleming agreed to deliver it, but not unless he could read it first. Having done so, he delivered it to the general, saying that "here was an 'eyes only' message for him that just arrived."

"Have you read it?" Short asked. At Fleming's affirmative, Short continued, "What are you doing delivering messages?"

"Well, the Signal Officer didn't want to come in here," explained Fleming. "He's read it, he didn't want to come in and deliver it himself because he knew you would be extremely angry about it." Whereupon he handed the paper to Short, who, just as predicted, "about went through the roof."[23]

Kimmel reacted with equal vigor when he read a copy that Cobb,

---

* See Chapter 5.

† See Chapter 27.

acting as the Army's messenger, brought to Fleet Headquarters. In a fury, the admiral flung it into his wastebasket.[24]

In all areas preparations were under way to meet the expected Japanese return engagement. Soon after Short received the Marshall message, General Murray of the 25th Infantry Division and his assistant division commander reported to Short at the advanced Headquarters "to inform him that the division was completely in position and had the first unit of fire at the guns."[25]

At Wheeler, "figuring that most of our airplanes were destroyed," Colonel Flood got hold of four Air Force officers who had been in the infantry and formed four infantry companies using Air Force personnel. "We put them around the field...to watch for anybody that might come in." Then he called Phillips, asking for "some troops to guard the airfield. We thought we might be able to get some planes up. Of course we didn't know what was coming." Phillips sent a battalion of infantry from Schofield, and Flood turned his ground personnel over to the major in command of the battalion.[26]

According to General Davidson, Wheeler's fighters were by no means out of the picture. By sunset he had, as he remembered, about a hundred aircraft capable of flying. He felt quite sure that if the enemy had come back that night, with that all-important element of surprise gone, his fighters could have polished off all their bombers.[27]

At Hickam, too, Hawaiian Air Force personnel served as ground defenders to protect the airfield and bomb dump in case of the anticipated Japanese landing.[28] Corporal Bongo was shocked at the amount of damage the enemy had inflicted at Hickam and nearby Pearl Harbor. He "expected the Japanese to continue the attack later the same day." He thought a quick follow-through could well succeed, "because everything was in utter confusion that first day." If they waited until Monday or Tuesday, however, the result might be different.[29]

Col. "Cush" Farnum, too, believed that a prompt landing might win the Japanese control of Hawaii. The Navy seemed to him demoralized. "They were like a defeated football team. They were down and out."[30] Colonel Farthing recalled, "Everybody thought the Japanese would be back and could not understand why they didn't land."[31]

General Martin seemed to age before Colonel Mollison's eyes. "The attack crushed Martin utterly," said his chief of staff. "He walked around like a corpse." The general was no coward, but an old ulcer had reactivated and robbed him of physical stamina. At about 1500, he stammered to Mollison, "What am I going to do? I believe I am losing the power of decision." Mollison tried to reassure, comfort, and encourage him, but he could not raise the general's spirits.[32]

Dunlop stole about 15 minutes to go home for a bite to eat and a cup of coffee. On his way, he mused, "We're going to get knocked off just as sure as hell!" He gave Mrs. Dunlop a brief rundown of the current situation and hurried back to his office just in time to take a message from Col. Hollis L. Mueller, commanding the mobile AA regiment, that all his units were in the field. They discussed the safety of the women and children. Mueller mentioned the cave outside Shafter. "There is room there now for about 500 women. But there are no comforts, for there is rubble all over the ground. But they will be protected by more than ten feet of rock on top of them."

"We'll send them up there as soon as possible," Dunlop declared.

His assistant, Major Thiebaud, spent the afternoon trying to identify the dead at Hickam Field, for many men had not been wearing their dog tags when they were killed. Immediate burial was essential. Between 1500 and 1600, some 400 Hickam men were buried at Schofield in a triple ceremony—Protestant, Catholic, and Jewish.[33]

Because "something, presumably Japanese bombs," had struck buildings and killed people in Honolulu, Col. W. A. Capron, the department ordnance officer, organized a bomb squad of three civilian ammunition technicians to investigate. They checked out every incident and came back with a discomfiting report. The missiles were neither Japanese bombs nor Army ammunition. "They were antiaircraft ammunition of another service...," Capron later explained delicately, "whose time fuses had failed to function in the air. This particular type of ammunition had a base fuse with a tracer that would function on impact, and it was those items which led to the belief that the Japanese had bombed the city."[34]

One incident hints that image was becoming a concern. Three men had been scheduled for duty at the Opana Station that morning, but only Private Lockard and Elliott had showed up.* Now an officer called in Lockard and sent him back to the unit for a statement to be signed by the two privates. He wanted Elliott to incorporate therein the name of the absent soldier. "It was put to me that they wanted to keep the records straight," Elliott stated. No one was supposed to operate the unit "unless the motorman was present to operate that motor," and neither

---

* See Chapter 7.

Lockard nor Elliott was a qualified mechanic. Elliott refused to include the absentee's name, and the report was written up using the noncommittal personal pronoun—"'we' did this and 'we' did that."[35]

The tasks, however distasteful and difficult, that faced the officers and men of Oahu's military establishment gave them something constructive to do and a sense of accomplishment. They knew what had happened and could act and plan accordingly. Their dependents had no such relief. As Mrs. Potts remarked, "All we got was rumors and the radio."[36] The radio could give them no direct news of their husbands, and the scuttlebutt only made matters worse. "Those terrible, dreadful rumors affected the women worse than anything else," said "Soldier" Burford. "People could scream because of them!"[37]

Elise Newton, wife of Admiral Newton, resolved to find out what she could. She was not in the best of health, and whenever the admiral went to sea, a chief petty officer named Peacock stood by to look after her. At about 1100, Mrs. Newton asked Peacock to go to Pearl Harbor, investigate, and let her know as much of the facts as were available.

As soon as he returned, about a dozen Navy wives, including Betty Smith, gathered in the Newton home to hear his story. Peacock, hat in hand, was "the most solemn person" Mrs. Smith had ever seen as he gave them the dreadful news. When he reached the end, his voice plunged with the weight of his words: "The whole American Navy has been sunk!" Then he seemed to brighten, and he added, "but Admiral Newton is out there and he'll get them!"

After the group broke up, Mrs. Smith and a Navy enlisted man spent much of the afternoon looking for Capt. Arthur Davis's wife. She had been ill, and Betty wanted to bring her to her home where she could take care of her. A trip to the Davis household proved fruitless. Finally, they located her in a nearby hospital. Assured that Mrs. Davis was in good hands, Betty returned to her quarters to prepare for what might happen next: another air attack, an enemy landing, or an uprising on Oahu. The authorities had repeatedly warned Navy wives that in case of an emergency the local Japanese might rise up and massacre American women. "We were genuinely fearful," she said.[38]

At about 1300, Captain Bruns told the women of his household that they must leave the Pearl Harbor area immediately. So Mrs. Bruns and her two daughters, Kathleen Cooper and Betty Bruns, drove off to join their friend, Trudy Kraft, in her apartment in downtown Honolulu. Kathleen left in tears and with the utmost reluctance. She had had no word of her husband's submarine, the *Pollack*, and all morning she had been deeply concerned on his behalf. She would much rather remain at home where Bud would know where to find her when—and if—he returned.

When they had to leave, however, she felt almost drained of emotion. "By this time practically everyone was numb," she recalled. Passing through the gate from Pearl Harbor was an unreal experience: traffic snarled into a huge knot, smoke billowing overhead, people rushing about feverishly.

The three women spent the afternoon with Mrs. Kraft, talking, planning, and wondering what had happened to the U.S. forces, and especially to their friends. The rumor cropped up that the water had been poisoned, but they drank it anyway. Over the radio they heard many sporadic military broadcasts that only added to their confusion and depression. At the back of their minds lay the possibility that the Japanese might take over the island.[39]

At Schofield, some time around 1400, someone came to the barracks where Mrs. Haynes was staying and advised the women there that it had been decided to let them go home. Mrs. Haynes thankfully hurried home and again tried to eat a meal—this time a long overdue lunch. As she was about to sit down, more soldiers interrupted her; they were rounding up the dependents again.[40]

To Mrs. Leard's barracks at Schofield came a representative from the Red Cross. The hospital had run out of bandages. Would the women roll some? Glad of something to do, the refugees sat down at bridge tables and pitched in, a few mothers watching the children. Even as they worked, many of these women were distraught; some could not help crying because they had no idea where their husbands were, and whether they were alive or dead. The inevitable crop of rumors sprang up in this dismal atmosphere. It was a relief to be told at about 1600 that they could go home. They were to black out one room and the bathroom and confine themselves to those two places.

No sooner had Mrs. Leard returned than a young wife from Wheeler came to her door. "Mrs. Leard, you are the only person I know here. Would you feed my two babies?" she implored. "I have just been back at Wheeler Field and a bomb has gone through the corner of my house." Mrs. Leard obligingly took in the two toddlers and fed them along with her own son, Bob.[41]

Among those moved to the cave outside Shafter were Dunlop's wife, Ruth, and her 81-year-old mother, Mrs. Lucy Ord Mason. A feisty woman who had lost her husband at the Battle of Wounded Knee in 1891, Mrs. Mason gave her twelve canaries enough food to last them for four days and then went with Ruth and the others.[42] Mrs. Short was among those at the cave. She had anticipated sailing the previous Friday aboard an Army transport to the mainland for a holiday visit to Oklahoma City with their son, a West Point cadet. But the sailing had been postponed.[43] Now she, Mrs. Dunlop, and other wives worked to clean up the forbidding cave, give it a semblance of human habitation, and improvise sanitary facilities. The shelter held only one water spigot to serve the needs of approximately 400 women and children.

The gallant manner in which the evacuees made the best of their dreary surroundings excited Dunlop's admiration. "It was one of the most heroic things I have ever seen," he said. He paid special tribute to Mrs. Mason. "She took it all in stride, cave and all, the discomforts and everything that went with them. She slept like a top every night. She was a real trooper—and she lived to be 93."[44]

General Short and Major Fleming visited "the tunnel," as Fleming called the cave. "Stay in there and pitch, Walter," Mrs. Short exhorted her husband. Mrs. Fleming produced her entire lunch for the major's inspection—a thick slice of ham between two slabs of bread. Then the two officers "wandered around chatting with the women and children, some of whom were kind of jittery." Later Mrs. Fleming left the shelter long enough to go home and collect her bridge tables and some from her neighbors "so the gals could start a 'tunnel tournament.'"[45]

The 200-odd women and children who had crowded the Bellingers' shelter on Ford Island gradually dwindled to about thirty. Mrs. Bellinger returned to her home, to discover that shrapnel and machine-gun bullets had punctured the roof. Thereafter, she shivered every time she heard an alarm, which she attributed to reflex action rather than actual fright. The Bellinger children, however, found all the alarms "better than the Fourth of July."[46]

At the Naval Hospital, the chief nurse made her rounds to formulate a schedule. Lt. Erickson went off duty at 1600. She did not feel tired, nor did many of her associates. "We were riding on nervous energy and wanted to keep right on going," she said. But she knew she must rest, because she was due back in the hospital later and must be alert and vigorous for whatever ordeals the night might bring.[47]

CHAPTER 32

"Jumpy and Trigger-Happy"

When Laurence Nakatsuka returned to the Honolulu *Star-Bulletin* offices, he "related with every evidence of satisfaction that the Japanese consul just had been taken over and he was glad to see that the Japs were locked up at this time." In the past, he had experienced a feeling "that he was being, as he expressed it, pushed around by the Japs at the consulate."[1]

Ironically enough, the consulate officials were among the more comfortably situated that evening. Van Kuren established them in an outer office that was "rather large, contained many large easy chairs, a carpeted floor and a desk." A guard of three men under Lieutenant Hasegawa was established in the building.

After nightfall, the staff was moved to the large lanai, "and chairs were placed there for their comfort." In both locations they enjoyed bathroom privileges. "Dinner was served to the members of the staff in the usual manner." They also had several Scotch-and-soda highballs, with fruits, nuts, and candies. But they did not go to bed that night. The police insisted that they remain fully clothed and ready to evacuate at any minute, in case of another attack. "I might add," Van Kuren wrote, "that this precaution was taken by every individual on the island."[2]

These Japanese had nothing to fear from a further attack on Oahu, even a landing party, except the possibility of a stray bomb striking the consulate compound. Far otherwise the American residents of whatever racial or national background.

Oahu figuratively tightened its belt and chinstrap. After conferring with Governor Poindexter and Colonel Fielder, Short announced at 1545 that martial law had been declared and that blackout of the island would begin at sundown.[3] Alfred L. Castle, head of the Red Cross, met with key workers at city hall while "shooting was still going on." Among those present was Mrs. Herman von Holt, in charge of the women volunteers. By 1400, Mrs. W. W. G. Moir had mobilized the forty women of the Motor Corps located all over Oahu and arranged 24-hour shifts to transport refugees to places of safety and run errands for the police and disaster council. On the lanai of historic Iolani Palace, the Red Cross set up a canteen under the direction of Mrs. Vernon Tenny and Mrs. Wayne Pflueger. There, food was served to various emergency workers.[4]

By 1850, Headquarters of the Hawaiian Air Force had recovered its collective composure sufficiently to send a radiogram report to General Arnold in Washington: Damage to Hickam and Wheeler was severe. Martin had remaining seven B-17s, six B-18s, eight A-20s, and forty pursuit planes. He urged Arnold to send "all possible reinforcement heavy bombardment fully equipped," plus additional fighters, dive bombers, and spare parts. "Additional ground personnel will be needed as large part of Air Corps troops are being used in close-in defense and anti-sabotage guards."[5]

The barracks at Hickam having been destroyed, many enlisted men had to bunk down under trees, set up pup tents, or sleep in the open under blankets. These men were understandably in a state of nerves, challenging anyone in sight, shouting at every shadow. Officers' quarters were full of enlisted men. Several settled in Colonel Farnum's home and drank his entire stock of potables except a bottle of apricot brandy. "But nobody minded," said Farnum. "This was war."[6]

Rumors ran riot. "The city of San Francisco is under attack." And even more mind-boggling, "Kansas City is under bombardment." That one startled Lieutenant Reeves into a mental "Jesus Christ, Kansas City! If the Japs have done that, we're sunk!"[7]

Fielder telephoned Bicknell with the startling information, "The Japanese are coming in again! They have a four-engine bomber."

"How in the hell could they be bringing in a four-engine bomber?" Bicknell demanded.[8]

What Fielder had seen—or heard about—could only have been one of Hickam's two B-17s which had been scouting. Capt. "Blondie" Saunder's Flying Fortress narrowly escaped being shot down when it landed, low on fuel.[9]

Captain Allen had the same experience. "Everyone was gun-happy and shooting at us when we landed." He climbed out into a dismal scene: The field was blacked out, a light tropical drizzle was falling, everyone was armed. "Someone had two Orientals at the end of a bayonet marching them off."

Tired and hungry, Allen headed for bomber Headquarters, to find that it had been moved to a quartermaster warehouse. "Rudolph's face almost dropped off when he saw me," Allen remembered. He had been gone so long that the general and his colleagues had given him up for dead.

Rudolph designated Allen and Saunders to lead two flights before dawn. The remaining B-17s were to take off at that time on an armed reconnaissance to the south, because the estimate was that the Japanese task force would return to the homeland by way of the Marshall Islands.

By this time ravenous, Allen went to the Officers' Club for dinner; it was closed. He tried a field kitchen; it had run out of food. So he proceeded to his quarters, only to stumble over a group of enlisted men who had eaten all his food and drunk all his liquor. Resignedly, he gave up hope of eating and settled down to sleep. [10]

A miniature battle broke out shortly after dark when Lieutenant Davis's outfit and a nearby unit began to take pot shots at one another for no apparent reason. "This was not just a stray shot here and there; it was a genuine firefight with a good amount of volume to it." Fortunately, there were no casualties.

A major came down to find out what the shooting was all about. As he and Davis started toward the scene, Davis fell back, as military courtesy demanded. Under the circumstances, the major was not interested in protocol and motioned for Davis to go ahead. [11]

Shortly after this situation simmered down, Davis received another of the directives that kept him and his party so well occupied that they had only about an hour's sleep the entire night: "There is a phosphorescent arrow on a bridge at a certain location pointing to Pearl Harbor and Hickam Field. Investigate." Davis did so and found nothing. [12]

Driving to the telephone company office on communications business, Captain Sampson of the Hawaiian Department was stopped several times. Guards even poked the barrels of their guns over the glass in his car door to make sure he would not pull anything before identifying himself. This was unnerving because, as he said, "Everyone was jumpy and trigger-happy."[13]

Private Michaud and his colleagues at Kaaawa expected the Japanese to return, and the prospect worried them, for their total armament consisted of one .45 caliber pistol and seven rounds of ammunition. Later they received a .30 caliber Enfield rifle each and a .30 caliber machine gun. Less welcome, they also were assigned a second lieutenant to take charge. "Unfortunately, his lack of experience did nothing to help our situation," Michaud wrote, "and when night came he kept seeing lights on the mountain behind us, and ordering our machine gunner to shoot them out. He shot that mountain full of lead, but the lights blazed on. It turned out that they were stars. He was obviously terrified. I suppose we all were, but I think the rest of us contained it better."[14]

Similar fear and lack of experience on the part of the young Reservists of the AA batteries at Kaneohe caused a nightmarish situation. By the same token, Avery later reflected somewhat cynically that "we who survived owe all our thanks to their lack of skill and experience." He was upstairs on the sleeping porch looking out to sea for signs of the Japanese landing parties, which he confidently expected, when at about 2000 the sentry who had been patrolling the beach with increasing nervousness finally lost his self-control. Avery "heard his fear-frenzied voice screech 'Halt!' and simultaneously he pulled the trigger." His shot passed through the wall "right between two men who sat on the floor leaning against the wall." It also "touched off a crazy spree of firing by both batteries." The scene burned itself into Avery's memory:

> Tracers could be seen going almost straight up or in an almost flat trajectory....They fired in all directions. At what, neither they nor anyone else knew. Every soldier who had a rifle was firing furiously. The Air Station siren sounded General Quarters but no one had a battle station so it didn't matter....Our phone rang; the Administration Building wanted to know if we were under attack by landing parties. Nobody knew....After a full ten minutes of this reckless, pell-mell firing their officers finally regained control and got the firing stopped—momentarily.[15]

The only casualty scored was at Fort Hase, just outside Kaneohe's main gate. There some soldiers wanted to see what was happening, "to watch the Japs come in," as one man said. One soldier "disliked the idea, declaring it to be too dangerous. He went to bed instead. And got a rifle bullet in the buttocks."[16]

The alarm on Kaneohe "aroused the curiosity of many civilians who drove their cars along that road to see what was happening." For reasons which Avery never understood, "the two AA batteries now brought their guns to bear on those autos and riflemen sniped at them until all were driven from the road. No casualties."[17]

To permit Kimmel and his staff to work after blackout began, the windows of his Headquarters were painted black. But the painters worked on the inside and fumes filled the offices. Because the windows could not be opened, there was no escape from the stuffy heat and blinding fumes. Captain Davis's eyes smarted so badly that he had to keep treating them with cold compresses to get any work done.[18]

Lieutenant East found the stifling heat bad enough, the general situation worse. "Make no mistake about it," he said bluntly, "people were frightened and if they say they weren't, they're damn liars." Reports poured in of Japanese landing parties at various locations, and the Navy authorities believed many of them. "They did not have too much faith in the Army to resist the Japanese or to size up the situation correctly."[19]

East's wife, Joan, was worried but did not really take in the entire picture. "I was too young and in a state of shock," she explained years later. However, she vividly remembered the blackout: "They even made us put little black covers over the radio dial at night." Nor did she forget the nasty rumors: The Japanese fleet was right off Oahu; Japanese troops had already landed. "We were told to fill our bathtubs so we would have drinking water."

The Easts lived in the Manoa valley, back in the hills, so Joan, her mother, and baby daughter did not have to leave their home. Instead, an evacuee moved in with them. This woman became stupid and hysterical with shock. Mrs. East "simply had to slap her to bring her out of it."[20]

Another service wife who did not have to evacuate was Mrs. Hodge, who was determined to carry her baby to term in spite of hostile Japanese and discouraging doctors:*

In the black, black dark that night with nothing but the radio pst-pst-psting and a rug thrown over it to keep out light, it was really

---

* See Chapter 11.

scary. All the men were gone and we women had to sit in the dark, listening to directives from the police over the radio.

The set buzzed with all sorts of strange noises and then a cop said, "Check enemy paratroopers landing in Manoa Valley...." And we heard noises crackling in the bushes outside the open door and were sure we were going to be raped by fixed bayoneted men!

A month later, when she triumphantly gave birth to a healthy baby, she was still expecting the Japanese to return to Oahu waters.[21]

Colonel Potts's home held eight women and seven children. They, too, feared that enemy paratroopers had landed, and the tropical-style house was difficult to lock up securely. "Can you imagine me sitting all night with a .38 revolver, ready to commit murder if necessary?" Mrs. Potts wrote to her sister on the mainland the next day. "I am in charge because the woman next to me is only 31 years old and the others very young."[22]

These women who stayed in their own or in neighbors' homes were fortunate, for those evacuated had unpleasant experiences. Mrs. Leard was blacking out her windows when an orderly came to the door and told her, "Get ready to move. You are going on busses." He did not know where. His instructions were: "Dress warmly. Take an extra pair of shoes, a change for the children, a robe, any concentrated food, a first aid kit, your valuables, one blanket apiece and one pillow apiece. And get to the barracks within ten minutes."

Just about that time Colonel Leard drove up with a stack of sandwiches from the Officers' Club. Mrs. Leard scooped them in and later served them to the women on the bus. They reached the barracks at about 6 p.m. One childless woman had brought her dog, Maggie, and cried bitterly when informed she could not take the dog to the shelter.[23]

During the afternoon, Mrs. Charles Davis received orders to proceed to a designated building for evacuation from the Schofield area. She donned a plain cotton maternity dress and packed some wearing apparel and cosmetics. She stowed the family silver into the suitcase, too, hoping that if the situation reached the point where she had to abandon most of her possessions, she could save at least the silverware. At the last minute she snatched up a woollen coat.

When she reached the meeting place, the atmosphere was confused and rumor-laden, but someone put the women to work rolling bandages. A major named Pierce seemed to be in charge, and the women, among themselves, promptly nicknamed him "Fierce Pierce" because he was ordering people around "like Simon Legree with a bull whip."

After what seemed an interminable wait, Mrs. Davis was herded with other dependents into a bus that set off for Honolulu. As it bumped over a narrow, winding road, the right rear wheel slipped into a ditch. Mrs. Davis was severely jolted, for she happened to be sitting over that wheel. Because of her pregnancy, the other women were very solicitous and tried to make her comfortable.

Passing near the Pearl Harbor area, the women could see warships burning in the distance. "It was a frightening, sickening sensation to realize what the Japanese had done and what they still might do," said Mrs. Davis, "and to think that hundreds of brave men had died that day on those ships or for all we knew were dying that very minute."

After several hours, her bus arrived at an elementary school, "bleak and blacked out."[24] Mrs. "Skinny" Haynes, ever alive to the ridiculous, noted sardonically that this was a school that had been scheduled for immediate evacuation in case of an attack.[25] The weather had turned rainy and chilly, and Mrs. Davis was thankful for her coat. She had no blanket, so it provided her only protection from the cold and from the bare wooden floor where she and her companions stretched out. She wondered how this experience would affect the life growing within her.[26]

General Wilson's wife was among those who crowded into a bus, the driver of which lost his way. Finally, he found his road again, only to be caught in a traffic jam and remain immobilized for an hour. Tracer bullets flashing through the darkness lent a very real terror to the general feeling of being trapped and helpless. Many of the women lost control of themselves and their children, screaming, crying, and mumbling prayers. "I wondered whether the driver, between the traffic and the passengers, didn't want to blow his brains out," Mrs. Wilson recalled.[27]

The atmosphere near Pearl Harbor and Honolulu, instead of simmering down with the passage of time, grew—if anything—worse. "After the attack Hawaii was flat on its ass," declared Grannis. "We had no defense left. Honolulu the night after the attack was a confused mess. The local Japanese stayed strictly off the streets. Some of them even got beat up." Grannis stayed aboard the *Antares* in Honolulu harbor. He heard a sentry shout, "Halt, who goes there?" When the man received no reply, he raised his gun and shot into the distance at what proved to be another guard. Luckily he had missed. Aghast, he yelled, "Hey, Joe, is that you?"[28]

"Everyone was trigger-happy," said Emil Johnson. "If you moved ten feet on Ford Island that night, you had a good chance of getting shot."[29] Armed guards had been stationed around the perimeter of the airfield, each sentry covering about 500 feet. "A life wasn't worth a nickel that night if a person wasn't damn careful," stated Chief Petty Officer Forrow.[30]

The situation was tailor-made for a tragic accident. At 2045, Lt. Fritz Hebel, leading the six fighters from the *Enterprise*,* notified the Ford Island tower that they were off Diamond Head and asked for landing instructions. He received clearance and was told to turn on navigation lights and then come in for a landing.[31] The Fourteenth Naval District notified "all ships present and Army anti-aircraft units. This notice was sent out several times because of the anxiety of Commander PatWingTwo about these planes."[32]

Captain Shoemaker put Cmdr. "Brig" Young on the voice radio at the control tower, figuring that if anyone could bring these planes in safely, he could, for the pilots would recognize the voice of the *Enterprise*'s air group commander.[33]

Storekeeper Rogo saw Hebel's flight approaching with running lights gleaming. He knew these must be American, "because the enemy wouldn't have their lights on."[34] Neither such common sense as Rogo's, such thoughtfulness as Shoemaker's, nor Admiral Bellinger's twice-repeated notification to all ships plus the Army stood a chance of prevailing against the overall tension, terror, and frustration. Virtually every AA gun on Oahu, both on ship and on shore, was manned by this time. "Kids were sitting on these guns who had been shot at all morning," Commander Johnson of the *West Virginia* explained, "and they were jittery and trigger-happy."[35] Commander Quynn, aboard the *Argonne*, saw the fighters coming in, recognized them as American, but had to ask himself, "Will anyone smack them?" Sure enough, as the planes winged over the *Pennsylvania* in drydock, the flagship opened fire.[36]

The Fourteenth Naval District Watch Officer Log confirmed that the *Pennsylvania* initiated the action.[37] And when the flagship led, almost everyone else followed. A lone voice of sanity spoke from the *Neosho*'s log: "Enemy planes reported. Anti Aircraft Battery did not fire, as Planes were believed friendly."[38] The *Curtiss* had received a report that six planes from the *Enterprise* were approaching Pearl Har-

---

* See Chapter 30.

bor from the south and assumed that these were the aircraft "approaching for landing." However, "the planes zoomed up from landing field and AA batteries from the whole fleet commenced firing on them." So the *Curtiss* sounded General Quarters and joined in.[39]

Seaman Osborne of the *Arizona* had transferred to the *Tennessee* and was aboard her when her guns opened up. "I thought for sure there was another raid starting," he remembered.[40] Seaman Eisnaugle had just gone off duty when the *Maryland* commenced firing. Eisnaugle and his comrades assumed the Japanese had come back. They did not think in terms of the *Enterprise*, for a rumor had spread through the *Maryland* that the carrier had been sunk at sea.[41]

Hickam Field was reported being bombed.[42] At almost the same time, Bellinger ordered cease fire. Within minutes Kimmel's Headquarters canceled the order.[43] Communications at the Ford Island tower were not working properly, and the incoming pilots could not hear Young's instructions.[44] Very shortly, all concerned realized that a ghastly mistake had been made, but it was too late for the unfortunate *Enterprise* men.

Hebel attempted to land at Wheeler, but his bullet-riddled fighter crash-landed and burned in a cane field near Aiea. Hebel survived the crash only to die the next day. Ens. Herbert Menges perished instantly when his plane smashed into a tavern at Pearl City and exploded. Ens. Gayle Herman spiraled down to Ford Island, under fire even after he landed. Miraculously, he was uninjured. The next morning he counted eighteen holes in his F4F. Ens. David Flynn swooped out to sea, hoping to return safely when the shooting had stopped. But on his way back his engine conked out and he parachuted to safety near Barber's Point. Ens. James Daniels adopted similar tactics and hovered near Barber's Point until he could land safely.[45]

Ens. Eric Allen's plane struck the water in the channel near Pearl City; Allen bailed out but was shot as he drifted down.[46] The minesweeper *Vireo* picked him up and took him to Riggs at the dispensary. Riggs tentatively diagnosed a ruptured liver. The pilot was in great pain, and the doctor had him rushed to the hospital, where he died almost immediately.[47]

Nor was this the end. A machine-gun bullet passed through the port side of the *Argonne* at frame 70 and instantly killed a seaman in the mess hall on the second deck. This man had taken refuge aboard the *Argonne* from the *Utah*. Another *Utah* man nearby also was hit but not killed. After receiving first aid, he was transferred to the Naval Hospital. Seaman 1st Class V. W. Nance from the *Nevada* was found lying on 1010 Dock with a machine-gun bullet in his left shoulder. He, too, was given first aid and sent to the Naval Hospital.[48]

Cmdr. Katsuji Watanabe, in command of the submarine *I-69*, on reconnaissance quite near southern Oahu, saw at 2101 "a very large flame heaving heavenward—a flame like a ship exploding in Pearl Harbor. After this very heavy antiaircraft followed." The flame probably came when Menges crashed in Pearl City. Then at 2241 the mother submarine *I-16* received a message from its midget submarine commander, Ensign Yokoyama, "Successful surprise attack." On this somewhat slender evidence the Japanese Navy concluded that at least three midget submarines had penetrated Pearl Harbor and, after the air raid, had inflicted severe damage, including the destruction of a capital ship.[49] Quickly the word spread that the minisubs had sunk the *Arizona*. During the spring of 1942, the Japanese Navy released this to the press, and the midget submariners were glorified as veritable gods, to the resentment of the fliers, who knew exactly when and under what circumstances the *Arizona* had exploded.[50]

So too did the Americans who could at least take comfort in the fact that the casualties aboard the ships had not died at the hands of their own countrymen.

CHAPTER 33

"At Last Came the Dawn"

Captain Allen heard "all the guns in Pearl Harbor go off" just as he had settled down fully clothed for a little sleep. He had only to put on his shoes before he headed for bomber Headquarters in the quartermaster warehouse. Several guards challenged him before the driver of an MP car picked him up and took him to his destination. There he found that his services as a bomber pilot would not be needed. No further attack was in progress; the Navy had shot down some of its own planes.

Deciding to sleep at Headquarters rather than return to his quarters, Allen spread out a mattress from the warehouse stock and instructed a clerk to wake him at 0230. Shortly after Allen stretched himself out, General Rudolph dragged up a mattress and collapsed on it. "He was completely gone."[1]

Lieutenant Ruff was making one of his runs between the *Nevada* and Kimmel's Headquarters during the *Enterprise* incident and later admitted, "Actually I was more afraid then of our jittery and trigger-happy American gunners than I was of the Japanese during the morning attack."

Unlike many of his colleagues, Ruff did not expect the Japanese to return. Plying between his own stricken battleship and the submarine base, he had an all-too-clear view of the destruction and could see no reason why they should come back.

Captain Scanland kept only a skeleton crew aboard the *Nevada* that night, and Ruff made arrangements for the rest of the men to bed down temporarily in an open-air theater at the Naval Base.[2]

When it came time to serve the evening meal at the Naval Hospital Admiral Calhoun was very proud to find that "practically every patient who was able to walk was absent. He had returned to his ship or any ship that he could catch and had gone to sea. They did not return to the hospital for several days."[3]

Aboard the *Argonne*, Calhoun's Filipino mess attendant, whom everyone called "Francisco," never left the admiral's side except to bring coffee and sandwiches.[4] Chief Petty Officer Rafsky, Calhoun's enlisted aide, "couldn't eat another sandwich." The death, destruction, and suffering he had witnessed affected him physically as well as psychologically.

WO Henry H. Raymond from the *Argonne* went over to the *Oklahoma*, heard tapping, and returned to the *Argonne* to report that there were further signs of life aboard the capsized battleship. A hastily organized rescue party was dispatched and brought out a few more trapped sailors.[5]

Small boats worked all night in the harbor trying to pull bodies out of the water. "Trigger-happy Marines were stationed all over the place," Admiral Furlong said. "They would even challenge the boats in the water and if they did not answer at once they would blaze away."

That night Furlong and Captain Train slept at the submarine base and had to move their cots inboard from the outside bulkhead because of the danger of being hit by stray bullets. "Things were popping all over the place. Everyone expected that 'the Japanese would land that night."[6]

Officers on Ford Island "expected the Japanese to take over. We were defenseless," reminisced Commander Coe. "I thought one infantry division could have taken over the whole island. What was very bad was the fact that the moon was so bright that night that it cast shadows. Under the mood and atmosphere of the time, rumors spread like wildfire."[7]

Reports from the Hawaiian Air Force came in until midnight and after. Shoemaker remembered them as being of this nature: "Many high," "Planes coming in," "Enemy craft standing in from the southwest." Said Shoemaker, "They were intermittent reports, just enough to shake one up good. And there wasn't a Goddamn thing we could do about it."[8]

Coe remembered that at about 2200 a report came in that Japanese invasion forces were landing at one of the forts below Hickam Field, with gliders taking them to the beach.[9] Certainly there was a flurry of excitement at about that time. At 2150 the 64th Coast Artillery reported that Pearl Harbor was "receiving naval bombardment," and at 2205 the Hawaiian Air Force noted, "Seven planes reported trying to land at ALA MOANA and are being fired on."[10]

This was approximately the time when an AA shell, falling on the campus of Punahau High School, disrupted the first-aid group which included Mrs. Cooper and her friend Mrs. Kraft. The school was directly across the street from the hotel where they were staying. Fearing that the enemy had come back and having no recourse but prayer, Mrs. Cooper and other Catholics present began to say the rosary. At the end of each decade, the non-Catholics echoed, "Me, too, O Lord!" No one had been hurt in the explosion, but it dug a large crater.[11]

Back on duty in the Naval Hospital only a short time, nurses Ruth Erickson and Violet Chlossey were working in the blacked-out surgical ward when this burst of shooting took place. Certain that the Japanese were staging another strike, they gasped in horror. But they had no time to indulge their fears, for the ward hummed with activity. So many patients had come in that beds almost filled the hospital corridors.[12]

At what he estimated to be 2100, Colonel Dunlop snatched a few minutes to visit the cave shelter to check on the situation and try to visit with his wife. As he walked around, calling softly, "Ruthie! Ruthie!" he saw hundreds of women and children huddled there with only a blanket or two apiece. The sight aroused mixed emotions in Dunlop. It was pathetic, yet somehow inspiring, for the refugees seemed to have everything under control and to be settling down stoically. He could not find his wife, but he knew she was safe and so went back to his office, where he worked the rest of the night.[13]

A number of Navy wives would be spending the night with Betty Smith. She moved her furniture out of the way, so that everyone would be able to move quickly in the blackout if an emergency arose. By nightfall, eight women had arrived, and Headquarters sent two enlisted men with rifles to guard them. One was exhausted and in deep distress, for he had worked much of the afternoon and evening helping to drag bodies out of the harbor. The women kept the radio on, trying to piece together from the military and police calls some picture of what was happening. At midnight they turned in, seeking rest on the beds, sofas, floors, or propped up in chairs. But worry, tension, and fear kept them awake.[14]

Around midnight, a base near Kaneohe "sounded an alarm and a searchlight battery on the hill overlooking the town of Kaneohe began sweeping the skies," Avery wrote. "The AA batteries now found it expedient to shell the searchlight batteries." When Avery asked about the incident the next day, a soldier told him that "they were only trying to enforce the order for complete blackout."[15]

A remarkably similar incident took place at the Pearl Harbor Navy Yard. In the black of night, someone threw a wrong switch, and every floodlight "for illuminating the lower fuel tank farm came on." Someone nearby leaned out a window and screamed, "Shoot those lights out!" Every man within hearing and armed with a rifle fired away. "It was like Coney Island on the Fourth of July." The lights went out, and tracer bullets lit up the sky. Then blackness fell again.[16]

At about 0100 on December 8, the buses carrying Mrs. Wilson's group ground to a halt near the Punchbowl at an old school, a Spanish-type structure with concrete floors. As the women stepped inside, the spooky atmosphere of an empty building at night added to their uneasiness. Mrs. Wilson supervised the refugees. Among her charges was a young wife who had just been delivered of a baby on December 6 and who, with her child, had been removed from the Schofield hospital to make way for the wounded. Having neither blankets nor mattresses, the women curled up in their coats on the cold floor.

Strict blackout prevailed. One of Mrs. Wilson's most difficult tasks was keeping the women from lighting cigarettes. Locked in the chill blackness, sleepless with anxiety and discomfort, many found the temptation to smoke almost irresistible.[17]

Aboard the destroyer-minelayer *Breese*, in open waters near Oahu, her skipper, Commander Stout, had a hunch that Japanese submarines might be lurking in the area, although so far he had not seen one. "It was as black as the inside of a hat," he said, "and we were running on dead reckoning. The whole area was blacked out. We would look ashore and not see a damn thing except the waves washing in." He stood near the bridge rail on the *Breese*'s starboard side, idly watching porpoises play around the ship. When he saw the breakers glistening against the night, he slowed *Breese* to 5 knots.

There, about 50 to 75 feet away, he saw a streak of phosphorescence in the water. "Well, here comes another porpoise," he thought. Then he saw that there were two, the second being about 150 feet ahead. They kept right on coming toward the *Breese* instead of turning away. Moreover, Stout saw bubbles coming from the first "porpoise," and he knew what he had to deal with: "It was a fish, all right, but not the type of fish I thought it was."

He believed that slowing his ship down saved her. "If I had continued on my normal speed, the torpedo would have hit me amidships. Whoever had done the shooting was pretty good, because he had a good solution on [the] *Breese*."

Turning the ship seaward, he avoided the torpedoes, but the *Breese*'s instruments did not pick up the submarine that had launched them. Although the *Breese* carried about seventy-two depth charges, he decided against loosing any of them at random. "There was no use dropping depth charges just for the hell of it, because people were jittery enough as it was. And they—our own people—might have started shooting at me."[18]

One cannot be certain, but the two torpedo tracks suggest that the *Breese* had attracted the attention of a midget submarine, possibly that of Ensign Yokoyama from the *I-16*, which was in that general area. If so, the midget's escape was temporary. At 0111, December 8, all communication ceased between Yokoyama and his mother submarine.

As prearranged, at 0330 on December 8, the mother subs reached the rendezvous point off the west coast of Lanai, but none of the mini-subs appeared. The big submarines searched for several days, but finally had to acknowledge that all the midgets had been destroyed.[19]

The *I-69*'s engines had been expending considerable energy, and Capt. Nobuki Nakaoka, in command of the Twelfth Submarine Squadron, of which the *I-69* was flagship, "felt keenly the need for recharging the batteries that night." So he directed Commander Watanabe "to set course...for the area southwest of Barber's Point," estimating that the U.S. antisubmarine patrol might be "comparatively lax" in that region. At 0145 on December 8, the *I-69* surfaced and began recharging her batteries while at battle speed. Later that morning she sighted two "patrol vessels" on her "port quarter and port beam respectively," some 3 miles away, and reversed course. "Pearl Harbor shone red in the sky, like a thing afire. It was already dawn...."

At 0536, Watanabe had to take her down, although recharging was incomplete. The destroyers dropped depth charges but were too far off to damage the *I-69*. About three and a half hours later, the undersea craft was caught in an antisubmarine net and spent 38 hours thus immobilized before her crew managed to free her. Understandably, Captain Nakaoka "was profoundly convinced that the *I-69*'s escape from danger was entirely due to Divine Providence."[20]

No such sense of celestial intervention buoyed up the spirits of Lieutenant Sakamaki and his crewman Inagaki as the sea lapped around the *I-24*'s minisub. Their last happy moment of the day came when, although their craft was stuck on a reef, they saw huge pillars of smoke over Pearl Harbor and assumed that the air attack had succeeded.[21] Not until about noon did they free the minisub from the reef, and then they discovered that their second—and last—torpedo was useless because of "a fatal injury to the torpedo-charging mechanism." As the afternoon wore on toward evening, Sakamaki checked the batteries and estimated that they did not have enough power to reach the pickup point some 2 miles southwest of the southwest point of Lanai. He entertained a last hope of ramming the submarine into a battleship, so decided to try again to penetrate the harbor. Later he reflected that he must have been half out of his mind, for he remembered nothing further until darkness fell. Then he realized that Inagaki was weeping, and he too broke into tears, "completely exhausted both in body and mind." Once more he tried to steer into Pearl Harbor; once more he failed. In desperation, he set course for Lanai and collapsed into deep sleep.[22]

He awoke again around midnight and felt a little better; the minisub's hatch had been open during these hours, so the air had cleared. At dawn he saw what he took to be Lanai and shook Inagaki awake, but the submarine had merely drifted off the Kaneohe-Bellows Field area. A final attempt to start the engine failed. After vibrating for a moment, it gave up, this time for good.

Setting the fuse to scuttle the minisub to keep it from falling into enemy hands, the two men jumped overboard. Sakamaki lost sight of Inagaki and had to face the fact that his good companion had drowned. No reassuring explosion told him that the submarine had blown up. Bitterly he realized that, to crown the day's frustrations, he had failed to destroy his minisub.

A breaker knocked him unconscious. He awoke on a beach to find an American soldier, Sgt. David M. Akui, standing over him. Sakamaki had just earned the dubious distinction of being the United States' prisoner of war No. 1. Dazedly he remembered that once he had been knocked unconscious in a soccer game; now he felt the same numbness of emotion and blankness of mind. He offered no resistance when put into an Army truck. Then he fell asleep again, awakening to find himself in a building in Honolulu.[23]

December 8 brought very little letup in Oahu's "alarums and excursions." At 0330, Captains Allen and Saunders were ready to lead their scheduled B-17 patrol when they received word that the Japanese were attacking Wheeler Field. General Rudolph ordered the B-17s to take off if they could do so before the Japanese reached Hickam, otherwise to stay on the ground. Of course, they took off with no difficulty and fruitlessly searched to the southwest for about 8 hours.[24]

At 0546, the *Whitney* fired "two rounds of 3 inch/.50 caliber and machine gun bursts at presumed enemy aircraft."[25] Probably this ship was one of those which contributed to the troubles of the remaining *Enterprise* planes. Commander Young was under orders to rejoin the *Enterprise* at sunrise with these aircraft. "Just prior to the time of our scheduled take-off, a utility plane (JRS) took off, and was immediately fired on by ships and other shore batteries." Although Young had arranged "to notify all hands of our scheduled departure and route to be taken to the *Enterprise*," takeoff had to be delayed for nearly an hour because of the continuous Navy AA fire. Eventually, matters calmed down sufficiently for them to leave with no further incident.[26]

Many on Oahu experienced genuine difficulty in believing that the Japanese had truly gone. Sergeant Crouse remembered vividly that as daybreak came, the first persons he and some of his fellow wounded saw were two Japanese. "I'm very sure every man thought the Japs had taken over," he wrote. The pair turned out to be a local Reservist doctor who had been called to active duty, and the woman had been with the Army Nurse Corps for several years.[27]

Early in the morning Capt. Freeland A. Daubin called Betty Smith. "We expect the Japanese to come back," he told her. "We expect another attack. Can you take care of my wife?" Mrs. Smith cordially agreed to add Mrs. Daubin to the group at her home.[28]

At the school near the Punchbowl, very few of Mrs. Wilson's group slept at all the night of December 7, in their worry about what the next day would bring. With the first trace of dawn they arose, stiff with cold. They could make out misty forms of men in uniform outside the school. The immediate thought of most of the women was, "My God! The Japanese! They have taken over Hawaii and we are their prisoners!" Then, as the dim light of early day brightened, they could see that these men were local militia sent to guard the schoolhouse.[29]

At 0200, Nurse Erickson again went off duty and retired with other nurses on her shift to a nearby building where women and children evacuees were trying to sleep, although they had no beds. Tension engendered by the rumor that the Japanese were taking over the island kept everyone awake.

She was never so glad to see a night end. "At last came the dawn and the realization that we had survived the night," she recalled. "No one could imagine what daylight meant to us. We could now see outside. Even the air was cleaner, purer. There was a feeling that we had made it. Our material possessions meant nothing. The fact that we were alive—that was the whole meaning. We had prayed many times, and we were grateful that our prayers had been answered."[30]

Mrs. Cooper's tour of duty at the improvised first-aid station ended at midnight, and she tumbled into bed, to fall into exhausted sleep. She awoke to a warm, bright morning. Since December 8 was a holy day, she attended mass at the nearby Sacred Heart church. She experienced an upsurge of confidence. The American flag still flew over Oahu, and soon they could go home to Pearl Harbor—the sooner the better for her, for she believed that at the naval base she could learn what had happened to her husband. In the meantime, she, her mother, and her sister responded to an urgent call for blood donors at Queen's Hospital.[31]

For some, daylight of December 8 brought home the full horror of the previous day. It gave Baker 1st Class Johnson of the *Tern* his first real chance to size up the destruction. "It was a terrible, unbelievable mess," he declared. "One of the worst parts about it was to see a body floating in the channel and know there is one of your buddies, and then call a small boat to come and fish him out or take him out yourself."[32]

That morning Coxswain Richard L. Frost of the *Tennessee* was assigned to a detail bringing the dead and wounded still on shipboard to a central pier for identification. "I can still see those poor guys," he said twenty-five years later, "in groups of four or five, blasted, burned and butchered by shrapnel, being towed by launches and whatever small craft was available. The worst part was when a body would start to disintegrate, and we would have to stop in the middle of the tow and re-lash."[33]

Honolulu newspapers announced that all unidentified boats ap-

proaching Oahu would be fired on, in case they should be enemy
craft. It was also feared that vessels of the local fishing fleet, "manned
predominantly by Japanese aliens," might have been rendezvousing
with Japanese ships. Unfortunately, quite innocuous fishing sampans
coming in had no way of receiving this warning.[34]

The *Kiho Maru*, a sampan with a captain and his crew of three,
including his 21-year-old son, had been fishing since December 4 between Kewalo Basin and Kahe Point. Her crew realized that "something was happening" when they saw the smoke over Pearl Harbor
but, having no radio, did not know what had taken place until that
night when another sampan pulled alongside with the information.
At daybreak the *Kiho Maru* steered for Diamond Head. Some 2 miles
off Barber's Point she joined three other fishing boats. At about 0900,
several aircraft that crewman Seiki Arakaki recognized as American
P-40s flew over. "Each picked out a target and attacked." Arakaki,
shot in the left leg, was the sampan's only survivor.

A boat believed to have been the *Shinei Maru* also lost three fish-
ermen, including a "Nisei kid from Kauai." The sampan *Miyojin Maru*
caught fire when a bullet punctured a fuel line. Her skipper,
Sannosuki Onishi, saved himself and his crew when he ordered all
hands over the side. Clinging to the hull, they were burned but not
shot.

After Kenji Takumi's *Sumiyoshi Maru* had been fired on by shore-
based machine guns, he steered away from land. He was some hundred yards from the other boats when the fighters appeared. He, too,
recognized them as American. His sampan was undamaged.

Later, the authorities told Arakaki and Onishi that the bullets found
in their craft were "enemy bullets." They knew otherwise, but made
no protest. At that time, discretion was decidedly the better part of
valor.[35]

General Davidson visited Kimmel in the latter's office that morning and found the admiral "quite low and discouraged." Davidson tried
to cheer him up by pointing out that basically he had not lost too
much—"just some old battleships and a few other craft. You still have
your carriers and cruisers." But Kimmel could take no comfort and
paced the floor in his distress. From time to time he walked to the
window and looked out on the dismal scene in Pearl Harbor. "Oh,
what a doleful sight!" he repeated. "Oh, what a doleful sight!"[36]

Rescue work continued on the *Oklahoma*. Eventually, Electrician's

Mate Thesman heard voices calling out. The rescue party first "was cutting for Radio Three which was not far away." Finally, the survivors could hear air hammers and chisels. Next the party came close enough that the trapped men could converse with the rescuers. Water was rising; Thesman thought he might open a manhole cover, but his rescuers advised not: Water or fumes might invade the room and kill them all.

"By now I began to feel a real sense of urgency, because if they didn't get to us before too much longer they could cross us off," said Thesman. "It was completely dark in the Steering Room and had been so for a long time. Waiting in the dark with all its eerie aspects can be a discouraging business."

Finally, they got word to open the manhole cover, which they did. They had to crawl forward through several passageways to reach the opening that had been cut in the hull. At about 1500 a motor launch took Thesman and his men out and to the hospital ship *Solace*, where each received a stiff drink of whiskey. "It was the first legal shot of booze I got in the Navy," Thesman remembered with a grin. Physical examinations showed only one injury in the group—one man had a sprained finger.[37]

At Fleet Headquarters, Major Shapley found orders directing him to return stateside aboard the *Neosho* and lost no time in boarding her. From the tanker, he witnessed men working on the *Oklahoma* and saw some of her survivors rescued. Shapley was impressed by the fact that the first thing they did when they got out of there was to kneel down and pray, "and I bet there wasn't one out of ten who had ever seen the inside of a church."[38]

After a night of fitful sleep, Mrs. Davis awoke early to the roar of planes, and for a terrified moment she thought they were Japanese. Later that morning friends took her to the home of Steven Derby in Honolulu. There she began to have labor pains. In the Kapiolani Maternity Hospital, at 1536, she gave birth to a baby girl and named her Carol for her husband, Charles.[39]

About half an hour later, the hospital telephoned Davis: "Congratulations, you are a father." The news astonished him, for he did not expect the newcomer for another two months. But he was delighted, not only to be a father for the first time, but to know that his wife was safe. Around 1900, he checked out an old staff car and drove to the hospital. There he looked on his first-born with the help of a flashlight covered with blue cellophane. "She was beautiful, even though she was two months premature," said Davis. "All other things seemed very insignificant at the time."[40]

The *Enterprise* entered Pearl Harbor at 1630. Those on her bridge watched in silence as she slipped past scene after scene of destruction. To Halsey the worst sight was the *Utah*, capsized in the berth the *Enterprise* would have been occupying on Sunday morning had weather conditions not delayed his task force. He muttered, "Before we're through with 'em, the Japanese language will be spoken only in hell!"

As soon as the *Enterprise* docked at 1743, Halsey commandeered a small boat and headed for Kimmel's Headquarters, pursued all the way by machine-gun bullets from still nervous American gunners. Kimmel and his staff had neither changed from their Sunday whites nor shaved. They appeared haggard, "but their chins were up." The rumor mill was still grinding them out, and one—that Japanese troops had just landed in gliders—aroused Halsey's mirth.

"What the hell is there to laugh at?" demanded Kimmel.

Halsey explained the incongruity: The nearest Japanese base was much too far away to tow gliders to Oahu, and the enemy would never waste carrier space on "any such nonsense."[41]

That particular rumor was still spooking around at 2247, when glider troops were reported "landing on salt flats near Fort Weaver; they are firing on them." A somewhat sheepish retraction came at 2315: The report was erroneous. "Firing was at an orange flare." Evidently the story persisted, for at 2342 came a second retraction: "Forts Weaver and Kam [Kamehameha] report that glider troops reports were in error, caused by confusion over PBY landing."[42]

A woman in the Manoa Valley telephoned G-2 and would speak to no one but Colonel Fielder. "In a very calm voice" she told him that "paratroopers were floating down in Manoa Valley." Fielder knew this could not be true, because no planes were in the air, but she seemed so positive that he asked her to take another look outside; he would hold the phone. She did so, and assured Fielder "that they were still coming down a short distance from her house." He thanked her and instructed her to be sure the house was well blacked out, to lock her doors and stay inside. He would send "a platoon of soldiers to capture the paratroopers." This satisfied his caller, and he heard no more from her. Fielder could only guess that she saw "the fleecy white clouds drifting across the moon."[43]

One of the more interesting tasks Fielder had over the next few days was his contact with Sakamaki. As that young man sat in a chair wrapped in an army blanket in Fort Shafter's guard house, he was one of the most miserable men in the Imperial Navy, in spirit if not in body. He was bitterly ashamed of his failure and that through his fault a valuable secret weapon had fallen into enemy hands. In fact, his mind blanked out much of the next two months: "I was not myself."[44]

The men of the U.S. National Guard who had captured him were of Japanese ancestry but did not speak Japanese, so he had to be questioned through an interpreter. At first he "folded his arms and refused to answer questions." But he soon broke his silence. He claimed that the only reason he did not commit suicide when he landed on shore was his hope of escaping to rejoin the Japanese Navy; moreover, he was in disgrace and did not want any information about himself sent to Japan. "My greatest mistake was being captured," he mourned. "This is the first time I have failed. Please do not advise Japan about this. Please kill me."[45] Needless to say, no one obliged.

At first the U.S. Navy tried to sink his submarine by plane, but when the bombs missed it, they evidently had second thoughts, for this new weapon merited close examination. So the Navy "picked it up and set it on the inside of the reef." Then the Army "sent a man out to put a rope around the conning-tower and towed it in." Said General Short with a touch of humor, "Some fellow from Texas, probably, lassoed it...."[46]

A few days later, Sakamaki wrote "To a Commanding Officer"— probably Fielder, who visited his cell. Fielder discovered that the guards had been harassing Sakamaki without laying a finger on him or even speaking to him. They used such tactics as "turning bright lights on at irregular intervals, dropping mess kits and other tin things on the concrete floor with an awful clatter, giving the prisoner only American food...." Fielder brought these measures to a halt, insisting that Sakamaki "was an officer of the Imperial Japanese Navy and would be treated as an honorable prisoner of war."

His eardrums no longer assaulted and his stomach full of Japanese food, Sakamaki naturally thought Fielder "a great guy" and talked to him quite freely through a Naval Intelligence interpreter. So far as Fielder could determine, his revelations were less than earthshaking.[47]

If Sakamaki's answers were half as confused as his letter, he must have baffled his interrogators considerably:

I thank you for your kindly visit of yesterday....I set out for Pearl Harbor with the purpose of sinking a battleship, but...although we were able to reach the mouth of the harbor by creeping underneath your bombs falling like rain...since the...accident was fatal to the submarine, we determined to proceed without hesitation to the surface of the water, and dashing into the harbor, and climbing the gangway ladder, hoped to leap onto the deck and die simultaneously with blowing up the enemy warship....

Due entirely to my inexpert navigation and strategy, my honor as a soldier has fallen to the ground. Thus I betrayed the expectations of our 100,000,000 [people] and became a sad prisoner of war disloyal to my country....

My willingness to die need not be mentioned; to be killed by one of your bullets of your country shall make me very happy. I pray for your country's lasting military success....

To the Japanese people, especially to officers like ourselves, becoming a prisoner of war is inexcusable. Of course, whether or not there is a record of the incident or not, I will commit suicide upon my return to my native land. Even though we are unarmed, to bite with teeth and fight to the last is the Japanese spirit....

Sakamaki asked that a copy of his "Last Will and Testament"— actually an apology for his failure—be forwarded to the Japanese Navy Department. He continued with a poem which he had composed on the day of his capture:

When cherry blossoms fall,

Let them fall!

Wet are its branches and leaves

With the sorrow of today!

...Last night, again scores of bayonets and muzzles were pointed at me from the front door and from the window and from above my head. However, righteousness won....I hope that all would be forgiven with my death....

I appreciate your many kindness shown me up to now, and I pray for your success in the war.[48]

Of course, it was no truer that "scores of bayonets and muzzles" were pointed at Sakamaki in his cell than that Sakamaki sincerely prayed for

American success in the war. But under the circumstances, one can understand why the man might be less than lucid.

He was quite right, however, in assuming that his fellow countrymen, especially his comrades in the Navy, would have little or no sympathy with him, for he had been captured rather than killed. Several months later, the Combined Fleet received word of his capture. Admiral Yamamoto called Captain Arima, staff Submarine Officer, into his cabin and "literally stormed. He got red in the face and stamped his feet on the deck in anger." He thought the Americans would get important information out of Sakamaki. Moreover, "according to the code of a Japanese warrior it was a disgrace to be captured."[49]

Meanwhile, another young Japanese was living out an even more fantastic episode. Between 1300 and 1400 on December 7, residents of Niihau Island, westernmost of the Hawaiian chain, saw two Japanese aircraft pass overhead. One of them continued on its way and disappeared, presumably crashing at sea.[50] Either it or its companion almost certainly was the "enemy single seat monoplane" that engaged the *Northampton* that morning west of Kauai.*

These fliers were headed for Niihau, because the Pearl Harbor planners had designated it as a rescue point. During the training period, Fuchida had told Genda that some method must be devised to rescue pilots whose planes were too badly damaged to reach the carriers. Genda agreed, and Fuchida consulted a sort of encyclopedia prepared by the Intelligence Section of the Naval General Staff. In the volume dealing with Hawaii, he came to Niihau and decided it fit the bill, being only 30 minutes' flight time from Oahu. Besides, according to his source, it had no American inhabitants. The island also had "a flat, meadow-like area on the west coast where planes could land with reasonable safety." So he recommended Niihau as the rendezvous point for damaged planes. This was approved, and arrangements were made to have a standard-sized submarine wait there to pick up stranded fliers.[51]

It would have been difficult to find under the American flag a less sophisticated corner of earth than Niihau. This privately owned island lacked telephones and radios. Its only communication with Kauai, some 20 miles to the northeast, was a weekly supply boat or an emergency beacon fire. Into this Polynesian paradise jarred Zero No. B11–120.[52] At the controls was Petty Officer Shigenori Saikaijo of the *Hiryu*, a grad

---

* See Chapter 29.

uate of the flying school at Kasumigaura.* He had participated in the first-wave attack against Wheeler. In strafing the base, he ran into American fire that seriously damaged his Zero. Unable to return to the *Hiryu*, he headed for Niihau.[53]

Upon touching down, Saikaijo "tried to zoom up again when its [his Zero's] undergear got caught in the fence wire, and the plane landed flat on the ground," with both wheels knocked off. Hauila Kaleohano, a Hawaiian who lived nearby, "saw that it wasn't an American plane, and thought it strange." He raced for the aircraft, disarmed the Japanese struggling with his safety belt, and pulled him unceremoniously out of the cockpit. In a brief scuffle, Kaleohano confiscated Saikaijo's map and papers.[54]

At first the intruder was "peaceful and friendly." He had no reason not to be, for his sole purpose in heading for Niihau was to contact the submarine supposed to be waiting nearby for such stragglers as himself. For their part, the islanders did not know about the attack on Pearl Harbor, so they did not put the interloper under strict security. At first he communicated by writing in English, but it soon developed that he spoke the language fluently.

His hosts wanted to send their Japanese guest to Kauai on the boat belonging to the Robinson family—owners of Niihau—but time passed and it did not come.[55] During the delay, Saikaijo evidently realized how important his documents could be to the Americans. For the ensuing few days he went to incredible lengths to get them back or destroy them. He secured the aid of the only two Japanese residents of Niihau—Ishimatsu Shintani, an alien, and Yoshio Harada, a nisei. He dispatched Shintani to Kaleohano with a bribe of $200 to give up the documents, claiming excitedly "that it was life and death and that Japan had forced him to take this action." When the Hawaiian refused, Shintani prudently disappeared.

Saikaijo and Harada then overpowered the guard, found firearms, and started a frantic search, shouting threats to shoot up the whole island unless the Hawaiians turned Kaleohano and the papers over to them. They even burned down Kaleohano's house when a search there failed

* To obtain enough pilots during, and to a certain extent before, the war, the Japanese Navy trained young high school graduates at a special school at Kasumigaura called *Yokaren*. There they received flying instructions almost exclusively, from which they graduated as Petty Officers (interview with Fuchida, February 27, 1964).

to uncover the documents. They also mounted two machine guns from the wrecked plane—which Saikaijo had set on fire—but two intrepid Hawaiians, Benehakaka Kanahele and Kashikila Kalimahuluhulu, captured the ammunition.

After further wild adventures, the two Japanese held up Kanahele and his wife. This was a mistake, for the huge Hawaiian and his wife promptly jumped Saikaijo. Harada pulled the woman loose, and the pilot blazed away at Kanahele, striking him in the groin, stomach, and leg.

"Then I got mad," said the Hawaiian. Seizing Saikaijo by the neck and leg, he smashed his head against a stone wall. Horrified at this drastic turn of events, Harada shot himself.[56]

The Niihau story received wide coverage in the Hawaiian press and in later accounts. It aroused mixed feelings. On the one hand, residents of the islands were delighted with the brave, loyal, and quick-witted Niihau Polynesians. On the other hand, the rapidity with which the two resident Japanese went over to the pilot's cause dismayed the islanders. The more pessimistic among them cited the Niihau incident as proof that one could not trust any Japanese, even if an American citizen, not to go over to Japan if it appeared expedient.[57] This thought did nothing to assuage the fears of Hawaiians of all races, who did not really rest easy again until after the battle of Midway in June of 1942.

CHAPTER 34

"Hostilities Exist"

The "news of war broke like a thunderclap as departing football fans encountered cab drivers and park employees" at the exits to Griffith Stadium after the Washington Redskins had trounced the Philadelphia Eagles.[1] A future four-star general, Lyman Lemnitzer, recalled that "the minute we were out of the stadium, the news went around like wildfire." But another full-general-to-be, Capt. George Decker, did not know what happened until, driving home with a friend, "we noticed as we passed the old Munitions Building that the soldiers were out in front of it with helmets on. When we got back to his house we turned on the radio and heard the news."[2]

By word of mouth, by radio, by telephone call, the information spread across the United States. Senator Alben W. Barkley, the majority leader, and his wife were driving back to Washington from Paducah, Kentucky. They had been somewhat isolated from events because of trouble with their car radio. The senator tinkered with it again as they neared Washington. This time the radio worked and brought them the incredible news. The Barkleys made all speed to their home, where they found Roosevelt's summons to the White House for a conference at 2045.[3]

Senator Thomas T. Connally, chairman of the Foreign Relations Committee, likewise heard the flash over his car radio during "a relaxing drive...into the hills of Maryland." He had spent much of the day at the home of Secretary of the Interior Harold L. Ickes at Olney, with Chief of Defense Mobilization Donald Nelson, and Supreme Court Justice Hugo Black. They had discussed the Japanese situation but agreed among themselves that no war with Japan appeared imminent. It was past 2000 when Connally reached his apartment and discovered his notice of the meeting. He bolted his supper and sped to the rendezvous.[4]

When U.S. Deputy Marshall Roy Webb telephoned to say, "the Japs are bombing Pearl Harbor," Senator Harry S. Truman was taking a nap in his hotel room in Columbia, Missouri.

"Are you sure you know what you're talking about, Roy?" asked Truman skeptically.

"It's on the radio."

"My goodness, man, this is war!" exclaimed the senator. "I've got to get to Washington."

However, at St. Louis he was held up for hours and did not reach Washington until 0530 the next day.[5] As he boarded his plane in St. Louis, he announced, "It's for the welfare of the country that we declare war and put Japan in its place."[6]

Secretary of Labor Frances Perkins and an assistant were "locked up in a room" in her club in New York City, working on an important report. They had seen no one else and had not turned on the radio. So when the White House Chief Operator, Miss Hackmeister, telephoned the President's summons to a Cabinet meeting at 2030, she was still ignorant of developments

"What's the matter, Hacky," she asked, "why the cabinet meeting tonight?"

"Just the war, what's in the paper," Miss Hackmeister answered, and hung up.

The taxi driver who took Secretary Perkins to her plane told her, "They said on the radio there was shooting somewhere." At the airport she joined forces with Vice President Henry A. Wallace and Postmaster General Frank C. Walker, neither of whom knew much more than she. Walker had been watching his children perform at a Sunday School concert.[7]

Holding hands, young lawyer Richard M. Nixon and his wife, Pat, emerged from a movie theater in Los Angeles and heard newsboys selling Pearl Harbor extras.[8]

Capt. (later General) Bruce Palmer, a member of the Fort Oglethorpe Georgia, polo team, had participated in a hunt and hunt breakfast early that morning. He heard the news over the radio when he went home. "I was immediately sent down to the stables to ride off to protect the dams in the Tennessee Valley—that was our mission. You see, we were afraid of sabotage....only a couple of days later it dawned on somebody that the enemy wasn't after that dam...."[9]

One of the last Americans of any official stature to hear about the attack was Ambassador Joseph C. Grew. At 0700 December 8 Tokyo time,* his bedside phone rang. It was Foreign Minister Togo's private secretary, claiming he had been trying to reach Grew since 0500. The ambassador remarked, "That is surprising, because the telephone is right beside my bed and it has not rung." The caller requested of Grew, "Please come over as soon as possible to see the Minister." Within half an hour Grew had presented himself at Togo's official residence.

The foreign minister entered, dressed in formal clothes, evidently from an audience with Emperor Hirohito. He slapped a document on the table, saying, "This is the Emperor's reply to the President." Grew did not accept this without a protest. "I have asked for an audience in order to present that memorandum, that message, to the Emperor personally."

Togo replied, "I have no wish to stand between you and the Throne." Then he read the document—the note transmitted by the fourteen-part message†—and asked Grew "to notice especially the last paragraph." He added: "In view of the fact that the conversations in Washington had made no progress it had been decided to call them off."

This did not seem unduly serious to Grew. "They had been called off before...and they had been resumed at a later date." So he answered, "Well, I am very sorry. I hope we can get them started again." Whereupon Togo "made a pleasant little speech," thanking Grew for his "cooperation for peace." He saw the ambassador off at the door. "He said not one single word about the attack on Pearl Harbor."

A few minutes after Grew returned to the Embassy, he heard newsboys calling out "Gogai! Gogai!" This meant a single-sheet special edition containing "an important piece of news." Grew sent out one of his secretaries to buy a copy. The extra told the ambassador that Japan had attacked the United States.[10]

He immediately instructed his naval attaché, Lt. Cmdr. Henri H. Smith-Hutton, to go to the Japanese Navy Department about four

---

* This was 1130 December 7 in Hawaii, 1700 December 7 in Washington.

† See Chapters 1 and 5.

blocks away to find out if the news was correct and, if so, when the Embassy would receive an official declaration of war.

Smith-Hutton experienced no delay in being ushered into the office of RADM Katsuhei Nakamura, senior aide to Navy Minister Shigetaro Shimada. "Unfortunately, the report of the attack is true," Nakamura replied when Smith-Hutton stated his errand. Nakamura added that the Foreign Office must issue the declaration of war; "he had no idea when it would be delivered."

Smith-Hutton had been "on friendly terms" with Nakamura for years. So he asked if he had known about the attack beforehand. Nakamura declared that he had not, and the attaché believed him. The admiral personally escorted Smith-Hutton to the Navy building's entrance. Each expressed the wish that the other "would live through the war." Both did so.[11]

Realizing what lay ahead, Grew destroyed his secret files. These were so arranged that the task could be accomplished "in a very few minutes." Thus all his papers and codes had been disposed of before the police came, about an hour later, and locked up the Embassy personnel in the compound.[12]

Reaction on the part of the rank and file of Americans ranged from the sublime to the ridiculous. Confidence ran high, so high that correspondent Fillmore Calhoun in Chicago wrote with some exasperation, "Whether rightly or wrongly, people seem to believe all the so-called experts' claims that Japan has only two bathtubs in the Navy, no money, no oil, and all Japanese fliers are so cross-eyed they couldn't hit Lake Michigan with a bomb."[13]

Eighty delegates to the Institute of Pacific Relations were meeting in Cleveland to discuss Oriental problems. Reporter Clayton Fritchey had never seen "a greater mixture of men and women and never heard a greater mixture of opinion—until the radio flashed out the stunning news." It interrupted the Sunday afternoon's roundtable discussion. "There was dead silence for two minutes. In those 120 seconds, 80 different opinions were resolved."[14]

In Pittsburgh, where a capacity crowd had gathered to hear Senator Gerald P. Nye, the news of Pearl Harbor arrived before this "America First" meeting began. Robert Hagy, covering the meeting for the Pittsburgh *Post-Gazette*, handed Nye the news item. It did not faze the isolationist senator, who merely remarked, "It sounds terribly fishy to me. Can't we have some details? Is it sabotage or is it open attack?

I'm amazed that the President should announce an attack without giving details."

Nye proceeded with the meeting as if nothing had happened, "with emphasis on denouncing Roosevelt as a warmonger." During one of the speeches, from an aisle seat toward the rear of the building, Col. Enrique Urrutia, Jr., chief of the Second Military Area of the Organized Reserve, burst out incredulously, "Can this meeting be called after what has happened in the last few hours? Do you know that Japan has attacked Manila, that Japan has attacked Hawaii?" A police escort saved him from a manhandling, hustling him out to the tune of yells: "Throw him out!" and "Warmonger!"

Nye was the last speaker, starting at about 1645. While he was talking, Hagy was called to the phone to receive the bulletin that Japan had declared war. He printed the news on a piece of paper, walked out on the platform, and laid it before Nye. "He glanced at it, read it, never batted an eye, went on with his speech." Not until the end of his talk, about 45 minutes later, did he break the news to his audience, adding, "I can't somehow believe this. I can't come to any conclusions until I know what this is all about. I want time to find out what's behind it. Previously I heard about bombings in Hawaii. Somehow, I couldn't quite believe that, but in the light of this later news, I must, although there's been many funny things before."[15]

Unconcerned with politics, thinking only of their sons, brothers, or sweethearts at Pearl Harbor or Manila, hundreds of women telephoned Dallas station WFFA, all asking the same questions: "Do you have the casualty list yet? When will it be broadcast?"[16]

But not even Pearl Harbor could alter everyone's mindset. "What's this I hear about Japan declaring war?" asked an irritated listener in Phoenix. "Have you got anything on the game between the Chicago Bears and the Cardinals? Aren't you getting anything besides that war stuff?" In Seattle, a housewife pouted, "Well, this spoils our day at home, my husband is being called down to the office." And in Palm Springs a young woman protested, "They couldn't have bombed Pearl Harbor. That Admiral I met in Coronado is in charge and he is a perfectly lovely person."[17]

When Secretary of War Stimson returned to his office from lunch, he "started matters going in all directions to warn against sabotage and to get punch into the defense move." Then he plunged into a series of conferences.[18]

At 1520, Roosevelt conferred with Secretary of State Hull and General Marshall in the White House.[19] This meeting was brief. Roosevelt charged Hull with maintaining close rapport and communications with the Latin American republics, and he discussed troop and airpower dispositions with Marshall.[20] As Roosevelt's personal physician, Admiral McIntire, noted, "The President, stunned and incredulous at first, quickly regained the poise that always marked him in moments of crisis. Closing his mind against the shock and grief of the disaster, he concentrated on plans for setting America's war effort in motion."[21]

Information concerning the situation on Oahu continued to pour into the White House, most of it from Stark. Such was the noise and confusion that Miss Tully had to resort to Roosevelt's bedroom phone to take down Stark's calls in shorthand. McIntire and several others peered over her shoulder as she transcribed her notes.[22]

At 1600, Stimson's special assistant, John J. McCloy, met in his room with the chiefs of the Army Services. Stimson joined them long enough to make them "a little pep-up talk about getting right to work in the emergency." But he spent most of his time in conference with Marshall and other associates. Their main subject of discussion was "the form of a declaration of war." All thought it possible that the United States "should declare war on Germany at the same time with Japan...." However, that was "an open question."[23]

At the same hour, Hull presided over a conference at the State Department with some of his key subordinates. They arranged for a press release concerning the Japanese note, and they also discussed the President's forthcoming address to Congress. During this meeting, a press report came in announcing that Japan had declared war on the United States. Although so far Japan had acted unilaterally, these men assumed that the Rome-Berlin-Tokyo axis would stand together. So they decided "that every American merchant vessel in the world should be notified of the existence of hostilities as it was feared that these vessels anywhere would be prey for German, Italian, or Japanese armed forces."

Hull was calm, but he expressed "with great emphasis his disappointment that the armed forces in Hawaii had been taken so completely by surprise." He was also "exceedingly bitter" toward Nomura and Kurusu. "He was contemptuous of them and mentioned their cowering attitude while they were in his office. On the other hand, he seemed to feel that they were not aware, when they arrived at the Department, that an attack had been made on Hawaii."[24]

Assistant Secretary of State Adolf A. Berle, Jr., grimly noted in his diary, "It was a bad day all around; and if there is anyone I would not like to be, it is Chief of Naval Intelligence." He ended his entry, "It is likely to be a wild night along the coast."[25]

At 1609, Baukhage went on the air over his direct line.* Without telling the public where he was, he broadcast all the information that Early supplied. In addition, he drew on his vast experience to provide background sketches of world leaders and events to rivet his hearers' attention between releases. He kept this up for almost nine hours.[26]

At 1700, Merriman Smith estimated that a good hundred reporters, radiomen, photographers, and their entourages, with assorted "Washington big shots," were trying to pack into the press room normally suited for about a dozen. The major New York papers flew in additional staffs to bolster their Washington complements. Unaccustomed to White House protocol, these men tried to monopolize private lines until the regulars posted large signs on the telephone booths that these were for the exclusive use of AP, UP, and INS.[27]

Shortly before 1700, Roosevelt called Miss Tully to his study. "Sit down, Grace," he said, lighting a cigarette. "I'm going before Congress tomorrow. I'd like to dictate my message. It will be short." He began calmly and slowly, speaking each word incisively and "carefully specifying each punctuation mark and paragraph." As she took his dictation, a corner of her mind reflected, "This is terrible for F.D.R. He has four sons who will have to go into it."[28]

Early that evening Roosevelt telephoned Governor Poindexter in Honolulu. Despite the telephone operator who kept interrupting, the governor got across the message that many had been killed and that Oahu badly needed food and planes. General Short had asked for martial law, and Poindexter was inclined to invoke it. This Roosevelt approved. Suddenly Poindexter's voice rose almost to a scream, and Roosevelt relayed to those with him, "My God, there's another wave of Jap planes over Hawaii right this minute."[29]

At 1758, Steve Early told the newsmen clustered in the press room that Roosevelt had just talked with Poindexter, who "confirms the report of heavy damages and loss of life there, including the city. He said that a second wave of planes was just then coming over." Since 1758 in Washington was 1228 in Honolulu, whatever planes Poindexter saw or heard were not Japanese.

---

* See Chapter 22.

At this time, photographers—both still and movie cameramen—were admitted to the press room, and klieg lights added heat to the general discomfort.[30] The *Christian Science Monitor*'s veteran correspondent, Richard L. Strout, described the scene as beyond anything he had ever witnessed:

> The telegraph boys fairly came out of the cracks, the floor was tangled with a black spaghetti of wires, the motion picture lights were on, cameras were busy, men were telephoning, a radio receiver blared (and rattled out static every time somebody dialed a number from the booths). Men with chattering hand motion-picture machines climbed over and under desks...and they were followed by others carrying glaring lamps on black cords.[31]

Meanwhile, crowds were gathering. They were neither overly large nor hysterical, but almost silent. Around 500 people, "mostly men with angry faces," congregated around the southeast entrance to the State Department, but they soon moved to the west entrance to the White House executive office where the action seemed to be. From time to time, White House police politely asked them to move along, but others soon took their places.[32]

Another crowd settled in front of the Japanese Embassy. When Domei correspondent Masuo Kato emerged, it parted to let him pass, but one man said to him, "You are the last son of a bitch we're going to let out." After some little difficulty, Kato hailed a cab, and realizing that he "was roaming about in enemy country at night," he drove to the home of a young woman, a State Department employee, with whom he had become well acquainted. She and her parents accepted him hospitably and urged him to stay for dinner. When he finally had to leave, his friends, fearing for his safety, walked home with him.[33]

Secretary of the Treasury Henry Morgenthau, Jr., was exceedingly worried about the President's safety, and at 1835 he discussed the problem with Assistant Secretary Herbert E. Gaston and Secret Service Chief Frank J. Wilson. The latter thought the augmented White House team could "handle the situation in pretty good shape." But Morgenthau wanted soldiers on the job, because the Japanese had already taken the United States by surprise that day. "No telling what they will do next.... How do you know what trick they might pull from within!"

Wilson suggested they would need two companies of 250 men each to cover the White House grounds on short details of 75 to 100 soldiers for each shift. Morgenthau phoned Roosevelt for permission. But on learning that the Secret Service had already doubled the guard force, the President decided that was enough.

At 1945, Morgenthau conferred with Gaston, General Counsel Edward H. Foley, Jr., and the latter's assistant, Bernard Bernstein, about the legal aspects of preventing Japanese from leaving the country. After Bernstein left, Gaston asked, "Did you get any information on the losses?"

"I was there when they phoned them in but I can't tell you," Morgenthau replied. "They were terrible."[34]

The President dined in his study with his secretary, his son James, and his confidant Harry Hopkins. "Harry looked just like a walking cadaver, just skin and bones," said Miss Tully. Roosevelt "did not talk about Pearl Harbor and he did not complain. It was an hour when he wanted to relax a bit," she explained.[35]

Among the dinner guests at the White House was newsman Edward R. Murrow, just back from England and already on his way to becoming an American institution. Roosevelt sent word for him to wait; he wanted "some information about Britain and the blitz."[36] Mrs. Charles S. Hamlin's dinner partner "was sure bombing would occur at once and that in the next 24 hours we could expect Washington and New York to be bombed."[37]

At 2040 the Cabinet met in the Oval Room. First to arrive was Secretary of Commerce Jesse Jones, at 2020. Then came Vice President Wallace, Postmaster General Walker, and Mrs. Perkins. Ickes came next, and as he approached the gate, he noticed the crowd gathered nearby. "They were quiet and serious...responding to that human instinct to get near the scene of action even if they could see or hear nothing."[38]

Falteringly at first, then with confidence, they began to sing "God Bless America" and "My Country, 'Tis of Thee." Correspondent Smith wondered whether Roosevelt and his Cabinet "could hear those unrehearsed songs coming spontaneously and from the hearts of the little people across his back lawn."[39]

The rest of the Cabinet followed in rapid succession—Secretary of Agriculture Claude Wickard, Morgenthau, Stimson, Hull, and Attorney General Francis Biddle. Last of all, Knox hurried in just at the appointed hour, 2030.[40]

Roosevelt opened by stating that "this was the most serious meeting of the Cabinet that had taken place since 1861:"[41] For the benefit of those who had just reached Washington, he summed up the situation as he knew it: Japanese bombers had struck Pearl Harbor and the airfields. Casualties were "extremely heavy"; three, possibly four, battleships had been sunk, two others badly damaged. Other smaller vessels had been destroyed.[42]

The President read aloud the draft of his message to Congress. Stimson entertained serious reservations about it. "The President's message..., while a very effective document, was not one of broad statesmanship. It really represented only the just indignation of the country at Japan's treachery in this surprise attack and not the full measure of the grievances we have against her as a confirmed law breaker and aggressor." Nor did it connect Japan with Germany. Stimson and Hull urged a broader, more detailed approach, not based "wholly on indignation at the surprise attack," but the rest of the group preferred the President's draft as presented.[43]

While they were meeting, leaders of the Congress were assembling for their briefing, scheduled for 2045. The Senate was represented by Barkley and Minority Leader Charles L. McNary, Warren R. Austin of the Military Affairs Committee, and Connally and Hiram W. Johnson of the Foreign Relations Committee. To the clustering reporters, Connally waxed grandiloquent:

> Let the Japanese Ambassador go back to his masters and tell them that the United States answers Japan's challenge with steel-throated cannon and a sharp sword of retribution....we shall repay their dastardly treachery with multiplied bombs from the air and accurate shells from the sea.[44]

Johnson, a leader of the isolationist faction, "stalked up the White House steps under the portico, stern and silent," wrote Strout. "All the reporters parted without one question, knowing that isolationism was over...."[45]

The House sent Speaker Sam Rayburn and Acting Majority Leader Jere Cooper. The House majority leader, John McCormack, was in Boston when he received Roosevelt's telephone call and could not reach Washington in time for the meeting. Minority leader Joseph W. Martin was there, as were Sol Bloom, chairman of the Foreign Affairs Committee, and committee member Charles A. Eaton.[46] The latter had rushed to the White House from Union Station, still carrying an overnight bag. He had a brief word for the reporters: The only thing left to do was declare war. "I think this will unite America. If it doesn't, what will?"[47]

The Cabinet members remained in the room during the President's briefing. "The effect on the Congress was tremendous," Stimson wrote in his diary. "They sat in dead silence and even after the recital was over they had very few words."[48]

Someone asked about Japanese casualties, but Roosevelt had no firm figures. He stressed, however, that "the principal defense of the whole west coast of this country and the whole west coast of the Americas has been very seriously damaged today."

He asked for and received authority for a concurrent resolution requesting him to address Congress at 1230 the next day. A little later he gave a remarkably accurate outline of how the Japanese task force might have managed to launch its planes undetected, observing, "In other words, at dark, last night, they might very well have been four hundred or five hundred miles away from the Island, and therefore out of what might be called a good patrol distance...."[49]

But Connally wanted no excuses. "Hell's fire," he exclaimed, "didn't we do anything?"

"That's about all," answered Roosevelt.

Connally turned to Knox. "Well, what did we *do?*" he demanded. "Didn't you say last month that we could lick the Japs in two weeks? Didn't you say that our navy was so well prepared and located that the Japanese couldn't hope to hurt us at all? When you made those public statements, weren't you just trying to tell the country what an efficient secretary of the navy you were?"

While Knox struggled for a suitable reply, Roosevelt spoke no word to help him, but sat with "a blank expression on his face." Connally continued to prod Knox. "Why did you have all the ships at Pearl Harbor crowded in the way you did?" Possibly with some vague idea of the antisubmarine net, he went on, "And why did you have a log chain across the mouth of the entrance to Pearl Harbor, so that our ships could not get out?"

"To protect us against Japanese submarines," Knox answered shakily.

"Then you weren't thinking of an air attack?"

"No," Knox answered.[50]

"Well, they were supposed to be on the alert," Connally said, "and if they had been on the alert....* I am amazed by the attack by Japan, but I am still more astounded at what happened to our Navy. They were all asleep. Where were our patrols? They knew these negotiations were going on." No one could answer that question; facts were too scarce.

Some discussion ensued about events in the Far East and the ways and means of defeating Japan eventually.[51] Just before he dismissed the delegation, Roosevelt asked Bloom how soon he would have the House war resolution ready. Bloom had a bad case of nerves. Although he appreciated the honor of introducing the resolution, he "shrank from exposing the Jews of a future generation to the possible charge that this war had been set in motion by a Jew." Therefore, he worked out with the House parliamentarian a plan relieving him of this responsibility. They arranged that, at McCormack's request, Speaker of the House Sam Rayburn should suspend the rules to pass the resolution and have the clerk read it.[52]

The reporters in the stone portico were unusually subdued as they waited for the nation's leaders to emerge. They were "rather awed and silent." To Strout, it was "like a cathedral there, with the world visible but shut out." At 2325 Hull came out. "He was kind and quiet and spoke mildly, wearily, with a touch of humor.

"Suddenly, the reporters were respectful." This was the man who had given the Japanese envoys their comeuppance that afternoon. As he entered his car, the group called out, "Good night, sir!"[53]

Morgenthau returned to the Treasury, where he met again with key associates. After a brief chat alone with Chief Wilson, Morgenthau returned and told his colleagues that only three men were guarding the rear of the White House. "And I told the President the guard was doubled. The whole back of the White House—only three men," he lamented. "Anybody could take a five ton truck with 20 men and they could take the White House without any trouble." This development flicked Morgenthau on the raw. He gave Edmund W. Starling, supervising agent of the White House Secret Service detail, "the most terrific dressing-down you ever heard of."

During the meeting, Morgenthau's wife and son came in, hoping to take him home. They waited while the men discussed a number of

---

* This break occurs in the transcript, indicating inaudibility.

technical problems. But whatever the subject, they always reverted
to one question: How had the attack been possible?

"Was it a terrible shock to the President?" asked Mrs. Morgenthau.

"Must be—must be," muttered her husband.

Under Secretary Daniel W. Bell reminded them, "Merle* mentioned when he flew back ten days ago what a wonderful target those ships would make at Pearl Harbor."

"That's what Stimson kept saying," remarked Morgenthau. "He kept mumbling that all the planes were in one place....

"They haven't learned anything here. They have the whole Fleet in one place—the whole Fleet was in this little Pearl Harbor base.... They never can explain this. They will never be able to explain it."[54]

The President's day had not ended. Some time after midnight, Murrow and William J. "Wild Bill" Donovan, chief of the Office of Strategic Services, came in for a brief talk. "Gray with fatigue," Roosevelt gave Murrow an earful on losses. "Several times the President pounded his fist on the table, as he told of the American planes that had been destroyed 'on the ground, by God, on the ground!'" Nevertheless, Roosevelt's self-control impressed Murrow. "I have seen certain statesmen of the world in time of crisis," he wrote later. "Never have I seen one so calm and steady. He was completely relaxed." He even inquired about mutual friends in London.[55]

At about 0100, Captain Roosevelt assisted his father into bed.[56] One hour later, Grace Tully, exhausted by all the excitement, worry, and work, and virtually "frozen in space and time," started homeward.[57]

As the White House began to stir the next day, a special detachment of Military Police had already set up sentry boxes, while extra details from the Metropolitan Police and Secret Service augmented the normal strength of the White House force. The beautiful old mansion was being measured for blackout curtains.[58]

Roosevelt arose "before the sun,...breakfasted briefly on black coffee and the latest dispatches." He studied and edited his speech, adding "the latest news as it came in from time to time during the morning." Just before he finished the final draft, Hopkins suggested, and the President approved, "the next to the last sentence expressing confidence that we would 'gain the inevitable triumph—so help us God.'"

In preparation for his address to Congress, Roosevelt, in his "old

---

* H. Merle Cochran was a technical assistant to Morgenthau.

blue cape," visited McIntire's clinic in the White House basement to
have his throat sprayed and to gargle. The physician was "well pleased
but not surprised, at the way the President had stood up to an unprece-
dentedly hectic day, long anxious night with but four hours' sleep."[59]

At 1207 he was wheeled "out of the south door of the Executive
Mansion and helped into his waiting limousine." The President was
unsmiling. He settled himself into the back seat beside his son James
and adjusted his naval cape around his morning dress. As the car
turned out of the White House grounds, a Secret Service man stood
on each running board; on either side moved an open Secret Service
car, agents on running boards, others inside with riot guns. Two other
vehicles full of watchers kept vigil before and behind the limousine.

Here and there people cheered their President, but it was nothing
like the spontaneous shouts of friendly approval that usually greeted him.
This was neither the time nor the place, and the crowd sensed it. The
President responded with a restrained smile and wave of his hand.[60] As
he passed, some of the spectators turned their faces toward the Capitol
Building, settling into the silence of a rage and determination too deep
for vocal expression.

The huge, gold-domed seat of government bristled as if under siege.
Marines with fixed bayonets guarded the entrance. Capitol police formed
the secondary line, reinforced by about 250 Washington city police—all
that could be spared—and Secret Service agents.[61]

At precisely 1209, Speaker Rayburn called the House to order.
Shortly thereafter, the Senate entered. In an impressive demonstration of solidarity, Democrat and Republican, liberal and conservative,
walked side by side. Vice President Wallace assisted aged Carter Glass
of Virginia. The Senate's Democratic and Republican party leaders,
Barkley and McNary, entered arm in arm.

After the Senate came the Supreme Court. Then Hull led in the
Cabinet. Appearing exhausted, the Secretary of State "looked almost
like a ghost risen for the occasion." Up in the gallery, in one of the
worst seats in the House, Mrs. Roosevelt, dressed in black with a
silver fox fur, peered down at the proceedings from behind a girder.
She had brought with her, among others, Mrs. Woodrow Wilson,
widow of the United States' last wartime leader.

Only a scattering of uniforms were in evidence—Jimmie Roosevelt,
Marshall, Stark, Maj. Gen. Thomas Holcomb, commandant of the Marine Corps, General "Hap" Arnold—perhaps a few others—as if

to emphasize that in the United States the civilian government exercised the awesome responsibility of sending the nation to war.

The President took the podium amid a thunder of applause, which he acknowledged with "a strained, sad smile." Then he settled his glasses firmly on his nose and opened a black looseleaf notebook, such as any American child took to school.[62] He spoke in a voice of steel:

> Yesterday, December 7, 1941—a date which will live in infamy— the United States of America was suddenly and deliberately attacked by the naval and air forces of the Empire of Japan...
>
> It will be recorded that the distance of Hawaii from Japan makes it obvious that the attack was deliberately planned many days or even weeks ago. During the intervening time the Japanese Government has deliberately sought to deceive the United States by false statements and expressions of hope for continued peace.
>
> The attack yesterday...has caused severe damage to American naval and military forces. I regret to tell you that very many American lives have been lost....
>
> No matter how long it may take us to overcome this premeditated invasion, the American people in their righteous might will win through to absolute victory....

At this point the entire assemblage leaped to its feet for a full minute of heartfelt applause. Roosevelt continued,

> Hostilities exist. There is no blinking at the fact that our people, our territory, and our interests are in grave danger.
>
> With confidence in our armed forces—with the unbounded determination of our people—we will gain the inevitable triumph—so help us God.

Once more he paused as the Congress and its guests applauded approval and agreement. Then he carried his speech to its climax: "I ask that the Congress declare that since the unprovoked and dastardly attack by Japan on Sunday, December 7, 1941, a state of war has existed between the United States and the Japanese Empire." Thus, technically, Roosevelt had not asked for a declaration of war, but for congressional ratification of a *fait accompli*.

Congress took only thirty-three minutes to vote. In the Senate the count was 82–0, in the House, 388–1.[63] Thus did the United States—united as never before—embark on the long, bloody war that would eventually end with Japan's leaders signing the Articles of Surrender aboard the battleship *Missouri* in Tokyo Bay.

NOTES

Introduction

1. *Newsweek*, December 12, 1966.

2. *Hearings before the Joint Committee on the Investigation of the Pearl Harbor Attack, Congress of the United States, Seventy-ninth Congress.* (Washington, D.C., 1946), Part 22, p. 321 (hereafter *PHA*).

Preface

1. Interview with Maj. Gen. Howard C. Davidson, July 6, 1962 (hereafter Davidson).

2. Interview with Lt. Gen. Allan Shapley, USMC, October 11, 1967 (hereafter Shapley).

3. Interview with Admiral Harold F. Pullen, September 12, 1964 (hereafter Pullen).

4. Interviews with Admiral Arthur C. Davis, January 30, 1963 (hereafter Davis) and Brig. Gen. William J. Flood, July 9, 1962 (hereafter Flood).

Chapter 1

"Time Was Running Out"

1. *Newsweek*, December 12, 1966, p. 36.

2. Washington *Post*, December 6, 1941.

3. Herbert Feis, *The Road to Pearl Harbor* (Princeton, N.J., 1950), p. 336 (hereafter *Road to Pearl Harbor*).

4. Washington *Post*, December 7, 1941.

5. *Newsweek*, December 12, 1966, p. 38.

6. Washington *Post*, December 6, 1941.

7. Diary of Henry L. Stimson, Yale University Library, New Haven, Conn., September 16 and December 6, 1941 (hereafter Stimson diary).

8. *PHA*, Part 14, p. 1246.

9. Ibid., Part 15, p. 1681.

10. Ibid., p. 1680.

11. Ibid., p. 1633; Part 2, pp. 443–44.

12. Ibid., Part 11, p. 5394.

13. Ibid., Part 2, p. 441.

14. Ibid., Part 3, p. 1121.

15. Comments prepared by Capt. Laurence F. Safford on Prange's then unpublished manuscript relating to Pearl Harbor (hereafter Safford comments).

16. *PHA*, Part 2, p. 818.

17. Ibid., Part 12, p. 238. The U.S. "invasion" of Dutch Guiana (Surinam) was neither sudden nor sinister. Since the summer of 1941, Washington had been in correspondence with Queen Wilhelmina and the Netherlands government in exile in London concerning the need to protect the bauxite mines at Paramaribo, which at the time furnished 60 percent of the requirements of the U.S. aluminum industry. The action was taken with the consent of the Netherlands government in exile and with the cooperation of Brazil, whose border touched Surinam. Cordell Hull, *The Memoirs of Cordell Hull*, Vol. 2 (New York, 1948), p. 1051 (hereafter *Hull Memoirs*).

18. *PHA*, Part 20, p. 4528.

19. Ibid., p. 4529.

20. Ibid., pp. 4530–31.

21. Ibid., pp. 4531–32.

22. Ibid., p. 4533.

23. Ibid., pp. 4533–34.

24. Ibid., pp. 4534–35.

25. Masuo Kato, *The Lost War* (New York, 1946), pp. 36–38 (hereafter *Lost War*).

26. *PHA*, Part 14, p. 1413. See Gordon W. Prange, *At Dawn We Slept* (New York, 1981), Chap. 57 (hereafter *At Dawn We Slept*).

27. Ibid., Part 12, pp. 238–39; Department of Defense, *The "Magic" Background of Pearl Harbor*, Vol. 4 (Washington, D.C., 1977), Appendix, p. A129 (hereafter *"Magic" Background*).

28. Kiyoaki Murata, "'Treachery' of Pearl Harbor," *Nippon Times*, June 8, 1956 (hereafter "Treachery").

29. *PHA*, Part 12, p. 245.

30. "Treachery."

31. *PHA*, Part 14, pp. 1413–15. The full set of messages appears in PHA, Part 12, pp. 239–45 and *"Magic" Background,* Vol. 4, Appendix, pp. A130–34. See *At Dawn We Slept,* Chaps. 57–59.

32. Ibid. The time of receipt of parts 9 and 10 is not given.

33. Ibid., Part 2, p. 900.

34. Ibid., Part 9, p. 4510.

35. Ibid., p. 4513.

36. Ibid., Part 14, pp. 1413–15.

37. Ibid., Part 9, p. 4015.

38. Ibid., Part 9, p. 4015.

39. Ibid., Part 11, p. 5271; Part 10, p. 4661.

40. Ibid., Part 14, p. 1238.

41. Unpublished biography of Stanley K. Hornbeck, Hornbeck Papers, Hoover Institution on War, Revolution and Peace, Stanford, Calif., Box 497 (hereafter Hornbeck biography).

42. *PHA*, Part 14, pp. 1240–44.

43. Ibid., pp. 1244–45.

44. A. A. Hoehling, *The Week Before Pearl Harbor,* (New York, 1963), pp. 134–35 (hereafter *Week Before*); VADM Ross T. McIntire, *White House Physician* (New York, 1946), p. 57. (hereafter *White House Physician*).

45. Eleanor Roosevelt, *This I Remember* (New York, 1949), pp. 232–33 (hereafter *This I Remember*).

46. Stimson diary, December 6, 1941.

47. Safford comments; *PHA*, Part 8, p. 3562.

48. Washington *Evening Star,* December 6, 1941.

Chapter 2

"Just Another Saturday"

1. Interview with RADM James M. Shoemaker, January 31, 1963 (hereafter Shoemaker).

2. War Diary of the First Destroyer Division, December 7, 1941 (hereafter 1st DD Div diary). All Japanese diaries cited herein were kept by Tokyo time regardless

of geographic location. Where appropriate, we have adjusted to reflect the Hawaiian military times.

3. War Diary of the Third Battleship Division, December 7, 1941 (hereafter 3d BB Div diary).

4. Diary of RADM Sadao Chigusa, December 7, 1941 (hereafter Chigusa diary). At the time, Chigusa was a lieutenant commander, the executive of the light cruiser *Akigumo*.

5. Interview with Capt. Mitsuo Fuchida, December 10, 1963 (hereafter Fuchida).

6. *PHA*, Part 6, p. 2728.

7. Chigusa diary, December 7, 1941.

8. Honolulu *Advertiser*, December 6, 1941; see also *PHA*, Part 30, p. 2975.

9. Interview with Capt. Robert H. Dunlop, Jr., November 16, 1963 (hereafter Dunlop Jr.).

10. Logs of *Allen* and *Chew*, December 6, 1941.

11. Interview with RADM William W. Outerbridge, September 8, 1970 (hereafter Outerbridge).

12. Log of *Monaghan*, December 6, 1941.

13. Interview with RADM William P. Burford, August 18, 1964 (hereafter Burford).

14. Log of *Neosho*, December 6, 1941.

15. Log of *Tangier*, December 6, 1941.

16. Log of *Argonne*, December 6, 1941.

17. Log of *Curtiss*, December 6, 1941.

18. Log of *Dobbin*, December 6, 1941.

19. Interview with Cleveland Davis, August 8, 1964 (hereafter Cleveland Davis).

20. Log of *Hulbert*, December 6, 1941.

21. Interview with RADM Milo F. Draemel, January 17, 1963 (hereafter Draemel).

22. Interview with RADM Herald F. Stout, August 2, 1964 (hereafter Stout).

23. Interview with Admiral George A. Rood, July 24, 1964 (hereafter Rood).

24. Interview with Draemel, January 17, 1963.

25. Log of *Vestal*, December 6, 1941.

26. Interview with Lt. Cmdr. B. C. Hesser, August 10, 1964 (hereafter Hesser).

27. Letter, William D. Osborne to Prange. This letter was undated, but from the context it apparently was written in 1964.

28. Interview with Shapley, October 11, 1976.

29. Log of *Maryland,* December 6, 1941.

30. Interview with Lt. Irwin H. Thesman, August 15, 1964 (hereafter Thesman). In December of 1941, Thesman was an electrician's mate 1st class aboard the *Oklahoma.*

31. Interview with Howard C. French, August 11, 1964 (hereafter French).

32. Interview with CWO-4 Edgar B. Beck, August 6, 1964 (hereafter Beck).

33. *Week Before,* pp. 199–200.

34. *PHA,* Part 10, p. 4835.

35. Interview with Admiral Edwin T. Layton, July 22, 1964 (hereafter Layton); *PHA,* Part 26, p. 236.

36. Interview with RADM William Rhea Furlong, November 16, 1962 (hereafter Furlong).

37. Interview with VADM William Ward Smith, November 29, 1962 (hereafter Smith).

38. Interview with Layton, July 22, 1964.

39. *PHA,* Part 26, p. 236.

40. Interview with Layton, July 22, 1964; *PHA,* Part 26, p. 237.

41. *PHA,* Part 22, pp. 380, 384.

42. Interview with Smith, November 29, 1962.

43. *PHA,* Part 6, p. 2536.

44. Ibid., p. 2531.

45. Ibid., pp. 2536–37.

46. Interview with Layton, July 22, 1964.

47. *PHA,* Part 6, p. 2793.

48. Ibid., Part 22, p. 191.

49. Ibid., Part 7, pp. 3103–04.

50. Chigusa diary, December 7, 1941. The 1st DD Div and 3d BB Div diaries also record this message.

51. 3d BB Div diary, December 7, 1941.

52. *PHA,* Part 23, p. 738.

53. Letter, Walter J. Curylo to Prange, March 3, 1964.

54. Letter, Guy C. Avery to Prange, December 1, 1963.

55. Ibid., December 16, 1963.

56. Interview with Maj. Gen. Brooke E. Allen, July 2, 1962 (hereafter Allen).

57. Interview with Col. Vernon H. Reeves, October 27, 1969 (hereafter Reeves).

58. *PHA*, Part 22, pp. 160–61.

59. Letter, Philippe A. Michaud to Prange, December 16, 1964.

60. Ibid.

61. Ibid.

62. Interview with Takeo Yoshikawa, July 16, 1950 (hereafter Yoshikawa).

63. *PHA*, Part 12, p. 269.

64. Ibid., p. 266; *"Magic" Background*, Vol. 4, Appendix, p. A151.

65. Interview with Yoshikawa, July 16, 1950.

66. *PHA*, Part 12, p. 269; *"Magic" Background*, Vol. 4, Appendix, p. A151.

67. Interview with Yoshikawa, July 16, 1950.

68. Interview with Layton, July 22, 1964.

69. Interview with Capt. Walter J. East, August 7, 1964 (hereafter East).

70. Interview with Layton, May 22, 1958.

71. Interview with Davis, January 30, 1963.

72. Interview with East, August 7, 1964.

CHAPTER 3

"An Air of Tenseness"

1. Unpublished manuscript, Mrs. Charles S. Hamlin, "Some Memories of Franklin Delano Roosevelt," Papers of Charles S. Hamlin, Box 358, Library of Congress (hereafter Hamlin mss.); *PHA*, Part 15, pp. 1633–34.

2. *PHA*, Part 20, p. 4535.

3. Ibid., pp. 4536–37.

4. *Lost War*, pp. 38–39.

5. "Treachery."

6. *PHA*, Part 8, p. 3899, corrected by Part 11, p. 5309.

7. Ibid., Part 8, pp. 3900–01.

8. Ibid., Part 11, p. 5556. Stark never did recall of his own knowledge where he was the night of December 6, 1941. It was Krick who pinpointed his whereabouts. See *At Dawn We Slept*, p. 719.

9. *PHA*, Part 4, p. 1971.

10. Ibid., Part 8, pp. 3900–01; see also Part 4, p. 1763.

11. Letter, Mrs. Alwin Kramer to Prange, December 3, 1970.

12. *PHA*, Part 8, p. 3901.

13. Ibid., Part 10, pp. 4661–62.

14. Ibid., pp. 4662–63.

15. Ibid., pp. 4663–64.

16. Kramer letter, op. cit.; *PHA*, Part 8, pp. 3902–03.

17. *PHA*, Part 8, p. 3907.

18. Kramer letter, op. cit.

19. *PHA*, Part 4, p. 1762; Part 11, pp. 5271.

20. Kramer letter, op. cit.

21. *PHA*, Part 4, pp. 1763–64; Part 11, p. 5272.

22. Ibid., Part 8, p. 3903–04.

23. Kramer letter, op. cit.

24. *PHA*, Part 9, p. 4513.

25. Ibid., pp. 4513–14.

26. Ibid., Part 2, pp. 925–26.

27. Ibid., Part 3, p. 1110. Marshall could not prove his whereabouts on the evening of December 6, 1941, which generated considerable controversy. But he was quite sure he had spent it at home with his convalescent wife, and we have accepted this. See Gordon W. Prange, *Pearl Harbor: The Verdict of History* (New York, 1985), p. 240 (hereafter *Verdict of History*).

28. Katherine Tupper Marshall, *Together: Annals of an Army Wife* (New York, 1946), p. 98 (hereafter *Together*).

29. *PHA*, Part 11, p. 5557.

30. Ibid., p. 5546.

31. Ibid., p. 5557.

32. Ibid., p. 5559.

33. Interview with Lt. Gen. Truman H. Landon, December 15, 1959 (hereafter Landon); *PHA*, Part 27, p. 96.

34. Interview with Landon, December 15, 1959.

35. *PHA*, Part 18, p. 2965.

36. Ibid., Part 27, p. 96.

37. Ibid., Part 22, p. 45; Part 18, p. 2965.

38. Chigusa diary, December 7, 1941; interview with Chigusa, November 18, 1964.

CHAPTER 4

"A Wonderful Evening"

1. Honolulu *Star-Bulletin*, December 7, 1941.

2. Interview with Brig. Gen. Robert H. Dunlop, October 10, 1963 (hereafter Dunlop).

3. *PHA*, Part 22, p. 384.

4. Interview with Curts, November 16, 1962.

5. Interview with Capt. Joseph J. Rochefort, August 26, 1964 (hereafter Rochefort).

6. Log of *Maryland*, December 6, 1941.

7. Log of *Monaghan*, December 6, 1941.

8. *PHA*, Part 7, pp. 2951, 3034–35; Part 18, p. 3191.

9. Ibid., Part 22, p. 303.

10. Letter, R. R. Moser to Prange, January 23, 1964.

11. Letter, William B. Daniels to Prange, January 14, 1965.

12. Ibid.

13. Ibid.

14. Ibid.

15. Letter, Michaud to Prange, December 6, 1964.

16. Interview with Col. Charles W. Davis, November 1, 1963 (hereafter Charles Davis); interview with Charles and Mrs. Davis, February 19, 1964.

17. *Military Press (Honolulu)*, December 7, 1961.

18. *PHA*, Part 35, p. 274.

19. Ibid., p. 275.

20. Ibid., Part 10, p. 5107.

21. Ibid., Part 35, p. 276; Part 10, p. 5106.

22. Ibid., Part 31, p. 3188.

23. Ibid., pp. 3188–89.

24. Ibid., Part 10, pp. 4870–71.

25. Interview with Bicknell, September 8, 1967; *PHA*, Part 10, pp. 5099–5100.

26. *PHA*, Part 10, p. 5108.

27. Interview with Bicknell, September 8, 1967; *PHA*, Part 10, p. 5100; Part 27, p. 738.

28. *PHA*, Part 28, pp. 1558, 1542.

29. Ibid., Part 7, p. 2977.

30. Interview with Bicknell, September 8, 1967; *PHA*, Part 10, pp. 5091, 5097.

31. *PHA*, Part 27, p. 738.

32. Ibid., Part 10, p. 5113; interview with Bicknell, September 8, 1967.

33. Interview with Yoshikawa, July 16, 1950; *PHA*, Part 35, p. 390.

34. *PHA*, Part 12, p. 270; Part 35, p. 390; *"Magic" Background*, Vol. 4, pp. A154–55. In both Part 12 and *"Magic" Background*, the word following "which entered port were" appears as a garble. It is shown as *Wyoming* in Part 35. This was Yoshikawa's error. He mistook the *Utah* for the *Wyoming*.

35. Interview with Yoshikawa, July 16, 1950; *PHA*, Part 35, p. 371.

36. *PHA*, Part 23, p. 632.

37. Interview with Shapley, October 11, 1967.

38. Interviews with Hesser, August 10, 1964, and Lt. Cmdr. Harley F. Smart, August 21, 1964 (hereafter Smart). He was an ensign aboard the *Vestal* in December of 1941.

39. Interview with John Crawford, August 8, 1964 (hereafter Crawford).

40. *PHA*, Part 22, p. 506.

41. Interview with RADM Lawrence E. Ruff, July 28, 1964 (hereafter Ruff).

42. Interview with Pullen, September 12, 1964.

43. *PHA*, Part 22, p. 507.

44. Ibid., p. 508.

45. Ibid., Part 20, p. 4482.

46. Interview with Furlong, November 9, 1963; *PHA*, Part 22, p. 594.

47. Interview with Crawford, August 8, 1964.

48. Interview with Furlong, November 9, 1963.

49. *PHA*, Part 23, pp. 745–46.

50. Ibid., Part 22, p. 589.

51. Interview with Emil Johnson, August 8, 1964 (hereafter Emil Johnson).

52. Log of *Neosho*, December 6, 1941.

53. Interview with Shoemaker, January 31, 1963.

54. *PHA*, Part 22, p. 565.

55. Interview with Capt. and Mrs. East, August 17, 1964.

56. Interview with Cmdr. Doir C. Johnson, July 25, 1964 (hereafter Johnson).

57. *PHA*, Part 22, pp. 286–87.

58. Ibid., Part 23, pp. 794–96.

59. Ibid., p. 818.

60. Ibid., Part 28, p. 1558.

61. Interview with Col. and Mrs. Emil Leard, October 17, 1963 (hereafter Leard).

62. *PHA*, Part 22, p. 156; Part 10, p. 4983.

63. Ibid., Part 22, p. 87; Honolulu *Star-Bulletin*, December 7, 1966.

64. Interview with Maj. Gen. Robert J. Fleming, Jr., June 24, 1977 (hereafter Fleming).

65. *PHA*, Part 6, pp. 2825–26.

66. Interview with Draemel, January 17, 1963.

67. Interview with Bicknell, September 8, 1967.

68. Interview with DeLany, November 2, 1962.

69. *PHA*, Part 6, pp. 2825–26.

70. Interview with Kimmel, November 29, 1963.

71. Letter, Michaud to Prange, December 16, 1964.

72. Interview with Reeves, October 27, 1969.

73. Interview with Allen, July 2, 1962.

74. Interview with Bicknell, September 8, 1967.

75. *PHA*, Part 18, p. 3015.

76. Interview with Brig. Gen. James A. Mollison, January 30, 1963 (hereafter Mollison).

77. Interview with Col. William C. Farnum, October 16, 1963 (hereafter Farnum).

78. Interview with Dunlop, October 10, 1963.

79. Interview with Brig. Gen. George R. Sampson, October 18, 1963 (hereafter Sampson).

80. Interview with Layton, July 22, 1964.

81. Interview with Capt. Minoru Genda, June 6, 1947 (hereafter Genda); Minoru Genda, *Shinjuwan Sakusen Kaikoroku* (Tokyo, 1972), pp. 271–72 (hereafter *SSK*).

82. Interview with Fuchida, December 10, 1963.

83. Interview with Iyozo Fujita, February 2, 1951 (hereafter Fujita).

84. Interview with Kyozo Ohashi, November 18, 1949 (hereafter Ohashi).

85. Interview with Minoru Yokota, February 23, 1951 (hereafter Yokota).

86. Interview with Fuchida, August 27, 1967.

87. Interview with Hanku Sasaki, October 24, 1950 (hereafter Sasaki); History Section, Hq, USAFFE, Tokyo, Japanese Monograph No. 102, "Submarine Operations December 1941–April 1952" (hereafter "Submarine Operations"). This monograph was compiled by Capt. Tatsuwaka Shibuya, who in 1941 was submarine staff officer, First Air Fleet.

88. Statement by Hanku Sasaki, October 30, 1950 (hereafter Sasaki statement).

89. Interview with Sasaki, October 24, 1950.

90. Sasaki statement.

91. Interview with Kazuo Sakamaki, October 19, 1947 (hereafter Sakamaki); Kazuo Sakamaki, *I Attacked Pearl Harbor* (New York, 1949), pp. 19–21 (hereafter *I Attacked Pearl Harbor*).

CHAPTER 5

"That Rather Hectic Morning"

1. December 7, 1941.

2. Washington *Post,* December 7, 1941.

3. December 7, 1941.

4. Indianapolis *Star,* December 7, 1941.

5. Washington *Post,* December 7, 1941.

6. San Antonio *Express,* December 7, 1941.

7. Washington *Sunday Star,* December 7, 1941.

8. IMTFE Exhibit No. 1224, June 23, 1946, Affidavit of Joseph Clark Grew (hereafter Grew affidavit); *PHA,* Part 2, pp. 569–70, 692–93, corrected by Part 5, p. 2481.

9. *PHA,* Part 14, p. 1415.

10. Ibid., Part 12, p. 245; *"Magic" Background,* Vol. 4, Appendix, p. A-134.

11. "Treachery."

12. *PHA,* Part 8, pp. 3907–08.

13. Ibid., pp. 3392–93.

14. Ibid., Part 11, pp. 5546–47; see also Part 5, p. 2132.

15. Ibid., Part 33, p. 865.

16. Ibid., pp. 858–59.

17. Ibid., Part 11, pp. 5273–74, 5282–83.

18. Ibid., Part 33, p. 858; Part 8, pp. 3907–08.

19. Ibid., Part 8, pp. 3907–08.

20. Ibid., Part 9, pp. 4516, 4523; Part 35, p. 98.

21. Ibid., Part 35, p. 98; Part 9, p. 4524. It is not certain exactly when or how Hull received the full fourteen-part message. John B. Schindel, in 1941 a second lieutenant in Bratton's section, informed Prange that he delivered it at about 0730 (interview with Schindel, July 14, 1956). However, Bratton's assistant, Lt. Col. C. C. Dusenbury, stated that he delivered it shortly before Hull met with Nomura and Kurusu (*PHA*, Part 35, p. 26). Hull's *Memoirs* indicate only that he received it that morning (*Hull Memoirs*, Part II, p. 1095). In any case, Knox had it when he conferred with Hull at 1000 on December 7, and it is obvious from the course of events that Hull knew the contents well before he met with the two Japanese diplomats that afternoon.

22. Grew affidavit; *PHA*, Part 2, p. 569.

23. Grew affidavit.

24. *PHA*, Part 2, p. 570.

25. Ibid., p. 692.

26. IMTFEC Exhibit No. 1225, July 30, 1946, Affidavit of Tateki Shirao; IMTFEC Document No. 2669A, "Extracts from Diary of Shirao, Tateki."

27. Grew affidavit; *PHA*, Part 2, pp. 570, 693.

28. *PHA*, Part 12, p. 248; *"Magic" Background*, Vol. 4, Appendix, p. A-129.

29. *PHA*, Part 14, p. 1416.

30. Ibid., Part 9, pp. 4517, 4524.

31. Ibid., p. 4527.

32. Ibid., p. 4571.

33. Ibid., p. 4548.

34. Ibid., pp. 4524, 4595; Part 3, p. 1114.

35. Ibid., Part 8, pp. 3908–09.

36. Ibid., pp. 3393–94.

37. Ibid., pp. 3910–11; Part 9, p. 4048.

38. Ibid., Part 9, pp. 4017–18; Part 12, pp. 248–49; *"Magic" Background*, Vol. 4, Appendix, pp. A-134–35.

39. *PHA*, Part 9, pp. 4050–51.

40. Ibid., p. 4018; Part 12, pp. 186–87; *"Magic" Background*, Vol. 5, pp. 55–56.

41. *PHA*, Part 8, p. 3909; Part 12, p. 251; *"Magic" Background*, Vol. 5, p. 57.

42. *PHA*, Part 9, pp. 3970–71; Part 8, p. 3920; Part 36, p. 343.

43. Ibid., Part 9, p. 4018; Part 12, p. 248; *"Magic" Background*, Vol. 4, Appendix, p. A-134.

44. *PHA*, Part 8, pp. 3909, 3437; Part 36, p. 27.

45. Ibid., Part 8, pp. 3430, 3909.

46. Ibid., Part 36, pp. 25–26.

47. Ibid., Part 8, p. 3396.

48. Ibid., p. 3437; Part 9, p. 4580.

49. Ibid., Part 8, pp. 3910–12; Part 9, pp. 4052–53.

50. Stimson diary, December 7, 1941.

51. Rose Page Wilson, *General Marshall Remembered* (Englewood Cliffs, N.J., 1968), p. 245.

52. *Together*, pp. 98–99.

53. *PHA*, Part 3, p. 1108.

54. Ibid., Part 9, p. 4525. Marshall did not remember talking with Bratton (Part 11, pp. 5175–76).

55. "Treachery."

56. *Lost War*, p. 57.

57. Gwen Terasaki, *Bridge to the Sun* (Chapel Hill, N.C., 1957), pp. 1–2 (hereafter *Bridge to the Sun*).

58. *PHA*, Part 9, p. 4525.

59. Ibid., Part 2, p. 933.

60. Ibid., Part 9, pp. 4517–18, 4552; Part 14, p. 1410.

61. Ibid., Part 29, pp. 2309–10.

62. Ibid., Part 9, p. 4518; Part 14, p. 1410.

63. Ibid., Part 14, p. 1410.

64. Ibid., Part 2, pp. 932–33.

65. Ibid., Part 9, p. 4518; Part 3, p. 1109; Part 14, pp. 1409–10.

66. Ibid., Part 5, p. 2132.

67. Ibid., Part 14, p. 1410.

68. Ibid., Part 5, pp. 2132–33.

69. Ibid., Part 9, p. 4519; Part 14, p. 1410.

70. Ibid., Part 34, p. 32; Part 23, p. 1105.

71. Ibid., Part 9, p. 4519.

72. Ibid., Part 14, p. 1334.

73. Ibid., Part 9, p. 4519; Part 14, p. 1411.

74. Ibid., Part 15, p. 1640.

75. Ibid., Part 34, p. 33; Part 27, pp. 109, 114; Part 23, p. 1103; Part 15, p. 1640.

76. Honolulu *Star-Bulletin,* December 7, 1941.

Chapter 6

"About to Launch a Blow"

1. Log of *California,* December 7, 1941.

2. Log of *Ramapo,* December 7, 1941; Samuel E. Morison, *The Rising Sun in the Pacific* (Boston, 1950), p. 119 (hereafter *Rising Sun*).

3. Log of *Ward,* December 7, 1941.

4. Interview with Outerbridge, September 8, 1970; Theodore Roscoe, *United States Destroyer Operations in World War II* (Annapolis, 1953), p. 45 (hereafter *Destroyer Operations*).

5. Interviews with Capt. Tatsuwaka Shibuya, July 17 and August 7, 1948 (hereafter Shibuya).

6. Interview with Capt. Takayasu Arima, November 21, 1948 (hereafter Arima).

7. Sei-Ichi Hohjo, "The Nine Heroes of Pearl Harbor Attack," *Contemporary Japan* (April, 1942), p. 578 (hereafter "Nine Heroes").

8. Log of *San Francisco,* December 7, 1941.

9. Log of *Maryland,* December 7, 1941.

10. See, for example, logs of *Maryland, Medusa, Pennsylvania, Phoenix, Raleigh,* and *San Francisco,* December 7, 1941.

11. See, for example, logs of *California, Helena, Maryland, Nevada, New Orleans, Raleigh, St. Louis,* and *Tennessee,* December 7, 1941.

12. Interview with Shibuya, August 7, 1948.

13. Interview with Genda, June 1, 1947.

14. Interview with Cmdr. Naohiro Sata, November 23, 1949 (hereafter Sata).

15. Interview with Cmdr. Hisao Shimoda, November 21, 1949 (hereafter Shimoda).

16. Interview with Genda, January 26, 1950.

17. 1st DD Div. diary, December 8, 1941.

18. Interview with RADM Sadatoshi Tomioka, January 26, 1948 (hereafter Tomioka). For full details of the showdown between Yamamoto and the Naval General Staff, see *At Dawn We Slept*, Chap. 37.

19. 1st DD Div. diary, December 8, 1941.

20. Diary of the Fifth Carrier Division, December 8, 1941 (hereafter 5th CV Div. diary).

21. Interviews with Shibuya, July 17 and August 7, 1948.

22. *Japan Times and Advertiser*, March 7, 1942; "Nine Heroes," p. 579.

23. Interviews with Shibuya, July 17 and August 7, 1948.

24. Interview with Arima, November 21, 1948.

25. *Japan Times and Advertiser*, March 7, 1942.

26. Interviews with Shibuya, July 17 and August 7, 1948.

27. Interview with Sakamaki, October 19, 1947; *I Attacked Pearl Harbor*, pp. 37–38.

28. Log of *Ward*, December 7, 1941.

29. Log of *Condor*, December 7, 1941; *PHA*, Part 37, pp. 1296, 1299; Part 39, p. 496.

30. Interview with Outerbridge, September 8, 1970; log of *Ward*, December 7, 1941; *PHA*, Part 36, pp. 55–56.

31. *PHA*, Part 36, p. 56; Part 37, p. 703; interview with Outerbridge, September 8, 1970.

32. *PHA*, Part 36, p. 56; log of *Ward*, December 7, 1941; interview with Outerbridge, September 8, 1970.

33. *PHA*, Part 39, p. 497.

34. Ibid., Part 13, p. 494; Part 39, p. 497.

35. Interview with Capt. Takahisa Amagai, October 5, 1949 (hereafter Amagai).

36. Interview with Heita Matsumura, January 8, 1965 (hereafter Matsumura).

37. Interview with Fujita, February 2, 1951.

38. Interview with Tamotsu Ema, May 27, 1950 (hereafter Ema).

39. Interview with Sata, November 23, 1949.

40. Interview with Yoshio Shiga, December 21, 1964 (hereafter Shiga); questionnaire which Shiga submitted at Prange's request (hereafter Shiga questionnaire). Although undated, this questionnaire was one of a group which Prange obtained in October of 1950.

41. Interview with Keizo Ofuchi, January 19, 1950 (hereafter Ofuchi).

42. Interview with Fuchida, December 10, 1963.

43. Interview with Jinichi Goto, January 17, 1950 (hereafter Goto).

44. Interview with Fuchida, December 10, 1963.

45. Ibid.

46. Interviews with Genda, January 26, 1950, and Goto, January 17, 1950.

47. Interview with Fuchida, December 10, 1963.

48. Interview with Sata, November 23, 1949; statement by Kazuyoshi Kitajima, October 18, 1950 (hereafter Kitajima).

49. Interview with Shiga, December 21, 1964.

50. Interviews with Amagai, October 5 and 19, 1949.

51. Interview with Ema, May 27, 1950.

52. Interview with Shimoda, November 21, 1949.

53. Interview with Ohashi, November 18, 1949. Ohashi mistakenly identified the *Shokaku*'s air officer as Shimoda, who held that position on the *Zuikaku*.

54. Interview with VADM Chuichi Hara, September 6, 1955 (hereafter Hara); statement by Hara, December 26, 1951.

55. Interview with Ohashi, November 18, 1949.

CHAPTER 7

"To the Point of Attack"

1. Interview with Lt. Col. Kermit A. Tyler, August 21, 1964 (hereafter Tyler); *PHA*, Part 22, pp. 220; Part 32, p. 341.

2. Interview with Tyler, August 21, 1964; *PHA*, Part 22, p. 223; Part 27, p. 569; Part 32, p. 344.

3. *PHA*, Part 22, p. 223.

4. Interview with Tyler, August 21, 1964; *PHA*, Part 32, p. 342.

5. *PHA*, Part 22, p. 230; Part 32, p. 342.

6. Interview with Tyler, August 21, 1964.

7. *PHA*, Part 22, pp. 226–27; Part 27, p. 618.

8. Interview with Tyler, August 21, 1964.

9. *PHA*, Part 27, p. 367.

10. Interview with Tyler, August 21, 1964; *PHA*, Part 27, p. 567; Part 32, p. 342, 349.

11. Interview with Tyler, August 21, 1964.

12. Ibid.; *PHA*, Part 27, p. 618; Part 29, p. 2121.

13. *PHA*, Part 27, pp. 528, 617, 623; Part 31, Item No. 4, illustrations following p. 3357.

14. Ibid.; Part 10, p. 5077; Part 32, pp. 476, 523–24.

15. Ibid., Part 10, pp. 5059–60.

16. Ibid., Part 32, p. 481.

17. Ibid., Part 27, pp. 518, 528, 617; Part 32, p. 477; Part 10, p. 5038.

18. Ibid., Part 27, pp. 518–19, 531.

19. Interviews with Genda, June 11; 1947 and November 3, 1950; *SSK*, p. 121, 1st DD Div diary, December 7, 1941.

20. Genda statement, June 11, 1947.

21. Interviews with Genda, December 26, 1947 and November 3, 1950; *SSK*, pp. 272–73.

22. Chigusa diary, December 8, 1941.

23. 2d BB Div diary, December 8, 1941.

24. Interview with Fuchida, December 10, 1963.

25. Interview with Amagai, October 5, 1949.

26. Interview with Fuchida, December 10, 1963.

27. Interview with Goto, January 17, 1950.

28. Matsumura statement, January 19, 1951.

29. Interviews with Amagai, October 5, 1949, and Genda, December 27, 1947.

30. Ofuchi statement, January 17, 1950.

31. Ibid.; interview with Fuchida, December 10, 1963.

32. Interview with Shiga, December 21, 1964; Shiga undated statement.

33. Statement by Kiyokuma Okajima, January 19, 1951 (hereafter Okajima).

34. Statement by Kazuo Muranaka, December 17, 1949 (hereafter Muranaka).

35. Interview with Fuchida, December 10, 1963.

36. Statement by Heijiro Abe, October 14, 1950 (hereafter H. Abe).

37. Statement by Takashi Hashiguchi, October 16, 1950 (hereafter Hashiguchi); interviews with Genda, December 28, 1947, and Fuchida, December 10, 1963.

38. Interviews with Fuchida, December 10, 1963, and Genda, December 28, 1947.

39. Statement by Iwakichi Mifuno, March 6, 1951 (hereafter Mifuno).

40. Interview with Ema, May 27, 1950.

41. Interviews with Fuchida, December 10, 1963, and Genda, December 28, 1947.

42. Interview with Goto, January 17, 1950.

43. Statement by Atsuki Nakajima, January 28, 1951 (hereafter Nakajima).

44. Statement by Ichiro Kitajima, October 18, 1950 (hereafter Kitajima).

45. Statement by Matsumura, January 19, 1951; interview with Matsumura, January 8, 1965.

46. Interview with Genda, December 27, 1947.

47. Ibid., November 3, 1950 and December 28, 1947; Hitoshi Tsunoda et al., *Hawai Sakusen* (Tokyo, 1967), p. 332 (hereafter *Hawai Sakusen*).

48. Interview with VADM Gunichi Mikawa, March 5, 1949 (hereafter Mikawa).

49. Chigusa diary, December 8, 1941.

50. Interviews with Fuchida, December 10, 1963, and Amagai, October 5, 1949.

51. Interviews with Genda, December 28, 1947 and November 3, 1950.

52. Statement by Ofuchi, January 19, 1950.

53. Interview with Genda, December 29, 1947; *SSK,* p. 264.

54. Interviews with Fujita, February 2, 1951, and Shiga, December 21, 1964.

55. Interview with Fuchida, December 10, 1963.

56. Interview with Fujita, February 2, 1951.

57. Interview with Genda, December 28, 1947.

58. Statement by Saburo Shindo, January 17, 1951 (hereafter Shindo); interview with Fuchida, December 10, 1963.

59. Interview with Genda, December 28, 1947.

60. Interview with Fuchida, December 10, 1963.

61. Statement by Zenichi Sato, October 19, 1950 (hereafter Sato).

62. Statement by Jozo Iwami, October 20, 1950 (hereafter Iwami).

63. Interview with Genda, December 28, 1947.

64. Interview with Fuchida, December 10, 1963.

65. Statement by Zenji Abe, October 19, 1950 (hereafter Z. Abe).

66. Interviews with Amagai, October 12, 1949 and October 19, 1950.

67. Interview with Genda, December 28, 1947. Some discrepancy exists as to the number of patrol planes. *Hawai Sakusen* (p. 327) stated that each of the four ships sent up one.

68. Interview with Amagai, October 12, 1949.

69. Ryusosuke Kusada, *Rengo Kantai* (Tokyo, 1952), p. 34 (hereafter *Rengo Kantai*).

70. Interview with Genda, December 28, 1947.

CHAPTER 8

"Suitable Dawn for the Epoch-Making Day"

1. Interview with Capt. Lawrence C. Grannis, July 24, 1964 (hereafter Grannis); log of *Antares*, December 7, 1941.

2. Interview with Grannis, July 24, 1964.

3. Log of *Antares*, December 7, 1941.

4. Interview with Grannis, July 24, 1964; *PHA*, Part 39, p. 498.

5. Walter Lord, *Day of Infamy* (New York, 1957), pp. 39–40 (hereafter *Day of Infamy*); *PHA*, Part 13, p. 494; interview with Grannis, July 24, 1964.

6. Interview with Outerbridge, September 8, 1970; *PHA*, Part 36, pp. 56–57.

7. *PHA*, Part 13, p. 494; Part 36, p. 57.

8. Interview with Outerbridge, September 8, 1970; log of *Ward*, December 7, 1941.

9. Report of W. W. Outerbridge, December 13, 1941, DD 139/A16–3/(759), located in Classified Operational Archives Branch, Naval History Division, Washington Navy Yard, D.C.; log of *Ward*, December 7, 1941.

10. *Day of Infamy*, p. 41; *PHA*, Part 13, p. 494; Part 39, pp. 498–99.

11. *PHA*, Part 36, pp. 57, 59; Part 37, p. 704. It is impossible to say just which of the midget craft met its fate in this incident, but it might well have been the *I-20* midget, with Hiroo in command, for he had been released very close to Oahu.

12. Statement by Mifuku, March 6, 1951.

13. Statement by Muranaka, December 17, 1949.

14. Statement by H. Abe, October 14, 1950.

15. Interview with Goto, January 17, 1950.

16. Statement by Matsumoto, January 19, 1950.

17. Interviews with Fuchida, March 4, 1948 and December 10, 1963.

18. Interview with Tyler, August 21, 1964.

19. *PHA*, Part 18, p. 3015; Part 22, p. 220.

20. Ibid., Part 31, following p. 3357, Item 4, Army Pearl Harbor Board Exhibits.

21. Ibid.

22. Letter from Michaud, December 16, 1964. As Michaud made no mention of the Kaaawa sightings in his very detailed letter, presumably the three men who had the 0400–0700 duty did not mention them.

23. *PHA*, Part 31, following p. 3357, Item 4, Army Pearl Harbor Board Exhibits.

24. Ibid., Part 10, pp. 5056, 5069; chart opp. p. 5058.

25. Interview with Tyler, August 21, 1964; *PHA*, Part 18, p. 3015; Part 22, pp. 220–21; Part 27, p. 568.

26. Log of *Antares*, December 7, 1941.

27. *PHA*, Part 36, p. 58; log of *Ward*, December 7, 1941.

28. Log of *Ward*, December 7, 1941.

29. *PHA*, Part 36, p. 59; interview with Outerbridge, September 8, 1970.

30. *PHA*, Part 37, p. 705.

31. Ibid., Part 36, p. 58.

32. Interview with Tyler, August 21, 1964; *PHA*, Part 22, p. 221.

33. *PHA*, 10, p. 5064; Part 27, p. 531.

34. Ibid., Part 32, pp. 478, 488.

35. Ibid., Part 27, pp. 520–21; Part 32, p. 488; Part 10, Record of Readings, opp. p. 5058.

36. Ibid., Part 10, p. 5046; Part 27, p. 521; Part 32, p. 489.

37. Ibid., Part 10, pp. 5031, 5041; Part 32, p. 489.

38. Ibid., Part 29, p. 2122.

39. Ibid., Part 32, p. 479.

40. Interview with Tyler, August 21, 1964.

41. *PHA*, Part 27, p. 569; Part 32, p. 345; interview with Tyler, August 21, 1964.

42. Several versions of Tyler's reply exist, including "Forget it." He informed Prange that he was quite certain that he did not use that expression, as such flippancy would have been uncalled for and out of character. Both to Prange (interview of August 21, 1964) and to the Roberts Commission (*PHA*, Part 22, p. 221), Tyler stated that his words were, "Well, don't worry about it."

43. *PHA*, Part 29, p. 2122.

44. Ibid., Part 27, p. 568; Part 10, Record of readings opp. p. 5058.

45. Mitsuo Fuchida, *Shinjuwan Sakusen No Shinso; Watakushi Wa Shinjuwan Joku Ni Ita* (Nara, Japan, 1949), pp. 155–56 (hereafter *Shinjuwan Sakusen No Shinso*; interview with Fuchida, March 4, 1948.

46. *PHA*, Part 27, p. 521; Part 32, p. 489; Part 10, Record of readings opp. p. 5058.

47. "Treachery."

48. *PHA*, Part 35, p. 211; *Day of Infamy*, p. 174.

49. *PHA*, Part 10, Record of readings opp. p. 5058.

50. *Rengo Kantai,*, p. 34.

51. *Shinjuwan Sakusen No Shinso*, pp. 161–64. In interview of March 4, 1948, Fuchida recalled that the scout reported six light cruisers, not ten.

52. *PHA*, Part 10, Record of readings opp. p. 5058.

53. Ibid., Part 32, pp. 479–80.

54. Ibid., Part 10, p. 5033.

CHAPTER 9

"We've Made It!"

1. *PHA*, Part 23, p. 1035.

2. Ibid., p. 1036.

3. Ibid., p. 1041.

4. Ibid., p. 1043. The Roberts Commission was the first of the official inquiries into Pearl Harbor. See *At Dawn We Slept*, Chap. 70.

5. *PHA*, Part 23, pp. 1036–37.

6. Ibid., Part 26, p. 209.

7. Ibid., Part 23, p. 1037.

8. Letter to Prange from Mrs. John B. Earle, October 16, 1964.

9. *PHA*, Part 23, p. 1052.

10. Ibid., p. 1038.

11. Ibid., Part 22, p. 499; Part 26, pp. 411–12.

12. Letter from Mrs. Earle, op. cit.

13. *PHA*, Part 23, pp. 1037–38.

14. Ibid., p. 1052.

15. Ibid., Part 26, p. 209; Part 32, p. 444; interview with Admiral Logan C. Ramsey, December 6, 1962 (hereafter Ramsey).

16. *PHA*, Part 26, pp. 209–10; interview with RADM Husband E. Kimmel, December 1, 1963 (hereafter Kimmel).

17. *Idaho Sunday Statesman* (Boise), December 2, 1956.

18. Interview with Mrs. Allen Haynes, November 23, 1970 (hereafter Mrs. Haynes).

19. Interview with Mrs. Davis, February 19, 1964.

20. Interview with Mrs. Smith, June 15, 1964.

21. *PHA,* Part 29, p. 1651.

22. Interview with Mrs. Frank Cooper, March 5, 1966 (hereafter Mrs. Cooper).

23. Honolulu *Star-Bulletin,* December 6 and 7, 1941.

24. Interview with Ruff, July 28, 1964.

25. Statement which Osborne prepared for the U.S.S. *Arizona* Memorial Foundation, courtesy Osborne (hereafter Osborne statement).

26. Interview with Capt. Ruth A. Erickson, September 7, 1971 (hereafter Erickson).

27. Col. C. B. Drake, "A Day at Pearl Harbor," *Marine Corps Gazette* (November 1965), pp. 64, 94 (hereafter "Day at Pearl Harbor").

28. Interview with Shapley, September 11, 1967.

29. Fleet Admiral William F. Halsey, USN, and Lt. Cmdr. J. Bryan, III, USNR, *Admiral Halsey's Story* (New York, 1947), p. 76 (hereafter *Admiral Halsey's Story*); *PHA,* Part 12, p. 345.

30. Interview with Shapley, September 11, 1967.

31. Capt. Joseph K. Taussig, Jr., "I Remember Pearl Harbor," *United States Naval Institute Proceedings* (December 1972), p. 18 (hereafter "I Remember").

32. Letter, Taussig to Prange, January 8, 1963.

33. "I Remember," p. 18.

34. Letter, Robert G. Crouse to Prange, November 24, 1964.

35. Interview with Allen, July 2, 1962.

36. *Military Press* (Honolulu), December 7, 1961.

37. Letter, Avery to Prange, December 16, 1963.

38. Interview with Rochefort, September 1, 1964.

39. Interview with Ema, May 27, 1950.

40. Interview with Toshio Hashimoto, April 20, 1950 (hereafter Hashimoto).

41. Statement by Mifuku, March 6, 1951.

42. Interview with Goto, January 17, 1950.

43. Statement by Matsumura, January 19, 1951.

44. Interviews with Fuchida, February 28, 1953 and December 10, 1963; *Shinjuwan Sakusen No Shinso,* p. 156; statement by Okajima, January 19, 1951.

45. Interviews with Fuchida, December 10 and 11, 1963.

46. Ibid., March 4, 1948 and December 11, 1963; *Shinjuwan Sakusen No Shinso,* pp. 158–61.

47. Interview with Fuchida, December 11, 1963; *Shinjuwan Sakusen No Shinso,* pp. 164–165.

48. *Japan Times and Advertiser,* January 2, 1942. This article did not name Fuchida, referring to him as "Commander X."

49. Interviews with Fuchida, March 4, 1948 and December 11, 1963.

50. Ibid., *Shinjuwan Sakusen No Shinso, pp. 170–72.*

51. Ibid., *Rengo Kantai,* p. 35.

CHAPTER 10

"Japanese! Man Your Stations!"

1. Interview with Goto, February 7, 1950.

2. Ibid., January 17 and February 7, 1950.

3. *PHA,* Part 26, p. 210.

4. Interview with Furlong, November 16, 1962.

5. *PHA,* Part 22, p. 595.

6. Letter from Mrs. Earle, October 16, 1964; interview with Mrs. Earle, September 22, 1970.

7. *Rising Sun,* p. 104.

8. Interviews with Goto, January 17 and 24, 1950.

9. Interview with Shiga, December 21, 1964.

10. Interviews with Goto, January 17 and 24, 1950.

11. Interview with Johnson, July 25, 1964.

12. After Action Report, *West Virginia,* statement of Lt. Cmdr. T. T. Beattie, December 14, 1941, Navy Record Office, Washington Navy Yard, D.C. (hereafter Beattie statement).

13. Statement by Matsumura, January 19, 1951; interview with Matsumura, January 8, 1965.

14. Statement by Nakajima, January 28, 1951.

15. Interview with Cleveland Davis, August 8, 1964.

16. *PHA,* Part 23, pp. 748–49; log of *Raleigh,* December 7, 1941.

17. "Supplementary Battle Report, Captain R. B. Simons, USN, Commanding USS RALEIGH, 7 December, 1941." (hereafter Simons report). Courtesy of W. L. Simons, the captain's brother.

18. Interview with Beardall, November 17, 1970; *PHA*, Part 23, p. 746.

19. Simons report.

20. Interview with Fuchida, March 4, 1948.

21. *PHA*, Part 22, p. 596.

22. Log of *Oglala*, December 7, 1941.

23. Log of *Helena*, December 7, 1941.

24. Washington *Post*, December 7, 1951.

25. Interview with Goto, January 24, 1950.

26. *PHA*, Part 23, pp. 723–24.

27. Interview with Irvin H. Thesman, August 12, 1964 (hereafter Thesman).

28. Stephen B. Young, "God, Please Get Us Out of This," *American Heritage*, Vol. 17, p. 50 (hereafter "Get Us Out").

29. *PHA*, Part 26, p. 210.

30. Interview with Kimmel, December 1, 1963.

31. Letter from Mrs. Earle, October 16, 1964; interview with Mrs. Earle, September 22, 1970; interview with Kimmel, December 1, 1963.

32. *Day of Infamy*, p. 71.

33. Interview with Crawford, August 8, 1964.

34. Interview with Shapley, October 11, 1967; William H. Ewing, "High Dive Off the Mainmast," Honolulu *Star-Bulletin*, December 7, 1961 (hereafter "High Dive").

35. *Day of Infamy*, p. 85.

36. Blake Clark, *Remember Pearl Harbor!* (New York, 1942), pp. 13–14.

37. *PHA*, Part 22, p. 533.

38. Honolulu *Star-Bulletin*, December 7, 1966.

39. *PHA*, Part 23, p. 829.

40. Interview with Ruff, July 28, 1964.

41. *PHA*, Part 29, pp. 2008–2010; Summary of Verbal Report Submitted to Colonel Bicknell and Lieutenant Dyson, U.S. Army, re: Attack on the Island of Oahu—December 7, 1941, Observer: Harold T. Kay, Army Pearl Harbor Board, Miscellaneous Document File, Box 8, PG 107, Records of the Office of the Secretary of War, National Archives, Washington, D.C. (hereafter Kay report).

42. Interview with Outerbridge, September 8, 1970.

43. Osborne statement.

44. Statement by Matsumura, January 19, 1951; interview with Matsumura, January 8, 1965.

45. Undated statement by Masanobu Ibusuki (hereafter Ibusuki).

46. Logs of *Hulbert* and *Thornton*, December 7, 1941.

47. Interview with Capt. William S. Finn, August 11, 1964 (hereafter Finn); log of *Dolphin*, December 7, 1941.

48. Log of *Selfridge*, December 7, 1941.

49. Logs of *PT 29* and *PT 30*, December 7, 1941.

50. Log of *Sacramento*, December 7, 1941.

51. Log of *Nevada*, December 7, 1941.

52. Interview with Fuchida, March 4, 1948; *Shinjuwan Sakusen No Shinso*, p. 187; 1st DD Div diary, December 18, 1941.

53. *Rengo Kantai*, p. 35.

54. Interview with Genda, November 30, 1950; *SSK*, p. 280.

CHAPTER 11

"Great Ships Were Dying"

1. Log of *Nevada*, December 7, 1941.

2. *PHA*, Part 23, p. 704. *Nevada's* log does not mention this kill, but Samuel Eliot Morison states that .50 caliber machine-gun fire accounted for this Japanese torpedo plane (*Rising Sun*, p. 109).

3. Statement by Kitajima, October 18, 1950.

4. "I Remember," p. 20.

5. Action Report of *Nevada*, contained in Action Report, Commander-in-Chief, United States Pacific Fleet, Serial 0479, 15 February 1942, Report of Japanese Raid on Pearl Harbor, 7 December 1941, Vol. III, Classified Operational Archives Branch, Naval History Division, Washington Navy Yard, D.C. (hereafter Action Report).

6. Letter from Taussig, January 8, 1963.

7. Honolulu *Advertiser*, December 7, 1966. Ross was awarded the Medal of Honor. He survived the attack and later received a commission.

8. Log of *Grebe*, December 7, 1941.

9. Seattle *Post-Intelligencer*, December 7, 1966.

10. Interview with Grannis, July 24, 1964.

11. Interview with Mrs. Cooper, March 5, 1966.

12. Honolulu *Advertiser*, December 6, 1970.

13. Interview with Erickson, September 7, 1971.

14. Interview with Kimmel, December 1, 1963.

15. Log of *California*, December 7, 1941.

16. Interview with Train, November 27, 1962.

17. "A Day at Pearl Harbor," p. 94.

18. *Rising Sun*, p. 112.

19. Honolulu *Advertiser*, December 7, 1966.

20. Ibid. All three men received the Medal of Honor, Jones and Reeves posthumously.

21. Log of *Detroit*, December 7, 1941.

22. Simons report. The log of *Utah* was lost when she capsized, but that of the seaplane tender *Tangier*, directly astern *Utah*, gave the time *Utah* sank as 0810.

23. Honolulu *Advertiser*, December 7, 1966. Tomich was posthumously awarded the Medal of Honor.

24. Interview with Stout, August 8, 1964.

25. Ibid.

26. Log of *Blue*, December 7, 1941, with "Addendum to 8–12 Watch of December 7, 1941," which Asher submitted to his skipper on December 11, 1941.

27. *PHA*, Part 23, pp. 696–97.

28. Interview with Rood, July 24, 1964.

29. Ibid.; interview with RADM Carl K. Fink, November 17, 1970 (hereafter Fink).

30. *PHA*, Part 23, pp. 724–25.

31. Honolulu *Advertiser*, December 7, 1966.

32. Interview with Beck, August 6, 1964.

33. "Get Us Out," pp. 50–51.

34. Statement by Cmdr. J. L. Kenworthy, December 16, 1941, Action Report, Vol. 3, Encl. E.

35. Interview with French, August 11, 1964.

36. Ibid.

37. Ibid. French said that Struther swam "over to the *West Virginia*"; however, the *West Virginia* was forward of the *Oklahoma*, so it is more likely that he swam to the *Maryland*, moored inboard of the *Oklahoma*, as did a number of his shipmates.

38. Ibid.

39. *PHA*, Part 23, p. 725.

40. Interview with Beck, August 6, 1964.

41. Philip N. Pierce, "Twenty Years Ago," *The Leatherneck* (December 1961), p. 79 (hereafter "Twenty Years Ago").

42. Letter from Mrs. Earle, October 16, 1964.

43. Interview with Thesman, August 15, 1964.

44. Ibid.

45. Interview with Yokota, February 23, 1951; article by Alf Pratte in Honolulu *Star-Bulletin*, December 7, 1966. Because of conflicting evidence on just when the Matson liner *Lurline* received the *Cynthia Olsen's* distress signal, some believe that this incident took place before the attack on Pearl Harbor. But Yokota was positive that he did not jump the gun, and it is unlikely that such an experienced submarine skipper followed the vessel all night only to lose patience at the last minute.

CHAPTER 12

"Through the Smoke and Flames"

1. Interviews with Fuchida, March 9, 1948 and December 11, 1963; *Shinjuwan Sakusen No Shinso*, p. 174.

2. Interview with Fuchida, December 11, 1963; *Shinjuwan Sakusen No Shinso*, p. 175.

3. Interview with Fuchida, December 11, 1963; *Shinjuwan Sakusen No Shinso*, pp. 176–178.

4. *Shinjuwan Sakusen No Shinso*, p. 178.

5. Interview with Hesser, August 8, 1964.

6. Log of *Vestal*, December 7, 1941.

7. Interview with Crawford, August 8, 1964.

8. Interview with Hesser, August 10, 1964.

9. Interview with Crawford, August 8, 1964.

10. Interviews with Hesser, August 10 and 14, 1964.

11. Interview with Fuchida, December 11, 1963.

12. Interview with Genda, December 25, 1974. Kanai was shot down during the attack on Wake Island. Some claim the bomb went down the stack, but this is incorrect.

13. Interview with French, August 11, 1964.

14. Interview with Fink, November 17, 1970.

15. Seattle *Post-Intelligencer*, December 7, 1966.

16. *Newsweek*, December 12, 1966, pp. 44, 49.

17. Osborne statement.

18. Interview with Shapley, October 11, 1967.

19. Ibid.

20. Interview with Earl C. Nightingale, November 5, 1970 (hereafter Nightingale).

21. Ibid.

22. Interview with Shapley, October 11, 1967.

23. Interview with Nightingale, November 5, 1970. In later years, Nightingale gave his son the middle name of Alan in honor of Shapley.

24. Interview with Shapley, October 11, 1967.

25. Interview with Nightingale, November 5, 1970.

26. Interview with Shapley, October 11, 1967. Shapley was awarded the Silver Star for gallantry based on Nightingale's report of the action.

27. Both officers were posthumously awarded the Medal of Honor. A body believed to be Kidd's was found on the boat deck at the foot of the bridge ladder. The captain's body was never found. (*PHA*, Part 23, p. 636). Some time after the attack, when the *Arizona* had cooled off, a party boarded her, found a pile of ashes on deck, and in the ashes an Academy class ring. They took it ashore and had a goldsmith clean it. Inside they could then read the name, Franklin Van Valkenburgh. The command sent it to his wife (Interview with Train, November 27, 1962).

28. *PHA*, Part 23, pp. 634–35. Fuqua was awarded the Medal of Honor.

29. Interview with Ruff, July 28, 1964.

30. Interview with Crawford, August 8, 1964.

31. Interview with Hesser, August 10, 1964.

32. Interview with Smart, August 21, 1964.

33. Interview with Hesser, August 10, 1964.

34. Interview with Smart, August 21, 1964.

35. Interviews with Hesser, August 10 and 14, 1964.

36. Interview with Mrs. Cassin B. Young, August 9, 1964.

37. Interview with Hesser, August 10, 1964. Young received the Medal of Honor for his heroism at Pearl Harbor. He was killed near Guadalcanal in 1942 (Honolulu *Advertiser*, December 7, 1966).

38. Interview with Hesser, August 10, 1964. The *Vestal*'s log of December 7, 1941, shows this torpedo as almost simultaneous with the *Arizona*'s explosion, but some moments must have elapsed, because Young was back aboard the *Vestal*.

39. Log of *Tennessee*, December 7, 1941.

40. *Rising Sun*, p. 106.

41. Beattie statement.

42. Statement by Lt. (jg) C. V. Ricketts, Action Report, Vol. 3, Encl E (hereafter Ricketts statement).

43. *Rising Sun*, p. 104.

44. Interview with Johnson, July 25, 1964; VADM Homer N. Wallin, USN (Ret), *Pearl Harbor; Why, How, Fleet Salvage and Final Appraisal* (Washington, D.C., 1968), pp. 233–34 (hereafter Wallin).

45. Sault St. Marie *Evening News*, December 7, 1961. Both Johnson and Matheson believed it was a fragment from this bomb that killed Bennion.

46. Statement by H. Abe, October 14, 1950.

47. Beattie statement.

48. Interview with Johnson, July 25, 1964; *Day of Infamy*, p. 132.

49. Ricketts statement. Bennion received the Medal of Honor posthumously.

50. Interview with Johnson, July 25, 1964.

51. *Day of Infamy*, pp. 131–32.

52. Interview with Johnson, July 25, 1964.

53. Honolulu *Star-Bulletin*, May 27, 1942.

CHAPTER 13

"A Terrible Hour"

1. Interview with Erickson, September 7, 1971.

2. *Newsweek*, December 13, 1966, p. 39.

3. Ibid.; The editors of the Army Times Publishing Company, *Pearl Harbor and Hawaii: A Military History* (New York, 1971), p. 50 (hereafter *Pearl Harbor and Hawaii*); *Day of Infamy*, p. 144.

4. Interview with Fuchida, December 11, 1963; *Shinjuwan Sakusen No Shinso*, p. 181. Fuchida was sure that his target was the *Maryland*, which was indeed the

fourth in line, and we have accepted his version. But the *Maryland*'s log for December 7, 1941, recorded no strikes until 0909, when she "Received one and possibly two bomb hits on forecastle on amidships line about frame 10...and about three near misses on each side and ahead of bow." This was during the second-wave attack. This suggests that the *Maryland*'s log was incorrect, not surprising under the circumstances. According to Fuchida, no horizontal bombers attacked ships in the second wave (Interview with Fuchida, January 6, 1949).

5. After Action Report, *Maryland*, statement of Seaman 1st Class Leslie Short, December 11, 1941, Naval Record Office, Washington Navy Yard, D.C.

6. Letter from Harlan C. Eisnaugle to Prange, November 24, 1964 (hereafter Eisnaugle).

7. Interview with Fuchida, December 11, 1963; *Shinjuwan Sakusen No Shinso*, pp. 182–83.

8. See Estimated Damage Report Map, *At Dawn We Slept*, p. 512.

9. Wallin, p. 192

10. Interview with Train, November 26, 1962.

11. *PHA*, Part 22, p. 533.

12. Ibid., p. 534. The *California*'s log for December 7, 1941, shows that Pye came aboard at 0845. However, the log also shows that the bombings which Pye described took place a good 15 minutes earlier.

13. Log of *California*, December 7, 1941.

14. Interview with Train, November 26, 1962.

15. Wallin, p. 225.

16. Interview with Johnson, July 25, 1964.

17. Statement by Cmdr. H. H. Hillenkoetter, Vol. 3, Encl. F, Action Report. Hillenkoetter was executive officer of *West Virginia*.

18. Interview with Ruff, July 28, 1964.

19. Interview with Kimmel, December 1, 1963.

20. Interview with Captain and Mrs. East, August 7, 1964.

21. Interview with Curts, November 16, 1962.

22. *PHA*, Part 26, p. 114.

23. Interview with Curts, November 16, 1962.

24. *PHA*, Part 24, p. 1365; Part 26, p. 210.

25. Interview with Curts, November 16, 1962.

26. *PHA*, Part 24, pp. 1365 and 1371.

27. Interviews with Curts, November 16, 1962, and Kimmel, December 1, 1963; *PHA*, Part 23, p. 899.

28. Interviews with Smith, November 14, 1962 and June 15, 1964. Mrs. Smith participated in the latter session.

29. *PHA*, Part 26, p. 65.

30. Interview with Davis, January 30, 1963.

31. Interview with DeLany, November 2, 1962.

32. *PHA*, Part 26, p. 84.

33. Ibid., Part 22, p. 511.

34. Interview with DeLany, November 2, 1962.

35. Interview with Davis, January 30, 1963.

36. Statement by Hashiguchi.

37. Statement by Kitajima, October 18, 1950.

38. Interview with Goto, January 24, 1950.

39. Statement by Matsumura, January 19, 1951; interview with Matsumura, January 8, 1965.

40. 1st DD Div diary, December 17, 1941.

CHAPTER 14

"This Is Not Drill"

1. Interview with Ramsey, December 6, 1962; *PHA*, Part 32, p. 444.

2. *PHA*, Part 32, pp. 438, 457.

3. Interview with Ramsey, December 6, 1962; Report of Patrol Wing Two Action Report, Vol. 1.

4. Interview with Ramsey, December 6, 1962; *PHA*, Part 32, pp. 445, 458.

5. St. Louis *Post-Dispatch*, December 18, 1941.

6. Interview with Ramsey, December 6, 1962.

7. Letter, Victor Kamont to Prange, November 9, 1964 (hereafter Kamont).

8. Interview with Thomas E. Forrow, August 16, 1964 (hereafter Forrow).

9. Letter, Jack Rogo to Prange, September 2, 1964 (hereafter Rogo).

10. Ibid.

11. Interview with Admiral Cecil D. Riggs, January 14, 1962 (hereafter Riggs).

12. Interview with VADM Charles Coe, January 23, 1963 (hereafter Coe).

13. Ibid.

14. Ibid.

15. Interview with Shoemaker, January 31, 1963.

16. *Admiral Halsey's Story*, p. 77.

17. *PHA*, Part 23, pp. 608, 620; Part 26, p. 330.

18. *Admiral Halsey's Story*, p. 81; *PHA*, Part 16, p. 2118.

19. *PHA*, Part 26, p. 330.

20. Interview with Shoemaker, January 31, 1963. Halsey wrote that Nichol was standing at a window in CinCPAC Headquarters when the *Arizona* blew up (*Admiral Halsey's Story*, p. 81). However, Young reported that he landed at about 0835 (*PHA*, Part 16, p. 2119), which was some time after the *Arizona* exploded.

21. *PHA*, Part 23, pp. 611–12; *Admiral Halsey's Story*, p. 78; *Rising Sun*, p. 121.

22. Interview with Forrow, August 16, 1964.

23. Letter from Kamont, November 9, 1964.

24. Interview with Shoemaker, January 31, 1963.

25. Ibid., log of *Neosho*, December 7, 1941.

26. Charles Rawlings and Isabel Leighton, "Fat Girl," *Saturday Evening Post*, February 6, 1943, p. 10.

27. Log of *Neosho*, December 7, 1941.

28. Interview with Shoemaker, January 31, 1943.

29. Interview with Ramsey, December 2, 1962.

CHAPTER 15

"Somebody Is Going to Pay for This"

1. Letter from Moser, January 23, 1964.

2. Interview with Admiral Harold M. Martin, November 10, 1970 (hereafter Martin).

3. *PHA*, Part 12, pp. 351–52; Part 23, pp. 738–40.

4. Interview with Martin, November 10, 1970.

5. Letter from Avery, November 4, 1963.

6. Ibid., December 16, 1963.

7. Ibid., November 4 and December 16, 1963.

8. Interview with Fuchida, December 11, 1963.

9. Letter from Avery, November 4, 1963.

10. Honolulu *Advertiser*, December 6, 1966. This issue printed highlights of Cmdr. H. M. Martin's report to Bloch on the activities at Kaneohe on December 7, 1941.

11. Letter from Avery, December 16, 1963.

12. Interview with Martin, November 10, 1970; *PHA*, Part 23, pp. 738–39.

13. Letter from Curylo, March 3, 1964.

14. Letter from Moser, January 23, 1964.

15. Letter, R. M. Richmond to Prange, November 26, 1963 (hereafter Richmond).

16. Interview with Dunlop, Jr., November 16, 1963.

17. Ibid. Dunlop could not recall the name of the Amish soldier.

18. Ibid.

19. Ibid.

20. *PHA*, Part 23, p. 739.

21. Letter from Moser, January 23, 1964.

22. *PHA*, Part 23, p. 739.

23. Interview with Martin, November 10, 1970.

24. Honolulu *Advertiser*, December 6, 1966.

25. Letter from Curylo, March 3, 1964.

26. Letter from Moser, January 23, 1964.

27. Interview with Martin, November 10, 1970.

28. Letter from Avery, December 16, 1963.

Chapter 16

"Tearing the Place to Pieces"

1. *PHA*, Part 27, p. 641.

2. Ibid., Part 22, pp. 291–92.

3. Interview with Mollison, January 30, 1963; *PHA*, Part 27, p. 431.

4. Interview with Maj. Gen. William E. Farthing, August 17, 1955 (hereafter Farthing).

5. *PHA*, Part 27, pp. 432–34, 437.

6. Interview with Farthing, August 17, 1955; *PHA*, Part 27, p. 434.

7. Interview with Landon, December 15, 1959.

8. Interview with Farthing, August 17, 1955; *PHA*, Part 22, p. 202; Part 12, p. 323.

9. Interview with Capt. William H. Heydt, January 10, 1971 (hereafter Heydt).

10. Letter from Crouse, November 24, 1964.

11. *PHA*, Part 22, p. 283.

12. Interview with Mollison, January 30, 1963.

13. *PHA*, Part 22, p. 304.

14. Ibid., p. 291.

15. Ibid., Part 27, p. 439.

16. Ibid., pp. 439–40; Answers by Farthing, November 12, 1962, to questionnaire by Prange (hereafter Farthing questionnaire).

17. Letter from Crouse, November 24, 1964.

18. Interviews with Mollison, January 30, 1963, and Allen, July 17, 1962.

19. Interview with Farnum, October 13, 1963.

20. Letter, Nicholas Bongo to Prange, June 9, 1964 (hereafter Bongo).

21. Interview with Reeves, October 27, 1969.

22. *PHA*, Part 22, pp. 304–05.

23. Statement by Mifuku, March 6, 1951.

24. *PHA*, Part 22, pp. 291–92.

25. Ibid., Part 27, p. 641.

26. Letter from Crouse, November 24, 1964.

27. *PHA*, Part 22, pp. 283–85.

28. Interview with Heydt, January 10, 1971.

29. *Military Press* (Honolulu), December 7, 1961.

30. Ibid.

31. *PHA*, Part 22, p. 134.

32. Interview with Mollison, April 15, 1961.

33. *PHA*, Part 22, pp. 193–94.

34. Interview with Mollison, April 15, 1961.

35. *PHA*, Part 22, p. 194.

36. Interview with Farnum, October 13, 1963.

37. Interview with Allen, July 17, 1962; *PHA*, Part 22, p. 124.

38. Interview with Lt. Col. Francis Gutzak, October 19, 1953 (hereafter Gutzak).

39. *Day of Infamy*, pp. 80, 113.

40. Interview with Gutzak, October 19, 1953.

41. Letter from Crouse, November 24, 1964.

42. Interview with Allen, July 17, 1962; *PHA*, Part 22, pp. 124, 127.

43. Statement by Mifuku, March 6, 1951.

44. Interview with Shiga, December 21, 1964.

45. Interview with Harry Rafsky, August 11, 1964 (hereafter Rafsky).

46. *PHA*, Part 22, p. 126.

47. Interview with Landon, December 15, 1959.

48. *Day of Infamy*, p. 110.

49. Interviews with Landon, December 15, 1959, and Mollison, April 15, 1963; *Day of Infamy*, p. 110.

50. Statement by Ibusuki, undated.

51. Interview with Landon, December 15, 1959.

52. Interview with Mollison, April '5, 1963.

53. Martin Caiden, *The Rugged, Rugged Warriors* (New York, 1966), p. 156.

54. Interview with Mrs. Cooper, March 5, 1966.

55. *PHA*, Part 28, p. 988.

56. Interview with Farthing, August 17, 1955.

57. Interview with Farnum, October 16, 1963.

58. *Newsweek*, December 12, 1966.

CHAPTER 17

"Bedlam and Bombs and Bullets"

1. *PHA*, Part 28, p. 1491.

2. Ibid., Part 29, p. 2114.

3. Interview with Flood, July 9, 1962.

4. Ibid.; interview with Davidson, July 6, 1962.

5. *PHA*, Part 22, pp. 108–09.

6. Ibid., Part 28, p. 1489; interview with Flood, July 9, 1962.

7. *PHA*, Part 12, p. 323.

8. Interview with Davidson, July 6, 1962.

9. *PHA*, Part 28, pp. 1486–87.

10. Ibid., Part 22, p. 260.

11. Interview with Flood, July 9, 1962.

12. *PHA*, Part 28, p. 1487.

13. Interview with Flood, July 9, 1962.

14. Interview with Davidson, July 6, 1962.

15. *PHA*, Part 22, pp. 257–60.

16. Interview with Maj. Gen. and Mrs. Durward S. Wilson and Mrs. Charles A. Kengla, January 23, 1963 (hereafter, respectively, Wilson, Mrs. Wilson, and Mrs. Kengla).

17. Lt. Col. Franklin Hibel, "Caught with Our Planes Down," *Air Force* (December, 1956), pp. 81–82 (hereafter "Caught with Our Planes Down").

18. Ibid., p. 82.

19. Interview with Ema, May 27, 1950.

20. Ibid.

21. Statement by Muranaka, December 17, 1949.

22. Interview with Flood, July 9, 1962.

23. Interview with Davidson, July 6, 1962.

24. Interview with Flood, July 9, 1962.

25. *PHA*, Part 22, pp. 258–59.

26. Ibid., pp. 117–18; interview with Davidson, July 6, 1962.

27. Chigusa diary, December 8, 1941; *Rengo Kantai*, p. 35.

28. *PHA*, Part 28, pp. 1049, 1051.

29. "Caught with Our Planes Down," p. 81; *PHA*, Part 22, pp. 249, 253, 255.

30. *PHA*, Part 22, pp. 250, 254.

31. Ibid., Part 28, pp. 1050–51.

32. Ibid., Part 22, pp. 249–50, 254–55.

33. Ibid., pp. 251–52, 254–55.

34. Ibid., Part 28, pp. 1572–73.

35. Ibid., Part 22, pp. 293–94.

36. "Twenty Years Ago," p. 27.

37. Ibid.

38. *PHA,* Part 12, p. 354.

39. Interview with Duane W. Shaw, March 19, 1960.

40. Statement by Okajima, January 19, 1951.

41. Statement by Muranaka, December 17, 1949.

42. Ibid.

43. Undated statement by Shiga.

44. "Twenty Years Ago," p. 28.

CHAPTER 18

"It's the Real Thing, Boys"

1. *PHA,* Part 22, p. 57.

2. Ibid., p. 134.

3. Interview with Dunlop, October 10, 1963.

4. *PHA,* Part 22, p. 134.

5. Ibid., p. 57.

6. Interview with Col. Russell C. Throckmorton, September 11, 1967 (hereafter Throckmorton).

7. Interviews with Maj. Gen. Morrill W. Marston, September 11, 1976 and May 31, 1977 (hereafter Marston).

8. Reply, January 11, 1977, to questionnaire which Prange submitted to Fleming (hereafter Fleming questionnaire).

9. *PHA,* Part 22, p. 185.

10. Interview with Throckmorton, September 11, 1967.

11. Interview with Dunlop, October 23, 1963.

12. Interview with Throckmorton, September 11, 1967.

13. Interviews with Dunlop, October 11 and 13, 1963.

14. Interview with Col. Kenneth E. Thiebaud, November 27, 1970 (hereafter Thiebaud).

15. Interview with Bicknell, September 8, 1967.

16. Ibid., September 7, 1967; *PHA,* Part 10, p. 5098.

17. *PHA*, Part 10, p. 5118.

18. Interview with Bicknell, September 8, 1967.

19. *PHA*, Part 27, p. 741.

20. Interview with Bicknell, September 8, 1967.

21. Interview with Brig. Gen. George P. Sampson, October 18, 1963 (hereafter Sampson).

22. Ibid.

23. *PHA*, Part 22, p. 59.

24. Indianapolis *Star,* December 14, 1941.

25. *PHA*, Part 22, pp. 159–61.

26. Ibid., pp. 154, 157.

27. Interview with the Wilsons, January 22, 1963.

28. Interview with the Leards, October 17, 1963.

29. Interview with Col. and Mrs. Allen F. Haynes, November 23, 1970 (hereafter Haynes).

30. Ibid.

31. Interview with Tyler, August 21, 1964; *PHA*, Part 18, p. 3015; Part 27, p. 569.

32. *PHA*, Part 10, pp. 5079–80; Part 27, pp. 533–34.

33. Ibid., Part 10, p. 5080; Part 27, p. 533.

34. Ibid., Part 32, p. 490; Part 10, p. 5033.

35. Ibid., Part 22, p. 273.

36. Ibid., pp. 277–78.

37. Ibid., p. 278.

38. Ibid., pp. 273–74, 279.

39. Ibid.

40. Interviews with the Charles Davises, November 1, 1963 and February 19, 1964.

41. *PHA*, Part 22, p. 299.

42. Ibid., p. 300.

43. Ibid., pp. 301–03.

44. Ibid., p. 265.

45. Ibid., pp. 262–64.

46. Ibid., p. 311.

47. Ibid., pp. 308–09.

48. Ibid., p. 307.

49. Letter from Daniels, January 14, 1965.

50. Ibid.

51. Ibid.

52. Ibid.

CHAPTER 19

"A Heart-Breaking Scene"

1. Interview with Capt. Paul C. Crosley, November 23, 1970 (hereafter Crosley).

2. Interview with Layton, July 22, 1964.

3. Interviews with Crosley, November 23, 1970, and Layton, July 22, 1964.

4. *PHA*, Part 26, p. 192.

5. Interviews with Layton, May 22, 1958 and July 22, 1964.

6. Ibid., July 22, 1964.

7. Interview with Rochefort, August 26, 1964.

8. Interview with Davis, January 30, 1963.

9. Interview with East, August 7, 1964.

10. Brig. Gen. Samuel R. Shaw, USMC (Ret.), "Marine Barracks, Navy Yard Pearl Harbor, December 1941," *Shipmate* (December, 1973), pp. 16, 18 (hereafter "Marine Barracks").

11. Ibid., p. 17.

12. *PHA*, Part 23, pp. 1095–97.

13. "Marine Barracks," p. 18.

14. *PHA*, Part 26, p. 237.

15. Ibid., pp. 237–38. Calhoun's action was well taken. The Roberts Commission had to devote considerable time to investigating lurid charges of drunkenness at Pearl Harbor.

16. Interview with RADM Allen G. Quynn, December 30, 1963 (hereafter Quynn).

17. Log of *Oglala*, December 7, 1941.

18. Interview with Mrs. Cooper, March 5, 1966.

19. Interview with Quynn, December 30, 1963.

20. Interview with Rafsky, August 11, 1964.

21. Ibid.

22. Interview with Quynn, December 30, 1963.

23. Honolulu *Star-Bulletin*, December 7, 1966.

24. *PHA*, Part 23, p. 635.

25. Statement by Ens. W. J. Bush, Action Report, Vol. 2, Encl E.

26. Interview with Hesser, August 10, 1964.

27. Interview with Shapley, October 11, 1967.

28. Osborne statement.

29. Interview with Coe, January 23, 1963.

30. Interview with Riggs, January 14, 1964.

31. Ibid.

32. Interview with Ramsey, December 6, 1962.

33. Letter from Kamont, November 9, 1964.

34. Interview with Forrow, August 16, 1964.

35. Interview with Erickson, September 7, 1971. Erickson eventually rose to the rank of captain and became director of the Navy Nurse Corps.

CHAPTER 20

"What Is Going to Happen Next?"

1. Interview with Grannis, July 24, 1964.

2. Ibid.

3. Log of *Helm*, December 7, 1941; *PHA*, Part 13, pp. 494–95.

4. Interview with Sakamaki, October 19, 1947.

5. Interview with Finn, August 11, 1964.

6. Honolulu *Advertiser*, December 7, 1966; log of *Henley*, December 7, 1941.

7. Interview with Stout, August 8, 1964; *PHA*, Part 24, p. 1583.

8. Log of *Zane*, December 7, 1941.

9. *PHA*, Part 23, p. 935; Part 24, p. 1370.

10. Log of *Curtiss*, December 7, 1941.

11. Log of *Medusa*, December 7, 1941; Simons report.

12. Simons report.

13. Log of *Monaghan,* December 7, 1941; *PHA,* Part 32, p. 309.

14. Interview with Burford, August 18, 1964.

15. Ibid.; log of *Monaghan,* December 7, 1941.

16. Log of *Curtiss,* December 7, 1941.

17. Log of *Tangier,* December 7, 1941.

18. Interview with Burford, August 18, 1964.

19. Log of *Medusa,* December 7, 1941.

20. Log of *Monaghan,* December 7, 1941.

21. *Rising Sun,* p. 115.

22. Interview with Burford, August 18, 1964; log of *Monaghan,* December 7, 1941.

23. Simons report; *PHA,* Part 32, p. 309.

24. Interview with Burford, August 18, 1964; log of *Monaghan,* December 7, 1941.

25. Log of *Dale,* December 7, 1941.

26. Log of *Ward,* December 7, 1941.

27. Interview with Sakamaki, October 19, 1947; *I Attacked Pearl Harbor,* pp. 40–41.

28. Log of *Blue,* December 7, 1941.

29. *PHA,* Part 23, p. 693.

30. Interview with Beck, August 6, 1964.

31. Interview with French, August 11, 1964.

32. *PHA,* Part 23, p. 635.

33. Log of *Vestal,* December 7, 1941.

34. Interview with Crawford, August 8, 1964.

35. Log of *Vestal,* December 7, 1941.

36. Log of *Oglala,* December 7, 1941; *PHA,* Part 22, p. 597.

37. *PHA,* Part 22, p. 597.

38. Interview with Ruff, July 28, 1964.

39. *Rising Sun,* p. 109.

40. Interview with Ruff, July 28, 1964.

41. Log of *Nevada,* December 7, 1941.

42. Interview with Ruff, July 28, 1964.

43. Interview with Emil Johnson, August 8, 1964.

44. After Action Report, *West Virginia,* statement of Lt. Cmdr. E. E. Berthold, December 14, 1941, Navy Record Office, Washington Navy Yard, D.C.

45. Interview with D. Johnson, July 25, 1964.

CHAPTER 21

"We Wanted to Fight"

1. Interview with Ramsey, December 6, 1962.

2. Interview with Coe, January 23, 1963.

3. Interview with Forrow, August 16, 1964.

4. *PHA,* Part 23, p. 739.

5. Ibid., p. 712.

6. Ibid., Part 24, p. 1961.

7. Ibid., Part 23, pp. 743–45.

8. Ibid., Part 22, pp. 249–50, 254.

9. Ibid., p. 257.

10. Interview with Bicknell, September 8, 1967.

11. Interview with Col. Wesley C. Wilson, September 20, 1956 (hereafter W. Wilson).

12. Ibid.

13. Interview with Throckmorton, September 11, 1967.

14. Interview with Dunlop, October 10, 1963.

15. *PHA,* Part 24, p. 1975.

16. Interview with Reeves, October 27, 1969.

17. Interview with Landon, December 15, 1959.

18. *PHA,* Part 22, p. 155.

19. Ibid., p. 125; interview with Allen, July 17, 1962.

20. Interview with Heydt, January 10, 1971.

21. *Military Press* (Honolulu), December 7, 1961.

22. Letter from Crouse, November 24, 1964.

23. *PHA,* Part 23, p. 818.

24. Honolulu *Advertiser,* December 9, 1941.

25. *Newsweek,* December 12, 1966, p. 39.

26. Gwenfread Allen, *Hawaii's War Years* (Honolulu, 1950), p. 9.

27. *Remember Pearl Harbor!*, p. 76.

28. Washington *Star*, December 7, 1976; *Newsweek*, December 12, 1966, p. 39. Inouye won the Distinguished Service Cross and lost his right arm serving in Italy with the famed Japanese-American 442d Regimental Combat Team. In 1962 he became the first American citizen of Japanese descent to be elected to the U.S. Senate.

29. *Newsweek*, December 12, 1966, pp. 39–40.

30. Ibid., p. 40. In later years, Miss Ogure married Brian Casey, political editor of the Honolulu *Advertiser.*

CHAPTER 22

"Terrible, Simply Terrible"

1. *White House Physician*, pp. 136–37.

2. David E. Lilienthal, *The Journals of David E. Lilienthal*, Vol. 1: *The TVA Years* (New York, 1964), pp. 506–07 (hereafter *TVA Years*); Grace Tully, *F.D.R., My Boss* (New York, 1949), p. 253 (hereafter *F.D.R., My Boss*).

3. *This I Remember*, pp. 232–33; Hamlin mss.

4. PHA, Part 8, pp. 3828–29, 3834–35.

5. Ibid., p. 3837; Robert E. Sherwood, *Roosevelt and Hopkins: An Intimate History* (New York, 1948), pp. 430–31 (hereafter *Roosevelt and Hopkins*).

6. "Treachery."

7. *Hull Memoirs*, Vol. 2, pp. 1095–96; *Roosevelt and Hopkins*, p. 431.

8. State Department Memorandum of Conversation, December 7, 1941, Hull Papers, Box 60; *Hull Memoirs*, Vol. 2, pp. 1096–97. Ballantine was a State Department expert on Far Eastern matters.

9. Typewritten manuscript of Nomura's diary which he gave to Prange (hereafter Nomura diary).

10. Interviews with Nomura, May 7 and 9, 1949.

11. *The Lost War*, pp. 57–59.

12. *Bridge to the Sun*, pp. 2–3.

13. VADM Frank E. Beatty, unpublished essay written in 1953, "Secretary Knox and Pearl Harbor," a copy of which Dr. Harry Elmer Barnes furnished Prange. This essay, with several minor and some major changes, appeared in *National Review* (December 13, 1966) under the title "The Background of the Secret Report." Prange used the unpublished copy.

14. Hamlin mss.

15. *This I Remember*, p. 233.

16. *The TVA Years*, p. 507.

17. Interview with Mrs. Stephen T. Early, December 13, 1970 (hereafter Mrs. Early); Papers of Stephen T. Early, Franklin D. Roosevelt Library, Hyde Park, N.Y., Box 35 (hereafter Early Papers).

18. The Correspondents of *Time, Life,* and *Fortune, December 7: The First Thirty Hours* (New York, 1942), pp. 9–10 (hereafter *First Thirty Hours; Newsweek,* December 15, 1949, p. 18; Washington *Post,* December 8, 1941; Early Papers, Box 35.

19. Interview with Mrs. Early, December 13, 1970.

20. Stimson diary, December 7, 1941.

21. Fred Blumenthal, "The White House Is Calling," Washington *Post,* July 7, 1957.

22. *F.D.R., My Boss,* p. 254; interview with Grace Tully, December 15, 1970 (hereafter Tully).

23. James Roosevelt and Sidney Shalett, *Affectionately, F.D.R.: A Son's Story of a Lonely Man* (New York, 1959), pp. 327–28 (hereafter *Affectionately, F.D.R.*).

24. A. Miles Hughey, "How We Got the News of Pearl Harbor," *American Legion Magazine* (December 1970), p. 21 (hereafter "How We Got the News"); interview with Tully, December 15, 1970.

25. A. Merriman Smith, *Thank You, Mr. President: A White House Notebook* (New York, 1946), pp. 112–15 (hereafter *Thank You, Mr. President*).

26. *F.D.R., My Boss,* p. 254; interview with Tully, December 15, 1970.

27. *PHA,* Part 14, p. 1411. Deane wrote that he reached Marshall at his quarters, where he was at lunch; however, Mrs. Marshall wrote that after the general left for his office that morning he did not return home until 1900. She heard the news of Pearl Harbor over the radio (*Together,* p. 99).

28. Interview with Lt. Col. John B. Schindel, August 3, 1956.

29. Letter, Safford to Lt. Cmdr. Charles C. Hiles, March 29, 1967, Papers of Lt. Cmdr. Charles C. Hiles, University of Wyoming, Laramie, Wy., Box 14 (hereafter Hiles Papers). In a telephone conversation on November 9, 1972, Safford told Prange virtually the same story. For the background of Safford's agitation, see *At Dawn We Slept,* Chap. 56, and *Verdict of History,* Chap. 19.

30. Washington *Post,* December 8, 1941; December 7, 1951; December 7, 1965; Washington *Star,* December 7, 1966; *Newsweek,* December 11, 1961.

31. Washington *Post,* December 8, 1941; December 7, 1951.

CHAPTER 23

"The Japanese Bombers Swarmed Down on Us Like Bees"

1. Interview with Fujita, February 2, 1951.

2. Statement by Ofuchi, January 19, 1950.

3. Statement by Shindo, January 17, 1951.

4. Statement by Z. Abe, January 19, 1950.

5. Statement by Ofuchi, January 19, 1950.

6. Statement by Iwami, October 20, 1950.

7. Interview with Fujita, February 2, 1951.

8. Interviews with Fuchida, March 4, 1948 and December 11, 1963; *Shinjuwan Sakusen No Shinso*, p. 187.

9. Statement by Z. Abe, October 19, 1950.

10. Statement by Sato, October 19, 1950.

11. Statement by Ofuchi, January 19, 1950.

12. Statement by Shindo, January 17, 1951.

13. Interviews with Fuchida, March 4, 1948 and December 10 and 11, 1963.

14. Statement by Ofuchi, January 19, 1950.

15. *Shinjuwan Sakusen No Shinso*, pp. 188–89.

16. Log of *Curtiss*, December 7, 1941.

17. Logs of *Medusa*, *Conyngham*, and *Tucker*, December 7, 1941.

18. The logs of both the *Tangier* and the *Zane*, December 7, 1941, show the time as 0850, but at that minute Shimazaki had not yet given his attack order.

19. Interview with Genda, December 29, 1947; *Day of Infamy*, p. 180.

20. Log of *Curtiss*, December 7, 1941.

21. Log of *Aylwin*, December 7, 1941.

22. Logs of *Patterson*, *Blue*, and *Tangier*, December 7, 1941.

23. Log of *Detroit*, December 7, 1941.

24. Simons report.

25. Interview with Stout, August 8, 1964.

26. Log of *Detroit*, December 7, 1941.

27. Log of *Raleigh*, December 7, 1941.

28. Simons report.

29. Log of *Raleigh*, December 7, 1941.

30. Log of *Curtiss*, December 7, 1941.

31. Log of *Avocet*, December 7, 1941.

32. Log of *Helena*, December 7, 1941.

33. Interview with Fuchida, December 10, 1963.

34. Interview with Ruff, July 28, 1964.

35. *PHA*, Part 23, p. 705.

36. Log of *Nevada*, December 7, 1941. The log shows this action at 0850; however, as noted, the attack did not begin until 0854.

37. *PHA*, Part 23, p. 720.

38. Ibid., Part 22, p. 534. The *Nevada*'s log for December 7, 1941, recorded receipt of Pye's signal at 0905.

39. Interview with Ruff, July 28, 1964.

40. Log of *Nevada*, December 7, 1941. Hill received the Medal of Honor posthumously (Honolulu *Advertiser*, December 7, 1966).

41. Interview with Ruff, July 28, 1964.

42. *PHA*, Part 23, p. 705.

43. Interview with Furlong, November 16, 1962; *PHA*, Part 22, p. 597.

44. Interview with Ruff, July 28, 1964.

45. Ibid.; log of *Nevada*, December 7, 1941.

46. Log of *Nevada*, December 7, 1941.

47. Statement by Ofuchi, January 19, 1950.

48. *PHA*, Part 22, p. 534.

49. Log of *California*, December 7, 1941.

50. *PHA*, Part 22, p. 534; interview with Train, November 26, 1962.

51. *Shijuwan Sakusen No Shinso*, p. 189.

52. Log of *Pennsylvania*, December 7, 1941. The log records this hit as being from a high-altitude bomb; however, Shimazaki's horizontal bombers did not participate in the action against ships.

53. *Rising sun*, p. 118.

54. *PHA*, Part 22, p. 596. The floating drydock had to be sunk to save it.

55. Interview with Smart, August 21, 1964.

56. Fleming questionnaire, January 11, 1977.

57. *PHA*, Part 23, p. 693.

58. Log of *Blue*, December 7, 1941.

59. *PHA*, Part 23, p. 693.

60. Ibid., p. 698.

61. Honolulu *Advertiser*, December 7, 1966; log of *Henley*, December 7, 1941.

62. Log of *Conyngham*, December 7, 1941.

63. Log of *Dale*, December 7, 1941.

64. Log of *Tucker*, December 7, 1941.

Chapter 24

"The Desperate Urgency"

1. Interview with Pullen, September 12, 1964.

2. Ibid.

3. Interview with Draemel, January 17, 1963. The *Detroit's* log does not show the time Draemel came aboard.

4. Log of *Dobbin*, December 7, 1941.

5. Log of *Curtiss*, December 7, 1941.

6. Interview with Stout, August 8, 1964.

7. Log of *Breese*, December 7, 1941.

8. Log of *Tangier*, December 7, 1941.

9. Log of *Raleigh*, December 7, 1941.

10. Simons report.

11. Seattle *Post-Intelligencer*, December 7, 1966.

12. Log of *Curtiss*, December 7, 1941.

13. Capt. Burdick H. Brittin, USN (Ret.), "We Four Ensigns," *United States Naval Institute Proceedings* (December 1966), pp. 106–09; Washington *Post*, December 7, 1951; log of *Aylwin*, December 7, 1941.

14. Log of *Montgomery*, December 7, 1941.

15. Log of *Cummings*, December 7, 1941.

16. Log of *Riegel*, December 7, 1941.

17. Logs of *Ramapo* and *New Orleans*, December 7, 1941.

18. Log of *San Francisco*, December 7, 1941.

19. Interview with Rood, July 24, 1964.

20. Log of *Honolulu*, December 7, 1941.

21. Log of *St. Louis*, December 7, 1941.

22. Interview with Rood, July 24, 1964.

23. Log of *St. Louis*, December 7, 1941; interview with Rood, July 24, 1964.

24. Interviews with Rood, July 24, 1964, and Fink, November 17, 1970.

25. Interview with Rood, July 24, 1964.

26. Interview with Smart, August 21, 1964.

27. Log of *Vestal*, December 7, 1941.

28. Interview with Hesser, August 14, 1964; log of *Vestal*, December 7, 1941.

29. Log of *Oglala*, December 7, 1941; interview with Furlong, November 9, 1963.

30. *PHA*, Part 22, p. 598.

31. Interview with Furlong, November 9, 1963; log of *Oglala*, December 7, 1941.

32. Log of *Sacramento*, December 7, 1941.

33. Log of *Tern*, December 7, 1941; interview with Emil Johnson, August 8, 1964.

34. Interview with Furlong, December 1, 1962.

35. Interview with Johnson, July 25, 1964. The *West Virginia's* log was lost in the attack, but that of the *Maryland* indicates that the *West Virginia* was abandoning ship at 0940.

36. Honolulu *Advertiser*, December 7, 1966; log of *Trevor*, December 7, 1941.

37. Interview with Pullen, September 12, 1964.

38. Log of *Reid*, December 7, 1941.

39. Interview with Pullen, September 12, 1964; log of Reid, December 7, 1941.

40. *Shinjuwan Sakusen No Shinso*, pp. 189–90.

Chapter 25

"A Mass of Twisted Wreckage"

1. Interview with Charles A. Russell, August 6, 1964. Hereafter Russell.

2. Letter from Rogo, September 2, 1964.

3. Interview with French, August 11, 1964.

4. Interview with Ramsey, December 6, 1962.

5. Interview with French, August 11, 1964.

6. Interview with Riggs, January 14, 1964.

7. Interview with Shoemaker, January 31, 1963. Among those agreeing that this bomb was a dud were Ramsey (interview of December 6, 1962) and French (interview of August 11, 1964).

8. Letter from Rogo, September 2, 1964.

9. Interview with Riggs, January 14, 1964.

10. Letter from Rogo, September 2, 1964.

11. Interview with Genda, December 29, 1947.

12. Interview with Fuchida, December 10, 1963.

13. Interview with Genda, December 29, 1947.

14. Ibid.

15. Ibid.

16. Interview with Fujita, February 2, 1951.

17. According to Genda, Iida's group was supposed to hit Bellows and Haleiwa after the attack on Kaneohe; however, something went wrong and Haleiwa was not hit. It seems most likely, therefore, that Iida led his men to Bellows first (interview with Genda, December 29, 1947).

18. *PHA*, Part 1, p. 51.

19. Ibid., Part 22, pp. 293–94.

20. Ibid., pp. 294–95.

21. Ibid., Part 23, p. 742.

22. Ibid., Part 28, p. 1571.

23. Ibid., Part 22, pp. 295–96.

24. Interview with Fujita, February 2, 1951.

25. Letter from Richmond, November 26, 1963.

26. *PHA*, Part 23, p. 740.

27. Letters from Avery, November 4, and December 1, 1963.

28. Letter from Moser, January 23, 1964.

29. *PHA*, Part 23, p. 740.

30. Finn recovered and later was commissioned. He received the Medal of Honor for his heroism at Kaneohe (Honolulu *Advertiser*, December 7, 1966; and *Military Press* [Honolulu], December 7, 1961).

31. Letter from Curylo, March 3, 1964.

32. Interview with Fujita, February 2, 1951.

33. Letters from Richmond, February 19, 1964 and November 26, 1963; letter from Avery, December 1, 1963.

34. Letter from Avery, November 4, 1963.

35. Interview with Fujita, February 2, 1951.

36. Letter from Avery, November 4, 1963.

37. Ibid.

38. Letters from Richmond, November 4 and 26, 1963; *Military Press* (Honolulu), December 7, 1961.

39. Interview with Fujita, February 2, 1951.

40. Letter from Moser, January 23, 1964.

41. *PHA*, Part 23, p. 740.

42. *Rising Sun*, p. 122.

43. Letter from Avery, November 4, 1963.

CHAPTER 26

"This Time Our Aim Was Better"

1. Interviews with Fujita, February 2, 1951, and Genda, December 29, 1947.

2. Interview with Fujita, February 2, 1951.

3. *PHA*, Part 22, p. 254.

4. Interview with Fujita, February, 2, 1951.

5. *Remember Pearl Harbor!*, pp. 31–32; San Francisco *Chronicle*, December 14, 1941. Sanders and Sterling were credited with one aircraft each.

6. *Remember Pearl Harbor!*, pp. 32–33; San Francisco *Chronicle*, December, 14, 1941.

7. *Remember Pearl Harbor!*, p. 31; San Francisco *Chronicle*, December 14, 1941.

8. Letter from Michaud, December 16, 1964.

9. Interview with Fujita, February 2, 1951. Fujita mentioned none of the losses the Americans claimed to have inflicted.

10. *PHA*, Part 22, p. 257.

11. Ibid., p. 118.

12. Ibid., p. 254; "Caught with Our Planes Down," p. 82.

13. *PHA*, Part 22, p. 250.

14. Ibid., p. 254.

15. Letter from Daniels, January 14, 1965.

16. *PHA*, Part 22, pp. 265–66. Captain Ebey testified that Fort Kamehameha's machine guns brought down two Japanese fighters. Ibid., p. 263.

17. Letter from Daniels, January 14, 1965.

18. *PHA*, Part 22, p. 305.

19. Ibid., p. 311.

20. Interview with Reeves, October 27, 1969.

21. *PHA*, Part 24, p. 1969.

22. Statement by Shindo, January 17, 1951; interview with Fuchida, December 10, 1963.

23. Statement by Iwami, October 20, 1950.

24. Statement by Sato, October 19, 1950.

25. *PHA*, Part 24, pp. 1969, 1975.

26. Interview with Allen, July 17, 1962.

27. *PHA*, Part 22, p. 284.

28. Interview with Farnum, October 15, 1963.

29. Ibid.

30. Interviews with Allen, July 17, 1962; *PHA*, Part 22, p. 125.

31. Interview with Allen, July 17, 1962; Ted R. Sturm, "Mission: War! (A B-17 on December 7, 1941)," *Airman* (December 1965), p. 41 (hereafter "Mission: War!").

32. Interview with Heydt, January 10, 1971.

33. Ibid.

34. Letter from Crouse, November 24, 1964.

35. Interview with Mollison, January 30, 1963.

36. Interview with Gutzak, October 19, 1953.

37. *PHA*, Part 27, p. 440. Japanese intelligence on Hickam may well have been out of date. Yoshikawa found security on that base quite tight and had difficulty in learning anything definite about it. Interview with Yoshikawa, September 10, 1955.

38. Statement by Ofuchi, January 19, 1950.

39. *PHA*, Part 22, p. 250.

40. Ibid., p. 254. Records credited Welch and Taylor with four planes in their first action, three in their second. Ibid., Part 1, p. 55.

CHAPTER 27

"A Mixed-Up Affair"

1. Interview with Erickson, September 7, 1971.

2. New York *Herald Tribune*, December 16, 1941; *Day of Infamy*, p. 193.

3. *Hawaii's War Years*, p. 29; *Day of Infamy*, pp. 193–94; *Idaho Sunday States-man* (Boise), December 2, 1956.

4. Letter, Robert G. Crouse, November 24, 1964.

5. *Military Press* (Honolulu), December 7, 1961.

6. *PHA*, Part 35, pp. 385, 871.

7. Interview with Richard M. Kotoshirodo, September 14, 1967 (hereafter Koto-shirodo); *PHA*, Part 35, p. 372.

8. Interview with Kotoshirodo, September 14, 1967.

9. Ibid.; *PHA*, Part 35, p. 372; interview with Yoshikawa, July 16, 1950.

10. Honolulu *Advertiser*, December 9, 1941.

11. Seattle *Post-Intelligencer*, December 7, 1966.

12. Indianapolis *Star*, December 14, 1941.

13. Interview with Mrs. Burford, August 8, 1964.

14. Los Angeles *Times*, March 1, 1942. When Mrs. Shea reached the mainland later in December of 1941, she found that "the entire book had to be censored. The war had changed every chapter..."

15. Interview with Col. and Mrs. Haynes, November 23, 1970.

16. Interview with Col. and Mrs. Leard, October 17, 1963.

17. *Military Press* (Honolulu), December 7, 1961.

18. Interview with Mollison, January 30, 1963.

19. *PHA*, Part 22, p. 47.

20. Ibid., p. 173.

21. Ibid., Part 35, p. 210.

22. Letter from Michaud, December 16, 1964.

23. *PHA*, Part 32, p. 480.

24. Ibid., Part 10, p. 5069.

25. Ibid., Part 27, p. 571.

26. Ibid., Part 18, p. 3015.

27. Ibid., Part 32, p. 346.

28. Ibid., Part 29, p. 2292.

29. Ibid., Part 22, p. 234.

30. Ibid., Part 23, pp. 936–37.

31. Interview with Layton, July 22, 1964.

32. *PHA*, Part 26, pp. 344–45.

33. Ibid., Part 23, p. 759.

34. Ibid., p. 609.

35. Ibid., p. 621.

36. Ibid.; *Admiral Halsey's Story*, p. 80.

37. *PHA*, Part 19, p. 3628.

38. Log of *Maryland*, December 7, 1941.

39. *PHA*, Part 24, p. 1146.

40. Interview with Layton, July 22, 1964.

41. *PHA*, Part 19, p. 3631.

42. Log of *Maryland*, December 7, 1941.

43. *PHA*, Part 12, p. 345.

44. Interview with Dunlop, October 10, 1963.

CHAPTER 28

"They Didn't Have Their Right Bearings"

1. Interview with Rood, July 24, 1964.

2. Interview with Fink, November 17, 1970.

3. Interview with Rood, July 24, 1964.

4. Log of *St. Louis*, December 7, 1941.

5. Ibid.; interview with Rood, July 24, 1964.

6. Log of *Blue*, December 7, 1941.

7. Interview with Rood, July 24, 1964. The log of the *St. Louis*, December 7, 1941, shows that the *Blue*, the *Phelps*, and the *Lamson* were the destroyers so ordered; however, the *Lamson* was with Task Force Twelve (*PHA*, Part 12, p. 345). The third destroyer was, as Rood stated, the *Monaghan*. Log of *Monaghan*, December 7, 1941).

8. *PHA*, Part 36, p. 59.

9. Log of *Ward*, December 7, 1941. The *Ward* was so badly damaged by kamikazes at Leyte Gulf that she had to be sunk. By one of the sad circumstances of war, Outerbridge, then in command of the *O'Brien*, had to sink his old destroyer. Samuel E. Morison, *Leyte, June 1944–January 1945* (Boston, 1958); Honolulu *Star-Bulletin*, December 7, 1977.

10. Log of *Wasmuth*, December 7, 1941.

11. Log of *Chew*, December 7, 1941.

12. Log of *Cummings*, December 7, 1941.

13. Log of *Breese*, December 7, 1941.

14. Log of *Trever*, December 7, 1941.

15. Honolulu *Advertiser*, December 7, 1966.

16. Log of *Trever*, December 7, 1941.

17. Honolulu *Advertiser*, December 7, 1966. The *Henley*'s log recorded the transfer at 1216.

18. Log of *California*, December 7, 1941.

19. *PHA*, Part 22, p. 534; Part 24, p. 1371.

20. Interview with Train, November 26, 1962; *PHA*, Part 22, p. 534.

21. Log of *California*, December 7, 1941.

22. Log of *Detroit*, December 7, 1941.

23. Simons report.

24. *PHA*, Part 24, p. 1371.

25. Log of *Detroit*, December 7, 1941; *PHA*, Part 24, p. 1372.

26. Log of *PT 20*, December 7, 1941.

27. Simons report.

28. Interview with Thesman, August 15, 1964.

29. Log of *Tern*, December 7, 1941.

30. Interview with Emil Johnson, August 8, 1964. In this interview Johnson gave the impression that the *Tern* was fighting fire on the *Arizona*. The *Tern*'s log makes clear that she was assisting the *West Virginia*.

31. Log of *Curtiss*, December 7, 1941.

32. *PHA*, Part 23, pp. 705–06.

33. Interview with Ruff, July 28, 1964.

34. Log of *Nevada*, December 7, 1941.

35. Log of *Reid*, December 7, 1941; interview with Pullen, September 12, 1964.

36. Interview with Grannis, July 24, 1964; log of *Antares*, December 7, 1941.

37. *PHA*, Part 22, p. 88.

38. Papers of Franklin D. Roosevelt, Franklin D. Roosevelt Library, Hyde Park, N.Y. Presidential Secretary's File (PSF), Box 85.

39. *PHA*, Part 22, pp. 591–92.

40. Papers of Frank Knox, Library of Congress, Washington, D.C., Box 7.

41. Memorandum of Conference with Col. Francis H. Miles, Jr., January 20, 1942, re Pearl Harbor, Papers of General of the Army George C. Marshall, George C. Marshall Research Foundation, Lexington, Va., Research File.

42. *PHA*, Part 22, p. 311.

43. Ibid., Part 29, pp. 2011–12.

44. Kay report.

45. Logs of *Tracy, Maryland, Sumner,* and *Pelias,* December 7, 1941.

46. Log of *Dolphin,* December 7, 1941.

47. Log of *Sicard,* December 7, 1941.

48. Logs of *Maryland* and *Conyngham,* December 7, 1941.

49. Log of *St. Louis,* December 7, 1941.

50. Log of *Helena,* December 7, 1941.

51. Logs of *Ramapo, Maryland,* and *Sumner,* December 7, 1941.

52. Log of *Pelias,* December 7, 1941.

53. Log of *Dewey,* December 7, 1941.

54. Log of *Pelias,* December 7, 1941.

55. Log of *Sicard,* December 7, 1941.

56. Log of *Sumner,* December 7, 1941.

57. Log of *St. Louis,* December 7, 1941.

58. Log of *Phoenix,* December 7, 1946.

CHAPTER 29

"What a Welcome Sight!"

1. Interviews with Hashimoto, April 20, 1950, and Shiga, December 21, 1964.

2. Statement by Muranaka, December 17, 1949.

3. The 3d BB Div diary recorded 0540 December 8, 1941 (Japan time), i.e., 1010 December 7, 1941, local. Matsumura kept figures of the landings which gave 0537 (1007) December 7. Statement by Matsumura, January 19, 1951.

4. Interview with Genda, December 30, 1947.

5. Interview with Goto, January 24, 1950.

6. Ibid.; interview with Genda, December 30, 1947.

7. Interview with Goto, January 24, 1950.

8. *SSK*, p. 281.

9. Undated statement by Ibusuki.

10. Interview with Shiga, December 21, 1964; undated statement by Shiga.

11. Statement by Kitajima, October 18, 1950.

12. Interview with Sata, November 23, 1949.

13. Statement by H. Abe, October 14, 1950.

14. Interview with Mikawa, March 5, 1949.

15. Statement by Okajima, January 19, 1951.

16. Interview with Amagai, October 12, 1949.

17. Interview with Hashimoto, April 20, 1950.

18. Interview with Amagai, October 12, 1949.

19. Statement by Matsumura, January 19, 1951.

20. Interview with Amagai, October 12, 1949.

21. Statement by Muranaka, December 17, 1949.

22. Statement by Capt. Takatsugu Jojima, July 17, 1951.

23. Interviews with Ohashi, November 24, 1949, and Shimoda, November 21, 1949.

24. Interview with Ohashi, November 18, 1949.

25. Statement by Mifuku, March 6, 1951.

26. Interview with Hara, September 6, 1955.

27. Interview with Ema, May 27, 1950.

28. Interview with Shimoda, November 21, 1949.

29. Statement by Matsumura, January 19, 1951.

30. Statement by Shindo, January 17, 1951.

31. Interview with Genda, December 29, 1947.

32. Statement by Ofuchi, January 19, 1950.

33. Statement by Z. Abe, October 19, 1950.

34. Interview with Sata, November 23, 1949.

35. Statement by Fujita, February 2, 1951.

36. Interview with Amagai, October 12, 1949.

37. Statement by Muranaka, December 17, 1949.

38. Chigusa diary, December 8, 1941.

39. Statement by Sato, October 19, 1941; and interview with Ohashi, November 18, 1949. Sato's account gives the impression that two dive bombers were involved, but Ohashi claims only one. Others support him, e.g., Mifuku in statement of March 6, 1951, and Jojima, in statement of July 17, 1951.

40. *PHA*, Part 22, p. 61

41. *Shinjuwan Sakusen No Shinso*, pp. 189–91; interview with Fuchida, December 11, 1963.

42. Interviews with Fuchida, March 4, 1948 and December 11, 1963.

43. *Shinjuwan Sakusen No Shinso*, pp. 187, 189.

44. *PHA*, Part 7, pp. 3069–70; Part 12, pp. 357–58; Part 22, pp. 60–61.

45. Statement by Matsumura, January 19, 1951.

46. *PHA*, Part 23, p. 743.

47. Ibid., Part 20, pp. 2119–20; Part 24, p. 1593.

48. Ibid., Part 22, p. 60.

49. Ibid., p. 194.

50. Ibid., Part 12, p. 345; Part 32, p. 426.

51. Ibid., Part 23, p. 609; *Rising Sun*, p. 215.

52. *PHA*, Part 22, p. 195.

53. Ibid., Part 24, pp. 1594–95.

54. Interview with Allen, July 17, 1962; *PHA*, Part 22, p. 125.

55. Honolulu *Advertiser*, December 7, 1966.

56. Interview with Allen, July 17, 1962; *PHA*, Part 22, p. 125.

57. *PHA*, Part 23, p. 683; Part 24, p. 1593.

CHAPTER 30

"Rumors Were Coming In Fast and Furious"

1. Letter from Rogo, September 2, 1964.

2. Interview with Riggs, January 14, 1962.

3. Interview with French, August 11, 1964.

4. St. Louis *Post-Dispatch*, December 18, 1941.

5. *PHA*, Part 22, p. 584.

6. Interview with Forrow, August 16, 1964.

7. Interview with Shoemaker, January 31, 1963.

8. Letter from Rogo, September 2, 1964.

9. Interview with Reeves, October 27, 1969.

10. Interview with Wesley C. Wilson, September 20, 1956.

11. Interview with Dunlop, October 10, 1963.

12. Log of *Maryland*, December 7, 1941.

13. "Marine Barracks," p. 19.

14. Ibid., p. 20.

15. Interview with Shapley, October 11, 1967.

16. Interview with Curts, November 16, 1964.

17. Interviews with Smith, November 14, 1962, and Kimmel, December 1, 1963.

18. Interview with Davis, January 30, 1963.

19. Interview with Layton, July 22, 1964.

20. *Hawaii's War Years*, p. 9.

21. Interview with Curts, November 16, 1964.

22. *PHA*, Part 19, pp. 3625, 3628.

23. Log of *Rigel*, December 7, 1941.

24. Log of *New Orleans*, December 7, 1941.

25. Log of *Maryland*, December 7, 1941.

26. Letter from Eisnaugle, November 24, 1964.

27. *PHA*, Part 19, p. 3629.

28. Interview with East, August 7, 1964.

29. *PHA*, Part 19, p. 3629.

30. *Day of Infamy*, p. 169.

31. *PHA*, Part 19, p. 3629.

32. Ibid., p. 3632.

33. Ibid., Part 24, p. 1598.

34. Ibid., p. 1650.

35. Ibid., Part 16, p. 2257.

36. Interview with Charles Davis, November 1, 1963.

37. Interviews with Wesley C. Wilson, September 20, 1956, and Gutzak, October 26, 1953. Both men remembered the cane field rumor.

38. Interview with Gutzak, October 26, 1953; *PHA*, Part 22, p. 505.

39. Interview with Charles Davis, November 1, 1963.

40. Log of *Sicard*, December 7, 1941.

41. Letter from Eisnaugle, November 24, 1964.

42. Interview with Emil Johnson, August 8, 1964.

43. Interview with Beck, August 6, 1964.

44. Interview with Crawford, August 8, 1964.

45. Interview with Hesser, August 14, 1964.

46. Interview with Doir Johnson, July 25, 1964.

47. *PHA*, Part 22, p. 591.

48. Log of *Nevada*, December 7, 1941.

49. Log of *Shaw*, December 7, 1941. Because of the *Shaw*'s explosion, only a portion of her log is available.

50. Log of *Dobbins*, December 7, 1941.

51. Simon report.

52. *PHA*, Part 22, p. 400.

53. Log of *Maryland*, December 7, 1941.

54. Log of *Case*, December 7, 1941.

55. Log of *Hulbert*, December 7, 1941.

56. Log of *Maryland*, December 7, 1941.

57. Interview with Outerbridge, September 8, 1970; log of *Ward*, December 7, 1941.

58. Log of *Chew*, December 7, 1941.

59. Log of *Detroit*, December 7, 1941.

60. Interview with Draemel, January 17, 1963; log of *Detroit*, December 7, 1941.

61. Interview with Rood, July 24, 1964; log of *St. Louis*, December 7, 1941.

62. Log of *Gamble*, December 7, 1941; History of USS GAMBLE, Division of Naval History, Washington Navy Yard, D.C.

63. *PHA*, Part 23, p. 610.

64. Ibid., Part 32, pp. 426–27.

65. Ibid., Part 26, p. 345.

66. Ibid., Part 23, p. 610.

67. Interview with Allen, July 17, 1962.

CHAPTER 31

"Everybody Thought the Japanese Would Be Back"

1. Letter from Avery, December 15, 1963.

2. Ibid.

3. Letter from Moser, January 23, 1964.

4. *Remember Pearl Harbor!*, pp. 79–80.

5. Interview with Reeves, October 27, 1959.

6. *PHA*, Part 28, p. 1620–21.

7. Interview with Kotoshirodo, September 14, 1967.

8. *Day of Infamy*, p. 170.

9. *PHA*, Part 23, p. 873.

10. "Report of Police Activities in Connection with the Japanese Consulate Subsequent to December 7th, 1941 and Up to February 8th, 1942," Capt. Benjamin Van Kuren, February 13, 1943 (hereafter Van Kuren report). Courtesy of Fielder.

11. Interview with Kotoshirodo, September 7, 1967.

12. Van Kuren report.

13. Interview with Yoshikawa, September 14, 1955.

14. Van Kuren report.

15. PHA, Part 22, p. 192.

16. Ibid., Part 23, p. 874.

17. Ibid., Part 35, pp. 371–72.

18. *Day of Infamy*, pp. 174–175.

19. *PHA*, Part 22, p. 217.

20. Ibid., Part 35, pp. 210, 214.

21. Interviews with Dunlop, October 10 and 23, 1963.

22. *PHA*, Part 35, p. 212.

23. Taped reminiscences of Maj. Gen. Robert J. Fleming, Jr., March 7 and 31, 1975, Hoover Institution on War, Revolution and Peace, Stanford, Calif., 94305 (hereafter Fleming tapes); Fleming questionnaire.

24. Interview with Kimmel, December 1, 1963; *PHA*, Part 35, p. 212.

25. *PHA*, Part 28, p. 1613.

26. Ibid., p. 1488.

27. Interview with Davidson, July 6, 1962.

28. Interview with Gutzak, October 26, 1953.

29. Letter from Bongo, June 9, 1963.

30. Interview with Farnum, October 16, 1963.

31. Interview with Farthing, August 11, 1955.

32. Interviews with Mollison, April 15, 1961 and January 30, 1963.

33. Interview with Dunlop, October 10, 1963.

34. *PHA*, Part 28, p. 1059.

35. Ibid., Part 10, p. 5044.

36. Indianapolis *Star*, December 14, 1941.

37. Interview with Mrs. Burford, August 19, 1964.

38. Interview with Mrs. Smith, June 15, 1964.

39. Interview with Mrs. Cooper, March 6, 1966.

40. Interview with Col. and Mrs. Haynes, November 23, 1970.

41. Interview with Col. and Mrs. Leard, October 17, 1963.

42. Interview with Dunlop, October 10, 1963.

43. St. Louis *Post-Dispatch*, December 8, 1941.

44. Interview with Dunlop, October 10, 1963.

45. Fleming questionnaire.

46. St. Louis *Post-Dispatch*, December 18, 1941.

47. Interview with Erickson, September 7, 1971.

Chapter 32

"Jumpy and Trigger-Happy"

1. *PHA*, Part 28, p. 1621.

2. Van Kuren report.

3. *PHA*, Part 19, p. 3626.

4. Honolulu *Star-Bulletin*, December 13, 1941.

5. *PHA*, Part 35, p. 210.

6. Interview with Farnum, October 16, 1963.

7. Interview with Reeves, October 27, 1969.

8. Interview with Bicknell, September 7, 1967.

9. Honolulu *Advertiser*, December 7, 1966.

10. Interview with Allen, July 17, 1962.

11. Interview with Charles Davis, November 4, 1963.

12. Ibid., November 1 and 4, 1963; *PHA*, Part 19, p. 3634.

13. Interview with Sampson, October 18, 1963.

14. Letter from Michaud, December 16, 1964.

15. Letter from Avery, December 15, 1963.

16. Ibid.

17. Ibid.

18. Interview with Davis, January 30, 1963.

19. Interview with East, August 7, 1964. Layton, too, recalled these rumors of Japanese commando landings on Oahu (interview of July 22, 1964).

20. Interview with Capt. and Mrs. East, August 17, 1964.

21. Honolulu *Advertiser*, December 6, 1970.

22. Indianapolis *Star*, December 14, 1941.

23. Interview with Col. and Mrs. Leard, October 17, 1963.

24. Interview with Col. and Mrs. Charles Davis, February 19, 1964.

25. Interview with Col. and Mrs. Haynes, November 23, 1970.

26. Interview with Col. and Mrs. Charles Davis, February 19, 1964.

27. Interview with Wilson, Mrs. Wilson and Mrs. Kengla, January 22, 1963.

28. Interview with Grannis, July 24, 1964.

29. Interview with Emil Johnson, August 8, 1964.

30. Interview with Forrow, August 16, 1964.

31. Cmdr. Edward P. Stafford, USN., *The Big E: The Story of the USS Enterprise* (New York, 1962), p. 20 (hereafter *Big E*). In *Rising Sun*, Morison mistakenly identified the evening flight as SBD's returning after being sent from Oahu to seek the Japanese (p. 121). We unwittingly perpetuated this error in *At Dawn We Slept* (pp. 570–71).

32. *PHA*, Part 24, p. 1650.

33. Interview with Shoemaker, January 31, 1963.

34. Letter from Rogo, September 2, 1964.

35. Interview with Doir Johnson, July 25, 1964.

36. Interview with Quynn, December 30, 1963.

37. *PHA*, Part 24, p. 1650.

38. Log of *Neosho,* December 7, 1941.

39. Log of *Curtiss*, December 7, 1941.

40. Osborne statement.

41. Letter from Eisnaugle, November 24, 1964.

42. *PHA*, Part 19, p. 3633; log of *Maryland,* Deember 7, 1941.

43. *PHA*, Part 24, p. 1650; logs of *Tangier* and *Maryland*, December 7, 1941.

44. *PHA*, Part 20, p. 2120.

45. *Big E*, p. 21; *Day of Infamy*, pp. 206–07; interview with Shoemaker, January 31, 1963.

46. Interview with Shoemaker, January 31, 1963; *Day of Infamy*, p. 206. *Big E* does not mention Ensign Allen.

47. Log of *Vireo*, December 7, 1941; interview with Riggs, January 14, 1962. Riggs did not recall the man's name, but from the location it almost certainly was Allen.

48. Log of *Argonne*, December 7, 1941.

49. Interviews with Shibuya, August 7 and 21, 1948. Arima confirmed that the midget submariner reporting on the night of December 7 was Yokoyama (interview, November 21, 1948). A report of *I-69's* actions on and following December 7, 1941, may be found in *PHA*, Part 13, pp. 505–11.

50. Interview with Fuchida, February 27, 1964.

CHAPTER 33

"At Last Came the Dawn"

1. Interview with Allen, July 17, 1962.

2. Interview with Ruff, July 28, 1964.

3. *PHA*, Part 22, p. 591.

4. Interview with Quynn, December 30, 1963.

5. Interview with Rafsky, August 11, 1964.

6. Interviews with Furlong, November 16, 1962 and November 9, 1963.

7. Interview with Coe, January 23, 1963.

8. Interview with Shoemaker, January 31, 1963.

9. Interview with Coe, January 23, 1963.

10. *PHA*, Part 19, p. 3634.

11. Interview with Mrs. Cooper, March 5, 1966.

12. Interview with Erickson, September 7, 1971.

13. Interview with Dunlop, October 10, 1963.

14. Interview with Mrs. Smith, January 15, 1964.

15. Letter from Avery, December 15, 1963.

16. "Marine Barracks," p. 20.

17. Interview with Wilson, Mrs. Wilson, and Mrs. Kengla, January 22, 1963.

18. Interview with Stout, August 12, 1964.

19. Interview with Shibuya, August 7, 1948.

20. Ibid.; *PHA*, Part 13, pp. 495, 506, and 510.

21. Interview with Sakamaki, October 19, 1947.

22. Ibid.; *I Attacked Pearl Harbor*, pp. 43–44.

23. Interview with Sakamaki, October 19, 1947; *I Attacked Pearl Harbor*, pp. 44–47; *Day of Infamy*, p. 214.

24. Interview with Allen, July 17, 1962.

25. Log of *Whitney*, December 8, 1941.

26. *PHA*, Part 20, pp. 2120–21.

27. Letter from Crouse, November 24, 1964.

28. Interview with Mrs. Smith, June 15, 1964.

29. Interview with Wilson, Mrs. Wilson and Mrs. Kengla, January 22, 1963.

30. Interview with Erickson, September 7, 1961.

31. Interview with Mrs. Cooper, March 5, 1966.

32. Interview with Emil Johnson, August 8, 1964.

33. *Newsweek*, December 12, 1966.

34. *Hawaii's War Years*, p. 41.

35. Honolulu *Star-Bulletin*, December 7, 1977.

36. Interview with Davidson, July 6, 1962.

37. Interview with Thesman, August 15, 1964.

38. Interview with Shapley, October 11, 1967.

39. Interview with Mrs. Davis, February 19, 1964.

40. Interview with Col. Charles Davis, November 4, 1964.

41. *Admiral Halsey's Story*, pp. 81–82; *PHA*, Part 16, p. 2075.

42. *PHA*, Part 24, p. 1651.

43. Notes by Fielder for a talk he delivered before the Rotary Club of Honolulu on December 7, 1966 (hereafter Fielder notes). Courtesy of Fielder.

44. *PHA*, Part 37, p. 1148; *I Attacked Pearl Harbor*, pp. 49–50.

45. Fielder notes; *PHA*, Part 37, p. 1148.

46. *PHA*, Part 7, p. 3069.

47. Ibid., Part 37, pp. 1149; Fielder notes.

48. *PHA*, Part 37, pp. 1149–50. Fielder gave Prange a copy of this letter.

49. Interview with Arima, November 21, 1948.

50. *PHA*, Part 24, p. 1449.

51. Interview with Fuchida, February 27, 1964.

52. *PHA*, Part 24, p. 1449; Andrew W. Lind, *Hawaii's Japanese: An Experiment in Democracy* (Princeton, N.J., 1946), p. 44.

53. Interview with Fuchida, February 27, 1964. According to another account, this pilot participated against Bellows in the second wave. Mutsuji Kohase, "A Hidden Episode Concerning Niihau Island," *Suiko* (October 1973).

54. *PHA*, Part 24, p. 1450.

55. Ibid., p. 1449; Part 35, p. 293.

56. *PHA*, Part 24, pp. 1449–52; Part 35, pp. 293–94; Honolulu *Advertiser* and *Star-Bulletin*, December 16, 1941. Kohase's highly romanticized account claimed that the two Japanese "sat on the sand beach facing each other and killed themselves with the last remaining two shots." Fuchida, too, perpetuated this suicide myth by writing that Saikaijo "found himself in a hopeless situation, finally killing himself after refusing to be captured as a prisoner." *Shinjuwan Sakusen No Shinso*, p. 191.

57. See in particular Intelligence "Conclusions," *PHA*, Part 35, p. 294.

CHAPTER 34

"Hostilities Exist"

1. Washington *Post*, December 8, 1941.

2. Ibid., December 12, 1976.

3. Alben W. Barkley, *That Reminds Me* (New York, 1954), p. 261.

4. Thomas T. Connally, *My Name Is Tom Connally* (New York, 1954), p. 248 (hereafter *Tom Connally*).

5. Washington *Post*, December 7, 1951.

6. Washington *Evening Star*, December 8, 1941.

7. Frances Perkins, *The Roosevelt I Knew* (New York, 1946), pp. 377–78.

8. *Newsweek*, December 12, 1966.

9. Washington *Post*, December 12, 1976.

10. *PHA*, Part 2, pp. 570–71; Grew Affidavit.

11. Capt. H. H. Smith-Hutton, USN (Ret.), "Tokyo, December, 1941," *Shipmate* (December 1973), p. 13.

12. *PHA*, Part 2, p. 766.

13. *First Thirty Hours*, p. 62.

14. Ibid., p. 53.

15. Ibid., pp. 31–36.

16. Ibid., pp. 86–87.

17. Ibid., pp. 88, 107, 118.

18. Stimson diary, December 7, 1941.

19. *PHA*, Part 15, p. 1634.

20. *Roosevelt and Hopkins*, p. 432.

21. *White House Physician*, p. 137.

22. *F.D.R., My Boss*, p. 254; interview with Tully, December 15, 1970.

23. Stimson diary, December 7, 1941.

24. "Conference in the Office of the Secretary of State, 4:00 to 6:00 p.m.," December 7, 1941, Papers of Cordell Hull, Library of Congress, Washington, D.C., Box 72–73.

25. Diaries of Adolf A. Berle, Jr., Franklin D. Roosevelt Library, Hyde Park, New York, December 7, 1941, Box 213.

26. "How We Got the News, p. 49; *First Thirty Hours*, p. 13.

27. *Thank You, Mr. President*, p. 115.

28. *F.D.R., My Boss*, p. 256; interview with Tully, December 15, 1970.

29. *F.D.R., My Boss*, p. 255; *Hawaii's War Years*, p. 35.

30. *First Thirty Hours*, pp. 15–16; Washington *Post*, December 8, 1941.

31. *Christian Science Monitor,* Decembr 7, 1951.

32. *First Thirty Hours,* p. 18; Washington *Post* and Washington *Evening Star,* December 8, 1941.

33. *Lost War,* pp. 61–63.

34. Diaries of Henry Morgenthau, Jr., Franklin D. Roosevelt Library, Hyde Park, N.Y., December 7, 1941, Box 470 (hereafter Morgenthau diaries).

35. *This I Remember,* p. 234; interview with Miss Tully, December 15, 1970.

36. Edward R. Murrow, *In Search of Light: The Broadcasts of Edward R. Murrow, 1938–1961* (New York, 1967), p. 108 (hereafter *In Search*).

37. Hamlin mss.

38. *First Thirty Hours,* p. 21; Harold L. Ickes, *The Secret Diary of Harold L. Ickes,* Vol. 3: *The Lowering Clouds 1939–1941* (New York, 1954), pp. 661–62.

39. *Thank You, Mr. President,* p. 116.

40. *First Thirty Hours,* p. 21.

41. Stimson diary, December 7, 1941.

42. *PHA,* Part 19, pp. 3503–04.

43. Stimson diary, December 7, 1941.

44. Washington *Post,* December 7, 1951.

45. *Christian Science Monitor,* December 7, 1951.

46. *First Thirty Hours,* pp. 45, 127.

47. Washington *Post,* December 8, 1941.

48. Stimson diary, December 7, 1941.

49. *PHA,* Part 19, pp. 3504–06. The transcript of Roosevelt's remarks at the Cabinet and congressional meetings of December 7 does not make a clear demarkation between the two.

50. *Tom Connally,* p. 249.

51. *PHA,* Part 19, pp. 3506–07.

52. Sol Bloom, *The Autobiography of Sol Bloom* (New York, 1948), p. 250.

53. *Christian Science Monitor,* December 7, 1951.

54. Morgenthau diaries, December 7, 1941, Box 470.

55. *In Search,* p. 109; Alexander Kendrick, *Prime Time: The Life of Edward R. Murrow* (Boston, 1969), p. 240.

56. *Affectionately, F.D.R.,* p. 328.

57. Interview with Tully, December 15, 1970.

58. *F.D.R., My Boss*, p. 259.

59. Washington *Post*, December 9, 1941; Samuel I. Rosenmann, *Working With Roosevelt* (New York, 1952), p. 307.

60. Washington *Post*, December 9, 1941; *First Thirty Hours*, pp. 181–83.

61. *First Thirty Hours*, p. 184–85; Washington *Post*, December 9, 1941; Washington *Evening Star*, December 8, 1941.

62. *First Thirty Hours*, pp. 190–92; Washington *Post*, December 9, 1941; Washington *Evening Star*, December 8, 1941.

63. Washington *Post*, December 9, 1941. The sole vote against the resolution was that of Jeanette Rankin, who had also voted against the declaration of war in 1917, at which time she had 49 others for company. On this occasion she insisted that Congress had acted precipitately, that there was no confirmation of the attack on Pearl Harbor. "The British," she said, "are such clever propagandists, that they might well have cooked up the story."

SELECTED BIBLIOGRAPHY

This bibliography includes only sources cited herein. For a comprehensive bibliography on Pearl Harbor, see At Dawn We Slept *and* Verdict of History.

Unpublished Sources in the Prange Files

Action Report, Commander-in-Chief, United States Pacific Fleet, Serial 047; 15 February 1942, Report of Japanese Raid on Pearl Harbor, 7 December 1941, Classified Operational Archives Branch, Naval History Division, Washington Navy Yard, D.C.

After Action Report, *Maryland*, statement of Seaman 1/c Leslie Short, December 11, 1941, Navy Record Office, Washington Navy Yard, D.C.

After Action Report, *West Virginia*, statement of Lt. Cmdr. T. T. Beattie, December 14, 1941, Navy Record Office, Washington Navy Yard, D.C.

Avery, Guy C. Letters to Prange, November 4, December 1, December 12, December 16, 1963, and February 16, 1964.

Beatty, VADM. Frank E. USN (Ret.), "Secretary Knox and Pearl Harbor." This article in altered form was published in *National Review* (December 13, 1966) under the title "The Background of the Secret Report." Courtesy of Dr. Harry E. Barnes.

Bongo, Nicholas. Letter to Prange, June 9, 1964.

Crouse, Robert G. Letter to Prange, November 24, 1964.

Curylo, Walter J. Letter to Prange, March 3, 1964.

Daniels, William B. Letter to Prange, January 14, 1965.

Earle, Mrs. John B. Letter to Prange, October 16, 1964.

Eisnaugle, Harlan C. Letter to Prange, November 24, 1964.

Farthing, Maj. Gen. William E. Reply, November 12, 1962, to questionnaire by Prange.

Fielder, Brig. Gen. Kendall J. Notes for talk delivered before the Rotary Club in Honolulu on December 7, 1966. Courtesy of Fielder.

Fleming, Maj. Gen. Robert J., Jr. Reply, January 11, 1977, to questionnaire by Prange.

―――. Taped reminiscences, March 7 and 31, 1975, Hoover Institution on War, Revolution and Peace, Stanford, Calif.

History of U.S.S. *Gamble*, Division of Naval History, Washington Navy Yard, D.C.

Kamont, Victor. Letter to Prange, November 9, 1964.

Kramer, Mrs. Alwin D. Letter to Prange, December 3, 1970.

Michaud, Philippe A. Letter to Prange, December 16, 1964.

Moser, R. R. Letter to Prange, January 23, 1964.

Osborne, William D. Letter to Prange, undated.

―――. Statement prepared for the U.S.S. Arizona Memorial Foundation. Courtesy of Osborne.

Outerbridge, W. W. Report, DD139/A16–3(759), Classified Operational Archives Branch, Naval Historical Division, Washington Navy Yard, D.C.

Richmond, R. M. Letter to Prange, November 26, 1963.

Rogo, Jack. Letter to Prange, September 2, 1964.

Safford, Capt. Laurence F., USN (Ret.). Comments on Prange's then unpublished manuscript pertaining to Pearl Harbor.

Summary of Verbal Report Submitted to Colonel Bicknell and Lieutenant Dyson, U.S. Army, re: Attack on the Island of Oahu—December 7, 1941, Observer: Harold T. Kay, Army Pearl Harbor Board, Miscellaneous Document File, Box 8, Record Group 107, Records of the Office of the Secretary of War, National Archives, Washington, D.C.

Supplementary Battle Report, Captain R. B. Simons, USN, Commanding, USS RALEIGH, 7 December, 1941. Courtesy of W. L. Simons.

Taussig, Capt. Joseph K., Jr., USN (Ret.). Letter to Prange, January 8, 1963.

Van Kuren, Benjamin. "Report of Police Activities in Connection with the Japanese Consulate Subsequent to December 7th, 1941 and up to February 8th, 1942," February 13, 1943. Courtesy of Fielder.

DIARIES

Some of these have been published in whole or in part; however, Prange worked exclusively from the unpublished versions.

Berle, Adolf A., Franklin D. Roosevelt Library, Hyde Park, N.Y.

Chigusa, RADM Sadao (courtesy of Admiral Chigusa).

Morgenthau, Henry, Jr., Franklin D. Roosevelt Library, Hyde Park, N.Y.

Nomura, Admiral Kichisaburo (courtesy of Admiral Nomura).

Stimson, Henry L., Yale University Library, New Haven, Conn.

War Diary, First Destroyer Division.

War Diary, Third Battleship Division.

War Diary, Fifth Carrier Division.

COLLECTED PAPERS

Early, Stephen T., Franklin D. Roosevelt Library, Hyde Park, N.Y.

Hamlin, Charles S., Library of Congress, Washington, D.C.

Hiles, Cmdr. Charles C., University of Wyoming Library, Laramie, Wyo.

Hornbeck, Stanley K., Hoover Institution on War, Revolution and Peace, Stanford, Calif.

Hull, Cordell, Library of Congress, Washington, D.C.

Knox, Frank, Library of Congress, Washington, D.C.

Marshall, General of the Army George C., George C. Marshall Research Foundation, Lexington Va. Xerox copies of official records in National Archives, Washington, D.C., WDCSA SGS (Secretariat) (1939–1941).

Roosevelt, President Franklin D., Franklin D. Roosevelt Library, Hyde Park, N.Y.

OFFICIAL PRIMARY SOURCES

Hearings Before the Joint Committee on the Investigation of the Pearl Harbor Attack, Congress of the United States, Seventy-Ninth Congress, Government Printing Office, Washington, D.C., 1946.

Japanese Monograph No. 102, *Submarine Operations, December 1941–April 1942,* prepared by Military History Section, Headquarters, Army Forces Far East, Tokyo, Japan. Prange files.

IMTFE Exhibit No. 1224, June 23, 1946, Affidavit of Joseph Clark Grew. Prange files.

IMTFE Exhibit No. 1225, July 30, 1946, Affidavit of Tateki Shirao. Prange files.

IMTFE Exhibit No. 2660A. Extracts from the Diary of Shirao, Tateki. Prange files.

Published Sources
Articles

Blumenthal, Fred. "The White House Is Calling." Washington *Post,* July 7, 1957.

Brittin, Capt. Burdick S. "We Four Ensigns." *United States Naval Institute Proceedings* (December 1966).

Drake, Col. C. B. "A Day at Pearl Harbor." *Marine Corps Gazette* (November 1965).

Ewing, William H. "High Dive Off the Mainmast." Honolulu *Star-Bulletin,* December 7, 1961.

Hibel, Lt. Col. Franklin. "Caught with Our Planes Down." *Air Force* (December 1956).

Hohjo, Sei-ichi. "The Nine Heroes of Pearl Harbor Attack." *Contemporary Japan: A Review of Far Eastern Affairs* (April 1942).

Hughes, A. Miles. "How We Got the News of Pearl Harbor." *The American Legion Magazine* (December 1970).

Kohase, Matsuji. "A Hidden Episode Concerning Niihau Island." *Suiko* (October 1973).

Murata, Kiyoshi. "'Treachery' of Pearl Harbor." *Nippon Times,* June 8, 1956.

Pierce, Philip N. "Twenty Years Ago." *The Leatherneck* (December 1961).

Rawlings, Charles, and Isabel Leighton. "Fat Girl." *Saturday Evening Post* (February 6, 1943).

Shaw, Brig. Gen. Samuel R., USMC (Ret.). "Marine Barracks, Navy Yard Pearl Harbor, December 1941." *Shipmate* (December 1973).

Smith-Hutton, Capt. H. H., USN (Ret.). "Tokyo, December, 1941." *Shipmate* (December 1973).

Sturm, Ted R. "Mission: War! (A B-17 on December 7, 1941)." *Airman* (December 1965).

Taussig, Capt. Joseph K., Jr. "I Remember Pearl Harbor." *United States Naval Institute Proceedings* (December 1962).

Young, Stephen B. "God, Please Get Us Out of This." *American Heritage* (Vol. 17).

Books

Allen, Gwenfread. *Hawaii's War Years.* Honolulu: University of Hawaii Press, 1950.

Barkley, Alben W. *That Reminds Me.* Garden City, N.Y.: Doubleday, 1954.

Bloom, Sol. *The Autobiography of Sol Bloom.* New York: G. P. Putnam's Sons, 1948.

Caidan, Martin. *The Rugged, Rugged Warriors.* New York: E. P. Dutton & Co., 1966.

Clark, Blake. *Remember Pearl Harbor!* New York: Modern Age Books, 1942.

Connally, Thomas T. *My Name Is Tom Connally.* New York: Crowell Publishing Co., 1954.

The Correspondents of *Time, Life,* and *Fortune. December 7, The First Thirty Hours.* New York: Alfred A. Knopf, 1942.

The Editors of the Army Times Publishing Co. *Pearl Harbor and Hawaii: A Military History.* New York: Walker and Company, 1971.

Feis, Herbert. *The Road to Pearl Harbor.* Princeton, N.J.: Princeton University Press, 1950.

Fuchida, Mitsuo. *Shinjuwan Sakusen No Shinso: Watakushi Wa Shinjuwan Joku Ni Ita.* Nara, Japan: Yamato Taimusu Sha, 1949.

Genda, Minoru. *Shinjuwan Sakusen Kaikoroku.* Tokyo: Yomiuri Shimbun, 1972.

Halsey, Fleet Admiral William F., USN, and Lt. Cmdr. J. Bryan, III, USNR. *Admiral Halsey's Story.* New York: McGraw-Hill Book Co., 1947.

Hoehling, A. A. *The Week Before Pearl Harbor.* New York: W. W. Norton & Co., 1963.

Hull, Cordell. *The Memoirs of Cordell Hull.* New York: Macmillan Co., 1948.

Ickes, Harold L. *The Secret Diary of Harold L. Ickes,* Vol. 3: *The Lowering Clouds 1939–1941.* New York: Simon & Schuster, 1954.

Kato, Masuo. *The Lost War.* New York: Alfred A. Knopf, 1946.

Kendrick, Alexander, *Prime Time: The Life of Edward R. Murrow.* Boston: Little, Brown & Co., 1969.

Lilienthal, David E. *The Journals of David E. Lilienthal,* Vol. 1: *The TVA Years.* New York: Harper & Row, 1964.

Lind, Andrew W. *Hawaii's Japanese: An Experiment in Democracy.* Princeton; N.J.: Princeton University Press, 1946.

Lord, Walter, *Day of Infamy.* New York: Holt, Rinehart & Co., 1957.

Marshall, Katherine T. *Together: Annals of an Army Wife.* New York: Tupper & Love, 1946.

McIntire, VADM. Ross T. *White House Physician*. New York: G. P. Putnam's Sons, 1946.

Morison, Samuel E. *Leyte (June 1944–January 1945)*. Boston: Little, Brown & Co., 1958.

———. *The Rising Sun in the Pacific*. Boston: Little, Brown & Co., 1948.

Murrow, Edward R. *In Search of Light: The Broadcasts of Edward R. Murrow, 1938–1961*. New York: Alfred A. Knopf, 1967.

Perkins, Frances. *The Roosevelt I Knew*. New York: Viking Press, 1946.

Prange, Gordon W. *At Dawn We Slept*. New York: McGraw-Hill Book Co., 1981.

———. *Pearl Harbor: Verdict of History*. New York: McGraw-Hill Book Co., 1985.

Roosevelt, Eleanor. *This I Remember*. New York: Harper & Brothers, 1949.

Roosevelt, James, and Sidney Shalett. *Affectionately, F.D.R.: A Son's Story of a Lonely Man*. New York: Harcourt, Brace & Co., 1959.

Roscoe, Theodore. *United States Destroyer Operations in World War II*. Annapolis, Md.: United States Naval Institute, 1953.

Rosenman, Samuel L. *Working with Roosevelt*. New York: Harper & Brothers, 1952.

Sakamaki, Kazuo. *I Attacked Pearl Harbor*. New York: Association Press, 1949.

Sherwood, Robert E. *Roosevelt and Hopkins: An Intimate History*. New York: Harper & Brothers, 1948.

Smith, A. Merriman. *Thank You, Mr. President: A White House Notebook*. New York: Harper & Brothers, 1946.

Stafford, Cmdr. Edward P., USN. *The Big E: The Story of the USS Enterprise*. New York: Random House, 1953.

Terasaki, Gwen. *Bridge to the Sun*. Chapel Hill, N.C.: University of North Carolina Press, 1957.

Tsunoda, Hitoshi, et al. *Hawai Sakusen*. Tokyo: Boeicho Boei, Kenshujo Senshishitsu, 1967.

Tully, Grace. *F.D.R., My Boss*. New York: Charles Scribner's Sons, 1949.

United States Department of Defense. *The "Magic" Background of Pearl Harbor*. Washington, D.C.: U.S. Government Printing Office, 1977.

Wilson, Rose Page. *General Marshall Remembered*. Englewood Cliffs, N.J.: Prentice-Hall, 1968.

MAGAZINES

Air Force

Airman

American Heritage

American Legion

Contemporary Japan

The Leatherneck

Marine Corps Gazette

Newsweek

Saturday Evening Post

Shipmate

Suiko

United States Naval Institute Proceedings

NEWSPAPERS

Chicago *Daily News*

Honolulu *Advertiser*

Honolulu *Star-Bulletin*

Idaho Sunday Statesman

Indianapolis *Star*

Japan *Times and Advertiser*

Los Angeles *Times*

Military Press (Honolulu)

New York *Herald Tribune*

St. Louis *Post-Dispatch*

San Antonio *Express*

San Francisco *Chronicle*

Seattle *Post-Intelligencer*

Washington *Evening Star*

Washington *Post*

SHIPS' LOGS

Allen (destroyer)

Antares (stores and supply ship)

Argonne (auxiliary)

Avocet (seaplane tender)

Aylwin (destroyer)

Blue (destroyer)

Breese (destroyer-minelayer)

California (battleship)

Case (destroyer)

Chew (destroyer)

Condor (minesweeper)

Conyngham (destroyer)

Cummings (destroyer)

Curtiss (seaplane tender)

Dale (destroyer)

Detroit (light cruiser)

Dewey (destroyer)

Dobbin (destroyer tender)

Dolphin (submarine)

Gamble (destroyer-minelayer)

Grebe (minesweeper)

Helena (light cruiser)

Helm (destroyer)

Henley (destroyer)

Honolulu (light cruiser)

Hulbert (destroyer)

Maryland (battleship)

Medusa (repair ship)

Monaghan (destroyer)

Montgomery (destroyer-minelayer)

Neosho (tanker)

Nevada (battleship)

New Orleans (heavy cruiser)

Oglala (minelayer)

PT 29 (motor torpedo boat)

PT 30 (motor torpedo boat)

Patterson (destroyer)

Pelias (submarine tender)

Pennsylvania (battleship)

Perry (minesweeper)

Phoenix (light cruiser)

Raleigh (light cruiser)

Ralph Talbot (destroyer)

Ramapo (tanker)

Ramsay (destroyer-minelayer)

Reid (destroyer)

Rigal (repair ship)

Sacramento (gunboat)

St. Louis (light cruiser)

San Francisco (heavy cruiser)

Selfridge (destroyer)

Shaw (destroyer)

Sicard (destroyer-minelayer)

Solace (hospital ship)

Sumner (auxiliary)

Tangier (seaplane tender)

Tennessee (battleship)

Tern (minesweeper)

Thornton (destroyer-seaplane tender)

Tracy (destroyer-minelayer)

Trever (destroyer-minesweeper)

Tucker (destroyer)

Vestal (repair ship)

Vireo (minesweeper)

Ward (destroyer)

Wasmuth (destroyer-minesweeper)

Whitney (destroyer tender)

Zane (destroyer-minesweeper)

INTERVIEWS

Dates of interviews appear in Notes.

Maj. Gen. Brooke E. Allen

Capt. Takehisa Amagai

Capt. Takayasu Arima

CWO-4 Edgar B. Beck

RADM William P. Burford

RADM Sadao Chigusa

VADM Charles Coe

Mrs. Frank Cooper

John Crawford

Capt. Paul C. Crosley

Maj. Gen. Howard C. Davidson

Admiral Arthur C. Davis

Col. Charles W. Davis

Mrs. Charles W. Davis

Cleveland Davis

RADM Milo F. Draemel

Brig. Gen. Robert H. Dunlop

Capt. Robert H. Dunlop, Jr.

Mrs. Stephen T. Early

Capt. Walter J. East

Mrs. Walter J. East

Tamotsu Ema

Capt. Ruth A. Erickson

Col. William C. Farnum

Maj. Gen. William E. Farthing

Capt. William S. Finn

Maj. Gen. Robert J. Fleming, Jr.

Brig. Gen. William J. Flood

Thomas E. Forrow

Howard C. French

Capt. Mitsuo Fuchida

Iyozo Fujita

Capt. Minoru Genda

Jinichi Goto

Capt. Lawrence C. Grannis

Lt. Col. Francis Gutzak

VADM Chuichi Hara

Toshio Hashimoto

Col. Allen P. Haynes

Mrs. Allen P. Haynes

Lt. Cmdr. B. C. Hesser

Capt. William H. Heydt

Cmdr. Doir C. Johnson

Emil Johnson

Mrs. Charles A. Kengla

RADM Husband E. Kimmel

Richard M. Kotoshirodo

Lt. Gen. Truman H. Landon

RADM Edwin T. Layton

Col. Emil Leard

Mrs. Emil Leard

Maj. Gen. Morrill W. Marston

Admiral Harold M. Martin

Heita Matsumura

VADM Gunichi Mikawa

Brig. Gen. James A. Mollison

Keizo Ofuchi

Kyoshi Ohashi

RADM William W. Outerbridge

RADM Harold F. Pullen

RADM Allen G. Quynn

Harry Rafsky

RADM Logan C. Ramsey

Col. Vernon H. Reeves

RADM Cecil D. Riggs

Capt. Joseph J. Rochefort

Admiral George A. Rood

RADM Laurence E. Ruff

Charles A. Russell

Kazuo Sakamaki

Brig Gen. George P. Sampson

Hanku Sasaki

Cmdr. Nachiro Sata

Lt. Col. John B. Schindel

Lt. Gen. Allan Shapley, USMC

Duane W. Shaw

Capt. Tatsuwaka Shibuya

Yoshio Shiga

Cmdr. Hisao Shimoda

RADM James M. Shoemaker

Lt. Cmdr. Harley F. Smart

VADM William W. Smith

Mrs. William W. Smith

RADM Herald F. Stout

Lt. Irwin H. Thesman

Col. Kenneth E. Thiebaud

Col. Russell C. Throckmorton

RADM Sadatoshi Tomioka

Miss Grace Tully

Lt. Col. Kermit A. Tyler

Maj. Gen. Durward S. Wilson

Mrs. Durward S. Wilson

Col. Wesley C. Wilson

Minoru Yokota

Takeo Yoshikawa

STATEMENTS

The following submitted written statements to Prange in lieu of or in addition to personal interviews.

Heijiro Abe, October 14, 1950

Zenji Abe, October 19, 1950

Minoru Genda, June 11, 1947

VADM Chuichi Hara, December 26, 1951

Takashi Hashiguchi, October 16, 1950

Masanobu Ibusuki, undated

Jozo Iwami, October 20, 1950

Takatsugu Jojima, July 17, 1951

Kazuyoshi Kitajima, October 18, 1951

Heita Matsumura, January 19, 1951

Iwakichi Mifuno, March 6, 1951

Kazuo Muranaka, December 17, 1949

Atsuki Nakajima, January 28, 1951

Keizo Ofuchi, January 17, 1950

Kiyakuma Okajima, January 19, 1951

Hanku Sasaki, October 30, 1950

Zenichi Sato, October 19, 1950

Yoshio Shiga, undated

Saburo Shindo, January 17, 1951

TABLE OF COMPARATIVE TIMES

Washington, D. C.	Hawaii	Tokyo
0600 December 6	0030 December 6	2000 December 6
0700	0130	2100
0800	0230	2200
0900	0330	2300
1000	0430	0000 December 7
1100	0530	0100
1200	0630	0200
1300	0730	0300
1400	0830	0400
1500	0930	0500
1600	1030	0600
1700	1130	0700
1800	1230	0800
1900	1330	0900
2000	1430	1000
2100	1530	1100
2200	1630	1200
2300	1730	1300
0000 December 7	1830	1400
0100	1930	1500
0200	2030	1600
0300	2130	1700
0400	2230	1800
0500	2330	1900
0600	0030 December 7	2000
0700	0130	2100
0800	0230	2200
0900	0330	2300
1000	0430	0000 December 8
1100	0530	0100
1200	0630	0200
1300	0730	0300
1400	0830	0400
1500	0930	0500
1600	1030	0600
1700	1130	0700
1800	1230	0800
1900	1330	0900
2000	1430	1000

Washington, D. C.	Hawaii	Tokyo
2100	1530	1100
2200	1630	1200
2300	1730	1300
0000 December 8	1830	1400
0100	1930	1500
0200	2030	1600
0300	2130	1700
0400	2230	1800
0500	2330	1900
0600	0030 December 8	2000
0700	0130	2100
0800	0230	2200
0900	0330	2300
1000	0430	0000 December 9
1100	0530	0100
1200	0630	0200
1300	0730	0300
1400	0830	0400
1500	0930	0500
1600	1030	0600
1700	1130	0700
1800	1230	0800
1900	1330	0900
2000	1430	1000
2100	1530	1100
2200	1630	1200
2300	1730	1300
0000 December 9	1830	1400
0100	1930	1500
0200	2030	1600
0300	2130	1700
0400	2230	1800
0500	2330	1900

EPILOGUE

Within four years of Pearl Harbor, Gordon W. Prange began working on the subject, and never ceased until his final illness thirty-seven years later. In that time, he conducted hundreds of interviews, read scores of books, articles and newspapers, and researched in the collected papers of many key personalities of this period. One has only to read the bibliographies of his Pearl Harbor volumes to have some idea of the scope, nature and volume of his sources. We suspect that if he had lived to be 100, he would still have been hard at it— one more collection to examine, one more book to read, one more person to interview.

In all those years of research, reading and interviewing, his enthusiasm never flagged. Without that quality, his work might have ended up awesomely documented but unbearably boring. But Prange had no use for the attitude that scholarship precluded readability. In addition to being absorbed in his subject, he loved the English language—its sweep and power, its capacity to convey nuances of meaning and shades of emotion. If his books achieved a respectable place on academic bookshelves, that would be well and good, but he also wanted them to be read and enjoyed by the general reading public. Nothing would have pleased him more than the reviews which mentioned that his books were enjoyable to read.

We were deeply honored when Prange entrusted us with his projects a short time before his death. He plunged us into a great adventure. When we took over, we found, as we had expected, manuscripts so bulging with documented facts, colorful incidents, and ma-

ture judgments that we realized our main task would be pruning and
some rearranging. The former was especially true of the first book,
At Dawn We Slept, where much interesting and important material
had to be cut to keep the book at a reasonable size. So we were delighted when it succeeded beyond our wildest hopes. The very kind
reception accorded this work opened the way to publishing *Pearl Harbor: Verdict of History*, and finally this account of eyewitness experiences.

We also felt obligated to conduct further research in documents
released since Prange's death. In so doing we were pleased but not
surprised to find that nothing therein contradicted or even outdated
Prange's judgments. What has surprised and to a degree disappointed
us is the deep-rooted tendency to regard Pearl Harbor as a political
problem for which blame must be allocated rather than as a military
engagement from which lessons should be learned. In a military or
naval engagement, there can be no evasion of responsibility. For example, in the recent U.S.S. *Stark* incident, no one seriously questioned that its skipper was a conscientious officer with a good record,
doing his duty as he saw it. But that was beside the point; he was in
command, hence responsible, and his removal from that post was inevitable. Not that his dismissal did, or should, answer all the questions raised by that unfortunate happening.

By the same token, the responsibility which the military and naval leaders on Oahu in 1941 cannot escape does not and should not
answer all the questions hovering about the name "Pearl Harbor."
The subject is endlessly fascinating, and many people are still looking
for a simplistic answer, a single key reason for the debacle. No doubt
they will still be doing so a century from now. We feel safe in pre-
dicting that they will never find it, for the American side of the story
is no clear-cut case of conspiracy or betrayal. There was a certain
amount of post-event scrambling for figurative lifeboats, but there is
no "smoking gun."

As the 46th anniversary approaches, we hope that the time will
soon come when finger-pointing can be set aside in favor of dispas-
sionate reflection, when the lessons of Pearl Harbor can be absorbed
and acted upon. If they cannot, a future generation may be compelled
to learn them the hard way. The general tenor of those lessons is the
appalling damage that can result from underestimating a potential enemy, misdirection of attention, improper use of intelligence, and fail-

ure to take seriously one's own Headquarters studies such as the Martin-Bellinger and Farthing reports which called the shots with uncanny accuracy and which were totally ignored in the event.

As Prange stressed, there was no willful villainy at Pearl Harbor, but considerable bungling and human error. If one persists in seeking a one-sentence solution, it may have been provided by one eyewitness when he testified, "They caught them asleep, by God!"

Donald M. Goldstein
Pittsburgh, PA

Katherine V. Dillon
Arlington, VA

Index

Cast of Characters

AMERICANS

Claude C. Bloch - Commandant 14th Naval District

George W. Bicknell - Lt. Col. Assistant G/2 Hawaiian Department

Patrick Bellinger - Rear Admiral, Chief of Naval Aviation / Martin Bellinger Report

Henry C. Clausen - Assistant Recorder of Army Board; Conducts follow-up inquiry

William E. Farthing - Commander 5th Bomb Group - Farthing Report

James Forrestal - Secretary of the Navy / May 1944 - September 1947

Leonard T. Gerow - Brig. Gen. Chief War Plans Division - War Department

J.C. Grew - U.S. Ambassador to Japan

William F. Halsey - Commander Air Craft Battle Force VADM

Thomas C. Hart - Admiral CINC Asiatic Fleet - conducts inquiry

Cordell Hull - Secretary of State

Frank Knox - Secretary of Navy

George C. Marshall - Chief of Staff, U.S. Army

Frederick Martin - Major General, Commanding Gen. of Hawaiian Air Force

Irving Mayfield - Head, District Intelligence Office

A.H. McCollum - Commander, Chief Far Eastern Section ONI

Sherman Miles - Brig. General, Acting ACS, Intelligence War Department

Henry J. Morthenthau - Secretary of the Treasury

James O. Richardson - Commander-in-Chief, U.S. Fleet - 1940

J.J. Rochefort - Commander, Chief Communications Section, 14th Naval District

Franklin D. Roosevelt - President

Walter C. Philips - Lt. Col. Chief of Staff, Hawaiian Department

Lawrence F. Stafford - Chief, Security Section, Communications Division, Navy Dept.

Robert L. Shivers - Special Agent in Charge, FBI, Honolulu

Walter C. Short - Lt. Gen., Commanding General, Hawaii Department

William Ward Smith - Capt. USN, Chief of Staff, Pacific Fleet

Harold R. Stark - Admiral, CNO

Harry S. Truman - President of U.S. - effective April 12, 1945

Richard K. Turner - RADM, Chief of War Plans, Navy Department

Elias M. Zacharias - Captain USN - Intelligence expert

JAPANESE

Takashige Egusa - Lt. Commander, Dive Bomber, Leader of First Air Fleet
Mitsuo Fuchida - Leader, Air Attack on Pearl Harbor
Minoru Genda - Commander, Air Staff Officer, First Fleet
    (Principle Planner for Pearl Harbor)
Hirohito - Emperor of Japan
Fumimaro Konoye - Premier, July 1940 to October 1941
Nagao Kita - Consular General at Honolulu
Saburo Kurusu - Special Envoy to Washington
Shigeharu Murata - Torpedo Bomber Leader, First Air Fleet
Osami Nagano - Admiral, Chief of Naval General Staff
Chuichi Nagumo - Commander-in-Chief, First Air Fleet
Kichisaburo Nomura - Ambassador to the United States
Takijiru Onishi - RADM, Chief of the Staff, 11th Fleet
Shigetaro Shimada - VADM, Navy Minister under Tojo
Saburo Shindo - Lt., Leader of second wave of fighters
Itaru Tachibana - Lt. Commander, Intelligence Expert - Naval General
    Staff
Shigenori Togo - Minister in Tojo's Cabinet
Hideki Tojo - War Minister, Konoye Cabinet, Premier - October 18, 1941
Sadatoshi Tomioki - Captain, Chief of Operations - First Air Fleet
Matome Ugaki - Chief of Staff (Rear Admiral), Combined Fleet - August 10,
    1941
Yasuji Watanabi - Captain, Staff Officer - Combined Fleet
Tamonon Yamaguchi - Rear Admiral, Chief of Second Carrier Division
Isoroku Yamamoto - Admiral, Commander-in-Chief - Combined Fleet
Takeo Yoshikawa - Chancellor of the Honolulu Consulate

Abbreviated Chronology of Key Events Relating to Pearl Harbor

1940

10 April—Fleet to Hawaii
June—Fall of France
Summer—Herron alert against "trans-Pacific raid"
August—U.S. breaks Purple code
September—Tripartite Pact
12 November—Taranto
November—Plan DOG (Europe first)

1941

7 January—Yamamoto writes Oikawa
23 January—Nomura sails for US
26 or 27—Yamamoto meets with Onishi
27—Grew message re rumor
1 February—Kimmel becomes CinCUS
1 February—ONI places "no credence in Grew message
7 February—Short becomes CG Hawaiian Dept.
early February—Genda becomes tactical planner of PH
27 March—ABC-1 agreement—strategy *if* US enters war
31 March—Martin-Bellinger report sent to DC
10 April—FDR draws patrol line in Atlantic
10 April—First Air Fleet formed
19–22 May—about 1/4 of Pacific Fleet transferred to Atlantic
22 June—Germany invades Russia
2 July—Imperial Conference
16 July—Konoye resigns, forms new cabinet
26 July—US freezes Japanese assets
1 August—US embargoes high octane gas
7 August—FDR & party to Argentia
20 August—Farthing report to DC
11–16 September—War games for PH etc.
24 September—Bomb plot message
9–13 October—Table maneuvers for PH
16 October—Konoye Cabinet falls
18 October—Tojo becomes Premier
18 October—Yamamoto threats to resign, NGS submits
5 November—Togo gives Nomura deadline of 25 November
15 November—Kurusu arrives in US

19 November—Winds message (East Wind Rain)
20 November—Japan presents Proposal B
21–25 November—Hull etc working on modus vivendi
21–26 November—Rendezvous at Hitokappu Bay
22 November—Togo extends deadline to 29th.
26 November—Japanese fleet sighted headed for Indochina
26 November—Hull Note
27 November—Kimmel & Short arrange to send fighter planes to Wake & Midway. *Enterprise* leaves
27 November—"war warning" messages to Kimmel and Short etc.
27 November—Short initiates anti-sabotage alert
1 December—FDR tells Halifax GB can count on US support
1 December—Imperial conference officially decides on war
1 December—IJN changes call signals for 2d time in one month.
2 December—CNO orders "three little ships" reconnaissance
2 December—Tokyo advises certain embassies and consulates to burn secret documents and destroy most codes.
2 December—Climb Mt. Niitaka
3 December—CNO informs CinCPAC etc of code orders
3 December—"Kita message" (Kuehn's proposed code
3 December—FDR tells Halifax GB can count on "armed support"
4 December—Nagumo orders sinking of enemy or neutral ships if necessary
5 December—*Lexington* leaves PH
6 December—1st 13 parts of 14-part message
6 December—FDR writes Emperor
7 December—*Enterprise* due in PH
7 December—Budapest-Tokyo message
7 December—Brooke-Popham message
7 December—14th part received
7 December—"One o'clock" message
7 December—Marshall advises Short of one o'clock msg.